Research Paradigms and Contemporary Perspectives on Human– Technology Interaction

Anabela Mesquita
School of Accounting and Administration of Porto, Polytechnic Institute of Porto, Portugal & Algorithm Research Centre, Minho University, Portugal

A volume in the Advances in Human and Social Aspects of Technology (AHSAT) Book Series

www.igi-global.com

Published in the United States of America by
IGI Global
Information Science Reference (an imprint of IGI Global)
701 E. Chocolate Avenue
Hershey PA, USA 17033
Tel: 717-533-8845
Fax: 717-533-8661
E-mail: cust@igi-global.com
Web site: http://www.igi-global.com

Library of Congress Cataloging-in-Publication Data

Names: Sarmento, Anabela, editor.
Title: Research paradigms and contemporary perspectives on human-technology
  interaction / Anabela Mesquita, editor.
Description: Hershey : Information Science Reference, [2017]
Identifiers: LCCN 2016046932| ISBN 9781522518686 (hardcover) | ISBN
  9781522518693 (ebook)
Subjects: LCSH: Social media. | Internet access. | World Wide Web.
Classification: LCC HM851 .R467 2017 | DDC 302.23/1--dc23 LC record available at https://lccn.loc.gov/2016046932

This book is published in the IGI Global book series Advances in Human and Social Aspects of Technology (AHSAT) (ISSN: 2328-1316; eISSN: 2328-1324)

British Cataloguing in Publication Data
A Cataloguing in Publication record for this book is available from the British Library.

For electronic access to this publication, please contact: eresources@igi-global.com.

Advances in Human and Social Aspects of Technology (AHSAT) Book Series

Ashish Dwivedi
The University of Hull, UK

ISSN:2328-1316
EISSN:2328-1324

MISSION

In recent years, the societal impact of technology has been noted as we become increasingly more connected and are presented with more digital tools and devices. With the popularity of digital devices such as cell phones and tablets, it is crucial to consider the implications of our digital dependence and the presence of technology in our everyday lives.

The **Advances in Human and Social Aspects of Technology (AHSAT) Book Series** seeks to explore the ways in which society and human beings have been affected by technology and how the technological revolution has changed the way we conduct our lives as well as our behavior. The AHSAT book series aims to publish the most cutting-edge research on human behavior and interaction with technology and the ways in which the digital age is changing society.

COVERAGE

- Technology Dependence
- Information ethics
- Technology Adoption
- Cyber Bullying
- Gender and Technology
- Technology and Freedom of Speech
- Human Rights and Digitization
- Technoself
- Cyber Behavior
- End-User Computing

IGI Global is currently accepting manuscripts for publication within this series. To submit a proposal for a volume in this series, please contact our Acquisition Editors at Acquisitions@igi-global.com or visit: http://www.igi-global.com/publish/.

The Advances in Human and Social Aspects of Technology (AHSAT) Book Series (ISSN 2328-1316) is published by IGI Global, 701 E. Chocolate Avenue, Hershey, PA 17033-1240, USA, www.igi-global.com. This series is composed of titles available for purchase individually; each title is edited to be contextually exclusive from any other title within the series. For pricing and ordering information please visit http://www.igi-global.com/book-series/advances-human-social-aspects-technology/37145. Postmaster: Send all address changes to above address. Copyright © 2017 IGI Global. All rights, including translation in other languages reserved by the publisher. No part of this series may be reproduced or used in any form or by any means – graphics, electronic, or mechanical, including photocopying, recording, taping, or information and retrieval systems – without written permission from the publisher, except for non commercial, educational use, including classroom teaching purposes. The views expressed in this series are those of the authors, but not necessarily of IGI Global.

Titles in this Series

For a list of additional titles in this series, please visit: www.igi-global.com

Enriching Urban Spaces with Ambient Computing, the Internet of Things, and Smart City Design
Shin'ichi Konomi (University of Tokyo, Japan) and George Roussos (University of London, UK)
Engineering Science Reference • copyright 2017 • 323pp • H/C (ISBN: 9781522508274) • US $210.00 (our price)

Handbook of Research on Individualism and Identity in the Globalized Digital Age
F. Sigmund Topor (Keio University, Japan)
Information Science Reference • copyright 2017 • 645pp • H/C (ISBN: 9781522505228) • US $295.00 (our price)

Information Technology Integration for Socio-Economic Development
Titus Tossy (Mzumbe University, Tanzania)
Information Science Reference • copyright 2017 • 385pp • H/C (ISBN: 9781522505396) • US $200.00 (our price)

Handbook of Research on Human-Computer Interfaces, Developments, and Applications
João Rodrigues (University of Algarve, Portugal) Pedro Cardoso (University of Algarve, Portugal) Jânio Monteiro (University of Algarve, Portugal) and Mauro Figueiredo (University of Algarve, Portugal)
Information Science Reference • copyright 2016 • 663pp • H/C (ISBN: 9781522504351) • US $330.00 (our price)

Human Development and Interaction in the Age of Ubiquitous Technology
Hakikur Rahman (BRAC University, Bangladesh)
Information Science Reference • copyright 2016 • 384pp • H/C (ISBN: 9781522505563) • US $185.00 (our price)

Examining the Evolution of Gaming and Its Impact on Social, Cultural, and Political Perspectives
Keri Duncan Valentine (West Virginia University, USA) and Lucas John Jensen (Georgia Southern University, USA)
Information Science Reference • copyright 2016 • 456pp • H/C (ISBN: 9781522502616) • US $190.00 (our price)

Handbook of Research on Human Social Interaction in the Age of Mobile Devices
Xiaoge Xu (Botswana International University of Science and Technology, Botswana)
Information Science Reference • copyright 2016 • 548pp • H/C (ISBN: 9781522504696) • US $325.00 (our price)

Defining Identity and the Changing Scope of Culture in the Digital Age
Alison Novak (Rowan University, USA) and Imaani Jamillah El-Burki (Lehigh University, USA)
Information Science Reference • copyright 2016 • 316pp • H/C (ISBN: 9781522502128) • US $185.00 (our price)

Gender Considerations in Online Consumption Behavior and Internet Use
Rebecca English (Queensland University of Technology, Australia) and Raechel Johns (University of Canberra, Australia)
Information Science Reference • copyright 2016 • 297pp • H/C (ISBN: 9781522500100) • US $165.00 (our price)

www.igi-global.com

701 E. Chocolate Ave., Hershey, PA 17033
Order online at www.igi-global.com or call 717-533-8845 x100
To place a standing order for titles released in this series, contact: cust@igi-global.com
Mon-Fri 8:00 am - 5:00 pm (est) or fax 24 hours a day 717-533-8661

To João, Pedro Ivo, Nuno Miguel and Joãozinho.
To my mother.

List of Reviewers

Elena Barcena, *Distance Learning Unit, Spain*
João Batista, *Universidade de Aveiro, Portugal*
Fernando Moreira, *Universidade Portucalense, Portugal*
Paula Peres, *Politécnico do Porto, Portugal*
Álvaro Rocha, *Universidade de Coimbra, Portugal*
Wen-Lung Shiau, *Ming Chuan University, Taiwan*
Alexandrina Sirbu, *Constantin Brancoveanu University, Romania*
Chia-Wen Tsai, *Ming Chuan University, Taiwan*

Table of Contents

Section 2
The Importance of Web Accessibility and Public Services

Section 3
Technology Acceptance and Satisfaction

Section 4
What Future is Hidden Behind IS/IT?

Detailed Table of Contents

Section 1
The Use of Social Media and its Impact in the Human Life Dimension

The proliferation of mobile phones and tablets shape a new arena for online commercial activity with unprecedented opportunities and challenges. In this omnipresent mobile environment, understanding consumer behavior constitutes a challenge for m-commerce vendors, as they seek to understand factors that affect it, positively and negatively, and to integrate social media in their mobile strategy and across mobile devices. This paper presents an exploratory qualitative research examining separately mobile phones and tablets and the use of social media, in the context of m-commerce. The results of our qualitative analysis show important factors for m-commerce and social media adoption and use, highlighting the similarities and differences between mobile phones and tablets. Our qualitative results also reveal factors having a negative effect to m-commerce, for both mobile devices. Business opportunities enabled by social media for m-commerce and how these can be leveraged in this promising multiple-device mobile context are also discussed.

Facebook is a major part of the lives of many consumers who share a considerable amount of information with friends, acquaintances, and commercial interests via the platform, leading to greater exposure to privacy risks. Training has been shown to be effective in reducing computer risk in a variety of contexts. This study investigates the effectiveness of training on consumer attitudes and behavioral intentions toward

Facebook privacy risk. The study highlights the importance of training consumers on how and why they need to protect their privacy. Findings suggest that training can reduce consumer risk, but effectiveness can vary across types of training. For example, Facebook's Privacy Tour was less effective than third party training videos in improving consumer vigilance. Implications of the findings for consumers and privacy advocates are discussed.

    Sylvaine Castellano, Paris School of Business, France
    Insaf Khelladi, ICN Business School, France

New opportunities and challenges are emerging thanks to the growing Internet importance and social media usage. Although practitioners have already recognized the strategic dimension of e-reputation and the power of social media, academic research is still in its infancy when it comes to e-reputation determinants in a social networks context. A study was conducted in the sports setting to explore the impact of social networks on the sportspeople's e-reputation. Whereas the study emphasized (1) the influence of social networks' perception on the sportspeople's e-reputation, and the neutral roles of (2) the motives for following sportspeople online, and (3) the negative content on the Internet, additional insights are formulated on maintaining, restoring and managing e-reputation on social networks. Finally, future research directions are suggested on the role of image to control e-reputation.

    Erika Melonashi, European University of Tirana, Albania

The present chapter aims to explore the relationship between social media and identity by reviewing theoretical frameworks as well as empirical studies on the topic. Considering the complexity of the concept of identity, a multidisciplinary theoretical approach is provided, including Psychological Theories, Sociological Theories and Communication Theories. These theories are revisited in the context of online identity formation and communication through social media. Different aspects of identity such as gender identity, professional identity, political identity etc., are discussed and illustrated through empirical studies in the field. Moreover, the role of social media as a factor that might either promote or hinder identity development is also discussed (e.g., phenomena such as cyber-bulling and internet addiction). Finally recommendations and suggestions for future research are provided, including the need for multidisciplinary theoretical frameworks to the investigation of the relationships between social media and identity.

    Jessica Lichy, IDRAC Business School, France
    Maher Kachour, IDRAC Business School, France

This study focuses on the Internet user behaviour of young people, at a time when information and communication technologies (ICT) are rapidly transforming how individuals behave and interact in the online environment. The intention is to put forward a snapshot of contemporary Internet user behaviour, with reference to social networking, and thus provide an overview and understanding of the various online activities undertaken by Generation Y and Generation Z in a non-Anglophone context. The study uses a mixed methods approach to gather data on the thoughts, experiences and behaviours of young Internet users in order to explain their social networking. The findings suggest commonality and disparity between Generation Y and Generation Z. They also reveal the extent to which certain national differences are less apparent when using social networks, suggesting that the widespread adoption of Internet technology is generating a somewhat 'standardised' Internet user behaviour.

Section 2
The Importance of Web Accessibility and Public Services

Chapter 6
Carlos Peixoto, INESC TEC and University of Trás-os-Montes and Alto Douro, Portugal
Frederico Branco, INESC TEC and University of Trás-os-Montes and Alto Douro, Portugal
José Martins, INESC TEC and University of Trás-os-Montes and Alto Douro, Portugal
Ramiro Gonçalves, INESC TEC and University of Trás-os-Montes and Alto Douro, Portugal

Accessibility has become increasingly important in information technology, particularly due to legislation pressure to make affordable public services to all. Being end-users and software companies those who have direct contact with accessibility problems, other stakeholders are committed to defining methods and change mentalities in Web accessibility implementation. In addition to a conceptual definition, this chapter presents entities views with responsibilities in the area, taking into account their work done in the past and the prospects for future. The understanding of the interaction between all these perspectives will help to realize the way it will go, which carries with it great challenges and opportunities, widely explored in this work.

Chapter 7
Maria José Angélico, Polytechnic of Porto, Portugal
Amélia Silva, Polytechnic of Porto, Portugal
Sandrina Francisca Teixeira, ISCAP/IPP, Portugal
Telma Maia, Câmara Municipal Valongo, Portugal
Anabela Martins Silva, University of Minho, Portugal

Local government is a political power close to citizens and constitutes a mainstay of democracy. Because of their mission, the guidelines promoted by local government must be embedded in strategies of accountability and public communication. In that sense, it is worthwhile to ask if "local government accountability is being an inclusive concept?" In Portugal, transparency of municipalities is being accessed through the Municipality Transparency Index (MTI). The study aim was to investigate whatever MTI measures accessibility. This study examined the availability of local government information on the website for a sample of 86 Portuguese municipalities and presented the results of a quantitative evaluation of the web accessibility based on W3C guidelines, using an automated tool. Based on the main concepts of transparency and accessibility, it explored static association between MTI and web accessibility. This study contributed to the discussion about transparency as a social value and is of great importance for local policy makers and civic movements in favor of disabled people.

Section 3
Technology Acceptance and Satisfaction

Chapter 8

T. S. Amer, Northern Arizona University, USA
Todd L. Johnson, Northern Arizona University, USA

Users of information technology often encounter "progress indicators" during their interactions. These graphics (e.g., progress bars) appear on computing screens as users wait for a task to complete to inform them of the progress being made toward completing the task. This study employed theoretical models from psychological research on human waiting to develop specific hypotheses related to the design of progress indicators. Three experiments tested these hypotheses. Experiment 1 revealed that participants preferred a linear progress bar to a cycling progress bar. Experiment 2 revealed that participants preferred a video progress indicator to a cycling progress bar, and they judged process duration to be shorter with the video progress indicator. Experiment 3 revealed that the video progress indicator yielded the best user experience. Systems designers can use these results to develop more effective user interfaces.

Chapter 9

A. Y. M. Atiquil Islam, Institute of Graduate Studies, University of Malaya, Malaysia

In the 21st century wireless internet technology has been extensively extending and contributing to various aspects of human lives. However, technological assessment and evaluation have been rarely taken place, especially to investigate the satisfaction among students in using wireless internet for learning and research purposes. As such, this study validates the Technology Satisfaction Model proposed by Islam in an academic context for estimating students' satisfaction and the moderating effect of gender in using wireless internet. The findings of SEM analyses attested that students' satisfaction was directly influenced by perceived ease of use and usefulness in using wireless internet and it was also indirectly affected by computer self-efficacy medicated by usefulness and ease of use, respectively. Additionally, computer self-efficacy had a significant direct influence on ease of use and usefulness. The results of invariance analyses also discovered that gender was not a moderating variable for technology satisfaction in an academic context.

Chapter 10

Anis Khedhaouria, Montpellier Business School, Montpellier Research in Management,
France
Adel Beldi, IÉSEG School of Management (LEM-CNRS 9221), France

In this chapter, we investigate the moderating effect of gender on the intention to continue using mobile Internet services (MIS) in an everyday life context. An extended model based on the technology acceptance theory is used to examine gender differences regarding MIS continuance intention in an everyday life context. A survey was conducted among 623 current MIS users to test the hypotheses using structural equation modeling approach. The findings show that female users expressed a stronger need for perceived usefulness and ease-of-use than male users, while male users expressed a significant need for perceived enjoyment. Interestingly, the stronger effect of perceived usefulness in females was contrary to prior TAM research. The observed gender differences suggest that MIS providers should consider gender when advertising and marketing MIS.

Section 4
What Future is Hidden Behind IS/IT?

Chapter 11

Steffen Roth, ESC Rennes School of Business, France
Carlton Clark, University of Wisconsin – La Crosse, USA
Jan Berkel, Independent Researcher, Puerto Rico

Using the updated Google Book corpus dataset generated in July 2012, we analyze the largest available corpus of digitalized books to review social macro trends such as the secularization, politicization, economization, and mediatization of society. These familiar trend statements are tested through a comparative analysis of word frequency time-series plots for the English, French, and German language area produced by means of the enhanced Google Ngram Viewer, the online graphing tool that charts annual word counts as found in the Google Book corpus. The results: a) confirm that the importance of the political system, religion, economy, and mass media features significant change in time and considerable regional differences and b) suggest that visions of economized or capitalist societies are intellectual artifacts rather than appropriate descriptions of society.

Chapter 12

Florin Popescu, University "Politehnica" of Bucharest, Romania
Cezar Scarlat, University "Politehnica" of Bucharest, Romania

More or less primitive homo sapiens have always secretly dreamt about, or plainly believed in immortality. All cultures had and still have beliefs, traditions, rituals, legends, old stories, and fairy tales about immortality. Unfortunately, as science and technology progressed, human immortality is a remote ideal yet. In addition, as technology development speeds up, it challenges the social nature of humankind; a possible result is people alienation. It is the purpose of this paper to propose a new prospective: opposed to the common feeling that technology alienates people – in their most intimate nature – the authors believe that modern technologies and human nature (defined by its innermost dream of immortality) converge. The ancient human dream of eternal life can be achieved through technology: i.e. human digital immortality. A day will come when the entire technical capabilities will allow personalities to be copied into a computer. Thus immortality could be provided in a virtualized form, heaven being replaced with a super computer.

Chapter 13

The intention of this chapter is to provide an overview on the subject of Human-Computer Interaction. The overview includes the basic definitions and terminology, a survey of existing technologies and recent advances in the field, common architectures used in the design of HCI systems which includes unimodal and multimodal configurations, and finally the applications of HCI. This chapter also offers a comprehensive number of references for each concept, method, and application in the HCI. Human–computer interaction is considered a core element of computer science. Yet it has not coalesced; many researchers who identify their focus as human–computer interaction reside in other fields. It examines the origins and evolution of three HCI research foci: computer operation, information systems management, and discretionary use. It describes efforts to find common ground and forces that have kept them apart.

Foreword

When my friend and colleague Anabela talked me about her book, my first idea was to try to create something that could give bright to a big hard work done by her and her article's mates. This was going to be a difficult work, because there were 13 (yes, 13) very interesting documents, and they will be read by people interested in actual problems in the use of mobile devices, internet, electronic commerce and new emerging technologies and trends.

When you are trying to write a book about some matter, the first think that comes to your mind is "Will be these things interesting for my colleagues? 'Cause they are for me!"

Anabela lives in an actual and complex world, travelling much of her time, not for enjoy but for work. Her job makes herself to contact with a lot of people working in same skills, problems, technologies and trends.

I would like to talk about my friend and her incredible and extensive work, but this can be done talking about the papers on this book, because they are a good extension of her work.

Analysing the titles is possible to see a wide variety of topics on the same subject or, probably I should say topics within topics, because the subject is the Human-Technology Interaction. And they go from a deep analysis of the gender problem in HTI to the new trends on these computer world.

And I would like to underline an idea that came to me reading the abstracts "Does the ubiquity and immortality came with internet?", what an estrange idea!. Is this weird?, no it is not. If we talk with our neighbours, we can observe that, normally, for them, our "obvious" computer world is a deep black hole for them, where too many things can be done, but they do not know how (sometimes me neither!). Then we live in many different worlds and we can be dead but we can be still alive.

Is it possible to discover some of these secrets reading this book?, yes, I think so!, I am sure!, only let me repeat 3 titles (randomly taken): "Technology Satisfaction in an Academic Context: Moderating effect of Gender", actual, fresh, with a deep analysis of a big actual problem as is the satisfaction and gender; another one "Insights into the culture of young Internet users – emerging trends: Move over Gen Y, here comes Gen Z!", might I repeat my epithets?, it's clear, we are moving so fast, and it is so important for us to be "plugged" to the reality of the world we are trying to prepare as professors, our students shouldn't go ahead of us, we should go before them to guide and help them on the way; other more "Exploring M-commerce and Social Media: A comparative Analysis of Mobile Phones and Tablets", more and more about actual problems and, yes!, solutions.

And, to put a little more of honey on your lips, please you should read the rest of this book.

Manuel Pérez Cota
University of Vigo, Spain

Preface

When a research paper is well written and the topic is important to help us to understand what are the concerns in today's society, it is our duty, as editors, to recover them and follow the trend in order to see the most update research and discussions. This is what was in our minds when this book was prepared. In fact, this publication – *Research Paradigms and Contemporary Perspectives on Human-Technology Interaction* – comprises some of the best articles published in the International Journal of Technology and Human Interaction in 2014. Authors were asked to improve and update all of them, incorporating the latest discussions and results. They are complemented with some original work that bring some light to this field. As said, it is our purpose to offer the reader the most recent research and discussion concerning the trends and advancements in the area of Human-Technology Interaction.

IJTHI

The first issue of the *International Journal of Technology and Human Interaction* appeared in 2005 due to the increasing research being done in the area where technology and human meet. At that time researchers understood that the success or failure of the implementation of technology, was not due to the technology itself but to interactions between the technology and the user. Furthermore, the problem of technology and human interaction covers all the fields and aspects of our lives, such as education, profession, private, leisure time, just to mention a few.

Taking this into consideration, the journal provides a platform for leading research that addresses issues of human and technology interaction in all domains. The journal aims therefore at publishing interdisciplinary research, including aspects from a wide variety of disciplines. These disciplines may range from more technical ones such as computer science, engineering or information systems to non-technical descriptions of technology and human interaction from the point of view of sociology, psychology, education, communication, management, marketing or even philosophy. The journal also aspires to provide a publication outlet for research questions and approaches that are novel and may find it difficult to be published in established journals following a rigid and exclusive structure. It is open to all research paradigms, being empirical or conceptual, but requires that they are accessible and reflected. Submissions of high quality syntheses across research in different specialties that are interesting and comprehensible to all members of the information systems community and related disciplines are also welcome.

The journal is open to several topics that may include (but are not limited to) the following:

- Adoption of online learning
- All issues related to the interaction of technology and humans, either individually or socially
- Anthropological consequences of technology use
- Ethical aspects of particular technologies (e.g., e-teaching, ERP, etc.)
- Experiential learning though the use of technology in organizations
- HCI design for trust development
- Influence of gender on the adoption and use of technology
- Interaction and conversion between technologies and their impact on society
- Intersection of humanities and sciences and its impact on technology use
- Normative questions of the development and use of technology
- Online Education
- Perceptions and conceptualizations of technology
- Phenomenology of e-government
- Philosophy of Technology
- Questions of computer or information ethics
- Relationship of theory and practice with regards to technology
- Responsibility of artificial agents
- Shaping of e-commerce through law and culture
- Social impact of specific technologies (e.g., biometrics, SCM, PGP, etc.)
- Social shaping of technology and human interaction research
- Technological risks and their human basis
- Technology assessment of software / hardware development
- Technology-Enhanced Learning
- Value of intellectual capital in knowledge management

and all other issues related to the interaction of technology and humans, either individually or socially.

The IJTHI is also attentive to the trends and changes in society and from time to time organizes special issues that cover, discuss and deal with special and particular topics.

Nevertheless the topics covered by the journal are not confined to those mentioned above. Editors are aware that this is a very dynamic field and are open to welcome new topics and discussions.

ABOUT THIS BOOK

Before inviting the reader to explore the articles in this book I would like to present some of the concerns that were covered by the several authors that decided to submit their work to this journal.

PERSPECTIVES ON HUMAN-TECHNOLOGY INTERACTION

Everyone agrees that nowadays information technology (IT) and information systems (IS) are part of our lives and many of the human actions are linked by IT/IS taking into consideration knowledge exchange using all means at men's disposal. Even if we consider individuals, professionals or social media as whole, interactions between the technology and humans are increasingly studied and exploited. The interests for exploring in-depth this subject are multiple and these concern (but are not limited to):

- Collecting information for research development and innovation purposes, in general or particular cases;
- Improving technologies in order to comply with human requirements aiming to develop more useful tools;
- Describing or predicting human behavior as IT/IS's consumers with the objective to improve technological abilities and /or influence attitude in different processes (e.g. decision making etc.) on the market;
- Establishing insights and new trends about human-technology interaction.

The collection of the selected articles from 2014 comprises studies and discussions about information technology, mainly in terms of mobile services, software or different websites' interface with people addressing topics such as: usability, convenience, intention to use, privacy concern, vigilance, information and human actions within a professional environment or social media.

Overall the works introduce themes that developed, in a lesser or greater way, the relationships between non-technical factors that influence information technology strategies at the confluence of marketing and social sciences within the technical ones.

An interdisciplinary approach is used in order to add emphasis on:

- Consumer's perception on mobile technology;
- Consumer's trust related to information technology;
- Knowledge exchange for software development;
- Social computing through urban informatics;
- Perceived or existent cost-benefit ratio associated information;
- Quality of the information shared;
- Technology acceptance and/or satisfaction effect through its usage;
- online reputation;
- E-Consumer or m-consumer behavior patterns;
- Society features and other social media related to technology information.

RESEARCH PARADIGMS

As for the research paradigms, the majority of the articles published in 2014 adopted a qualitative approach with some case studies, observation and interviews and content analysis. Nevertheless, the use of questionnaires and quantitative analysis was also used but in a lesser proportion. Some of the best examples are presented in the selection in this book.

THE STRUCTURE OF THIS BOOK

One of the most dynamic areas of modern development is information systems and their use and impact in our daily lives. Each year, month, not to say day, we witness the emergence of new technologies, or new features and characteristics of older technologies that, in some way change the way we communicate, interact, express ourselves, play, and work. In this book, we present 13 works that illustrate how things are changing in today's world.

Section 1: The Use of Social Media and its Impact in the Human Life Dimension

We cannot deny that social media has impact in our lives. We use it to communicate, to interact, to have access to information before taking decisions. We use it to keep in touch with family and friends. To be consumers. In order to bring some light to this discussion, we selected five articles dealing with different topics and perspectives. The first one, Chapter 1, "Exploring M-Commerce and Social Media: A Comparative Analysis of Mobile Phones and Tablets," presents an exploratory qualitative research examining separately mobile phones and tablets and the use of social media, in the context of m-commerce. Results show factors with both positive and negative impact. Authors also discuss business opportunities enabled by social media for m-commerce.

Chapter 2, "The Impact of Online Training on Facebook Privacy," deals with the Facebook exposure to privacy and security risk and Facebook vigilance. Results show that narcissists, younger users and women face more risks than men since they are more active in the social media.

Chapter 3, "Play It Like Beckham! The Influence of Social Networks on E-Reputation – The Case of Sportspeople and Their Online Fan Base," explores the creation of e-reputation among sportspeople and its determinants.

Chapter 4, "Search Media and Identity: Understanding Identity Communication and Creation through Social Media," explores the relationship between social media and identity by reviewing theoretical frameworks and empirical studies on the topic.

Finally, Chapter 5, "Insights into the Culture of Young Internet Users: Emerging Trends – Move Over Gen Y, Here Comes Gen Z!," focuses on the internet user behaviour of young people. The aim is to understand the online behaviour ad activities undertaken by Generation Y and Generation Z

Section 2: The Importance of Web Accessibility and Public Services

Web accessibility is one of the concerns when it comes to public services and e-government. What kind of information should be available to citizens? In which format? And due to the diversity of the target, how should this be done in order to meet everyone's expectations and needs? These are some of the questions that cross our minds when we talk about web accessibility. In this section, we selected 2 chapters that discuss this problem and offer one possible solution to each of the problems being solved.

For instance, in Chapter 6, "A Multi-Perspective Theoretical Analysis to Web Accessibility," authors discuss the problem and present entities views with responsibility in the area. The understanding of the interaction between all the perspectives involved help to realize the way it will go, which carries with it great challenges and opportunities widely explores in this work.

Chapter 7, "Web Accessibility and Transparency for Accountability: The Portuguese Official Municipal Websites," examines the availability of local government financial reports on the website for a sample of 86 Portuguese municipalities of varying size and presents the results of a quantitative evaluation of the web accessibility levels of official municipal websites homepages based on W3C Guidelines, using an automatic tool.

Section 3: Technology Acceptance and Satisfaction

In this section, reader may find a selection of articles dealing with more technical aspects having impact on human behaviour and response.

In Chapter 8, "Information Technology Progress Indicators: Research Employing Psychological Frameworks," authors examine employed theoretical models from psychological research on human waiting to develop specific hypotheses related to the deisgn of progress indicators.

Chapter 9, "Technology Satisfaction in an Academic Context: Moderating Effect of Gender," studies the satisfaction among students in using wireless internet for learning and research purposes.

Finally, Chapter 10, "Continuance Use Intention of Mobile Internet Services: Does Gender Matter?," explores the moderating effect of gender on the intention to continue using internet services in an everyday context. Gender differences are examined. Findings show that female users expressed a stronger need for perceived usefulness and ease-of-use than male users, while male users expressed a significant need for perceived enjoyment.

Section 4: What Future is Hidden behind IS/IT?

Can the past predict the future? Can we have a glimpse of what can be based on what we have done? The last section contains two papers that discusses trends related with concepts related with society and our desire of being immortal while human. The last papers wraps the discussion around human computer interaction by summing up the genesis of the field, the enablers and constrainers, the perspectives and approaches in order to give the reader a comprehensive overview of this area.

In Chapter 11, "The Fashionable Functions Reloaded: An updated Google Ngram View of Trends in Functional Differentiation (1800 – 2000)," using the updated Google Book corpus dataset generated in July 2012, authors analyze the largest available corpus of digitalized books to review social macro trends such as the secularization, politicization, economization and mediatization of society.

Chapter 12, "Human Digital Immortality: Where Human Old Dreams and New Technologies Meet," proposes a prospective opposed to the one that advocates that technology alienates people. Authors believe that modern technology and human nature converge.

Finally, Chapter 13, "Design of Human-Computer Interaction Systems with Directions and Applications: Human-Computer Interaction," provides an overview on the subject of Human-Computer Interaction.

Before closing this preface, I would like to say that these papers represent a small part of what can be seen and read in the *International Journal of Technology and Human Interaction* (IJTHI). They represent the hard work of some of our researchers, a little bit from all over the World. They also represent a big effort to bring to the reader what the most recent and updated is being done in those areas. I hope that you enjoy reading them as much as I enjoyed preparing this compilation for you.

Anabela Mesquita
CICE – ISCAP/IPP and Algoritmi Centre, Portugal

Acknowledgment

As editor I would like to acknowledge the help of those involved in the collation and review of this book, without whose unstinting support the project could not have been completed. A further special note goes to all staff of IGI Global whose contribution throughout the whole process has been invaluable. Thanks to all those who provided constructive and comprehensive reviews.

Special thanks go to Chia-Wen Tsai, my co-editor-in-chief of the *International Journal of Technology and Human Interaction*, whose help and support in the development of the journal as well as of this book is sincerely very valuable.

Thank you all.

Anabela Mesquita
CICE – ISCAP/IPP and Algoritmi Centre, Portugal

Section 1
The Use of Social Media and its Impact in the Human Life Dimension

Chapter 1
Exploring M–Commerce and Social Media:
A Comparative Analysis of Mobile Phones and Tablets

Panagiota Papadopoulou
University of Athens, Greece

ABSTRACT

The proliferation of mobile phones and tablets shape a new arena for online commercial activity with unprecedented opportunities and challenges. In this omnipresent mobile environment, understanding consumer behavior constitutes a challenge for m-commerce vendors, as they seek to understand factors that affect it, positively and negatively, and to integrate social media in their mobile strategy and across mobile devices. This paper presents an exploratory qualitative research examining separately mobile phones and tablets and the use of social media, in the context of m-commerce. The results of our qualitative analysis show important factors for m-commerce and social media adoption and use, highlighting the similarities and differences between mobile phones and tablets. Our qualitative results also reveal factors having a negative effect to m-commerce, for both mobile devices. Business opportunities enabled by social media for m-commerce and how these can be leveraged in this promising multiple-device mobile context are also discussed.

INTRODUCTION

Mobile commerce presents tremendous growth, following and even outpacing the hype of electronic commerce. As smartphones and tablets gain increasing adoption, mobile users can engage in commercial activities anytime, anywhere. According to recent studies, mobile devices, phones and tablets, rapidly gain e-commerce purchase share in 2016 at the expense of desktop computers (Custora Ecommerce Pulse, 2016). Mobile commerce revenue continuously increases year by year, reaching 150 billions of US dollars with purchases on mobile phones and tablets being predicted to double by 2018 (Norton, 2015).

Although m-commerce was initially based on smartphones, the more recent advent of tablets has extended the mobile market, adding a new dynamic channel for online transactions and purchases that

DOI: 10.4018/978-1-5225-1868-6.ch001

contributes to the further development of m-commerce. The percentage of the e-commerce traffic originating from mobile devices, including both smartphones and tablets is 39% for the last quarter of 2015 (Monetate Ecommerce Quarterly, 2016). Orders from mobile channels account for 30% of all e-commerce orders, with 20% coming from smartphones and 10% from tablets (Custora Ecommerce Pulse, 2016). Mobile phones and tablets together constitute a very powerful tool for m-commerce and have become an integral part of the mobile environment.

Social media favour such progression in the way consumers behave with their smartphones and tablets. Social media offer new opportunities for marketing and sales to companies, especially since they can be used anytime, anywhere thanks to mobile devices. Facebook, Twitter as well as more recent social media which focus on images, video or sounds, i.e. rich media, such as Instagram, Pinterest or Snapchat, are widely used globally, with the latter gaining increasing adoption compared to the other two. Their simple interface that easily shows important and recent information with brief content comprising images, short text or videos makes them a powerful tool to enhance sales. Mobile devices and social media, as well as their combination, provide strong business opportunities for a vivid and effective communication with customers.

Consumer behaviour has fundamentally changed since the prevalence of smartphones and tablets in daily activities and habits. The advent and adoption of tablets has further reinforced the power of mobile consumers. With easy access to user reviews, expert opinions, price comparisons, and other emerging facilities, consumers are enabled to make thorough assessments of available products and services in an increasing number of categories. For marketers, this suggests a need for a totally new way of thinking about how to influence consumers. The challenge also holds for information systems developers, as m-commerce websites and social media have to be carefully implemented and used in order to become effective marketing tools. Therefore, these two groups of actors, marketers and information systems developers, have to work "hand in hand".

The aim of this paper is to investigate the use of m-commerce and social media on mobile phones and tablets and how m-commerce can benefit from social media and location-based applications in each of these devices. In this direction, we present an exploratory qualitative study on consumer perceptions and behaviour in using m-commerce, mobile social media and their combination, in both mobile phones and tablets. Based on the interviews conducted for the study, we seek to understand factors that affect m-commerce as well as the use of social media on mobile devices and for m-commerce, comparing mobile phones and tablets. A discussion of our findings concludes the paper.

SMARTPHONES VS TABLETS

The worldwide adoption of smartphones and tablets as well as their continuous use, independent of time and place constitute typical characteristics of contemporary life. Undoubtedly smartphones prevail in terms of ownership and usage on a global scale compared to tablets. According to recent studies, 78% of Internet users own a smartphone while tablet owners are 47%. Mobile phone adoption is widespread, especially in young population, with smartphones being preferred by mobile Internet users aged 16-24, while tablets are more popular in older and more mature populations (Mander, 2015).

As mobile commerce experience becomes increasingly familiar to users of mobile devices, evidence shows that mobile users tend to proceed in conducting purchases online more from tablets than from smartphones. M-commerce revenues are expected to be higher through tablets, estimated to reach 87 billions USD, than through smartphones, for which revenues are projected to 60 billions USD (Statista, 2015). Tablets present an impressively higher conversion rate compared to smartphones. According to Monetate Ecommerce Quarterly (2016), the conversion rate to add-to-basket/cart and sale was 3.75% for tablets and 1.53% for smartphones.

Tablets seem to sit in the middle of mobile phones and traditional desktop or laptop computers. Combining features of both types of devices, they offer the mobility and portability of a mobile phone with an easy-to-read and use screen of a desktop/laptop. Tablets seem to offer a richer user experience than smartphones in terms of the content that can be made available to the user such as videos and photos of large size and high quality. Moreover, a tablet might allow for more interactivity and aesthetic appeal when browsing an m-commerce website than a smartphone.

Although tablets seem to excel in relation to smartphones, because of their shape and size they cannot be practically used in any occasion, with the same ease as smartphones, especially comparing the place and the time of the day that they are used. Whereas smartphones are smaller and lighter and thus used in the street as well as anywhere, anytime, tablets seem to be more restricted in their usage, and are used mostly indoors or at home, as shown in Norton (2015). In a similar vein, studies show that the peak usage of tablets is between 7 pm and 10 pm whilst smartphones are used continuously throughout the duration the day (Husson, 2014).

On the other hand, smartphones seem to gain ground again against tablets. The average smartphone screen size has risen to 6 inches, rendering the available display area more suitable and convenient, if not ideal, for reading. The biggest smartphones are similar to small tablets. More mobile applications are designed for smartphones than for tablets. Smartphones have a better average battery life than tablets. They have better quality cameras than tablets and are more convenient for taking photos. The distinction between tablets and smartphones gradually blurs, as phone screen size increases and tablet screen size decreases (Taylor, 2015).

With smartphones and tablets having different characteristics which create different opportunities and different challenges, it is imperative to examine the use of both of these devices, juxtaposing consumers perceptions and behavior on mobile phones and tablets. A comparative approach is needed in order to facilitate the comprehension of how each mobile device can be separately used in m-commerce and in conjunction with social media and how these devices should be treated by online vendors as an integral part of their m-commerce strategy.

SMARTPHONES, TABLETS AND SOCIAL MEDIA

Mobile users are increasingly accessing social networks using their mobile devices. A study among mobile users in the USA, Canada, UK, France, and Germany found that most had accessed social networks using a mobile device, ranging from 94% for those 18-29 years old to 75% of those 50-64 years old (Adobe 2013). In fact, Facebook, the leader of social networks, was the second most visited web site that was accessed by smartphones and was the top smartphone app in the USA (ComScore, 2013). In the end of 2015, more than half of Facebook users accessed Facebook only via a mobile device and projections show that by 2018 over 75% of Facebook users worldwide will access Facebook through their mobile phone (Statista, 2016a). Overall 60% of consumers' time spent on social media is on mobile devices, smartphones and tablets (Adler, 2014). In the US these figures are higher with 67% of the time spent on social media being on smartphones and 12% on tablets (Statista, 2016b). Social media becomes the top Internet activity, with the average mobile Facebook user spending about 30 minutes per day on the social network (Statista, 2016a).

The increasing adoption of mobile technology and social media in all customer segments sets the ground for location-based services, enabling the successful targeting of customers, in the right place at the right time. Through location-based services, a consumer can receive a location-based alert about a special offer available for one hour only on his/her favourite wine when he or she is close to a wine retailer, assuming the consumer has opted in. As 71% of social media users accept to share their location, there is a challenge for online vendors to seize the potential offered by location-based marketing (Banks, 2015; Taylor, 2015). In this vein, mobile vendors should take advantage of the location data and the real time interaction enabled by the combined use of mobile devices and social media, in order to understand consumer behaviour and develop tailored offers and advertising messages.

However, while location-based services may be attractive to marketers, permission from the consumer needs to be taken into consideration. Even with permission, marketers need to manage their mobile marketing such that the communications are not seen as too intrusive (Lamarre, Galarneau & Boeck, 2012). This applies equally to m-commerce. Mobile phones and tablets are very popular and accompany their owner in almost all everyday activities, regardless of time and space. Because many decisions related to shopping or other actions are made on the move, in various occasions, such as in restaurants, airports, retail stores, these devices can facilitate decision-making and purchases since people usually have them in their hands. The information search related to a product or service sometimes may lead to a purchase and sometimes may not, but can still be critical to a purchase.

The speed of evolution of social media and mobile devices does not always allow companies to realize the implications of new consumer behavior trends or to cope with the challenges they face in the mobile web market. Thus, there is a need to carefully examine and understand how mobile phones and tablets and social media can effectively be used for m-commerce, considering the different requirements and possibilities of each mobile device.

INTEGRATING SOCIAL MEDIA IN M-COMMERCE

The potential benefits of m-commerce for generating sustainable profits need further exploration when used in conjunction with social media. In order to achieve profitability and sustainability in the highly competitive m-commerce environment, companies should understand consumer behavior in mobile devices and how it is intertwined with the use of social media on these devices. The combination of social media with mobile devices can be extremely powerful for m-commerce. The enormous social media user base can be leveraged to increase mobile vendors' customer base. M-commerce companies need to integrate social networks in their business strategy from both a technical and marketing perspective, offering a new compelling customer experience than can generate traffic and sales. Social media is not only a mobile commerce tool but there is an emerging tendency for convergence of social media and commerce, as consumers increasingly conduct purchases through social media (Evans, 2016)

At the same time concerns regarding privacy in m-commerce remain the same as in e-commerce, since they both involve transactions in an online environment. In the mobile context, privacy concerns could be considered as even higher risk, taking into account the use of social media, location-based applications and the information that is collected and can be available through them. Establishing trustworthiness remains very important for online companies in the mobile environment, and social media can help in this direction allowing for positive word-of-mouth. Thanks to their ease of use, social media can encourage shoppers to provide positive ratings and recommendations about the goods or services of a vendor on its public social media's page, an action which could be rewarded.

Whether m-commerce will surpass electronic commerce in growth and scope remains to be seen, with privacy being a central axis for its adoption. Using their mobile device for numerous activities consumers share information, without being as reluctant as when using a laptop for example. They also offer websites the possibility to locate them, and thus, vendors can target them more easily. This tendency and willingness of users to disclose information through social media and location-based applications seems to create a paradox in terms of privacy concerns in m-commerce.

People freely give out information, for example when they upload a picture from their mobile phone or tablet to their social media, in order to drive traffic to their website or to their social media page. This is so important that some social media such as Snapchat, Pinterest or Instagram use pictures as the basis of their business model. With their heaviest users being teenagers and young adults, most of them addicted to their smartphones and tablets, these social media seem important to take into account in an m-commerce strategy. They constitute promising platforms for customer engagement and retention which can help an m-commerce website and its products to be known in a target audience, representing opportunities for both consumer-focused and business-to-business companies. These social media allow an m-commerce website to connect directly with current and future consumers—developing a relationship that leads to sales, as consumers tend to buy from retailers they feel like they can relate to and "know" the brand: When you show the product as best as you can, providing good quality of image compression and fast downloading, customers tend to feel in a better situation with the seller since nothing is hidden.

Transparency on social media such as Instagram, Pinterest or Snapchat allows online vendors to build a relationship with their customers as well as drive traffic to their website. For instance, Instagram can help to target a particular audience and engage the latter in a conversation, in order to develop a relationship that can lead to very good word-of-mouth and to loyalty. In a highly saturated e-commerce world, savvy consumers tend to buy from retailers they know and trust and social media can be used as a shortcut to build that feeling.

Given the early stage of research, commonly accepted prescriptions for the future of social media and m-commerce have not yet been established. In this direction, this paper attempts an exploratory qualitative approach of m-commerce and social media adoption and their joint potential, examining mobile phones and tablets.

RESEARCH METHOD

Our research method includes two separate studies which have been conducted in order to gain a cumulative understanding of consumer perceptions and behaviour related to the use of mobile devices, social media and m-commerce; the first study focused on the use of mobile phones and the second study focused on the use of tablets. An exploratory qualitative approach was applied for both studies. Qualitative research is generally used to interpret meanings of a matter of interest or to gather further insight on the matter (Myers, 1997). In the attempt to gain an in-depth understanding of the topics under study and since, to our knowledge, research combining social media and m-commerce in mobile phones and tablets is scarce, an exploratory qualitative approach, with a survey-based method using short interviews seemed appropriate.

The main objective of this research is to investigate the use of m-commerce and the use of social media on mobile devices, mobile phones and tablets, and if and how users are influenced in shopping on m-commerce websites by using these social applications. In this direction, the studies have been conducted asking questions related to the following topics:

- Use of social media on mobile devices,
- Mobile phones and tablets,
- Use of mobile devices for shopping,
- Emotions and feelings felt following the visit of a mobile commerce website,
- Factors affecting behaviour with mobile devices and social media and
- Perception of an "ideal" m-commerce website.

Questions were structured and open, allowing for short duration interviews. Every interview, the duration of which ranged from 20 to 25 minutes, was analyzed resulting in verbatims and coded answers. We adopted a neutral attitude when interviewing the respondents so as not to influence their answers. Participants were questioned without being allowed to look at their mobile phone or tablet. This was to ensure that they answered only using their memory to access the information reinforcing their use of the combination of social media and m-commerce websites of their choice.

Participants

We used two samples for our research, one sample for collecting data on mobile phones and one for data collection about tablets. The samples comprise students aged 18-31 years, from various countries, equally divided into male and female. Sample selection was primarily based on qualitative criteria, with a mix of age, gender and socio-professional background, in order to obtain a homogeneous sample.

We used "theoretical sampling," also called "theoretical saturation," to attain the right number of interviewees. This method refers to the continuation of sampling and data collection until no new conceptual insights are generated. At this point, repeated evidence for conceptual categories were provided, using keywords (Bloor & Wood, 2006). We began interviewing students and, at some point, the interviewees' answers were repeated so there was no more need to interview more. Therefore, following the criteria of data saturation (Mucchielli, 1991, p.114), we interviewed 21 participants for mobile phones and 18 participants for tablets.

Students are deemed suitable as a sample even if their use has often been questioned in terms of their appropriateness. They share many characteristics with the profile of mobile Internet users' population. As shown by several studies, mobile Internet and social media users tend to be young adults, with the use of social networking and internet on smartphones within the age groups of 18–29 years rising up to 91% (Smith, C, 2015). In addition, the main age group of online consumers, spending more time and money in online commerce is 18-34 (Smith, A, 2015). Hence, although our sample presents a bias towards younger subjects, it can arguably be acceptable as representative of mobile users.

Data Analysis

Data were analyzed using a content analysis technique by coding the responses after transcription of the interviews. Due to the sensitivity of the subject matter and the possibility of interviewees having eventually difficulties expressing their emotions, the transcriptions were verbatim to enable accurate interpretation of responses (Jennings, 2005). Transcripts included speech hesitations, such as ''ohhh'' and ''euhhh'' where appropriate; paralinguistic features of speech were also recorded to help to qualify meaning (Gillham, 2005).

The qualitative data from the transcripts were analysed with a table, in which all the questions extracted from the interview guide were written. The data from each sample were analyzed separately, using one table for the mobile phone sample and one table for the tablet sample. A table file was used for each respondent, in both samples. Rows in this table indicated the different themes or constructs emerged from the interview guide. If a construct appeared while reading the transcript of a respondent's interview, a "1" figure was placed in a result column, in the row of the particular construct. Subsequently, we summarised the results from our respondents in order to have a cumulative understanding of the answers collected. We grouped the "result" columns of all our respondents in a final table, where each construct had at least a "1". This corresponded to a set of 21 columns for mobile phone sample and 18 columns for the tablet sample, either with "1" figures or empty. In this way, each construct had a score for each respondent's table. Then the respondents tables were concatenated in a summary one, for each sample, enabling us to use the "1" columns to add rows and finally write the results obtained from the addition of "1" figures.

In order to apply the content analysis properly, coding must effectively be done by multiple coders who are oblivious of research questions, and inter-coder reliability must be checked to demonstrate consistency of coding (Miles & Huberman, 1994). For this reason, two coders, blind to the research questions, were hired. Inter-coder reliability was checked to reinforce the reliability of this technique.

The interview transcripts were then coded and analyzed thematically using KH Coder[1], a content analysis software program, in order to validate the results of the method based on matrices and tables used to condense the qualitative data. For this purpose, the texts of the interviews were concatenated into a single document. With the text thereby captured, the verbatim analysis was performed thanks to the "KH-Coder" software enabling to rapidly identify themes and their relations and calculate the co-occurrence frequency of themes. This method permitted us to compare the results from our tables with those obtained from KH-Coder. No significant differences were found between them, reinforcing the validity of our coding and analysis. It also enabled us to formulate assumptions linking answers and respondents profiles.

RESULTS

In this section, we present the results of the exploratory qualitative analysis of the interview data, following the method explained previously. The results are presented for mobile phones and tablets with regard to the emerged categories of themes and related topics. A summary of the results for each device and their comparison is presented in Table 1 and Table 2 respectively.

Table 1. Summary of results by device

Theme	Construct	Mobile Phone	Tablet
Use of mobile devices	**SMS** **WWW** **Social media** **GPS**	■ Sending short messages ■ Surf the Internet (look for information) ■ Finding "information when needed" ■ Social media ■ Global Positioning System (GPS) "ON"	■ WWW ■ Information search ■ Social media ■ GPS
Use of social media on mobile devices	**Social media on mobile device**	■ Use them on their mobile phone to ■ contact their community ■ Get in touch with people ■ Stay in contact with people	Use them on their tablet to keep connected with community
	Social media and location-based services	■ Received an invitation for a commercial proposal ■ Contacted via Bluetooth with offers	■ Not received an invitation for a commercial proposal ■ Positive attitude for promotions
Use of mobile devices for M-commerce	**Use of mobile device for shopping**	■ not very common ■ prefer laptop ■ low ease-of-use ■ connection speed ■ high security and privacy concerns	■ common ■ preferred for shopping over mobile phone ■ convenience ■ larger screen ■ low security and privacy concerns
	Reputation	■ It has been heard from friends ■ Other people have already tested it	■ the website is well known and guaranteed ■ consumers advice
	Privacy	It respects our privacy when sharing information	Allow tracking when I trust the website
	Security	■ Presence of https ■ When there is a special safe paying system like paypal	Secure payment mechanism
	Products and services	■ Useful information ■ Lots of offers ■ Satisfying service ■ Benefits for using it ■ Product variety ■ Prices	■ Cheaper price ■ Interesting promotions ■ Large choice of products ■ Up-to-date ■ delivery
	Design and Intaraction	■ Appealing ■ Simplicity ■ User friendly ■ Aesthetics ■ Design is professional ■ Fast ■ practical ■ The website functions without problems on my mobile ■ Adapted for the screen of my mobile phone	■ Ease of use ■ Convenience ■ the time it takes to do a command, ■ ergonomics ■ Interactivity ■ interesting, relaxing interface ■ clear, light website
	Negative	■ slowness of the mobile website ■ difficulty of access ■ Website is not intuitive ■ I cannot read it on my mobile ■ It is dangerous for the security ■ Presence of advertisings ■ Offer of "bad products"	■ difficulty to navigate website ■ poor functionality ■ too complicated interface ■ when there is too much advertisement, too much information ■ difficult to quickly find what I am looking for

Use of Mobile Devices

Mobile Phones

All respondents own a mobile phone and are registered on one or several social media, such as Facebook, Twitter, YouTube and LinkedIn. Their activities on their mobile phone vary. The most common use of mobile phones is for surfing the Internet, followed by sending of messages (SMS) and use of the Global Position System (GPS). Respondents also use their mobile phone to go on Facebook and other social media, however, they do not seem to prefer to use mobile applications for social media.

When we asked respondents about what they think is important to use their mobile phone for apart from making calls and sending SMSs, most of them referred to the possibility to contact their community "for Facebook" (10/21). Respondents are also interested in using their mobile phone "to get in touch with people", while others mentioned the possible "use of the Internet" either in general, or more specifically, with the intention to "find information."

Tablets

Similarly, to mobile phone users, tablet users are also registered on one or several social media. Their activity on their tablet is for surfing the Internet, including using their social media and for using the GPS. The GPS of their tablet is "on" for a third of the respondents. When they use their tablet in conjunction with the GPS, they say "it helps me find my way to places and shows me where I am relative to where I want to go". Others find it "easier than a map and you can easily find any location", "to get the shop near by". We then asked them to explain why they didn't use this function, and their answers show various reasons. They may prefer their phone or laptop for this functions, or simply don't know what is the GPS option. Others don't use it "because of tracking issues and privacy". One person answered that it was "too complex" whereas another mentioned that "I just use it as a habit and I think it is convenient". An important reason comes from the connection: "I don't have 3G / 4G on it. It works just with wifi."

Use of Social Media on Mobile Devices

Mobile Phones

According to the interviews, social media help respondents to "keep informed" (4/21) and they are "easy to use" (2/21) as well as "interactive" (2/21). Respondents mentioned they were "happy to save time" (2/21) thanks to "convenience" (4/21) and finding "information when needed" (3/21). An "easy" use of their application (3/21), being "funny" (2/21), making them "free" (2/21), or helping them "not to feel lonely" (2/21) describes what respondents emotionally get with this type of application. Social media on the mobile phone also help them to reach "happiness" (2/21) and satisfy their "curiosity" (2/21), bringing "pleasure" (1/21) and "excitement" (1/21) to their everyday life. According to the respondents, social media must be "intuitive", for example permitting "an easy access to videos on Youtube" or "handy, easier to use than the usual homepage you have" (1/21). As respondents said, what would make them want to use social media on their mobile would be using social media on mobile to be "funny" (1/21), "quick" (1/21), "pleasant" (1/21), "useful" (1/21) and also the "aesthetics" (1/21).

Respondents were also asked to describe their experience and express their opinion about social media and location-based services on the mobile phone, when used by businesses to contact them. Only 3/21 respondents received an invitation for a commercial offer issued from a business thanks to the combined use of their GPS and social media. 2/21 referred to an experience they encountered and mentioned for example: "when I was on Facebook, a friend posted a link that I wanted to visit in order to take advantage of the same offer". Another one says "I have an application regarding stores, so I receive sometimes discounts and then when I am in the shop when I want to use the discount rate, I just show the message". Thus, some respondents already benefit from the conjoint use of social media and GPS embedded on their mobile phone. Bluetooth was also mentioned by one respondent: "I've been contacted via Bluetooth with offers when I was in shopping malls". In addition, respondents (6/21) referred to the use of SMS as a vehicle for being reached on their mobile phone. One of them said: "I receive SMS which offers me something if I answer to the SMS". Among these commercial proposals, 4/21 of respondents accepted them.

Tablets

Tablet users also use social media on their tablet in order to get informed about their social network community. They want to "be in touch." They enjoy using social media but they are not constantly connected on them. We narrowed the study to asking respondents to describe their experience and express their opinion about social media and location-based services on tablet, as used by businesses to contact them. Nobody among the 18 respondents had received an invitation for a commercial offer issued from a business thanks to the combined use of their GPS and social media, for example a message with an offer inviting them while walking in the street to come in a restaurant in order to drink a glass of wine. We then asked them what they thought of such an opportunity to get a free glass of wine. Here again, answers vary, ranging from people disliking this idea (5/18) to people finding it "very relevant" (13/18). People in favor of such a way of getting in touch mainly think that "it is a really good way to reach your possible customers by using social media suitably." On the other hand, negative answers mentioned the tracking aspect: "I can pay for my own wine. I don't like my Internet activity being tracked by someone else to receive a bunch of offers. Also, free wine is usually not that good." Privacy seems important for our sample of respondents. "It is a bit intrusive but depending upon if I have time I might check it out for curiosity sake." For some of them, it's a question of time: "As long as I have time, I may go have a try." When we asked them what they think about receiving this invitation through their mobile (smartphone/tablet), the majority showed privacy concerns, summarized by one respondent "I think that this restaurant is spying me."

In order to conclude with this topic, we asked our respondents what they thought about the use of this technology for promotion. Most of them think that "it is a great innovation which needs to be tested more in the real world and advertised more" while others think that "it's the modern form of flyers". But when our respondents were asked if the invitation they would receive could please them, most of them responded negatively, finding it "really annoying, too aggressive" and "kind of disturbing". Only 2/18 found that "it is an instant way to do the promotion, it's also very convenient both for buyers and sellers."

Use of Mobile Devices for M-Commerce

Among the 21 respondents, mobile shopping does not seem to be common. Respondents mainly use their mobile phone to buy music for iTunes and train tickets. They don't find it practical to make purchases from their mobile phone, preferring to use their laptop mainly for convenience purposes or due to confidentiality concerns.

In contrast, tablets are used for mobile commerce; the majority of respondents (11/18) use their tablets for shopping on Internet, a few times a month or between once and twice a year.

Shopping on Mobile Phone vs Computer

When respondents were asked about their preference regarding using their mobile phone rather than their computer to shop online, several topics emerged as important: ease of use, convenience, speed and security. Three respondents answered: "I feel more comfortable on a laptop" and another one found it "easier". For one respondent, "it just doesn't come to my mind to use it for this kind of things like shopping". In addition, a respondent referred to the speed of use in favor of the laptop instead of a mobile phone explaining: "I often have a better wifi connection with my laptop, so I don't want to waste time shopping with my mobile". As far as security is concerned, a respondent answered: "I am afraid that it´s more risky to give away my data on the mobile (credit card)" and another one said that shopping on its mobile phone "looks less secure."

On the other hand, other respondents replied that they would prefer to shop on their mobile rather than their laptop. Two respondents found using their laptop for shopping "less convenient". The speed of use has been mentioned too since the mobile "seems quicker", and also offers the "feeling of freedom". As it can be noted, perceptions of convenience, ease-of-use and speed can vary and be either positive for mobiles or positive for laptops, with respect to their use for shopping.

Shopping on Tablet vs. Mobile Phone

Shopping on tablets appears to be more preferable than shopping on mobile phones. Most respondents, 62% evaluated shopping on tablets positively, with their answers ranging from "important" to "very important" while 34% of the respondents rated shopping on tablets as "not important at all". This result shows that tablets can be viewed as more suitable for shopping than mobile phones, because of their ease-of-use and convenience, which is higher, thanks to their larger screen size, enabling a better user interaction and experience. Comparing mobile phones and tablets, 50% of the respondents think that their attention would not be the same if they had a mobile phone instead of a tablet. This further highlights the importance of the screen that is easier to use on tablets for online shopping activities.

Reputation

Mobile Phones

When respondents were questioned about what encourages them to trust a particular social media/ application over another, we observed that peer recommendations represent an important reason. Thereby, when "it is popular" (6/21) especially into the network of the respondent, when the "social media / m-commerce" application "has been heard from friends", 7/21 respondents seem more interested in the m-commerce website. Reputation is thus fundamental in the mobile market world. If "other people have already tested it", "when many other people trust it and have it" and "the people who use it and how often they use it" seem to be important for respondents. Reputation is also a factor for revisiting a mobile website, according to "the clients they have" (2/21). The m-commerce website "must be well-known" by 2/21 respondents in order to remain loyal to it.

Tablets

In a similar vein, reputation is also an important factor that encourages respondents to buy on a particular website when they use a tablet. As it was mentioned in the interviews, respondents would make a purchase from an m-commerce website on their tablet if "the website is well known and guaranteed". "Consumers' advice" would also be a reason for visiting a particular m-commerce website for tablet users. Describing their ideal shopping experience on tablet, respondents mentioned that the m-commerce website that they would use would be an "historical website" which is "known for its good service", which would be a reason to build loyalty for these customers.

Privacy and Security

Mobile Phones

Privacy and security concerns were found to be present in the mobile environment. "If it respects our privacy when sharing info" (4/21) while allowing to "stay in contact with people" (4/21), respondents are inclined to install a social media application or visit an m-commerce website. "Security" is important for 4/21 respondents and if "it looks safe (presence of https)" (1/21). Like for e-commerce, "when there is a special safe paying system like Paypal" (3/21) respondents accept to try to use a new m-commerce website. Security and privacy are considered necessary, as the "security/privacy level is high" in ideal m-commerce websites for 4/21 respondents, with a "secure website" being important for m-commerce for 3/21 respondents.

Tablets

Security and privacy issues are also considered by tablet users in their m-commerce activity, particularly regarding the payment mechanism and the credit card and personal data disclosed to a website. Regarding the topic of privacy, we asked our sample if they would allow a company to know where they are and make offers to them according to their location. A representative answer summarizes respondents view: "I generally switch off location tracking with my apps except where warranted. With this type of app where the customer gets discounts, I am happy for the app to track where I am." For those who leave the GPS functionality switched on, some respondents mentioned: "It's ok for me. Because if I allow the company to know where I am it's because I trust it." The feeling of privacy being violated seems again very important in this particular case.

Design and Interaction

Mobile Phones

Topics linked to the human-mobile interaction also emerged. 3/21 respondents evocate the "ease of use" as a condition for m-commerce. An "appealing" interface (2/21) with "simplicity" (5/21) and "user friendliness" (3/21) creates trust, with the latter, in particular, being mentioned as a factor making an m-commerce website ideal. In addition, "professionalism" (2/21) and the fact that the "design is professional" (1/21) seem important aspects for m-commerce. Speed is also essential as respondents would trust a website if "it's fast" (1/21), while they would also remain loyal to a "fast website" (2/21).

Similarly, factors related to ergonomics encourage users to re-visit a particular website on their mobile phone: "if it is practical" (6/21), "if the website functions without problems on my mobile" (4/21), if it is "easy to load" (4/21) and if the mobile website is "adapted for the screen of my mobile phone" (2/21). This is reinforced by 5/21 of the respondents who said that the m-commerce website should be "easy to use on a mobile phone" in order to remain loyal to it. Loyalty will also be based on a "good structure" for 1/21 respondent, on differentiation from other websites, being "something new" for 1/21.

Tablets

Ease-of-use emerges as a very important factor for tablets as well, affecting their usage. "Ease of use" and "convenience" were common answers from this sample, when respondents were asked what encourages them to buy on a particular website when they use a tablet. Similarly, ease of use was also mentioned by 67% of the respondents as an answer to which factors would encourage them to visit a particular website again when they used a tablet. Other factors that are important in influencing participants' intention to purchase or re-visit a website on their tablet include "the time it takes to do a command, faster" (32%) and "ergonomics" (32%) concerns.

Respondents were also questioned about what made them spend more time on a specific website when they used a tablet. Answers converge towards the same aspect: ease-of-use. They distinguish websites that are the "larger ones that are hard to navigate with a phone." "Interactivity and ergonomics" also reveal to be important assets to consider, in order to facilitate the visit of a website on a tablet. The use of tablets during particular times of the day also appears in answers such as the importance to give to "interesting, relaxing" interfaces, which will not interfere with the time spent with a tablet. An "easy-to-read" interface thanks to large fonts, short lines of text, large interlines and beautiful and large pictures reinforces this opportunity tablets can offer to users, in comparison to smaller screens of mobile phones. Other respondents emphasized the responsive aspect of the website, which should be taken into account for the design of m-commerce websites, mentioning "a clear, easy to use, light website" which would be essential for an ideal shopping experience on a tablet.

Products and Service

Mobile Phones

The website usefulness in terms of the offered service and products was also deemed as important. As respondents mentioned, they would revisit an m-commerce website "if I find useful information" (4/21) or if the website contains a "lot of offers". Other respondents based their judgment on the service received: "if I am satisfied" is foremost the necessary condition for 4/21 respondents, while if I am "happy with the service" is mentioned by 3/21 respondents. A "fast delivery" is important for 2/21 and if "I received the goods I bought on time" for 1/21. M-commerce website applications that offer benefits to the user such as 2/21 respondents say they "have advantages using it" will encourage the customers to remain loyal to an m-commerce website. The products offered on the m-commerce website were also found to be an important factor, affecting loyalty. A website with "many products" or a "large variety of products" (3/21) and "good products" and "prices lower than in a shop" (2/21) drives respondents' loyalty.

Tablets

The usefulness of the website and the prices of the products or services are important factors affecting purchases from m-commerce websites on tablets. Respondents are encouraged to buy on a particular website when they use a tablet "if the offer meets what I am looking for." For 66% of the respondents the possibility to find "cheaper prices" was the most important factor that would encourage them to visit a particular website again when they used a tablet. Making purchases from an m-commerce website on tablet is also encouraged by the possibility that "promotions are more interesting online", which seems important for 34% of the respondents. Other aspects such as "price, promotion" were also mentioned as answers about reasons for visiting a particular m-commerce website. Describing what an "ideal shopping experience on tablet" could be, our respondents mentioned the necessity for an m-commerce website to offer "a large choice of products" and provide an "up-to-date" content, with "auction availability". Aspects related to the service provided by the m-commerce website were also found to be significant, as it was mentioned that apart from "good prices", the ideal m-commerce website should have a "fast delivery" and "great conditions of delivery".

Negative Factors

Mobile Phones

On the other hand, some respondents are negative towards m-commerce and social media, as they "don't trust them at all" and "don't give much information to them" (2/21). Several factors seem to discourage users from re-visiting a particular website on their mobile phone. The most commonly mentioned factor relates to the "slowness" of the mobile website (5/21). If the "website is not intuitive" (3/21) or if the user has "difficulty of access" to it (3/21), it does not help to be used for m-commerce transactions. Once again, ergonomics appear as an important concern since a "not user friendly" application will hinder the use of the mobile website for 2/21 respondents. "If I cannot read it on my mobile […] it discourages me" reported 2/21 respondents. Other factors were related to unreliability of the m-commerce website (2/21), and "if it is dangerous for the security" (2/21). In addition "advertisings" (2/21) or offers of "bad products" were also mentioned as negative elements discouraging the revisiting of an m-commerce website by 2/21 respondents.

Finally, two respondents were negative towards loyalty, stating that "I cannot imagine being loyal to any m-commerce website" without specifying on which aspects they are against being loyal. This shows the importance of web analytics tools, also included in recent social media, enabling vendors to determine which of their contents drive the most click-throughs in their m-commerce website. The efficient measurement of the reach of the content of the m-commerce website and social media associated with it can help m-commerce vendors understand mobile consumer behavior and adapt to it.

Tablets

Although tablets seem to offer more convenience in their use for m-commerce and social media than mobile phones, tablet respondents expressed several negative comments regarding m-commerce and social media when using this device. Among the reasons which make our respondents quit a website when they use a tablet, is the difficulty to navigate it, combined with poor functionality or a too complicated interface. When the "interface is not user friendly" or "when there is too much advertisement, too much information," respondents can become "bored" because of an "ugly website", which is "not easy to navigate", and which is "not responsive design" making it "difficult to quickly find what I am looking for". Concerns in relation with human-machine interaction aspects are underlined by respondents, in line with their m-commerce purchase habits on tablets.

Table 2. Summary of comparison between devices

Use	Mobile phones and tablets are used for web browsing, information search, social media and GPS, with the latter being more preferred to be used on mobile phones than tablets. In addition, mobile phones are also used for calls and sms. Mobile phones are used more frequently than tablets, as they are used many times on a daily basis and in diverse locations, compared to tablets which are used less often and mostly at home, in line with Muller et al. (2015). GPS is used more on mobile phones than tablets, which can be attributed to the ubiquitous use of mobile phones. This implies that location-based services and applications should be primarily designed for mobile phone users.
Social media	Social media are used on both mobile phones and tablets. Mobile users use social media for contacting their community and social interaction. The use of social media combined with GPS for location-based services is quite common among mobile phone users but not in tablet users. Although tablet and mobile users do not have much experience of location-based offers and promotion messages, they seem to be positive towards them, as long as companies respect their privacy.
Shopping	Shopping on tablets appears to be more common than mobile phones. Mobile phones users opt for using their laptop for shopping because of the lack of convenience and slow connection of mobile phones. Shopping on mobile phones is also considered to be risky in terms of security and privacy. Tablets are used for online shopping and are preferred over mobile phones because of the ease-of-use emanating mainly from their larger screen size.
Reputation	Reputation is an important factor for mobile shopping both for mobile phone as well as for tablet users. A web site or application has to be well known in order to be trusted, with recommendations from friends and popularity among their friend network or in general being important, especially for mobile phone users.
Design	Mobile phone and tablet users want websites that are easy to use and navigate, fast, simple and appealing. Mobile phones, because of their screen size limitations create more difficulties in online activities and raise more requirements related to design and interaction issues. Tablets enable easy to read text and pictures that can be better viewed and enjoyed.
Privacy/ security	Privacy and security issues concern both mobile phone and tablet users. Respect of privacy and secure payment are the basic requirements of mobile users for engaging in m-commerce activity. Security and privacy concerns appear to be higher on mobile phones than tablets, possibly because of the insecurity created by the small size of the device.
Products and services	Useful information, variety and quality of products, attractive offers and promotions, cheap prices and fast delivery are the elements sought by mobile phone and tablet users in order to visit and spend time on an m-commerce website or make purchases. In either case, the number of products/services, the information given, the offers and the overall experience should meet the needs of mobile users.
Negative factors	Mobile phone and tablet users are negatively influenced by reading and navigation difficulties as well as excessive advertising. Reading and navigating problems are more important for mobile phone users, because of the smaller display area. At the same time, tablet users are more concerned with the nice appearance of the m-commerce website.

DISCUSSION

Following the presentation of the qualitative results of the exploratory study, a discussion of the findings is needed providing implications regarding the adoption and use of m-commerce and social media in mobile phones and tablets.

The most common requirement emanating from our results for social media and m-commerce is ease-of-use, in both mobile phones and tablets. Ease of use is a key factor for visiting a website, for making purchases on a particular website, encouraging users to visit a website again, and for spending more time on a website. Therefore, ease-of-use should be the design foundation of m-commerce websites so as to enable a pleasant shopping experience that will attract and keep mobile customers. A user friendly, easy-to-use interface, adaptable to the mobile device screen is essential in order to offering an interaction that will lead to purchases, repeat visits and loyalty.

Interface design is of high importance for both mobile phones and tablets. In particular, the demand for ease-of-use is higher in mobile phones because of the restrictions of the screen size. Designers should try to override these difficulties by offering websites and applications with fonts and text that is easy to read. They should also facilitate mobile user interaction by including buttons or other types of clickable interface areas that are easy to select, touch and manipulate through a touch screen of such small size. In parallel, mobile vendors should leverage the possibilities by the larger screen size of tablets and adapt their mobile website/application design to it, using multimedia content that can offer an advanced mobile customer experience. However, this should not happen at the expense of loading time of the online content, as, according to our findings, tablet users, as well as mobile phone users, do not enjoy slow interaction and trust and visit m-commerce websites which are fast in their usage and response. Photos, videos and other interactive media should thus be prudently applied, otherwise there is a risk that they will have a negative effect and thus a richer content, instead of being appealing, encouraging online transactions, will be deterrent to commercial activity for mobile consumers.

The importance of design and interaction as indispensable variables to be considered for social media and m-commerce is further highlighted by the fact that the negative factors emanating from the interviews against social media and m-commerce for mobile phone and tablet users were primarily associated with issues such as difficulty to read or navigate and complicated interfaces. Therefore, m-commerce vendors need to provide a pleasant and frictionless mobile user experience that can lead to purchases and avoid customer and revenue loss.

A good reputation is also found to be necessary for mobile phone and tablet users for visiting m-commerce websites and proceeding to purchases. Online vendors should thus invest in developing and maintaining their reputation, by creating it and preserving it during interaction with their customers, including the provision of guarantees regarding security and privacy. In this direction, social media can play a fundamental role as a reputation mechanism. Social media magnify the good quality of an m-commerce website, as satisfied customers become brand advocates. However, at the same time, customers will also tell others about a negative experience on social media. This is why social media must be taken into account when planning an m-commerce strategy. Consumers can be fast and effective to punish those who are slow to respond to questions or fail to deliver their purchases on time, for example. Marketers that stumble stand to lose business to rivals and become vulnerable to negative social buzz or negative e-Word-of-Mouth (e-WOM).

Based on our findings, it seems important for companies engaging in m-commerce to exploit the potential of social media in order to become known, increase their customer base and provide more interactive communication, gaining customer trust. Therefore, m-commerce companies should leverage the high reach, richness and interactivity of social media in order to promote positive awareness and reputation. Using social media, m-commerce vendors should also engage customers to become active participants in their marketing strategy. Social media should be used to offer a vivid and personalised mobile experience to mobile consumers so that they become members of a brand community and support the company with their loyalty, engaging in repeat purchases, as well as with referrals and viral content messages.

Respecting privacy is also essential for social media and m-commerce, in both mobile phones and tablets, and is part of a customer engagement strategy, mainly attained by having an explicit policy about the collection and use of customer data and by adhering to it. Another approach, which could possibly address the issue of privacy concerns, could be the use of personal or private data during a short period of time only. The general rule of Internet sharing thanks to social media, merely lies on the fact that if one puts something on the web, it will be there forever – even if it is deleted later. It could be reassuring to know that the content uploaded on social media will not remain there for ever and will be automatically deleted soon after it has been viewed. One of the unique key factors of success about Snapchat for example, is this "self-destructing" feature of photos. A few seconds after photos have been viewed, they disappear. This feature could be used by companies incorporating social media in their business model for promotional purposes. When a company promotes a product for a short period of time, a consumer chatting with a friend by sending photos can use this feature where the photo is instantly deleted seconds after it has been opened by the recipient to add some pressure on the scarcity of a product for example. Even if is still possible to capture content and save it permanently, m-commerce companies could efficiently use social media in this way to gain profit, and to increase customer trust and feeling of privacy.

M-commerce vendors should also take into account the range and quality of available products and services as well as their price, their delivery and the quality of the information provided. Although such issues are known from the e-commerce period, our findings remind us of their importance in the mobile setting. In addition, m-commerce vendors should bear in mind that the number of product choices offered and the amount of product information presented cannot follow a "the more the better" approach and should be appropriately selected and formatted so that they can effectively displayed on mobile devices, especially on the small screens of mobile phones.

Our results also imply that further research is needed to cover additional aspects that should be taken into account regarding use patterns and characteristics of mobile phones and tablets in terms of the location and the time of the day each device is used, as well as the combination with other activities, for example while watching television (Holz et al., 2015). These are factors that need to be considered for developing an m-commerce website and a mobile marketing strategy, especially when encompassing social media.

Another issue that deserves attention is the combination of multiple devices for performing commercial-specific activities and switching between devices in order to accomplish a task. For instance, in the context of hotel booking, Murhpy et al. (2016) found that customers search on several devices, including smartphones and tablets, but most reservation are made on PCs or laptops. Decision-making and shopping process can be split to different steps which can be accomplished in different devices before a purchase is completed. Preference of device for particular tasks and stages of transaction needs to examined and accommodated in website design and marketing strategies.

CONCLUSION

This paper presented an exploratory qualitative study examining consumers' perceptions and behaviour regarding the use of mobile phones and tablets for commercial transactions as well as the combination of social media and m-commerce. Our analysis shows that there is a growing use of social media on both mobile devices and a positive disposition towards m-commerce, especially when it is combined with social media. The most important factors that affect m-commerce and social media adoption and use can be summarized to interface design aspects, such as ease of use, ergonomics, professional appearance and speed, reputation from others that use them, products/services provided, privacy and security as well as device-specific factors mostly related to the convenience they offer for m-commerce and social media.

Having highlighted positive as well as negative factors related to the adoption of m-commerce and social media for m-commerce purposes for both devices, we believe that this research helps to improve the academic and practical understanding of how m-commerce and social media can be used in the mobile context, and how social media could be leveraged if not reinforced for m-commerce.

Our understanding of social media adoption for m-commerce has taken into account the insights from existing and future consumers and some pre-existing knowledge associated with social media-related business practices. The results of this exploratory research are indicative of the theoretical as well the managerial implications of this topic, especially the joint use of m-commerce and social media. Our data indicate that the critical links between the social media and customers will not be achieved without a deep understanding that trust, sharing tools to reinforce the reputation of an m-commerce asset and ease-of-use reveal to be key factors of success. This learning approach is essential during the adoption stage, at which m-commerce vendors should test actions on several media and monitor social activity in response to them. There is enormous potential for combining social media with the company website as a mode of sale referral and relationship development so long as customer requirements are seen as paramount. Our findings suggest ways in which social media could contribute to reach m-commerce objectives, by taking into account ease-of-use and design, reputation and privacy/security.

In addition, our data analysis shed a light on the similarities and differences between mobile phones and tablets regarding their use for m-commerce and social media. The special characteristics of each device can allow for different possibilities and opportunities and in parallel cause different problems and difficulties. Designing successful m-commerce websites and social media applications becomes a very demanding task in the multiple devices mobile setting. The advantages and disadvantages of each type of device should be taken into account for an integrated m-commerce and social media strategy, while at the same time enabling a differentiation between devices and among activities.

However, our research barely opens this prescriptive agenda and is not without limitations. Even though the sample size could look small, we thoroughly followed theoretical sampling to attain the right number of interviewees. Analysing comments and advice given by consumers on websites, twitter feeds, social media pages or fora in relation to a particular product, brand or service, could serve as a first step to understand more accurately what is shared by customers. Active m-commerce users browse and purchase a few items on the mobile web but many companies still do not have the proper interface and many consumers may still prefer a bigger screen than smartphones and tablets. As a result, it is not easy to link user comments from social media, or advice from peers to their browsing and purchasing history.

Further research is needed, firstly to interview more customers via mobile devices in order to use the "theoretical saturation" technique not only to social media and smartphone and tablet users but also and overall to existing m-customers. It would also be interesting to extend this study and its results with a confirmatory study, examining the factors affecting consumer perceptions and behaviour as well as the interrelationships among them. Studying the differences that pertain between shopping via smartphone, tablet, glasses or watches as mobile devices embedding social media should also bring interesting findings to the literature. The combination of the different mobile devices in consumer behaviour and social interaction and how each device can be used in various stages of the buying process and in various social media are also essential to be examined by researchers and practitioners, Finally, the efficacy of simultaneously employing geographical and contextualized targeting strategies in a mobile context could also be the topic of future research focused on the combined use of social media for m-commerce purposes.

REFERENCES

Adler. (2014). *Social Media Engagement: The Surprising Facts About How Much Time People Spend On The Major Social Networks*. Available at http://www.businessinsider.com/social-media-engagement-primer-2014-10

Banks, R. (2015). Location based mobile marketing. *Mobile Industry Review*. Available at http://www.mobileindustryreview.com/2015/02/location-based-mobile-marketing.html

Berthon, P. R., Pitt, L. F., Plangger, K., & Shapiro, D. (2012). Marketing meets Web 2.0, social media, and creative consumers: Implications for international marketing strategy. *Business Horizons*, *55*(3), 261–271. doi:10.1016/j.bushor.2012.01.007

Bloor, M., & Wood, F. (2006). *Keywords in Qualitative Methods: A Vocabulary of Research Concepts*. London: Sage Publications. doi:10.4135/9781849209403

Davis, F. D. (1989). Perceived Usefulness, Perceived Ease of Use, and User Acceptance of Information Technology. *Management Information Systems Quarterly*, *13*(3), 319–340. doi:10.2307/249008

eMarketer. (2013). *Tablets, smartphones drive mobile commerce to record heights*. Retrieved from http://www.emarketer.com/newsroom/index.php/emarketer-tablets-smartphones-drive-mobile-commerce-record-heights/

Evans, M. (2016). *Social media becomes more of a mobile commerce tool worldwide*. Available at http://www.mobilepaymentstoday.com/blogs/social-media-becomes-more-of-a-mobile-commerce-tool-worldwide/

Gillham, B. (2005). *Research Interviewing*. Maidenhead, UK: Open University Press.

Husson, T. (2014). *The Smartphone & Tablet Experience webinar*. Forrester Research.

Jennings, G. (2005). 'Interviewing: a focus on qualitative techniques. In B. Ritchie & P. Burns (Eds.), *Tourism Research Methods: Integrating Theory with Practice* (pp. 99–118). Cambridge, UK: CABI. doi:10.1079/9780851999968.0099

Lamarre, A., Galarneau, S., & Boeck, H. (2012). Mobile Marketing and Consumer Behavior Current Research Trends. *International Journal of Latest Trends in Computing*, *3*(1), 1–9.

Lenhart, A., Purcell, K., Smith, A., & Zickuhr, K. (2011). *Social Media and Young Adults*. Pew Internet & American Life Project. Retrieved from the Internet on February 2011 at http://www.pewinternet.org/Reports/2010/Social-Media-and-Young-Adults.aspx

Mander, J. (2015). *North America lags for smartphone ownership*. Available at http://www.globalwebindex.net/blog/north-america-lags-for-smartphone-ownership

Miles, M. B., & Huberman, A. M. (1994). *Qualitative Data Analysis: An Expended Sourcebook*. Thousand Oaks, CA: Sage Publications.

Moovweb. (2016). *7 Mobile Commerce Trends for 2016*. Available at http://www.moovweb.com/blog/mobile-commerce-trends-2016/

Mucchielli, A. (1991). *Les méthodes qualitatives, Que sais-je*. Paris: Presses Universitaires de France.

Murphy, H. C., Chen, M.-M., & Cossutta, M. (2016). An investigation of multiple devices and information sources used in the hotel booking process. *Tourism Management*, *52*, 44–51. doi:10.1016/j.tourman.2015.06.004

Myers, M. D. (1997, June). Qualitative Research in Information Systems. *Management Information Systems Quarterly*, *21*(2), 241–242. doi:10.2307/249422

Ngai, E. W. T., & Gunasekaran, A. (2007). A review for mobile commerce research and applications. *Decision Support Systems*, *43*(1), 3–15. doi:10.1016/j.dss.2005.05.003

Norton, S. (2015). *Forrester: Mobile Phone and Tablet E-Commerce to More Than Double by 2018*. Available at Wall Street Journal online edition: http://blogs.wsj.com/cio/2014/05/12/forrester-mobile-phone-and-tablet-e-commerce-to-more-than-double-by-2018/

Pelet, J.-É., Khan, J., Papadopoulou, P., & Bernardin, E. (2014). *Determinants of effective learning through social networks systems: an exploratory study. In Higher Education in the MENA Region: Policy and Practice*. IGI Global.

Quarterly, M. E. (2016). *Ecommerce Quarterly, Q4*. Available at monetate.com/research/

Smith, A. (2015). U.*S. Smartphone Use in 2015*. PewResearchCenter. Available at http://www.pewinternet.org/2015/04/01/us-smartphone-use-in-2015/

Smith, C. (2015). The surprising facts about who shops online and on mobile. *Business Insider*. Available at http://www.businessinsider.com/the-surprising-demographics-of-who-shops-online-and-on-mobile-2014-6

Statista. (2015). *U.S. mobile retail commerce revenue 2013-2019, by device*. Available at http://www.statista.com/statistics/249894/mobile-retail-commerce-revenue-in-the-united-states-by-device/

Statista. (2016a). *Statistics and facts about mobile social networks*. Available at http://www.statista.com/topics/2478/mobile-social-networks/

Statista. (2016b). *Distribution of time spent on social media content in the United States as of December 2015, by platform*. Available at http://www.statista.com/statistics/444986/social-content-platform-time-usa/

Taylor, B. (2015). *5 ways the smartphone is conquering the tablet.* Available at http://www.pcworld.com/article/2889275/phones/5-ways-the-smartphone-is-conquering-the-tablet.html

Taylor, R. J. (2015). *3 Steps for Location-Savvy Social Media Marketing.* Available at http://www.convinceandconvert.com/social-media-strategy/social-location/

ENDNOTE

[1]   KH Coder is a free software for quantitative content analysis or text mining invented by Koichi Higuchi. It is also utilized for computational linguistics. More information can be found here: http://koichi.nihon.to/psnl/en/

Chapter 2
The Impact of Online Training on Facebook Privacy

Karen H. Smith
Texas State University, USA

Francis A. Méndez Mediavilla
Texas State University, USA

Garry L. White
Texas State University, USA

ABSTRACT

Facebook is a major part of the lives of many consumers who share a considerable amount of information with friends, acquaintances, and commercial interests via the platform, leading to greater exposure to privacy risks. Training has been shown to be effective in reducing computer risk in a variety of contexts. This study investigates the effectiveness of training on consumer attitudes and behavioral intentions toward Facebook privacy risk. The study highlights the importance of training consumers on how and why they need to protect their privacy. Findings suggest that training can reduce consumer risk, but effectiveness can vary across types of training. For example, Facebook's Privacy Tour was less effective than third party training videos in improving consumer vigilance. Implications of the findings for consumers and privacy advocates are discussed.

INTRODUCTION

George Orwell's book *1984* (Orwell, 1949) described a society where the government constantly monitored its people, effectively eliminating citizens' privacy. Today, citizens willingly give up their privacy through social networks. In 2010 Mark Zuckerberg, founder of Facebook, declared that the "age of privacy is over" (Sarrel, 2010). Social networks have increased the amount of personal and identity information that is freely shared on the Internet. People often disclose too much personal information on social media such as Facebook, where privacy is not assured (Waters & Ackerman, 2011). People expose information about themselves by making personal information available to others to see and use. This exposure also

DOI: 10.4018/978-1-5225-1868-6.ch002

occurs by revealing preferences and habits. Knowledge of these preferences and habits allows intruders to detect behavioral patterns that can be used to predict courses of action (Shaw, 2009).

By incurring risky behavior, people do not only risk their personal information; but also information about others and perhaps even about the institutions that they represent. There is a need for better information security, especially privacy, awareness and education to improve protective behavior of users (Mensch & Wilkie, 2011; Okenyi & Owens, 2007). Therefore, it is in the best social interest that individuals are trained to protect their information. This study explores the idea that people can be trained to protect their privacy and poses the idea that peoples' attitudes and behavior intentions can be used to measure training effectiveness. Two key questions are:

- Can training reduce privacy risks?
- In addition, what attitudes and behavior intentions are impacted?

This study seeks to answer these questions.

On the Internet, there are multiple venues by which people expose private information, such as:

- Facebook,
- Twitter,
- MySpace,
- Instagram,
- Blogs, and others.

For this study, we have chosen Facebook due to its popularity (Madden, Lenhart, Cortesi, Gasser, Duggan, Smith, & Beaton, 2013), because it is a major part of many users' lives (Debatin, Lovejoy, Horn, & Hughes, 2009), and because these users share a considerable amount of information with friends, acquaintances, and commercial interests via the platform. Furthermore, Facebook has not been known as a protector of user privacy (Kuczerawy & Coudert, 2010). However, Facebook introduced a privacy education feature in 2012, the Facebook Privacy Tour (FPT), because of lawsuits and recommendations from user protections agencies in the U.S. and abroad. FTP features four screen shots about how to access privacy settings and was implemented for new users who go through the screen shots when they initially sign up for Facebook (Martinez, 2012). The research presented here tests the effectiveness of the FPT screen shots, as well as two additional training videos, in changing users' attitudes and behaviors toward protecting their privacy on Facebook.

Individuals can control disclosure and recipients of their personal information, but due to frequent modification to privacy policies, many users are unaware of who can access their information and for what purposes it can be used. One study found that if users do not take the time to investigate and educate themselves on the changes found in privacy policies, their perceived privacy settings are often times inconsistent with their actual settings (Butler, McCann, & Thomas, 2011). Furthermore, privacy policies and privacy controls may be confusing to many users. For example, Facebook's original privacy policy was written for Web-users with a minimum of two years of college education (Jafar & Abdullat, 2011). Thus, it is important to empirically investigate how users utilize social network privacy settings in order to inform the public.

User vigilance (Ramsey & Venkatesan, 2010; Reisz, 2005) is the best means of protecting privacy has been discussed a number of times. In order to be vigilant, users must understand the risks they face by exposing their personal information on social media and what they can do to reduce these risks. Smith, Mendez, and White (2014) operationalized the constructs of Facebook exposure and Facebook vigilance, and found that greater exposure on Facebook is associated with less vigilance. Because education increases preventative behavior (Albrechtsen & Hovden, 2010; D'Arcy, Hovav, & Galletta, 2009), training in the importance and application of social network privacy settings may enhance user vigilance. Yet, no research known to the authors has been conducted on the effectiveness of training with respect to Facebook privacy.

This research looks at attitudinal and behavioral variables that may be positively affected by privacy training. An experiment was designed to test the effectiveness of three types of Facebook training: the Facebook Privacy Tour and two third-party videos chosen from YouTube. Effectiveness was assessed in terms of user attitudes (privacy concern and privacy self-efficacy), as well as behavioral intentions (Facebook exposure, Facebook vigilance, and intention to disclose personal information). This study extends prior research by

1. Measuring the impact of training on both attitudes and behavioral intentions;
2. Examining and comparing the effectiveness of three types of facebook training available to users;
3. Examining the impact of narcissism and demographic variables on the dependent variables; and
4. Discussing implications of study outcomes.

LITERATURE REVIEW

Users need a better understanding of potential threats from Web activity and what to do about them. Without understanding how people's own behavior could expose their sensitive personal information and behavioral patterns to intruders, it is difficult to realize the need to protect personal information. People are the weakest link in security (Kirkpatrick, 2006); therefore, security is a people issue (Rezgui & Marks, 2008). It is important for social media users to understand that their behavior could lead to situations from which it is very difficult to recover (i.e., identity theft) - "Do something stupid online and you won't get the toothpaste back in the tube" (Davies, 2008). Our study considers the effect that training would have in influencing user behavior with respect to keeping their personal information secure while using social media. Gage (1996) reiterated the need for training that has been stressed over the years since 1984 when personal computers first came on the market (Grau, 1984). In the 1990's, training prevented a lot of fraud from occurring (Brown, 1990). The risky behavior, which leads to the disclosure of personal information, could also affect business institutions; especially when their employees are the ones incurring into such behavior. By 2000, corporations recognized the need to get people motivated in the area of information security (Siponen, 2000). Business management has realized the important role of training of training their employees to keep information safe. A survey of businesses from various fields found that the majority of organizations had formal policies and procedures for training their employees on Internet security, and the author stressed the importance of making sure employees actually follow security practices such as preventing access to passwords by coworkers (Kieke, 2006).

Most of this research has examined the use of employee training programs in business privacy; however, it is likely that user training can similarly reduce adverse consequences of a personal nature. For example, ransomware encrypts a user's computer files and then demands payment for decryption (Luo & Liao, 2007). Most ransomware infections come from a user opening an unknown e-mail attachment or careless browsing and download from a malware-embedded Web page. The best countermeasure for this malware is training (Luo & Liao, 2007). Likewise, training about how to understand and strengthen their privacy settings on Facebook can result in greater security and privacy for users.

Throughout information systems studies, the term "privacy concerns" has been used to conceptualize the general concerns that reflect individuals' inherent worries about possible loss of information privacy (Xu, Dinev, Smith, & Hart, 2011). Within the context of the Internet use and online privacy concerns, the relationship between user self-efficacy and privacy concerns is not clear (Yao, Rice, & Wallis, 2007). This study poses that, an effective training to prevent privacy breaches will results in changes to the realization of self-efficacy and privacy concerns of the user. Based on prior research, a model (see Figure 1) is developed that shows the constructs and their proposed relationships in this study. In this model, there are two types of outcomes examined because of Facebook training:

- Changes in attitudes (i.e., privacy concerns and self-efficacy) and
- Changes in behavior (i.e., exposure, vigilance, intention to disclose).

The first attitude of interest is privacy concern, or the degree to which a user is concerned about his or her information being private and secure. The second, self-efficacy, is an attitude about the self that embodies the user's perceived ability to protect himself on Facebook. Three behavioral constructs,

- Facebook exposure,
- Facebook vigilance, and
- Intention to disclose personal information,

are also proposed as outcomes. Facebook exposure captures the frequency and amount of activity of a user on Facebook, whereas disclosure represents the types of information a user may post. Facebook vigilance is the extent to which the user limits access to information on Facebook. Finally, since demographic variables and the narcissism personality construct have been shown to influence Facebook use, these are included in the model as influencing the relationships between training and outcomes. The following sections discuss each construct in the model and develop the hypotheses.

Privacy Concern

Definitions of privacy include:

- "The right to be let alone" (Warren & Brandeis, 1890),
- An individual's right to determine the information about him/her that is given to others (Schoeman, 1984),
- "A condition of limited access to identifiable information about individuals" (Smith, 1993),
- And "the legal rights or general expectations of individuals, groups, or institutions to determine for themselves when and to what extent information about them is communicated to others" (Baltzan & Phillips, 2008).

Figure 1. Model of Expected Outcomes of Training

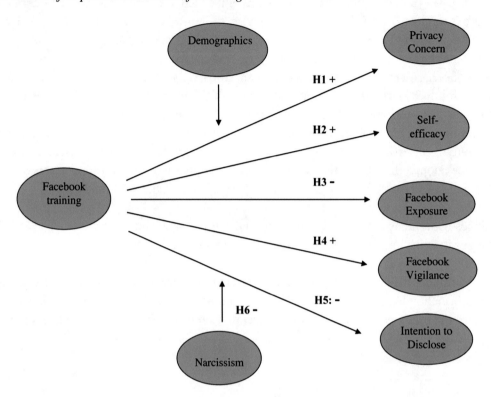

Miyazaki and Fernandez (2001) have shown that high levels of Internet experience lead to more concerns regarding privacy. Some of the concerns individuals have regarding information privacy include the following:

1. Too much personal data are being collected by businesses;
2. Much of the personal information maintained by organizations is inaccurate;
3. Personal information is often used for undisclosed purposes; and
4. Corporations are failing to protect personal information (Stewart & Segars, 2002).

When users click on ads, most social networks fail to obscure user names or identification numbers linked to their profiles (Steel & Vascellaro, 2010). Users of social networks provide many personal details, and the sites allow access to these details. As a result, personal details such as items purchased and credit card expenditures can end up on the Internet (Massari, 2010; Armano, 2010). In addition, social networking sites often generate phishing e-mails, which attempt to obtain personal information by impersonating a reliable source (Wagley, 2008).

Kuczerawy and Coudert (2010) found problems in the way privacy tools are used (or not used). Such problems result from uneducated users, the ambiguity of the privacy settings, and the confusion stemming from regular changes to the platform. Users' lack of awareness, along with complexity of the tool and lack of transparency are major factors shaping concerns among privacy advocates about Facebook. Practices, such as default privacy settings of "public" and selling user profile information to third party marketing companies, put users at risk. Yet, many users do not know how to strengthen their privacy settings or even know that they should strengthen settings. Therefore, privacy training should open users' eyes to potential risks and increase privacy concern, leading to the first hypothesis:

H1: Facebook privacy training increases privacy concern.

Dinev and Hart (2004) found that users' privacy concerns are driven by two factors. The first, users' perceived ability to control access to their personal information, is a form of self-efficacy. The second, perceived vulnerability to security and privacy breaches is similar to information exposure on Facebook and vigilance in protecting one's privacy. Self-efficacy in the current research is the ability of users to exercise vigilance in protecting their privacy on Facebook. Thus, we now turn to a discussion of self-efficacy, exposure, and vigilance on Facebook.

Self-Efficacy

Self-efficacy involves individuals' beliefs about whether they can control outcomes (Bandura & Wood, 1989), and is a major predictor of performance (Vasquez-Colina, 2005). In the context of the present study, self-efficacy is an individual's belief in his or her own ability to carry out a particular response to a threat, such as being able to install and use security software on a computer. Claar and Johnson (2012) found that self-efficacy was positively related to computer security software usage. Furthermore, self-efficacy was found to have the strongest relationship with intention and behavior in a meta-analysis of studies to predict health behavior (Milne, Sheeran, & Orbell, 2000).

LaRose and Rifon (2007) developed a scale specifically measuring privacy self-efficacy, which is users' perceived ability to protect their privacy on the Internet. Since Facebook training enhances users' knowledge about how to protect oneself through Facebook privacy settings, hypothesis 2 was developed:

H2: Facebook privacy training increases privacy self-efficacy.

Facebook Exposure and Facebook Vigilance

Smith, Mendez and White (2014) conceptualized and operationalized Facebook exposure and Facebook vigilance to enhance our understanding of social media users. They defined Facebook exposure "as the opportunity for privacy and security breaches" (Smith, Mendez, & White, 2014). Facebook users have a variety of ways in which they expose their information to security and privacy risk, including:

- Facebook profile,
- Status updates,
- Adding friends (or friends of friends who actually may be strangers),
- Joining groups,
- Checking in to events, and
- Engaging with third-party apps such as games.

In other words, increased activity on Facebook creates greater opportunities for privacy breaches. For example, every status update is a post of additional information the user wants to share with others but could be used in negative ways, such as identity theft. As users add friends, their information exposure can increase exponentially, depending on how many "friends of friends" there are for each friend added. Posting vacation pictures while on a trip allows friends to share your fun, and checking-in at bars and restaurants is beneficial in locating friends who might be interested in getting together at the mall or at a movie. However, these actions allow location tracking, which could alert burglars that the user is not at home. Informing users that the risks they face go up with increased activity on Facebook may persuade them to reduce their exposure on Facebook. Therefore:

H3: Facebook privacy training decreases Facebook exposure.

Drawing from human factors research, Smith, Mendez, and White (2014) defined vigilance as "the extent to which users stay focused, attentive, and alert to potential security and privacy risks on Facebook by restricting who can access and post to their Facebook accounts." Facebook claims that it wants users to control their experiences so they can express themselves freely (Facebook, 2012), and Facebook does provide tools for users to control their privacy settings. However, many users may be unaware of the importance and even the existence of these tools.

The default privacy setting for Facebook is "public." Thus, users must change their settings to eliminate access by everyone on the Internet. To protect themselves, Facebook users must adequately configure their privacy settings. In addition, they must stay vigilant because updates to the Facebook platform can change users' privacy settings, as happened in 2009 when Facebook made changes that resulted in most privacy settings being set to public (Collins, 2010). In fact, Facebook has made changes to its policies several times without informing users, raising concerns from users as well as privacy authorities (Kuczerawy & Coudert, 2010). In 2012, Facebook began testing a "want" button that would generate "wish lists" of products on users' Facebook pages; and it has been suggested that brands could promote to users with such wish lists for a fee (Kasriel, 2012).

Applications (apps) have a special ability to reach personal information through friends who use the apps. Thus, applications used by a Facebook user's friends can collect information from the Facebook user himself despite never using the app (Butler et al., 2011). Furthermore, privacy settings for applications reside in a different window than other security settings and are sometimes unknown to users.

Privacy settings on social networking sites can protect users (Kuczerawy & Coudert, 2010). Facebook users, who are vigilant, are better protected against intrusion. Yet, users must understand how they can limit access to their information. In addition, users must realize the importance of their own vigilant behavior in protecting themselves from "the data collection race that quickens all around us" (Norberg, Horne, & Horne, 2007). Training can enhance users' knowledge of these tools and their importance, leading to hypothesis 4:

H4: Facebook privacy training increases Facebook vigilance.

Disclosure of Personal Information

While Facebook exposure measures the level of activity of users on Facebook, the construct does not capture the types of information posted. Disclosure has been defined as sharing previously unknown information (Buchanan, Joinson, Paine, & Reips, 2007). Although users express concern about their privacy, they still tend to disclose a lot of information online. In fact, actual disclosure behaviors are often greater than users' intended disclosure, leading to a privacy paradox (Nadkarni & Hofmann, 2012). The paradox occurs for a number of different categories of information including demographics and preferences, as well as financial and personally identifying information.

According to Waters and Ackerman (2011), users are motivated for disclosing information such as sharing with others, keeping up with trends, and showing off. In addition, they may receive special offers or gifts. In fact, disclosure is usually required for users to access free goods or services or to have these products personalized (Joinson, Reips, Buchanan, & Schofield, 2010). The types of information users disclose on Facebook vary:

- From trivial (e.g., favorite snacks and TV shows)
- To identifiers (e.g., birthday and street address)
- To highly sensitive information (e.g., medical history and sexual orientation).

However, LaRose and Rifon (2007) found that when information about potential negative outcomes of privacy disclosures was communicated to users, it made them less inclined to supply personally identifying information. Therefore:

H5: Facebook privacy training decreases disclosure on Facebook.

Narcissism

Several studies have found that narcissists are more active on Facebook, reflecting the need to promote themselves (Buffardi & Campbell, 2008), as well as the needs to belong and for self-presentation (Nadkarni & Hofmann, 2012). Individuals high on the narcissism personality scale have extremely positive views of self in terms of attractiveness, intelligence, leadership, and other qualities. Often such views are overstated (Raskin & Terry, 1988). Buffardi and Campbell (2008) found that narcissists:

- Used attractive profile pictures,
- Posted "fun" photos,
- Posted self-promoting and entertaining quotes,
- And engaged in greater social interaction.

Another study (Carpenter, 2012) found those high in the exhibitionism dimension of narcissism reached a wider audience by having more friends and were more likely to accept strangers as friends. In addition, those high in entitlement/exploitativeness dimensions were more likely to monitor what others post about them and retaliate against those who post negative comments. Narcissism was also found to have a significant positive relationship with Facebook exposure and a significant negative relationship with Facebook vigilance (Smith et al., 2014). Because of this, the authors concluded that narcissists might be at greater risk than others. Furthermore, while privacy training should benefit most users, narcissists' need to promote themselves to others may interfere with the benefits of training. Therefore:

H6: Facebook privacy training becomes less effective as narcissism increases.

Demographic Variables

Several studies have found effects of demographic variables on privacy attitudes and behavior. For example, Joinson et al. (2010) found that women tended to protect their privacy more than males and older users had greater privacy concern than younger users. Nosko, Wood, and Molema (2010) found that age is an important factor determining disclosure; as age of the respondent increased, the amount of personal information disclosed decreased. Although this study did not find any evidence suggesting that gender is a factor related to disclosure, Joinson et al. (2010) did find that disclosure was related to gender and age. Finally, Smith, Mendez, and White (2014) found that age is associated with Facebook exposure and Facebook vigilance, and that gender is associated with Facebook exposure. In summary, we expect demographics to play a major role in this study, so they will be incorporated into the analyses.

Types of Facebook Privacy Training

In November 2012, Facebook added a "Privacy Tour" for users who open new Facebook accounts as suggested by the Irish Data Protection Commissioner's Office after an audit of Facebook's policies and practices; Facebook had also settled a lawsuit with the FTC in August of that year. The tour was touted as promoting the Facebook's privacy protection tools (Martinez, 2012). The Facebook Privacy Tour is composed of four slides or screen shots titled

1. Who Sees What You Share,
2. How Tagging Works,
3. How You Connect With Friends, and
4. Sharing with Apps, Games, and Websites.

These slides showed "how" to set these privacy settings. There were no accompanying audio or video presentations. In addition, there was no information as to why these settings are important. The four screen shots appear in Appendix A.

Believing the tour to be rather ineffectual, the researchers searched YouTube for instructional videos on Facebook privacy settings. Two videos of about 2 minutes and 5 minutes were chosen as experimental stimuli to compare to the Facebook Privacy Tour. More on how the videos were coded and chosen appears in the Method section. Because the third-party videos went into greater depth than the Facebook Privacy Tour, hypothesis 7 was developed:

H7: Facebook's Privacy Tour is less effective than third-party videos from YouTube in reducing Facebook exposure and increasing Facebook vigilance.

METHOD

The reported study is a quasi-experimental design with three levels of the experimental treatment:

- *Facebook Privacy Tour* (FB),
- *Video 1* (V_1) (Abner, 2015), and
- *Video 2* (V_2) (Pinkerton, 2015).

A matched sample design was used to assess the dependent variables both before and after the treatments. There was a three-week delay period between completion of pre-surveys and the post-surveys. All data were collected during spring and fall of 2014.

Sample

A nationwide panel of 204 adult Facebook users in the United States served as participants and were recruited through a major research firm (Luth Research) and paid for their participation. The overall sample, as well as each treatment group, was evenly split between male and female. Participants ranged in age from 18 to 81 years old, with a median age of 47 years old. The sample ethnic composition resulted in:

- 52.5% white,
- 23.0% black,
- 20.6% Hispanic, and
- 3.9% mixed or other ethnicities, which closely follows the distribution of the U.S. population.

Other demographics include:

- 51.5% married,
- 30.4% single,
- 15.2% divorced,
- 2.9% widowed;
- 18.2% with high school education or less,
- 34.8% with some college,
- 33.3% with bachelor degrees,
- 13.7% with master degrees; and median income between $50,000 and $59,999.

Stimuli and Procedure

YouTube searches for "privacy videos" yielded a large number of hits, from which we selected seventeen that addressed the issue of adjusting Facebook privacy settings. A panel of three reviewers compared the videos based on their features relative to exposure (e.g., profile changes, apps, friends), vigilance (e.g., access to profile, tagging), and mode of execution (e.g., voice, duration). Reviewers in the panel determined which features are present or absent for each video. They also noted level of quality and execution characteristics (e.g., the accent of the presenter). Reviewer responses were evaluated and found to be highly consistent. Based on this information, two videos of differing lengths were chosen that presented the most features of interest to our study. Table 1 shows a comparison of the three treatments (i.e., Facebook Privacy Tour, video 1 and video 2) on the features of exposure, vigilance, and execution.

The Facebook Privacy Tour (FPT) is not a video, but a set of four screen shots. As compared to the publicly available videos (V_1 and V_2), the FPT offers instruction on various aspects of exposure (i.e., changing profiles and friends). V_2 addresses the issue of exposure to applications, whereas FPT and V_1 do not address this property. On aspects of vigilance, the FPT lacks some features that the videos have,

Table 1. Main features of Facebook Privacy Tour and third party videos

Features Discussed	FB Privacy Tour	Treatment V1	V2
Exposure			
Changing Profile	yes		
Applications			yes
Friends	yes		
Vigilance			
Gear		yes	yes
Accessibility to profile	yes	yes	yes
Engine Search		yes	yes
Wall Posting	yes	yes	yes
Tag Posting	yes	yes	
Ads Control			yes
Apps Control	yes		yes
Execution			
Format	Slides	Video	Video
Duration	*NA*	2:40 mins	4:50 mins
Audio	None	Male Voice	Female Voice
URL/Link		https://youtu.be/klMLZKFHFzw_	https://youtu.be/sWPV7DPWxzY_

such as discussion of the gear (settings tool), protection against being discovered by a search engine, and advertisement control measures. The FPT is self-paced, administered as fast as the user reads the screen shots. The videos are timed; however, it is possible to rewind and review any part of the videos. V_1 takes longer to watch than V_2. The FPT lacks sound, whereas both videos are narrated. A male narrates V_1, whereas a female narrates V2.

Subjects completed the pre-survey online. After a three-week rest period, subjects were shown one of the three training conditions (i.e., FPT, V_1, V_2), followed by the post-survey. Items concerning narcissism were only gathered at pre-survey stage since our pre-tests verified that the experimental conditions had no effect on narcissism. Items in the post-survey for Facebook exposure and Facebook vigilance were slightly reworded to assess subjects' future behaviors with respect to privacy settings. For example, one item for Facebook exposure was reworded from "How often do you change your Facebook status?" to "How often do you plan to change your Facebook status?"

In order to assess the potential for demand effects, an open-ended request to "Please describe what you think this study was about" at the end of the survey. Most responses mentioned Facebook and privacy issues, but none mentioned privacy education or training. An additional two items were used to examine whether taking the pre-survey affected respondents; these results are discussed in the results section.

Measures

The six primary measures were drawn or adapted from prior research and the reliability coefficients (Cronbach's **α**) met the standard for the social sciences of 0.70 or higher (Nunnally, 1978). Narcissism was measured using 20 items from the Narcissistic Personality Inventory scale (Smith, Mendez, & White, 2014; Raskin, & Terry, 1988), and privacy concern was drawn from Dinev and Hart (2004). Items measuring intention to disclose personal information and privacy self-efficacy were drawn from LaRose and Rifon (2007).

The measure of Facebook exposure was adapted for this study by adding two activities ("How often do you log out of Facebook" and "How often do you 'check-in' to locations on Facebook") to the seven items measured in Smith, Méndez and White (2014)

- (i.e., frequency of status updates, profile updates, and access by phone;
- and number of apps installed, invitations to events, Facebook groups, and friends).

The eight items for Facebook vigilance were drawn directly from Smith, Mendez and White (2014), which they developed based on: the privacy settings in Facebook (e.g., who can look up your profile, send you Facebook messages, and see or post on your wall) using a 5-point response scale based on Facebook setting alternatives:

1. Public,
2. Friends of Friends,
3. Friends,
4. Custom (specific groups, lists), and
5. Only Me.

A response of "Public" represents the least vigilant setting because anyone on Facebook could see the content; whereas the response "Only Me" is the most vigilant of all settings because this setting allows no one else to access to the content.

Pre-measures for privacy concern, Facebook exposure, Facebook vigilance, intention to disclose, and self-efficacy were subtracted from the corresponding post-measures to compute a difference score for each variable. If the subject's score on the variable went up after the experimental treatment, the difference variable was positive; otherwise, it was negative. It was expected that Facebook exposure and disclosure would decline after the treatments, so the difference scores would be negative. Also, it was expected that privacy concern, Facebook vigilance, and self-efficacy would increase after the training, so the difference scores would be positive. Because pre-tests showed no significant effect of treatment, narcissism was only computed at pre-measure. For each variable, Table 2 presents the number of items and Cronbach alpha values, along with means and standard deviations for the pre-measures, post-measures, and difference scores. Finally, demographic variables (age, gender, ethnicity, education, income, and marital status) were measured only at the beginning of the study. Age was measured with an open-ended question; ethnicity and marital status were measured with nominal scales; and education and income were measured with ordinal scales. The models in this study control for the demographic variables and narcissism, since previous studies have found evidence that these variables (especially, age, gender, and narcissism) are related to the dependent variables. By design, gender was evenly split for each treatment. In addition, the other demographic variables are distributed evenly across treatment conditions.

Table 2. Number of items, reliabilities, means, and standard deviations of pre- and post-measures and difference scores

	# of Items	Cronbach Alpha	Means (Standard Deviations)		
			Pre-Measure	Post-Measure	Difference
Narcissism	20	.888	3.73	N/A	N/A
			(0.88)		
Privacy Concern	11	.944	4.57	4.87	.30***
			(1.39)	(1.34)	(.99)
Self-Efficacy	10	.898	4.85	4.74	-.11*
			(1.07)	(1.10)	(.71)
Facebook Exposure	9	.774	2.32	2.16	-.16***
			(0.80)	(.71)	(.50)
Facebook Vigilance	8	.842	2.77	2.97	.20***
			(0.75)	(.74)	(.66)
Intention to Disclose	15	.894	3.31	12.76	-.55***
			(1.17)	(1.07)	(.98)
N			204	204	204

Note: Significant differences from 0 are indicated by: * p < .05; ** p < .01; *** p < .001.

RESULTS

Hypothesis Tests

To test H_1-H_5 for effects of Facebook training, t-tests evaluating the null hypothesis that the mean difference score was equal to zero were conducted for the sample as a whole. Results are presented in the last column of Table 2. As expected, Facebook exposure (mean = -.16, p < .001) and disclosure (mean = -.55, p < .001) declined, while privacy concern (mean = .30, p < .001) and Facebook vigilance (mean = .20, p = .000) increased. Thus, by rejecting the null hypotheses, there is support for H1, H3, H4, and H5. H2 was not supported since self-efficacy actually declined after Facebook training (mean = -.11, p = .035), suggesting that participants felt less able to protect their privacy after the training. The significant difference was in the wrong direction.

H_6 states that Facebook privacy training becomes less effective with greater narcissism. Bivariate correlations between narcissism and the difference scores for Facebook exposure and Facebook vigilance were used to test this hypothesis. Since a negative score indicates effectiveness for Facebook exposure, a positive relationship between narcissism and Facebook exposure difference score would support H_6. In other words, we would expect the higher the narcissism, the smaller the decline in Facebook exposure. For Facebook vigilance, the opposite is expected. A negative correlation between narcissism and Facebook vigilance would be expected because the higher the narcissism, the smaller the increase in Facebook vigilance. Nevertheless, results were the opposite of expectations, refuting H_6. The data suggest that, in fact, the higher the narcissism, the more effective the training (r = -.146, p = .037 for Facebook exposure; and r = .173, p = .013 for Facebook vigilance).

H$_7$, stating Facebook's privacy tour would be less effective than the two third-party videos in changing the levels of exposure and vigilance, was not supported. To test this hypothesis, repeated measures ANOVA were conducted for each measure (i.e., exposure and vigilance). The analyses tested whether there were differences before and after the training (time) and whether there were differences between training methods (treatments). As can be seen in Table 3, Facebook exposure was reduced and vigilance was increased for all three training conditions. However, no evidence of differences between types of training were found between the third-party videos nor between the videos and the Facebook privacy tour. That is, the Facebook privacy tour was as effective as the videos in reducing Facebook exposure and increasing vigilance. Sage and Baldwin (2015) found similar results; performance differed little between a self-paced slideshow and videos. This suggests that training can be effective, and that effectiveness may not depend on the method used.

Table 3. Difference of scores overall and by treatment

	Mean Difference Scores (S.D.)			
	Overall	**Facebook Privacy Tour**	**Video 1**	**Video 2**
Facebook Exposure	-.16	-.16	-.20	-.13
	(.50)	(.53)	(.56)	(.41)
Facebook Vigilance	.20	.16	.21	.22
	(.66)	(.72)	(.67)	(.59)
N	204	68	68	68

Table 4. Analysis of variance with repeated measures for exposure and vigilance

Measure: Facebook Exposure				
Source	**SS**	**df**	**MS**	**F**
Time	2.698	1	2.698	21.333***
Treatments	0.102	2	0.051	0.403
Measure: Facebook Vigilance				
Source	**SS**	**df**	**MS**	**F**
Time	3.995	1	3.995	18.156***
Treatments	0.076	2	0.038	0.172

Note: ***p < .001.

Narcissism

As expected, based on prior findings, narcissism was significantly related to several variables. First, age and narcissism had a significant negative correlation (r = -.172, p = .014), suggesting that younger participants are more narcissistic than older participants. In addition, significant positive relationships with narcissism were found for pre-exposure (r = .392, p = .000) and pre-disclosure (r = .326, p = .000), as well as a significant negative relationship for vigilance (r = -.178, p = .011). This suggests that narcissists are more exposed and disclose more information, yet are less vigilant on social media. Because of these trends, it is an important finding that narcissists may be very responsive to privacy training.

Effects of Demographic Variables

To test for demographic effects, a multivariate analysis of covariance was conducted using the pre-measures of the six primary variables; with gender, ethnicity, and marital status as fixed factors; and age, education, and income as covariates. With the exception of age (Wilks' Lambda = .832, F = 4.174, p < .001), there were no significant multivariate results at the .05 level. Tests of between-subjects effects showed a significant relationship between age and only one variable, pre-Facebook exposure (F = 30.457, p < .001). Additional analyses highlight the importance of age. Younger participants were more narcissistic (r = -.172, p = .014), more exposed on Facebook (r = -.383, p = .000) and less vigilant (r = .146, p = .038).

CONCLUSION

Discussion

This study has shown Facebook privacy training has desirable impacts: increased privacy concern and Facebook vigilance, as well as lower Facebook exposure and intention to disclose personal information on Facebook. Also, all three types of training (Facebook privacy tour and third party videos from YouTube) reduced Facebook exposure. Therefore, it can be said that training is a factor that significantly contributes to greater privacy of users on Facebook. These findings are consistent with prior research that warnings and training can enhance protective behaviors (Albrechtsen & Hovden, 2010; LaRose & Rifon, 2007). Training may improve user privacy since the user learns how and why to limit disclosure. Trained users can minimize risks because of these changes in behavior, resulting in a safer environment (Kirkpatrick, 2006). However, users must constantly be reminded to remain vigilant as social media platforms evolve and privacy settings can automatically change (Kuczerawy & Coudert, 2010). Therefore, user training should be ongoing.

Interestingly, results showed that training reduced privacy self-efficacy in the present study. This may turn out to be a favorable result since LaRose and Rifon (2007) found that, after being warned about potential negative consequences of information disclosure, users with low self-efficacy were actually less likely to disclose personal information than those with high self-efficacy. They suggested that users with high privacy self-efficacy might discount the risk associated with disclosure of information since they believe they are capable of protecting themselves. Perhaps, self-efficacy declines because training highlights how much users do not know and how much they cannot control.

Another factor to consider is vigilance. User vigilance in protecting privacy has been discussed a number of times (Ramsey & Venkatesan, 2010; Reisz, 2005) and has now been operationalized in order to assess user risk. In order to be vigilant, users must understand the risks they face by exposing their personal information on social media and how they can reduce these risks by strengthening their privacy settings. Findings from the present study suggest that training in the importance and application of social network privacy settings can enhance user vigilance. Also, when comparing the main features of the training stimuli in this study, one can see that the videos had more features than the Facebook privacy tour. This is particularly true for the features related to vigilance. This may help explain why the videos were more effective in enhancing vigilance than the Facebook privacy tour.

Finally, there is narcissism. Consistent with prior research, narcissism was significantly related to Facebook exposure and vigilance, intent to disclose and self-efficacy. A surprise was the result that training appeared to be more effective in reducing exposure and enhancing vigilance for narcissists. Based on the findings of Smith, Mendez, and White (2014) that narcissists may be at greater risk, perhaps training is the answer to reducing that risk:

Privacy issue is more complicated and to a great extent, worsened by vendors' intentional tracking, information collection and usage without user permission. Thus, the effect of privacy training is limited and the expectation should be realistic (Reviewer's comment).

Implications

This research has several implications for privacy advocates. First, and foremost, the study highlights the importance of training users on how and why they need to protect their privacy. Reliance on Facebook and other social networks to provide this information falls short of the goal of protecting users. Since third-party videos were effective in decreasing exposure and increasing vigilance, perhaps government agencies, such as the Bureau of Consumer Protection of the Federal Trade Commission, should provide such training on their websites and promote the use of such videos among users.

Second, even though many users understand the need for privacy protection, they may lack vigilance until they experience privacy incidents (Debatin et al., 2009). Therefore, training should go beyond privacy settings and include solutions for reacting to events, such as privacy invasions or security breaches.

Third, age groups need to be considered in designing training programs. For example, Johnson (2007) found that middle-aged users tend to have the greatest concern for privacy, thus, might be more receptive to training than other groups. Hence, there is motivation to use privacy tools. The youngest Facebook users have grown up with technology and do not tend to fear it, so they must be made to understand the need for privacy settings in the first place. Finally, the older group, over 75, may not need more training since they may not use Facebook as much.

Finally, it is important for users to keep up with changes in their social network platforms. In January 2015, Facebook introduced Privacy Basics, an interactive guide to answer questions such as untagging yourself from photos, unfriending people, and blocking others from seeing certain content. This enhancement has the goal of improving users' experiences on Facebook. At the same time, Facebook's terms of service, data policy, and cookies policy all changed as well (E. Egan, email to Facebook users from Facebook's Global Chief Privacy Officer, 2015).

FUTURE RESEARCH

The current study found that training lowered privacy self-efficacy, yet also reduced intent to disclose information. This is consistent with findings of LaRose and Rifon (2007), that users with lower self-efficacy were less likely to disclose information, but inconsistent with another study where college students with higher self-efficacy were significantly more likely to practice information privacy behaviors and had significantly higher protective behavioral intentions (Yoon, Hwang, & Kim, 2012). However, there was no training in latter study and the behavioral intentions (e.g., I will take precautions against information privacy violations) and protective behaviors (e.g., I immediately delete suspicious emails without reading them) were different from the present study. Thus, although training may lead to lower self-efficacy and less disclosure, other security practices may be affected differently. Perhaps future research examining a wider range of protective behaviors could untangle these relationships and resolve the discrepancy. Experiments manipulating self-efficacy after training occurs would allow a careful observation of the resultant effects on disclosure and other protective behaviors.

Survey research yields important insights, yet relies on self-reported data. Future research could assess actual behavior on social networks after training. Furthermore, the present study did not look at specific invasions of privacy or security breaches. White (2012) and White (2015) found that as users engaged in behaviors that are more protective after training, they reported more security incidents. Possible explanations are that training

1. Enhances the recognition of incidents;
2. Increases confidence in dealing with security, leading to greater risk-taking on the computer; and/or
3. Increases the amount of time spent on the computer, resulting in more opportunities for security incidents (White, 2015).

Future experiments using real or hypothetical attacks could test the effects of training on vigilance, as well as on the frequency of security incidents encountered.

Another future experiment would be to see if group interaction during training could enhance its effectiveness. The employee training used by Albrechtsen and Hovden (2010) consisted of small-size workshops and stressed employee participation, dialogue, and collective reflection in groups, rather than a top-down approach such as emails and presentations by management. This type of group training was very effective in promoting protective behaviors of employees. Since Facebook is a social phenomenon, encouraging group interaction during training may enhance success.

REFERENCES

Abner, B. (2015, February 15). *Privacy Settings on Facebook*. Retrieved from https://youtu.be/klML-ZKFHFzw

Albrechtsen, E., & Hovden, J. (2010). Improving information security awareness and behaviour through dialogue, participation and collective reflection. An intervention study. *Computers & Security*, *29*(4), 432–445. doi:10.1016/j.cose.2009.12.005

Armano, D. (2010). Why social sharing is bigger than Facebook and Twitter. *Harvard Business Review Blog*. Retrieved from http://blogs.hbr.org/cs/2010/04/why_social_sharing_is_bigger_than_facebook.html

Baltzan, P., & Phillips, A. (2008). *Business driven information systems*. McGraw-Hill/Irwin.

Bandura, A., & Wood, R. (1989). Effect of perceived controllability and performance standards on self-regulation of complex decision making. *Journal of Personality and Social Psychology, 56*(5), 805–814. doi:10.1037/0022-3514.56.5.805 PMID:2724068

Brown, C. P. (1990). Crimes of the Vault. *Security Management, 34*(1), 31.

Buchanan, T., Joinson, A. N., Paine, C., & Reips, U. D. (2007). Looking for medical information on the Internet: self-disclosure, privacy and trust. *He@lth Information on the Internet, 58*(1), 8-9.

Buffardi, L. E., & Campbell, W. K. (2008). Narcissism and social networking web sites. *Personality and Social Psychology Bulletin, 34*(10), 1303–1314. doi:10.1177/0146167208320061 PMID:18599659

Butler, E., McCann, E., & Thomas, J. (2011). Privacy setting awareness on Facebook and its effect on user-posted content. *Human Communication, 14*(1), 39–55.

Carpenter, C. J. (2012). Narcissism on Facebook: Self promotional and anti-social behavior. *Personality and Individual Differences, 52*(4), 482–486. doi:10.1016/j.paid.2011.11.011

Claar, C. L., & Johnson, J. (2012). Analyzing home PC security adoption behavior. *Journal of Computer Information Systems, 52*(4), 20–29.

Collins, J. C. (2010). Fortify Your Facebook Privacy Settings: Don't Let the Window into Your Personal Life Sully Your Professional Reputation. *Journal of Accountancy, 209*(6), 42.

DArcy, J., Hovav, A., & Galletta, D. (2009). User awareness of security countermeasures and its impact on information systems misuse: A deterrence approach. *Information Systems Research, 20*(1), 79–98. doi:10.1287/isre.1070.0160

Davies, R. (2008, September 26). *Media Perspective: Take a Big Pinch of Salt with What You Read on the Internet*. Retrieved from http://www.campaignlive.co.uk/news/849444/

Debatin, B., Lovejoy, J. P., Horn, A. K., & Hughes, B. N. (2009). Facebook and online privacy: Attitudes, behaviors, and unintended consequences. *Journal of Computer-Mediated Communication, 15*(1), 83–108. doi:10.1111/j.1083-6101.2009.01494.x

Dinev, T., & Hart, P. (2004). Internet privacy concerns and their antecedents-measurement validity and a regression model. *Behaviour & Information Technology, 23*(6), 413–422. doi:10.1080/01449290410001715723

Facebook. (2012). *Safety and Privacy*. Retrieved from http://newsroom.fb.com/content/default.aspx?NewsAreaId=36

Gage, D. (1996). Companies need more security training programs, study finds. *Info World Canada, 21*(3), 24–25.

Grau, J. (1984). Security Education: Something to Think About. *Security Management, 28*(10), 25–31.

Jafar, M. J., & Abdullat, A. (2011). Exploratory analysis of the readability of information privacy statement of the primary social networks. *Journal of Business & Economics Research, 7*(12).

Johnson, B. R. (2007). *A mixed-methods study of the influence of generational consciousness on information privacy concern.* ProQuest.

Joinson, A. N., Reips, U. D., Buchanan, T., & Schofield, C. B. P. (2010). Privacy, trust, and self-disclosure online. *Human-Computer Interaction, 25*(1), 1–24. doi:10.1080/07370020903586662

Kasriel, D. (2012). Protecting privacy in our digital age: A growing consumer priority. *Passport: Euromonitor International, 1.*

Kieke, R. (2006). Survey shows high number of organizations suffered security breach in past year. *Journal of Health Care Compliance, 8*(5), 49–68.

Kirkpatrick, J. (2006). Protect your business against dangerous information leaks. *Machine design, 78*(3), 66.

Kuczerawy, A., & Coudert, F. (2010, August). Privacy settings in social networking sites: Is it fair? In *IFIP PrimeLife International Summer School on Privacy and Identity Management for Life* (pp. 231–243). Springer Berlin Heidelberg.

LaRose, R., & Rifon, N. J. (2007). Promoting i-safety: Effects of privacy warnings and privacy seals on risk assessment and online privacy behavior. *The Journal of Consumer Affairs, 41*(1), 127–149. doi:10.1111/j.1745-6606.2006.00071.x

Luo, X., & Liao, Q. (2007). Awareness Education as the key to Ransomware Prevention. *Information Systems Security, 16*(4), 195–202. doi:10.1080/10658980701576412

Madden, M., Lenhart, A., Cortesi, S., Gasser, U., Duggan, M., Smith, A., & Beaton, M. (2013). Teens, social media, and privacy. Pew Research Center, 21.

Martinez, J. (2012). Facebook Unveils Privacy Education Feature for New Users. *Hillicon Valley: The Hill's Technology Blog.* Retrieved from http://thehill.com/policy/technology/265639-facebook-unveils-privacy-education-feature-for-new-users

Massari, L. (2010). Analysis of MySpace user profiles. *Information Systems Frontiers, 12*(4), 361–367. doi:10.1007/s10796-009-9206-8

Mensch, S., & Wilkie, L. (2011). Information security activities of college students: An exploratory study. *Academy of Information and Management Sciences Journal, 14*(2), 91.

Milne, S., Sheeran, P., & Orbell, S. (2000). Prediction and intervention in health-related behavior: A meta-analytic review of protection motivation theory. *Journal of Applied Social Psychology, 30*(1), 106–143. doi:10.1111/j.1559-1816.2000.tb02308.x

Miyazaki, A. D., & Fernandez, A. (2001). Consumer perceptions of privacy and security risks for online shopping. *The Journal of Consumer Affairs, 35*(1), 27–44. doi:10.1111/j.1745-6606.2001.tb00101.x

Nadkarni, A., & Hofmann, S. G. (2012). Why do people use Facebook? *Personality and Individual Differences, 52*(3), 243–249. doi:10.1016/j.paid.2011.11.007 PMID:22544987

Norberg, P. A., Horne, D. R., & Horne, D. A. (2007). The privacy paradox: Personal information disclosure intentions versus behaviors. *The Journal of Consumer Affairs, 41*(1), 100–126. doi:10.1111/j.1745-6606.2006.00070.x

Nosko, A., Wood, E., & Molema, S. (2010). All about me: Disclosure in online social networking profiles: The case of FACEBOOK. *Computers in Human Behavior, 26*(3), 406–418. doi:10.1016/j.chb.2009.11.012

Nunnally, J. C. (1978). *Psychometric Theory*. New York: McGraw-Hill.

Okenyi, P. O., & Owens, T. J. (2007). On the anatomy of human hacking. *Information Systems Security, 16*(6), 302–314. doi:10.1080/10658980701747237

Orwell, G. (1949). *Nineteen Eighty-Four. A novel*. New York: Harcourt, Brace & Co.

Pinkerton, M. (2015, May 5). *How to Make a Facebook Page Secure*. Retrieved from https://youtu.be/sWPV7DPWxzY

Ramsey, G., & Venkatesan, S. (2010). Cybercrime strategy for social networking and other online platforms. *Licensing Journal, 30*(7), 23–27.

Raskin, R., & Terry, H. (1988). A principal-components analysis of the Narcissistic Personality Inventory and further evidence of its construct validity. *Journal of Personality and Social Psychology, 54*(5), 890–902. doi:10.1037/0022-3514.54.5.890 PMID:3379585

Reisz, S. (2005). Knowledge and Vigilance: Key Ingredients to Information Security. *Catalyst*, 18-23.

Rezgui, Y., & Marks, A. (2008). Information security awareness in higher education: An exploratory study. *Computers & Security, 27*(7), 241–253. doi:10.1016/j.cose.2008.07.008

Sage, K. D., & Baldwin, D. (2015). Childrens Use of Self-Paced Slideshows: An Extension of the Video Deficit Effect? *Journal of Research in Childhood Education, 29*(1), 90–114. doi:10.1080/02568543.2014.978919

Sarrel, M. (2010). Stay Safe, Productive on Social Networks. *eWeek*.

Schoeman, F. D. (1984). *Philosophical dimensions of privacy: An anthology*. Cambridge University Press. doi:10.1017/CBO9780511625138

Shaw, J. (2009). The Erosion of Privacy in the Internet Era. *Harvard Magazine*, 38–43.

Siponen, M. T. (2000). A conceptual foundation for organizational information security awareness. *Information Management & Computer Security, 8*(1), 31–41. doi:10.1108/09685220010371394

Smith, H. J. (1993). Privacy policies and practices: Inside the organizational maze. *Communications of the ACM, 36*(12), 104–122. doi:10.1145/163298.163349

Smith, K., Mendez, F., & White, G. L. (2014). Narcissism as a predictor of Facebook users privacy concern, vigilance, and exposure to risk. *International Journal of Technology and Human Interaction, 10*(2), 78–95. doi:10.4018/ijthi.2014040105

Steel, E., & Vascellaro, J. E. (2010). Facebook, MySpace confront privacy loophole. *The Wall Street Journal, 21*.

Stewart, K. A., & Segars, A. H. (2002). An empirical examination of the concern for information privacy instrument. *Information Systems Research*, *13*(1), 36–49. doi:10.1287/isre.13.1.36.97

Vasquez-Colina, M. D. (2005). *Relationships among demographic variables, organizational culture, interpersonal self-efficacy and perceived job performance*. Academic Press.

Wagley, J. (2008). Social Sites: More Foe Than Friend? *Security Management*, *52*(5), 54.

Warren, S. D., & Brandeis, L. D. (1890). The right to privacy. *Harvard Law Review*, *4*(5), 193–220. doi:10.2307/1321160

Waters, S., & Ackerman, J. (2011). Exploring privacy management on Facebook: Motivations and perceived consequences of voluntary disclosure. *Journal of Computer-Mediated Communication*, *17*(1), 101–115. doi:10.1111/j.1083-6101.2011.01559.x

White, G. L. (2012). Information Security Education Relationships on Incidents and Preventions: Cyber Assurance Literacy Needs. In *Proceedings of the Information Systems Educators Conference ISSN* (Vol. 2167, p. 1435).

White, G. L. (2015). Education and Prevention Relationships on Security Incidents for Home Computers. *Journal of Computer Information Systems*, *55*(3), 29–37. doi:10.1080/08874417.2015.11645769

Xu, H., Dinev, T., Smith, J., & Hart, P. (2011). Information privacy concerns: Linking individual perceptions with institutional privacy assurances. *Journal of the Association for Information Systems*, *12*(12), 798.

Yao, M. Z., Rice, R. E., & Wallis, K. (2007). Predicting user concerns about online privacy. *Journal of the American Society for Information Science and Technology*, *58*(5), 710–722. doi:10.1002/asi.20530

Yoon, C., Hwang, J. W., & Kim, R. (2012). Exploring Factors That Influence Students' Behaviors in Information Security. *Journal of Information Systems Education*, *23*(4), 407.

Chapter 3
Play It Like Beckham!
The Influence of Social Networks on E-Reputation – The Case of Sportspeople and Their Online Fan Base

Sylvaine Castellano
Paris School of Business, France

Insaf Khelladi
ICN Business School, France

ABSTRACT

New opportunities and challenges are emerging thanks to the growing Internet importance and social media usage. Although practitioners have already recognized the strategic dimension of e-reputation and the power of social media, academic research is still in its infancy when it comes to e-reputation determinants in a social networks context. A study was conducted in the sports setting to explore the impact of social networks on the sportspeople's e-reputation. Whereas the study emphasized (1) the influence of social networks' perception on the sportspeople's e-reputation, and the neutral roles of (2) the motives for following sportspeople online, and (3) the negative content on the Internet, additional insights are formulated on maintaining, restoring and managing e-reputation on social networks. Finally, future research directions are suggested on the role of image to control e-reputation.

INTRODUCTION

It takes 20 years to build a reputation and five minutes to ruin it. If you think about that, you'll do things differently. - Warren Buffet

Today, there are more than 3.2 billion Internet users globally (International Telecommunication Union, 2015), making them able to see whatever happens online. One of the major abilities of the Internet, beyond its mass communication technology dimension, is its bi-directionality (Dellarocas, 2003). The

DOI: 10.4018/978-1-5225-1868-6.ch003

Internet allows firms to reach a very large audience at low cost and individuals to diffuse their personal thoughts, opinions and reactions, making them available to any Internet user (Dellarocas, 2003).

Social media are global, open, transparent, non-hierarchical, interactive and real-time, and are completely shifting individuals' behaviors and expectations (Dutta, 2010). Online social platforms are used by billions of people around the world, making them a genuine phenomenon. The leading social networks worldwide ranked by number of active users are:

- Facebook (1.5 billion users),
- WhatsApp (900 million users), and
- QQ (860 million users) (Statista, 2016a).

Almost two-thirds of American adults use social networking sites. 35% of 65-year-olds and older is doing the same. Such behavior has entirely rebuilt the way people get and share information about everything related to their every day's life (Perrin, 2015).

The top ten Twitter accounts having the highest number of followers worldwide belong mainly to celebrities from the music industry, except Obama's account which is ranking third with more than 70 million followers. The most viewed YouTube channels worldwide per month are those of:

- Music stars (David Guetta and Justin Bieber), and
- Labels (T-Series),
- YouTubers (Ryan ToysReview and Family Fun Pack), and
- Nursery videos (LittleBabyBum) (Statista, 2016b).

Sportspersons have well grasped the social media phenomenon. Indeed, almost all websites of sports clubs have links to their Twitter, Facebook, YouTube official pages and accounts. Moreover, soccer players are a typical example of this social medial mania. As of April 2016, Cristiano Ronaldo has more than 41.5 million followers on Twitter, followed by Kaka (24.5 million) and Neymar (21.6 million). Other sports are not left out. Players such as Rafael Nadal (9.2 million followers) and Serena Williams (6.1 million followers) are topping the ranking of most followed Twitter accounts in tennis. Sprinters such Usain Bolt is nearing 4 million followers and F1 pilots such as Lewis Hamilton is having more than 3.2 million followers. Soccer players (Cristiano Ronaldo and Lionel Messi) and clubs (FC Barcelona and Real Madrid) are listed in the top ten most popular Facebook pages based on number of fans (Statista, 2016c).

Sports events are having their share of fame. The retirement of Sir Alex Ferguson in 2013 was the third most tweeted event after the reelection of Barack Obama and the resignation of Pope Benedict. The 2014 World Cup was of the top of conversations on Twitter, generating more than 670 million tweets worldwide (TwitterData, 2014). However, sports events are also having their share of shame. During the 2012 London Olympic Games, several athletes were banned from the competition because of their misbehavior on the Internet. The FIFA corruption crisis in 2015 and the tennis player Maria Sharapova's doping scandal in 2016 were also large online bad buzzes. Finally, it's worth mentioning that an anti-doping database Twitter account (@Dopinglist) was created in September 2008, displaying the most complete database of athletes sanctioned for doping.

The sports industry grows faster than global GDP on average (Kearney, 2011). It is expected to achieve global revenues of US$ 145.3 billion (PricewaterhouseCoopers, 2011). When it comes to social media, it is increasingly used by the sports world, with Facebook, YouTube and Twitter being the most privileged platforms to exchange with fans and online communities (Rothschild, 2011).

Even though social media help to increase the lead generation, to monitor conversation about their brand while mimicking the competition (Rothschild, 2011), social media is still a conundrum for sports firms because of their double-edge facet (Sanderson, 2011). On one hand, athletes can break news, share public and private information, and interact with their fan base via online social platforms. This gives to athletes a feeling of control over the content released. On the other hand, when debatable content is posted by athletes, sports firms become clueless in front of the bad buzz generated by unlimited online users (Sanderson, 2011).

Sports events do not only occur on stadiums but also on the virtual sphere. While athletes represent real business opportunities – sponsorship accounts for more than 30% of the total sports market (Price-waterhouseCoopers, 2011) – a video on YouTube, a picture on Facebook or a tweet can ruin the reputation of sportspeople. Hence, what athletes say online appears to be of great deal for their e-reputation.

So far, few studies have analyzed the concept of e-reputation (Chun & Davies, 2001), and fewer articles have investigated the extent to which social media influences the reputation online (Castellano & Dutot, 2013). Indeed, while 87% of firms' executives rate reputation risk as a top strategic risk (Deloitte, 2014), 56% of global consumers use research engines (e.g., Google, Yahoo!) as the first step of their purchasing journey (PricewaterhouseCoopers, 2014). Moreover, almost 80% of global consumers are influenced by social media in their decisions to buy products (PricewaterhouseCoopers, 2016), and more than 50% of web-consumers frequently use Facebook in their purchasing journey (PricewaterhouseCoopers, 2015). Nevertheless, knowing that more than one-quarter of crises spread internationally within an hour; and over two-thirds within 24 hours, it takes about 21 hours for firms to respond to bad buzzes; and more than half of bad news remains in the spotlights, a month after their first release. Also, only one firm out of ten was well-prepared to manage a crisis, 40% of firms have no contingency plan, and the situation is worse when it comes to manage a behavioral crisis (Freshfields, Bruckhaus, & Deringer, 2013). In short, e-reputation is no longer the affair of some marketing and communication professionals. It became a wider concern which pushed insurance companies, training centers and standardization institutions to develop offers and solutions to address individuals' as well as firms' concerns (Alloing, 2013).

Hence, it is paramount to understand the perception of fans regarding the online reputation of their favorite athletes and to explore how sportspeople manage their relationship with their community through social media in general and social networks more specifically. The aim of this chapter is fourfold:

1.   Investigate the perception of online communities of sportspersons' e-reputation,
2.   Understand the factors that might affect athletes' e-reputation,
3.   Formulate further insights on how to maintain, restore and manage e-reputation, and
4.   Propose future directions on the role of image to control e-reputation.

In the next paragraphs, a background exploring e-reputation in a social networks context is presented, followed by the investigation of the growing importance of social networks in the sports industry in general and the specific case of the French context. The chapter concludes with key recommendations and future research areas on e-reputation and image management.

BACKGROUND: E-REPUTATION IN A SOCIAL NETWORKS CONTEXT

Understanding e-reputation and its perception issues on social networks requires defining the concepts that have been widely used in the professional world but still need clarification on the academic level.

The Social Networks' Era

From Social Media to Social Networks

Social media represent the production, consumption and sharing of information through social interaction mostly on the Internet (Castellano & Dutot, 2013). Therefore, the growing importance of the Internet and of social media has many consequences. For instance, from marketing perspective, social media have a great impact on consumer-to-consumer communications (Mangold & Faulds, 2009). In management, Kaplan & Haelein (2010) emphasize the opportunities and benefits for decision makers deriving from the social media usage. For example, the use of blogs or virtual teams positively influences the collaborative projects and ultimately the performance of the firm.

Social media are various (Kaplan & Haelein, 2010). Among them, social network sites (also called social networking sites or social networks) which are "web-based services that allow individuals to:

1. Build a public or semi-public profile within a bounded system,
2. Articulate a list of other users with whom they share a connection, and
3. View and traverse their list of connections and those made by others within the system." (Boyd & Ellison, 2007, p. 211).

In short, social networking sites are the applications which connect strangers in the virtual sphere (Kaplan & Haelein, 2010), while allowing them to make visible their social links (Boyd & Ellison, 2007).

Social networks are the most popular online places worldwide. Indeed, more than 90% of online adults have an account on at least one social network site (GlobalWebIndex, 2016). In addition, individuals spend almost one hour and a half per day on their social networks, making their social networking accounts for almost 30% of their daily Internet activities (GlobalWebIndex, 2016). Also, the high user engagement on social networks highlights its universal appeal and emphasizes this global cultural phenomenon (comScore, 2011). Nevertheless, the fact that all users, through their social networks, share messages, links, videos, pictures, or even games with other members from the same network, they are creating a community with a multi-directional content. Additionally, the average digital consumer has about 7 social accounts (GlobalWebIndex, 2016). This makes social networks perfect places to observe and analyze individuals' opinions regarding a subject whether it is a person, a brand, a firm or an official institution (Cuvelier & Aufaure, 2011).

People use social networks to communicate and maintain relationships, to update others and get updates on activities and situations, to store events, or to post testimonials (Dwyer et al., 2007). People also use social networks for the enjoyment they feel, for the number of peers they collect as well as for the usefulness they perceive (Lin & Lu, 2011).

Social Networks Diversity and Challenges

Social networks are tremendously diverse. One way to usually categorize social networks is to consider the manner people use them. Some social networks are used to nurture the social connections (e.g., Facebook, Twitter, Google+, Myspace). Others are used to share multimedia contents (e.g. YouTube, Flickr, Pinterest). Some social networks are used for professional purposes such as finding job or business opportunities (e.g. LinkedIn, Viadeo) or to connect with counterparts of the same area of expertise (e.g., Classroom 2.0, Nurse Connect). Individuals also use social networks to connect with informational communities and get information related to their daily issues (e.g., Super Green Me, Do-It-Yourself Community). Other individuals target educational social networks to interact with students and professors (e.g., The Student Room, ePALS School Blog) or academic-specific social networking to share research and look for peer-reviews (e.g., Academia.edu). Finally, people also use social networks for their hobbies such as gardening (Oh My Bloom), or scrapbooking (My Place at Scrapbook.com) (White, 2012).

Social networks can be utilized in several ways which makes them so popular and at the same time raises several challenges for individuals as well as for the firms. For individuals, social networks question the privacy and trust principles which guide their willingness to share content and develop new social connections (Dwyer et al., 2007). More specifically, young individuals (i.e. children and adolescents) are highly concerned by cyberbullying and online harassment, sexting, as well as dealing with self-esteem and being addicted to the online life (O'Keeffe et al., 2010). Additional challenges related to individuals' online presence on social networks are setting the right boundaries between their personal and professional spheres and audiences, selecting the right content to disclose (Dutta, 2010), as well as managing the digital footprint.

Social networks also represent challenges that firms need to take into account. First, because many forms of user-generated contents emerged on the Internet, the credibility of the information shared on social networks is questioned (Castillo et al., 2011). Second, an overload of information flourished on social networks, which make it more difficult for followers to find the right information in the right social network (Bian et al., 2008). Third, the fact that individuals in online communities can very easily register, disappear and re-register under completely different identities with almost no costs, is problematic to handle (Dellarocas, 2003). Fourth, managers and decisions makers are not aware to the full extent of the influence of social networks on the firm's survival and on their sales because Internet users can use social networks as media to create, share or modify content on the Internet (Kietzmann et al., 2011). Fifth, because of the myriad social networks, firms cannot be active in all of them, to avoid making their efforts be meaningless and diluted. Hence, firms will need to select the most efficient and relevant social networking platforms to their target groups and to their messages (Kaplan & Haelein, 2010).

Nevertheless, one of the major challenges in using social networks is the reputational risk. The reputation might be at risk because of information leakage, piracy, data loss, etc. (Shullich, 2011). Moreover, losing reputation affects competitiveness, market positioning, stakeholders' trust and loyalty, and the legitimacy of operations (Aula, 2011). Consequently, firms lose the control of the information they and other Internet users create and diffuse. Overall, ignoring the relevance of the Internet on reputation management is no longer possible.

From Reputation to E-Reputation

Reputation and the Internet

Reputation is a "lasting perception held of an organization by an individual, group or network that forms a collective system of beliefs and opinions that influences people's actions with regards to an organization." (Balmer, 2001). Reputation is defined as "a summary of one's past actions within the context of a specific community, presented in a manner that can help other community members make decisions with respect to whether and how to relate to that individual" (Dellarocas, 2010, p. 34). It reflects the extent to which users can identify their standing and the standing of others (Kietzmann et al., 2011).

Frombrun (1996) highlighted key attributes of reputation that might be affected by the Internet and social media, more specifically social networks. First, reputation is based on perceptions. Because perception is subjective, reputation is to some extent out of the hands of the corporation (Brown et al., 2006). Therefore, when taking into account the Internet, the perception of virtual sphere individuals hold influences reputation. For example, if individuals are not technology savvy, their perception of IT-based products or services will be biased in comparison to individuals who appreciate such products and services. Consequently, the perception people have of social media and social networks influences the perception they have of a firm's reputation online. Second, reputation represents the aggregate perception of all its audiences (Fombrun, 1996). Both internal and external stakeholders' perception forms the overall reputation. However, previous studies pointed out that reputation is often issue specific; and that an organization can have a different reputation per stakeholder group constituents (Brown et al., 2006). Internet users can represent a new category of stakeholders. Consequently, their motivation to create and follow user-generated content can influence the perceived reputation they form towards the evaluated entity. Information is spread faster on the Internet by online communities. Such communities are empowered as they can create and diffuse information of the Internet. Third, reputation can be positive or negative (Wartick, 2002). Similarly, the retention of online information, based on user-generated content, can also be positive and negative. Because of limited cognitive capacity and because of an overload of information, the retention of information is limited. One can assume that people tend to better remember events with negative content. Therefore, one can deduce that especially on the Internet, the retention of negative content is higher than the retention of positive content. Fourth, reputation is stable and enduring (Wartick, 2002), but it does not prevent from change. Several authors implicitly or explicitly refer to the notion of time in their definition of reputation. Building a reputation takes time (Mahon, 2002; Rhee & Haunschild, 2006; Roberts & Dowling, 2002) and one can question whether the time issue is relevant on the Internet. Fifth, reputation summarizes relevant past actions (Dellarocas, 2010). Reputation links the past to the future as it results of a firm's past actions and future prospects (Fombrun, 1996). However, the Internet changed the rules of the game. While traditional reputation takes time to be built, e-reputation is immediate. One can deduce that the past and the immediate dimensions of reputation are both needed to be taken into consideration. Sixth, reputation is a matter of trust, a very difficult attribute to guarantee in an Internet setting. Hence, social media rely on automatic tools that aggregate user-generated information to ensure trustworthiness (Kietzmann et al., 2011). Finally, with the Internet, people are connected, and they want to know everything, from everywhere and at any time. Therefore, firms such as Twitter fit these new trends. People are motivated to follow other people on the Internet based on exclusivity of information, develop some kind of virtual proximity, etc. One can deduce that Internet users' motivations influence their perceptions of e-reputation.

Perspectives on E-Reputation

E-reputation, online reputation, cyber reputation, web reputation, and digital reputation are some of the several terms used to designated different practices, technologies or professional services (Alloing, 2013). E-reputation is viewed by the practitioners as "the image Internet users have about a company or a person based on information published on the web, on what is said by the others, on the messages diffused by various users (customers, competitors, employees, etc.), or by the footprints left involuntarily." (Frochot & Molinaro, 2008, p. 13). In the academic world, e-reputation refers to the elements of reputation which are derived specifically from electronic contacts (Chun & Davies, 2001). The e-reputation of an object is defined as "the reputation built on a set of perceptions that stakeholders have on that object, based on any information circulating on the Net." (Paquerot et al., 2011, p. 281).

E-reputation shares many common features with reputation (i.e. image, opinion, identity) but differs in the formation process using Internet in general or social media in particular (Alloing, 2013). E-reputation is often related to electronic Word-of-Mouth. The latter refers to positive or negative statement individuals express about products, brands or firms, and diffuse them on Internet (Hennig-Thurau et al., 2004). E-reputation is also often related to image. E-reputation refers to an overall image formed by an Internet user about an object. E-reputation is also the result of the several images formed by Internet users about an object and that are restituted by them to the Internet (Alloing, 2013). Finally, e-reputation is often related to digital identity. The latter helps to manage the e-reputation through highlighting the attributes that influence online users' perceptions about a firm (Alloing, 2013).

Putting reputation and e-reputation into perspective allows inferring the following features. E-reputation is first based on the perception of the evaluating audience. Second, e-reputation is strongly linked to social networks, considered as the most popular platforms for the expression and diffusion of opinions (Alloing, 2013). Third, online communities represent stakeholders that evaluate online reputation. Fourth, the retention of negative online content is higher than the retention of positive one. Fifth, the motivation of the multiple constituencies varies, which influences their perception of e-reputation. In addition, positive and negative elements need to be considered when analyzing perceived reputation. Finally, because reputation is built over time and e-reputation is immediate, two dimensions of reputation need to be considered: the present dimension ('awareness' as the creating stage of reputation); and the past dimension ('image' as the management stage of reputation). Awareness is the short-term initial stage of reputation whereas image is the long-term development stage of reputation.

THE GROWING IMPRORTANCE OF SOCIAL NETWORKS IN THE SPORTS INDUSTRY

Studies on Sports and Social Networks in the French Context

The image of an athlete is important since it can help to receive the support of the general public. In addition, sportspersons are ambassadors of their own sports. They also represent brands as a mean of celebrity endorsement. They carry specific values and can become heroes for a whole generation.

The impact of social networks on athletes' e-reputation in the French context has previously been investigated. Interviews with three sports experts were conducted. These experts explained that different elements play a significant role for sportspersons on social networks, such as:

1.	The frequency of social networks usage,
2.	The opinion towards social networks,
3.	The reasons to follow (or not) athletes on social networks,
4.	The number of athletes and sports followed on social networks,
5.	The need for athletes to be present on social networks,
6.	The role of social networks for athletes,
7.	The 'memory' of the internet by giving a positive example (and respectively a negative example)
8.	Involving a social network and an athlete and/or a sports event (open-ended question to assess the top of mind), and
9.	The reasons to stop following an athlete on social networks.

While it takes many years to build traditional reputation (offline), e-reputation is more instantaneous as social media spread information rapidly. Therefore, when analyzing e-reputation, it seems pertinent to differentiate short-term and long-term e-reputation (see table 1).

In addition, when it comes to factors that influence e-reputation in the sports context, table 2 further displays the elements mentioned by the three experts. Overall, it is important to differentiate factors that are related to the use of social networks in general, to the sports discipline itself, or to the athlete him/herself and his/her behavior on the Internet, and within or outside of sports fields. Each factor, and/or the combination of these factors can potentially influence the sportspeople's e-reputation (see table 2).

Table 1. Dimensions of e-reputation

Variable	Dimensions	
e-reputation	Short-term: awareness	Long term: Image

Source: *(Castellano et al., 2014)*

Table 2. Elements that influence athletes' e-reputation

Variable	Dimensions	
Perception of Social Network	Positive perception: • An opportunity. • A new media. • An entertainment.	Negative perception: • A danger. • Not useful.
Motivation for following sportsmen on social networks	• Sport (the specific discipline). • Sportsman's personal information. • "Proximity" developed with the athlete. • Type of information shared online, which is rather 'exclusive'.	
Motivation for not following sportsmen on social networks	• Social networks-related reasons. • Sport-related reasons. • Sportsman-related reasons.	
Retention of Information	• Positive negative elements of information retention.	• No retention • Partial retention (participants remember the name of the sportsman or the event mentioned on social networks). • Full retention (name both the name of a sportsman and a particular event or comment he/she made on social networks).

Source: (Castellano et al., 2014)

The above-mentioned elements were used to create an online survey and test corresponding hypotheses in order to investigate the relationship between social networks and e-reputation in the sports context. Among the 155 respondents who participated to the online questionnaire 44% were male and 56% female; most of them (53%) were below 25 years old, 19% between 26 and 30, 16% between 31 and 45, and 12% above 45.

Concerning the attitude towards social networks, the results showed that 84% of the respondents connected on social networks several times a day. First, social networks represent an unprecedented way to create some proximity between an athlete and his/her community. The respondents felt closer to the sportspersons (37%) and they had a sense of interactivity. It is also interesting to notice that respondents mostly looked for sports news (88%), but also for some more personal information about the athlete, and to gain some kind of exclusivity (72%). Second, according to the respondents, social networks represent a new relationship between athletes, sports, and fans. Although, most respondents did not follow sportspersons on social networks (60%), among the remaining 40%, half of them followed between 1 and 4 athletes, 12% between 5 and 10. Surprisingly, half of them followed 10 or more athletes. They mainly followed soccer, tennis, swimming and rugby. Third, most respondents said that athletes must be present on social networks (66%). The main reason evoked was to manage their image and e-reputation. Results showed that when the interactivity increased, so did the level of e-reputation.

However, the results also showed the dark side of social networks. Only 4% did not find them useful. But, 40% of them considered social networks as dangerous, even for a professional use. The privacy issue for instance has been already mentioned in previous studies (Boyd & Ellison, 2007). Finally, when it comes to top of mind illustrations related to athletes and social networks, respondents unexpectedly rather remembered positive examples in comparison to negative examples. Positive examples are for instance, posting the picture of a new born kid (Gerald Piqué from FC Barcelona and his famous wife Shakira). It can also be sharing a victory online. This showed that social networks cannot mainly be associated with short-term memory. Whatever an athlete can write or share, people will tend to remember it.

The results of the study showed that the way people perceive social networks influences e-reputation, both present-based (awareness) and past-based (image) e-reputation. In addition, the study also found that both short and long-term e-reputation derives from the combination between the perception of social networks and the motivation to use them. However, the underlying motivations to use social networks do not influence short and long-term e-reputation. Finally, the study found that respondents recall equally positive and negative information on the Internet. Women tend to remember positive events (mean = 0.37) over negative events (0.19). For men, a difference was noticed (retention means: positive = 0.5 and negative = 0.48). However, the mean difference for men is not significant. Overall, some results supported previous research (the double-edge of social networks), while others were counter-intuitive (Internet has a memory).

Initial Perspectives on Social Networks and E-Reputation

The main objective of this study was to explore the relationship between social networks and online reputation. More specifically, the study aimed at investigating the perception of online communities of sportspersons' e-reputation, and understanding the factors that affect such perception in line with previous research (Chun & Davis, 2001; Castellano & Dutot, 2013).

First, regarding the perception of online communities of sportspersons' e-reputation, results showed that fans and communities pay attention to the information that exists and that circulates online. Internet users do not only remember negative information (e.g., bad buzz), and the retention of positive events is higher. Internet has a memory for good news! Bad buzz can quickly be replaced by other types of information. However, the retention of information (both positive and negative) is limited as Internet users tend not to remember many things.

Second, the perception of social networks influences the e-reputation of sportspersons. When social networks are positively perceived, audiences tend to have a better awareness and image of the athlete. However, when social networks are negatively perceived, audiences tend to have negative perception of athletes' reputation. More specifically, technical problems of social networks (e.g., access issues, saturated networks), or the limited use of such networks have a negative impact on athletes' e-reputation. In addition, the literature also identified limits of social networks. Privacy and vulnerability (Baker, Gentry & Rittenburg, 2005; Aguirre et al., 2012) represents two main dangers of social networks and the Internet in general. Such dangers affect people's perception of e-reputation.

Third, athletes cannot only perform on the field, but also in the virtual scene in order to increase their potential revenues and sponsorship contracts. No matter the type of motivation to follow sportspersons on the Internet, such motivations have no influence on the sportspeople's e-reputation. Therefore, several questions arise regarding the type of information that athletes can share, and the new ways of communication with their online communities to consider. Another option is to reconsider the relationship with online audiences in order to increase e-reputation (Boyd et al., 2010).

Fourth, the interaction effect between perception and motivation has an impact on e-reputation. The combination of positive perception of social networks and the right motivation to use them was found to be the winning combination. It is not the number of tweets or provocative contents that matter but rather the right tweet for the right audience at the right time that matters to build and keep a high e-reputation.

Overall, e-reputation in the sports industry results from factors related to social networks, to the sports and to the sportspeople. Throughout the empirical investigation in the sports industry, online communities and fans were found to perceive differently the signals sent (videos, posts, tweets, etc.) by sportspersons. These aggregate perceptions form the overall e-reputation of an athlete. These athletes are the ambassadors of their sports and they often represent brands. It is therefore crucial for them to control their image in order to build and manage their e-reputation.

SOLUTIONS AND RECOMMENDATIONS

Maintain E-Reputation

First, the manner how sportspersons maintain good e-reputation on social networks is illustrated through the example of David Beckham. David Beckham created the Footwork Productions Limited in 1996 in order to manage his image. Such a strategy proved to be successful as he earned 31.5 million euros in 2012. Early 2013, David Beckham signed with the French football team Paris Saint-Germain, where he ended his career on May, 23rd, 2013. Even though his professional sport activities are over, David Beckham is still very active and he possesses many followers on social media and social networks. His presence on social networks kept on growing after he retired from football. For instance, his Facebook page has 54 million fans, and his latest post has been viewed more than one million times, with more than 11,000 likes in less than 24 hours. These numbers signal high level of interests from his audience all over the world. Similarly, his Twitter account has more than 610,000 followers, and his Instagram account is followed by 22 million users with only 350 publications.

How to explain this constant growth on social media from a retired professional sportsman? Managing efficiently one's presence online would ultimately have an impact on e-reputation.

The type of information shared and social networks used are further examined. For instance, the example of a picture posted on both Facebook and Instagram for David Beckham to celebrate the birthday of his famous wife Victoria Beckham is very instructive. Posted on Facebook on April 20th, 2016, the picture has almost 800,000 likes, 6,830 comments and 6,860 shares. On Instagram, there were 5923 comments and 805,000 likes. Such use of cross-social networks dynamics creates a spillover effect, and ultimately represents exponential visibility on social networks.

Besides cross social networks presence, another mean to keep a high level of visibility in the case of David Beckham is connected to the diffusion of information not directly related to sports activities. For instance, out of the 20 latest posts on Facebook, 6 were directly related to sports (i.e., meeting former Real Madrid team players, sponsorship activities with Adidas, celebrating Kobe Bryant career, tribute to Johan Cruyff, etc.). This means that more than 75% of the content posted was not related to sports. Among them, 4 posts were related to promotional activities (i.e., celebrity endorsement with the fashion brand H&M). Also, 8 additional posts were related to his family. Beckham's sons appeared on 6 of these 8 family posts. This strategy is not surprising as recent articles online explained that David has full control of his son Brooklyn's social media accounts (Shenton, 2015). Even though it is quite difficult to control what is said about oneself online, it is of strategic importance to at least have a certain control on one's official social network accounts.

Overall, the reputation and e-reputation of sportspersons are not only built on the sports arenas but also on a virtual field, either through cross social networks dynamics or through activities not directly related to sports. However, even though the case of David Beckham illustrates how to maintain high levels of e-reputation, the virtual sphere rather emphasizes the negative impact of the Internet on online reputation.

Restore E-Reputation

Online reputation management is about controlling the information shown on the Internet (specifically search engines) in order to manage what is visible to the general public (The Armchair Athletes, 2016). When typing the keywords 'athletes + reputation' on the most popular Internet search engine, the first five results emphasize the negative influence of the Internet on sportspersons' online reputation. These results specifically mention terms such as:

- 'Risks',
- 'Terrible reputation',
- 'E-Reputation in question',
- 'Bad reputation', and
- 'Coach killer reputation'.

As the David Beckham example exhibited, sportspersons should not only pay attention to their behavior on the real sports fields, but also to the virtual arena. Hence the question of maintaining high reputation and e-reputation, but also repair e-reputation in times of crisis should be further investigated.

There is a double-edge of being present on social networks. On the one hand, social networks can help to increase e-reputation. Teddy Riner, the first and only judoka to have won 8 World Championships gold medals, is very present on social media. He considers that there is no barrier between him and his 'friends' on the virtual sphere. For instance, Facebook is a good mean to keep in touch with his fans. That's the way he manages his image and closeness with his online communities, while preserving his private life simultaneously (Dixte, 2012). Other sportsmen consider that Twitter decreases physical distances and increases the opportunity to share information with fans. On the other hand, social networks give sportspersons little room for error because of the endless scrutiny. Online reputation problems can arise in different ways. They can be related to misleading news, outdated information, and other poisonous materials that populate the Web (The Armchair Athletes, 2016). Below are some examples of such problems:

- Sportspersons may wish to provide exclusive news but ultimately disclose private or secret information. For example, football player Eden Hazard gave the name of his new club while the news was not yet official. Eden gained 250,000 followers on Twitter, but was very much criticized by his new club at the same time.
- Sportspersons are not in full control of what is said about them online. Fox Sports posted in 2012 a message on their Latin American Twitter site and declared that Lionel Messi died. A 'hashtag' stating '#RIP Messi' was also included with the post (RecoverReputation, 2016).
- When sportspersons do not themselves post and monitor the news on their own official accounts, mistakes out of their control can damage their reputation. When famous Dutch football player Johan Cruyff (among the top 10 players of all time) passed away, Morgan Schneiderlin a French football player posted his tribute on Instagram - but sadly not only put up a picture of the wrong person but also spelled Cruyff's name wrong. The e-reputation of the French football player was damaged even though the tribute was posted by the community manager, not directly by the player, and the PR never publicly apologized (Bourdet, 2016).
- Finally, while sportpersons tend to better control established Internet-based media, they need to pay particular attention to new types of social networks. For instance, the football player Serge Aurier wanted to interact with fans through Periscope. At some point, he insulted his coach and the video was spread through the live video streaming app. New networks, apps, features, etc. increase interactivity and speed of information for the best but also for the worst. The video was posted by many YouTubers and got more than 1.5 million views. However, the video of Serge Aurier apologies on the official YouTube channel of his football club reached only 75,000 views. This examples shows some asymmetry between the damage done and attempts efforts to restore e-reputation.

Overall, it will always be better to avoid controversies and bad buzz as they can drag on for long periods of time (Miller, 2011). This consequently provides sportspersons new and challenging means to act and react efficiently and successfully on the Internet. The correct interaction with general audiences (fans, online communities, experts, business analysts, etc.) is crucial when it comes to e-reputation. In addition, sportspersons must ensure that all communication channels are covered accordingly so as to easily convey the information they wish to address. Those "new technologies enable audiences to move from a passive stage to an active one, playing, therefore, a dynamic role and allowing public controversies and crises." (Hearit, 1999, p. 303).

FUTURE RESEARCH DIRECTIONS: THE ROLE OF IMAGE TO CONTROL E-REPUTATION

When it comes to better understanding e-reputation dynamics, the previous illustrations show that maintaining high levels of e-reputation and restoring damaged e-reputation seem to be the main challenges and provide complementary perspective to examine issues related to e-reputation.

Internet users can influence each other and affect other users' perception of the sportsperson (Siano et al., 2011). As reputation is based on perceptions, it is to some extent outside the control of the sportsperson (Brown et al., 2006), especially with the development of the Internet because it is more difficult to distinguish or differentiate between official information posted by the athlete, and subjective interpretations deriving from information on blogs and social networks, for which sources of information are difficult to identify. For instance, positive or negative Word-of-Mouth would spread faster on the Internet because sportspersons cannot control such messages. Immediate and sudden online reactions and comments can boost or destroy the e-reputation of sportspersons faster than ever (Ory, 2009).

Because it becomes more challenging for the sportspeople to control what is said about them, they need to rely on stronger anchor points in order to protect their e-reputation. One of these points is their image, which can be defined as the general impression that audiences hold and which is directly linked to reputation.

For some scholars, image and reputation are interchangeable (Dowling, 1994). Other scholars differentiate image and reputation (Chun & Davies, 2001). Image is based on the perception of external audiences only whereas reputation is based on the perception of all audiences, both external and internal (Chun & Davies, 2001). Many authors implicitly or explicitly refer to the notion of time in their definition of reputation (Fombrun, 1996; Gotsi & Wilson, 2001), as evaluations are formed over time by repeated impressions of image, whether positive or negative (Gray & Balmer, 1998). In short, better managing one's image can better help to manage e-reputation.

Crisis Communication to Restore E-Reputation

A crisis is defined as "any emotionally charged situation that, once it becomes public, invites negative stakeholder reaction and thereby has the potential to threaten the financial wellbeing, reputation, or survival." (James & Wooten, 2005, p. 142). A crisis can be described as a chain of events that can have negative consequences on reputation (online and offline) (Bloch, 2012). Crisis can escalate and spread even more rapidly than before.

The Internet can act as "an agent that accelerates the crisis news cycle and breaks geographical boundaries." (Gonzalez-Herrero & Smith, 2008, p. 144). This "gives the crisis a new viral dimension although the same crisis would most probably occur at a slower pace without the existence of the Internet." (Gonzalez-Herrero & Smith, 2008, p. 145). "It is often the handling of a crisis that leads to more damage than the crisis event itself." (James & Wooten, 2011, p. 61).

Sometimes, the sports-related activity is not the core of the online discussions anymore, but rather the numerous social media reactions. Once the e-reputation is hurt on social media, the sportspersons' eagerness to defend themselves just makes the whole thing worst, or even funnier. Specifically, sportspersons try to "change or delete information available on the Internet, [which] will lead to a greater diffusion of information that would be kept confidential in case of no manipulation. That is called the Streisand effect." (Liarte, 2013, p. 103). Consequently, the more control sportspersons try to have on the Internet, whether it is on their brand image in general or a specific situation, the greater the negative consequences. "By monitoring the blogosphere and quickly correcting rumours that could be perceived as facts, companies were able to prevent the crisis from escalating to mainstream media." (Crush, 2006, as cited in Gonzalez-Herrero & Smith, 2008, p. 147).

E-Reputation Management

Online reputation management is an ongoing process (Jones et al., 2009). Sportspersons must monitor and participate to online activities, and they also measure their impact on their e-reputation.

In the age of social media, almost every public figure has dealt with a mocking tweet at one time or another. Today, it is not only the sports performances that are discussed online, but also the private life of these sportspersons, their links to celebrities in other industries (music, movies, etc.), or even make personal judgements of their look, their behavior outside of the sports fields, etc. (Depta, 2016).

A online monologue is no longer efficient. With the development of Web 2.0, sportspersons need to engage in virtual discussions with their online communities. A good e-reputation mainly depends on the right balance between "blogs, social networks, wikis, podcasts, mail groups, newsgroups, forums and chat rooms." (Jones et al., 2009, p. 930). In addition, image and e-reputation are now co-created with all types of audiences (fans, experts, etc.), leading to online communities. These online conversations need to be managed and coordinated efficiently. Overall, "when used effectively the Internet is the best tool for improving reputation that has yet been created." (Valor, 2009, quoted in Jones et al. 2009, p. 9).

Finally, some firms specialized in creating; managing and monitoring e-reputation in the sports industry are also being more and more established. Communication and PR firms, such as SportMarket© and Digidium©, aim to monitor information online. They screen the tone of the discussions online, whether positive or negative. They even provide follow-ups and recommendations based on the specific objectives of their clients who are professional sportspersons but also sports clubs and even agents.

New Perspectives on Managing E-Reputation on Social Networks

The digital era changed the traffic and the speed of information diffusion, as new technologies are creating an acceleration phenomenon. New challenges occur nowadays, companies are much more fragile with the faster diffusion of information on Internet, and crises arise more often. Social media and blogs have further fragmented the audience, which makes it more difficult for sportspersons to manage their communication on social networks. Different audiences can voice their opinion in a much easier and effortless way on social networks. Such dynamics can have an influence on the sportspeople's image and e-reputation.

For example, one particularity of e-reputation is that information spreads much faster among many more people than ever before. How is this happening within the sports sphere? The Facebook might appear to be privileged for regular daily conversation. During sports events such as the Olympic Games and football competitions, blogs represent interesting means to spread and analyze some information. Still, Twitter tops all social networks to comment sports events, whether the audience discusses sports brands or sportspersons. Interestingly, depending on the type of sports events, audiences will rather tend to be ethnocentric (i.e., discuss teams and/or sportspersons from their own country), such as during football competitions, while audiences tend to mention sportspersons from different countries during events such as the Olympic Games, which shows the truly global dimension of such sports events, with overall rather positive comments (Martins, 2012). Twitter is a pertinent way to develop a brand – in the case of professional athletes, they are the brand – and to interact with online communities by forming a connection with their fans. Sportspersons can use their Twitter accounts to give themselves more exposure for endorsements. But negative reactions from social networks can cost sportspersons / brands dearly. If the athlete as a brand is thought of to be controversial, then audiences are less likely to become associated with that athlete / brand.

CONCLUSION

In this chapter, the authors aimed at analyzing the factors that influence the perception of athletes' e-reputation, which is mainly observed on social networks. Many types of social networks exist and people tend to spend more and more time to discuss their favorite topics and sports is among them. Athletes are considered celebrities and online communities share their opinions on what athletes say, what is said by other Internet users, and any information published on the Web that overall form the e-reputation of athletes. Fans and online communities perceive the online reputation of athletes based on characteristics related to the specificities of the social networks, of the sports or sports event under scrutiny, and of the athletes themselves.

The Internet provides many opportunities from communication perspectives, such as greater interactivity, greater diffusion of information, wider reach, etc. Very few athletes such as David Beckham rather have a positive image and high reputation online. In fact, there are some risks in communicating through social networks, mainly because of the lack of control on the virtual sphere. These dangers are related to the diversity and sometimes conflicting types of audiences, and to the new types of apps and virtual tools recently created. When the e-reputation is damaged, negative consequences can appear on many levels – sponsorship contracts cancelled, lower sports-related performance, etc. – which requires a communication strategy to be defined. Sometimes, the management of the crisis is worse than the origin of the crisis itself. Communication crisis is a key to restore e-reputation on social networks and bring back good relationships between the athlete and the fans.

REFERENCES

Aguirre, M. E., Mahr, D., de Ruyter, K., Wetzels, M., & Grewal, D. (2012). The Impact Of Vulnerability During Covert Personalization – A Regulatory Mode Approach. *41st EMAC Conference.*

Alloing, C. (2013). *Processus de veille par infomédiation sociale pour construire l'e-réputation d'une organisation. Approche par agents-facilitateurs appliquée à la DSIC de La Poste* (Doctoral dissertation). Université of Poitiers.

Aula, P. (2010). Social media, reputation risk and ambient publicity management. *Strategy and Leadership*, *38*(6), 43–49. doi:10.1108/10878571011088069

Baker, S. M., Gentry, J. W., & Rittenburg, T. L. (2005). Building Understanding of the Domain of Customer Vulnerability. *Journal of Macromarketing*, *25*(2), 128–139. doi:10.1177/0276146705280622

Bloch, E. (2012). *Communication de crise et media sociaux. In Collection: Fonction de l'Entreprise.* Paris: Dunod.

Bourdet, A.-S. (2016). *Bourdes des sportifs sur les réseaux sociaux: c'est pas moi, c'est mon CM!* Retrieved April 24, 2016, from http://www.lequipe.fr/Football/Article/Bourdes-des-sportifs-sur-les-reseaux-sociaux-c-est-pas-moi-c-est-mon-cm/646602

Boyd, B. K., Bergh, D. D., & Ketchen, D. J. (2010). Reconsidering the Reputation-Performance Relationship: A Resource-Based View. *Journal of Management, 36*(3), 588–609. doi:10.1177/0149206308328507

Boyd, D. M., & Ellison, N. B. (2007). Social network sites: Definition, history, and scholarship. *Journal of Computer-Mediated Communication, 13*(1), 210–230. doi:10.1111/j.1083-6101.2007.00393.x

Brown, T. J., Dacin, P. A., Pratt, M. G., & Whetten, D. A. (2006). Identity, intended image, construed image, and reputation: An interdisciplinary framework and suggested terminology. *Journal of the Academy of Marketing Science, 34*(2), 99–106. doi:10.1177/0092070305284969

Castellano, S., & Dutot, V. (2013). Une analyse de l'e-réputation par analogie ou contraste avec la réputation: Une approche par les médias sociaux. *Revue Française du Marketing, 243*, 35–51.

Castellano, S., Khelladi, I., Chipaux, A., & Kupferminc, C. (2014). The Influence of Social Networks on E-Reputation: How Sportspersons Manage the Relationship with Their Online Community. *International Journal of Technology and Human Interaction, 10*(4), 65–79. doi:10.4018/ijthi.2014100105

Chun, R., & Davies, G. (2001). E-reputation: The role of mission and vision statements in positioning strategy. *The Journal of Brand Management, 8*(4), 315–333. doi:10.1057/palgrave.bm.2540031

comScore. (2011). *It's a Social World. Social Networking Leads as Top Online Activity Globally, Accounting for 1 in Every 5 Online Minutes.* Retrieved April 20, 2016, from http://www.comscore.com/Insights/Press-Releases/2011/12/Social-Networking-Leads-as-Top-Online-Activity-Globally

Cuvelier, E., & Aufaure, M. A. (2011). A buzz and e-reputation monitoring tool for twitter based on Galois Lattices. In *Conceptual Structures for Discovering Knowledge* (pp. 91–103). Springer Berlin Heidelberg. doi:10.1007/978-3-642-22688-5_7

Dellarocas, C. (2003). The digitization of word of mouth: Promise and challenges of online feedback mechanisms. *Management Science, 49*(10), 1407–1424. doi:10.1287/mnsc.49.10.1407.17308

Dellarocas, C. (2010). Online reputation systems: How to design one that does what you need. *MIT Sloan Management Review, 51*(3), 33.

Deloitte. (2014). *Global survey on reputation risk.* Reputation@Risk.

Depta, L. (2016). *25 People Sports Social Media Hilariously Called Out, Part 1.* Retrieved April 24, 2016, from http://bleacherreport.com/articles/2630187-25-people-sports-social-media-hilariously-called-out-part-1

Dixte, M. (2012). *La e-réputation sportive se joue sur tous les terrains.* Retrieved April 20, 2016, from http://blog.youseemii.fr/la-e-reputation-sportive-se-joue-sur-tous-les-terrains

Dowling, G. (1994). *Corporate Reputations.* London: Kogan Page.

Dutta, S. (2010). What's your personal social media strategy? *Harvard Business Review*, *88*(11), 127–130. PMID:21049685

Dwyer, C., Hiltz, S., & Passerini, K. (2007). Trust and privacy concern within social networking sites: A comparison of Facebook and MySpace. *AMCIS 2007 Proceedings*, 339.

Fombrun, C. J. (1996). *Reputation: realizing value from the corporate image*. Boston, MA: Harvard Business School Press.

Freshfields Bruckhaus Deringer. (2013). *Containing a crisis. Dealing with corporate disasters in the digital age*. Author.

Frochot, D., & Molinaro, F. (2008). *Livre blanc sur l'e-réputation*. Paris: Les Infostratèges.

GlobalWebIndex (2016). *Social summary. Quarterly report on the latest trends in social networking*. Author.

Gonzalez-Herrero, A., & Smith, S. (2008). Crisis communications management on the Web: How Internet-based technologies are changing the way public relations professionals handle business crises. *Journal of Contingencies and Crisis Management*, *16*(3), 143–153. doi:10.1111/j.1468-5973.2008.00543.x

Gotsi, M., & Wilson, A. M. (2001). Corporate reputation: Seeking a definition. *Corporate Communications: An International Journal*, *6*(1), 24–30. doi:10.1108/13563280110381189

Gray, E. R., & Balmer, J. M. T. (1998). Managing Corporate Image and Corporate Reputation. *Long Range Planning*, *31*(5), 695–702. doi:10.1016/S0024-6301(98)00074-0

Hearit, K. M. (1999). Newsgroups, activist publics, and corporate apologia: The case of Intel and its Pentium chip. *Public Relations Review*, *25*(3), 291–308. doi:10.1016/S0363-8111(99)00020-X

Hennig-Thurau, T., Gwinner, K. P., Walsh, G., & Gremler, D. D. (2004). Electronic word-of-mouth via consumer-opinion platforms: What motivates consumers to articulate themselves on the Internet? *Journal of Interactive Marketing*, *18*(1), 38–52. doi:10.1002/dir.10073

International Telecommunication Union. (2015). *ICT facts and figures*. Geneva: ITU.

James, E. H., & Wooten, L. P. (2005). Leadership as (Un)usual: How to display competence in times of crisis. *Organizational Dynamics*, *34*(2), 141–152. doi:10.1016/j.orgdyn.2005.03.005

James, E.H. & Wooten, L.P. (2011). Crisis Leadership and Why It Matters. *European Financial Review*, 60-64.

Jones, B., Temperley, J., & Lima, A. (2009). Corporate reputation in the era of Web 2.0: The case of Primark. *Journal of Marketing Management*, *25*(9-10), 927–939. doi:10.1362/026725709X479309

Kearney, A. T. (2011). *The Sports Market; Major trends and challenges in an industry full of passion*. Retrieved April 20, 2016, from https://www.atkearney.com/documents/10192/6f46b880-f8d1-4909-9960-cc605bb1ff34

Liarte, S. (2013). Image de marque et Internet: Comprendre, éviter et gérer leffet Streisand. *Décisions Marketing*, *69*(69), 103–110. doi:10.7193/dm.069.103.110

Lin, K. Y., & Lu, H. P. (2011). Why people use social networking sites: An empirical study integrating network externalities and motivation theory. *Computers in Human Behavior*, *27*(3), 1152–1161. doi:10.1016/j.chb.2010.12.009

Martins, D. (2012). *E-réputation marques et sportifs: les JO plus « sociaux » que l'Euro*. Retrieved April 24, 2016, from http://www.synthesio.com/fr/blog/francais-e-reputation-marques-et-sportifs/

Miller, S. (2011). *Lessons in social media brand reputation: observing athletes on Twitter*. Retrieved April 24, 2016, from http://www.cision.com/us/2011/06/brand-reputation-social-media/

OKeeffe, G. S., & Clarke-Pearson, K. (2011). The impact of social media on children, adolescents, and families. *Pediatrics*, *127*(4), 800–804. doi:10.1542/peds.2011-0054 PMID:21444588

Ory, W. (2009). *La réputation de l'entreprise ne se limite pas à Internet*. Retrieved April 24, 2016, from http://www.marketing-professionnel.fr/outil-marketing/reputation-entreprise-depasse-internet-perception-globale-marque.html

Paquerot, M., Queffelec, A., Sueur, I., & Biot-Paquerot, G. (2011). L'e-réputation ou le renforcement de la gouvernance par le marché de l'hôtellerie? *Management & Avenir*, (5), 280-296.

Perrin, A. (2015). *Social networking usage: 2005-2015*. Pew Research Center. Retrieved April 24, 2016 from http://www.pewinternet.org/2015/10/08/2015/Social-Networking-Usage-2005-2015/

PricewaterhouseCoopers. (2011). *Changing the game. Outlook for the global sports market to 2015*. Author.

PricewaterhouseCoopers. (2014). *Consommateurs connectés. La distribution à l'ère digitale. 4ème étude mondiale sur les web-acheteurs*. Author.

PricewaterhouseCoopers. (2016). *Global total retail survey. They say they want a revolution*. Author.

RecoverReputation. (2016). *Who Should Manage Your Online Reputation For Athletes, Tennis Players*. Retrieved April 24, 2016, from http://www.recoverreputation.com/who-should-manage-your-online-reputation-for-athletes-tennis-players/

Rothschild, P. C. (2011). Social media use in sports and entertainment venues. *International Journal of Event and Festival Management*, *2*(2), 139–150. doi:10.1108/17582951111136568

Sanderson, J. (2011). To tweet or not to tweet: Exploring Division I athletic departments social-media policies. *International Journal of Sport Communication*, *4*(4), 492–513. doi:10.1123/ijsc.4.4.492

Shenton, Z. (2015). *David Beckham reveals he has full control over son Brooklyn's social media accounts*. Retrieved April 24, 2016, from http://www.mirror.co.uk/3am/celebrity-news/david-beckham-reveals-full-control-6472971

Siano, A., Vollero, A., & Palazzo, M. (2011). Exploring the role of online consumer empowerment in reputation building: Research questions and hypotheses. *Journal of Brand Management*, *19*(1), 57–71. doi:10.1057/bm.2011.23

Socialbakers. (2016). *David Beckham Facebook statistics*. Retrieved April 20, 2016, from http://www.socialbakers.com/statistics/facebook/pages/detail/84218631570-david-beckham

Statista. (2016a). *Leading social networks worldwide as of April 2016, ranked by number of active users (in millions)*. Retrieved April 20, 2016, from http://www.statista.com/statistics/272014/global-social-networks-ranked-by-number-of-users/

Statista. (2016b). *Most viewed YouTube channels worldwide as of March 2016, by monthly views (in millions)*. Retrieved April 20, 2016, from http://www.statista.com/statistics/373729/most-viewed-youtube-channels/

Statista. (2016c). *Most popular Facebook fan pages as of April 2016, based on number of fans (in millions)*. Retrieved April 20, 2016, from http://www.statista.com/statistics/269304/international-brands-on-facebook-by-number-of-fans/

The Armchair Athletes. (2016). *Online Reputation Management*. Retrieved April 24, 2016, from http://www.thearmchairathletes.com/services/online-reputation-management/

TwitterData. (2014). *Insights into the #WorldCup conversation on Twitter*. Retrieved April 20, 2016, from https://blog.twitter.com/2014/insights-into-the-worldcup-conversation-on-twitter

Wartick, S. L. (2002). Measuring corporate reputation: Definition and data. *Business & Society, 41*(4), 371–393. doi:10.1177/0007650302238774

White, M. G. (2012). *What Types of Social Networks Exist?* Retrieved April 20, 2016, from http://socialnetworking.lovetoknow.com/What_Types_of_Social_Networks_Exist

KEY TERMS AND DEFINITIONS

E-Reputation: The reputation that derives from electronic contacts on the Internet.

Image: Overall public perceptions and beliefs over organizations, institutions, individuals, etc. based on their experience and observation.

Reputation: Past and present signals that influence the overall evaluation – either positive or negative – that different audiences hold towards organizations, institutions, individuals, etc.

Social Media: Social media represent the production, consumption and sharing of information through social interaction mostly on the Internet.

Social Network: Social networks represent one type of social media that connect different audiences on the virtual sphere in order to reach different purposes.

Chapter 4

Social Media and Identity:
Understanding Identity Communication and Creation through Social Media

Erika Melonashi
European University of Tirana, Albania

ABSTRACT

The present chapter aims to explore the relationship between social media and identity by reviewing theoretical frameworks as well as empirical studies on the topic. Considering the complexity of the concept of identity, a multidisciplinary theoretical approach is provided, including Psychological Theories, Sociological Theories and Communication Theories. These theories are revisited in the context of online identity formation and communication through social media. Different aspects of identity such as gender identity, professional identity, political identity etc., are discussed and illustrated through empirical studies in the field. Moreover, the role of social media as a factor that might either promote or hinder identity development is also discussed (e.g., phenomena such as cyber-bulling and internet addiction). Finally recommendations and suggestions for future research are provided, including the need for multidisciplinary theoretical frameworks to the investigation of the relationships between social media and identity.

INTRODUCTION

'Men have become the tools of their tools'; this rather strong affirmation of Thoreau (1854, p.54) dates almost two centuries ago; however paradoxically it is also much relevant in today's high-tech world. People nowadays live in a world which allows them to do things that their ancestors did not even dare to dream; thanks to technology individuals today are more powerful and controlling than ever. Life is made easier, the world goes faster, and efficiency of performance is ever-growing. These changes could not leave unaffected the personal and social domains; communication, work, friendship/intimate relationship formation, and even the concept of self have all been subject to change. Whether change is radical to the point of making men 'the tools of their tools', is however a debatable issue. In this context social

DOI: 10.4018/978-1-5225-1868-6.ch004

media probably represents the best example showing how several basic human face-to-face activities have been transferred into the online world.

Social media is a concept used to refer to a category of new digital media phenomena including social network sites such as:

- Facebook,
- Twitter,
- LinkedIn,

Photo and video sharing sites such as:

- Instagram,
- MySpace,
- YouTube,
- Flickr,

Location based services such as Foursquare, etc.

Despite the within group diversity, all social media include interactive communication, networking and content sharing (Lüders, 2008). Hence, the primary purpose of social media would be that of facilitating social connections, by overcoming barriers of distance or time. In this perspective, social media might be regarded as an enhancement tool, allowing people to connect and create a much larger network than that in real life. Providing accessibility to individuals living continents apart, social media greatly empowers human agency, aiding the social, cultural or professional development. Indeed, there have been suggestions that actually social media might greatly stimulate creativity (Bruns, 2008; Lüders, 2007; Thumin, 2008). According to Bruns (2008) the user in social media is also an active content producer. Moreover, Livingstone (2008) and Lundby (2008) define the communication process as story-telling or self-expression, while other authors such as Liu (2007) consider it as taste performance (information on interests, likes and dislikes). Beirut (2009) argues that many people see social media as a means of broadcasting problems, voicing debates or supporting causes. Relationships have also been found between social media use and the creation of self-concept or social relationships (Sponcil & Gitimu, 2013). Bechmann and Lomborg (2012) focus on developmental aspects and argue on the positive impact of the multiple expressive facets of social media, which allow users not only to express but also to explore themselves through content sharing.

The creative function of social media might be best understood in the context of a comprehensive theoretical framework proposed by Kietzmann et al. (2011). Authors suggested seven main building blocks of social media, including:

- Conversations,
- Sharing,
- Presence,
- Relationships,
- Reputation,
- Groups, and
- Identity.

The sharing building block represents exchange of content with other users, while presence implies mere knowledge of accessibility of users (where people are, whether they are available). The relationship block on the other hand, refers to the types of connections between users, which in most cases also determine the kind of content to be shared. A typical example provided by Kietzmann et al. (2011) is that of LinkedIn, which enables users to see links with others and calculate how 'far' they are from selected targets (e.g., a future collaborator); expansion of the existing network provides the user with increasing opportunities for finding collaborators, future employers etc. The reputation building block is also particularly relevant in LinkedIn, considering the professional nature of this network. Conversely, the conversation building block might be best illustrated through Skype, whose basic function would be that of maintaining existing relationships by enabling conversation. The groups functional block is related to identity formation since online groups mimic groups in real life, i.e., people joint by a common purpose, common characteristics etc. Moreover, a user might also create his/her groups based on types of relationships with others (friends, followers, fans etc.) (Kietzmann et al., 2011). Finally the identity building block, characterizes social media that require a personal profile; hence specific characteristics of users are provided sometimes to a great level of detail. The identity block represents one of the most important blocks since in most social networks it largely influences other blocks too; for instance the creation of an identity (profile) is a prerequisite to establish relationships (friends in Facebook), form links (in LinkedIn), engage in conversations (Skype), create groups etc.

Online identities provide an interesting topic of research especially because they raise important questions on the psychological realities of social media users. Is identity merely revealed or also created and re-created in social media? According to Mendelson and Papacharissi (2010) the version of the self, presented in social media is refined and polished, demonstrating that individuals are self-aware of presenting themselves in front of an audience. Hence social media is revelatory to some extent, while at the same time obeying to the social constraints dictated by presentation in front of an audience. On the other hand, the social constraints of the online medium are perceived to be smoother compared to real life. Along this line of thought Joinson (2001) proposed that social media might in fact facilitate more honest and open communication as compared to real life settings. Also, Turkle (1995) suggests that internet provides a freedom similar to that of playground children; it allows experimentation with different aspects of identity (even opposite ones), which is quite difficult to do in real life due to social constraints. Individuals are much freer to express themselves online because they can more easily avoid the cost of not obeying social norms and expectations in this medium. Nonetheless, the anonymity and freedom of the online world raises important questions on the degree to which users might construct false identities, present enhanced versions of the self, or adopt totally imaginary identities altogether (Stone, 1996). Along these lines, two emerging phenomena requiring further analyses include cyber-bullying and internet addiction; recent research suggests interactions between several aspects of identity and these two phenomena, especially in terms of explanatory factors and processes involved.

The present chapter aims to discuss identity in the social media context. The research question guiding the following analysis is:

- 'How is identity created and communicated through social media?'

Multi-disciplinary theoretical approaches from psychology, sociology, and communication studies will be analyzed and confronted in an effort to understand how identity is presented and created in online contexts. Empirical studies will be also reviewed and examples will be provided on several dimensions of identity (e.g., gender, professional, ethnic identity etc); finally two emerging phenomena including cyber-bullying and internet addiction, will be discussed in the contexts of threatening factors in online contexts. The chapter concludes with recommendations and suggestions for future research.

BACKGROUND

Identity has been a topic of great theoretical and research interest in several fields including, psychology, sociology, and communication. Identity represents a very complex concept especially in terms of operational definitions provided. Brewer and Gardner (1996) have distinguished between three dimensions of identity including:

- Individual,
- Interpersonal and
- Group dimensions.

The individual dimension comprises personal characteristics, which make the individual unique and different from others. The interpersonal dimension refers to that aspect of identity which is defined through relationships, while the group dimension refers to aspects of identity derived from identification with a specific group. The group identity dimension discussed by Brewer and Gardner (1996) builds on the social identity theory, proposed by Tajfel and Turner (1979), where self-identity as well as self-esteem largely depend on group participation; thus self-concept and esteem are provided by group membership rather than individual features (Hogg, Terry, & White, 1995; Hogg & Abrams, 1999; Turner & Oakes, 1986; Turner, Hogg, Oakes, Reicher, &Wetherell, 1987).

Baumeister (1999), on the other hand points out two important dimensions of identity including the stability/continuity of certain features over time and a set of core differences from others. In this context, Simon (2004) maintains that the list of characteristics defining a person's identity could be infinite; for instance it might include:

- Physical characteristics,
- Personality traits,
- Behavioral patterns,
- Social roles,
- Political membership,
- Particular abilities etc.

Nonetheless, he also provides a major conceptual distinction between personal and group/collective identities. Also in synthesizing his view, he considers identity both as the outcome of interaction with the social context and a crucial factor guiding social interaction in turn.

One of the most popular and stable theories of human development, Erikson's theory of psychosocial development, conceptualizes identity as an achievement at the end of adolescence. More specifically Erikson suggests that in the stage of 'Identity vs. Role Confusion' adolescents' main task is that of developing a sense of self (Erikson, 1968). In order to achieve this, they need to experiment with feelings of independence and self-control, as well as beliefs, desires, and interests. Exploration within intrapersonal and interpersonal domains, acquire major importance in this context (Berman, Schwartz, Kurtines, & Berman, 2001). Building on Erikson's theory, Marcia (1980) suggests that role confusion is a normal occurrence, as almost all adolescents experience mixed ideas and feelings about their social roles. However, the identity crisis is solved if the adolescent is given enough time and space to work properly with identity issues (a psychosocial moratorium) (Marcia, 1980).Thus a healthy sense of self is developed if individuals manage to find a balance between personal desires, beliefs, and interests on the one hand, and social demands (family, peers etc.) on the other. Highlighting the importance of individual-context transaction, Bosma and Kunnen (2001) have provided an encompassing transactional model of the process of identity development. Thus optimal identity development requires a balance between assimilation and accommodation of information, being at the same time constant and change-able through continuous transactions with the environment.

While developmental psychology theorists have focused on the process of identity formation, hu-manistic theorists like Rogers have shifted perspectives towards the way identity is presented in social contexts. Rogers suggested a conceptual distinction between the present self, the ideal self and the true self. The present self refers to the way the individual presents himself in the social context. The ideal self refers to images of a perfect idealized self, which might be motivation and guide for the individual's future behavior. However, the most important dimension according to Rogers, is the true self, a version of the self which fully exists in the present but is not fully expressed due to external social constraints (criticism, judgment etc.) (Rogers, 1951). Along the same lines, Higgins (1987) has proposed a three-dimensional model including:

- The actual,
- The ideal and
- The 'ought' self.

The actual self and ideal self are similar to what was proposed by Rogers; the 'ought self 'on the other hand, includes a series of attributes one must possess, especially in connection to specific prescribed social roles.

Similarly, the sociological perspective of Goffman (1959) addresses the issue of self-presentation in everyday life by highlighting the importance of impression management processes. The front stage/backstage approach suggests that each individual holds in fact a double identity; when in front of an audience, the individual displays a self which is in line with social expectations, norms and values. Thus individuals monitor the impression they want to give to others, conveying just what is 'appropriate'. On the other hand, the back stage identity refers to the self without the audience, free from social constraints and expectations. Goffman (1959) suggests that the true self is actually revealed in this private zone, and is audience-free (similar to Rogers' true self).

Shifting perspectives into transactional dimensions, theorists of communication science have sug-gested two main approaches including the Identity Management Theory (Cupach & Imahori, 1993; Imahori & Cupach, 2005) and Communication Theory of Identity (Hecht, 1993; Hecht, Warren, Jung, & Krieger, 2004). The Identity management theory of communication, considers relational and cultural aspects as determinant in creating identities while communicating. This theory is largely based on face to face communication and suggests that successful communication requires constant negotiation of aspects of identity between communicators. According to this theoretical viewpoint identity cannot be stable because individuals create and recreate their identities while communicating in social contexts.

Similarly, the Communication Theory of Identity posits a reciprocal relationship between identity and communication; communication is a product of identity while at the same time it constructs, sustains or modifies identity. This theory suggests that there are four layers of identity (Personal, Enacted, Relational, and Communal layers) which interact with each other (e.g., Hecht, 1993; Hecht, Jackson, &Ribeau 2003).The personal layer refers to the individuals' view of self, including thoughts and emotions. The enacted layer conceptualizes identity as what is expressed in terms of communication (performance) while the relational layer conceives identity in terms of social interaction (identifying with others, taking specific roles). Finally the communal level draws attention towards group membership and belonging (i.e., group identity).

To summarize, it might be stated that depending on the perspective of each specific field, identity might be considered as a three-dimensional construction of self, as a developmental outcome, a set of self-presentation characteristics (to an audience or to the self), a product of communication/social interaction etc. Nonetheless, it is quite evident that these views are not conflicting but rather compensatory or overlapping, thus allowing for a multidimensional understanding of such a complex concept as identity. The following section aims to transfer these theories originally proposed for real life contexts, to online contexts. Ways in which online identities are presented or constructed will be critically evaluated in the context of empirical research on social media.

CREATING AND COMMUNICATING IDENTITY IN ONLINE CONTEXTS

Mapping Theories of Identity in Online Contexts: The Case of Social Media

The ways identity is created and presented through social media has been subject to much research interest. In line with Goffman's front stage/back stage theory (Goffman, 1959), Robinson (2007) argues that self- presentation concerns are very present in online contexts too; thus the self-presented online, rarely matches the actual self. In this context, social media provide a front stage, in which individuals are fully aware of being observed, evaluated, discussed and even criticized; obviously the self which is displayed under these conditions, is one that is socially approved (unlikely to be criticized) (Zhao, Salehi, Naranjit et al., 2013). Along these lines, Zhao et al. (2013) propose a model which accommodates social media data (Facebook) into three different regions:

- A performance region, which organizes new data by having impression management techniques in mind (other people are observing),
- An exhibition region referring to future and long term presentations of self,
- And a personal region, serving as an archive for important and meaningful personal events.

Although work on impression management and privacy is not new (e.g., Armstrong, Gosling, Weinman, & Marteau, 1997; Robinson, 2007; Tufekci, 2008) authors provide a new way of upraising both, by adding a new dimension, i.e., temporality. Indeed, authors argue that the accumulation of personally relevant information over time might serve as an external memory drive, to which people can refer time after time (Cosley, 2012; Greengard, 2012). A related term is that of "digital possessions" or past content which is highly meaningful to the self or others (Marshall & Shipman, 2011; Odom et al., 2012). Along these lines a reflective or sense-making process of the content displayed has been suggested to occur (Hangal & Heer, 2011; Zhao & Cosley, 2012; Peesapati et al., 2010).

This research actually suggests that Goffman's Theory of Self Presentation and the Identity Management Theory of Communication might be successfully transferred in the online environment. Thus identity is not stable, but rather continuously created through social interaction, having nonetheless self-presentational concerns in mind. However, an important difference between real and online worlds, which might require further research, refers to the accessibility of past personally relevant information in the online context exactly the way it was at the time (e.g., Timeline in Facebook). In this sense, the online environment provides 'an external memory drive', which is quite different from the actual human memory. Indeed the reconstructing character of human memory has been widely accepted by now (i.e., each time an event is being remembered, it is at the same time re-interpreted and thus different from the original) (Schacter, Norman, & Koutstaal, 1998); thus future research might be directed towards examining the processes and consequences of individuals 'diving' into past identities, especially in terms of discrepancies with existing memories (i.e., what they remember vs. what it actually was).

Along the same lines, Humphreys (2011) suggests that social media might also serve as archives of places visited over time, an aspect which is considered as contributing to identity continuity and serving self-flattering or ego boosting purposes. Patil et al. (2012) and Barkhuus et al. (2008) also suggest that advertising of locations provides important information on the life-style of an individual, which in turn is an aspect closely related to self-concept and identity. Schwartz and Halegoua (2014) assert that places and spaces are actually markers of identity which are strategically chosen to convey desired messages to audiences and the presentation of place/location (Sutko & de Souza e Silva, 2011; de Souza e Silva & Frith, 2012) is just a form of constructing identity based on locations visited. Apart from the accumulation of 'memories' for future reference, presentation of place also points towards another phenomenon, originally suggested by Rogers, 'the idealized version of the self'. Indeed social media provide the means to broadcast how wonderful or perfect some experiences might be, an aspect which is clearly easier to do in this context as compared to real life. Also in line with the Communication Theory of Identity (Hecht, 1993; Hecht et al., 2003) advertising locations, actually contributes to the enacted layer of identity (i.e., identity equals performance) or the relational one (connections with individuals sharing similar experiences, e.g., visiting the same place). However, the contribution to the personal layer seems to be less obvious, and could represent an interesting direction for future research.

Yet another example, which raises important self-presentation concerns, is online dating. Ellison, Heino, and Gibbs, (2006) propose that users of these sites are actually engaged in a process of fighting for equilibrium between impression management and presentation of the 'real self'. These findings are in line with research on real-life dating, which suggests that self-presentation concerns are actually high in this setting. Deception largely occurs in real life too as people frequently lie about themselves in order to impress, be liked by others, achieve something etc. (Rowatt et al., 1998). In other words, what happens in the online medium might just be a reflection of what happens in real life, with conditions being slightly different (Rowatt, Cunningham, & Druen, 1998). One very interesting finding reported by Ellison et al. (2006) concerns a strategy reported by some users who presented themselves as improved future versions of the self (reflecting motivation and goals which were planned but not yet achieved, e.g., thinner than they actually were). Walther (1996) suggests that self-censorship might be easier to achieve in online contexts considering the higher levels of control as compared to real life (lack of non-verbal cues, plenty of time to reflect etc.). Thus, opportunity and conditions for misrepresentations and deceit in online contexts are much more favorable than those in real life (Bowker & Tuffin, 2003; Cornwell & Lundgren,

2001; Joinson & Dietz-Uhler, 2002). An important question to consider here is whether given the opportunity (online context), all individuals would be more prone to deceive on aspects of their identity. Or does the proneness to deception differ, depending more on individual traits rather than contextual ones? So far there is actually some evidence of continuity rather than discrepancy between online and offline identities, suggesting that personal traits seem to be more relevant than context (Beirut, 2009).

The issue of continuity and especially congruency between offline and online identities becomes particularly relevant in the context of professional identities. Although the personal-professional role strain exists in offline as well as online contexts, some characteristics of the latter (availability, visibility, anonymity) might further highlight the strain (Kirkup, 2010; Veletsianos & Kimmons, 2013; Kimmons & Veletsianos, 2014). The question of where to draw the line when it comes to sharing information online, has great practical significance especially for scholars, physicians or other professions directly working with people (e.g., DeCamp, Koenig, & Chisolm, 2013; Moran, Seaman, & Tinti-Kane, 2012). Reflecting back on suggestions by Brewer and Gardner (1996) these categories of professionals in social networks are constantly engaged into solving conflicts between individual and relational identities, an aspect which certainly deserves future examination (e.g., does distortion of individual identity occur to protect relational identity?).

While acknowledging the fact that conscious censuring or distortion of information might occur in online contexts (lack of additional sensory information or body language), there is a need to also address the phenomenon of unconscious disclosure. Thus, a category of information especially emotional in nature constantly leaks through the posts, thoughts, pictures etc. According to Kaplan and Haenlein (2010) disclosure in social networks obeys generally to the same principles like face-to-face behavior, i.e., unconscious feelings find their way out although it might not be evident straight away. Moreover, such unconscious behavioral patterns become more obvious if followed over time (specific patterns might be identified). For instance studies have investigated relationships between self-reports of personality traits (offline) and characteristics of online profiles of users (Back et al., 2010); results revealed that variables such as number of friends, profile detail or profile photo style were strongly related to self-efficacy with regard to impression management (Krämer, & Winter, 2008). Hence the study presents information that does not derive from user statuses but other characteristics of the profile, which are also indicative, although in an indirect fashion of who the person is.

Even so, the way that identity is expressed through language has attracted much research interest (Sumner, Byers, & Shearing, 2011; Holtgraves, 2011; Iacobelli, Gill, Nowson, & Oberlander, 2011). Language has been used as a marker of personality in several contexts (Ireland & Mehl, 2014; Kramer, 2010; Schwartz et al.,2013). For instance, Yarkoni (2010) found relationships between the agreeableness trait and the word 'hug', while Holtgraves (2011) reported a link between the neurotic trait and the use of acronyms. Another example refers to gender identity marks in language, e.g., studies have reported a greater use of emoticons or emotional words by women as compared to men (Rao, Yarowsky, Shreevats, 2010). Language data from Twitter accounts have also enabled very accurate predictions of gender as reported by Burger et al. (2011) (gender prediction for over 184,000 Twitter authors). Indeed men's and women's speeches seem to differ in terms of being either more informative (men) or more involving (women) (e.g., Argamon et al., 2003; Biber, 1995; Herring & Paolillo 2006; Newman, Groom, Handelman, & Pennebaker, 2008; Schler et al., 2006). Kinship terms are more frequently used by women than men (Bamman, Eisenstein, & Schnoebelen, 2014) while communication about hobbies, sports, career achievements is more frequent among men (Bamman et al., 2014). Style differences have also been reported by several authors, suggesting that men, differently from women prefer a style which is more explicit (Heylighen & Dewaele, 2002; Nowson, Oberlander, & Gill, 2005). Reflecting back on theories of communication discussed previously, it might be argued that there is at least some consistency between some broad markers of identity such as gender and personality traits and language expression in social media.

Moreover, it has been suggested that the online environment might in fact provide a context where individuals express their true self much easier than in real life (Bargh, McKenna, & Fitzsimons, 2002). For instance Bargh et al. (2002) showed that 'the true' self-concept was more accessible to memory (shorter reaction time) during online communications rather than face to face interactions. Conversely, the present self was more accessible to memory in real life context communications. The definition of true self that authors use is similar to that of Rogers, i.e., a version of the self which fully exists in the present but is just not fully expressed (Rogers, 1951). Thus in line with Rogers' theory, social contexts which buffer the individual from negative feedback (in this case online environment as compared to face-to-face interaction) boosts the expression of the true self (rather than 'ideal self' or 'ought' self). A supporting example here is the study by Craig and McInroy (2014) who reported that social media might be greatly helpful especially to homosexual and bisexual adolescents/ youth for exploring aspects of gender identity. Moreover, authors argue that exploration of gender identity online (mainly through association to similar others) greatly facilitates expression of self in real contexts. Reflecting back on theories of development (Erikson, Marcia) it might be argued that social media would be particularly relevant in identity development at least during crucial developmental stages such as adolescence. Apparently dimensions such as exploration or experimentation might be more easily pursued online, especially because of aspects such as anonymity. Moreover, feeling the presence (even virtual) of similar others, seems to be quite important too.

Indeed the association to similar others and group participation have been considered as an important dimension of social media use (Bennet & Segerberg, 2011; Papacharissi, 2009). Users with similar interests are more likely to be friends in social media (Aiello, Barat, Schifanella, Catutto, Marchines, & Menczer, 2012), a phenomenon which in real life has been coined as homophily, referring to similarity between people who are socially connected (Aral, Muchnik, & Sundararajan, 2009; Bisgin, Agarwal, & Xu, 2012; McPherson, Smith-Lovin, & Cook, 2001; Thelwall, 2008). Gilbert and Karahalios (2009) outline further similarities between real life groups and online groups by suggesting that trust and group belonging are present in online settings too. For instance, ethnic identity is particularly relevant in the case of minority groups, and possible threats to it might be transferred to real life behavior (McGuire, McGuire, Child, & Fujioka, 1978; Pratt, Hauser, Ugray, & Patterson, 2007; Spence, Lachlan, Spates, & Lin, 2013). Ethnic identity might be selectively displayed by users, since self-presentation is purposeful and strategic (e.g., connect to similar others) (Antheunis & Schouten, 2011; Phinney, 1990; Walther, Van Der Heide, Kim, Westerman, & Tong, 2008). Similarly, social media provides the means to express and strengthen political identity, e.g., there is evidence revealing relationships between the extent of social media use and increased political participation/activity (e.g., Pearce & Kendzior, 2012; Schmalz, Colistra, & Evans, 2015; Valenzuela, et al., 2012; Valenzuela, 2013). In all examples provided, association with similar others, rebuilds group identity, and enforces its' several dimensions. Reflecting back to theories of communication, group identity provides a good example of how identity is created through communication, and also transferred from online contexts to real life behavior.

To summarize, evidence to date suggests that existing theories of identity might be quite useful in explaining identity expression and construction through social media. Self-presentation concerns, true vs. ideal self, personal/public area, recreation through communication etc. are all theoretical concepts which might be well transferred to the virtual context. In line with theories of communication, human development, impression management etc., individuals engage in continuous transactions between self-expression and self-censuring, to communicate their identities. The correspondence between real and online identity is fairly good, at least for the dimensions examined (e.g., gender, personality traits etc.) but more complex aspects of identity might however produce different results. Indeed several aspects which characterize particularly virtual contexts such as:

- Anonymity,
- Availability,
- Visibility,
- Information storage,
- Massive positive/negative feedback etc. Are particularly important to consider.

In this context, two emerging phenomena, which need further discussion include cyber-bullying and internet addiction. The following section provides a general overview of these two issues especially as related to identity presentation and construction.

The Threatened Self: Addiction and Cyber-Bullying

Quite similarly to real life, identity presentation in the online environment is also subject to continuous threats; some common examples in both contexts include:

- Criticism,
- Disapproval,
- Labeling,
- Fun making,

while outcomes range from distortion of identity dimensions with the purpose of fitting social expectations to escape/social isolation. Nonetheless differently from real life, characteristics of online contexts such as visibility of content and anonymity might greatly amplify the extent of the threat (e.g., number of people seeing the comments, videos etc.)

Cyber-bulling, or bulling in online settings refers to a set of online behaviors harming or harassing individuals (Campbell, 2005). This emerging phenomenon especially among young people, is considered as harmful (if not more so) than bulling in real life contexts. Indeed the extensive audience in online contexts and the rapidity of information transmission magnify the harming effect and might quite easily result in fatalities (e.g., suicide attempts). The negative psychological outcomes, such as low self-esteem and self-efficacy, negative view of the self and the world, depression, anxiety etc. are all aspects which 'mutilate' the various dimensions of identity (Thornberg, 2015). Indeed attacks on virtual identity might produce real life threats, ranging from distortion to destruction of several dimensions of identity depending on the specific developmental stage. Along these lines, Campbell (2005) has maintained that research on cyber-bulling, and especially the profiles of bullies and their victims, is still scarce. Particularly interesting questions to be examined in future research might include:

- How do theories explaining bullying account for this phenomenon in the virtual context?

- Is there a real life-online context continuity (are bullies in real life online bullies and vice-versa?) or does the virtual context specifically promote this behavior?

Apart from cyber-bullying yet another threat to identity is addiction; the addictive potential of social media has been suggested by several researchers and there is increasing evidence that social media users might display behavioral profiles similar to victims of other types of addiction (e.g., gambling) (Kuss & Griffiths, 2011). Characteristics include increasingly more time spent online, highly frequent checking of online content, deficits in social/professional life because of time spent online etc. (Echeburua & de Corral, 2010; Young, 1999). Kuss and Griffiths (2011) in their comprehensive review on social media addiction, suggest that positive outcomes associated with social media use, might incite individuals into more extensive and frequent use. While authors argue that research on social media addiction is quite scarce (especially when compared to computer gaming or other types of internet addiction), they suggest that several personality characteristics might increase vulnerability, e.g., sociability, narcissism, extraversion etc. (Cain, Pincus, & Ansell, 2008; Campbell, Bosson, Goheen, Lakey, & Kernis, 2007; La Barbera, La Paglia, & Valsavoia, 2009). For instance, an imbalanced sense of self, which consistently demands social attention and admiration used to explain the relationship between social media addictive behavior and narcissism. This explanation is very close to the self-medication model of addiction, suggesting that individuals engage in the specific addictive behavior to regulate dysfunctional affective states (Khantzian, 2003). Particularly interesting would be the exploration of narcissism through new emerging phenomena such as selfie-mania (pictures of oneself) and the way this behavior is related to issues of self-image and self-adoration.

On the other hand, individual identity has been found to be an important risk or protective factor from addiction; e.g., it has been shown that the diffuse/avoidant identity style might be an important risk factor for drug addiction (Côté & Levine, 2002; Hojjat et al., 2015; White et al., 2003). Although research on identity styles and social media addiction is still missing, future research in this direction would be particularly interesting. Moreover, there is some evidence connecting relational aspects of identity with higher vulnerability to addiction (e.g., Internet addiction among those with insecure parental attachment) (Lin, Ko, &Wu, 2011; Severino & Craparo, 2013). Although there is still no specific evidence on social media addiction, it might be suggested that a troubled relational identity, might increase the vulnerability of the individual especially considering great social benefits provided by social networks.

To conclude cyber-bullying and addiction comprise two important aspects, which are only recently being investigated. Research suggests some connection between aspects of identity presentation/construction and addiction or cyber-bullying. These studies are actually a reminder that despite some particular features, the online context seems to be in many ways a reflection of human psyche on the one hand and social interactions on the other. Virtual identities:

- Have self-presentation concerns,
- Long for group participation,
- Want their needs to be satisfied,
- Create and re-create themselves over and over again.

In this way, social media provides just a different context to do those same things people do in the real world, search for approval, promote the self, create connections, or even bully others and get addicted. Sometimes these processes are more pronounced, other times more subtle than the real world; sometimes they appear quite different but the essence, the very core seems to be quite the same: human.

RECOMMENDATIONS AND FUTURE RESEARCH DIRECTIONS

The investigation of the social media-identity relationship represents only one aspect of the complex human-technology interaction. Even so, this dyad encloses one of the most central quests of all times, 'Who am I?' Philosophers, writers, and scientists have all reflected on the self, on identity and its' meaning. In today's modern world, technology is apparently an integral part of the self and social media comprises a substantial role too. As already discussed through the chapter, identity is both expressed and created through social media, in several complex interactions. Considering the complexity and novelty of the topic recommendations are mainly directed towards researchers, followed by educators and finally managers.

Recommendations for researchers are largely based on existing evidence on the types of studies on the specific topic; most of the research reviewed in this chapter has been guided by single and often times simplistic theoretical concepts/perspectives. In this context, a major recommendation for researchers is the consideration of a multidisciplinary theoretical framework which combines social, psychological and communication theories in an effort to disentangle the social media-identity dyad. The complexity of the problem, and still persistent debate especially on identity definition and expression, demand for theoretical perspectives which combine knowledge from several disciplines. Since multidisciplinarity is a challenge for every single researcher, collaboration through the construction of multidisciplinary teams might be quite useful. For instance, a research team including experts in communication, psychoanalysis and linguistics in conjunction might take a step further existing research on identity by using language content analysis. Along the same lines, future research might also broaden perspectives to also include unconscious mechanisms (and not only conscious ones) through which identity is displayed in social media. Research from cognitive psychology and neuroscience might enrich the investigation even further by providing ways to measure automatic processing and so on.

As regards recommendations for educators and education researchers, the social media-identity dyad provides a source of both theoretical and practical relevance. For instance, the effects of social media use in the fulfillment of specific developmental tasks provide an important direction for future research in education and development. Indeed, research on the role of social media on identity formation is quite scarce as compared to studies on identity communication. Social media does in fact represent an important social factor to be considered, along the traditional list of social factors which influence development (parents, peers, culture etc.). Also the way educators might use social media to promote development and education might be an important aspect of great practical significance (e.g., uploading of teaching materials, group discussions etc.) (Selwyn & Stirling, 2016).

Particularly important in educational contexts is the examination of cyber-bullying (paralleling the phenomenon of bullying in the classroom) as well as the extent to which it relates to real-life behavior or influences. This issue might be quite important to examine especially among youth. Several questions might be examined such as the possible continuity between real and virtual identities; is this phenomenon a desperate quest for identity, a search for a sense of self transferred to a different medium? From a practical perspective education on social media use in general and problems related to it might be particularly important (e.g., discussion of types of content sharing, privacy etc.).

Finally, an interesting direction for future research, which at the same time might have important practical managerial significance, refers to organizational identity (e.g., Whetten, 2006). Although this aspect was beyond the scope of the present review (the focus was on individual identity), evidence on the obvious advantages of constructing group identity through social media (reaching all group members in minimal time; sharing and communicating instantly) suggests that this aspect might be important to consider in future research as well as practice; indeed there is already some evidence on the efficiency of social media as a tool to promote and strengthen organizational identity (e.g., Young, 2013).

Ultimately the human-technology interaction raises important questions, and answers are far from being simple and straight forward. Nonetheless, a close collaboration between social scientists and technology developers is mandatory, not only for understanding the factors and processes involved but also for designing well-informed programs and policies, which promote rather than hinder human development across all its dimensions.

CONCLUSION

Technology has become an integral part of everyday life; it is ever-present and widely used across the most common activities. It has entered the daily routine with prepotency and has invariably affected psycho-social realities. The present chapter focused on a fragment of the human-technology interaction by discussing the social media-identity relationship. It was argued that social media serves a range of different functions such as:

- Communication,
- Creation,
- Enhancement or distortion of several aspects of identity.

Parallels have been drawn between theorists and researchers from different fields (psychology, sociology, developmental studies, communication etc.) into understanding how individuals communicate some aspects of their identity online, hide or distort some others, and still create or recreate some more. Referring to existing empirical research, it was suggested that theories on identity presentation and construction across several disciplines (Goffman's theory, Communication theories, Rogers' model etc.) fare quite well in explaining these same processes in the online environment; although the medium is different, basic principles guiding self-presentation and social interaction (although virtual) are considered to be quite similar. Indeed it has been argued on the general existence of continuity between real and virtual identities, at least in terms of some basic personality traits (e.g., neuroticism, narcissism), or characteristics such as gender, profession or ethnic group belonging. What is particularly important is that connection with like-minded others in these settings, might help building or enhancing aspects of identity especially during critical developmental. However, cases of discrepancies are present too and are suggested as serving similar purposes as incongruence in real life, i.e., self-presentation concerns drive instrumentally different behaviors depending on context. Two emerging phenomena including cyber-bullying and internet addiction were discussed in the context of the harming and distorting effects on identity presentation and construction, while suggesting the great need for future research into these problems. To conclude it might be argued that social media actually has an important impact on identity presentation and creation, ranging among the several other major social influences (parents, teachers, friends, etc). Indeed social media today represents an important social factor, whose role and influence on human development and quality of life in general are still being investigated. Reflecting back on the opening remark by Thoreau, fortunately people have not yet become the tools of their tools, but the struggle is far from being absent…

REFERENCES

Aiello, L. M., Barrat, A., Schifanella, R., Cattuto, C., Markines, B., & Menczer, F. (2012). Friendship prediction and homophily in social media. *ACM Transaction on the Web*, *6*(2), 9.

Alvi, S., Downing, S., & Cesaroni, C. (2015). The self and the 'selfie': Cyber-bullying theory and the structure of late modernity. In S. R. Maxwell & S. L. Blair (Eds.), *Violence and crime in the family: Patterns, causes, and consequences* (pp. 383–406). Emerald Group Publishing. doi:10.1108/S1530-353520150000009016

Antheunis, M. L., & Schouten, A. P. (2011). The effects of other-generated and system-generated cues on adolescents perceived attractiveness on social network sites. *Journal of Computer-Mediated Communication*, *16*(3), 391 406. doi:10.1111/j.1083-6101.2011.01545.x

Aral, S., Muchnik, L., & Sundararajan, A. (2009). Distinguishing influence-based contagion from homophily-driven diffusion in dynamic networks. *Proceedings of the National Academy of Sciences of the United States of America*, *106*(51), 21544–21549. doi:10.1073/pnas.0908800106 PMID:20007780

Argamon, S. A., Koppel, M., Fine, J., & Shimoni, A. R. (2003). Gender, genre, and writing style in formal written texts. *Text*, *23*(3), 321–346. doi:10.1515/text.2003.014

Armstrong, D., Gosling, J., Weinman, J., & Marteau, T. (1997). The place of inter-rater reliability in qualitative research: An empirical study. *Sociology*, *31*(3), 597–606. doi:10.1177/0038038597031003015

Back, M., Stopfer, J., Vazire, S., Gaddis, S., Schmukle, S., Egloff, B., & Gosling, S. D. (2010). Facebook profiles reflect actual personality, not self-idealization. *Psychological Science*, *21*(3), 372–374. doi:10.1177/0956797609360756 PMID:20424071

Bamman, D., Eisenstein, J., & Schnoebelen, T. (2014). Gender identity and lexical variation in social media. *Journal of Sociolinguistics*, *18*(2), 135–160. doi:10.1111/josl.12080

Bargh, J. A., McKenna, K. Y., & Fitzsimons, G. M. (2002). Can you see the real me? Activation and expression of the true self on the Internet. *The Journal of Social Issues*, *58*(1), 33–48. doi:10.1111/1540-4560.00247

Barkhuus, L., Brown, B., Bell, M., Sherwood, S., Hall, M., & Chalmers, M. (2008). From awareness to repartee: Sharing location within social groups. In *Proceedings of the 2008 Conference on Human Factors in Computing Systems* (pp. 497-506). Florence: ACM Press. doi:10.1145/1357054.1357134

Baumeister, R. F. (1999). Self-concept, self-esteem, and identity. Self-concept, self-esteem, and identity. In V. J. Derlega, B. A. Winstead, & W. H. Jones (Eds.), *Personality: Contemporary theory and research* (2nd ed.; pp. 339–375). Chicago: Nelson-Hall Publishers.

Bechmann, A., & Lomborg, S. (2012). Mapping actor roles in social media: Different perspectives on value creation in theories of user participation. *New Media & Society, 15*(5), 765–781. doi:10.1177/1461444812462853

Beirut. (2009). *Why do people really tweet? The psychology behind tweeting!* Retrieved April 15, 2016, from http://blog.thoughtpick.com/2009/08/why-do-people-really-tweet-the-psychology-behind-tweeting.html

Bennett, W. L., & Segerberg, A. (2011). Digital media and the personalization of collective action: Social technology and the organization of protests against the global economic crisis. *Information Communication and Society, 14*(6), 770–799. doi:10.1080/1369118X.2011.579141

Biber, D. (1995). *Dimensions of register variation: A cross-linguistic comparison.* Cambridge, UK: Cambridge University Press. doi:10.1017/CBO9780511519871

Bisgin, H., Agarwal, N., & Xu, X. (2012). A study of homophily on social media. *World Wide Web (Bussum), 15*(2), 213–232. doi:10.1007/s11280-011-0143-3

Bosma, H. A., & Kunnen, E. S. (2001). Determinants and mechanisms in ego identity development: A review and synthesis. *Developmental Review, 21*(1), 39–66. doi:10.1006/drev.2000.0514

Bowker, N., & Tuffin, K. (2003). Dicing with deception: People with disabilities' strategies for managing safety and identity online. *Journal of Computer-Mediated Communication, 8*(2). doi: 10.1111/j.1083-6101.2003.tb00209.x

Brewer, M. B., & Gardner, W. (1996). Who is this we? Levels of collective identity and self representations. *Journal of Personality and Social Psychology, 71*(1), 83–93. doi:10.1037/0022-3514.71.1.83

Bruns, A. (2008). *Blogs, Wikipedia, Second Life, and beyond: From production to produsage.* New York: Peter Lang.

Burger, J. D., Henderson, J., Kim, G., & Zarrella, G. (2011). Discriminating gender on Twitter. In *Proceedings of the Conference on Empirical Methods in Natural Language Processing*(pp.1301–1309). Edinburgh, UK: Association for Computational Linguistics.

Cain, N. M., Pincus, A. L., & Ansell, E. B. (2008). Narcissism at the crossroads: Phenotypic description of pathological narcissism across clinical theory, social/personality psychology, and psychiatric diagnosis. *Clinical Psychology Review, 28*(4), 638–656. doi:10.1016/j.cpr.2007.09.006 PMID:18029072

Campbell, M. A. (2005). Cyber bullying: An old problem in a new guise? *Australian Journal of Guidance & Counselling, 15*(01), 68–76. doi:10.1375/ajgc.15.1.68

Campbell, W. K., Bosson, J. K., Goheen, T. W., Lakey, C. E., & Kernis, M. H. (2007). Do narcissists dislike themselves deep down inside? *Psychological Science, 18*(3), 227–229. doi:10.1111/j.1467-9280.2007.01880.x PMID:17444918

Castells, M. (2009). *Communication power.* Oxford, UK: Oxford University Press.

Cornwell, B., & Lundgren, D. C. (2001). Love on the Internet: Involvement and mis-representation in romantic relationships in cyberspace vs. real space. *Computers in Human Behavior, 17*(2), 197–211. doi:10.1016/S0747-5632(00)00040-6

Cosley, D., Sosik, V. S., Schultz, J., Peesapati, S. T., & Lee, S. (2012). Experiences with designing tools for everyday reminiscing. *HCI*, *27*, 175–198.

Côté, J. E., & Levine, C. G. (2002). *Identity formation, agency, and culture: A social psychological synthesis*. Mahwah, NJ: Lawrence Erlbaum.

Craig, S. L., & McInroy, L. (2014). You can form a part of yourself online: The influence of new media on identity development and coming out for LGBTQ youth. *Journal of Gay & Lesbian Mental Health*, *18*(1), 95–109. doi:10.1080/19359705.2013.777007

Cupach, W. R., & Imahori, T. T. (1993). Identity management theory: Communication competence in intercultural episodes and relationships. In R. L. Wiseman & J. Koester (Eds.), *Intercultural communication competence* (pp. 112–131). Newbury Park, CA: Sage.

de Souza e Silva, A., & Frith, J. (2012). Mobile interfaces in public spaces: Locational privacy, control, and urban sociality. New York: Routledge.

DeCamp, M., Koenig, T., & Chisolm, M. (2013). Social media and physicians online identity crisis. *Journal of the American Medical Association*, *310*(6), 581–582. doi:10.1001/jama.2013.8238 PMID:23942675

Echeburua, E., & de Corral, P. (2010). Addiction to new technologies and to online social networking in young people: A new challenge. *Adicciones*, *22*, 91–95. PMID:20549142

Eckert, P. (2008). Variation and the indexical field. *Journal of Sociolinguistics*, *12*(4), 453–476. doi:10.1111/j.1467-9841.2008.00374.x

Ellison, N., Heino, R., & Gibbs, J. (2006). Managing impressions online: Self-presentation processes in the online dating environment. *Journal of Computer-Mediated Communication*, *11*(2), 415–441. doi:10.1111/j.1083-6101.2006.00020.x

Erikson, E. (1968). *Identity, youth and crisis*. New York: W. W. Norton Company.

Gilbert, E., & Karahalios, K. (2009). Predicting tie strength with social media. In *CHI '09: Proceedings of the 27th annual SIGCHI conference on Human Factors in Computing Systems* (pp. 211-220). New York, NY: ACM Press. doi:10.1145/1518701.1518736

Goffman, E. (1959). *The presentation of self in everyday life*. New York: Anchor.

Greengard, S. (2012). Digitally possessed. *Communications of the ACM*, *55*(5), 14–16. doi:10.1145/2160718.2160725

Hangal, S., Lam, M., & Heer, J. (2011). MUSE: Reviving memories using email archives. In *Proceedings of ACM User Interface Software & Technology (UIST)* (pp.75–84). Santa Barbara, CA: ACM.

Hecht, M. L. (1993). A research odyssey: Towards the development of a communication theory of identity. *Communication Monographs*, *60*(1), 76–82. doi:10.1080/03637759309376297

Hecht, M. L., Warren, J., Jung, J., & Krieger, J. (2004). Communication theory of identity. In W. B. Gudykunst (Ed.), *Theorizing about intercultural communication* (pp. 257–278). Newbury Park, CA: Sage.

Herring, S. C., & Paolillo, J. C. (2006). Gender and genre variation in weblogs. *Journal of Sociolinguistics, 10*(4), 439–459. doi:10.1111/j.1467-9841.2006.00287.x

Heylighen, F., & Dewaele, J. (2002). Variation in the contextuality of language: An empirical measure. *Foundations of Science, 7*(3), 293–340. doi:10.1023/A:1019661126744

Higgins, E. T. (1987). Self-discrepancy: A theory relating self and affect. *Psychological Review, 94*(3), 319–340. doi:10.1037/0033-295X.94.3.319 PMID:3615707

Hogan, B. (2010). The presentation of self in the age of social media: Distinguishing performances and exhibitions online. *Bulletin of Science, Technology & Society, 30*(6), 377–386. doi:10.1177/0270467610385893

Hogg, M., & Abrams, D. (1999). Social identity and social cognition: Historical background and current trends. In D. Abrams & M. Hogg (Eds.), *Social identity and social cognition* (pp. 1–25). Malden, MA: Blackwell Publishers.

Hogg, M. A., Terry, D. J., & White, K. M. (1995). A tale of two theories: A critical comparison of identity theory with social identity theory. *Social Psychology Quarterly, 58*(4), 255–269. doi:10.2307/2787127

Hojjat, S. K., Golmakani, E., Bayazi, M. H., Mortazavi, R., Khalili, M. N., & Akaberi, A. (2015). Personality traits and identity styles in methamphetamine-dependent women: A comparative study. *Global Journal of Health Science, 8*(1), 14–20. doi:10.5539/gjhs.v8n1p14 PMID:26234975

Holtgraves, T. (2011). Text messaging, personality, and the social context. *Journal of Research in Personality, 45*(1), 92–99. doi:10.1016/j.jrp.2010.11.015

Humphreys, L. (2012). Connecting, coordinating, cataloguing: Communicative practices on mobile social networks. *Journal of Broadcasting & Electronic Media, 56*(4), 494–510. doi:10.1080/08838151.2012.732144

Iacobelli, F., Gill, A. J., Nowson, S., & Oberlander, J. (2011). Large scale personality classification of bloggers. In *Proceedings of Affective Computing and Intelligent Interaction:Fourth International Conference* (pp. 568–577). Memphis, TN: Springer-Verlag.

Imahori, T. T., & Cupach, W. R. (2005). Theorizing about intercultural communication. *Sage (Atlanta, Ga.)*.

Ireland, M. E., & Mehl, M. R. (2014). Natural language use as a marker of personality. In T. M. Holtgraves (Ed.), *Oxford Handbook of Language and Social Psychology* (pp. 201–218). Oxford, UK: Oxford University Press.

Joinson, A. N. (2001). Self-disclosure in computer-mediated communication: The role of self-awareness and visual anonymity. *European Journal of Social Psychology, 31*(2), 177–192. doi:10.1002/ejsp.36

Kaplan, A., & Haenlein, M. (2010). Users of the world, unite! The challenges and opportunities of social media. *Business Horizons, 53*(1), 59–68. doi:10.1016/j.bushor.2009.09.003

Kaplan, A., & Haenlein, M. (2011). The early bird catches the news: Nine things you should know about micro-blogging. *Business Horizons, 54*(2), 105–113. doi:10.1016/j.bushor.2010.09.004

Khantzian, E. J. (2003). Understanding addictive vulnerability: An evolving psychodynamic perspective. *Neuro-psychoanalysis*, *5*(1), 5–21. doi:10.1080/15294145.2003.10773403

Kietzmann, J. H., Hermkens, K., McCarthy, I. P., & Silvestre, B. S. (2011). Social media? Get serious! Understanding the functional building blocks of social media. *Business Horizons*, *54*(3), 241–251. doi:10.1016/j.bushor.2011.01.005

Kimmons, R., & Veletsianos, G. (2014). The fragmented educator: Social networking sites, acceptable identity fragments, and the identity constellation. *Computers & Education*, *72*, 292–301. doi:10.1016/j.compedu.2013.12.001

Kirkup, G. (2010). Academic blogging: Academic practice and academic identity. *London Review of Education*, *8*(1), 75–84. doi:10.1080/14748460903557803

Kramer, A. (2010). An unobtrusive behavioral model of gross national happiness. In: *Proceedings of the Conference on Human Factors in Computing Systems* (pp. 287–290). Atlanta, GA: ACM. doi:10.1145/1753326.1753369

Krämer, N. C., & Winter, S. (2008). Impression management 2.0. The relationship of self-esteem, extraversion, self-efficacy, and self-presentation within social networking sites. *Journal of Media Psychology*, *20*(3), 106–116. doi:10.1027/1864-1105.20.3.106

Kuss, D. J., & Griffiths, M. D. (2011). Online social networking and addiction—A review of the psychological literature. *International Journal of Environmental Research and Public Health*, *8*(9), 3528–3552. doi:10.3390/ijerph8093528 PMID:22016701

La Barbera, D., La Paglia, F., & Valsavoia, R. (2009). Social network and addiction. *Cyberpsychology & Behavior*, *12*, 628–629. PMID:19592725

Lin, M. P., Ko, H. C., & Wu, J. Y. W. (2011). Prevalence and psychosocial risk factors associated with internet addiction in a nationally representative sample of college students in Taiwan. *Cyberpsychology, Behavior, and Social Networking*, *14*(12), 741–746. doi:10.1089/cyber.2010.0574 PMID:21651418

Liu, H. (2007). Social network profiles as taste performances. *Journal of Computer-Mediated Communication*, *13*(1), 252–275. doi:10.1111/j.1083-6101.2007.00395.x

Livingstone, S. (2008). Taking risky opportunities in youthful content creation: Teenagers use of social networking sites for intimacy, privacy and self-expression. *New Media & Society*, *10*(3), 393–411. doi:10.1177/1461444808089415

Lüders, M. (2007). *Being in mediated spaces. An enquiry into personal media practices* (Doctoral Thesis). University of Oslo, Norway.

Lüders, M. (2008). Conceptualizing personal media. *New Media & Society*, *10*(5), 683–702. doi:10.1177/1461444808094352

Marcia, H. E. (1980). Identity in adolescence. Handbook of Adolescent Psychology, 9(11), 159-187.

Marshall, C. C., & Shipman, F. M. (2011). Social media ownership: Using twitter as a window onto current attitudes and beliefs. *Proceedings of the Conference on Human Factors in Computing Systems* (pp. 1081–1090). Vancouver: CHI 2011. doi:10.1145/1978942.1979103

McGuire, W. J., McGuire, C. V., Child, P., & Fujioka, T. (1978). Salience of ethnicity in the spontaneous self-concept as a function of ones ethnic distinctiveness in the social environment. *Journal of Personality and Social Psychology*, *36*(5), 511–520. doi:10.1037/0022-3514.36.5.511 PMID:671213

McPherson, M., Smith-Lovin, L., & Cook, J. M. (2001). Birds of a feather: Homophily in social networks. *Annual Review of Sociology*, *27*(1), 415–444. doi:10.1146/annurev.soc.27.1.415

Mendelson, A., & Papacharissi, Z. (2010). Look at us: Collective narcissism in college student Facebook photo galleries. In Z. Papacharissi (Ed.), *The networked self: Identity, community and culture on social network sites*. Routledge.

Moran, M., Seaman, J., & Tinti-Kane, H. (2012). *Blogs, wikis, podcasts, and Facebook: How today's higher education faculty use social media*. Boston, MA: Pearson Learning Solutions.

Mukherjee, A., & Liu, B. (2010). Improving gender classification of blog authors. In: *Proceedings of the Conference on Empirical Methods in natural Language Processing* (pp. 207–217). Association for Computational Linguistics.

Newman, M., Groom, C., Handelman, L., & Pennebaker, J. (2008). Gender differences in language use: An analysis of 14,000 text samples. *Discourse Processes*, *45*(3), 211–236. doi:10.1080/01638530802073712

Nowson, S., Oberlander, J., & Gill, A. J. (2005). Weblogs, genres and individual differences. In B. G. Bara, L. Barsalou, & M. Bucciarelli (eds.) *Proceedings of the 27th Annual Conference of the Cognitive Science Society*, (pp. 1666–1671). Lawrence Erlbaum Associates.

Odom, W., Sellen, A., Harper, R., & Thereska, E. (2012). Lost in translation: Understanding the possession of digital things in the Cloud. In *Proceedings of the Conference on Human Factors in Computing Systems* (pp. 781–790). Austin, TX: ACM. doi:10.1145/2207676.2207789

Papacharissi, Z. (2009). The virtual geographies of social networks: A comparative analysis of Facebook, LinkedIn and ASmallWorld. *New Media & Society*, *11*(1-2), 199–220. doi:10.1177/1461444808099577

Patil, S., Norcie, G., Kapadia, A., & Lee, A. (2012). Check out where I am! Location-sharing motivations, preferences, and practices. In *Proceedings of Conference on Human Factors in Computing Systems* (pp. 1997-2002). Austin, TX: ACM.

Pearce, K. E., & Kendzior, S. (2012). Networked authoritarianism and social media in Azerbaijan. *Journal of Communication*, *62*(2), 283–298. doi:10.1111/j.1460-2466.2012.01633.x

Peesapati, S. T., Schwanda, V., Schultz, J., Lepage, M., Jeong, S., & Cosley, D. (2010). Supporting everyday reminiscence. In *Proceedings of Conference on Human Factors in Computing Systems* (pp. 2027–2036). Atlanta, GA: ACM.

Phinney, J. S. (1990). Ethnic identity in adolescence and adulthood: A review of research. *Psychological Bulletin*, *108*(3), 499–514. doi:10.1037/0033-2909.108.3.499 PMID:2270238

Pratt, J. A., Hauser, K., Ugray, Z., & Patterson, O. (2007). Looking at human–computer interface design: Effects of ethnicity in computer agents. *Interacting with Computers, 19*(4), 512–523. doi:10.1016/j.intcom.2007.02.003

Rao, D., Yarowsky, D., Shreevats, A., & Gupta, M. (2010). Classifying latent user attributes in Twitter. In *Proceedings of the 2nd International Workshop on Search and Mining User-Generated Contents* (pp. 37-44). New York: ACM. doi:10.1145/1871985.1871993

Robinson, L. (2007). The cyberself: The self-ing project goes online, symbolic interaction in the digital age. *New Media & Society, 9*(1), 93–110. doi:10.1177/1461444807072216

Rogers, C. (1951). *Client centered therapy.* Boston: Houghton Mifflin.

Rowatt, W. C., Cunningham, M. R., & Druen, P. B. (1998). Deception to get a date. *Personality and Social Psychology Bulletin, 24*(11), 1228–1242. doi:10.1177/01461672982411009

Schacter, D. L., Norman, K. A., & Koutstaal, W. (1998). The cognitive neuroscience of constructive memory. *Annual Review of Psychology, 49*(1), 289–318. doi:10.1146/annurev.psych.49.1.289 PMID:9496626

Schler, J., Koppel, M., Argamon, S., & Pennebaker, J. W. (2006). Effects of age and gender on blogging. In *Proceedings of AAAI Spring Symposium on Computational Approaches for Analyzing Weblogs* (pp.199–205). AAAI.

Schmalz, D. L., Colistra, C. M., & Evans, K. E. (2015). Social media sites as a means of coping with a threatened social identity. *Leisure Sciences: An Interdisciplinary Journal, 37*(1), 20–38. doi:10.1080/01490400.2014.935835

Schwartz, H. A., Eichstaedt, J. C., Kern, M. L., Dziurzynski, L., Ramones, S. M., Agrawal, M., & Ungar, L. H. et al. (2013). Personality, gender, and age in the language of social media: The open-vocabulary approach. *PLoS ONE, 8*(9), e73791. doi:10.1371/journal.pone.0073791 PMID:24086296

Schwartz, R., & Halegoua, R. G. (2014). The spatial self: Location-based identity performance on social media. *New Media & Society, 17*(10), 1643–1660. doi:10.1177/1461444814531364

Selwyn, N., & Stirling, E. (2016). Social media and education ... now the dust has settled. *Learning, Media and Technology, 41*(1), 1–5. doi:10.1080/17439884.2015.1115769

Severino, S., & Craparo, G. (2013). Internet addiction, attachment styles, and social self-efficacy. *Global Journal of Psychology Research, 1*, 9–16.

Simon, B. (2004). *Identity in modern society. A social psychological perspective.* Oxford, UK: Blackwell.

Spence, P. R., Lachlan, K. A., Spates, S. A., & Lin, X. (2013). Intercultural differences in responses to health messages on social media from spokespeople with varying levels of ethnic identity. *Computers in Human Behavior, 29*(3), 1255–1259. doi:10.1016/j.chb.2012.12.013

Sponcil, M., & Gitimu, P. (2013). Use of social media by college students: Relationship to communication and self-concept. *Journal of Technology Research, 4*, 1–13.

Stone, A. R. (1996). *The war of desire and technology at the close of the mechanical age.* Cambridge, MA: MIT Press.

Sumner, C., Byers, A., & Shearing, M. (2011). Determining personality traits & privacy concerns from Facebook activity. *Black Hat Briefings*, 1–29.

Sutko, D. M., & de Souza e Silva, A. (2011). Location-aware mobile media and urban sociability. *New Media & Society, 13*(5), 807–823. doi:10.1177/1461444810385202

Tajfel, H., & Turner, J. C. (1979). An integrative theory of intergroup conflict. In W. G. Austin & S. Worchel (Eds.), *The social psychology of intergroup relations* (pp. 33–47). Monterey, CA: Brooks/Cole.

Thelwall, M. (2008). Homophily in MySpace. *Journal of the American Society for Information Science and Technology, 60*(2), 219–231. doi:10.1002/asi.20978

Thoreau, H. D. (1854). *Walden.* Springer.

Thornberg, R. (2015). School bullying as a collective action: Stigma processes and identity struggling. *Children & Society, 29*(4), 310–320. doi:10.1111/chso.12058

Thumin, N. (2008). 'It's good for them to know my story': Cultural mediation as tension. In K. Lundby (Ed.), *Digital storytelling, mediatized stories: Self-representations in New Media* (pp. 85–104). New York: Peter Lang.

Tufekci, Z. (2008). Grooming, gossip, Facebook and MySpace. *Information Communication and Society, 11*(4), 544–564. doi:10.1080/13691180801999050

Turkle, S. (1995). *Life on the screen: Identity in the age of the internet.* New York: Simon and Schuster.

Turner, J. C., Hogg, M. A., Oakes, P. J., Reicher, S. D., & Wetherell, M. S. (1987). *Rediscovering the social group: A self-categorization theory.* Basil Blackwell.

Turner, J. C., & Oaks, P. J. (1986). The significance of the social identity concept for social psychology with reference to individualism, interactionism, and social influence. *The British Journal of Social Psychology, 25*(3), 237–252. doi:10.1111/j.2044-8309.1986.tb00732.x

Valenzuela, S. (2013). Unpacking the use of social media for protest behavior: The roles of information, opinion expression, and activism. *The American Behavioral Scientist, 57*(7), 920–942. doi:10.1177/0002764213479375

Valenzuela, S., Arriagada, A., & Scherman, A. (2012). The social media basis of youth protest behavior: The case of Chile. *Journal of Communication, 62*(2), 299–314. doi:10.1111/j.1460-2466.2012.01635.x

Veletsianos, G. (2012). Higher education scholars participation and practices on twitter. *Journal of Computer Assisted Learning, 28*(4), 336–349. doi:10.1111/j.1365-2729.2011.00449.x

Veletsianos, G. (2013). Open practices and identity: Evidence from researchers and educators social media participation. *British Journal of Educational Technology, 44*(4), 639–651. doi:10.1111/bjet.12052

Veletsianos, G., & Kimmons, R. (2013). Scholars and faculty members lived experiences in online social networks. *The Internet and Higher Education, 16*(1), 43–50. doi:10.1016/j.iheduc.2012.01.004

Walther, J. B., Van Der Heide, B., Kim, S. Y., Westerman, D., & Tong, S. T. (2008). The role of friends appearance and behavior on evaluations of individuals on Facebook: Are we known by the company we keep? *Human Communication Research, 34*(1), 28–49. doi:10.1111/j.1468-2958.2007.00312.x

Whetten, D. A. (2006). Albert and Whetten revisited: Strengthening the concept of organizational identity. *Journal of Management Inquiry, 15*(3), 219–234. doi:10.1177/1056492606291200

White, J. M., Wampler, R. S., & Winn, K. I. (1998). The Identity Style Inventory: A revision with a sixth-grade reading level (ISI-6G). *Journal of Adolescent Research, 13*(2), 223–245. doi:10.1177/0743554898132007

Yarkoni, T. (2010). Personality in 100,000 Words: A large-scale analysis of personality and word use among bloggers. *Journal of Research in Personality, 44*(3), 363–373. doi:10.1016/j.jrp.2010.04.001 PMID:20563301

Young, J. (2013). A conceptual understanding of organizational identity in the social media environment. *Administration in Social Work, 14*, 518–530.

Young, K. (1999). Internet addiction: Evaluation and treatment. *Student BMJ, 7*, 351–352.

Zhao, O. J., Ng, T., & Cosley, D. (2012). No forests without trees: Particulars and patterns in visualizing personal communication. *Proceedings of iConference* (pp. 25–32). Ontario: ACM.

Zhao, X., Salehi, N., Naranjit, S., Alwaalan, S., Voida, S., & Cosley, D. (2013). The many faces of Facebook: Experiencing social media as performance, exhibition and personal archive. *Proceedings of Conference on Human Factors in Computing Systems* (pp. 1-10). Paris: ACM. doi:10.1145/2470654.2470656

KEY TERMS AND DEFINITIONS

Cyber-Bullying: Purposeful harming or harassing behavior occurring in online contexts.

Gender Identity: Identification with several characteristics associated with the specific gender.

Identity: A concept of the self, associated with particular, unique characteristics, which make the individual different from others.

Impression Management: Process through which individuals control the impressions they make on others.

Internet Addiction: Compulsive use of internet, greatly interfering with normal every-day functioning.

Multidisciplinary Approach: Theoretical approach drawing on several disciplines.

Online Identity: Dimensions of identity displayed in online contexts.

Social Media: Digital media of social character, aiming to create or facilitate communication between individuals (e.g. Facebook, Twitter etc).

Chapter 5
Insights into the Culture of Young Internet Users:
Emerging Trends – Move Over Gen Y, Here Comes Gen Z!

Jessica Lichy
IDRAC Business School, France

Maher Kachour
IDRAC Business School, France

ABSTRACT

This study focuses on the Internet user behaviour of young people, at a time when information and communication technologies (ICT) are rapidly transforming how individuals behave and interact in the online environment. The intention is to put forward a snapshot of contemporary Internet user behaviour, with reference to social networking, and thus provide an overview and understanding of the various online activities undertaken by Generation Y and Generation Z in a non-Anglophone context. The study uses a mixed methods approach to gather data on the thoughts, experiences and behaviours of young Internet users in order to explain their social networking. The findings suggest commonality and disparity between Generation Y and Generation Z. They also reveal the extent to which certain national differences are less apparent when using social networks, suggesting that the widespread adoption of Internet technology is generating a somewhat 'standardised' Internet user behaviour.

INTRODUCTION

The difficulty of researching technology advancements is that the accelerating rate and evolving patterns of past usage do not reflect or predict current usage. When investigating the culture of young Internet users in a rapidly changing society, the challenge is two-fold:

- It requires both constant monitoring of the Internet user behaviour of this age group and an informed awareness of technological developments.

DOI: 10.4018/978-1-5225-1868-6.ch005

Building on the work of Lichy and Kachour (2014; 2016) which discusses emerging trends in Internet user behaviour from a cross-cultural and intergenerational perspective, this study responds to the call for more research in this area. This study therefore investigates the factors that determine the Internet consumption of younger Internet users, the so-called Generation Y and Generation Z, with reference to web 2.0 technologies. Set in an international context, the study aims to further our understanding of the key factors that influence the consumption of web 2.0 technologies, particularly social networking sites (SNS). Specifically, the objective of the study is to test the extent to which certain variables may determine Gen Y and Gen Z Internet user behaviour with reference to web 2.0 technologies, by comparing two distinct non-Anglophone settings: France and Russia over a 5-year period, 2011-2016. Our study is inspired by the work of Simonson (2015) who contends that the current Internet environment presents us with an environment that connects many previously disconnected elements, such as the ratings and reviews of millions of other consumers, and by the response from Kozinets (2016) who underscores the need to carefully examine actual occurrences of phenomena to guide the selection or creation of variables, data, constructs, and relations.

Understanding How Younger Generations Drive Creative Destruction

By drawing on the literature of technology adoption and acceptance, it is possible to provide a framework for understanding Internet user behaviour. Although the literature tends to consider 'young' Internet users as a homogeneous group (Lichy, 2011), there are many divers representations of user behaviour in the online environment (Sobkowicz, 2013; Liébana-Cabanillas, Ramos de Luna and Montoro-Ríos, 2015).

Generally speaking, younger Internet users are more comfortable with embracing technological change than older or more experienced Internet users (Dean, 2008), and are able to take advantage of high-tech innovation (Venkatesh, Thong & Xu, 2012). Younger Internet users tend to be less concerned about the security issues of cyberspace (Chen & Zahedi, 2016). They are driving the pace of change by demanding more powerful technology and by challenging current management thinking. Seemingly confident, independent and goal-oriented, they are transforming the modus operandi of business, for example by introducing new channels for providing information or distribution (Wu, Ray & Whinston, 2008), introducing lean start-up concepts distribution (Blank, 2013), or by integrating a virtualised workplace (Wang & Haggerty, 2011) alongside the existing structure.

Advances in information and communication technologies (ICT) affect the way in which the Internet is consumed, in other words, new technology generates new Internet user behaviour. The challenge for businesses is to develop an innovative business model which can meet the changing needs and wants of consumers, bearing in mind that consumer expectations and behaviour are constantly evolving. Technology and consumer behaviour have always been in constant evolution but the difference nowadays is that the rapid pace of technological development and the increasing sophistication of consumer preferences are shortening product life cycles. The challenge is further magnified by the fact that today's business environment is both global and virtual, crossing linguistic and cultural boundaries. Digitisation has drastically changed the communication process by shifting media from mass to social. Business concepts are constantly evolving; changing the traditional definition of a market as new ICT are introduced, creating new consumer behaviour, new philosophy and calling for new business models. In the current information-driven economy, much of what is taught in business schools today is likely to be obsolete within less than eighteen months' time. New theories and models are required to help understand the complex dynamics of change within society and within business.

The Generation Divide

The notion of generational difference was first put forward by Mannheim (1952) who considered a generational cohort to be a group raised in the same general chronological, social and historical context. Thus, the position in time and the impact of certain common experiences and events are fundamental in formulating generational cohort commonalities (Cheng, Chan, & Chan, 2008; Loroz & Helgeson, 2013). Mannheim's (1952) perspective on generations has been refined over recent decades to consider that generational cohorts have attitudinal, preferential, emotional and dispositional similarities. Consequently, the Internet is consumed in different ways by each generation (Gouteron, 2004).

Much has been published in academic literature and in the international business press about the adoption and usage of digital technology by Generation Y (Gen Y) and Generation Z (Gen Z), many of whom grew up surrounded by ICT. While dates very somewhat in the literature, it is believed that Gen Y were born in the late 70s/ early 80s and Gen Z in the mid-90s (Clarke, Marks & Miller, 2006; Kim-Choy & Holdsworth, 2012; Dhopade, 2016). The younger Internet users have been dubbed with various labels including 'Generation Facebook', 'Generation Connected' and 'Generation Why Not' for Gen Y and 'Generation Now', 'iGeneration' and 'Screenagers' for Gen Z. The work of Issa and Isaias (2016) and Wilkinson (2016) suggests that the Internet has enabled Gen Y and Gen Z to develop advanced skills such as:

- Problem-solving,
- Proactive study,
- Information gathering, and
- Heightened global awareness;

and has enhanced communication and collaboration with their peers and family. On the other hand, the Internet has introduced negative factors such as decreasing physical contact and physical activities; it has reduced the need to think, concentrate and use memory skills while increasing depression, isolation and laziness, an over-reliance on search engines such as Google and the expectation to be entertained. It is too soon to comment on the effect of having had instant access to highly mediatised information on global terrorism, financial insecurity and corporate malpractice. However, it is clear that Gen Z are accustomed to mature technology (iPad and iPhone) and that they have been influenced by the economically challenging times in which they grew up (Bernier, 2015).

As experienced Internet users, these young adults stand out from previous generations in their dependency on ICT for communicating, working and socialising. For example, Shekhawat and Rathore (2014) suggest that young adults who use the Internet for communicating and information search have a higher level of self-esteem and satisfaction with life compared to non-users. Gen Y and Gen Z can be described as the generations who have broken with traditional thinking to develop new models – both professionally and recreationally – facilitated by their familiarity with ICT. They may at times appear unconcerned or unaware of the potential dangers of divulging too much data online (van de Pas & van Bussel, 2015), believing that employers and recruiters cannot use personal data retrieved online (Benraïss-Noailles & Viot, 2012). Despite being digitally literate, there are a number of online activities that younger Internet users should know not to engage in, but still do, such as falling victim to a phishing scam, trusting a self-generated company product review or believing fake reviews (Malbon, 2013).

Career-wise, there is no shortage of role models for today's youth; from seniors like Richard Branson to younger pioneers like Facebook founder Mark Zuckerberg (born in 1984) who in 2010 was one of the world's youngest billionaires. Despite the competitiveness of the job market, young adults are leveraging social media technology to benefit career development via sites like Branchout and Silp which allow people to discover career opportunities through their friends and to facilitate introductions into organisations that they want to work with. Rising stars of the younger generation include Nick D'Aloisio who taught himself code at 12, created the news app Summly at 15, and sold it to Yahoo for $30 million in 2014 aged 18. Another is Beth Reekles who at 18 years old won a three-book contract with Random House publishers after her first book *The Kissing Booth* was released online - and shared 19 million times. And in 2014, DreamWorks awarded a multi-million-dollar film contract to 15-year-old Maya Van Wagenen for her memoir about school dynamics, *Popular, Vintage Wisdom for a Modern Greek*.

Gen Y and Gen Z have grown up surrounded by technology at home and at school (Beard & Dale, 2008). These young adults can be described as experienced Internet users who use technology to get information from each other, rather than from traditional institutions like corporations. Adept at media multitasking, they are at ease using digital technology to enhance their daily activities - but this does not necessarily mean that they will use the Internet for every activity. Moore (2012) suggests that while young Internet users are adept at using technology for research and interactive purposes they tend to buy in stores, presenting opportunities for multiple channel marketers and challenges for those who market online exclusively. Thus, understanding what Gen Y and Gen Z actually do online is an increasingly complex task, since greater interactivity generates a greater diversity of ideas and content. The task of teaching and managing Gen Y and Gen Z presents a new challenge.

The literature puts forward the view that young Internet users represent a cohort of like-minded, similar-aged individuals who behave in a fairly predictable manner in terms of both offline consumer behaviour and Internet user behaviour. The generational divide can be critiqued for propelling the myth that a particular behaviour can be ascribed to a certain generation; there are often as many differences between generations as within a generation (Lichy, 2012). Caution must be exercised when simplifying the behaviour of a whole generation in the way that Prensky (2001) did when he coined the term digital native in 2001 to refer to the 'new' students of that era. The term 'Millennial' is equally ambiguous; Gorman, Nelson and Glassman (2004) state that opinions differ on whether the digital divide among the 'Millennial' generation is growing or shrinking – although there is some variation in the definition of precisely when the Millennial Generation began, with estimates ranging from 1977 (Tapscott, 1998) to 1982 (Howe & Strauss, 2000). Researchers often present a narrow or over-simplified view of each generation – for example Muñoz-Leiva, Hernández-Méndez and Sánchez-Fernández (2012).

Within the same cohort, there can be considerable variety owing to geo-demographic differences (Wang & Wang, 2010). These differences merit closer attention. Firstly, many assumptions have been made about age and digital competence based on the notion that constant exposure to technology since birth will enable young people to be able to use it effectively. Segmenting a population by age overlooks the reality that individuals of a particular age-bracket cannot be categorised into a homogeneous segment. It is unwise to assume that everyone within a certain generation has the same digital skills and Internet access. Secondly, regarding the gender split, the Pew Internet study (2013) suggests that men and women are equally likely to use social networking tools, and that age is not a determining factor for younger generations of Internet users. Much research has been published on gender differences in psychology literature but comparatively less has been undertaken from a consumer behaviour perspective, despite the fact that "gender is one of the most common forms of segmentation used by marketers" (Tifferet & Herstein, 2012, p. 176). Lastly, concerning geographic location, it is thought that socio-spatial setting - or neighbourhood - can cause digital inequality (Hargittai, 2010), in other words there is a belief that there is disparity between urban and suburban Internet users - as opposed to urban versus rural. This lack of information highlights a specific difficulty in gathering data beyond borders and within different neighbourhoods.

Ongoing technological developments have engendered a new culture of Internet usage as Gen Y and Gen Z reveal their consumer values, beliefs and behaviour, distinguishing themselves from older generations (Kopanidis & Shaw, 2014). In order to engage with young adults, organisations need to have a clear understanding of the expectations and lifestyles of Gen Y and Gen Z, many of whom take for granted 24/7 connectivity for both professional communication and social interaction (Luck & Mathews, 2010). Instant response is now the norm; there is low tolerance for slow communication in today's digital society. As mobile and virtual technologies modify patterns of consumer behaviour particularly among young consumers, organisations need to transform their business model to address the emerging wants and needs of this segment. Understanding Internet user behaviour can help organisations engage with younger consumers, using technology to enhance their experience and build e-loyalty. Today's consumers expect transparency and collaboration. Digital technologies, particularly social media, have enabled organisations to interact, co-produce and co-create with customers. The consumer as a producer is now a common feature of many business models (Dong et al., 2015). Through co-creation, organisations can engage with consumers and explore together with them their emotions, feelings and memories while generating deep insights (Ind, Iglesias & Schultz, 2013). In reality though, co-creating remains a major challenge (Vernette & Hamdi-Kidar, 2013) since there is a general lack of understanding as to how an organisation can use co-creation to build relationships and generate value.

The dynamic pace of technological developments is reflected in new lexicon, such as 'web 2.0 technologies', 'social media' and 'social networking' (Snead, 2013). These terms are often used interchangeably by Internet users to refer to the second generation of web access and use, described as participatory, interactive, pervasive and integrated. Web 2.0 technologies include:

- Social networking sites or SNS (such as Facebook and MySpace),
- Blogs, micro-blogging (Twitter),
- Multi-media sharing (such as YouTube and Flickr) and
- Mash-up of data.

In the current online environment, the market is crowded and constantly evolving. The emergence of local SNS reflects national efforts to challenge the global giants, namely Twitter, Google+ and Facebook, by exploiting cultural difference (or patriotism). An early report published by the French media watchdog INA (*l'Institut National de l'Audiovisuel*) illustrates the extent to which local SNS target a cultural niche market (see Table 1):

Data available in the public domain - such as blogs like Coëffé (2014) and the social media analytics platform, Socialbakers - provide further insights into SNS trends. However, Internet users have responded to the information presented by questioning the accuracy. It seems that while national reports are published less frequently, they are generally more accurate than non-government data concerning Internet user behaviour, and thus reflect the difficulty of collecting valid data on SNS usage. Nevertheless, the

Table 1. Summary of popular social networking sites

Pure-Players (American)	Groups (American)	Local Networks	Specialist Networks
Facebook Twitter Bebo Hi5 Friendster Netlog Tumblr Vine	Myspace (News Corp) Orkut (Google) Google Buzz Yahoo Pulse Windows Live	Skyrock (France) Badoo (Italy) Tuenti (Spain) VKontakte (Russia) Odnoklassniki (Russia) As7ab Maktoob (Middle East) Hyves (Netherlands) StudiVZ (Germany) Cyworld (South Corea) Iwiw (Hungary) Nasza-Klasa (Poland) Lidé (Czech Republic) Mixi (Japan) One (Latvia & Lithuania) Qzone, Renren, 51.com, Kaixin001 (China) Wretch (Taiwan) Zing.vn (Vietnam)	YouTube (Google), DailyMotion, Soundcloud, Last.fm (CBS), Blip.fm, Pandora, Flickr (Yahoo), Fotolog, Classmates.com, Copainsdavant, Ning, LinkedIn, Viadeo, Ziki, Plaxo, Jigsaw, Livejournal, Yelp, Habbo, Flixster, FourSquare

Source: (Adapted from Smyrnaios,2011; Sareah,2015; eBIZ, 2016)

Global Web Index (2013) confirms an ongoing shift in the use of SNS, with consumers continuing to migrate from localised platforms to global networks, at the expense of local services. Mobile messaging apps such as WhatsApp and Viber are increasingly popular. The fact that each app has a unique advantage (Viber has superior voice calls and WhatsApp is better for text and picture messaging) makes it attractive for users to have both. Moreover, the apps are easy to switch between and are cost-effective for communicating via long-range Wi-Fi, as opposed to fixed wireless or satellite Internet access. Other popular mobile messaging apps on the market include:

- LINE,
- WeChat,
- Kakao Talk,
- ChatON and
- BBM (Smith, 2014).

The adoption of smartphones has increased the time users spend connected to social networks, particularly among the 18-29 year olds (Pew Internet, 2013; Xia, 2015). In today's global village, understanding how Gen Y and Gen Z consume the Internet is becoming increasingly complex; the online environment is continually fragmenting into new segments that transcend geographic borders, cultures and languages. Hence the choice of a non-Anglophone sample for this study: Russia and France.

Examining Internet User Behaviour

From a cross-cultural perspective, it is worth noting the difficulties of obtaining trustworthy data on Internet user behaviour in certain markets - such as Russia - where local firms dominate the online environment. Relying on media commentators such as the *Russian Internet Forum* (2012) and Oshkalo (2014), it appears that the market in Russia is segmented into four main local SNS:

- 73% of Russian Internet users access Одноклассники ('Classmates' in Russian, rebranded as 'OK'),
- 62% Вконтакте (VKontakte, referred to as VK),
- 31% Moj mir,
- 18% Facebook (an increase from 5% in 2010),
- 9% Twitter (increased from 2% since 2010),
- 3% Livejournal (gradually decreasing).

Prior to the availability of Facebook in Russian - June 2008 – there were only 90 000 users across Russia. The uptake of Facebook in Russia remains low. This disinterest can be partly explained by the fact that there are very powerful local competitors, namely 'VK' and 'OK'. Government control of social media is a further barrier. New legislation allows Russian security services to intercept any communication - from the biggest email service *Mail.ru* to the social network 'VK' *(*Soldatov & Borogan, 2015), intensifying the current regulation that requires all bloggers with 3,000 or more daily readers to register with the government (Stone, 2014). In this setting, blogs provide an alternative public sphere for civic discussion and organisation that differs significantly from that provided by the mainstream media, television and government (Etling, Roberts, & Faris, 2014).

'OK' and 'VK', both launched in 2006, are market leaders in Russia but competition is strong. VK shares many similarities to Facebook (with the added feature of music piracy). It is available in several languages; popular among Russian-speaking users worldwide especially in Russia, Ukraine, Kazakhstan, Moldova, Belarus and Israel. Like other social networks, VK allows users to:

- Message contacts publicly or privately,
- Create groups, public pages and events,
- Share and tag images, audio and video, and
- Play browser-based games.

Users can also upload and download video and audio files via the VK Tracker application, and view thousands of pirated copies of domestic and foreign films dubbed into Russian. Commentators believe that Facebook has only a small niche in Russia because the majority of Russians communicate with other Russian people. Nevertheless, interest is growing as Facebook benefits from the network effect:

- The way in which the technology manages the high volume of connections (Zeichick, 2008).

Russia is one of the few countries in which its own national networks are more popular than foreign networks. Over the next 5 years, it is likely that foreign networks may reach only 4th or 5th place. The majority of Gen Y and Gen Z Internet users in Russia have not yet adopted Facebook because they are satisfied with using 'OK' and 'VK'. Furthermore, it would be hypocritical to ignore the extent to which 'VK' and other social networks have played a major part in the intense and coordinated disinformation campaign surrounding the Ukraine crisis (Euromaidan Press, 2014) and other geopolitical incidents (Dannenberg, Cilluffo & Cardash, 2014).

Turning our attention to France, Fauconnier (2012) and Auffray (2013) identify various characteristics of French Internet users on social networks. Over four-fifths of Internet users in France, approximately 20 million people, have joined a social network. Although there are no statistics to distinguish between those who have set up an account and those who regularly use social networks, almost 50% French Internet users claim to be on Facebook. Other popular SNS include:

- Windows Live (40%),
- *Copains d'Avant* (37%),
- *Trombi* (18%),
- Picasa (14%),
- Google+ (12%),
- Viadeo (9%),
- Twitter (8%) and
- LinkedIn (8%) (IFOP, 2012).

In 2011, the average French Internet user belonged to 2.8 social networks; down from 2.9 in 2010. Almost a fifth of all French Internet users follow brands on social networks, trusting online information more than traditional print media. Less than 11% will post a comment online but 25% would use a social network to boycott a company. There is still a preference for offline shopping among young French consumers rather than shopping online, contrary to the emerging trends in other countries (Pujol, 2014).

In addition to the French preference for 'home-grown' technology, many people distrust Facebook-sponsored ads (La Fonderie, 2012). Meeting customer expectations is therefore a challenge in France, particularly at a time when Facebook prepares to launch a new service which would allow users to create short advertisements that appear in their friends' news feeds notifying them of everything from apartment rentals to furniture sales to job boards - in short, very similar to Craigslist. The emphasis is on exchanging information and facilitating 'open' communication across the ever-growing Facebook community. In contrast to the Craigslist business model of broadcasting ads, Facebook will display ads that are relevant to the users that might be interested. The change in Facebook's business model reflects a move away from relying on corporate sponsorship. While this service is outside the scope of the current study, it highlights the fast pace of change and draws attention to the different approaches used by Facebook to create an online community. It will be interesting to see the extent to which Internet users in different cultural markets adopt (or opt out of) this new service.

Methodology

Focusing on Gen Y and Gen Z Internet user behaviour with reference to web 2.0 technologies, this study explores the extent to which their behaviour may be influenced by certain variables that are typically used for classifying individuals into 'homogenous' user groups (i.e. age, gender and socio-spatial setting). The data was collected in three phases (mid-2011, mid-2013, early 2016) in order to explore the evolution of trends in the usage of SNS among young Internet users and to complement earlier data on Gen Y by adding Gen Z. The researchers used a convenience sample of over 400 international undergraduates at two distinct locations, Lyon (France) and St Petersburg (Russia), selected on the basis that they are both second cities. Software 'R' was used to analyse the survey data.

The decision to research each location separately is to advance intercultural factor. Indeed, we conducted two studies in two different cities/ countries (St Petersburg in Russia vs. Lyon in France). It is clear that the geopolitical, economic, cultural, democratic and social contexts vary greatly between these two regions of the world. Our goal is to verify whether the considered explanatory factors of the use of SNS vary by changing the spatial dimension. On other words, the intercultural factor can impact the SNS usage and consumer behavior (measured here by the time spent on these networks). Furthermore, we also discussed the chronological evolution of user behaviour by conducting our study longitudinally over three distinct periods 2011/2013/ and more recently in 2016.

In 2011, face-to-face surveys were administered to obtain general information about the Internet user behaviour of Gen Y to understand how they engage with ICT. The survey questions were purposely broad in order to elicit information on their routine Internet behaviour, including:

- The sites and services used for studying and for leisure,
- Time spent updating personal profile,
- Time spent communicating on SNS and related sites.

Space was provided at the end of the survey for the participants to add any further commentary, if they wished, about using web 2.0 technologies. To explore the existence of a relationship between certain variables, personal information was also requested - namely gender, age group, type of residential neighbourhood (urban, sub-urban, rural or semi-rural) and permanent country of residence. Participants were required to indicate when they first began using the Internet. Nearly 60% of the participants used the Internet prior to 2000; the results therefore reflect the behaviour of proficient Internet users.

The same survey was administered once again in mid-2013 in Lyon and St Petersburg with the aim of exploring evolution in Internet user behaviour among the Gen Y cohort. Following the collection and analysis of the survey data, a forum was organised in September 2013 with Gen Y Internet users to give the participants in each location (Lyon and St Petersburg) an opportunity to discuss and comment on the findings. This second phase enabled validation of the initial data gathered in the survey. The discussion and comments were transcribed and translated into English by the authors, then checked by a native proof-reader.

In the final phase, six focus groups were held in February 2016 with Gen Z Internet users in each location (three in Lyon and three in St Petersburg) to investigate their social networking habits and opinions on ICT. The focus groups centred on the use of contemporary ICT by Gen Z. The intention was not to compare generational differences per se (given that ICT evolves so rapidly) but to investigate the thoughts, experiences and behaviours of younger Internet users relating to the themes raised by Gen Y in the forum of 2013 and also present-day issues surrounding ICT. Online commentators – such as Viard (2016) and Ropars (2016) - provide quantitative data (taken from the SNS providers) on the growth of SNS and Internet user behaviour. However, these sites make no distinction between 'active users' and 'inactive users', fake profiles and people who have several profiles on the same SNS. This oversight produces inaccurate data, failing to present a realistic and authentic snapshot of Gen Z usage. Consequently, the purpose of focus groups was to contribute qualitative information concerning how Gen Z engage with ICT and SNS, on other words, their thoughts, experiences and behaviours.

Focus groups were used in order to obtain detailed information about the range of ideas and feelings that Internet users have about using SNS. This method is frequently used in qualitative research to illuminate the differences in perspective between groups of individuals through social interaction of a group (Kitzinger, 1994). One of the distinct features of focus-group interviews is its group dynamics; hence the type and range of data generated through social interaction is often deeper and richer than the data obtained from one-to-one interviews (Thomas et al., 1995).

Results

The numerical study is based on the survey which was administered to over 100 students at each location in 2011, then repeated in 2013. It focuses on five key questions:

- Time spent (hours/week) using web 2.0 technologies,
- Age group,
- Neighbourhood,
- Date of first entry on SNS,
- Gender.

Note that 'time spent (hours/week) using web technologies' is a quantitative variable which can be seen as a measure of consumption. 'Date of first entry on SNS' is also a quantitative variable which represents loyalty and consumer engagement in the context of the early SNS; it is worth noting that Internet users switch between multiple specialised apps rather than use a single app for a range of functions. 'Age group' is a categorical variable with five modalities/ classes:

- 18-20,
- 21-23,
- 24-26,
- 27-29 and
- +30,

'gender' is a categorical variable with two modalities:

- Male and
- Female,

and finally 'neighbourhood' is also a categorical variable, with four modalities:

- Urban,
- Sub-urban,
- Rural and
- Semi-Rural.

Numerical Study for Lyon

The variables are analysed differently depending on their nature; quantitative or categorical. The observed data of 'time spent using web 2.0 technologies' in 2011 vary from 1 to 25, with a sample mean of 18.15 and a sample standard deviation of 4.34; the observed data from 2013 vary from 1 to 24, with a sample mean of 16.12 and a sample standard deviation of 3.95. In contrast, the observed data of 'date of first entry' on SNS from 2011 vary from 1 to 5, with a sample mean of 2.68 and a sample standard deviation of 1; the observed data in 2013 vary also from 1 to 5, with a sample mean of 3.38 and a sample standard deviation of 0.97. The categorical variables are summarised in the following frequency tables (see Table 2, Table 3 and Table 4):

Data Modelling

'Time spent using web 2.0 technologies' is considered an explained (or dependent) variable, denoted by y, and age group, gender, neighbourhood, and date of first entry on SNS are explanatory variables,

Table 2. Summary of categorical variables (Lyon)

Variable	Modality	Frequency	Variable	Modality	Frequency
Age group 2011	18 -20	40%	Age group 2013	18 -20	11%
	21-23	44%		21-23	61%
	24-26	13%		24-26	25%
	26-29	2%		26-29	2%
	30 +	1%		30 +	1%
Variable	**Modality**	**Frequency**	**Variable**	**Modality**	**Frequency**
Neighbourhood 2011	Urban	57%	Neighbourhood 2013	Urban	42%
	Sub-urban	21%		Sub-urban	38%
	Rural	7%		Rural	4%
	Semi-rural	15%		Semi-rural	16%
Variable	**Modality**	**Frequency**	**Variable**	**Modality**	**Frequency**
Gender 2011	Female	59%	Gender 2013	Female	62%
	Male	41%		Male	38%

Table 3. Estimates of unknown parameters and standard deviations in 2011 (Lyon sample)

Parameter	Estimate	Standard Deviation	P-value
B_0	2.89498	0.09824	<2e-16
B_1	-0.06847	0.03007	0.0350
B_2	-0.07497	0.04867	0.2247
B_3	0.04397	0.02094	0.0354
B_4	0.02793	0.02343	0.1778

Table 4. Estimates of unknown parameters and standard deviations in 2013 (Lyon sample)

Parameter	Estimate	Standard Deviation	P-value
B_0	3.101223	0.133877	< 2e-16
B_1	-0.011622	0.035708	0.746
B_2	-0.002471	0.052253	0.439
B_3	0.024285	0.023758	0.306
B_4	-0.102761	0.025569	4.8e-05

denoted respectively by x_1, x_2, x_3, and x_4. The five modalities of the age group variable are encoded from 1 to 5 as follows:

- $1 \leftarrow$ from 18 to 20 years
- $2 \leftarrow$ from 21 to 23 years
- $3 \leftarrow$ from 24 to 26 years
- $4 \leftarrow$ from 27 to 29 years
- $5 \leftarrow$ 30 years and over,

Similarly, the four modalities of the neighbourhood variable are encoded from 1 to 4 as follows:

- $1 \leftarrow$ urban
- $2 \leftarrow$ sub-urban
- $3 \leftarrow$ rural
- $4 \leftarrow$ semi-Rural,

Finally, the modalities of the gender variable are encoded from 0 to 1 as following:

- $0 \leftarrow$ Female
- $1 \leftarrow$ Male

Since the explained variable is a count data type (which takes non-negative integer values, i.e. 0, 1, 2 …), it is not suitable to use the linear regression model (based on normal distribution) to describe the relationship between the explained variable and the explanatory variables. Furthermore, the logistic regression model cannot be used because the explained variable is not a binary variable, i.e. takes 0 or 1. For the surveys considered in our study, we asked participants to indicate the weekly number of hours spent on the SNS (without pre-set intervals/classes). Thus, this observed variable, denoted by y, is indeed a discrete variable. Moreover, we considered 'time spent on SNS' as our dependent variable which could be explained by the following variables: age group, gender, neighbourhood, and date of first entry on SNS. Thus the explanatory variables are denoted respectively by x_1, x_2, x_3, and x_4. Given the integer nature of the dependent variable and the fact that the values of the empirical mean and variance are significantly close, it fully justified the use of the Poisson regression model (one of the most prominent log-linear models for the integer-valued variables) to fit the data. Therefore, for all $i = 1…n$, the authors assume that y_i follows a Poisson distribution with a parameter λ_i given by

$$\text{Log } (\lambda_i) = \beta_0 + \beta_1 x_{1,i} + \beta_2 x_{2,i} + \beta_3 x_{3,i} + \beta_4 x_{4,i}, \tag{1}$$

where β_0, β_1, β_2, β_3 and β_4 are the unknown regression coefficients. Note that these parameters can be estimated by using Maximum likelihood method. In this study, software R is used for the estimation of the parameters and testing their significance. The Poisson regression model is applied to the observed data from 2011. Note that in 2011 the values of the empirical mean and variance are significantly close, validating our choice of Poisson regression to fit the data. The following table gives estimates of the unknown parameters with the associated standard deviations (Table 3):

Furthermore, using an ANOVA type test, at the 5% level, one can see that β_0, β_1, and β_3 are statistically significant (see the p-value results in Table 3).

Regarding the data observed in 2013, the values of the empirical mean and variance are also significantly close, which validates our choice of Poisson regression to fit the data. The following table gives estimates of the unknown parameters with the associated standard deviations (Table 4):

Thus, an ANOVA type test shows here that β_0 and β_4 are both statistically significant at the 5% level (see the p-value results in Table 4).

Comparing Consumption of the Internet

Here, the focus is on studying the chronological evolution of time spent (hours/week) using web 2.0 technologies by the participants. To do this, it is necessary to subtract the time spent using web 2.0 technologies in 2013 from time spent using web 2.0 technologies in 2011, which can be seen as a new variable. Note that, the sample mean equals -2.31 and the sample standard deviation equals 1.28. Let 'm' be the unknown mean of this new variable. The following univariate test is performed:

H_0: m $\geq$ -2 against H_1: m < -2.

Using a standard test based on the Normal distribution, one can reject the null hypothesis, at the 5% level. Hence, one can deduce that, between 2011 and 2013, the average time of SNS usage has decreased by at least two hours per week per person.

Numerical Study for St Petersburg

Once again, the variables are analysed differently depending on their nature, quantitative or categorical. The observed data of 'time spent using web 2.0 technologies' from 2011 vary from 1 to 29, with a sample mean of 16:53 and a sample standard deviation of 4.04; the observed data in 2013 vary from 1 to 24, with a sample mean of 18.69 and a sample standard deviation of 4.31. Moreover, the observed data of 'date of first entry' on web 2.0 technologies from 2011 vary from 1 to 5, with a sample mean of 2.4 and a sample standard deviation of 0.86; the observed data from 2013 vary also from 1 to 6, with a sample mean of 2.96 and a sample standard deviation of 1.12. The categorical variables are summarized in the following frequency tables (see Table 5, Table 6, and Table 7):

Data Modelling

Here, time spent using web 2.0 technologies is considered as explained variable, denoted by y, and age group, gender, neighbourhood plus date of first entry on SNS are explanatory variables, denoted respectively by x_1, x_2, x_3, and x_4. In order to analyse the data, using the same arguments as for the Lyon sample, the Poisson regression model is used, defined by (**1**). The table below (Table 6) gives estimates of the unknown parameters with the associated standard deviations for the observed data from the St Petersburg sample in 2011.

Furthermore, using an ANOVA type test, at 5% level, one can see that β_0, β_1, β_2, and β_3 are statistically significant (see the p-value results in Table 6). Applying the Poisson regression model to observed data from 2013 gives the following estimation:

Table 5. Summary of categorical variables (St Petersburg)

Variable	Modality	Frequency	Variable	Modality	Frequency
Age group 2011	18 -20	21%	Age group 2013	18 -20	5%
	21-23	53%		21-23	51%
	24-26	18%		24-26	31%
	26-29	6%		26-29	11%
	30 +	2%		30 +	2%
Variable	**Modality**	**Frequency**	**Variable**	**Modality**	**Frequency**
Neighbourhood 2011	Urban	61%	Neighbourhood 2013	Urban	43%
	Sub-urban	23%		Sub-urban	36%
	Rural	6%		Rural	3%
	Semi-rural	10%		Semi-rural	18%
Variable	**Modality**	**Frequency**	**Variable**	**Modality**	**Frequency**
Gender 2011	Female	48%	Gender 2013	Female	63%
	Male	52%		Male	37%

Table 6. to show the estimates of unknown parameters and standard deviations in 2011 (St Petersburg sample)

Parameter	Estimate	Standard Deviation	P-value
B_0	2.873477	0.105626	< 2e-16
B_1	-0.109227	0.028917	0.000159
B_2	0.107085	0.051066	0.035994
B_3	0.050444	0.025119	0.044619
B_4	0.008229	0.029049	0.776954

Table 7. Estimates of unknown parameters and standard deviations in 2013 (St Petersburg sample)

Parameter	Estimate	Standard Deviation	P-value
B_0	2.97985	0.10545	<2e-16
B_1	-0.03751	0.02846	0.188
B_2	0.07835	0.04844	0.106
B_3	-0.02949	0.02182	0.177
B_4	0.02364	0.02126	0.266

Therefore, using an ANOVA type test, at the 5% level, one can see that β_0 is the only parameter statistically significant (see the p-value results in Table 7).

Consumption Comparison of Internet

Here, the focus is on studying the chronological evolution of time spent (hours/week) using web 2.0 technologies for the St Petersburg sample. To do this, it is necessary to subtract the time spent using web 2.0 by the participants in 2013 from 2011, which can be seen as a new variable. Note that, the sample mean equals 2.36 and the sample standard deviation equals 1.54. Let 'm' be the unknown mean of this new variable. The following univariate test is performed:

H_0: m ≤ 2 against H_1: m > 2.

Using a standard test based on the Normal distribution, one can reject the null hypothesis, at the 5% level. Hence, one can deduce that the time spent using web 2.0 technologies has increased by two hours per week per person.

Post-Survey Forum

Following the statistical analysis, a forum was organised in September 2013 to give the participants in each location (Lyon and St Petersburg) an opportunity to comment on the findings, particularly the finding that the Lyon-based population were spending less time on SNS in 2013 compared to 2011 (for further details, see earlier paragraph on the consumption comparison of Lyon sample), and that conversely the St Petersburg-based population were spending more time on web 2.0 technologies in 2013 compared to 2011 (for further details, see paragraph above on the consumption comparison of St Petersburg sample).

The comments raised by participants during the forum were transcribed and manually sorted thematically using Template Analysis (King, 2004a,b; King & Horrocks, 2010) to generate a number of major themes (see Table 8). Full and equal attention was given to each comment with the aim of identifying interesting aspects that formed the basis of repeated themes. Coloured highlighter pens were used to make notes on each transcript being analysed; attention was paid to surrounding data in order to avoid losing context. Two additional academics were asked to analyse the transcripts independently in order to reduce bias while developing the themes. Consensus was reached on a number of central themes which can be described as:

- Lassitude,
- Distrust,
- Boredom, and
- Deviant user behaviour of SNS (from Internet users in France) and fascination,
- Novelty,
- Access to information, and
- Freedom of speech (from Internet users in Russia).

The comments provide a deeper insight into how young people consume web 2.0 technologies, their attitudes and thoughts, at a specific moment in time.

Findings of Focus Groups with Gen Z

To gain an insight into contemporary Internet user behaviour of Gen Z, it was decided to organise focus groups rather than a forum for the third phase of the investigation. The intention was to encourage debate among the participants by creating smaller group discussions. In contrast to the comments raised by the Gen Y participants of the 2013 forum including lassitude, distrust, boredom, and deviant user behaviour of SNS (from Internet users in France) and fascination, novelty, access to information, and freedom of speech (from Internet users in Russia), there was noticeable commonality in the comments raised from Gen Z Internet users in France and Russia, suggesting convergence in Internet usage. The comments raised by the Gen Z participants of the 2016 focus groups naturally reflect an evolution in technology

Table 8. Comparative summary of the themes put forward by each sample in response to the results of the survey data

Lyon-Based Comments	St Petersburg-Based Comments
- social networks are less of a novelty factor now - many other apps being used such as WhatsApp - growing interest in other new innovations in digital technology - 'voting with feet': each time FB changes the privacy settings, people are 'switching off' (cancelling membership) or opting-out of the new settings - Greater awareness of negative aspects of using social networks, people are more conscious of the risks involved (e.g. personal identity theft, voyeurism, media reports of "just a waste of time", privacy scares, hacking into sites, etc.) - too much advertising and marketing on social networks - if one friend leaves FB for a few weeks (to get away from being "too much in the public eye") then this triggers off a group of 20 or 30 close friends copying - younger, experienced users can navigate around a site quicker and find what they want faster, so they spend less time on networks; searches are more targeted - with dynamic change, users don't stay on one medium for long; consumers are very fickle with a short attention span, it only takes one person to criticize a site and everyone moves on to the next big 'wow' - Social networks are just a fad, another way of identifying with other people. It shows how much we are just "pack animals" - even the investors are bored with Facebook; the share price is not healthy	- people are fascinated with a virtual window on the world - the novelty factor still attracts new users to join social networks in Russia - the participants claim to enjoy discovering and using online social networks; this is to be expected since social networks were launched later on the Russian market - the perceived benefits of using social networks outweigh the drawbacks such as loss of privacy or hacking into accounts to send out spam and adverts - social networks reflect a modern way of living where young Internet users can connect with like-minded people around the world - users are attracted by free music and video sharing - social networks are also used to 'troll' or harass popular figures (such as authors) with the intention of causing deliberate anguish to their immediate entourage - ordinary individuals can become opinion leaders - social networks provide a platform for gregarious people to broadcast information worldwide on the minute changes in their life - social networks offer a channel for free communication (particularly among the emerging middle classes) in a previously censored environment, but are increasingly used to fuel social unrest, propaganda and political uprising

and ensuing user behaviour (see Table 9 for a detailed summary in Appendix). The common themes discussed by Internet users in France and Russia include:

- The choice of profile photos on SNS,
- Personal identity,
- Brand communities the use/abuse of status updates,
- The necessity for instant communication,
- The insincerity of SNS,
- The opportunities for business, government and policy makers,
- Deviant user behaviour.

There were no discernible differences that could be attributed to geographic setting. The dominant theme seemed to be a growing awareness of the many different categories (or typologies) of Internet users and subcultures of SNS users, generating different behaviour in terms of how a user consumes the Internet. Neither group of Gen Z participants mentioned SNS as a channel for virtual team work, and neither group referred to SNS as a resource for international collaboration. It was overwhelming evident that the participants rely heavily on SNS for communicating 24/7. They appreciate being in constant contact with other users and sharing information. The general consensus is that SNS have changed the way we live beyond recognition, bringing about changes in society, business and everyday life. Gen Z understand the limitations of modern technology too, citing addictions and deviant user behaviour.

Concerning the Lyon participants:

1. The choice of appropriate profile picture is very important for Gen Z: whether to choose a self-portrait or avatar, what tone of message it should denote, how often it should be changed, when to use a selfie or a professional photographer. The nature and regularity of posting videos was equally discussed.

2. Status updates are considered to be more personal/ revealing than a profile photo since more intimate information is shared; Gen Z frown upon a user who posts too many status updates (or too often) as it is seen as synonymous with attention-seeking.

3. Gen Z distinguish between status updates (*what I am doing now*) and personal opinions (*what I think*). While Gen Z acknowledge the commoditisation of their data, they nevertheless enjoy sharing personal views and judgements. They understand the limitations of sharing data, and the need to keep some opinions offline such as sexual suggestiveness and over-sharing of drunkenness, racism or homophobia – all of which are seen as a social media '*no no*'. When a user asks others to 'PM' (send a private message), Gen Z commented that this behaviour is a veiled cry for help/attention.

4. Gen Z perceive the non-sharing 'old' generations (Gen Y and Gen X) as uninformed or wary of sharing personal and professional information via SNS. However, the reasons why Gen Y and Gen X may choose to *not* divulge information were beyond the comprehension of the Gen Z participants who believe it has something to do with age.

5. Gen Z see the value of SNS for following favourite brands and for building brand communities. It was noted that some users deliberately "like" a brand (whether or not they consume the brand) in order to convey a certain lifestyle or sense of belonging.

6. Gen Z are aware of certain undesirable traits that are manifested on SNS including instability, attention-seeking, self-centredness, vanity or sycophantic behaviour.

7. Gen Z think that this behaviour stems from users who have become 'victims' of social network dependency - in order to get noticed they typically include their friends into their posts by mentioning them or publishing photos of them then tagging each person.

8. Despite the drawbacks, the participants wholeheartedly agreed that modern lifestyle depends entirely on broadcasting via SNS and to a lesser extent via online reviews – replacing physical interaction. Gen Z voiced a clear need for constant communication and sharing of information with a wide network of people.

9. This level of dependency can, for some users, be seen as a social crutch; they put pressure on themselves to be seen as part of a group/ community, in an attempt to capture the attention of other users. In some cases, they may have more friends on SNS than in real life.

10. Not having an account on SNS is considered strange behaviour; being part of an online community - Snapchat, Instagram, Twitter, Vimeo and Pinterest - is considered essential by Gen Z.

Concerning the St Petersburg participants:

1. SNS reflect users' *abilities to function in the modern world*; some may post too much or too little but, most importantly, they have a virtual presence. Suspicion is raised when an individual claims not to be part of a SNS,

2. A user may show appreciation of another user, an event or brand by clicking 'like'; it has been noticed that some users will deliberately "like" because they aspire to a certain social standing or a particular professional/ political affiliation.

3. Consciously or otherwise, *people's goals are revealed through the personal brand* that they create via SNS; a user will build a profile to facilitate personal, social or professional advancement. While self-marketing is socially acceptable, it is increasingly difficult to distinguish between the real person and the embellished profile. Similarly, it is impossible to ascertain if a user genuinely "likes" a person or product – or whether the user has "liked" for the sake of their personal goals.

4. Gen Z participants are aware that the information on a user's personality, interests, values, network and even social class can be deciphered for marketing purposes and wonder about calculating a '*social network worth'* or yardstick *to identify opinion leaders* for each user based on the amount and value of contacts a person has.

5. While the ethics of such a calculation are questionable, it is obvious that Gen Z users willingly divulge or *share information about personal values* and *personal information.*

6. Gen Z recognise the *different segments of consumer behaviour* on SNS; citing the use of Twitter for politicians and journalists, in contrast to Snapchat and Periscope for younger, more outgoing users. Gen Z are also aware of the extent to which consumer behaviour is graphically revealed via SNS, for example, when a user posts about the work-life balance or any 'hidden' traits (party animal, drinker, smoker).

7. Users will intentionally *associate with key figures* on SNS so as to make their views publically known and to confirm the groups with which they wish to be identified - be this social, political, corporate or professional. Users also post about the various communities to which they belong - such as religious affiliation or sports clubs - to augment their personal/professional identity (unless prevented by confidentiality clauses). Gen Z seem aware that this type of data will be commoditised and used by business and government alike.

8. To conceal many of the *'hidden' traits* that are publicly broadcast via SNS – intentionally or not - users generally manage their identity (and therefore privacy) by adopting either the "Chinese Wall" approach (when a person creates two individual online accounts to separate their personal and professional accounts) or the "Living Brand" approach (when a person uses a single account for communicating the personal, professional and company brand).

9. Gen Z acknowledge that it is *essential to keep a profile updated regularly* because SNS are a recognised multi-way channel of communication. Updates may take the form of a description or photo of what the user did or ate that day, or a personal view on something the user finds interesting such as politics, science or business. For Gen Z, updates indicate that a person likes not only to socialise with others in real life but also to share the experience and emotion with others online by posting *daily* statuses and photos. These updates serve the purpose of communicating with one's entourage and inspiring/ taking inspiration from others.

10. Gen Z hold that changing status or profile too frequently is a sign that a person is conceited, shallow or seeking attention in order to feel less insecure/unstable. In this respect, Gen Z consider that *SNS provide a fake veneer that hides an inferiority complex,* on the basis that a person lacking empathy or self-esteem in real life will publicise positive posts to generate affection or acceptance. Gen Z can discern that some users have an ostentatious view about their own talents and abilities, or that they suffer from an inflated view of their own talents. Pretentious users are seen as flippant in their decisions, in an attempt to present a confident image of themselves to other people but failing

completely. Over-sharing can denote an inferiority complex, according to Gen Z, signifying that the views of others matter more than one's own views – in addition, some people post positive (and never negative) information in order to boast about their lives because they crave the attention.

Gen Z believe that there are nowadays many different categories and subgroups of Internet users; people often belong to more than one user group. The participants in Lyon and St Petersburg differ in the factors that they consider to be most characteristic in their description of the various user groups (see Table 10 for a detailed summary in Appendix):

The Lyon participants listed the key typologies of users as:

- The inactive/ passive voyeur
- The social butterfly
- The active and dynamic interactor
- The NO-profile-picture-User / "Flower" – profile picture
- The Professional User / Hobby-Promoters
- The I-don't-care-for-that-account-but-I-have-one – User / young-utility-user
- The addicted user

The St Petersburg participants listed the key typologies of users as:

- The stalker
- The bling-bling
- The over-sharer
- The geek
- The messenger user
- The clubber
- The *I-am-so-popular* one

Discussion of Findings

The findings of the 2011 and 2013 survey suggest that there was no distinctive relationship between 'time spent using web 2.0 technologies' and gender, or between 'time spent using web 2.0 technologies' and socio-spatial setting (or neighbourhood). Age did exert some influence over 'time spent using web 2.0 technologies' in 2011 but this association was imperceptible in 2013. Thus, gender, socio-spatial setting and age exert very little or no influence over the time Gen Y spent using web 2.0 technologies in 2013. It seems more logical to define Internet users by how they use the technology. The issues raised by the Lyon-based population (for example privacy issues and voyeurism) were not apparent among the St Petersburg-based population. Confirming the Teens & Social Networks Study (2010), the Internet users in France revealed lassitude of Facebook – or 'Facebook fatigue'– however there was no indication that Russian Internet users were leaving Facebook or using it less, in favour of attractive alternative sites. Some younger users are choosing to leave Facebook as older relatives join, in preference for sites that allow pseudonyms such as Tumblr and Twitter, or for messaging apps like Line, Viber and Snapchat that are more suited for conversations between small groups of friends (Cookson, 2013).

The findings of the forum underscore the extent to which VK in Russia is benefitting from the network effect; although the business model does have a number of limitations, it nevertheless attracts a high volume of Russian Internet users who want to connect and communicate with other Russian Internet users, and consequently VK is the market leader in Russia – with twice as many users as Facebook. There are, however, mounting concerns over data security on VK; many accounts have been hacked into to send viruses and spam, revealing its indifferent approach to preventing hacking. DeMartino (2014) believes that VK is under the control of two Russian oligarchs who are known to have close ties with Putin.

From a user perspective, VK is less user-friendly than Facebook, requiring the user to navigate from page to page if they want to chat online or check the news feed. On VK, alerts about comments on pictures are emailed to user only, and not always on time. Whereas on Facebook, a notification is sent immediately to the user's main page when another user comments on status or pictures. VK does not allow users to be logged in and appear offline, which is inconvenient if users do not want to reply to messages instantly or to be noticed online. VK is an open copy of Facebook in colour and layout, offering basic functions and few apps, but it attracts new users and retains existing ones through offering pirated copies of domestic and foreign films dubbed into Russian. Users can also upload and download video and audio files via the VK Tracker application – a key feature of VK over Facebook. The average VK user enjoys the availability of online entertainment via VK, in preference to joining Facebook that offers numerous applications, ads, extra features and international appeal – but no online pirated films and music. Many Russians prefer VK but feel obliged to have a Facebook account for prestige, social identity or international networking. Although Facebook leads the way in terms of business approach, Facebook and VK complement and compete with each other.

Reflecting on the survey and forum results, a defining factor has emerged between 2011 and 2013. There seems to have been a shift in Gen Y expectations as consumers of the Internet. This can be partly explained by the notion that Internet users in France are increasingly blasé, cautious or disinterested in social networks; and perhaps by the fact that Gen Y grew up with concerns about data privacy and Internet security. Facebook is the leading social network in many countries but in France and Russia, Facebook is failing to engage with Gen Y Internet users, for different reasons. VK offers greater value for Russian-speaking Internet users than Facebook. In France, Skyrock.com seems more popular than Facebook. For the French, Facebook needs to find the balance between passive listening and the complete loss of privacy in order to attract new users. Thus, it can be concluded that the availability of the same technology worldwide – social networks – does not automatically bring about the same Internet user behaviour. Users differ in the amount of personal information that they are willing to share and the features that they expect from a social network. In the 2013 study, it seems that an external factor – possibly the cultural context – has an impact on the choice of SNS and Gen Y user behaviour.

The focus group results indicate that convergence is taking/ has taken place in Internet user behaviour among Gen Z. Commonality is noticed in the responses given by the French participants and the Russian participants. When asked how they (and their friends) engage with ICT, Gen Z described in detail what they do on SNS and how it relates to what others do on SNS. Their descriptions and comments discussed in the focus groups can be grouped 20 categories to reveal key themes (10 for each setting). The themes cited by Gen Z (from most to least discussed) include:

- Choice of profile picture,
- Status updates,

- Personal opinions,
- The non-sharing 'old' generations (Gen Y and Gen X),
- Online brand communities,
- Undesirable traits,
- Social network dependency,
- Modern lifestyle of broadcasting via social media,
- SNS as a 'social crutch', and
- The abnormality of not belonging to a SNS – for the Lyon participants.

Similarly, for the St Petersburg participants, the themes discussed include:

- SNS as measure of ability to function in the modern world,
- The use of "like",
- Personal identity/brand,
- "Social network worth"/ opinion leaders,
- Sharing information,
- Segmentation of SNS consumer behaviour,
- Connecting with key figures,
- 'Hidden' traits,
- Profile updates,
- SNS as a fake veneer.

From these broad themes, the Gen Z participants drew up typologies of users, reflecting on the traits they observe on SNS. The Lyon sample labelled each typology of SNS users as:

- Inactive/ passive voyeur,
- Social butterfly,
- Active and dynamic interactor,
- NO-profile-picture-User / "Flower" – profile picture,
- Professional User / Hobby-Promoters,
- I-don't-care-for-that-account-but-I-have-one – User / young-utility-user, and
- The addicted user.

In contrast, the St Petersburg put forward:

- Stalker,
- Bling-bling,
- Over-sharer,
- Geek,
- Messenger user,
- Clubber, and
- The *I-am-so-popular* one.

Although the typology labels differ in semantics, there is commonality in how Gen Z perceive their generation's use of SNS. From the perspective of Internet user behaviour, the typologies could be simplified into:

- Over-active,
- Active,
- Under-active,
- Deviant, and
- Inactive.

However, the typology labels suggested by the Gen Z participants provide a more evocative illustration of the activities undertaken by younger Internet users.

In this sample, Gen Z is seemingly comfortable with the virtual world; they are likely to have always had Internet access at school and home. Throughout their relatively short lives, many technological developments have taken place – including:

- Internet telephony,
- Cellular phones,
- Smartphones,
- Streaming video and
- Social networking.

Technological obsolescence is, to them, a *fait accompli* to replace the 'old' with the 'new' which is invariably 'better, smaller and cheaper'. Having (and using) the latest technology is important for Gen Z. The expectation for constant innovation seems to be a way of life for young Internet users, differentiating Gen Z from their parents' or grandparents' generations who typically would have been more wary of 'marketing spin' and more cost-conscious. Our investigation suggests that Gen Y and Gen Z have different Internet user behaviour. Gen Z relies on the Internet and social media to look for content and social networking across many different apps. They are influenced by online videos and aware of other users. While Gen Y wholeheartedly embrace a digital lifestyle, Gen Z seem more aware of the bigger picture of what Internet users are doing and why.

CONCLUSION

The genesis of this investigation stems from a comparative study in two non-Anglophone countries (France and Russia) concerning Internet usage among young adults (Gen Y) between 2011 and 2013. The 2011 data from the French sample (Lyon) revealed that 'age' and 'neighbourhood' influence the duration of usage. This finding can be partially explained by the infrastructure of ICT provision in France and also by the generation to which the sample belong. However, by 2013 the influence of 'age' and 'neighbourhood' had been replaced by 'date of first usage' as the determinant factor of Internet usage. It was also noticed that over this period of time, SNS usage had decreased by an average of two hours per week per person. This finding, combined with the data from the ensuing forum, points strongly to the emergence of 'SNS lassitude' among the French sample.

In contrast, the 2011 data from the Russian sample (St Petersburg) showed that 'age', 'gender' and 'neighbourhood' influenced the duration of Internet usage. By 2013, none of these factors can be used to explain usage. This finding can be partly explained by the rapid developments in ICT, and by the ongoing evolution in Internet user behaviour. Unlike the Lyon sample, the 'date of first usage' seems to have had minimal impact on the Russian sample as far as Internet user behaviour is concerned - which implies that young adults are able to keep pace with advances in ICT despite lack of prior experience of usage. Moreover, it was noticed that SNS usage among the St Petersburg sample had increased by an average of two hours per week per person. The forum offered further insight into this finding, in particular a growing awareness and uptake of non-Russian SNS among young Internet users in Russia. The popularity of global SNS in Russia reflects the open-mindedness of Gen Y who desire to communicate across different languages and cultures.

The findings of the focus groups with Gen Z support the notion that SNS usage in particular, and Internet user behaviour in general, seem to be converging over time. Geographic location seems to bear little influence on the way in which young adults consume the Internet, contrary to previous generations who traditionally had reservations about leaving their (cultural or technological) comfort zone. Certainly, Gen Z seem more aware of the dangers (and opportunities) of Internet usage than older users but they have found coping strategies and consequently appear more comfortable with ICT.

Our study contributes to the existing literature including the work of Issa and Isaias (2016) and Wilkinson (2016) on the activities undertaken online by Gen Y and Gen Z, by revealing intergenerational and cross-cultural aspects of social media usage in a non-Anglophone context. Such knowledge is important for businesses, policy makers and academics in order to broaden our understanding of technology usage among young adults. In the workplace, Gen Y and Gen Z present a challenge; managers need to learn how to train and motivate these younger digital-savvy employees so that their strengths become a benefit to the company. Taken as a whole, the findings suggest some commonality among Gen Y and Gen Z in their connected lifestyle and use of social media. However, whereas Gen Y demonstrated a certain apprehension with using social networks in 2013, concerned by loss of privacy and voyeurism for example, Gen Z seems very comfortable in 2016 sharing detailed personal information via several different social networks. In contrast to Gen Y, Gen Z is able to manage the drawback of divulging personal data in order to reap the benefits of 24/7 connectivity. While Gen Z readily share information across multiple SNS, they maintain an awareness of the dangers of over-sharing. The findings also reveal the extent to which certain national/cultural differences reported in the literature are less apparent when using social networks, suggesting that the widespread adoption of Internet technology is generating a somewhat 'standardised' Internet user behaviour.

Over the last 5 years the popularity of using SNS has waned among Gen Y. This loss of interest can be partly attributed to the growing discontent that users feel concerning intrusive marketing efforts, and partly because users are uncomfortable about third parties having access to personal information. There are nowadays many networks and messaging apps to choose from, including micro-blogs and forums where privacy/security is easier to maintain. While Gen Y may appear to be turning away from certain SNS, older Internet users – for example the grandparents of Gen Y – are joining SNS in order to stay in touch with friends and relatives. The net effect of a growing online population is that there will be ongoing fragmentation of user groups and user behaviour.

For businesses, fragmentation poses a problem for ensuring effective communication. Internet users are increasingly irritated by being bombarded with digital content. With the steady growth in the number of Internet users, greater interactivity will lead to greater diversity of ideas, content and Internet user behaviour. Managing online customers will require continual monitoring of developments in digital technology and user behaviour. As Gen Z prepares to enter the world of work, more changes can be expected regarding the use and role of technology. Younger Internet users will accelerate the rate of innovation; they expect to use the latest interactive, mobile technology for work, learning and socialising. In the workplace, Gen Z are likely to use the corporate software in tandem with their own devices; however, the notion of 'BYOD' (bring your own devices) raises further issues for data security and leaks.

From a training and learning perspective, younger Internet users often have a better understanding of ICT than the teachers - many of whom are experiencing difficulty in shifting from 'sage on the stage' to 'guide on the side'. However, whereas the younger generation may understand ICT at a utilitarian level (for example, how to use a piece of software for its intended purpose), it is debatable whether they can use ICT beyond that level or indeed for reflective thinking and problem-solving. Clearly, more research is needed to provide a framework that explains the evidence within the context of a changing world.

The Internet is used widely within (and across) generations and beyond borders. It is a diverse medium that conforms to the notion of a global village and illustrates a key feature of post-modernity, manifested in the popular use of social networking. The findings of this study underscore two key points; firstly, there is a certain convergence in the way younger Internet users consume ICT and SNS - irrespective of cultural and linguistic barriers. Secondly, the study draws attention to the way in which the accelerating pace of technological change interacts with transnational convergence and globalisation to generate 'augmented' Internet user behaviour, which is not nationally differentiated. Both these points require agility and flexibility in business thinking and business models.

The literature that pre-dates the digital revolution continues to play a key role in academia - to explain how the business world and individuals functioned prior to web 2.0 in a largely offline environment. However, some theories are now outdated and inapplicable in today's globalising society – such as the traditional concepts that use notions of culture and linguistic difference to anticipate consumer behaviour. This study puts forward that the essentialist view of cultural difference has no predictive value in today's global online business environment. Ongoing and further research is now needed for understanding the constant changes in ICT and the ensuing Internet user behaviour. Keeping track of dynamic change is the biggest challenge. Our next step is to widen the enquiry to other geographic markets in order to provide a wider insight into the culture of young Internet users in a rapidly changing society.

REFERENCES

Auffray, C. (2013). *Social networks: 20 million French Internet users connect daily*. Retrieved August 17, 2014, from http://www.zdnet.fr/actualites/reseaux-sociaux-20-millions-d-internautes-francais-se-connectent-tous-les-jours-39791743.htm

Beard, J., & Dale, P. (2008). Redesigning Services for the Net-Gen and Beyond: A Holistic Review of Pedagogy, Resource, and Learning Space. *New Review of Academic Librarianship, 14*(1-2), 99–114. doi:10.1080/13614530802518941

Benraïss-Noailles, L., & Viot, C. (2012). Social media in recruitment strategies. *French Management Journal, 38*(224), 125–138.

Bernier, L. (2015). Getting ready for gen Z. *Canadian HR Reporter, 28*(19), 1–16.

Blank, S. (2013). Why the Lean Start-Up Changes Everything. *Harvard Business Review, 91*(5), 65–72.

Chen, Y., & Zahedi, F. M. (2016). Individuals' Internet Security Perceptions and Behaviors: Polycontextual Contrasts between the United States and China. *Management Information Systems Quarterly, 40*(1), 205–A12.

Cheng, S.-T., Chan, W. C., & Alfred, C. M. (2008). Older peoples realisation of generativity in a changing society: The case of Hong Kong. *Ageing and Society, 28*(5), 609–627. doi:10.1017/S0144686X07006903

Clarke, J. T., Marks, J. G., & Miller, J. J. (2006). Mind the Gap. *Archives of Dermatology, 142*(7), 927–947. PMID:16847215

Coëffé, T. (2014). *15 Social Networks that have surpassed 100 million users*. Retrieved August 19, 2014, from http://www.blogdumoderateur.com/reseaux-sociaux-100-millions

Cookson, R. (2013). *'Facebook fatigue' stirs investor concern*. Retrieved August 20, 2014, from http://www.ft.com/cms/s/0/8b7ab90e-bc91-11e2-b344-00144feab7de.html#axzz3Ar8SttQN

Dannenberg, R., Cilluffo, F. J., & Cardash, S. L. (2014). *Putin's Russia: A Geopolitical Analysis HSPI Issue Brief 24*. Retrieved March 22, 2016, from https://cchs.gwu.edu/sites/cchs.gwu.edu/files/downloads/Issue%20Brief-Putin's%20Russia-%20A%20Geopolitical%20Analysis.pdf

Dean, D. H. (2008). Shopper age and the use of self-service technologies. *Managing Service Quality, 18*(3), 225–238. doi:10.1108/09604520810871856

DeMartino, I. (2014). *VKontakte (The 'Facebook of Russia') Creator: The Site Is Controlled By Putin's Friends*. Retrieved March 22, 2016, from http://www.business2community.com/social-buzz/vkontakte-facebook-russia-creator-site-controlled-putins-friends-0856559#S43uUUkoLJjdM4tp.99

Dhopade, P. (2016). How To... Support Generation Z. *Benefits Canada, 40*(2), 22–23.

Dong, B., Sivakumar, K., Evans, K. R., & Zou, S. (2015). Effect of Customer Participation on Service Outcomes: The Moderating Role of Participation Readiness. *Journal of Service Research, 18*(2), 160–176. doi:10.1177/1094670514551727

eBIZ. (2016). *Top 15 Most Popular Social Networking Sites*. Retrieved March 18, 2016, from http://www.ebizmba.com/articles/social-networking-websites

Etling, B., Roberts, H., & Faris, R. (2014). *Blogs as an Alternative Public Sphere: The Role of Blogs, Mainstream Media, and TV in Russia's Media Ecology*. Retrieved March 24, 2016, from https://cyber.law.harvard.edu/node/95699

Euromaidan Press. (2014). *Russian aid to Ukraine is actually Russian military, social network reveals*. Retrieved August 20, 2014, from http://euromaidanpress.com/2014/08/11/russian-aid-to-ukraine-is-actually-russian-military-social-network-reveals

Fauconnier, F. (2012). *Prepare a Facebook ad service*. Retrieved November 8, 2013, from http://www.journaldunet.com/ebusiness/le-net/facebook-petites-annonces-1112.shtml

Fonderie, L. (2012). *Facebook sponsored ads*. Retrieved June 26, 2013, from http://www.lafonderie-idf.fr/facebook-sponsored-ads-3471.html

Global Web Index. (2013). *Social platforms GWI.8 update: Decline of Local Social Media Platforms.* Retrieved March 13, 2013, from http://globalwebindex.net/thinking/social-platforms-gwi-8-update-decline-of-local-social-media-platforms

Gorman, P., Nelson, T., & Glassman, A. (2004). The Millennial Generation: A Strategic Opportunity. *Organizational Analysis, 12*(3), 255–270, 339–340.

Gouteron, J. (2004). Using the segmentation nostalgia: The age of the internet mediate consumption: Comparative Study of chronological age and subjective age. *The Journal of Management Science: Management and Management, 39*(208), 81–94.

Hargittai, E. (2010). Digital Na(t)ives? Variation in Internet Skills and Uses among Members of the Net Generation. *Sociological Inquiry, 80*(1), 92–113. doi:10.1111/j.1475-682X.2009.00317.x

Howe, N., & Strauss, W. (2000). *Millennials rising: The next great generation.* New York: Random House.

IFOP. (2012). *Observatoire des Réseaux Sociaux.* Retrieved March 16, 2013, from http://www.ifop.com/media/poll/2050-1-study_file.pdf

Ind, N., Iglesias, O., & Schultz, M. (2013). Building Brands Together: Emergence and Outcomes of Co-Creation. *California Management Review, 55*(3), 5–26. doi:10.1525/cmr.2013.55.3.5

Internet, P. (2013). *Pew Internet: Social Networking (full details).* Retrieved March 15, 2013, from http://pewinternet.org/Commentary/2012/March/Pew-Internet-Social-Networking-full-detail.aspx

Issa, T. B. T., & Isaias, P. (2016). Internet factors influencing generations Y and Z in Australia and Portugal: A practical study. *Information Processing & Management, 52*(4), 592–617. doi:10.1016/j.ipm.2015.12.006

Kim-Choy, C., & Holdsworth, D. K. (2012). Culture and behavioural intent to adopt mobile commerce among the Y Generation: Comparative analyses between Kazakhstan, Morocco and Singapore. *Young Consumers, 13*(3), 224–241. doi:10.1108/17473611211261629

King, N. (2004a). *Using Interviews in Qualitative Research. In Essential Guide to Qualitative Methods in Organizational Research* (pp. 11–22). London: Sage Publications.

King, N. (2004b). *Using Templates in the Thematic Analysis of Text. In Essential Guide to Qualitative Methods in Organizational Research* (pp. 256–270). London: Sage Publications.

King, N., & Horrocks, C. (2010). *Interviews in Qualitative Research.* London: Sage Publications.

Kitzinger, J. (1994). The methodology of focus groups: The importance of interactions between research participants. *Sociology of Health & Illness, 16*(1), 103–121. doi:10.1111/1467-9566.ep11347023

Kozinets, R. V. (2016). Amazonian Forests and Trees: Multiplicity and Objectivity in Studies of Online Consumer-Generated Ratings and Reviews, A Commentary on de Langhe, Fernbach, and Lichtenstein. *The Journal of Consumer Research, 42*(6), 834–839. doi:10.1093/jcr/ucv090

Lichy, J. (2011). Internet user behaviour in France and Britain: Exploring socio-spatial disparity among adolescents. *International Journal of Consumer Studies, 35*(4), 470–475. doi:10.1111/j.1470-6431.2010.00955.x

Lichy, J. (2012). Towards an International Culture: Gen Y Students and SNS? *Active Learning in Higher Education*, *13*(2), 101–116. doi:10.1177/1469787412441289

Lichy, J. & Kachour, M. (2014). Understanding the culture of young Internet users in a rapidly changing society. *International Journal of Technology and Human Interaction*, *10*(4), 1-18.

Lichy, J., & Kachour, M. (2016). Understanding how students interact with technology for knowledge-sharing: The emergence of a new social divide in France. *International Journal of Technology and Human Interaction*, *12*(1), 90–112. doi:10.4018/IJTHI.2016010106

Liébana-Cabanillas, F., Ramos de Luna, I., & Montoro-Ríos, F. (2015). User behaviour in QR mobile payment system: The QR Payment Acceptance Model. *Technology Analysis and Strategic Management*, *27*(9), 1031–1049. doi:10.1080/09537325.2015.1047757

Loroz, P. S., & Helgeson, J. G. (2013). Boomers and Their Babies: An Exploratory Study Comparing Psychological Pro files and Advertising Appeal Effectiveness across Two Generations. *Journal of Marketing Theory and Practice*, *21*(3), 289–306. doi:10.2753/MTP1069-6679210304

Luck, E., & Mathews, S. (2010). What Advertisers Need to Know about the iYGeneration: An Australian Perspective. *Journal of Promotion Management*, *16*(1-2), 134–147. doi:10.1080/10496490903574559

Malbon, J. (2013). Taking Fake Online Consumer Reviews Seriously. *Journal of Consumer Policy*, *36*(2), 139–157. doi:10.1007/s10603-012-9216-7

Mannheim, K. (1952). The Problem of Generations. In P. Kecskemeti (Ed.), *Essays on the Sociology of Knowledge* (pp. 276–322). London: Routledge & Kegan Paul.

Moore, M. M. (2012). Interactive media usage among millennial consumers. *Journal of Consumer Marketing*, *29*(6), 436–444. doi:10.1108/07363761211259241

Muñoz-Leiva, F., Hernández-Méndez, J., & Sánchez-Fernández, J. (2012). Generalising user behaviour in online travel sites through the Travel 2.0 website acceptance model. *Online Information Review*, *36*(6), 879–902. doi:10.1108/14684521211287945

Oshkalo, A. (2014). *Odnoklassniki.ru rebrands into OK*. Retrieved July 11, 2014, from http://www.russiansearchtips.com/category/social-media-in-russia/

Prensky, M. (2001). Digital natives, digital immigrants. *NCB University Press*, *9*(5), 1–6.

Pujol, J. (2014). *Generation Y prefer the malls to shop online*. Retrieved August 15, 2014, from http://pro.01net.com/editorial/622412/la-generation-y-prefere-les-centres-business-to-e-purchases

Ropars, F. (2016). Blog du Modérateur [online] 11 février. Retrieved March 24, 2016, from http://www.blogdumoderateur.com/usage-reseaux-sociaux-11-18-ans/

Russian Internet Forum. (2012). *Российский Интернет Форум. Выходные данные. Дизайн и разработка - Internet Media Holding*. Retrieved November 06, 2012, from http://2012.russianinternetforum.ru/get/40074/876/

Sareah, F. (2015). *Interesting Statistics for the Top 10 Social Media Sites*. Retrieved March 17, 2015 from http://smallbiztrends.com/2015/07/social-media-sites-statistics.html

Shekhawat, D., & Rathore, P. S. (2014). Internet usage in college: A comparison of users and non users in relation to self-esteem and satisfaction with life. *Indian Journal of Positive Psychology*, *5*(2), 216–222.

Simonson, I. (2015). Mission (Largely) Accomplished: Whats Next for Consumer BDT-JDM Researchers. *Journal of Marketing Behavior*, *1*(1), 9–35. doi:10.1561/107.00000001

Smith, B. (2014). *The instant messaging shootout: BBM, WhatsApp, Line, WeChat and Viber*. Retrieved August 17, 2014, from http://gearburn.com/2014/03/the-instant-messaging-shootout-bbm-whatsapp-line-wechat-and-viber/

Smyrnaios, N. (2011). *Social networks: reflection of cultural differences?*. Retrieved December 17, 2012 from http://www.inaglobal.fr/numerique/article/les-reseaux-sociaux-reflet-des-differences-culturelles#intertitre-8

Snead, J. T. (2013). Social media use in the U.S. Executive branch. *Government Information Quarterly*, *30*(1), 56–63. doi:10.1016/j.giq.2012.09.001

Sobkowicz, P. (2013). Quantitative Agent Based Model of User Behavior in an Internet Discussion Forum. *PLoS ONE*, *8*(12), e80524. doi:10.1371/journal.pone.0080524 PMID:24324606

Stone, J. (2014). *Russian Internet Censorship, Social Media Crackdown Make It Easy for Putin to Stay Popular*. Retrieved 02 March, 2016, from http://www.ibtimes.com/russian-internet-censorship-social-media-crackdown-make-it-easy-putin-stay-popular-1651078

Tapscott, D. (1998). *Growing up digital: The rise of the net generation*. New York: McGraw-Hill.

Teens & Social Networks Study. (2010). *Objective: To understand teens' experience with social networking and communities*. Retrieved December 17, 2012, from http://fr.scribd.com/doc/33751159/Teens-Social-Networks-Study-June-2010

Thomas, L., MacMillan, J., McColl, E., Hale, C., & Bond, S. (1995). Comparison of focus group and individual interview methodology in examining patient satisfaction with nursing care. *Social Sciences in Health*, *1*, 206–219.

Tifferet, S., & Herstein, R. (2012). Gender differences in brand commitment, impulse buying, and hedonistic consumption. *Journal of Product and Brand Management*, *21*(3), 176–182. doi:10.1108/10610421211228793

van de Pas, J., & van Bussel, G.-J. (2015). 'Privacy Lost - and Found?' The information value chain as a model to meet citizens' concerns. *Electronic Journal of Information Systems Evaluation*, *18*(2), 185–195.

Venkatesh, V. L., Thong, J., & Xu, X. (2012). Consumer Acceptance and Use of Information Technology: Extending The Unified Theory Of Acceptance and Use of Technology. *Management Information Systems Quarterly*, *36*(1), 157–178.

Vernette, E., & Hamdi-Kidar, L. (2013). Co-creation with consumers: Who has the competence and wants to cooperate? *International Journal of Market Research*, *55*(4), 2–20. doi:10.2501/IJMR-2013-047

Viard, R. (2016). *Ranking Social Networks*. Retrieved March 24, 2016, from http://www.webmarketing-conseil.fr/classement-reseaux-sociaux/

Wang, H.-Y., & Wang, S.-H. (2010). User Acceptance Of Mobile Internet Based On The Unified Theory Of Acceptance And Use Of Technology: Investigating The Determinants And Gender Differences. *Social Behavior and Personality*, *38*(3), 415–426. doi:10.2224/sbp.2010.38.3.415

Wang, Y., & Haggerty, N. (2011). Individual Virtual Competence and Its Influence on Work Outcomes. *Journal of Management Information Systems*, *27*(4), 299–333. doi:10.2753/MIS0742-1222270410

Wilkinson, D. (2016). *Who are 'Generation Z' and what it means for your organisation*. Retrieved March 23, 2016, from https://www.linkedin.com/pulse/who-generation-z-what-means-your-organisation-david-wilkinson

Wu, D., Ray, G., & Whinston, A. B. (2008). Manufacturers Distribution Strategy in the Presence of the Electronic Channel. *Journal of Management Information Systems*, *25*(1), 167–198. doi:10.2753/MIS0742-1222250107

Xia, F., Hsu, C., Liu, X., Liu, H., Ding, F., & Zhang, W. (2015). The power of smartphones. *Multimedia Systems*, *21*(1), 87–101. doi:10.1007/s00530-013-0337-x

Zeichick, A. (2008). Facebook's Combinatorial Challenge. *Technology Review*, *111*(4), 47.

APPENDIX

Table 9. Focus group comments on how Gen Z use social network sites

	Common Themes Discussed
Lyon	• The *choice of a person's portrait picture* shows activity and real-time location, both socially and professionally. Some profile pictures are anonymous or professional-looking. Some selfies and pictures of events reveal the owner, others are anonymous. Professional photographers are used by people for self-marketing whereas selfies are posted from iPhone owners. Selfies are more common for showing vacation pictures, seasonal greetings, different events, parties, festivals, pets, babies, sports, arts and family members. Video posts are usually own videos but sometimes videos about hobbies, and funny videos, event videos and news videos. • *Status updates* are more private, showing people's whereabouts, what are they thinking or doing at that moment, for example views on job applications, summer jobs, their love life, political ideas, society, and reflections on how the day has generally gone. Statuses are very mood revealing, more common among outgoing people (who like to share information) than among observer-bystander people (who are more voyeuristic). • *Personal opinions* are often shared openly via social networks. Some users share far too many details of their lives ('too much information'), revealing their consumer profile and making it possible for businesses to anticipate their needs & wants and to calculate how much money a user is spending based on information posted; business can be too intrusive. • Some users thrive on creating sensation/ suspense by throwing out a wild statement via SNS then posting "For more information PM (private message) me!!" • *'Old' generations* (namely Gen Y and Gen X) are more wary of SNS; they don't share much information and prefer to keep their lives private, as well as their social views and political views, • People follow their favourite brands via social networks; SNS are ideal for building *brand communities* – but people tend to "like" certain upmarket brands to give the impression that they are part of that community whereas they are not really consumers of that brand. • Social networks can provoke *undesirable traits* in some people such as instability, attention-seeking, egotistical, vanity or sycophantic shallow behaviour. • Some people feel the need to seek attention and compliments from friends to increase their own self-esteem, by posting everything you do and feel on Facebook. For example, among our Facebook friends, there are girls who would post a picture like "look how hot/ sexy I am" with the most seductive look on their faces and quite a lot of makeup on. Or boys who would post a picture like "do you want to touch my triceps" (wearing sleeveless tops which according to them looks very sexy and striking a pose for the camera), or "you can only imagine what kind of catch I am". By focusing on physical attributes, they are trying to show how much time they spend taking care of themselves. They behave like that because they want to know the opinion of others and in this way be more influential. Those people are *'victims' of social network dependency;* they always include their friends into their lives by mentioning them in posts or publishing photos of them. • The *modern lifestyle depends entirely on broadcasting via SNS* and to a lesser extent via online reviews, not necessarily exchanging information with other users physically. There is a constant need to share/ broadcast personal information to family, (close) friends and acquaintances. A person's profile is an important way to present oneself, requiring time and effort to keep the profile updated by sharing both significant as well as mundane events daily/weekly. It can be seen as a convenient exchange of important information, with the possibility of communicating and connecting with a high number of people simultaneously. • For some people, social networks are a *social crutch*; they generate self-inflicted pressure (a 'herding' instinct) to be part of a group/ community and then capture the attention of other users. Pictures, status updates and information – when wisely picked – can easily be directed in a way as desired by the presenter. Nowadays, it seems to be more valuable – or at any rate it plays a great role - to have (more) friends on SNS than in real life. Since people have access to private data, anyone can get an impression of your personality at the click of a mouse (although, in real life, you might not be that person as depicted, at all). • *Not having an account on SNS is considered as strange behaviour* (I have heard lines like "Really, how do you survive like that?", "Seriously? I don't believe you!"). A person wants to be up-to-date and to know what is going on in cyberspace, to follow global trends, funny videos and news that goes viral. Long story short: be part of this community. With a rising number of social media tools like Snapchat, Instagram, Twitter, Vimeo, Pinterest and so on it is hard to stay off SNS. It's fun and provides a great platform for people striving for success and popularity by frequently updating their information and changing status and profile picture) – it draws attention.

continued on following page

Table 9. Continued

	Common Themes Discussed
SPb	• Social networks represent a range of *abilities to function in the modern world* by virtual presence – from OTT (over the top) users to 'off the radar' users (i.e. no intention/ability to use SNS or no understanding). Suspicion is raised when an individual claims not to be part of a SNS, • Users *"like"* a person/event/brand to denote the lifestyle they wish at have; a "like" reflects the social standing or professional/ political inclination, • *People's goals are revealed through the personal brand* that they build on SNS: for a promotion? For a better job? For advancement in their political career? For prestige among their friends? It is difficult to distinguish between what they have genuinely "liked" and what they have "liked" for the sake of their personal goals. • People who post information impulsively are more straightforward to deduce marketing-wise; their SNS posts provide an insight into their personality, interests, values, network and even social class. One of the most interesting of these is the analysis of a person's network; based on the amount and value of contacts a person has could be used for calculating some sort of a *"social network worth"* for everyone. • On SNS, there seems to be more and more friends who want to *share information about personal values* like family relationships or their healthy lifestyle, but many subcultures of people who "like" brands or professional groups, • Measuring the number social contacts per user, SNS could be used as a marketing yardstick *to identify opinion leaders* and game changers, • These days, everybody participates in social media and in countless SNS, one way or another. By ignoring this channel raises questions: Are you technologically illiterate? Unsocial? Some sort of a rebel against the system? • People are constantly feeding the SNS with *personal information* about themselves and companies are increasingly interested to utilize this knowledge. • Different SNS are clearly targeted to and used by *different segments* of the population. For example, Twitter is used a lot by politicians and journalists, while Snapchat and Periscope are more typical for the younger and more outgoing personalities. • What people do on SNS shows their *consumer behaviour:* their work-life balance, their lifestyle, attitudes and values, and their 'hidden' traits (party animal, drinker, smoker), • Users deliberately *associate with key figures* in society or politics (radical or moderate) to identify with their own views. They also post about other groups that they belong to (corporate or community), religious affiliations (from strongly religious to atheist), sports clubs etc. to complement the personal/ professional identity (however the amount of detail will vary depending on where they work). This level of information is of use to businesses, insurance companies and government officials. • Many of the *'hidden' traits* of a person are revealed via SNS (party person, drinker, smoker, etc) - intentionally and not. Users generally manage their identity (and therefore privacy) on one of two ways; the "Chinese Wall" approach (when a person creates two individual online accounts to separate their personal and professional accounts) and the "Living Brand" approach (people use a single account for personal, professional and company brand). • It is *essential to keep your profile updated regularly* because SNS are a multi-way channel of communication. Usually, users post a status change on Facebook which is either a description/photo of what he/she did or ate that day or a view on something he/she is interested in (e.g. political views, scientific research, etc.) to denote that the person is outgoing, sociable and open to new experiences. The updates imply that people like to socialise with others in real life, but also they like to actually share their experiences and emotions with others online by posting statuses and photos. It is normal to post a daily status/photo on Facebook about your everyday activities or intellectual view on current events to try to communicate with others and get inspired from others. • At the same time, frequent profile changes can indicate that a person is conceited, shallow or seeking attention from others to feel less insecure/ unstable. *SNS provide a fake veneer to hide an inferiority complex.* It may be that the person lacks empathy in real life or they lack self-esteem, so they choose to publicise something positive about themselves to get love and acceptance. It can also mean they have an ostentatious view about their own talents and abilities, or that they suffer from an inflated view of their own abilities. They may be very flippant in their decisions, trying to present an image of themselves to other people as completely confident and knowledgeable but the truth is that there are not at all. In fact, they do that to exist, to enhance their image by trying to appear effortlessly perfect, like if everything was under control. Some people post about anything all day long and sometimes it goes so far that they talk about their private lives. But it just shows how much of an inferiority complex the person has. In such a case, the views of others matter more and that shows a lack of self-confidence. Also, there are people that post a lot to show off their lives because they need all sorts of attention. They only want to show the good and not share the bad.

Table 10. How subjects would segment Internet/ SNS usage for Gen Z users?

Lyon	• *The inactive/ passive voyeur* o These users are registered but log-in almost never and have an observer role rather than a user role. In terms of profile photo, usually passive users do not have one or if they do, they keep it the same for a long period of time. There are also people who do not reveal any real information about themselves - even the name is not their real one. Their profile photos are usually avatars. Moreover, they don't feel the necessity to publish a status or maybe they just do not know how to publish. They are present on SNS only to stay informed of what other people do and not to inform others of their life. In this category, we can find mostly seniors (+55) and also introvert people. For example Arianna's mum has just created a Snapchat account to be informed about Arianna's daily life far away from her. Otherwise she would have never created the account. • *The Social Butterfly:* o This kind of user mainly communicates with friends or family and contributes to simple activities according to their needs. They change their profile photo occasionally (approximately once per month) and they publish a status and interact with publications quite often. In this category we can find people who belong to generations X and Y. For example "A's" mum changes her Facebook photo approximately once a month and publishes status weekly according to her lifestyle (i.e. animals, children…) • *The Active and Dynamic Interactor:* o This kind of users is always connected and ready to answer or interact instantly with other people. They are used to changing their profile photo often (approximately once a week) and they perform a high frequency of statuses. Advanced users do not just exist; they use SNS for different purposes, such as socializing, debating, and contributing. This category regroups especially people who belong to generation Z. For example Arianna's little sister (who is 13 years old) publishes at least 1 video per day on her page. Another example, "B's" friend changes her profile picture weekly just because she wants to get noticed and she is looking for attention. These people are using SNS actively, changing profile picture and status weekly. They usually want to share some events in their lives in order to keep in touch with persons they are close to. Their behaviour can easily turn into addiction. • *The NO-profile-picture-User / "Flower" – profile picture:* o This kind of user is a person, who uses SNS just to make use of the utility that it provides. They are using SNS to keep in touch with people close them – often relatives. The no-profile-picture-user usually cares for data. Old people and people new to SNS are often this type of user. Most of them are not teenagers anymore. People that are not showing profile-picture belong to this group as well. • *The Professional User / Hobby-Promoters:* o Professionals on SNS (such as LinkedIn or Twitter) use it in a commercial way. Their goal is to make the account look as reliable and serious as possible. On profiles of this kind of user, you will never find any "hangover pictures". The behaviour of semi-professional Hobby-Promoters is similar to the professional users. He/she wants other people to follow his hobby, so you might find whatever is interesting to that group (including party pictures). There is set pattern for updating profile picture or status but the information is usually up-to-date. • *The I-don't-care-for-that-account-but-I-have-one – User / young-utility-user:* o Unlike the No-profile-picture-user this type of user has a profile picture (sometimes out of date) and like all other types before no status, because it is just not of interest to him / her. Many of this kind of users are young, but, sharing the whole life on SNS is not the way they handle their SNS-presence. • *The Addicted User:* o No further explanations needed. Symptoms: changing status and profile picture far too often. You will notice them …
SPb	• *The Stalker:* o This person never posts or comments. This person reads everything, so he/she knows about what is going on. He/she spends (a lot of) time on a SNS when he/she gets bored, to waste his/her time or because he/she is curious. He/she is just on SNS it to observe and stalk his/her friends and even other people who are not friends. • *The Bling-Bling:* o This person likes to show that he/she has money, a high level living. He/she shows him/herself having fun on vacation, in big luxurious cars, huge fine watches, even shows money bills. And he/she likes his own posts, photos and videos. Of course, his/her profile picture is…. Himself/herself, never anyone else or a close friend because there probably are no close friends. • *The Over-Sharer:* o This person posts a lot of information, usually via Instagram. Most of the time, he/she shares something. But if we take a closer look to the timeline, we will only see shared things - articles, photos videos, and locations – that have been taken from other people's pages. Nothing posted is ever original or even ground-breaking. • *The Geek:* o This person is always online, knows about everything, likes to post all day long, tags friends on photos and videos, comments everything, answers within 30 seconds on iMessenger. When you send him/her a link about something to share a funny stuff, he/she is generally snaps back "Yep nice I already saw it 2 weeks ago" – but we all know that it can't be true! • *The Messenger User:* o This person subscribed to Facebook a couple years ago and is now tired of it. But he/she keeps the account for chatting with friends and acquaintances on messenger. They no longer post or comment anymore. He/she doesn't even wish anyone 'happy birthday' anymore! • *The Clubber:* o When this person posts it's for sharing via different SNS an event to go to. His/her friends post photos of him/her completely drunk, or out in a club with of course a glass (in some case a bottle) in his/her hand. He/she is tagged on funny drunk pictures on Snapchat, Periscope and Instagram. • *The I-am-so-popular One:* We all know this person. He/she has 5000+ Facebook friends. He/she doesn't even know a tenth of them!

Section 2
The Importance of Web Accessibility and Public Services

Chapter 6
A Multi–Perspective Theoretical Analysis to Web Accessibility

Carlos Peixoto
INESC TEC and University of Trás-os-Montes and Alto Douro, Portugal

José Martins
INESC TEC and University of Trás-os-Montes and Alto Douro, Portugal

Frederico Branco
INESC TEC and University of Trás-os-Montes and Alto Douro, Portugal

Ramiro Gonçalves
INESC TEC and University of Trás-os-Montes and Alto Douro, Portugal

ABSTRACT

Accessibility has become increasingly important in information technology, particularly due to legislation pressure to make affordable public services to all. Being end-users and software companies those who have direct contact with accessibility problems, other stakeholders are committed to defining methods and change mentalities in Web accessibility implementation. In addition to a conceptual definition, this chapter presents entities views with responsibilities in the area, taking into account their work done in the past and the prospects for future. The understanding of the interaction between all these perspectives will help to realize the way it will go, which carries with it great challenges and opportunities, widely explored in this work.

INTRODUCTION

Information and Communication Technologies (ICT) represent a good opportunity to reduce the exclusion of people with some sort of disability. As a result, the Web can be viewed as leverage for increasing communication possibilities and users' autonomy. On the other hand, Internet is making the world more connected and globalized. Organizations, in this context, are present not only in their own national territory but in the entire world.

Continuous change in how users make use of Web applications is an irreversible fact, perceivable in the increasingly complexity associated with the available content and the existing needs for it to be dynamic and personalized. By merging this reality with the need to make the referred content more ac-

DOI: 10.4018/978-1-5225-1868-6.ch006

cessible to all, one can clearly understand that entities and organizations, such as development agencies, education institutions and governments, have a very important role in this process.

With the above in mind, from our point of view, a broader analysis to the Web accessibility topic is need in order to understand how the various entities and organizations perspective the topic. This is even critical when the scientific and professional communities, with common interests in Web accessibility, have difficulties in interacting, find consensus and sharing information and solutions.

The purpose of this study is to try to clarify the perspectives of the various relevant stakeholders associated with Web accessibility, and doing so by performing an extensive literature review. During the research project a set of perspectives was achieved and considered the most relevant to the topic:

1. End users;
2. Organizations;
3. Governmental entities;
4. Education institutions; and
5. Associative entities.

This paper was organized into six sections. Section 1 is the introduction and the second section provides the main theoretical concepts. Web accessibility according to the various aforementioned perspectives is characterized in Section 3. Section 4 contains a set of challenges and opportunities in the context of Web accessibility. Finally, the last section of the chapter presents the achieved conclusions, limitations and future work.

WEB ACCESSIBILITY: CONCEPTS AND PERSPECTIVES

Internet has been growing in size and complexity since its inception. Some arguments explain that this is because of its decentralized property, where anyone can contribute without there being a central authority to dictate what can and cannot be published (Lopes, Gomes & Sedge, 2010). With the integration of the Web in people's daily lives cannot be ignored potential accessibility barriers, as these barriers make this important resource inaccessible to a certain set of users (Van der Geest & Velleman, 2014).

WHO (2014) stated a disabled person covers impairment, limited activity or restricted participation. Still, according to data collected by the same organization there are over one billion people with type of disability, which amounts to 15% of the world population. At the European level, according to data collected by the European Union, there are more than 80 million citizens in the same context (EU-FRA, 2015).

The exclusion in the use of IT is not a single issue only of those people with disabilities. There is another group of users who have constant difficulties in interacting with the Web, the elderly (Arch, 2008). As society ages there is a serious probability of people suffering from some sort of disability, whether temporary or not (Díaz-Bossini & Moreno, 2014). This is even more relevant when considering that in 2050 the number of people with more than 60 years old is going to triple (United Nations, 2008).

Despite the various definitions associated with the term, accessibility is assumed as the ability of a person with disabilities have access to a particular service / product or perform a certain activity in the same way that a person without a disability would do. Accessibility is a topic that can be applied to various areas, and the area of ICT, an area in which this concept has been more debated and publicized (Gonçalves, Martins, Branco & Barroso, 2013).

In the technological context, the term accessibility means 'people with disabilities should perceive, understand, navigate and interact with the Web and that should contribute to the Web' (W3C, 2005). This concept evaluates how easily different sets of users, regardless of their constraints whether physical or on the surrounding environment, can access the content on a website (Mankoff, Fait, & Tran, 2005).

In the same context Iwata, Kobayashi, Tachibana, Shirogane, and Fukazawa (2013) says Web accessibility refers to the construction of a website, where all users can access to their information, regardless of their age and physical limitations, they can easily navigate in their site. In contrast, Aizpurua, Arrue, and Vigo (2015) report that a website can follow all the recommended standards in order to gain better understanding and yet this effort is not sufficient because developers can consider the site accessible and users hold a different perception about the accessibility the site. The same authors also claim that a Web site designed to be compatible with the appropriate standards can fail if users do not experience this accessibility.

Henry, Abou-Zahra, and Brewer (2014) studied the role of accessibility in the universal web and affirm the fundamental project of Web has the potential to be worked by all people, taking into account, their hardware, software, language, culture, location or physical and mental capacity. To achieve these goals there are different disciplines that focus on specific technical aspects, such as multi modality, internationalization and accessibility for people with disabilities.

Today, Web accessibility, or lack of it, can be a serious obstacle to integration into society and not only with regard to individual interactions. Organizations are very powerful modern institutions that enjoy many of the legal rights of human beings, so it is only permissible for corporate web sites are accessible to everyone, even to those who are in the minority (Gonçalves, Martins, Pereira, Oliveira & Ferreira, 2013). In contrast, Web accessibility can also be very advantageous for companies because the number of users who visit the site will increase, which in the business aspect can result in an increase in sales effect for the organization (Noh Jeong, You, Moon, & Kang, 2015).

Martínez, De Andres, and García (2014) say Web accessibility is a technological innovation able to improve the relationship between an organization and all its stakeholders, not just those with disabilities. This happens because one of the key principles is to design websites and software flexible enough to meet different user needs, preferences and situations. The same perspective is approached by Sanchez-Gordón and Moreno (2014) when they stated that accessible technologies are technologies that users can adapt to suit their visual, auditory, cognitive deficiencies, dexterity and also their interaction preferences.

In addition, Web accessibility will also benefit people who use the Internet in special conditions, such as whom using text-only devices, which are in places where the network quality is relatively poor, or users connecting to the Internet through smart phones, tablets or Web-TV and using the same in a context where their eyes, ears or hands are interfered with by factors such as walking, driving or traveling in a quite difficult (Rau, Zhou, Sun, & Zhong, 2014). Web accessibility will improve the Internet user experience in all these conditions which will be beneficial not only for people but also for the Web service providers (Gonçalves, Martins, Pereira, Santos & Cota, 2013). These efforts have resulted in a number of different solutions, the most relevant being the regulations and recommendations that have been published and which provided development tools, evaluation and appropriate Web content classification (Gonçalves, Martins, & Branco, 2014).

In the 1990s, there were already information regarding Web accessibility and were available in companies like IBM and organizations such as the Trace Research and Development Centre (Henry, 2002).

However, the organization stood out most in this area was the World Wide Web Consortium (W3C), which is managed through the voluntary participation of members of the industry and universities and is basically oriented on two primary principles:

- "Web for all" and
- "Web on everything" (W3C, 2015).

In 1997, the W3C established the Web Accessibility Initiative to promote a corporate environment with Web content accessible to people with disabilities (WAI, 2005). Later, in May 1999 the WCAG 1.0 (Web Content Accessibility Guidelines 1.0) became the recommendation developed by WAI as a global standard for accessibility and design of Web content (W3C, 1999). This recommendation is a set of 14 guidelines, each containing clear key points about HTML form a total of 65 checklists, divided into three levels based on their importance and scope (Kuzma, 2009). However, implementation of this set of guidelines the W3C / WAI has received extensive comments since represented the first time that there was an international standard for Web accessibility, and this feedback reflected the need to update the recommendation (Brewer, 2004). Subsequently, in December 2008 the second version was created, the most current WCAG guidelines, WCAG 2.0 (Wentz et al., 2014).

The current version of the referred guidelines was defined according to several layers of conceptualization, including:

- Principles,
- General strategies,
- A set of techniques to promote web accessibility and
- Complex documentation set with all accessibility flaws and potential errors (W3C, 2008).

There are some studies in which the goal passes to deepen the process of migrating from one version to the other and even demonstrate the main differences between them (Bradbard & Peters, 2010; Li Yen Lu, & Lin, 2012).

In parallel, ISO (International Organization for Standardization) also introduced some regulations regarding Web accessibility, such as ISO TS-16071, ISO 9241-111 (ISO 2003, 2006), and the most relevant standard is the ISO 9241 -171 (ISO 2008) which was achieved through the development and evolution of the previous and aims not only the implementation of a set of rules that must be met, but also help the public and organizations create content accessible on its Web platforms (Gonçalves et al., 2015).

As these guidelines used by most countries, even so there are some who choose to create their own rules and methods. An example of these countries is the USA who created the "Section 508". In particular, this policy has served as an impetus for public libraries to facilitate the use of its websites and electronic resources. However, there are two issues at stake:

- One is the lack of perception and the other is the limited budget (Yi, 2015).

There are also studies for other countries that seek to demonstrate the laws and regulations regarding Web accessibility will follow the same (Leitner & Strauss, 2008; Sánchez-Gordón & Moreno, 2014).

A MULTI-PERSPECTIVE VISION OF WEB ACCESSIBILITY

In a field in constant evolution, the understanding between different stakeholders engaged on this subject can be tricky and complex. As a result, there is an increase difficulty for the inherent community in sharing knowledge and reaching agreements and understandings, which makes it even more difficult for people outside the community to realize what is at stake in terms of requirements, legislation and activities. With this in mind, an attempt to analyse the Web accessibility topic from the perspective of the various stakeholders was made. The chosen perspectives were drawn from Gonçalves, Martins, Pereira, Santos, et al. (2013), and are the following:

1. Governmental perspective;
2. Educational perspective;
3. Business Perspective;
4. Institutional perspective; and
5. End users' perspective.

Governmental Perspective

Government authorities have the capacity and the obligation to create laws and regulations, while taking the task of monitoring the implementation of laws and act accordingly on their practice. Therefore, the area of Web accessibility is no exception and has to be adequate rules that must be exercised by those in charge, and the government is the entity that has the duty to manage the whole process and above all to be an example in their sites web. Many countries have demonstrating evident interest in finding laws and policies that work in Web accessibility area. In America Section 508 was established as the standard mostly followed in other continents is the W3C WCAG 2.0 guidelines. However, there is still a lack of legislation or irregular adoption of the same, and there are communities that are trying to fill this gap, setting standards and promoting their implementation. In this perspective Andreasson and Snaprud (2014) discuss the efforts of a community called European Internet Inclusion Initiative (EIII) in order to support greater digital inclusion in the public sector.

Policy issues related to fragilities in the laws regarding the government's electronic services are a problem where discrimination exists in relation to the on line environment is huge and attitudes taken by the responsible authorities are not necessary (Jaeger, 2004). To achieve adequate levels of accessibility is necessary for the government to establish formal laws and appropriate guidelines to the local context and then adapt existing and force by law enforcement or other additional mechanisms monitoring these guidelines (Al-Khalifa, 2012).

In some research the concern of the authors is to understand whether government agencies are developing their web presence affordable to all the people and at the same time realize that they are being established standards that can be followed by other organizations or public, or private (White, Goette, & Young, 2015).USA is a country that has developed great efforts in this field, where several projects have been developed in order to understand how they behave different states as concerns the accessibility of their government websites. (Lazar et al., 2010).

The provision of government services via mobile applications (m-government) has had a significant growth in recent years. In this context, it is also crucial that the applications are accessible to all people. Sierra, Carvalho, Ferreira, Vaz, and Freire (2015) present a case study with the evaluation of four government mobile applications in Brazil. The article discusses the methodological adaptations of WCAG 2.0 in the context of mobile and its limitations. The results showed many basic accessibility problems, which highlights the importance of promoting research accessibility in mobile applications.

Karkin and Janssen (2014) conducted a study which evaluate government websites in Turkey for the municipalities, not a common perspective of values as the content, privacy, usability and quality, but from a perspective of public values such as:

- Accessibility,
- Transparency,
- Openness,
- Dialogue and
- Balancing of interest.

The evaluation showed that websites perform better with regard to common values than the public values, justified by the fact that websites are built on providing functionality instead of holding public values.

Certain approaches to Web sites reviews have shown that there are other ways of perceiving their evolution. Hanson and Richards (2013) developed a study where the aim was to understand the changes of accessibility indicators over a period of 14 years in order to understand whether there was progress in this period. The conclusion is that the sites have a low level of compliance with WCAG 2.0 standards, although improvements are evident, at least in some success criteria, which can be a side effect of good coding practices and will improve the accessibility of Web sites.

Government websites are one of the main sources of information for people. Parmanto and Yu (2011) evaluated a set of US government websites and compared with the federal government sites and random e-commerce sites. The results showed that though the US government and the federal government provide the service more accessible, yet the barriers are huge and it is very difficult for a person with some kind of trouble navigating the 3 groups.

Nietzio, Olsen, Eibegger, and Snaprud (2010) a different concept presented with the aim of improving the development process of governmental sites. This project called eGovMon aims to bridge the gap between high levels of benchmarking and accessibility improvements that are implemented in isolation. This concept is based on several pillars:

- An on-line scanner that provides reviews,
- A community that serves to help managers of sites and finally,
- Regular and updated publication of benchmarking for managing the progress and improvements over time.

Some studies make a comprehensive analysis, the government websites in various groups of countries, such as the European Union (Goodwin, Susar, Nietzio, Snaprud, & Jensen, 2011). These studies used various terms of comparison to developed countries and developing countries (Kuzma, 2010), continents (Kuzma, Yen, & Oestreicher, 2009) or even sets of comparison between countries a particular continent (Costa et al., 2013). Mostly these researches reveal that there are serious issues of accessibility in e-government sites, even those whose governments claim compliance with international accessibility standards.

Completed a bibliographic review you can see that there is a serious gap in the whole system when we talk on Web accessibility theme. It is easy to see that government institutions are not to assign the required value that the subject requires and the problem increases exponentially every day and every created Web site. It is extremely important that the responsible entities look to your web presence responsibly and judiciously with accessibility concerns. Only then, after resolving its internal problem can act careful way in other sectors.

Educational Perspective

Educational institutions, where universities and polytechnic institutes have a leading role, have a very important part in the continuous improvement of mission of the Web accessibility levels. These institutions are the ones with the knowledge and skills needed to develop, transmit and stimulate the best practices and techniques on the topic in question.

Van Rooij and Zirkle (2016) developed a work which describe the results of a collaborative case study that addresses one hand, the design and development of on-line educational experiences and other accessibility thereof. These issues are discussed simultaneously with the development of an on-line course and are taken a few lessons, particularly from the perspective of students in the same. Finally, the authors share their experience in order to sustainable collaborative processes are created for successful on-line initiatives.

There is a problem when two areas like Web accessibility and education intersect, is to realize what are the challenges and directions that have to take and above all who is working to implement the entire system. Linder, Fontaine-Rainen, and Behling (2015) also presented a study, performed in the United States, on the current institutional practices, structures, resources and policies that are necessary to ensure on-line accessibility for all students, with the key finding better articulate who is responsible for the process of on-line accessibility initiatives.

Education is a social process and consequently before moving any content learning to students is absolutely critical that teachers have accurate knowledge of what they convey. As the Web a recent area accessibility is necessary to train teachers on the content they are teaching, an example of such initiatives is presented by Santarosa, Comfort, and Neves (2015) promoting a course where the areas of accessibility and usability are part of the curriculum of training.

Despite laws and policies imposed it is still difficult to educational institutions recognize the rights for equal benefit of persons with disabilities on their Web sites. With this in mind it is urgent that these institutions adopt good accessibility practices in its on-line platforms, which has not been the case (Zap & Montgomerie, 2013). Failure by the university Web designers to use these guidelines reveals the unwillingness of institutions to follow in accordance with a universal Web.

In order to achieve organizational changes necessary to ensure that the accessibility challenges are effectively fulfilled, it requires a cultural change in educational institutions. Cooper (2013) reflected on the process of promoting this cultural change within an Open University and found that the importance of being clear about the roles and responsibilities in promoting accessibility for educators is huge. At the same time, educators must be provided with the necessary support to enable them to assume that responsibility.

In order to better understand the depth state of accessibility in education, a study was conducted by Ringlaben, Bray, and Packard (2014) where the sample were not public universities but to assess the websites of special education university departments, or institutions where their audience is none other than the disabled people. The results were catastrophic and showed that 97% of the pages have many problems of accessibility in which 39% of which are serious.

Distance education has grown significantly in recent decades and in parallel the need to meet the standards of accessibility of on-line courses increases. Several studies have focused their interest in this subject in order to determine if students with disabilities are satisfied with the respective institutions and the courses act in accordance with their capabilities in order to understand if these learning environments can be academically well- successful (Roberts, Crittenden, & Crittenden, 2011).

Wijayaratne and Singh (2010) explored the level of accessibility of Web sites of the Association of Asian Open Universities and realized that on-line learning tools are behind compared to Western countries. The purpose of this study is to highlight the importance of accessibility to educational institutions, which are to despise a wide range of users with large barriers in their platforms. Some countries have specified laws that legally oblige the institutions of higher education to have their Web sites accessible, as is the case of the US with the Americans with Disabilities Act (ADA). With this in mind are developed studies designed to assess the extent and effectiveness of the implementation of these accessibility policies in universities (Bradbard, Peters, & Caneva, 2010). The results show that while most universities apply these laws, they have serious deficiencies. In the case of ADA authors report that probably many schools are in breach and run the risk a judicial process by a disabled person.

In Portugal, the Web accessibility in educational institutions has also been the focus of many researchers. Gonçalves, Martins, Pereira, Santos et al. (2013) assessed the compliance of all high schools in the country with the WCAG 2.0 standard and found that there are serious problems that limit the availability of the mentioned sites and their content promoting serious implications in the educational context of students. Through these results the authors created a model that aims to improve the accessibility levels within the Portuguese spectrum.

Although all problems, research suggests some possible solutions. One can go through the potential generic pedagogical tools such as the theories of learning and learning projects can help teachers to develop materials and activities accessible. Seale and Cooper (2010) analysed these tools and argue that they can have potential, but its influence and too general and abstract. The authors also argue that the key is the teachers learn to use design tools because its potential is more concrete and influence the content of the design process is much higher.

Reviewed literature summary, we conclude that education and Web accessibility are two areas where it is critical that there is communion to achieve the objectives, not only related to educational institutions, as well as the future of all other sectors. It is essential that education to work as a sustainable basis for all Web accessibility implementation system and is through education that begins the process of learning an area that requires effective and robust training. That said, it is urgent that educational intuitions change their stance regarding this issue, with a profound change in their culture, their way of acting, in their curriculum programs and the platforms they manage.

Business Perspective

In this set of perspectives, we identified the companies as a major actor in the mission to improve Web accessibility levels. As business entities to express corporate social responsibility (CSR), Web accessibility is an integral part of this obligation in order to demonstrate the commitment to provide the same equal opportunities. In our view the business outlook should be divided into two distinct areas:

- The non-technological companies and
- Enterprises of information technology in which fits the perspective of programmers.

Even though, there is a highlight of the Internet in people's lives, most of the Web presence of organizations in the private sector does not yet meet the contemporary accessibility standards. Leitner, Strauss, and Stummer (2015) conducted a case study in order to find the motivations of organizations to implement or reject the accessibility standards. The authors realized that motivation varies according to several factors such as:

- The size and complexity of the business,
- The organizational sector,
- Corporate culture and
- The degree of complexity of web presence.

In the daily activity of a company there is a key element: employees. Providingh Web accessibility can be an important element in the CSR to demonstrate and employees can play a vital role in this process. Oh and Chen (2014) proposes a model which shall examine the intention of the employees to exert pressure, as concerns the accessibility is influenced by three psychological needs:

- The need for belonging,
- Control, and
- Meaningful existence.

In some sectors of activity, the importance of the Internet takes on a large scale. One of these sectors is the bank which has developed some research with the focus of this very Web accessibility. According to Martínez et al. (2014) three factors are associated with Web Accessibility adoption in banks:

- Operating factors,
- Size, and
- The organization's CSR strategy.

After a case study the authors conclude that both operating factors, such as database size, does not seem to influence the Web Accessibility adoption. On the other hand, the commitment to CSR, the results indicate significant influence on the adoption of accessibility.

As is evident, companies have a social citizenship behaviour that should take into account, with the leaders of organizations to fulfil this role. The world's largest companies to be a good example by setting standards to be followed by smaller companies. Gonçalves, Martins, Pereira, and Oliveira et al. (2013) evaluated the websites of the 250 largest companies in the Forbes list and found a considerable number of accessibility errors on all sites of the chosen group, demonstrating a level of compliance with the decidedly down guidelines.

Web accessibility in business is not just an ethical dimension issue or equal opportunities, but also an economic dimension as it excludes a group of consumers with economic potential. Rocha, Bessa, Gonçalves, Peres, and Magalhães (2012) focused on characterizing the economic value of people with disabilities so that companies realize what they are losing monetarily when their Web presences are inaccessible to a number of people. With specific data that used the authors demonstrated a very high amount of money that companies are losing.

Lorca, Andrees, and Martínez (2012) conducted a study on Web accessibility levels of a sample of 600 European companies. The researchers' findings are that both the size of the company and the culture of the country in which it operates have a considerable effect associated. A fact that proves this argument is that large British companies are likely to have the highest levels of Web accessibility and this comes from the fact that English law has high levels of individualism, low power distance and low uncertainty avoidance, and all these issues promote innovation (such as Web accessibility).

Organizations of information technologies, which include developers also have an important role to play in this process. While there are numerous regulations and standards for accessibility for the development of appropriate interfaces, it is still quite difficult to achieve, and more to maintain high levels of quality in the development process. This difficulty is due to several factors such as the lack of adequate development of methods, tools used and the professional's training of development (Miñón, Moreno Martínez, & Abascal, 2014).

In order to be included in accessibility is vital development process that developers acquire habits of developing accessible Web sites, more precisely in the techniques and methods used by them. In spite of the literature review show that Web accessibility is important in the work of these people, it happens that the actions are somewhat limited, either due to their own causes of the individual as their limited perception on the subject, his empathy, and especially the lack of related to the Web accessibility experience, whether due to external reasons, mainly relating to firms in which they operate, where the main reason is due to the fact that developers have lack of control / power in relation to positive or negative ramifications of Web accessibility (Putnam et al., 2012).

Web accessibility is increasingly desired by customers, where many development companies listed the same as one of the techniques offered in their services. As such, evaluation studies to the websites of these companies are carried out in order to see if these companies have accessibility as a service to incorporate in your on-line presence. These studies demonstrate that despite the homepage these websites contain the compliance icon with the guidelines, it has no impact on actual accessibility of the homepage and also does not reflect the current state of the entire site, as it may have been modified several times since the validation happened (Gilbertson & Machin, 2012).

Lopes, Van Isacker, and Sedge (2010) effected an investigation to try to understand the motivations, concerns and difficulties of web developers when the topic is Web accessibility. The answers showed that in half of the people surveyed the topic has effect on his work, recognizing some awareness of the guidelines and standards accessibility, but only a more theoretical format. Overall the majority expressed the need for greater knowledge about the functional limitations of the disabled as well as assistive devices. However, the largest proportion (85%) was attributed by those who indicated the need for advanced training in Web accessibility area.

Still in the same direction, a similar study to the previous with the difference being only specific to a group of programmers from a recognized software development company was analysed. The conclusions were that the design, testing and find appropriate technology, are the hardest aspects in producing an accessible application. Although programmers have access to information and training, testing and technological solutions are time-consuming to implement, and the lack of time is a limiting factor in the development of projects (Trewin, Cragun, Swart, Brezin, & Richards, 2010).

In light of the knowledge gained through the existing literature, it is clear that organizations, despite being aware that Web accessibility has assumed increasing importance globally, does not give it the proper value. Although all ethical and cultural values that arise, it should be noted that individuals with some kind of trouble have a high economic value and it is absolutely imperative that companies understand that they are losing that amount to devalue this set of people.

Institutional Perspective

Associations are organizations whose mission is achieving a common goal of all participants thereof. In the case of web accessibility, this setting is no exception, and associations related to the theme, which may or may not have been created under that system, must have the ability to not only sensitize the world to the subject and must also submit active participation in the discovery of information and knowledge.

One of the associations that have made more efforts in this area is the Web Accessibility in Mind (WebAIM), which has helped build a large community of programmers, specialized people in the Web, people with disabilities and others who share the goal of making the Web more accessible. The major contribution of this community based on sharing resources and information on-line ensuring the knowledge, technical skills, tools and leadership strategies that enable organizations to make their own content accessible to people with disabilities (WebAIM, 2015).

As already discussed in this chapter, the professionals who develop their work in Web accessibility of the area are very important parts in the process. Thus one of the associations that have had great impact is the International Association of Accessibility Professionals (IAAP), which is to end the association of individuals and organizations with a focus on accessibility or in the process of building their skills and strategies. The purpose of this association is to help accessibility professionals to develop and advance their careers in order to help organizations integrate accessibility into their products and infrastructure (IAAP, 2015).

By another hand, there are assistive technologies that are very important tools in providing help to people with particular needs. Thus was created the Assistive Technology Industry Association (ATIA) that represents the common interests of business, government, education and agencies. Their mission is to serve as the collective voice of the assistive technology industry to best products are delivered to people with disabilities (ATIA, 2015).

There are also associations not being created exclusively for the purpose of Web accessibility, begin to focus their attention on the subject. The US Public Policy Council of ACM (USACM) is an association that unites the US government, the computing community and the entire American public, which in recent years has been looking at Web accessibility as a major theme. Aims of the council are:

- To increase awareness,
- Develop tools, and
- Extend the accessibility standards minimizing the regulatory burden (USACM, 2015).

Another country that has shown interest in the subject through their associations is Australia. The Web Australian Industry Association (AWIA) representing all the Web industry, both from an ethical point of view and professional, regularly organizes events related to Web accessibility where the topic is discussed thoroughly in order to find the best solutions, for both for the industry and for end users (AWIA, 2015).

According to what has already been reported, education and Web accessibility are two fields that to work properly necessarily have to cooperate among themselves. With this in mind, there are also associations for educational purposes that do not discard the Web accessibility. An example is the Association for the Advancement of Computing in Education (AACE) which has the mission to advance information technology in education and e- learning in its practical application. For this Web accessibility functions as a central pillar for the association in your research (AACE, 2015).

We verified the existence of a considerable number of associations approaching Web accessibility, some of them created exclusively for this purpose and others who realized the increasingly urgent necessity of the theme and the need to adapt. It is good to realize that within the associations the path already begun, however there is still much to go and it is essential that not only appear more entities concerned, as well as those that already exist, to make themselves heard more impactful to be successful in the goals that propose to achieve.

End Users Perspective

The last perspective to be analysed is the end users. We attribute great importance and emphasis to this group because obviously the whole scope of this work and Web accessibility in global revolves around these individuals, who may benefit if the objectives are achieved. As such it cannot exclude these people from intervening in the process of achieving better levels of accessibility, it is essential to acquire all the feedback and experience that they gather and use this valuable knowledge when developing new platforms.

Internet users are a highly heterogeneous entity, with different needs and requirements, where individuals with a disability may have many problems. With this in mind are created adaptive software systems to facilitate the interaction of people with all the information around them. The possibilities for exploring new methods and accessibility techniques to make adaptive Web for these users is a key point, since recent studies indicate that even when the guidelines are implemented, there is little evidence that people with disabilities gain better accessibility indexes (Raufi, Ferati, Zenuni, Ajdari, & Ismaili, 2015).

Research on inclusive design has contributed to a rich and wide range of publications and initiatives, forming an emerging knowledge base in this area. Understanding the needs and characteristics of the knowledge of the users, added a new dimension to the research task. For this purpose, there are works that focus on knowledge of inclusive design, involving the end users, in order to help the developers in their work. Research programs are used to illustrate the understanding of these needs and developed tools in order to evaluate its effectiveness (Dong, McGinley, Nickpour, & Cifter, 2015).

Factors such as the physical constraints, experience of using and accessibility barriers that websites have, are very important when observing users' behaviour on a particular Web site. This process of adaptation has been much investigated in recent times and the findings show that will as the interaction progresses the user gets higher completion rates of tasks, developing more techniques of exploitation, which makes them more qualified, independent and autonomous. These metrics can be considered learning indicators to be explored in order to intervene appropriately in the interface (Vigo & Harper, 2014).

Blind users are the most affected by this exclusion and is a challenge for them to seek information effectively on the Web. Xie, Babu, Jeong, Joo, and Fuller (2014) effected a case study with blind people in digital libraries in order to find possible solutions help in the interaction. The authors concluded that the keyboard focus location advertising, shortcut keys to exit out the current location of the cursor and descriptive summaries in relation to the overall site structure can be incorporated into digital libraries in order to improve the accessibility levels.

Ferati, Raufi, Kurti, and Vogel (2014) conducted a study which grouped people with different levels of visual impairment in different countries to compare their needs. The results showed that the cultural dimension of their country of origin and the context of use plays a crucial role in making the content accessible, and WCAG guidelines alone are often insufficient. Furthermore, it is necessary to evaluate the visual impairment level of the user before applying any technical adaptation.

Blind users interact with sites in different ways and it is necessary to analyse each case in particular to understand how they can eliminate these barriers. Pascual, Ribera, Granollers, and Coiduras (2014) performed an evaluation at two sites with similar content but different accessibility levels in three groups of users with different vision impairment. It was noted that all users showed better mood when interacting with the site accessible. An interesting fact is that the blind users when interact with the site inaccessible, complained much less than the low vision individuals and those without any difficulty. One possible explanation for this phenomenon is the daily interaction that blind users are always using the Web.

The evaluation of a website respect of its availability is an essential part of the whole process. Automatic ratings are the most common and which has higher utilization rate, however there are some barriers that are only detected with the participation of users. So it is important to study the behavior of these people in order to identify features and develop protocols that assessors and experts should consider in the performance of expert assessment (Capra, Ferreira, Silveira, & Ferreira, 2012).

Power, Freire, Petrie, and Swallow (2012) conducted an empirical study in collaboration with blind users and came to the conclusion that even though the developers correctly implement the current guidelines WCAG, there is little evidence that people with disabilities may have fewer problems. These results indicate that it is time to change the Web accessibility paradigm and define a much wider set of principles, in addition to the guidelines, which is based on users and knowledge that can be transmitted by them and used as valuable feedback by developers.

The question of accessibility on the Internet is not just for blind people, older users also have an important role in the information society. Yao, Qiu Huang, Du and Ma (2011) investigated the technological accessibility problems of this group and concluded that the reason for these difficulties is linked to:

- The lack of promotion by government entities enabling environments,
- Lack of involvement of the rest of the community,
- Lack of support the newest members of the family, and
- Little capacity autonomous learning of the elderly.

With older people as the focus of research Sayago and Blat (2009) effected an ethnographic study of daily interactions over a period of three years, concluded that the greatest barriers these people face are the difficulty in memorizing the steps, understanding the terms used on the Web and use of the computer by the mouse, despite the will to use it. Regardless of these limitations the inclusion and independence are two conditions desired by these users.

Audits and evaluations the Web is becoming ever more complicated and time consuming due to the increasing number of compliance criteria to be tested. As a consequence, Yesilada, Brajnik, and Harper (2011) tested 61 common barriers with different groups of users to try to reduce the compliance criteria and showed that 58% of them are common among users of mobile applications and users with disabilities. Another interesting aspect is that the most serious barriers are similar for users with low vision and users with motor disabilities.

Lopes, Van Isacker, et al. (2010) conducted a questionnaire to users who deal daily with accessibility problems either people with disabilities or elderly people, and realized that they all claim that increasingly Web and mobile applications are raising severe obstacles in their tasks. Even so, they continue to use your computer or smartphone on a daily basis, relying often with dependence on friends to help them. The group has explicitly stated that the main improvement that they desire is the better compatibility between assistive technologies and websites.

As result of this research, we can see how it is absolutely essential we include in this work the perspective and knowledge of end users can assign. End user are relevant throughout Web Accessibility process as their feedback is what makes work of programmers more focused to the needs of those will use. Thus all are benefited and are not wasted later features in practice does not serve as useful.

CHALLENGES AND OPPORTUNITIES

The demand for sophisticated Web interfaces, able to interact with everyone without any exceptions, using autonomous reactions, and meeting the needs of different users, has produced high expectations from ICT. Progressing towards understanding and modelling these computational tools is crucial in the behaviour of Human-Computer Interaction-systems in order to achieve social and economic benefits.

Laws and Regulations

Web accessibility depends on the combined efforts of several components, such as software development tools, developers and the content itself, and this interaction can sometimes be complicated. There are several organizations that recognize these difficulties and provide technical and functional indications directed to each of these elements, even though not always consensual and accepted transversally. In the case WCAG 2.0 it means that the automated validation and correction, preferred by programmers, cannot be considered as the only (or main) form to validate content and web platforms developed.

Based on previously explained, and after an analysis and reflection on the existing literature, we can see that there is a set of technical / functional regulations or indications homogeneously accepted by all and that programmers can easily follow. Such limitation brings a huge challenge to organizations and scientific community who wish to focus in this context, whereas its impact is immense, forcing the need to make a previous work of cross-examination before we even be able to think of technological developments or new solutions (Harper & Chen, 2012).

Current mass acceptance of mobile devices has also been creating a new set of issues to the already immensely complex problem of Web accessibility. This stems from the fact that most of the regulations and technical and operational indications are not directed at the development of content and platforms for mobile devices. Presented this fact, from our point of view it will be necessary to provide further clarification and regulations on how best to develop mobile applications accessible to all.

Web Accessibility in Education

After reviewing the existing literature Web accessibility in education it is possible to verify that there is a considerable gap in terms of know-how lack of progress in terms of different areas. This view is reinforced by arguments of several researchers (Seale, 2013), whereby an update to the teaching support systems and a thematic implementation of "Web accessibility" in study programmer focused and comprehensive manner.

Online learning has the ability to open the door of education to those who have the technology to participate. However, when it comes to inclusion rise up some barriers. These problems need to be solved quickly, but it is necessary to investigate the real needs of these students and their interaction with these platforms in order to achieve concrete objectives and to really improve your experience (Burgstahler, 2015).

Education is considered one of the main actions to improve integration of people with functional diversity in society, more accurately through the higher education institutions. Both the administrations of higher education institutions, as their teachers need to understand concepts in Web accessibility issues in order to carry out a more inclusive learning and quality. In fact, today's students will be professionals in the future, and when we invest now in their education about Web accessibility, we invested in an improvement of inclusion levels of long-term Web platforms.

Restrepo, Benavidez, and Gutiérrez (2012), present the idea to include lectures on the subject in educational institutions or even change the curriculum in the most appropriate courses, thematic instilling applying Web accessibility techniques, and thus teach students the techniques and methodologies appropriate to the creation of accessible Web content, may be the best option. Although there are some studies in this regard (Fuertes, González, & Martinez, 2012), is plenty of space for research in this area, as there are great challenges, both on the content being taught or about the most appropriate way of teaching.

Web Accessibility in Companies

We have seen, in recent years, some positive signs of how companies look at Web accessibility, however in light of the research we conducted, the adoption of Web accessibility by organizations (either when they are developing their own web content, either when they are developing Web content and platforms for others) is still very scarce (Gilbertson & Machin, 2012).

For many companies, websites are priority in the services they provide, then improve the accessibility levels of the same is urgent. Even so the challenges do not exhaust here and there are much deeper issues that need a comprehensive investigation. The challenges are immense, ranging from realizing that the reasons why organizations use this technology to analyse and try to change the perception that these are the social and economic value inherent in Web accessibility.

Nevertheless, for organizations are absolutely crucial to inform all the potential that Web accessibility can bring them in order to make themselves understood to companies that Web accessibility should not be an obligation, but a way to reach new audiences and reach more quality to those who are already loyal.

Collaborative Accessibility Web

Web content is under the control of the owners of Web sites and therefore are those who have the responsibility to make your content accessible. Given this basic assumption of accessibility, users should be able to demonstrate their discontent and even contribute with knowledge and help the owners of websites. So some windows of opportunities and challenges open, whereas are very few platforms where users can report problems of interaction and navigation, and those that implement this feature have very slow registration process and low success rate.

purpose to connect users and owners through platforms creating a social network so that these groups can share their experiences, report problems in real time and even serve as a platform to attract new users through the services affordably, it may be one way. However other directions may be taken into account, and the researchers are of utmost importance in this context, as it is necessary to realize a conceptual point of view of how it can integrate users and owners of websites so that they can collaborate.

Web Accessibility in Mobile Applications

The growing use of mobile devices has been overwhelming and today this type of systems has become one of the means most used by people to access services and information on-line. In this context it is extremely important that these resources are accessible to the entire community. Focused on this thought, it is possible to say that there is much work to be done in this area to achieve satisfactory levels of accessibility.

As argued by Leitner, Strauss, and Stummer (2015) the research possibilities in the framework of accessibility in mobile applications are varied. The challenges start right in designing accessible applications, where many problems still exist, as Although we already have some regulations of support do not yet exist any firm base to serve as a support to the developers of these platforms. On the other hand, the evaluation as to the accessibility of mobile applications already on the market is still an open challenge as a result of lack of regulation and technologies and support tools.

Researchers can also go through the studies with users with limitations, with the objective of analyse the problems arising from the use of mobile platforms in order to adjust and define recommendations for mobile accessibility based not only on assumptions, but on evidence empirical. This work has enormous relief, for it is through the results of this research that mobile application developers can direct their focus and work on developing truly accessible applications.

CONCLUSION

Web accessibility is an increasingly important topic both from a technological and from a more human perspective. This relevance is largely drawn from current Web users needs and the necessity to develop (Web) software and platforms that allow for a universal access and use.

Although most of the accessibility problems can be anticipated by users or programmers, there is another set of questions that can only be identified during the development stages. Nevertheless, it is increasingly accepted that the Web accessibility is also a critical topic for all organizations, including those who produce and provide Web content.

Social agencies with responsibility in education, associations or in government activities, should also help in triggering an accessible Web. This can be done from various perspectives: the development of regulations; the creation of a moral and social mindset towards the Web accessibility topic, and so many others. Besides these more direct actions, these entities can also help shape positive perceptions on stakeholders and web developers in order to increase the perception on the topic and the awareness on the necessity.

Despite the existing amount of scientific and technical work on the Web accessibility topic, perceivable through a literature analysis, it is still possible to identify a knowledge gap on the subject that should be analysed and aimed.

This chapter intends to document a multi-perspective vision on the Web accessibility topic and with this try to help creating a global perception on the subject and, in parallel, help both the scientific community and the organization to better understand the related issues and how to contribute to an overall improvement on websites accessibility levels, hence transforming this technology into an inclusive one.

REFERENCES

W3C. (1999). *Web Content Accessibility Guidelines 1.0.* Retrieved 25/11/2015, 2015, from http://www.w3.org/TR/WAI-WEBCONTENT/

W3C. (2005). *Introduction to Web Accessibility.* Retrieved 15/11/2015, 2015, from http://www.w3.org/WAI/intro/accessibility.php

W3C. (2008). *Web Content Accessibility Guidelines (WCAG) 2.0.* Retrieved 25/11/2015, 2015, from http://www.w3.org/TR/WCAG20/

W3C. (2015). *About W3C.* Retrieved 25/11/2015, 2015, from http://www.w3.org/Consortium/

AACE. (2015). *About AACE.* Retrieved 27/12/2015, 2015, from http://www.aace.org/about.htm

Aizpurua, A., Arrue, M , & Vigo, M. (2015). Prejudices, memories, expectations and confidence influence experienced accessibility on the Web. *Computers in Human Behavior, 51,* 152-160. doi:10.1016/j.chb.2015.04.035

Al-Khalifa, H. (2012). The accessibility of Saudi Arabia government Web sites: An exploratory study. *Universal Access in the Information Society, 11*(2), 201–210. doi:10.1007/s10209-010-0215-7

Andreasson, K., & Snaprud, M. (2014). *The European e-government web accessibility divide.* Paper presented at the Proceedings of the 8th International Conference on Theory and Practice of Electronic Governance.

Arch, A. (2008). *Web Accessibility for Older Users: A Literature Review.* Retrieved 15/11/2015, 2015, from http://www.w3.org/TR/2008/WD-wai-age-literature-20080514/

ATIA. (2015). *About ATIA - Information.* Retrieved 26/12/2015, 2015, from http://www.atia.org/

AWIA. (2015). *Web Accessibility.* Retrieved 26/12/2015, 2015, from https://www.webindustry.asn.au/news-and-events/events/web-accessibility

Bradbard, D., & Peters, C. (2010). Web Accessibility Theory and Practice: An Introduction for University Faculty. *Journal of Educators Online, 7*(1), n1.

Bradbard, D., Peters, C., & Caneva, Y. (2010). Web accessibility policies at land-grant universities. *The Internet and Higher Education, 13*(4), 258–266. doi:10.1016/j.iheduc.2010.05.007

Brewer, J. (2004). *Web accessibility highlights and trends.* Paper presented at the 2004 international cross-disciplinary workshop on Web accessibility (W4A). doi:10.1145/990657.990667

Burgstahler, S. (2015). Opening Doors or Slamming Them Shut? Online Learning Practices and Students with Disabilities. *Social Inclusion, 3*(6).

Capra, E., Ferreira, S., Silveira, D., & Ferreira, A. (2012). Evaluation of Web Accessibility: An Approach Related to Functional Illiteracy. *Procedia Computer Science, 14*, 36–46. doi:10.1016/j.procs.2012.10.005

Cooper, M. (2013). Making online learning accessible to disabled students: an institutional case study. *Approaches to Developing Accessible Learning Experiences: Conceptualising Best Practice*, 103.

Costa, D., Fernandes, N., Neves, S., Duarte, C., Hijón-Neira, R., & Carriço, L. (2013). *Web accessibility in Africa: a study of three African domains. In Human-Computer Interaction–INTERACT 2013* (pp. 331–338). Springer.

Díaz-Bossini, J., & Moreno, L. (2014). Accessibility to Mobile Interfaces for Older People. *Procedia Computer Science, 27*(0), 57–66. doi:10.1016/j.procs.2014.02.008

Dong, H., McGinley, C., Nickpour, F., & Cifter, A. (2015). Designing for designers: Insights into the knowledge users of inclusive design. *Applied Ergonomics, 46*, 284-291. doi:10.1016/j.apergo.2013.03.003

EU-FRA. (2015). *People with disabilities*. Retrieved 28/11/2015, 2015, from http://fra.europa.eu/en/theme/people-disabilities

Ferati, M., Raufi, B., Kurti, A., & Vogel, B. (2014). *Accessibility requirements for blind and visually impaired in a regional context: An exploratory study*. Paper presented at the Usability and Accessibility Focused Requirements Engineering (UsARE), 2014 IEEE 2nd International Workshop on. doi:10.1109/UsARE.2014.6890995

Fuertes, J., González, Á., & Martínez, L. (2012). Including Accessibility in Higher Education Curricula for ICT. *Procedia Computer Science, 14*, 382–390. doi:10.1016/j.procs.2012.10.044

Gilbertson, T., & Machin, C. (2012). *Guidelines, icons and marketable skills: an accessibility evaluation of 100 web development company homepages*. Paper presented at the international cross-disciplinary conference on web accessibility. doi:10.1145/2207016.2207024

Gonçalves, R., Martins, J., & Branco, F. (2014). A Review on the Portuguese Enterprises Web Accessibility Levels–A Website Accessibility High Level Improvement Proposal. *Procedia Computer Science, 27*, 176–185. doi:10.1016/j.procs.2014.02.021

Gonçalves, R., Martins, J., Branco, F., & Barroso, J. (2013). *Web Accessibility–From the Evaluation and Analysis to the Implementation–The anoGov/PEPPOL Case. In Universal Access in Human-Computer Interaction. User and Context Diversity* (pp. 664–673). Springer.

Gonçalves, R., Martins, J., Branco, F., Pereira, J., Rocha, T., & Peixoto, C. (2015). *AccessWeb Barometer: A Web Accessibility Evaluation and Analysis Platform*. Paper presented at the INTERNET 2015 - The Seventh International Conference on Evolving Internet, St. Julians, Malta.

Gonçalves, R., Martins, J., Pereira, J., Oliveira, M., & Ferreira, J. (2013). Enterprise Web Accessibility Levels Amongst the Forbes 250: Where Art Thou O Virtuous Leader? *Journal of Business Ethics, 113*(2), 363–375. doi:10.1007/s10551-012-1309-3

Gonçalves, R., Martins, J., Pereira, J., Santos, V., & Cota, M. (2013). Can I Access my School Website? Auditing Accessibility of the Portuguese Teaching Institutions Websites. *Journal of Universal Computer Science, 19*(18), 2639–2655.

Goodwin, M., Susar, D., Nietzio, A., Snaprud, M., & Jensen, C. (2011). Global web accessibility analysis of national government portals and ministry web sites. *Journal of Information Technology & Politics*, *8*(1), 41–67. doi:10.1080/19331681.2010.508011

Hanson, V., & Richards, J. (2013). Progress on website accessibility?. *ACM Transactions on the Web*, *7*(1), 2. doi:10.1145/2435215.2435217

Harper, S., & Chen, A. (2012). Web accessibility guidelines. *World Wide Web (Bussum)*, *15*(1), 61–88. doi:10.1007/s11280-011-0130-8

Henry, S. (2002). *Understanding web accessibility. In Constructing accessible web sites* (pp. 6–31). Springer. doi:10.1007/978-1-4302-1116-7_2

Henry, S., Abou-Zahra, S., & Brewer, J. (2014). *The role of accessibility in a universal web.* Paper presented at the 11th Web for All Conference. doi:10.1145/2596695.2596719

IAAP. (2015). About IAAP. Retrieved 26/12/2015, 2015, from http://www.accessibilityassociation.org/

ISO. (2003). *TS 16071: 2003: Ergonomics of human-system interaction–Guidance on accessibility for human-computer interfaces.* Geneva, Switzerland: International Standards Organisation.

ISO. (2006). *9241-110: 2006. Ergonomics of human system interaction-Part 110: Dialogue principles.* ISO.

ISO. (2008). *9241-171 (2008) Ergonomics of humansystem interaction--Part 171: Guidance on software accessibility.* ISO.

Iwata, H., Kobayashi, N., Tachibana, K., Shirogane, J., & Fukazawa, Y. (2013). Web accessibility support for visually impaired users using link content analysis. *SpringerPlus*, *2*(1), 116. doi:10.1186/2193-1801-2-116 PMID:23667799

Jaeger, P. (2004). The Social Impact of an Accessible E-Democracy Disability Rights Laws in the Development of the Federal E-Government. *Journal of Disability Policy Studies*, *15*(1), 19–26. doi:10.1177/10442073040150010401

Karkin, N., & Janssen, M. (2014). Evaluating websites from a public value perspective: A review of Turkish local government websites. *International Journal of Information Management*, *34*(3), 351–363. doi:10.1016/j.ijinfomgt.2013.11.004

Kuzma, J. (2009). Regulatory compliance and web accessibility of UK parliament sites. *Journal of Information Law & Technology*, *2*, 1–15.

Kuzma, J. (2010). *Global E-government web accessibility: a case study.* Academic Press.

Kuzma, J., Yen, D., & Oestreicher, K. (2009). *Global e-government web accessibility: an empirical examination of EU, Asian and African sites.* Academic Press.

Lazar, J., Beavan, P., Brown, J., Coffey, D., Nolf, B., Poole, R., & Weber, K. (2010). *Investigating the accessibility of state government web sites in Maryland. In Designing Inclusive Interactions* (pp. 69–78). Springer.

Leitner, M., & Strauss, C. (2008). *Exploratory case study research on web accessibility*. Springer. doi:10.1007/978-3-540-70540-6_70

Leitner, M., Strauss, C., & Stummer, C. (2015). Web accessibility implementation in private sector organizations: Motivations and business impact. *Universal Access in the Information Society*, 1–12.

Li, S., Yen, D., Lu, W., & Lin, T. (2012). Migrating from WCAG 1.0 to WCAG 2.0–A comparative study based on Web Content Accessibility Guidelines in Taiwan. *Computers in Human Behavior*, *28*(1), 87–96. doi:10.1016/j.chb.2011.08.014

Linder, K., Fontaine-Rainen, D., & Behling, K. (2015). Whose job is it? Key challenges and future directions for online accessibility in US Institutions of Higher Education. *Open Learning: The Journal of Open, Distance and e-Learning*, 1-14.

Lopes, R., Gomes, D., & Carriço, L. (2010). *Web not for all: a large scale study of web accessibility*. Paper presented at the 2010 International Cross Disciplinary Conference on Web Accessibility (W4A). doi:10.1145/1805986.1806001

Lopes, R., Van Isacker, K., & Carriço, L. (2010). *Redefining assumptions: accessibility and its stakeholders. In Computers Helping People with Special Needs* (pp. 561–568). Springer. doi:10.1007/978-3-642-14097-6_90

Lorca, P., Andrées, J., & Martínez, A. (2012). Size and culture as determinants of the web policy of listed firms: The case of web accessibility in Western European countries. *Journal of the American Society for Information Science and Technology*, *63*(2), 392–405. doi:10.1002/asi.21650

Mankoff, J., Fait, H., & Tran, T. (2005). *Is your web page accessible?: a comparative study of methods for assessing web page accessibility for the blind*. Paper presented at the SIGCHI conference on Human factors in computing systems. doi:10.1145/1054972.1054979

Martínez, A., De Andrés, J., & García, J. (2014). Determinants of the Web accessibility of European banks. *Information Processing & Management*, *50*(1), 69–86. doi:10.1016/j.ipm.2013.08.001

Miñón, R., Moreno, L., Martínez, P., & Abascal, J. (2014). An approach to the integration of accessibility requirements into a user interface development method. *Science of Computer Programming*, *86*, 58–73. doi:10.1016/j.scico.2013.04.005

Nietzio, A., Olsen, M., Eibegger, M., & Snaprud, M. (2010). *Accessibility of eGovernment web sites: towards a collaborative retrofitting approach. In Computers Helping People with Special Needs* (pp. 468–475). Springer. doi:10.1007/978-3-642-14097-6_75

Noh, K., Jeong, E., You, Y., Moon, S., & Kang, M. (2015). A study on the current status and strategies for improvement of web accessibility compliance of public institutions. *Journal of Open Innovation: Technology, Market, and Complexity*, *1*(1), 1–17. doi:10.1186/s40852-015-0001-0

Oh, L., & Chen, J. (2014). Determinants of employees intention to exert pressure on firms to engage in web accessibility. *Behaviour & Information Technology*, *34*(2), 108–118. doi:10.1080/0144929X.2014.936040

ONU. (2008). *World Population Prospects: The 2008 Revision*. Retrieved 15/11/2015, 2015, from http://www.un.org/esa/population/publications/wpp2008/wpp2008_highlights.pdf

Pascual, A., Ribera, M., Granollers, T., & Coiduras, J. (2014). Impact of Accessibility Barriers on the Mood of Blind, Low-vision and Sighted Users. *Procedia Computer Science, 27*(0), 431–440. doi:10.1016/j. procs.2014.02.047

Power, C., Freire, A., Petrie, H., & Swallow, D. (2012). *Guidelines are only half of the story: accessibility problems encountered by blind users on the web.* Paper presented at the SIGCHI conference on human factors in computing systems. doi:10.1145/2207676.2207736

Putnam, C., Wozniak, K., Zefeldt, M., Cheng, J., Caputo, M., & Duffield, C. (2012). *How do professionals who create computing technologies consider accessibility?* Paper presented at the 14th international ACM SIGACCESS conference on Computers and accessibility. doi:10.1145/2384916.2384932

Rau, P., Zhou, L., Sun, N., & Zhong, R. (2014). Evaluation of web accessibility in China: Changes from 2009 to 2013. *Universal Access in the Information Society*, 1–7.

Raufi, B., Ferati, M., Zenuni, X., Ajdari, J., & Ismaili, F. (2015). Methods and Techniques of Adaptive Web Accessibility for the Blind and Visually Impaired. *Procedia: Social and Behavioral Sciences, 195*, 1999–2007. doi:10.1016/j.sbspro.2015.06.214

Restrepo, E., Benavidez, C., & Gutiérrez, H. (2012). The Challenge of Teaching to Create Accessible Learning Objects to Higher Education Lecturers. *Procedia Computer Science, 14*, 371–381. doi:10.1016/j. procs.2012.10.043

Ringlaben, R., Bray, M., & Packard, A. (2014). Accessibility of American University Special Education Departments Web sites. *Universal Access in the Information Society, 13*(2), 249–254. doi:10.1007/s10209-013-0302-7

Roberts, J., Crittenden, L., & Crittenden, J. (2011). Students with disabilities and online learning: A cross-institutional study of perceived satisfaction with accessibility compliance and services. *The Internet and Higher Education, 14*(4), 242–250. doi:10.1016/j.iheduc.2011.05.004

Rocha, T., Bessa, M., Gonçalves, R., Peres, E., & Magalhães, L. (2012). Web Accessibility and Digital Businesses: The Potential Economic Value of Portuguese People with Disability. *Procedia Computer Science, 14*, 56–64. doi:10.1016/j.procs.2012.10.007

Sánchez-Gordón, M., & Moreno, L. (2014). Toward an integration of Web accessibility into testing processes. *Procedia Computer Science, 27*, 281–291. doi:10.1016/j.procs.2014.02.031

Santarosa, L., Conforto, D., & Neves, B. (2015). Teacher Education and Accessibility on E-Learning System: Putting the W3C Guidelines into Practice. *Teaching Education, 4*(01).

Sayago, S., & Blat, J. (2009). *About the relevance of accessibility barriers in the everyday interactions of older people with the web.* Paper presented at the 2009 International Cross-Disciplinary Conference on Web Accessibililty (W4A). doi:10.1145/1535654.1535682

Seale, J. (2013). *E-learning and disability in higher education: accessibility research and practice.* Routledge.

Seale, J., & Cooper, M. (2010). E-learning and accessibility: An exploration of the potential role of generic pedagogical tools. *Computers & Education, 54*(4), 1107–1116. doi:10.1016/j.compedu.2009.10.017

Serra, L., Carvalho, L., Ferreira, L., Vaz, J., & Freire, A. (2015). Accessibility Evaluation of E-Government Mobile Applications in Brazil. *Procedia Computer Science, 67*, 348–357. doi:10.1016/j.procs.2015.09.279

Trewin, S., Cragun, B., Swart, C., Brezin, J., & Richards, J. (2010). *Accessibility challenges and tool features: an IBM Web developer perspective.* Paper presented at the 2010 international cross disciplinary conference on web accessibility (W4A). doi:10.1145/1805986.1806029

USACM. (2015). *Web Accessibility.* Retrieved 26/15/2015, 2015, from http://usacm.acm.org/accessibility/category.cfm?cat=23&accessibility

van der Geest, T., & Velleman, E. (2014). Easy-to-read Meets Accessible Web in the E-government Context. *Procedia Computer Science, 27*, 327–333. doi:10.1016/j.procs.2014.02.036

van Rooij, S., & Zirkle, K. (2016). Balancing pedagogy, student readiness and accessibility: A case study in collaborative online course development. *The Internet and Higher Education, 28*, 1–7. doi:10.1016/j.iheduc.2015.08.001

Vigo, M., & Harper, S. (2014). A snapshot of the first encounters of visually disabled users with the Web. *Computers in Human Behavior, 34*, 203–212. doi:10.1016/j.chb.2014.01.045

WAI. (2005). *Web Accessibility Initiative (WAI).* Retrieved 25/11/2015, 2015, from http://www.w3.org/WAI/

WebAIM. (2015). *About WebAIM.* Retrieved 27/12/2015, 2015, from http://webaim.org/about/

Wentz, B., Lazar, J., Stein, M., Gbenro, O., Holandez, E., & Ramsey, A. (2014). Danger, danger! Evaluating the accessibility of Web-based emergency alert sign-ups in the northeastern United States. *Government Information Quarterly, 31*(3), 488–497. doi:10.1016/j.giq.2014.02.010

White, J., Goette, T., & Young, D. (2015). Measuring the Accessibility of the US State Government Web Sites. *Communications of the IIMA, 5*(1), 4.

WHO. (2014). *Disability and health.* Retrieved 15/11/2015, 2015, from http://www.who.int/mediacentre/factsheets/fs352/en/

Wijayaratne, A., & Singh, D. (2010). Is there space in cyberspace for distance learners with special needs in Asia? A review of the level of Web accessibility of institutional and library homepages of AAOU members. *The International Information & Library Review, 42*(1), 40–49. doi:10.1080/10572317.2010.10762841

Xie, I., Babu, R., Jeong, W., Joo, S., & Fuller, P. (2014). *Blind Users Searching Digital Libraries: Types of Help-seeking Situations at the Cognitive Level.* Academic Press.

Yao, D., Qiu, Y., Huang, H., Du, Z., & Ma, J. (2011). A survey of technology accessibility problems faced by older users in China. *Universal Access in the Information Society, 10*(4), 373–390. doi:10.1007/s10209-011-0222-3

Yesilada, Y., Brajnik, G., & Harper, S. (2011). Barriers common to mobile and disabled web users. *Interacting with Computers, 23*(5), 525–542. doi:10.1016/j.intcom.2011.05.005

Yi, Y. (2015). Compliance of Section 508 in public library systems with the largest percentage of under-served populations. *Government Information Quarterly*, *32*(1), 75–81. doi:10.1016/j.giq.2014.11.005

Yu, D., & Parmanto, B. (2011). U.S. state government websites demonstrate better in terms of accessibility compared to federal government and commercial websites. *Government Information Quarterly*, *28*(4), 484–490. doi:10.1016/j.giq.2011.04.001

Zap, N., & Montgomerie, C. (2013). *The status of web accessibility of Canadian universities and colleges: A follow-up study 10 years later.* Paper presented at the World Conference on Educational Multimedia, Hypermedia and Telecommunications.

KEY TERMS AND DEFINITIONS

Challenges: A demanding or stimulating task.

Characterization: A characteristics and peculiarities description.

Disability: A disadvantage or deficiency, especially a physical or mental impairment that interferes with or prevents normal achievement in a particular task.

Guidelines: A rule or instruction that shows or tells how something should be done.

Multi-Perspective: Relative to more than one perspective.

Opportunities: A chance for advancement or progress.

Web Accessibility: Use of Web environments, products and services by anyone, regardless of their limitations.

Chapter 7
Web Accessibility and Transparency for Accountability:
The Portuguese Official Municipal Websites

Maria José Angélico
Polytechnic of Porto, Portugal

Sandrina Francisca Teixeira
ISCAP/IPP, Portugal

Amélia Silva
Polytechnic of Porto, Portugal

Telma Maia
Câmara Municipal Valongo, Portugal

Anabela Martins Silva
University of Minho, Portugal

ABSTRACT

Local government is a political power close to citizens and constitutes a mainstay of democracy. Because of their mission, the guidelines promoted by local government must be embedded in strategies of accountability and public communication. In that sense, it is worthwhile to ask if "local government accountability is being an inclusive concept?" In Portugal, transparency of municipalities is being accessed through the Municipality Transparency Index (MTI). The study aim was to investigate whatever MTI measures accessibility. This study examined the availability of local government information on the website for a sample of 86 Portuguese municipalities and presented the results of a quantitative evaluation of the web accessibility based on W3C guidelines, using an automated tool. Based on the main concepts of transparency and accessibility, it explored static association between MTI and web accessibility. This study contributed to the discussion about transparency as a social value and is of great importance for local policy makers and civic movements in favor of disabled people.

INTRODUCTION

Over the last two decades, accountability and transparency in public administration are two interrelated issues that have gained a huge relevance in political discourse. These issues are now inevitable for discussion in developed societies.

DOI: 10.4018/978-1-5225-1868-6.ch007

- How well are public resources being used?
- What are the outputs and the outcomes of public resources?
- Are citizens' needs being satisfied in an effective and efficiency way?

These are some of the key questions involved. Therefore, one can say that there is no real democracy without real accountability. By being accountable, it means to provide information about what is being done, in what way, with which motivations and how much it costs. In other words, it means being transparent and practicing good governance (Arnold & Garcia, 2011).

More than any other organization, public entities has a vast list of stakeholders.

- Citizens,
- Customers,
- Suppliers,
- Government bodies,
- Political bodies,
- Civil movements,
- Consumer advocates,
- Environmentalists,
- Special interest groups and
- Media are just some of them.

The importance of each stakeholder depends on its attributes of power, urgency and legitimacy (Austen et al., 2008; Flak & Dertz, 2006). Normally, social minorities face some difficulties in being recognized as important stakeholders.

In an instrumental approach, this question may be of little relevance. However, if one follows a political perspective, then there are some moral or philosophical guidelines that should command the way public entities manage their stakeholders (Fontaine et al., 2006; Donaldson & Preston, 1995). Disabled people represent a minority of the population, but each person is a citizen, no matter what are their physical conditions. Therefore, developed societies should ask themselves if their public entities are being accountable for all.

Local government is the political structure most closed to day-to-day citizens. Because of their mission and their activities, the moral or philosophical guidelines promoted by local government must be embedded in the processes and strategies of accountability and public communication. There is no doubt that the way public bodies communicate with their stakeholders has changed a lot over the two decades. Technology and the Internet have driven social life changes. The digital era arrived to Portuguese public administration some years ago. Nowadays in most Portuguese municipalities, citizens can apply for public local services through the respective websites. In the other hand, local governments use websites and other digital instruments to inform and communicate with their citizens.

In Portugal, the transparency of municipalities is being assessed through the "Municipality Transparency Index" (MTI). This index was created by an independent body and is published annually. The variable measures are grouped in seven dimensions and the data source of the MTI is mainly digital information. This study critically analyzed the MTI. The aim was to investigate whatever MTI measures accessibility. Considering that the MTI is based on digital information, it investigated web accessibility of municipal websites. Besides, since the economic and financial dimension is a structural pillar of the concepts of transparency and accountability, the study focused on that dimension and investigated if the operationalization of these concepts is being inclusive.

On the other side, the websites have changed their scope and functionality in the last decade as the result of technological improvements (Shah, 2007). The increasing usage of the Internet by municipalities to interact with citizens through web-based services led to thinking about the accessibility barriers for disabled people. Web accessibility is defined as "usability of a product, service, environment or facility by people with the widest range of capabilities" by ISO/TS 16071 and is reviewed on ISO 9241 (ISO/TS 16071, 2003; ISO 9241-171, 2008). As defined by the World Wide Web Consortium (W3C),

Web accessibility means that people with disabilities can use the web. More specifically, web accessibility means that people with disabilities can perceive, understand, navigate and interact with the web and that they can contribute to the web. Web accessibility also benefits others including older people with changing abilities due to aging.

The W3C proposed metrics to evaluate web accessibility. It defined three conformity levels (A, AA and AAA) that can be assessed by reviewing the Web Content Accessibility Guidelines (now WCAG 2.0) (Nielsen, 2006). Level A is the minimal requirement for a website to be accessible for a group of users with lesser handicaps. Such orientations, though not mandatory for non-public websites, started orienting and promoting a new level of accessibility in the websites managed by webmasters, certified with the affixation of one of the W3C logotypes.

In September, 2007, Resolution 155/2007 was created by the Committee of Portuguese Ministers. It defines orientations for web accessibility of administration public websites in Internet accessibility for citizens with special needs. This resolution recognizes that the previous "97/99 Resolution" didn't have real effects. With this new legislation, it was defined that the informative sites should follow the Level A of the WCAG 1.0, on a three months schedule after the date of the publication, while the transactional sites should follow Level AA on a six months schedule.

This study presented preliminary results of an accessibility evaluation of municipal websites through an adaptation of the WCAG Evaluation Methodology to allow the usage of an automated tool. This measure of web accessibility is than compared with transparency measure (IMT) in other to investigate if local government accountability is being practices in an inclusive way, i.e., are the websites of the most transparent municipalities accessible? It is the main research question of this study.

This article is structured as follows. In the next section, the background concepts and the methodology, namely data collection and data analyses, are presented. The next section presents and discussed the empirical results and findings. Finally, the main conclusions, contributions and limitations of the study are reviewed.

BACKGROUND

Nowadays, most of that information is provided and freely available in the official websites of public bodies. The Internet created new opportunities for social interactions. The potential benefits of the use of digital communication for social development are well recognized. Public bodies like local governments use the Internet to communicate with their stakeholders in a simple, rapid and effective way. However, sometimes people just assume that the Internet is accessible for everybody. This is a wrong assumption.

For instance, in Portugal in 2012, only 66% of households had access to broadband service and 62% of people between 16 and 74 years old use computers. Even if the ICT penetration rate is 100%, one must guarantee that digital applications used by public entities, like public websites, are accessible for everyone. In the public arena, accountability should be for all. At the core of the accountability process lays a "moral ideal". So, if public bodies use websites as a mechanism to provide information then, this mechanism should be accessible to everyone, no matter what are their physical limitations.

Accountability and Transparency

Accountability is normally treated as an abstract ideal. Politicians' narratives often refer to accountability in an ambiguous and unprecise way. Accountability is a plural concept that can have different meanings depending on the actors, on the context and on the purposes and there is no single concrete and operative definition (Bovens, 2007, 2010; Ebrahim, 2003; Murtaza, 2012; Samuel, 1992). Actually, accountability can be discussed as an objective vs. a subjective concept (Cutt and Murray, 2000). It can be analyzed in its external (explicit) or internal (implicit) dimensions (Ebrahim, 2003; Walker, 2002). It can follow a downward vs. upward model (Jacobs & Wilford, 2010; O'Dwyer & Unerman, 2010; Wellens & Jegers, 2014). It can be approached as a political (Weingart, 1999), a normative (Ebrahim, 2009), an instrumental (Moynihan, 2003) or a functional (O'Dwyer and Unerman, 2007) issue. Moreover, accountability is a relational concept. It has an implicit relationship between an entity/organization and its stakeholders. Taking in that there are multiple stakeholders, one can sustain that there are also multiple accountabilities (Cavill & Sohail, 2007; Ebrahim, 2010; Volkmann, Tokarski, & Ernst, 2012). This multiplicity of relations happens within a certain social and economic context and each one has its own dynamic. These dynamic influences are influenced by the context in which they happen. Indeed, the accountability process should solidify the rights of citizens by promoting their active participation in decision-making and getting them to debate and influence decisions of common interest. This collaborative attitude can only be effective if information is shared (Warren, 2007; Jordan, 2007; Hardina, 2011).

In the context of social nonprofit organizations, Jäger (2014) identified six main approaches. However, these theoretical approaches are commons, or at least extensive, to all kind of organization. The biggest changes is the answer to the question "To whom is the organization accountable?" as it is shown in table 1.

We do not interpret these approaches as blocked perspectives. By the contrary, they are rooted in gradual concept. However, the strategies, processes and mechanisms of accountability adopted by the organization are not neutral. They are influence by, and can also influence, the context and the behaviors of the actors involved. How does an organization archives accountability depend on the shared values and social meaning? Accountability is therefore a social construct. Accountability mechanisms are part of the means by which organizations inform, negotiate and consult stakeholders on a number of aspects concerning their performance and mission. The development of information and communications technology (ICT) has been an important incitement to the divulgation of information in the public sector. It has empowered the citizens because it stimulates participation in public affairs and its embeddedness into everyday community life and interconnectivity (Grimmelikhuijsen & Welch, 2012; Fleisch, 2004; Hilty et al., 2004; Hildebrandt, 2008; Koops et al., 2009; Meister et al., 2008).

In the public sphere, both political and administrative entities are exposed to public scrutiny. Therefore, accountability is always associated with the provision of information about public resources management, responsibility for the process and the consequences of the management. In other words, there is no accountability without transparency. In the context of this study, transparency is seen as a component

Table 1. Approaches of local government accountability

Accountability Approaches	Core Concept	To Whom is the Local Government Accountable?	How does it Achieve Accountability?
Normative approach	Normative/ethical	Society	Moral obligation to provide justifications for the way the local government aims at achieving its mission.
Relational approach	Embeddedness stakeholder	• Relationships among organizational actors embedded in a social and institutional environment • Particular sets of stakeholders	• Negotiate criteria measures and interpretation of success • Legitimacy is socially constructed
Stakeholder approach	External stakeholder	• Specific stakeholders such as politicians, bureaucratic directors, government agencies, public organizations, decision makers, institutional supporters, staff, local citizens, nonprofit organizations, representatives of civil society, wider public • The stakeholders maps	• Multiple approach to satisfy different expectations of stakeholders • Public as legitimating reference body balances all stakeholders relation as important sum
Rule-based approach	Legality	• Specific set of stakeholders • Technical stakeholders	• Objective standards of assessment • Predictable and legal stream of information
Strategic approach	Strategy	• Local citizens to guarantee their vote in future elections • Political organizations to gain their support in political options	• Tools to provide arguments to support the organization' mission • Information on outcomes achieved calculi expectations local government fulfills with its services
Learning approach	Organizational learning	Local government for improvement its effectiveness	• Learning how to improve activities in order to achieve local government mission • Creating a culture of accountability that is built on mission and purpose

Source: (Adapted from Jäger, 2014)

of accountability. Following the definition of proposed by T/A Initiative (2016), "Transparency is a characteristic of governments, companies, organizations and individuals that are open in the clear disclosure of information, rules, plans, processes and actions". Indeed, there is no effective accountability without transparency. These two concepts reinforce each other. However, the concept of transparency is narrower than the concept of accountability. It is about information accessible in a timely and user-friendly manner (Eijffinger & Hoeberichts, 2002; Hess, 2007)

The positive impact of information accessibility and public communication on society's development is widely recognized. Seminal work of Schramm (1970) brought some evidences on that. The access to information is understood as a precondition for social development. Summarizing the argument, there is no real development without democracy, there is no democracy without free transparency on public management, and there is no transparency without access to information (Sen & Mendes, 2000). In this line of thought, the relation between information accessibility and citizenship is easy to understand (Bezzon, 2004; Di Felice, 2008; Carniello, 2015) The local government communication in the digital environment is a huge opportunity for providing easy and free access to information and develop the capability of citizens' participation in public affairs and in the work of government (Bingham, Nabatchi, & O'Leary, 2005).

The present paper is mainly exploratory. As stated above, it focus on transparency for everyone and interpret inclusiveness as a moral value that should be promoted by public organizations. In such context, it is useful to think on accountability in a normative manner. More specifically, the study pretends to set out web accessibility a criterion by which transparency of Portuguese local municipalities is judged.

Web Accessibility

According to the W3C, web accessibility is "an universal web access, independent of hardware, software, network infrastructure, language, culture, geographical localization an user capabilities" (ISO 9241-171, 2008).

The universal availability of web resources is essential for disabled people to guarantee equal opportunities of access to digital services and information provided by the government. Websites can offer barriers to different types of disabilities:

- Visual, auditory and cognitive impairments present different accessibility challenges that must be addressed by governments (W3C, 2016).

The basic principles of web accessibility allow improving web access not only for disabled people but also for any other individuals that otherwise could be excluded by software, hardware or cultural differences (W3C, 2012).

The Web Accessibility Initiative (WAI) defines guidelines for the assessment of accessibility levels of websites, helping not only to improve web accessibility, but also facilitating the development of tools for reviewing and even repairing websites. The WAI also advocates the importance of web accessibility and contributes to the education of web developers (WAI, 2016).

The WAI developed the Web Content Accessibility Guidelines (WCAG) (Reid et al., 2008). Its main purpose is to provide a development guide for the web and its contents, guiding it to an accessible design and reducing the barriers to information access (Reid et al., 2008). Four basic principles define the basis of the proposed metrics:

Principle 1: Perceivable.
   Information and user interface components must be presented to the users in a perceivable way.
Principle 2: Operable.
   User interface components and navigation must be operable.
Principle 3: Understandable.
   Information and operation of the user interface must be understandable.
Principle 4: Robust.
   Content must be robust enough that it can be reliably interpreted by a wide variety of user agents, including assistive technologies.

These principles are refined in the guidelines (see Appendix 1, Tables 7, 8, 9 and 10). Each guideline has a set of satisfaction criteria that can be audited with manual inspections or using automated tools. Websites can be categorized according to their accessibility rating, that is, their agreement with the WCAG 2.0 principles, guidelines and satisfaction criteria (Reid et al., 2008). These website accessibility levels are:

Level A: Fulfills all satisfaction criteria present in the initial level.

Level AA: Satisfies all the criteria in Level A and AA or provides an alternative version compliant with this level.

Level AAA: Satisfies all criteria in Levels A, AA and AAA, or provides an alternative version compliant with this level.

RESEARCH METHODOLOGY

The main challenge posed to any researcher in this field is creating conditions so that citizens can consult the accountability, increasing literacy in the area and promoting the active participation of residents in political life.

The initial question that needed to be answered to build such a model could be phrased as follows:

- "Are official websites transparent and web accessible for all?"

Questions

To provide an operational answer (necessarily open and comprehensive) to the previous question, three sub-questions included in Table 1 should first be answered.

Sample and Data Collection

To answer the above questions, the study used data from differences sources depending on the variables, as shown in Table 3.

Design of the Research

The study was conducted in three steps, each one related to one of the three research questions. The two first steps are independent from each other. The third step explores the relation between transparency and web accessibility.

Table 2. Research Questions

Q1 – Focus on Transparency Is the information available in the websites transparent enough?
Q2 – Focus on Web Accessibility Are the official websites available for all?
Q3 – Focus on Relation Between Transparency and Accessibility Is there any statistical relation with the MTI on official websites available for all?

Table 3. Data sources

Variables	**Data Sources**
Transparency	Secondary data TIAC website (http://poderlocal.transparencia.pt/)
Accessibility	Primary data The data resulted from the analysis of 86 municipal websites (see table 13) using the automatic tool - Achecker.

Step 1: Focus on Transparency

The study used data available from the Municipal Transparency Index (MTI). It was created by the Transparência e Integridade Associação Cívica (Civic Association for Transparency and Integrity - TIAC). With the creation of the MTI, TIAC aimed to contribute for a better democracy.

The MIT is composed of 76 indicators grouped in seven dimensions:

- Dimension A
  - Information about the political structure and the organizational structure of the local bodies, their members and functions. It considers eighteen indicators.
- Dimension B
  - Information about the political options, strategic and operational plans. It considers thirteen indicators.
- Dimension C
  - Information about taxes, fees, tariffs, prices and rulebooks. It considers five indicators.
- Dimension D
  - Information about the relation with society. It considers eight indicators.
- Dimension E
  - Information about public contracts. It considers ten indicators.
- Dimension F
  - Information about economic and financial performance. It considers twelve indicators.
- Dimension G
  - Information about the urbanization options. It considers ten indicators.

As one can see by this list of dimensions, the index does not have any dimension related to accessibility, any kind of accessibility. Moreover, from the list of the seventy-six indicators, there is not any to measure web accessibility.

Indeed, the authors of the index considered it relevant if the information is available but ignore whether it is accessible to all. That means that a municipality can be classified as transparent even if it ignores some of their citizens.

Step 2: Focus on Web Accessibility

The methodology used in this study was based on the W3C WCAG 2.0 recommendations. Due to the number of sites to inspect, the first approach was to use an automated inspection tool. The AChecker Tool (AChecker Website, 2011) was chosen for use. It is an online inspection tool of the WCAG 2.0 recommendations (Reid et al., 2008). This tool checks single HTML pages for conformance with accessibility standards to ensure the content can be accessed by everyone.

The next part, W3C WCAG 2.0 Recommendations, presents the sequence of actions performed and the adaptations necessary for this particular study.

1. **Phase One:** Define the evaluation goals

a. Define the compliance level of the evaluation. In this study, it was decided to perform an evaluation at the AAA level. Define the tool that will support the evaluation. The study opted to perform an automatic evaluation using AChecker (see http://achecker.ca/checker/index. php.). It is frequently used by researchers, such as Gambino, O., Pirrone, R. & Giorgio (2016) and Marques, L. F. C. et al. (2016).

2. **Phase Two:** Explore the pages of the websites
   a. Identify which are the main pages of the portal. This study opted to focus on the home page of each official website. The criteria used for the pages selection was the URL provided by the municipality. However, in later stages, the study will be extended to other pages that provide financial reports. It analyzed all the websites of the municipalities of the NUT II – Portugal North1, eighty-six, in April 2016.

3. **Phase Three:** Sample page selection
   a. As the study had exploratory characteristics, it did not use a survey to define the web pages to analyze; the analysis was restricted to the home page.

4. **Phase Four:** Define the document for data registration.
   a. This study used a spreadsheet to consolidate the data generated by AChecker. In the AChecker tool it is possible to select the compliance level to evaluate (A, AA or AAA). It is also possible to choose the specification to use: WCAG 1.0, WCAG 2.0. In this study the A, AA and AAA levels were evaluated, based on the WCAG 2.0 specification (ISO 9241-171, 2008; ISO/TS 16071, 2003).

5. **Phase Five:** Evaluate the selected page sample.
   a. The home page for each site was analyzed by AChecker. A summary report of the analysis was generated by the tool, containing the number of known problems to be corrected and other aspects, namely HTML validation and CSS validation. The report information was categorized by each WCAG 2.0 checklists.

Step 3: Focus on Relation Between Transparency and Web Accessibility

The MTI does not include any dimension or even an indicator to measure accessible. This is an important limitation of the index. A developed society cannot ignore minorities. If accountability is a social construct, i.e., it lies on core common values and meanings, and if a society ignores its group of disabled people, then no matter how much information is provided, there will be no real democracy. Based on that, the study explored static association between MTI (each of its dimension and indicators) and web accessibility looking for any potential (possible), or even indirect, measures of accessibility.

ANALYSIS AND DISCUSSION OF RESULTS

Transparency

As stated above, the study used secondary data available on the TIAC website. But before carrying out the data analysis, its reliability was tested. To do so, the study collected fifteen of the seventy-six indicators from each of the eighty-six websites under investigation. It then compared the data collected with information available in the MTI database. The reliability was highly satisfactory because a 99%

Table 4. Descriptive statistics related to transparency

	N	Average	Standard Deviation	Minimum	Maximum
Guidelines with error	66	3.20	2.25	.00	8.00
Number of errors	66	53.48	118.44	.00	675.0
Municipal Transparency Index	66	48.18	20.16	7.97	94.23
Municipal Transparency Ranking	66	33.50	19.20	1	66
Dimension A	66	44.26	24.46	7.14	100
Dimension B	66	36.90	18.10	.00	71.43
Dimension C	66	45.45	28.67	.00	100
Dimension D	66	48.80	24.31	14.29	100
Dimension E	66	28.57	34.68	.00	92.86
Dimension F	66	81.60	20.32	.00	100
Dimension G	66	50.32	22.39	.00	92.86

match was obtained. This procedure provided a high confidence level. In table 4 it is summarized some descriptive statistics related to transparency:

Web Accessibility

The eighty-six websites were evaluated using AChecker by inputting the URL of each official municipal website in the tool and then analyzing each one.

The results for each satisfaction criteria were grouped as follows:

1. **Problem:** The tool detected at least one problem that implies that the criteria cannot be satisfied.
2. **Errors Number:** The tool detected error numbers by guideline.
3. **Not Applicable:** The website did not have elements to allow the evaluation of the reviewed satisfaction criteria.

Three main analyses were performed. In the first one, a ranking of the municipalities was built by the number of problems presented in the thirty-eight satisfaction criteria reviewed (see Table 13, Appendix 3).
In the second one, this question was answered:

- What are the most violated guidelines among the municipalities?

This analysis sought to gather information about the compliance to accessibility principles.
The eighty-six websites were analysed (NUT II – North municipalities). NUT II – North consists of a total of 86 municipalities:

- 10 of Alto Minho;
- 6 of Cávado;
- 8 of Ave;

- 17 of the Porto Metropolitan Area;
- 6 of Alto Tâmega;
- 11 of the Tâmega and Sousa;
- 19 of the Duero;
- 9 of Trás-os-Montes.

We decided to begin by examining this NUT but we intend to extend the study to all NUTS II.

The AChecker tool did not read the HTML code of 20 websites (see Table 13, Appendix 3). When we checked the homepage we received the message: HTTP 504: "Gateway Timeout". This is an HTTP status code and this error means that one server did not receive a timely response from another server that it was accessing while attempting to load the web page or fill another request by the browser

Figure 1 shows the website numbers and percentages with certification, according to the logotype presented in the home page.

Even though the analysis was realized in public entities, it was verified that web accessibility isn't a concern for municipal managers as 76% of the websites do not have W3C certification. For the others, 19% of the websites have certification level A, 3% have certification level AAA and 2% have certification level AA.

Table 5 presents a summary ranking of the municipalities by the number of problems presented in the thirty-eight satisfaction criteria reviewed. The information present in Table 5 can be viewed in more detail in Table 13, Appendix 3.

To complement table 5, it is presented information about error numbers by guideline in table 6. When the number is 0, the guideline does not exist in the table.

According to results of the automated analysis, it was verified that the tool detects at most guidelines with errors. It was also verified that there are websites with 0 errors. However, the local managers hadn't

Figure 1. Number of websites with different web accessibility

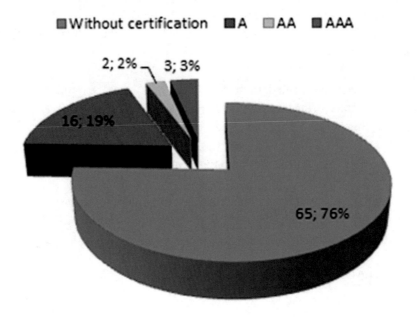

Table 5. Number of guidelines with errors

		Number of Websites	Percentage	Cumulative percentage
Number of guidelines with error	0	10	15.2%	15.2%
	1	7	10.6%	25.8%
	2	10	15.2%	40.9%
	3	9	13.6%	54.5%
	4	12	18.2%	72.7%
	5	8	12.1%	84.8%
	6	4	6.1%	90.9%
	7	3	4.5%	95.5%
	8	3	4.5%	100.0%
Total		66	100.0%	

asked for the certification at that moment. Moreover, there were 2 websites where the WC3 certification logotype (website of Vinhais and Oliveira de Azeméis, level A and AAA, respectively) and the tool did not read the HTML code (see Table 13, Appendix 3).

This table data allows one to state that the most violated guidelines by the municipalities are 1.1.1 Non-text content (Lvl A) and 1.4.3 Contrast (Minimum) (Lvl AA) – Perceivable principle – and 2.1.1 Keyboard (Lvl A) - Operable principle. These errors are easy to solve and a very useful feature for some tools such as readers for blind people. Also, an automated review of this feature consists of a low cost evaluation. This implies that with few resources, a great improvement in the official websites could be made.

In 2014, the Association for the Promotion and Development of Information Society (APDSI) released a study to determine the state of the 1000 biggest small and medium companies of Portugal (Gonçalves, 2015), according to the norms of WCAG 2.0 (see Figure 2).

While assessing the motives of the low adhesion to the W3C certification, the authors of the APDSI study came to the following conclusions:

1. Low sensibility for the subject by enterprises, top managers and web development professionals.
2. Feasibility on the application of the norms (W3C). There are several complaints present in some studies about the nature of some norms and the effort involved in their application.
3. Legislation.
4. Shows lack of information.

Even though the current study was made in the public sector and the APDSI's study focused on the private sector, it was verified that the problem was common to both.

Transparency and Web Accessibility

The basic assumption of MTI is that to be really free and democratic, a society needs to have institutions that are transparent in their action and provide information with such attributes as:

Table 6. Number of satisfaction criteria with problems for each WCAG guideline

Principle	Guidelines WCAG 2.0	Number	Minimum	Maximum	Average	Standard Deviation
1. Perceivable	1.1.1 Non text content (Level (lvl) A)	66	0	624	42.54	114.57
	1.4.3 Contrast (Minimum) (Lvl AA)	66	0	128	11.02	25.37
	1.3.1 Info and Relationships (Lvl A)	66	0	21	3.22	4.86
	1.4.4 Resize text (Lvl AA)	66	0	63	2.52	9.51
	1.4.6 Contrast (Enhanced) (Lvl AAA)	66	0	235	5.30	34.64
2. Operable	2.1.1 Keyboard (Lvl A)	66	0	80	4.70	15.13
	2.4.4 Link Purpose (In Context) (Lvl A)	66	0	42	1.67	6.25
	2.4.6 Headings and Labels (Lvl AA)	66	0	3	0.30	0.73
	2.4.2 Page Titled (Lvl A)	66	0	1	0.02	0.15
3. Understandable	3.3.2 Labels or Instructions (Lvl A)	66	0	13	2.09	2.62
	3.1.1 Language of Page (Lvl A)	66	0	2	0.46	0.84
	3.2.2 On Input (Lvl A)	66	0	10	0.22	1.47
4. Robust	4.1.1 Parsing (Lvl A)	66	0	1	0.22	0.42

Figure 2. Study Results (Adapted from Gonçalves, 2015)

Elements/Websites

2 742,34

Average Errors/Elements

0,7

Average		Standard Deviation		Minimum		Maximum	
A	604	A	540	A	0	A	3161
AA	99	AA	98	AA	0	AA	546
AAA	203	AAA	200	AAA	0	AAA	1019

- Relevant,
- Intelligible,
- Reliable,
- Complete,
- Timely and
- Easy to access (TIAC, 2016).

However, when TIAC refer to "easy to access", it ignores that disabled people have special needs. Considering Internet information, those needs are easy to satisfy. It is a question of kindness. There is no need for extra money to be kind. If public entities are aware of that, then with little effort it is possible to practice accountability in an inclusive way.

We explore data looking for statistic relations between Web accessibility and each of the seven dimensions pondered in MTI. Once the study had two alternatives measures of web accessibility, it explored the statistical associations between these alternatives measures.

As was expected, it found a high positive association between the Web accessibility measured by the number of errors and the Web accessibility measured by the guidelines with error (r =,873; ρ<, 001).

The study went further in data exploration by looking for statistical relations between web accessibility and each of the seven dimensions pondered in MTI.

As we can see in table 7, there is a low positive association between web accessibility (number of errors) and Municipal Transparency Index; Dimension C; Dimension D and Dimension F. In all cases, evidences of association are too weak to deserve further investigation. Moreover, when we investigate each of the indicator which compose the dimensions under analyse, we did not find any significate association.

The Table 8 results are different from those shown in Table 7. Indeed, while in Table 7 Dimension C, D and F have significant association with web accessibility, Table 8 only shows low positive association between web accessibility (measured by the number of guidelines with errors) and the Dimension C. Once again, the associations are very low. Even so, for each of the indicators that compose those dimensions, there were not found any significant associations. When one considers the MTI or the position in the ranking, a significant association was also found, but it the statistic association is low. Besides, there is no theoretical support that justifies additional investigation. Consequently, one can conclude that the actual MTI does not measure web accessibility.

These results reinforce the argument that it is important to introduce an indicator of web accessibility in the MTI. Developed society can no longer ignore any kind of discrimination against individuals with disabilities. It makes no sense to classify a local government as highly transparent if this transparency is not accessible for everyone. Thus, we recommend a revision of MTI by including a measure of web accessibility. As stated in Americans with Disabilities Act of 1990, Amendments Act of 2008, "physical and mental disabilities in no way diminish a person's right to fully participate in all aspects of society, but that people with physical or mental disabilities are frequently precluded from doing so because of prejudice, antiquated attitudes, or the failure to remove societal and institutional barriers".

CONCLUSION

By definition, local government is a political power close to citizens and constitutes a mainstay of democracy. In Portugal, it is playing a vital role in the local development dynamic. Portuguese local

Table 7. Relations Between number of errors and MTI dimensions

Questions	N	Correlation Coefficient (*r*)	Comments
Is there any statistical relation between web accessibility (number of errors) and municipal transparency index?	**66**	**.247***	**Low positive association**
Is there any statistical relation between web accessibility (number of errors) and municipal transparency ranking?	66	-.238	Not significant
Is there any statistical relation between web accessibility (number of errors) and transparency on political and organizational structures (Dimension A)?	66	.192	Not significant
Is there any statistical relation between web accessibility (number of errors) and transparency on strategic and operational plans (Dimension B)?	66	.197	Not significant
Is there any statistical relation between web accessibility (number of errors) and transparency on taxes and prices policy (Dimension C)?	**66**	**.287***	**Low positive association**
Is there any statistical relation between web accessibility (number of errors) and transparency on relation with society (Dimension D)?	**66**	**.297***	**Low positive association**
Is there any statistical relation between web accessibility (number of errors) and transparency on public contracts (Dimension E)?	66	-.075	Not significant
Is there any statistical relation between web accessibility (number of errors) and transparency on economic and financial performance (Dimension F)?	**66**	**.267***	**Low positive association**
Is there any statistical relation between web accessibility (number of errors) and transparency on urbanizations options (Dimension G)?	66	.233	Not significant

Significance of correlation coefficient: * $p < .05$; ** $p < .01$; *** $p < .001$

1. Pearson´s coefficient for all variables, except for MT Ranking for which it was calculated the Spearman´s coefficient.

Table 8. Relations between number of guidelines with errors and MTI dimensions

Questions	N	Correlation Coefficient (*r*)	Comments
Is there any statistical relation between web accessibility (guidelines with error) and municipal transparency index?	**66**	**.287***	**Low positive association**
Is there any statistical relation between web accessibility (guidelines with error) and municipal transparency ranking?	66	-.226	Not significant
Is there any statistical relation between web accessibility (guidelines with error) and transparency on political and organizational structures (Dimension A)?	66	.227	Not significant
Is there any statistical relation between web (guidelines with error) and transparency on strategic and operational plans (Dimension B)?	66	.194	Not significant
Is there any statistical relation between web accessibility (guidelines with error) and transparency on taxes and prices policy (Dimension C)?	66	.277	Not significant
Is there any statistical relation between web accessibility (guidelines with error) and transparency on relation with society (Dimension D)?	**66**	**.280***	**Low positive association**
Is there any statistical relation between web accessibility (guidelines with error) and transparency on public contracts (Dimension E)?	66	.211	Not significant
Is there any statistical relation between web accessibility (guidelines with error) and transparency on economic and financial performance (Dimension F)?	66	.232	Not significant
Is there any statistical relation between web accessibility (guidelines with error) and transparency on urbanizations options (Dimension G)?	66	.234	Not significant

Significance of correlation coefficient: * $p < .05$; ** $p < .01$; *** $p < .001$

2. Pearson´s coefficient for all variables, except for MT Ranking for which it was calculated the Spearman´s coefficient.

governments are adopting the web as a primordial mechanism to provide and disseminate information and communicate with citizens. This option is perceived by society as synonymous with transparency and trust (Song & Lee, 2016). However, public accountability is, or should be, an inclusive concept.

This study aimed to contribute to the discussion about transparency as a social value. Currently, Portuguese transparency in local government is being assessed through the MTI. This study argued that the components of MTI must be revised to include specific indicators of web accessibility. The results data showed that there is a low association between the MTI and web accessibility. The results reinforced the study arguments that it is urgent to redesign the MTI.

Considering web accessibility assessment, the study proposed an adaptation of the WCAG Evaluation Methodology to apply an automated inspection of municipality websites based on the defined satisfaction criteria. Although this approach can be considered incomplete, important information can be gathered with a low cost and little effort. The study results showed that municipal websites with the worst evaluations violate 8 of the criteria without a need of further analysis.

The study found out that the most violated principle is perceivable. It also reviewed the usefulness of the study approach, concluding that automated reviews can help to improve the Perceivable principle, while little value is added in the evaluation of the Operable principle, which needs manual reviews for conclusive results.

Future work should focus extending to all NUTS II and on reviewing other sections of websites besides the home page. Also, the authors are conducting manual reviews to fulfil the original WCAG Evaluation Methodology recommendations. In the future, they will compare the manual and automated approaches to find possible relationships between their results.

REFERENCES

W3C website. (2012). *Introduction to Web Accessibility*. Retrieved Mach 23, 2016, from http://www.w3.org/WAI/intro/accessibility.php

W3C website. (2016). *Designing for Inclusion*. Retrieved Mach 1, 2016, from https://www.w3.org/WAI/users/Overview.html

Achecker Website. (2011). Retrieved Mach 2, 2016, from http://achecker.ca/checker/index.php

Americans with Disabilities Act of 1990, Amendments Act of 2008

Arnold, A.-K., & Garcia, H. (2011). *Generating genuine demand for accountability through communication. The World Bank communication for governance & accountability program (commgap) external affairs*. Washington, DC: World Bank.

Besson, L. (2004). *Análise político-sociológica do reencontro da sociedade civil brasileira com a cidadania e a democracia segundo a perspectiva da comunicação pública. OLIVEIRA, MJ da C. Comunicação pública*. Campinas: Alínea.

Bingham, L. B., Nabatchi, T., & OLeary, R. (2005). The new governance: Practices and processes for stakeholder and citizen participation in the work of government. *Public Administration Review, 65*(5), 547–558. doi:10.1111/j.1540-6210.2005.00482.x

Bovens, M. (2007). Public Accountability. In E. Ferlie, L. E. Lynn Jr, & C. Pollitt (Eds.), *The Oxford Handbook of Public Management*. doi:10.1093/oxfordhb/9780199226443.003.0009

Bovens, M. (2010). Two Concepts of Accountability: Accountability as Virtue and as a Mechanism. *West European Politics*, *33*(5), 946–967. doi:10.1080/01402382.2010.486119

Carniello, M. F. (2015). Proposta Metodológica de Avaliação de Comunicação Governamental Digital. *Revista Observatório*, *1*(2), 101–116. doi:10.20873/uft.2447-4266.2015v1n2p101

Cavil, S., & Sohail, M. (2007). Increasing strategic accountability: A framework for international NGOs. *Development in Practice*, *17*(2), 231–248. doi:10.1080/09614520701196004

Cohen, J., Cohen, P., West, S., & Aiken, L. (2013). *Applied multiple regression/correlation analysis for the behavioral sciences*. Routledge.

Donaldson, T., & Preston, L. (1995). The stakeholder theory of the corporation: Concepts, Evidence, and Implications. *Academy of Management Review*, *20*(1), 65–91.

Dos Santos, M. J., Carniello, M. F., & Oliveira, E. A. D. A. Q. (2013). Comunicação digital na gestão pública dos municípios da RMVP: Acesso à informação, transparência e mecanismos de participação. *Revista Brasileira de Desenvolvimento Regional*, *1*(1), 167–184.

Ebrahim, A. (2003). Accountability in Practice: Mechanisms for NGOs. *World Development*, *31*(5), 813–829. doi:10.1016/S0305-750X(03)00014-7

Ebrahim, A. (2009). Placing the Normative Logics of Accountability in Thick Perspective. *The American Behavioral Scientist*, *52*(6), 885–904. doi:10.1177/0002764208327664

Ebrahim, A. (2010). *The Many Faces of Nonprofit Accountability*. Working Paper 10 -069. Harvard Business School.

Eijffinger, S. C., & Hoeberichts, M. (2002). Central bank accountability and transparency: Theory and some evidence. *International Finance*, *5*(1), 73–96. doi:10.1111/1468-2362.00088

Di Felice (2008). D*o público para as redes: a comunicação digital e as novas formas de participação social*. São Caetano do Sul: Difusão, 2008.

Fleisch, E. (2004). Business impact of pervasive technologies: Opportunities and risks. *Human and Ecological Risk Assessment*, *10*(5), 817–829. doi:10.1080/10807030490513838

Fontaine, C., Haarman, A., & Schmid, S. (2006). *Stakeholder Theory of the MNC*. Retrieved April 23, 2016, from http://www.edalys.fr/documents/Stakeholders%20theory.pdf

Gonçalves, R. (2015). *Fórum para a Sociedade de Informação – Acessibilidade Web*. Retrieved June 20, 2016, from http://www.apdsi.pt/uploads/news/id950/01%20-%20Ramiro%20Goncalves%20-%20Bar%C3%B3metro%20da%20Acessibilidade%20Web%2020132015%20-%20Estado%20da%20Acessibilidade%20Web.pdf

Grimmelikhuijsen, S., & Welch, E. (2012). Developing and Testing a Theoretical Framework for Computer-Mediated Transparency of Local Governments. *Public Administration Review*, *72*(4), 562–571. doi:10.1111/j.1540-6210.2011.02532.x

Hardina, D. (2011). Are Social Service Managers Encouraging Consumer Participation in Decision Making in Organizations? *Administration in Social Work*, *35*(2), 117–137. doi:10.1080/03643107.2011.557583

Hess, D. (2007). Social reporting and new governance regulation: The prospects of achieving corporate accountability through transparency. *Business Ethics Quarterly*, *17*(03), 453–476. doi:10.5840/beq200717348

Hildebrandt, M. (2008). Ambient intelligence, criminal liability and democracy. *Criminal Law and Philosophy*, *2*(2), 163–180. doi:10.1007/s11572-007-9042-1

Hilty, L. M., Som, C., & Koehler, A. (2004). Assessing the Human, Social and Environmental. Risks of Pervasive Computing. *Journal of Human and Ecological Risk Assessment*, *10*(5), 853–874. doi:10.1080/10807030490513874

ISO 9241-171:2008. (2008). *Ergonomics of human-system interaction -- Part 171: Guidance on software accessibility*. Retrieved April 2, from http://www.iso.org/iso/home/store/catalogue_ics/catalogue_detail_ics.htm?csnumber=39080

ISO/TS 16071:2003. (2003). *Ergonomics of human-system interaction -- Guidance on accessibility for human-computer interfaces*. Retrieved March 30, from http://www.iso.org/iso/catalogue_detail.htm?csnumber=30858

Jacobs, A., & Wilford, R. (2010). Listen First: A Pilot System for Managing Downward Accountability in NGO. *Development in Practice*, *20*(7), 797–811. doi:10.1080/09614524.2010.508113

Jäger, U. (2014). *Managing Social Businesses: Mission, Governance, Strategy and Accountability*. Basingstoke, UK: Palgrave MacMillan.

Jordan, L. (2007). A rights -based approach to accountability. In Global Accountabilities: participation, pluralism, and public ethic (pp. 151-167) New York: Cambridge University Press.

Koops, B. J., Hildebrandt, M., & Jaquet-Chiffelle, D. O. (2010). Bridging the accountability gap: Rights for new entities in the information society? *Minnesota Journal of Law Science & Technology*, *11*(2), 497–561.

Marques, L. F. C., Guilhermino, D. F., de Araújo Cardoso, M. E., da Silva Neitzel, R. A. L., Lopes, L. A., Merlin, J. R., & dos Santos Striquer, G. (2016, July). Accessibility in Virtual Communities of Practice Under the Optics of Inclusion of Visually Impaired. In *International Conference on Universal Access in Human-Computer Interaction* (pp. 14-26). Springer International Publishing. doi:10.1007/978-3-319-40250-5_2

Meister, M., Pias, M., Topfer, E., & Coulouris, G. (2008). Application Scenarios for Cooperating Objects and their Social, Legal and Ethical Challenges. In *Adjunct Proceedings of First International Conference on The Internet of Things*.

Moynihan, D. P. (2003). Normative and instrumental perspectives on public participation citizen summits in Washington, DC. *American Review of Public Administration*, *33*(2), 164–188. doi:10.1177/0275074003251379

Murtaza, N. (2012). Putting the Lasts First. *The Case for Community-Focused and Peer-Managed NGO Accountability Mechanisms, 23,* 109–125.

Nielsen, J., & Loranger, H. (2006). *Web usability.* New Riders.

ODwyer, B., & Unerman, J. (2007). From functional to social accountability: Transforming the accountability relationship between funders and non governmental development organisations. *Accounting, Auditing & Accountability Journal, 20*(3), 446–471. doi:10.1108/09513570710748580

ODwyer, B., & Unerman, J. (2010). Enhancing the role of accountability in promoting the rights of beneficiaries of development NGOs. *Accounting and Business Review, 40*(5), 451–471. doi:10.1080/0 0014788.2010.9995323

Reid, L.G., Vanderheiden, G., Cooper, M., & Caldwell, B. (2008). *Web Content Accessibility Guidelines (WCAG) 2.0.* W3C.

Samuel, P. (1992). Accountability in public services: Exit, voice and control. *World Development, 20*(7), 1047–1060. doi:10.1016/0305-750X(92)90130-N

Sen, A., & Mendes, R. (2000). *Desenvolvimento como liberdade.* São Paulo: Companhia das Letras.

Shah, B. P., & Shakya, S. (2007). Evaluating the web accessibility of websites of the central government of Nepal. ACM Press. doi:10.1145/1328057.1328154

Song, C., & Lee, J. (2016). Citizens' Use of Social Media in Government, Perceived Transparency, and Trust in Government. *Public Performance & Management Review, 39*(2).

T/A Initiative. (2016). Retrieved from www.transparency-initiative.org/about/definitions

Volkmann, C., Tokarski, K. O., & Ernst, K. (2012). *Social entrepreneurship and social business. An Introduction and Discussion with Case Studies.* Wiesbaden: Gabler.

Walker, P. (2002). Understanding Accountability: Theoretical Models and their Implications for Social Service Organizations. *Social Policy and Administration, 36*(1), 62–75. doi:10.1111/1467-9515.00270

Warren, J. (2007). *Service User and Carer Participation in Social Work.* Glasgow, UK: Learning Matters Ltd.

Web site WAI. (2016). *Web Accessibility Initiative (WAI).* Retrieved Mach 5, 2016, from http://www.w3.org/WAI

Weingart, P. (1999). Scientific expertise and political accountability: Paradoxes of science in politics. *Science & Public Policy, 26*(3), 151–161. doi:10.3152/147154399781782437

Wellens, L., & Jegers, M. (2014). Beneficiary participation as an instrument of downward accountability: A multiple case study. *European Management Journal, 32*(6), 938–949. doi:10.1016/j.emj.2014.03.004

KEY TERMS AND DEFINITIONS

Accountability: Means ensuring that officials in public, private and voluntary sector organizations are answerable for their actions and that there is redress when duties and commitments are not met. Accountability is an institutionalized (i.e. regular, established, accepted) relationship between different actors. One set of people/organizations are held to account ('accountees'), and another set do the holding ('accounters'). There are many ways in which people and organizations might be held to account. (Transparency and Accountability Initiative)

AChecker: Is an open source Web accessibility evaluation tool. It can be used to review the accessibility of Web pages based on a variety international accessibility guidelines.

Transparency: Means to act visibly, predictably and understandably to promote participation and accountability. Simply making information available is not sufficient to achieve transparency. Large amounts of raw information in the public domain may breed opacity rather than transparency. Information should be managed and published so that it is relevant, accessible, timely and accurate (Transparency and Accountability Initiative)

Web Accessibility Initiative (WAI): Brings together people from industry, disability organizations, government, and research labs from around the world to develop guidelines and resources to help make the Web accessible to people with disabilities including auditory, cognitive, neurological, physical, speech, and visual disabilities." (W3C, 2016)

Web Accessibility: Means that people with disabilities can perceive, understand, navigate, and interact with the Web, and that they can contribute to the Web. Web accessibility also benefits others, including older people with changing abilities due to aging.

Web Content Accessibility Guidelines (WCAG) 2.0: Covers a wide range of recommendations for making Web content more accessible. Following these guidelines will make content accessible to a wider range of people with disabilities, including blindness and low vision, deafness and hearing loss, learning disabilities, cognitive limitations, limited movement, speech disabilities, photosensitivity and combinations of these. Following these guidelines will also often make your Web content more usable to users in general" (W3C, 2008).

APPENDIX 1

Table 9. WCAG 2.0 checklists

Principle	Guideline		Level
1. Perceivable	1.1 Text Alternatives	1.1.1 Non-text Content	A
	1.2 Time-based Media	1.2.1 Audio-only and Video-only (Pre-recorded)	A
		1.2.2 Captions (Pre-recorded)	A
		1.2.3 Audio Description or Media Alternative (Pre-recorded)	A
		1.2.4 Captions (Live)	AA
		1.2.5 Audio Description (Pre-recorded)	AA
		1.2.6 Sign Language (Pre-recorded)	AAA
		1.2.7 Extended Audio Description (Pre-recorded)	AAA
		1.2.8 Media Alternative (Pre-recorded)	AAA
		1.2.9 Audio-only (Live)	AAA
	1.3 Adaptable	1.3.1 Info and Relationships	A
		1.3.2 Meaningful Sequence	A
		1.3.3 Sensory Characteristics	A
	1.4 Distinguishable	1.4.1 Use of Colour	A
		1.4.2 Audio Control	A
		1.4.3 Contrast (Minimum)	AA
		1.4.4 Resize text	AA
		1.4.5 Images of Text	AA
		1.4.6 Contrast (Enhanced)	AAA
		1.4.7 Low or No Background Audio	AAA
		1.4.8 Visual Presentation	AAA
		1.4.9 Images of Text (No Exception)	AAA
	2.1 Keyboard Accessible	2.1.1 Keyboard	A
		2.1.2 No Keyboard Trap	A
		2.1.3 Keyboard (No Exception)	AAA
	2.2 Enough Time	2.2.1 Timing Adjustable	A
		2.2.2 Pause, Stop, Hide	A
		2.2.3 No Timing	AAA
		2.2.4 Interruptions	AAA
		2.2.5 Re-authenticating	AAA
	2.3 Seizures	2.3.1 Three Flashes or Below Threshold	A
		2.3.2 Three Flashes	AAA

continued on following page

Table 9. Continued

Principle	Guideline		Level
	2.4 Navigable	2.4.1 Bypass Blocks	A
		2.4.2 Page Titled	A
		2.4.3 Focus Order	A
		2.4.4 Link Purpose (In Context)	A
		2.4.5 Multiple Ways	AA
		2.4.6 Headings and Labels	AA
		2.4.7 Focus Visible	AA
		2.4.8 Location	AAA
		2.4.9 Link Purpose (Link Only)	AAA
		2.4.10 Section Headings	AAA
3. Understandable	3.1 Readable	3.1.1 Language of Page	A
		3.1.2 Language of Parts	AA
		3.1.3 Unusual Words	AAA
		3.1.4 Abbreviations	AAA
		3.1.5 Reading Level	AAA
		3.1.6 Pronunciation	AAA
	3.2 Predictable	3.2.1 On Focus	A
		3.2.2 On Input	A
		3.2.3 Consistent Navigation	AA
		3.2.4 Consistent Identification	AA
		3.2.5 Change on Request	AAA
	3.3 Input Assistance	3.3.1 Error Identification	A
		3.3.2 Labels or Instructions	A
		3.3.3 Error Suggestion	AA
		3.3.4 Error Prevention (Legal, Financial, Data)	AA
		3.3.5 Help	AAA
		3.3.6 Error Prevention (All)	AAA
4. Robust	4.1 Compatible	4.1.1 Parsing	A
		4.1.2 Name, Role, Value	A

APPENDIX 2

Guidelines Definition by Level

Table 10. Level A guidelines definition (A)

Guideline	Summary
1.1.1 – Non-text Content	Provide text alternatives for non-text content
1.2.1 – Audio-only and Video-only (Pre-recorded)	Provide an alternative to video-only and audio-only content
1.2.2 – Captions (Pre-recorded)	Provide captions for videos with audio
1.2.3 – Audio Description or Media Alternative (Pre-recorded)	Video with audio has a second alternative
1.3.1 – Info and Relationships	Logical structure
1.3.2 – Meaningful Sequence	Present content in a meaningful order
1.3.3 – Sensory Characteristics	Use more than one sense for instructions
1.4.1 – Use of Colour	Don't use presentation that relies solely on colour
1.4.2 – Audio Control	Don't play audio automatically
2.1.1 – Keyboard	Accessible by keyboard only
2.1.2 – No Keyboard Trap	Don't trap keyboard users
2.2.1 – Timing Adjustable	Time limits have user controls
2.2.2 – Pause, Stop, Hide	Provide user controls for moving content
2.3.1 – Three Flashes or Below	No content flashes more than three times per second
2.4.1 – Bypass Blocks	Provide a 'Skip to Content' link
2.4.2 – Page Titled	Use helpful and clear page titles
2.4.3 – Focus Order	Logical order
2.4.4 – Link Purpose (In Context)	Every link's purpose is clear from its context
3.1.1 – Language of Page	Page has a language assigned
3.2.1 – On Focus	Elements do not change when they receive focus
3.2.2 – On Input	Elements do not change when they receive input
3.3.1 – Error Identification	Clearly identify input errors
3.3.2 – Labels or Instructions	Label elements and give instructions
4.1.1 – Parsing	No major code errors
4.1.2 – Name, Role, Value	Build all elements for accessibility

Table 11. Level AA guidelines definition (Intermediate)

Guideline	Summary
1.2.4 – Captions (Live)	Live videos have captions
1.2.5 – Audio Description (Pre-recorded)	Users have access to audio description for video content
1.4.3 – Contrast (Minimum)	Contrast ratio between text and background is at least 4.5:1
1.4.4 – Resize Text	Text can be resized to 200% without loss of content or function
1.4.5 – Images of Text	Don't use images of text
2.4.5 – Multiple Ways	Offer several ways to find pages
2.4.6 – Headings and Labels	Use clear headings and labels
2.4.7 – Focus Visible	Ensure keyboard focus is visible and clear
3.1.2 – Language of Parts	Tell users when the language on a page changes
3.2.3 – Consistent Navigation	Use menus consistently
3.2.4 – Consistent Identification	Use icons and buttons consistently
3.3.3 – Error Suggestion	Suggest fixes when users make errors
3.3.4- Error Prevention (Legal, Financial, Data)	Reduce the risk of input errors for sensitive data

Table 12. Level AAA guidelines definition (Advanced)

Guideline	Summary
1.2.6 – Sign Language (Pre-recorded)	Provide sign language translations for videos
1.2.7 – Extended Audio description (Pre-recorded)	Provide extended audio description for videos
1.2.8 – Media Alternative (Pre-recorded)	Provide a text alternative to videos
1.2.9 – Audio Only (Live)	Provide alternatives for live audio
1.4.6 – Contrast (Enhanced)	Contrast ratio between text and background is at least 7:1
1.4.7 – Low or No Background Audio	Audio is clear for listeners to hear
1.4.8 – Visual Presentation	Offer users a range of presentation options
1.4.9 – Images of Text (No Exception)	Don't use images of text
2.1.3 – Keyboard (No Exception)	Accessible by keyboard only, without exception
2.2.3 – No Timing	No time limits
2.2.4 – Interruptions	Don't interrupt users
2.2.5 – Re-authenticating	Save user data when re-authenticating
2.3.2 – Three Flashes	No content flashes more than three times per second
2.4.8 – Location	Let users know where they are
2.4.9 – Link Purpose (Link Only)	Every link's purpose is clear from its text
2.4.10 – Section Headings	Break up content with headings
3.1.3 – Unusual words	Explain any strange words
3.1.4 – Abbreviations	Explain any abbreviations
3.1.5 – Reading Level	Users with nine years of school can read your content
3.1.6 – Pronunciation	Explain any words that are hard to pronounce
3.2.5 – Change on Request	Don't change elements on your website until users ask
3.3.5 – Help	Provide detailed help and instructions
3.3.6 – Error Prevention (All)	Reduce the risk of all input errors

APPENDIX 3

Ranking of the Municipalities

Table 13. Ranking of the municipalities by the number of problems presented in the thirty-eight satisfaction criteria reviewed

ID	Certification	Municipality	URL	Analyzed with AChecker Tool	Number of error guideline	% error guideline
41		Baião	http://www.cm-baiao.pt	Y	0	0,00%
63	A	Carrazeda de Ansiães	http://www.cm-carrazedadeansiaes.pt	Y	0	0,00%
94	AA	Fafe	http://www.cm-fafe.pt	Y	0	0,00%
155		Monção	http://www.cm-moncao.pt	Y	0	0,00%
193		Penafiel	http://www.cm-penafiel.pt	Y	0	0,00%
214		Póvoa de Lanhoso	http://www.mun-planhoso.pt/	Y	0	0,00%
215		Póvoa de Varzim	http://www.cm-pvarzim.pt	Y	0	0,00%
226		Sabrosa	http://www.cm-sabrosa.pt	Y	0	0,00%
268		Torre de Moncorvo	http://www.torredemoncorvo.pt	Y	0	0,00%
304	A	Vimioso	http://www.cm-vimioso.pt	Y	**0**	0,00%
34		Arouca	http://www.cm-arouca.pt	Y	1	0,47%
90		Esposende	http://www.cm-esposende.pt	Y	1	0,47%
145		Melgaço	http://www.cm-melgaco.pt	Y	1	0,47%
167		Murça	http://www.cm-murca.pt	Y	1	0,47%
189		Paredes	http://www.cm-paredes.pt	Y	1	0,47%
190		Paredes de Coura	http://www.cm-paredes-coura.pt	Y	1	0,47%
275		Valença	http://www.cm-valenca.pt	Y	1	0,47%
26		Amarante	http://www.cm-amarante.pt	Y	2	0,95%
31	AAA	Arcos de Valdevez	http://www.cmav.pt	Y	2	0,95%
33		Armamar	http://www.cm-armamar.pt	Y	2	0,95%
53	A	Bragança	http://www.cm-braganca.pt	Y	2	0,95%
110		Gondomar	http://www.cm-gondomar.pt	Y	2	0,95%
157		Mondim de Basto	http://www.cm-mondimdebasto.pt	Y	2	0,95%
204	AAA	Ponte da Barca	http://www.cmpb.pt	Y	2	0,95%
233	AA	Santa Maria da Feira	http://www.cm-feira.pt	Y	2	0,95%
286	A	Vila do Conde	http://www.cm-viladoconde.pt	Y	2	0,95%
295		Vila Nova de Gaia	http://www.cm-gaia.pt	Y	2	0,95%
54	A	Cabeceiras de Basto	http://www.cabeceirasdebasto.pt	Y	3	1,42%
77	A	Chaves	http://www.chaves.pt	Y	3	1,42%
142	A	Matosinhos	http://www.cm-matosinhos.pt	Y	3	1,42%

continued on following page

Table 13. Continued

ID	Certification	Municipality	URL	Analyzed with AChecker Tool	Number of error guideline	% error guideline
150	A	Miranda do Douro	http://www.cm-mdouro.pt/	Y	3	1,42%
179	AAA	Oliveira de Azeméis	http://www.cm-oaz.pt	Y	3	1,42%
263		Tarouca	http://www.cm-tarouca.pt	Y	3	1,42%
283		Vieira do Minho	http://www.cm-vminho.pt	Y	3	1,42%
288	A	Vila Flor	http://www.cm-vilaflor.pt	Y	3	1,42%
153		Moimenta da Beira	http://www.cm-moimenta.pt	Y	3	1,42%
52		Braga	http://www.cm-braga.pt	Y	4	1,90%
69		Castelo de Paiva	http://www.cm-castelo-paiva.pt	Y	4	1,90%
89		Espinho	http://www.cm-espinho.pt	Y	4	1,90%
130		Lousada	http://www.cm-lousada.pt	Y	4	1,90%
132	A	Macedo de Cavaleiros	http://www.cm-macedodecavaleiros.pt	Y	4	1,90%
151		Mirandela	http://www.cm mirandela.pt	Y	4	1,90%
152	A	Mogadouro	http://mogadouro.pt/	Y	4	1,90%
238	A	Santo Tirso	http://www.cm-stirso.pt	Y	4	1,90%
241		São João da Pesqueira	http://www.sjpesqueira.pt	Y	4	1,90%
292	A	Vila Nova de Cerveira	http://www.cm-vncerveira.pt	Y	4	1,90%
294		Vila Nova de Foz Côa	http://www.cm-fozcoa.pt	Y	4	1,90%
305	A	Vinhais	http://www.cm-vinhais.pt	Y	4	1,90%
13	A	Alfândega da Fé	http://www.cm-alfandegadafe.pt	Y	5	2,37%
14		Alijó	http://www.cm-alijo.pt	Y	5	2,37%
42		Barcelos	http://www.cm-barcelos.pt	Y	5	2,37%
114	A	Guimarães	http://www.cm-guimaraes.pt	Y	5	2,37%
136		Maia	http://www.cm-maia.pt	Y	5	2,37%
210		Porto	http://www.cm-porto.pt	Y	5	2,37%
274		Vale de Cambra	http://www.cm-valedecambra.pt	Y	5	2,37%
298		Vila Pouca de Aguiar	http://www.cm-vpaguiar.pt	Y	5	2,37%
103		Freixo de Espada à Cinta	http://www.cm-freixoespadacinta.pt	Y	6	2,84%
123		Lamego	http://www.cm-lamego.pt	Y	6	2,84%
139		Marco de Canaveses	http://www.cm-marco-canaveses.pt	Y	6	2,84%
196		Penedono	http://www.cm-penedono.pt	Y	6	2,84%
205		Ponte de Lima	http://www.cm-pontedelima.pt	Y	7	3,32%
276		Valongo	http://www.cm-valongo.pt	Y	7	3,32%
307		Vizela	http://www.cm-vizela.pt	Y	7	3,32%
159		Montalegre	http://www.cm-montalegre.pt	Y	8	3,79%
234		Santa Marta de Penaguião	http://www.cm-smpenaguiao.pt	Y	8	3,79%

continued on following page

Table 13. Continued

ID	Certification	Municipality	URL	Analyzed with AChecker Tool	Number of error guideline	% error guideline
293		Vila Nova de Famalicão	http://www.vilanovadefamalicao.org	Y	8	3,79%
27		Amares	http://www.cm-amares.pt	N		
51		Boticas	http://www.cm-boticas.pt	N		
60		Caminha	http://www.cm-caminha.pt	N		
75		Celorico de Basto	http://www.mun-celoricodebasto.pt/	N		
78		Cinfães	http://www.cm-cinfaes.pt	N		
96		Felgueiras	http://www.cm-felgueiras.pt	N		
147		Mesão Frio	http://www.cm-mesaofrio.pt	N		
186		Paços de Ferreira	http://www.cm-pacosdeferreira.pt	N		
199		Peso da Régua	http://www.cm-pesoregua.pt	N		
221		Resende	http://www.cm-resende.pt	N		
223		Ribeira de Pena	http://www.cm-rpena.pt	N		
240		São João da Madeira	http://www.cm-sjm.pt	N		
249		Sernancelhe	http://www.cm-sernancelhe.pt	N		
262		Tabuaço	http://www.cm-tabuaco.pt	N		
265		Terras de Bouro	http://www.cm-terrasdebouro.pt	N		
272		Trofa	http://www.mun-trofa.pt	N		
278		Valpaços	http://www.valpacos.pt	N		
281		Viana do Castelo	http://www.cm-viana-castelo.pt	N		
299		Vila Real	http://www.cm-vilareal.pt	N		
302		Vila Verde	http://www.cm-vilaverde.pt	N		

[1] NUT II – North - Nomenclature of Territorial Units for Statistics. Portugal is divided into 7 different NUTS II, corresponding to its regions: North; Centre; Lisbon Metropolitan Area; Alentejo; Algarve; Autonomous Region of the Azores; and Autonomous Region of Madeira.

Section 3
Technology Acceptance and Satisfaction

Chapter 8
Information Technology Progress Indicators:
Research Employing Psychological Frameworks

T. S. Amer
Northern Arizona University, USA

Todd L. Johnson
Northern Arizona University, USA

ABSTRACT

Users of information technology often encounter "progress indicators" during their interactions. These graphics (e.g., progress bars) appear on computing screens as users wait for a task to complete to inform them of the progress being made toward completing the task. This study employed theoretical models from psychological research on human waiting to develop specific hypotheses related to the design of progress indicators. Three experiments tested these hypotheses. Experiment 1 revealed that participants preferred a linear progress bar to a cycling progress bar. Experiment 2 revealed that participants preferred a video progress indicator to a cycling progress bar, and they judged process duration to be shorter with the video progress indicator. Experiment 3 revealed that the video progress indicator yielded the best user experience. Systems designers can use these results to develop more effective user interfaces.

INTRODUCTION

Users of information technology (IT) often encounter "progress indicators" during their interactions. Progress indicators are graphics that appear on the computer screen as a user waits to complete a task, such as downloading a file, saving a file, or updating software. The purpose of progress indicators is to inform the user of the progress that is being made as the task moves toward completion. Progress indicators can take different forms, such as a spinning disk, a bar that moves across the screen, or a textual message (for example, "26% completed") (Amer & Johnson, in press; Conrad, Couper, Tourangeau,

DOI: 10.4018/978-1-5225-1868-6.ch008

& Peytchev, 2010; Cooper & Reiman, 2003; Galitz, 2007; Shneiderman, Plaisant, Cohen, & Jacobs, 2009). Because progress indicators are common features in IT environments, it is not only important to understand which form, content, and movement patterns maximize the quality of the user experience but also to understand the problems users experience in such interactions (Galitz, 2007; Ghafurian & Reitter, 2016; Hohenstein et al., 2016; Shneiderman et al., 2009; Villar, Callegaro, & Yang, 2013).

Systems designers program progress indicators for display when time consuming operations interrupt the user interface for longer than a few seconds. In such circumstances users can become impatient if the interface provides no indication that some underlying process is functioning. Therefore, a progress indicator informs the user that the system is still operating and is not waiting for a response from the user before processing continues. Progress indicators often move in a manner that is directly proportional (linear) to the amount of work that has been completed. However, factors such as varying speeds of disk and memory access, processor speed, and bandwidth may alter the time and rate of movement. Consequently, progress indicators often exhibit non-linear behaviors, such as:

- Acceleration,
- Deceleration, and
- Stalls.

Regardless of the movement pattern of the progress indicator, the user must wait while the underlying computing process completes. Waiting is, therefore, a common aspect of the user experience when encountering progress indicators.

This paper applies theoretical models from psychological research on human waiting and perception to develop specific hypotheses related to the design of progress indicators, and it reports the results of several experiments that were carried out to test those hypotheses. These findings can be used to better understand the impact of a progress-indicator design on the user experience.

RELATED LITERATURE

Prior research has investigated the design features of progress indicators in different contexts to determine appropriate parameters and user perceptions. These efforts have largely been experimental in nature and examined participants' perceptions of preference, process duration, and other factors (Amer & Johnson, in press). One area of concentrated work investigated the use of progress indicators in online surveys (Villar et al., 2013; Conrad et al., 2010; Matzat, Snijders, & van der Horst, 2009; Sarraf & Tukibayeva, 2014). The emphasis of that research was to study the effect of alternative progress-indicator designs to reduce "drop-off rates"—that is, to minimize the probability that a respondent will not complete a survey after starting. Villar et al. (2013) used meta-analytics of 32 published manuscripts that examined three types of progress indicators:

- Constant (moving linearly),
- Fast-to-slow, and
- Slow-to-fast.

Their results indicate that using a constant-moving progress indicator does not significantly reduce drop-offs, and that effectiveness of the progress indicator varies depending on the speed of the indicator:

- Fast-to-slow indicators reduced drop-offs, whereas slow-to-fast indicators increased drop-offs.

These results may be explained by a sense-of-progress psychological framework of waiting (to be discussed below):

- A progress indicator that moves quickly at the beginning of the task may give users the impression that there is a greater movement toward task completion (a sense of progress), which improves user satisfaction.

Additional research has examined other progress-indicator design features in contexts other than participants completing online surveys. Crease and Brewster (1998) added sounds to progress bars and found that users preferred progress bars with sound cues over progress bars without sound cues. Harrison, Amento, Kuznetsov, and Bell (2007), and Harrison, Yeo, and Hudson (2010) examined progress bars with nonlinear movement and "ribbed" and "pulsating" visual features. While no specific theoretical framework was used in the design of these progress bars, the authors found that participants perceived that progress bars that paused took longer than those that did not. Order effects may have confounded some of their results as the participants tended to prefer (i.e., perceive as faster) whichever progress bar they experienced first.

Hamada, Ohnishi, and Köppen (2011) attempted to find a relationship between progress bar colors and perceptions of process duration during a waiting period. They prepared six combinations of colors:

- Blue/red for the progress bar's foreground color, and
- Cyan/orange/gray for its background color.

No specific theoretical model was referenced in the design or the choice of the color combinations, and the data reported no difference in subjective perceptions across participants. The authors hypothesized that the results were possibly due to the small sample size of only 10 participants and the order effects in the presentation of the experimental trials. Ohtsubo and Yoshida (2014) examined 10 alternative shapes of progress indicators, including the length and thickness of progress bars and ring-shaped progress indicators. The most robust finding was that a progress indicator in the shape of a quarter ring was perceived to complete faster than a progress indicator in the shape of a half ring or full ring. The Ohtsubo and Yoshida (2014) study was one of a few that invoked psychological theories to guide the research effort—an approach also taken in this study. Similarly, Paul, Komlodi, and Lutters (2015), and Jung, Sirkin, Turgut, and Steinert (2015) appealed to psychological concepts of multitasking and expectations, respectively. While these studies are only tangentially related to progress indicators, they highlight the usefulness of applying an understanding of human decision-making in the study of human-computer interaction.

Other research has examined issues and factors similar to perception-based research on progress indicators (Amer & Johnson, in press). Hurter, Girouard, Riche, and Plaisant (2011) explored the possibility of using "active progress bars," which allow users to switch to temporary (secondary) activities when a primary activity requires them to wait. Using the results of survey data, they proposed samples of secondary-activity applications, combining existing applications with a normal progress bar. The secondary activities included entertainment activities (for example, games) and work activities, such as allowing the user to manage a to-do list. The researchers' idea to add secondary activities was a way to fill the time users spend waiting for the primary activity to complete. Hohenstein et al. (2016) studied the effect of animated loading screens on perceived wait time as compared to a progress bar and passive animation. Their findings indicate that perceived wait time is shorter and user satisfaction is higher with an interactive animation than with a progress bar or passive animation. Milicevic, Zubrinic, and Zakarija (2008) constructed a model representing structured query language (SQL) query behavior to estimate the duration of database queries. The model incorporated query parameters such as pages scanned, device interrupts, and system calls during database queries. Model estimates of query duration could then be used to display percent-done progress indicators (for example, "26% completed"). The idea was to accurately communicate query duration to improve the user experience during waiting.

Kortum, Peres, and Stallmann (2011) and Garcia and Peres (2012) examined auditory progress indicators as an alternative to visual progress indicators. In both studies, participants were asked to listen to three alternative auditory stimuli during waiting periods:

- Pure tones (sine wave),
- Musical patterns (cello), and
- A continuous, electronically generated musical scale.

Participants' time estimation and preferences were measured across waiting durations. The results indicated that auditory progress indicators can influence both the accuracy of time estimation and user preferences.

WAITING

Waiting is a common aspect of the user experience which is addressed across the disparate studies cited above (Amer & Johnson, in press). Hohenstein et al. (2016) note that one of the most fundamental aspects of perceived software performance is waiting time. Harrison et al. (2010) suggest that in some user interfaces both novice and expert users have no choice but to watch progress indicators while they wait until a given activity is completed before moving forward with a task. Hurter et al. (2011) emphasized the design of progress indicators within a taxonomy of waiting-period contexts. Kortum et al. (2011) investigated the design of auditory progress indicators on users' perception of the duration of wait (on-hold) time, and Garcia and Peres (2012) examined users' accuracy estimating the remaining wait time. Indeed, a key role of a progress indicator is to provide users with feedback as they wait for a task to complete (Conrad et al., 2010). This experience is similar to other waiting experiences, such as waiting in physical queues at a bank or waiting in queues for operator assistance while on the telephone. Psychologists have examined these types of waiting scenarios from the perspective of psychological frameworks. The authors of this study propose that applying psychological frameworks of human waiting not only can shed light on the design of progress indicators but also perhaps more tightly focus research efforts and explain some of the varied findings in prior work on progress indicators.

For example, Amer and Johnson (in press) applied the "temporal-expectancy" framework of waiting (Klapproth, 2010) to users' experience with progress indicators. Under this framework, temporal expectations regarding waiting duration may influence people's perceptions of how pleasant the waiting experience is. Prior experience plays a key role in setting temporal expectations. That is, people will base their expectation of how long the wait will be based upon experience. This theoretical framework was applied to a situation where a computer user was exposed to a progress bar that begins, moves consistently, but then stalls just prior to the completion of the task. This so-called "stalling progress bar" appears surprisingly often during computer interactions. Applying the temporal-expectancy framework to this waiting scenario would indicate that a user's expectation of the waiting time is set during the initial movement of the progress bar but is then disrupted by the stalling of the bar just prior to completion. In other words, the disruption causes the actual waiting duration to deviate from the expected duration established when the progress bar moved to the point of stall. Thus, the user's expectation of the finish time is lengthened by the stall, which results in a negative affective response (Klapproth 2010). Experimental results indicate that participants preferred a linear progress bar (a progress bar that moves consistently) over a stalling progress bar, and they judged process duration to be shorter with the linear progress bar. When a stalling progress bar was accompanied by an explanatory message, participants' perceptions of the stalling progress bar improved.

Study Objectives

This study extends prior research and draws upon two additional theoretical models from psychological research on human waiting experiences to develop specific hypotheses related to the design of progress indicators. Specifically, the authors applied the "sense-of-progress framework" of waiting and the "subjective-sense-of-time" framework of waiting to investigate alternative design attributes of progress indicators (Munichor & Rafaeli, 2007; Peevers, McInnes, Morton, & Jack, 2009; Weiss, Rafaeli, & Munichor, 2008; Wittmann, 2015; Maister, 2005). These theoretical frameworks were applied to progress indicators that were comprised of specific parameters that were predicted to improve the user experience in terms of both affective response and perceptions of process duration. Two experiments tested these hypotheses, and the results provide robust support for the predictions set forth by both psychological frameworks. In addition, a third experiment that compared the two frameworks indicated that the application of the subjective-sense-of-time framework to the design of a video progress indicator resulted in the best user experience.

HYPOTHESIS

Sense-of-Progress Framework

The sense-of-progress framework argues that the affective response during a waiting scenario is regulated by the perceived distance between an individual's current position and goal. Progress toward the goal is necessary for user satisfaction (Carver & Scheier, 1990, 1998; Munichor & Rafaeli, 2007; Weiss et al., 2008). A person waiting for a task to complete views the completion of the task as the goal. Therefore, a positive reaction should result if the individual perceives that progress is being made toward the completion of the task. This notion has been supported by research on people waiting in physical queues and in phone queues. Carmon and Kahaneman (1996) found that providing a sense of movement in a simulated queue reversed the negative reactions of participants. Soman and Shi (2003) noted that better service evaluations result if consumers can actively see the rate of progress—that is, they observe a queue that physically moves as consumers are serviced. Munichor and Rafaeli (2007) reported results of an experiment with participants who waited in a phone queue. When participants were informed about their location in the queue (for example, "You are fourth in line"), there were lower call-abandonment rates and more positive call evaluations.

Applying the sense-of-progress framework to IT progress indicators is appropriate given that progress indicators provide IT users with information about the progress that is being made as the task moves toward completion. Accordingly:

H1: A progress indicator that provides a user with a sense of progress about task completion will be preferred to a progress indicator that does not provide a sense of progress about task completion.

Subjective-Sense-of-Time Framework

The subjective-sense-of-time framework contends that people possess subjective mental timers that focus on the passage of time (Zakay & Hornik, 1991). Time is perceived to pass more slowly when attention is focused primarily on time rather than on something else (Block, 1990; Munichor & Rafaeli, 2007; Wittmann, 2015). Factors that draw attention away from the passage of time are argued to halt mental timers, which reduce the perceived passage of time and increase satisfaction. Empirical studies of physical waiting have demonstrated a negative relationship between perceived waiting time and customer satisfaction (for example, Katz, Larson, & Larson, 1991; Munichor & Rafaeli, 2007; Taylor, 1995; Tom & Lucey, 1997). Maister (2005) articulates this notion as "occupied time feels shorter than unoccupied time." Maister goes on to note how restaurants occupy waiting customers by handing out menus for them to peruse while they wait in line. Likewise, time spent in phone queues is often filled with music to distract the person who is waiting from noticing the passage of time.

As with the sense-of-progress framework, the application of the subjective-sense-of-time framework to progress indicators would be appropriate for a progress indicator designed to draw IT users' attention away from the passage of time. Accordingly:

H2: A progress indicator that draws a user's attention away from the passage of time will reduce the perception of task duration versus a progress indicator that does not draw a user's attention away from the passage of time.

The negative relationship between the perceived passage of time instilled by a progress indicator and user satisfaction with that progress indicator is expressed as follows:

H3: A progress indicator that draws a user's attention away from the passage of time will be preferred to a progress indicator that does not draw a user's attention away from the passage of time.

RESEARCH METHODOLOGY AND DESIGN

Methodology Overview

Laboratory experiments were conducted to test these hypotheses. One experiment examined the predictions of the sense-of-progress framework (H1), and a second experiment examined the predictions of the subjective-sense-of-time framework (H2 and H3). A third experiment compared the two frameworks to determine which of the two resulted in a better user experience. In all three experiments, different groups of participants sat individually at computers in a laboratory setting and responded to prompts that were displayed on a computer screen. The programmed data-elicitation instrument controlled the presentation of the experimental factors, optimally ordering and randomizing the variables to prevent order effects. In a within-subject design, participants viewed all possible configurations of progress indicators that were designed with features to provide either a sense of progress (Experiment 1) or that drew the participants' attention away from the passage of time (Experiment 2) while they downloaded files from a central server. Experiment 3 compared the two frameworks. All data collected was sent to a file stored on a central server.

Computerized Procedure and Task

The computerized data-collection program was coded using Windows Forms and Windows Presentation Foundation for the user interface. The C# programming language was used to control the forms and to write the data collected to a database file. The program displayed a series of screens, which provided all participants with information about the task and elicited and recorded their responses. The program was structured so participants could not backtrack as they progressed through the program, and it controlled the order of the progress indicators presented to the participants to prevent order effects in the data collected. Participants convened at a pre-established time in a computer lab where the authors provided instruction. Each participant sat individually at a computer within the lab, and when instructed, accessed the data-collection program from a central server. The participants completed the task in its entirety during one sitting, which lasted approximately 15 minutes.

EXPERIMENT 1: SENSE OF PROGRESS

Participants and their Task

The authors recruited 63 upper-division students from a large university to complete the first experiment. The participants were provided with a nominal level of extra-credit course points (approximately two percent of the total course points) as an incentive to complete the exercise. The selected participants were deemed appropriate for this study because the psychological concepts of waiting should apply to decision-makers of all ages and backgrounds. Table 1 shows the age and sex of these participants. For example, data from Table 1 indicates that the majority of the participants were male and younger than 25 years of age.

Table 1. Age and sex of participants in experiment 1

Age	
< 18	0
18 to 20	8
21 to 23	32
24 to 26	7
27 to 30	12
31 to 40	4
> 40	0
Sex	
Male	47
Female	16

At the start of the exercise, participants were informed that the purpose of the study was to obtain feedback as they downloaded files. Next, they read through a scenario on their computer screens, which explained that they would download several files from a central server. There was no mention of progress indicators. After reading the scenario, the participants answered three multiple-choice questions about the scenario. The multiple-choice questions were designed to ensure that the participants understood the contextual information presented in the scenario. The participants were not able to continue the exercise until they had answered the scenario-related questions correctly. More than 90 percent of the multiple-choice questions were answered correctly on the first attempt.

The scenario described a very common file-downloading situation in which the participant was interacting over a computer network. This scenario provided a reasonable context within which to assess the progress indicators. Presenting the scenario provided a common frame of reference within which the participants could respond to questions and judgments. The common frame of reference also increased the external validity of the results. Responses were not linked to any individual participant, but each participant's completion of the exercise was recorded in order to provide that person with extra-credit course points.

Progress Indicators Utilized

One of two types of progress indicators was displayed on the computer screen as each file downloaded. The first progress indicator, shown in Figure 1(a), was a linear progress bar where the bar advanced consistently (linearly) throughout the downloading period. This progress indicator gave the participants a sense of progress because the consistently advancing bar was perfectly correlated with the duration of the download. The bar moved faster during shorter downloading periods and slower during longer downloading periods. This progress indicator communicated a sense of progress to the user in a manner that is similar to how people are informed about their location in a phone queue (for example, "You are fourth in line.") (Munichor & Rafaeli, 2007).

The second progress indicator was a "cycling" progress bar as shown in Figure 1(b). The movement of this progress bar showed no advancement during the downloading period as the colored band within

Figure 1. Progress indicators used in the sense-of-progress experiment
a. **Linear Progress Bar**: *Instills a sense of progress as the consistently advancing bar is perfectly correlated with the duration of the download.*
b. **Cycling Progress Bar**: *Does not instill a sense of progress as the cycling nature of the progress bar is not correlated with the duration of the download.*

(a)   (b)

the boundary of the bar simply cycled back and forth continuously until the download completed. The cycling of the colored bar did not correlate with the downloading duration—the movement pattern repeated in the same back and forth manner throughout. Therefore, this progress indicator did not provide participants with any sense of progress. Both the linear and cycling progress bars are available in the Windows Development software, and, therefore, they were identical in form to the progress bars utilized by Windows systems developers. In addition, these two types of progress bars are commonly employed in Apple software and other software.

The experiment incorporated five different duration periods for the progress bars:

- 10 seconds,
- 20 seconds,
- 30 seconds,
- 40 seconds, and
- 50 seconds.

Therefore, each participant received a total of 10 different progress bars while downloading 10 different files:

- Five were linear, and
- Five were cycling.

The order of the presentation of the durations and progress bars was completely randomized for each participant to prevent order effects.

Results

Each participant responded to questions after completing the 10 file downloads. Three of the questions captured data regarding the participant's preference for one of the two progress indicators he or she experienced, and one question addressed the participant's perception of the sense-of-progress instilled by the two progress indicators. Table 2 displays the results for the 63 participants. The data in the top panel of Table 2 indicates that the participants had a strong preference for the linear progress bar:

- Approximately 90 percent of the participants said they preferred this progress indicator.

Table 2. Results of the sense-of-progress experiment (63 participants)

Elicitations Regarding Preferences		
	Linear Progress Bar	**Cycling Progress Bar**
1. For which progress indicator did you find the wait to be the most PLEASANT?	57	6
2. Which progress indicator would you LIKE TO ENCOUNTER in other file-download, waiting situations?	53	10
3. Which progress indicator would you PREFER to see when you are downloading files?	59	4
Elicitation Regarding Sense of Progress		
	Linear Progress Bar	**Cycling Progress Bar**
1. Which progress indicator communicated to you that you were MAKING PROGRESS, that is, that you were advancing to the completion of the download?	63	0

Moreover, 100 percent identified the linear progress bar as the progress indicator that communicated that participants were making progress and advancing to the completion of the file download. Taken together, these results provide strong support for hypothesis H1:

- That a progress indicator providing a user with a sense of progress about task completion will be preferred to a progress indicator that does not provide a sense of progress about task completion.

A binomial statistical analysis was carried out to compare the data collected in the experiment to a random selection by the participants of one of the two progress indicators. The probability that the data displayed in Table 2 resulted from random draws from a binomial distribution was less than .01 for all measures, which indicated that the results were statistically significant.

EXPERIMENT 2: SUBJECTIVE SENSE OF TIME

Participants and Their Task

The authors recruited 41 different upper-division students from a large university to complete the second experiment. As with Experiment 1, the participants were provided with a nominal level of extra course points as an incentive to complete the exercise, and they were deemed appropriate for this study because the psychological concepts of waiting should apply to decision-makers of all ages and backgrounds. Table 3 indicates that the participants were demographically similar to the participants in Experiment 1. The instructions given to participants and the downloading exercise were the same as in Experiment 1, but the progress indicators displayed in the study were different.

Progress Indicators Utilized

One of two types of progress indicators were displayed on the computer screen as each file downloaded. The first progress indicator, shown in Figure 2(a), was a group of short, silent videos of gymnasts performing gymnastic routines. This video progress indicator served to draw attention away from the

Table 3. Age and sex of participants in the subjective-sense-of-time experiment

Age	
< 18	0
18 to 20	7
21 to 23	25
24 to 26	5
27 to 30	3
31 to 40	1
> 40	0
Sex	
Male	26
Female	15

passage of time in a way that is similar to how customers waiting in restaurants are occupied by reading menus and people in phone queues are occupied by listening to music or other content while on-hold (Maister, 2005; Munichor & Rafaeli, 2007). Other video content could have been used, but gymnastics content was selected based on the belief that most people find viewing gymnastic and acrobatic feats to be interesting and absorbing, especially without sound accompaniment.

The second progress indicator was the cycling progress bar utilized in Experiment 1 (see Figure 2(b)). The movement of this progress bar showed no advancement during the downloading period but simply cycled back and forth continuously until the download was completed. This progress indicator did not give study participants any information about progress toward task completion because its cycling nature was not correlated with the downloading time— the movement pattern repeated in the same back and

Figure 2. Progress indicators used in the subjective-sense-of-time experiment: Disclaimer: This image is a still frame taken from a video.
a. **Video Progress Indicator***: Draws attention away from the passage of time because users are occupied by watching the video.*
b. **Cycling Progress Bar***: Provides users with no information about progress toward task completion so they are more likely to focus on the passage of time as the file downloads.*

(a)

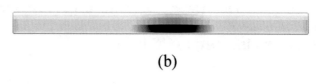

(b)

forth manner throughout. As in Experiment 1, five different duration periods for the progress indicators were incorporated into the experiment:

- 10 seconds,
- 20 seconds,
- 30 seconds,
- 40 seconds, and
- 50 seconds.

Therefore, each participant received a total of 10 different progress indicators while downloading 10 different files:

- Five indicators were different gymnastic videos (i.e., athletes performing different exercises, such as balance beam, a floor exercise, and vault), and
- Five were cycling progress bars.

The order of the presentation of the durations and progress indicators was completely randomized for each participant to prevent order effects.

Results

Each participant responded to questions after completing the 10 file downloads. One of the questions captured data about how participants perceived the download speed of the two progress indicators they experienced, and two of the questions captured data regarding the participant's preference for one of the two progress indicators. Table 4 displays the results for the 41 participants. The data in Table 4 indicates that 28 of the 41 participants (68 percent) perceived that the video progress indicator downloaded files faster, although the download times were identical across both progress indicators. The responses to the preference questions revealed that approximately 92 percent of the participants preferred the video progress indicator to the cycling progress indicator. As with the first experiment, a binomial statistical analysis was completed to compare the data collected in the experiment to a random selection by the participants of one of the two progress indicators. The probability that the data displayed in Table 4 resulted from random draws from a binomial distribution was less than .01 for all measures. Taken together, these results provide support for hypothesis H2 and H3:

Table 4. Results of the subjective-sense-of-time experiment (41 participants)

Elicitations Regarding Download Speed and Preference		
	Video Progress Indicator	**Cycling Progress Bar**
1. Which downloaded the files FASTEST?	28	13
2. For which progress indicator did you find the wait to be the most PLEASANT?	39	2
3. Which progress indicator would you LIKE TO ENCOUNTER in other file-download, waiting situations?	37	4

- That a progress indicator that draws a user's attention away from the passage of time will reduce the perception of task duration relative to a progress indicator that does not draw a user's attention away from the passage of time, and it will be preferred.

EXPERIMENT 3: COMPARING THE FRAMEWORKS

Having confirmed the hypotheses predicted by both the sense-of-progress and subjective-sense-of-time frameworks, a third experiment was structured to compare the two frameworks. The third experiment utilized the progress indicators that resulted in the best user experience from the first two experiments:

- A linear progress indicator and
- A video progress indicator.

No a priori expectations were formulated relative to this comparison as neither framework is theoretically known to dominate. Accordingly, the following research question was posited:

R1: Will a progress indicator that draws a user's attention away from the passage of time be preferred to a progress indicator that provides a user with a sense of progress about task completion?

Participants and Their Task

The authors recruited a new set of 56 upper-division students from a large university to complete the third exercise. They were demographically similar to the participants utilized in the first two experiments. Again, the participants were provided with a nominal level of extra-credit course points as an incentive to complete the exercise. The instructions provided to the participants and the downloading exercise were the same as in Experiment 1 and Experiment 2. The progress indicators displayed in this experiment were the same ones used in the first two experiments.

Progress Indicators Utilized

One of two types of progress indicators was displayed on the computer screen as each file downloaded. The first progress indicator, shown in Figure 1(a), was the linear progress bar utilized in Experiment 1 where the bar advanced consistently (linearly) throughout the downloading period. The second progress indicator, shown in Figure 2(a), was the group of short, silent videos of gymnasts performing gymnastic routines as utilized in Experiment 2. As in Experiments 1 and 2, five different duration periods for the progress indicators were incorporated into the experiment:

- 10 seconds,
- 20 seconds,
- 30 seconds,
- 40 seconds, and
- 50 seconds.

Therefore, each participant received a total of 10 different progress indicators while downloading 10 different files:

- Five indicators were linear progress bars, and
- Five indicators were different gymnastic videos.

The order of the presentation of the durations and progress indicators were completely randomized for each participant to prevent order effects.

Results

Each participant responded to questions after completing the 10 file downloads. One of the questions captured data about the participant's perceptions of the download speed of the two progress indicators they experienced, and two of the questions captured data regarding the participant's preference for one of the two progress indicators. Table 5 displays the results for the 56 participants. The data in Table 5 indicates that 37 of the 56 participants (66 percent) perceived that files downloaded faster with the video progress indicator, although the download times were identical across both progress indicators. The responses to the preference questions revealed that approximately 87 percent of the participants would prefer the video progress indicator to the linear progress indicator. Again, the probability that the data displayed in Table 5 resulted from random draws from a binomial distribution was less than .01 for all measures. Taken together, these results reveal that the video progress indicator based upon a subjective-sense-of-time framework was preferred over the linear progress indicator based upon the sense-of-progress framework. The video progress indicator both reduced the perception of task duration and was preferred.

FINDINGS AND DISCUSSION

This study investigated the application of two psychological models of waiting to progress indicators in IT environments. The experimental results indicate that progress indicators can be designed to enhance the user's waiting experience and that certain design features should be avoided. Specifically, participant's preferred progress indicators that gave them a sense that they were making progress toward completing a

Table 5. Results of experiment comparing frameworks (56 participants)

Elicitations Regarding Download Speed and Preference		
	Video Progress Indicator	**Linear Progress Bar**
1. Which downloaded the files FASTEST?	37	19
2. For which progress indicator did you find the wait to be the most PLEASANT?	50	6
3. Which progress indicator would you LIKE TO ENCOUNTER in other file-download, waiting situations?	48	8

computing task. Study results also demonstrated that a progress indicator that draws the user's attention away from the passage of time is perceived to shorten the process duration and is preferred. Moreover, the data indicate that a "cycling" progress indicator, utilized in both experiments, is the least preferred in this context. Finally, the video progress indicator outperformed both the cycling and linear progress bars in terms of both user perception of process duration and preference. These results have implications for both research and practice.

CONCLUSION

Implications

These models can be used to explain some prior research findings. For example, the sense-of-progress framework may explain results reported by Villar et al. (2013) who found that participants were less likely to "drop-off" (i.e., abandon) completing online surveys if the progress indicator began moving quickly at the beginning of the task rather than if it began moving slowly at the beginning of the task. Such a progress bar that moves quickly at the beginning of the task may give users the impression that there is a greater movement toward task completion. Likewise, some of the results reported by Harrison et al. (2007, 2010) may be explained by the sense-of-progress framework. The longer perceived downloads of a pausing progress bar found by Harrison et al. (2007, 2010) may have resulted from a break in the users' sense of progress caused by the pause.

The findings by Crease and Brewster (1998), Hurter et al. (2011), and Hohenstein et al. (2016) might be supported by the subjective-sense-of-time framework. Crease and Brewster's (1998) research findings that adding sounds to progress bars improved usability and increased user preference when compared to progress bars without sound cues may have resulted from the sound cues drawing the participant's attention away from the passage of time as predicted by the subjective-sense-of-time framework. Similarly, Hurter et al.'s (2011) notion of "active progress bars," whereby users can switch to temporary (secondary) activities when a primary activity requires them to wait may increase user satisfaction. This would be supported by the subjective-sense-of-time framework as the temporary activity draws the user's attention away from the passage of time. Finally, Hohenstein et al.'s (2016) finding that users' are more satisfied with an interactive animation than with a progress bar or passive animation also may have resulted from the animation drawing the participants' attention away from the time they spent waiting. Additional research may be able to examine these factors in relation to the theoretical frameworks more precisely.

Systems designers can use the results reported in this paper to improve the user interface by incorporating appropriate characteristics in the design of progress indicators. Based upon the data in this study, designers should avoid the "cycling" progress indicator. This indicator provides neither a sense of progress toward the completion of a task nor any information regarding the duration of the waiting time. Therefore, it leaves users with a sense of uncertainty. If possible, users should be provided with information that will enable them to understand the status of the completion process. Moreover, a video progress indicator may be the best progress indicator to use during waiting experiences.

LIMITATIONS AND FUTURE RESEARCH

The current research has a few limitations that warrant discussion. First, the participants used in the study were relatively young and more than half were male. This could limit the generalizability of the results. However, there were no significant differences in the data attributable to gender, and the results reported are relatively robust. Second, the task completed by the participants involved file downloads. Task variables may alter the results. For example, tasks such as online shopping and transaction processing may have an impact on the type of progress indicator users prefer. Third, the video content employed in the video progress indicator could have an impact as well. The authors thought that gymnastics content would appeal to most users, but this may not be the case. Video content may be irrelevant or unappealing for some users, and perhaps changing the video content might change the preference results. Finally, there may be other explanations for the superiority of the video progress indicator other than the subjective-sense-of-time framework. For example, a video may be generally more interesting because it provides the user with additional content.

Future research can provide additional insights related to the limitations noted above. In general, applying these and other frameworks of waiting to IT progress indicators provides useful design-parameter insights. Future research could investigate the application of other waiting frameworks to progress indicators and the user waiting experience in IT environments. Maister (2005) notes that uncertain waiting times are perceived to be longer than known, finite waiting durations. This fact may have implications for IT interface design, such as structuring the system to provide information about waiting time in a manner that reduces user uncertainty. Other types of progress indicators, such as offering a textual message (for example, "26% completed") as the task moves toward completion could also be investigated.

As an illustration, a preliminary experiment was conducted to compare a linear progress bar to a simple digital display of the percentage completion of a file download. That is, a digital count-up from 0% to 100% as the file downloaded. Prior work and theory would indicate that users would prefer a linear progress bar over a digital percentage display as the graphical nature of the linear progress bar is more efficient for providing data about temporal and spatial orderings (Amer, 1991; VanderPlas & Hofmann, 2016; Vessey, 1991). The experimental procedure employed was identical to the procedures described above. The 78 new participants were demographically similar to those who participated in this study's experiments. Results indicate that, consistent with the theoretical predictions, 69.2% of the participants preferred the linear progress bar to the display of a count-up digital percentage, a statistically significant difference. Here again, applying psychological theories and frameworks provided useful insights about alternative progress-indicator designs.

REFERENCES

Amer, T. (1991). An experimental investigation of the effects of multi-cue financial information display on decision making. *The Journal of Information Systems*, 5(2), 18–34.

Amer, T., & Johnson, T. (in press). Information technology progress indicators – Temporal expectancy, user preference, and the perception of process duration. *International Journal of Technology and Human Interaction*.

Block, R. (Ed.). (1990). *Cognitive models of psychological time*. Florence, KY: Psychology Press.

Carmon, Z., & Kahaneman, D. (1996). *The experienced utility of queuing: Experience profiles and retrospective evaluations of simulated queues.* Working paper. Durham, NC: Fuqua School of Business, Duke University.

Carver, C., & Scheier, M. (1990). Origins and functions of positive and negative affect: A control-process view. *Psychological Review, 97*(1), 19–35. doi:10.1037/0033-295X.97.1.19

Carver, C., & Scheier, M. (1998). *On the self-regulation of behavior.* Cambridge, UK: Cambridge University Press. doi:10.1017/CBO9781139174794

Conrad, F., Couper, M., Tourangeau, R., & Peytchev, A. (2010). The impact of progress indicators on task completion. *Interacting with Computers, 22*(5), 417–427. doi:10.1016/j.intcom.2010.03.001 PMID:20676386

Cooper, A., & Reimann, R. (2003). *About face 2.0: The essentials of interaction design.* Hoboken, NJ: Wiley Publishing, Inc.

Crease, M., & Brewster, S. (1998). Making progress with sounds – The design and evaluation of an audio progress bar. In *ICAD98 Proceedings of the 1998 International Conference on Auditory Display.* Swinton, UK: British Computer Society, 1–5.

Galitz, W. (2007). *The essential guide to user interface design.* Hoboken, NJ: Wiley Publishing, Inc.

Garcia, A., & Peres, C. (2012). Auditory progress bars: The effects of feedback, endpoint, and free response on estimations of time remaining. In *Proceedings of the Human Factors and Ergonomics Society Annual Meeting 2012.* doi:10.1177/1071181312561335

Ghafurian, M., & Reitter, D. (2016). Impatience induced by waiting: An effect moderated by the speed of countdowns. In *Proceedings of the Designing Interactive Systems.* Brisbane, Australia: ACM. doi:10.1145/2901790.2901830

Hamada, K., Yoshida, K., Ohnishi, K., & Köppen, M. (2011). Color effect on subjective perception of progress bar speed. In *Proceedings of the Third International Conference on Intelligent Networking and Collaborative Systems.* Iizuka, Japan: Kyushu Institute of Technology. doi:10.1109/INCoS.2011.65

Harrison, C., Amento, B., Kuznetsov, S., & Bell, R. (2007). Rethinking the progress bar. In *Proceedings of the 20th Annual ACM Symposium on User Interface Software and Technology.* New York, NY: ACM. doi:10.1145/1294211.1294231

Harrison, C., Yeo, Z., & Hudson, S. (2010). Faster progress bars: Manipulating perceived duration with visual augmentation. In *Proceedings of the 28th Annual SIGCHI Conference on Human Factors in Computing Systems.* New York, NY: ACM. doi:10.1145/1753326.1753556

Hohenstein, J., Kahn, H., Canfield, K., Tung, S., & Cano, R. (2016). Shorter wait times: The effects of various loading screens on perceived performance. In *Proceedings of the 2016 CHI Conference Extended Abstracts on Human Factors in Computing Systems.* doi:10.1145/2851581.2892308

Hurter, C., Girouard, A., Riche, N., & Plaisant, C. (2011). Active progress bars: Facilitating the switch to temporary activities. In *Proceedings of the 2011 Annual Conference on Human Factors in Computing Systems.* New York, NY: ACM, (pp.1963–1968). doi:10.1145/1979742.1979883

Jung, M., Sirkin, D., Turgut, M., & Steinert, M. (2015). *Displayed uncertainty improves driving experience and behavior: The case of range anxiety in an electric car.* UI Impact on Performance & Decisions. CHI 2015, Seoul, Republic of Korea. doi:10.1145/2702123.2702479

Katz, K., Larson, B., & Larson, R. (1991). Prescription for the waiting-in-line blues: Entertain, enlighten, and engage. *Sloan Management Review, 32*(2), 44–53.

Klapproth, F. (2010). Waiting as a temporal constraint. In J. A. Parker, P. A. Harris & C. Steineck (Eds.), Time: Limits and Constraints (pp. 179-198). Leiden, The Netherlands: Koninklijke Brill NV. doi:10.1163/ej.9789004185753.i-378.70

Kortum, P., Peres, S., & Stallmann, K. (2011). Extensible auditory progress bar design: Performance and aesthetics. *International Journal of Human-Computer Interaction, 27*(9), 864–884. doi:10.1080/10447318.2011.555310

Maister, D. H. (2005). *The psychology of waiting lines.* Retrieved from www.davidmaister.com

Matzat, U., Snijders, C., & van der Horst, W. (2009). Effects of different types of progress indicators on drop-out rates in web surveys. *Social Psychology, 40*(1), 43–52. doi:10.1027/1864-9335.40.1.43

Milicevic, M., Zubrinic, K., & Zakarija, I. (2008). Dynamic approach to the construction of progress indicator for a long running SQL queries. *International Journal of Computers, 4*(2), 489–496.

Munichor, N., & Rafaeli, A. (2007). Numbers or apologies? Customer reactions to telephone waiting-time fillers. *The Journal of Applied Psychology, 92*(2), 511–518. doi:10.1037/0021-9010.92.2.511 PMID:17371095

Ohtsubo, M., & Yoshida, K. (2014). How does shape of progress bar effect time evaluation. *IEEE 2014 International Conference on Intelligent Networking and Collaborative Systems.* Salerno, Italy: University of Salerno. doi:10.1109/INCoS.2014.85

Paul, C., Komlodi, A., & Lutters, W. (2015). Interruptive notifications in support of task management. *International Journal of Human-Computer Studies, 79*, 20–34. doi:10.1016/j.ijhcs.2015.02.001

Peevers, G., McInnes, F., Morton, H., Matthews, A., & Jack, M. (2009). The mediating effects of brand music and waiting-time updates on customers satisfaction with a telephone service when put on-hold. *International Journal of Bank Marketing, 27*(3), 202–217. doi:10.1108/02652320910950196

Sarraf, S., & Tukibayeva, M. (2014). Survey page length and progress indicators: What are their relationships to item nonresponse? *New directions for institutional research, 161,* 83–97. Retrieved from http://wileyonlinelibrary.com

Shneiderman, B., Plaisant, C., Cohen, M., & Jacobs, S. (2009). *Designing the user interface: Strategies for effective human-computer interaction* (5th ed.). Upper Saddle River, NJ: Prentice Hall.

Soman, D., & Shi, M. (2003). Virtual progress: The effect of path characteristics on perceptions of progress and choice. *Management Science, 49*(9), 1229–1250. doi:10.1287/mnsc.49.9.1229.16574

Taylor, S. (1995). The effects of filled waiting time and service provider control over the delay on evaluations of service. *Journal of the Academy of Marketing Science, 23*(1), 38–48. doi:10.1007/BF02894610

Tom, G., & Lucey, S. (1997). A field study investigating the effect of waiting time on customer satisfaction. *The Journal of Psychology*, *131*(6), 655–660. doi:10.1080/00223989709603847

VanderPlas, S., & Hofmann, H. (2016). Spatial reasoning and data displays. *IEEE Transactions on Visualization and Computer Graphics*, *22*(1), 459–468. doi:10.1109/TVCG.2015.2469125 PMID:26390492

Vessey, I. (1991). Cognitive fit: A theory-based analysis of the graphs versus tables literature. *Decision Sciences*, *22*(2), 219–240. doi:10.1111/j.1540-5915.1991.tb00344.x

Villar, A., Callegaro, M., & Yang, Y. (2013). Where am I? A meta-analysis of experiments on the effects of progress indicators for web surveys. *Social Science Computer Review*, *31*(6), 744–762. doi:10.1177/0894439313497468

Weiss, L., Rafaeli, A., & Munichor, N. (2008). Proximity to or progress toward receiving a telephone service? An experimental investigation of customer reactions to features of telephone auditory messages. *Advances in Consumer Research. Association for Consumer Research (U. S.)*, *35*, 791–792.

Wittmann, M. (2015). Modulations of the experience of self and time. *Consciousness and Cognition*, *38*, 172–181. doi:10.1016/j.concog.2015.06.008 PMID:26121958

Zakay, D., & Hornik, J. (1991). *How much time did you wait in line? A time-perception perspective* (Working Paper No. 20/91). Tel Aviv, Israel: The Leon Recanati Graduate School of Business Administration, Tel Aviv University.

Chapter 9
Technology Satisfaction in an Academic Context:
Moderating Effect of Gender

A. Y. M. Atiquil Islam
Institute of Graduate Studies, University of Malaya, Malaysia

ABSTRACT

In the 21st century wireless internet technology has been extensively extending and contributing to various aspects of human lives. However, technological assessment and evaluation have been rarely taken place, especially to investigate the satisfaction among students in using wireless internet for learning and research purposes. As such, this study validates the Technology Satisfaction Model proposed by Islam (2014) in an academic context for estimating students' satisfaction and the moderating effect of gender in using wireless internet. The findings of SEM analyses attested that students' satisfaction was directly influenced by perceived ease of use and usefulness in using wireless internet and it was also indirectly affected by computer self-efficacy medicated by usefulness and ease of use, respectively. Additionally, computer self-efficacy had a significant direct influence on ease of use and usefulness. The results of invariance analyses also discovered that gender was not a moderating variable for technology satisfaction in an academic context.

INTRODUCTION

Scientists have been discovering, updating, spreading and implementing the innovative communication technologies throughout the world, where internet technology is one of them playing an imperative role to maximize the human-computer interaction. According to the recent statistics of International Telecommunications Union (ITU) carried out in 2010, the internet penetration reaches 30.1 per hundred residents (ITU 2010). However, the substantial disparity between developing and developed countries in terms of internet penetration has also been uncovered through the same study, where a large proportion of 71.6% residents in developed countries turn out to be internet users, while no such high figure has been perceived in developing countries (Afacan, Er & Arifoglu, 2013). Comparing with the situation

DOI: 10.4018/978-1-5225-1868-6.ch009

in 1968, the US Department of Defense used only one computer to link its four sites. Available figures show that usage of internet has increased dramatically around the globe from West to East. Researchers provided a parameter of economic and social benefits of internet usage by identifying the contribution made by internet in:

- Increasing job productivity,
- Technology updates,
- Social networks (Gaudreau, Miranda & Gareau, 2014; Hamid, Waycott, Kurnia & Chang, 2015; Dutot, 2014; Lichy & Kachour, 2014; Dineva & Koufteros, 2002),
- Information access (Islam, 2016; Bouzaabia, Bouzaabia & Capatina, 2016; Islam, 2014; Islam 2011a; Islam, 2011b; Dineva & Koufteros, 2002; Zejno & Islam, 2012; Nwagwu, Adekannbi, & Bello, 2009; Ani, 2010; Zamani-Miandashti, Memarbashi & Khalighzadeh, 2013) and
- The effectiveness of learning and research outcomes (Islam, 2014; Islam 2011b).

Their findings demonstrated that Internet contributes immensely for economic, social and educational development. According to Ani (2010), as a contemporary worldwide tool, the internet plays a role in reaping a better educational outcome of diverse nations, especially in developing countries. Furthermore, with the arrival of information era, the innovation of education has been brought up following the utilization of information technology in educational area. Thus, as an essential educational instrument, internet has been investigated and utilized by researchers and teachers in numerous countries in recent years (Chun, 2014). Despite these benefits received from internet, there are huge social problems created arising from its usage (Hashim, Alam & Siraj, 2010). Subsequently, cautious steps are needed to ensure more benefits are received through the use of the internet by reducing its negative impact. On the other hand, Nwagwu, Adekannbi & Bello (2009) claimed that the difficulty of slowness of access to internet information is a common scenario, primarily because of low bandwidth.

In line with this technological development, International Islamic University Malaysia (IIUM) has also provided the infrastructure of wireless internet to its community, thereby helping the learners in getting access to their subject related materials and keeping up with the current information updates. On the other hand, students can surf the internet and get its access through their laptops, desktop computers, mobile phone and personal digital assistant (PDA). Though widely adopted, there are many aspects of the usage and implementation of this technology that need to be studied and empirically documented. While wireless internet access has been provided for quite some time now at IIUM, there are still many barriers that limit the successful integration and usage of this emerging educational technology within its environment. Especially, technology satisfaction is one of the vital issues which limit students' success in using wireless internet for their learning and research purposes in higher education. Along this line, researchers recently stated that student satisfaction is commendable of examination because it is critical to academic achievement and success (Kuo, Walker, Schroder & Belland, 2014). As such, the purpose of this study is to validate the Technology Satisfaction Model (TSM) proposed by Islam (2014) in an academic context for estimating students' satisfaction and the moderating effect of gender in using wireless internet for learning and research purposes in higher education.

LITERATURE REVIEW

Since internet works as micro but important branch of technology, the technology acceptance Model (TAM) invented by Davis (1989) was used to measure the acceptance of Internet usage. TAM was working with some criticism as regard the context of internet needs some particular focus. Comprehending this reality, scholars have been working for the development and validation process on acceptance of internet since early 1990s (Taylor & Todd, 1995; Venkatesh & Morris, 2000; Yousafzai, Foxall & Pallister, 2007; Shamdasani, Mukherjee, & Malhotra, 2008; Legris, Ingham, & Collerette, 2003; Ahmad, Basha, Marzuki, Hisham, & Sahari, 2010; Islam, 2011b; Chun, 2014; Shroff, Deneen, & Ng, 2011; Hong, Hwang, Hsu, Wong, & Chen, 2011).

There are abundance of literatures that have examined the relationships among variables related to technology acceptance (Mezghani & Ayadi, 2016; Khedhaouria & Beldi, 2014; Dutot, 2014; Chen & Lan, 2014; Aljuaid, Alzahrani, & Islam, 2014; Islam, 2011a; Kaba & Osei-Bryson, 2013; Kreijns, Vermeulen, Kirschner, van Buuren, & van Acker, 2013; Moses, Wong, Bakar, & Rosnaini, 2013; Zejno & Islam, 2012; Shroff et al., 2011; Shittu, Basha, Rahman, & Ahmad, 2011; Lee, Hsieh, & Hsu, 2011; Teo & van Schalk, 2009; Teo, 2009; Liu, Liao, & Pratt, 2009; Dash, Mohanty, Pattnaik, Mohapatra, Sahoo, & Sundar, 2011). As such, numerous theoretical models have been propounded to provide detail explanations on users' intention to use technology, and actual technology use (Venkatesh, Morris, Davis, & Davis, 2003). Following the introduction of the TAM, the model has been widely used to explain computer-usage behavior and factors associated with acceptance of technology. According to the model, the technology adoption is influenced by the user's intention to use which consequently is determined by his or her attitudes towards technology. Perhaps, user's perceptions— perceived ease of use (PEU) and perceived usefulness (PU) determine the variability in these attitudinal and behavioural dimensions (Ahmad et al., 2010). While PEU reveals the degree to which technology might be free of efforts in its application, PU on the other hand indicates the extent to which technology usage can help in improving users' performance in order to enhance one's task (Davis, Bagozzi, & Warshaw, 1989). The suggested TAM indicates that, behavioral intention mediates the influence of the two extrinsic motivation components, namely; PEU and PU as presented in Figure 1.

According to Ahmad et al. (2010), TAM has attracted the interest of decision makers, researchers and practitioners due to the fact that, it is simple, robust and reasonable. Though, it has unanimously

Figure 1. Technology Acceptance Model (Davis et al., 1989)

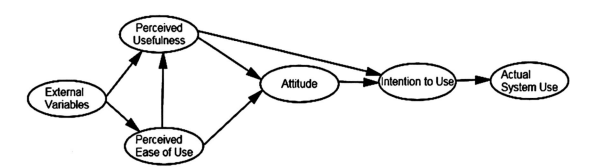

gained empirical support in terms of its strength through applications and validations in assuming the use of information systems (Davis, 1993; Taylor & Todd, 1995; Venkatesh & Morris, 2000), previous meta-analyses demonstrates that, if various overriding issues are considered, it could be resolved through proper understanding in this case (Ma & Liu, 2004; Schepers & Wetzels, 2007; Yousafzai et al., 2007).

Additional studies on factors related to technology acceptance and refinement of acceptance models that can facilitate its generalizability have been suggested (Sun & Zhang, 2006; Thompson, Compeau, & Higgins, 2006). Considering the evolving new technologies, perceived ease of use and perceived usefulness, they are not the only suitable constructs that determine technology acceptance (Thompson et al., 2006). Many researchers have shown that, including more dimensions with other IT acceptance models in order to enhance its specificity, and explanatory utility would perform better for a particular context and focus (Agarwal & Prasad, 1998; Mathieson, 1991). More so, there is suggestion by previous researchers (Legris et al., 2003) that, TAM deserves to be extended by integrating additional factors that could facilitate the explanation of more than 40 percent of technology acceptance and usage. Against this backdrop, Islam (2014) developed and validated the Technology Satisfaction Model (TSM) as shown in Figure 2, incorporated two additional intrinsic motivation attributes namely, satisfaction and self-efficacy into the original TAM. The TSM (2014) discovered significant direct and indirect causal relationships between the constructs, namely, computer self-efficacy (CSE), perceived ease of use (PEU), perceived usefulness (PU) and satisfaction (SAT). Later on, Islam, Leng, and Singh (2015) tested the efficacy of the TSM for assessing research databases in higher education. Their findings were consistent with the original TSM (Islam, 2014). Recently, the Technology Adoption and Gratification (TAG) model has been developed and validated by Islam (2016) based on three existing models, namely,

- TSM,
- TAM and
- Online Database Adoption and satisfaction (ODAS) (Islam, 2011a), while TSM was the especially most critical one.

Figure 2. Technology Satisfaction Model (Islam, 2014)

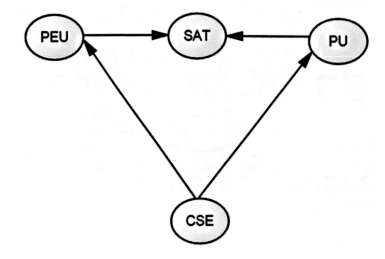

CONSTRUCTION OF HYPOTHESES

The perceived ease of use in technology acceptance is highly recognized in TAM invented by Davis et al. (1989). However, the TSM (Islam, 2014), ODAS model (Islam, 2011a) and TAG model (Islam, 2016) discovered that perceived ease of use was one of the most critical antecedents of students' and lecturers' satisfaction or gratification in using ICT facilities (Islam, 2016), wireless internet (Islam, 2014; Islam, 2011b) and online research databases (Islam, 2011a; Islam et al., 2015) for their teaching, learning and research purposes in higher education. Similarly, Islam (2011a) revealed that perceived ease of use was found to be most significant predictor compared to the behavioural intention that influences on the students' satisfaction in using the online research database. More preciously, perceived ease of use had a significant direct influence on satisfaction (Islam, 2016; Islam, 2014, Masrek & Gaskin, 2016; Islam et al., 2015; Islam, 2011a; Islam, 2011b; Lee & Park, 2008). Cheok and Wong (2015) predicted a significant relationship between perceived ease of use and e-learning satisfaction but there was no empirical evidence. Szymanski and Hise (2000) and Dabholkar and Bagozzi (2002) respectively revealed that, convenience and ease of use are important antecedents of e-satisfaction. In a related study, Shamdasani et al. (2008) regarded ease of use as one of the factors of service quality and investigated its impact on consumer satisfaction in using self-service internet technologies. Along this line, Huang (2008) indicates that, the impact of e consumers' perceived ease of use mediated by their behavioral attitude on their satisfaction are statistically significant. On the other hand, Islam (2016) revealed that lecturers' perceived ease of use had a significant indirect influence on their gratification mediated by intention to use of ICT facilities for teaching and research purposes in higher education. Thus, this study posits:

H1: Perceived ease of use (PEU) will have a significant direct influence on students' satisfaction (SAT) in using wireless internet.

The TSM explored that students' satisfaction was directly influenced by their perceived usefulness of wireless internet (Islam, 2014) and online research databases (Islam et al., 2015) in higher education. In line with this finding, the TAG model (Islam, 2016) also confirmed the direct relationship between lecturers' perceived usefulness of ICT facilities and their satisfaction. However, the ODAS model (Islam, 2011a) discovered that, perceived usefulness had a statistically significant indirect influence on satisfaction mediated by intention to use online research database. According to Huang (2008), perceived usefulness was found to have an impact on consumer satisfaction mediated by their behavioral attitudes, while researchers indicated the relationship between perceived usefulness and satisfaction in using mobile technology (Lee & Park, 2008) and web digital library (Masrek & Gaskin, 2016). In addition to this, in the extant literature, numerous studies existed vis-à-vis the effect of perceived usefulness on intention to use (Davis et al., 1989; Hanafizadeh, Behboudi, Koshksaray & Tabar, 2014; Terzis, Moridis, Economides & Rebolledo-Mendez, 2013; Hong et al., 2011; Chun, 2014). On the other hand, Cheok and Wong (2015) reported that, perceived usefulness might directly affect teachers' e-learning satisfaction in teaching. This argument is corroborated by Islam (2016) who exhibited that, Malaysian and Chinese lecturers' perceived usefulness had a significant indirect influence on their satisfaction mediated by intention to use of ICT facilities for teaching and research purposes. It is thus hypothesized that:

H2: Perceived usefulness (PU) will have a significant direct influence on students' satisfaction (SAT) in using wireless internet.

Self-efficacy has been described as one's view regarding how well one can carry out different courses of actions in various prospective situations embedded with many uncertain and stressful elements (Bandura & Schunk, 1981). This was further corroborated by Aiken (1993), who was of the opinion that, self-efficacy represents the expected capability in learning or performing certain behaviors of a person that will lead to desirable outcomes in a certain condition. Regarding learning procedures, Schunk (1991) suggested that, it expresses students' judgment about their cognitive competence to achieve particular academic goals. In the perspective of internet usage, it stands for user's confidence to organize and implement courses of internet actions that are important to come up with some specific targets. Suggestions that self-efficacy influences the decision as to whether or not to carry out a task including the effort made in implementing it and the degree of determination required in achieving it has been justified by researchers (Bandura, 1977; Bandura & Schunk, 1981; Delcourt & Kinzie, 1993). It has effect on how people think, feel and their behavior (Bandura, 1986, p393). Adding self-efficacy as an intrinsic motivation attribute further enriches the understanding of how and why technology is used (Ahmad et al., 2010). Later on, the TAG (Islam, 2016) model, TSM (Islam, 2014; Islam et al., 2015) and ODAS model (Islam, 2011a) found computer self-efficacy is the most imperative dimension for measuring users' technological adoption and their satisfaction or gratification in higher education. According to a study conducted among university students, Agarwal and Karahanna (2000) revealed computer self-efficacy to be an important antecedent of perceived ease of use and it was highly influenced by an individual's ingenuity with information system. In light of this, current researches showed that computer self-efficacy had significant direct influence on perceived usefulness (Chow, 2016) and ease of use (Islam, 2016; Islam et al., 2015; Islam, 2014; Chun, 2014).

Based on the findings in the previous research on the relationship between computer self-efficacy and behavioral intention to use or infusion (Wu, Chang & Guo, 2008; Ahmad et al., 2010), and latter with individual satisfaction (Huang, 2008; Shamdasani et al., 2008), it is inferred that there is a relationship between computer self-efficacy and satisfaction through the mediating effect of an individual's behavioral intention. Subsequently, Islam (2011a) revealed the presence of significant indirect relationship between computer self-efficacy and satisfaction through the mediating influence of intention to use online research database. Along this line, researchers also demonstrated that computer self-efficacy had significant indirect influence on satisfaction mediated by perceived ease of use and usefulness, respectively (Islam, 2016; Islam, 2014; Islam et al., 2015). Additionally, Malaysian and Chinese lecturers' computer self-efficacy had also significant indirect influence on their intention to use of ICT facilities for teaching and research purposes mediated by perceived usefulness and ease of use, respectively (Islam, 2016). On the other hand, Ahmad et al. (2010) indicated that computer self-efficacy indirectly influences faculty's use of computer mediated technology through perceived usefulness and intention to use. Against this backdrop, the following hypotheses are derived:

H3: Computer self-efficacy (CSE) will have a significant direct influence on perceived usefulness (PU) of wireless internet.

H4: Computer self-efficacy (CSE) will have a significant direct influence on perceived ease of use (PEU) of wireless internet.

H5: Computer self-efficacy (CSE) will have a significant indirect influence on students' satisfaction (SAT) mediated by perceived usefulness (PU) of wireless internet.

H6: Computer self-efficacy (CSE) will have a significant indirect influence on students' satisfaction (SAT) mediated by perceived ease of use (PEU) of wireless internet.

At the beginning of technological era, researchers claimed that the rate of use or adoption of technology varied based on gender issue. Male users were assumed to be more active in using technological facilities compared to female. However, in the 21st century, gender issues have been changed. For instance, Islam (2011b) explored that gender was not a moderating variable in using wireless internet facility for their learning and research purposes in higher education. Similarly, Ahmad et al. (2010) articulated that gender did not influence faculty's use of technology to facilitate learning and teaching. Their findings also recommended that the gender gap in technology uptake between female and male users is gradually diminishing. In a recent study, Khedhaouria and Beldi (2014) evaluated the moderating influence of gender. Their findings indicated that female users showed a stronger necessitate for perceived ease of use and usefulness compared to male, whereas male users indicated a significant necessitate for perceived enjoyment in using mobile internet services. Furthermore, researchers revealed gender differences in terms of internet self-efficacy, learning motivation and performance (Chang, Liu, Sung, Lin, Chen, & Cheng, 2014), and latter between internet self-efficacy and source of internet self-efficacy (Chuang, Lin, & Tsai, 2015). It is thus hypothesized that:

H7: Gender will have a moderating effect on students' satisfaction in using wireless internet in higher education.

METHODOLOGY

In this study, the data were sourced using a survey questionnaire which was administered on students of a comprehensive public university in Malaysia. In the process, the researcher (Islam, 2014) was able to collect a total of 285 students from five faculties

- (Education,
- Islamic Revealed Knowledge and Human Sciences,
- Engineering,
- Information and Communication Technology, and
- Economics & Management Sciences)

who were equally selected using quota sampling technique by focusing on the students that have laptops as well as wireless internet connection at IIUM. They consisted of 45% male and 55% female students, most of whom (86%) were between 21 to 30 years of age, and represented 67% local and 33% international students. This study also included:

- 72% undergraduate,
- 23% master and
- 5% PhD students.

The sample size is considered adequate for the application of Structural Equation Modeling (SEM) to address the objectives of this study as supported by Hair, Black, Babin and Anderson (2006). The data for the study were given inputs in using SPSS version 16.0. The structural relationships among the various constructs in the TSM were analyzed using AMOS software version 18.0.

Table 1. Constructs measured in the questionnaire

Construct	Source Adapted from:	Number of items
Perceived Ease of Use (PEU)		10
Perceived Usefulness (PU)		11
Computer Self-efficacy (CSE)	Islam, 2014	10
Satisfaction (SAT)		6
Total items		37

Research Instrument

The instrument consisting of 37 items measuring the four constructs pertaining to students' satisfaction of the wireless internet – perceived ease of use, perceived usefulness, computer self-efficacy and satisfaction – was adapted from the previous study conducted by Islam (2014) to assess the moderating effect of gender. The reliability and validity of the instrument were estimated by Rasch model using Winsteps version 3.49 (Islam, 2014). To measure perceived ease of use, perceived usefulness, and computer self-efficacy, this study used a 5-point Likert scale of 1 to 5, with 1 being strongly disagree and 5 being strongly agree. To measure satisfaction, the study applied the 1-to-5 scale to represent very unsatisfied (1) and very satisfied (5). The number of items for each construct is presented in Table 1.

RESULTS

The three-stage results of the structural equation modeling that address the objectives of the study are described in this section. It first evaluated the results of validated Confirmatory Factor Analysis (CFA) for 4 measurement models and then estimated the full-fledged structural model of TSM. Finally, in order to test the moderating effect of gender, the two-stage of invariance analyses were conducted, namely, configural and metric.

Validating the Measurement Models

Confirmatory Factor Analysis (CFA) was run for each of the 4 measurement models namely, CFA-1 (CSE), CFA-2 (PEU), CFA-3 (PU) and CFA-4 (SAT); in each case, a few items were removed one at a time due to the violation of estimation. The revised 4 CFA models for each of these latent constructs showed an adequate fit to the empirical data:

[CFA-1: ($\chi2$ ($df=2$) = 3.344; $p = 0.188$; RMSEA = 0.049; CFI = 0.996; TLI = 0.988);

CFA-2: ($\chi2$ ($df=2$) = 3.411; $p = 0.182$; RMSEA = 0.050; CFI = 0.989; TLI = 0.966);

CFA-3: ($\chi2$ ($df=5$) = 13.969; $p = 0.016$; RMSEA = 0.079; CFI = 0.966; TLI = 0.933;

CFA-4: ($\chi2$ ($df=2$) = 3.751; $p = 0.153$; RMSEA = 0.056; CFI = 0.993; TLI = 0.979).

ESTIMATING THE TECHNOLOGY SATISFACTION MODEL (TSM)

The structural equation modeling was adopted to examine the TSM, which integrates the four measurement models of the latent constructs, namely,

- Perceived ease of use (PEU),
- Perceived usefulness (PU),
- Computer self-efficacy (CSE) and
- Satisfaction (SAT).

The majority of the items exhibited in this model have a loading greater than 0.67, with only five items demonstrating loadings ranging from .34 to .49 (SE10, PEU4, PEU6, PEU10 and SAT1). The overall statistical analyses revealed a satisfactory fit of the model to the empirical data:

- Chi-square, $\chi 2$ (df=115) = 286.558; p< 0.001; RMSEA = 0.072; CFI = 0.862; TLI = 0.837.

However, CFI and TLI were found to be slightly lower from the recommended (Byrne, 2000) value (above 0.90) as shown in Figure 3. As such, the TSM requires to be revised.

Figure 3. Technology Satisfaction Model (TSM)

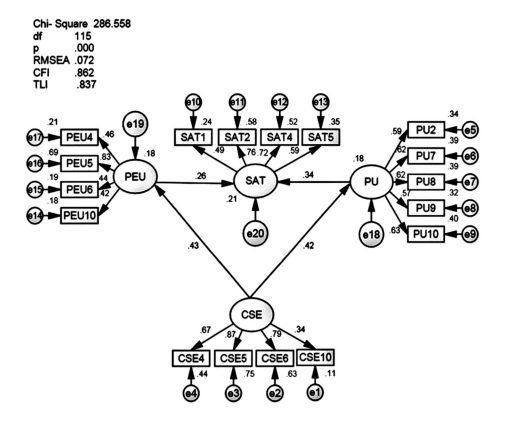

The Revised Technology Satisfaction Model (TSM)

In the third stage, the TSM was revised and estimated so as to examine its overall adequacy. The results indicated that the parameters of the revised model were free from offending estimates. The magnitude of the factor loadings and path coefficients were statistically significant. The overall goodness-of-fit statistics of the model showed a satisfactory fit to the data:

- The Chi-square, $\chi 2$ (*df*=50) = 112.547; *p*< 0.001; RMSEA = 0.066; CFI = 0.928; TLI = 0.905 as supported by Byrne (2000).

The TSM was evaluated according to the standardized path coefficients, as shown in Figure 4. As expected, hypotheses H1 and H2 were supported with both perceived ease of use ($\beta = 0.39$, *p*<0.001) and perceived usefulness ($\beta = 0.26$, *p*<0.001) demonstrating significant direct influence on students' satisfaction. Similarly, hypotheses H3 and H4 were accepted, the findings revealed that computer self-efficacy had a significant positive direct effect on perceived usefulness ($\beta = 0.41, p$<0.001) and perceived ease of use ($\beta = 0.40, p$< .001).

In addition, hypothesis H5 and H6 were also supported, the results discovered that computer self-efficacy had a statistically significant indirect influence on satisfaction mediated by perceived usefulness

Figure 4. Technology Satisfaction Model (TSM)

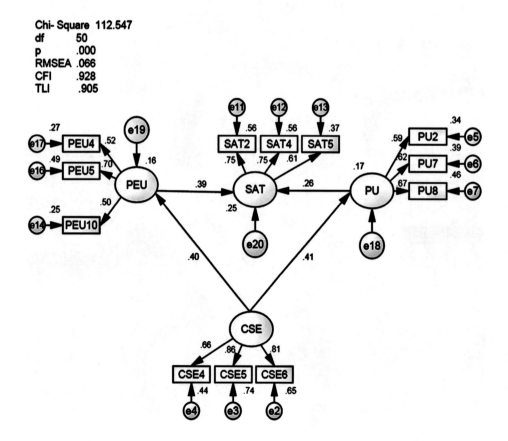

(Chi-square, $\chi 2 = 1.793$, $p = 0.036$) and computer self-efficacy also showed a significant indirect influence on students' satisfaction mediated by perceived ease of use (Chi-square, $\chi 2 = 2.152$, $p = 0.015$) as conducted by the Sobel test (Sobel, 1982). Moreover, all path coefficients of the casual structure were practically important, while the strongest value of the standardized path coefficient of computer self-efficacy on perceived usefulness was 0.41. The data indicated that computer self-efficacy was moderately more influential factor in the TSM in affecting the students' perceived usefulness, perceived ease of use and satisfaction in using wireless internet. All the standardized factor loadings of TSM were greater than .50. Table 2 presents the 12 valid items, their loadings, mean, standard deviation, and Cronbach's alpha.

The Moderating Effect of Gender

The second purpose of this study is to measure the moderating effect of gender in using wireless internet for learning and research purposes in higher education. To achieve this aim, the original pool of data was separated based on the moderating variable, which is gender. Two different sets of data files were created for male and female respondents. In order to estimate gender-invariant, a two-stage analysis such as configural and metric invariance, was performed on the male ($n1 = 127$) and female ($n2 = 158$) respondents individually. Firstly, the validation of the revised TSM was conducted using a total of 127 male respondents. The results of TSM for male respondents demonstrated that the overall fit statistics indicated a satisfactory fit to the data as revealed by the following fit indices:

Table 2. Measurement of the variables of the revised TSM

Constructs	Items	Item Measure	Loadings	*M*	*SD*	α
Perceived Usefulness	PU2	Using the Wireless Internet enables me to download learning materials from the internet.	0.59	3.729	1.031	0.653
	PU7	Wireless Internet helps me access online database to enhance my research.	0.62	3.656	1.031	
	PU8	Using Wireless Internet allows me to obtain multimedia facilities.	0.67	3.512	1.019	
Perceived ease of Use	PEU4	With Wireless Internet, I find it easy to access online database to do research.	0.52	3.361	1.134	0.672
	PEU5	It is easy for me to become skillful in navigating the Internet using Wireless facility.	0.70	3.473	1.053	
	PEU10	Wireless Internet is easy to use.	0.50	3.305	1.163	
Computer Self-efficacy	CSE4	I have the skills required to use Wireless Internet to enhance the effectiveness of my learning.	0.66	3.915	0.945	0.817
	CSE5	I know how to save and print journals/articles from online research database using Wireless Internet.	0.86	3.926	0.999	
	CSE6	I can easily go through the steps of downloading software.	0.81	3.782	1.028	
Satisfaction	SAT2	Overall I am satisfied with the Wireless Internet service provided at the university.	0.75	2.582	1.118	0.751
	SAT4	I am satisfied with wireless service provided by the Information Technology Division (ITD).	0.75	2.743	1.178	
	SAT5	I am satisfied to access Wireless Internet from the Hostel.	0.61	2.203	1.138	

- The Chi-square, $\chi2$ (df=50) = 83.262; p= 0.002; RMSEA = 0.073; CFI = 0.924; TLI = 0.900.

The hypotheses of the TSM for male respondents were tested according to the standardized path coefficients, as shown in Figure 5. The hypothesis H1 was supported with perceived ease of use ($\beta = 0.51, p = 0.006$) indicating significant direct influence on male students' satisfaction in using wireless internet for their learning and research purposes in higher education. However, the hypothesis H2 was not supported with perceived usefulness ($\beta = 0.17, p = 0.226$) demonstrating insignificant direct influence on male students' satisfaction. Similarly, hypotheses H3 and H4 were accepted, the findings revealed that male students' computer self-efficacy had a significant direct effect on perceived usefulness ($\beta = 0.45, p = 0.002$) and perceived ease of use ($\beta = 0.34, p = 0.021$), respectively. Nevertheless, hypotheses H5 and H6 were not supported, the results showed that male students' computer self-efficacy had a statistically insignificant indirect influence on satisfaction mediated by perceived usefulness (Chi-square, $\chi2 = 0.920, p = 0.178$) and computer self-efficacy also showed an insignificant indirect influence on male students' satisfaction mediated by perceived ease of use (Chi-square, $\chi2 = 1.558, p = 0.059$) as conducted by the Sobel test (Sobel, 1982). Although, all path coefficients of the casual structure were practically important and the strongest value of the standardized path coefficient of perceived ease of use on satisfaction was 0.51. The data exhibited that perceived ease of use was a moderately more influential factor in the TSM in affecting the male students' satisfaction in using wireless internet for their learning and research purposes. The majority of the standardized factor loadings were greater than .62, with only three items demonstrating loadings ranging from .43 to .57, representing statistically significant indicators. Meanwhile, approximately 32% of the variability of male students' satisfaction in using wireless internet for their learning and research purposes was explained by the exogenous variable (CSE) and the two mediator variables (PU and PEU) collectively, as shown in Figure 5.

Secondly, the validity of the revised TSM was tested using a total of 158 female participants. The findings of TSM for female participants explored that the overall fit indices showed an adequate fit to the data as indicated by the following fit statistics:

- The Chi-square, $\chi2$ (df=50) = 86.955; p= 0.001; RMSEA = 0.069; CFI = 0.919; TLI = 0.893.

All the hypotheses of the TSM for female participants were estimated in accordance with the standardized path coefficients, as shown in Figure 6. The hypothesis H2 was accepted with perceived usefulness ($\beta = 0.36, p = 0.008$) confirming significant direct influence on female students' satisfaction in using wireless internet for their learning and research purposes in higher education. However, the hypothesis H1 was not supported with perceived ease of use ($\beta = 0.23, p = 0.084$) indicating insignificant direct influence on female students' satisfaction. In the meantime, hypotheses H3 and H4 were accepted, the results exhibited that female students' computer self-efficacy had a significant direct effect on perceived usefulness ($\beta = 0.40, p = 0.001$) and perceived ease of use ($\beta = 0.43, p = 0.000$), respectively. Moreover, hypothesis H5 was supported, the findings discovered that female students' computer self-efficacy had a statistically significant indirect influence on satisfaction mediated by perceived usefulness (Chi-square, $\chi2 = 1.693, p = 0.045$). Whereas computer self-efficacy revealed an insignificant indirect influence on female students' satisfaction mediated by perceived ease of use (Chi-square, $\chi2 = 1.266, p = 0.102$) as conducted by the Sobel test (Sobel, 1982). All the path coefficients of the casual structure were practically important and the strongest value of the standardized path coefficient of computer self-efficacy on perceived ease of use was 0.43. The data confirmed that computer self-efficacy was moderately

Figure 5. Technology satisfaction model for male respondents

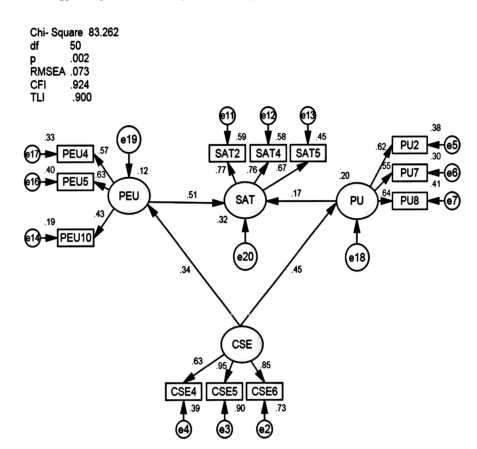

more dominant predictor in the TSM in affecting the female students' perceived ease of use of wireless internet. The standardized factor loadings were ranging from .48 to .83, demonstrating statistically significant items. Additionally, almost 21% of the variability of female students' satisfaction in using wireless internet for their learning and research purposes was clarified by the two mediator variables (PU and PEU) and an exogenous variable (CSE) collectively.

Thirdly, after confirming the validity of the TSM for male and female respondents, the configural and metric invariance analyses were conducted using both groups of data, respectively. The configural invariance analysis required to group the male and female data together to analyze two different models, which are named as "male" and "female", by using unstandardized estimates without constraining the structural paths. The findings derived a baseline Chi-square value. Subsequently, the findings for unconstrained male and female models were discovered to be consistent with the data and the overall fit indices found to be similar for both models as shown in Figure 7. Although the chi-square ($\chi2$) and degree of freedom (*df*) values had to be equal for both models as required by the configural invariance analysis as well as in order to proceed with metric invariance analysis.

Next, to conduct the metric analysis, the structural paths of the model were constrained to be equal for the male and female groups. The findings for constrained male and female models were found to be consistent with the data and the chi-square ($\chi2$) and degree of freedom (*df*) values were similar for both models as shown in Figure 8.

Figure 6. Technology satisfaction model for female respondents

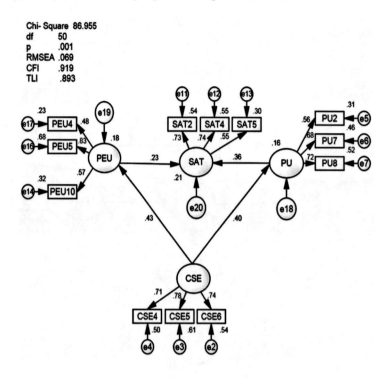

Figure 7. The Unconstrained Model

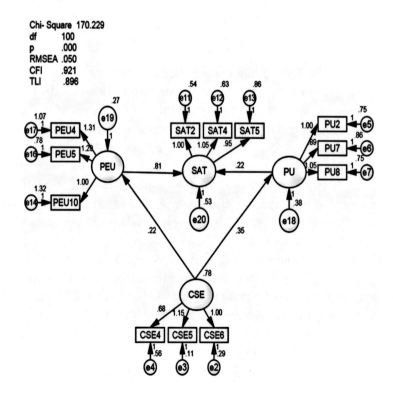

Figure 8. The Constrained Model

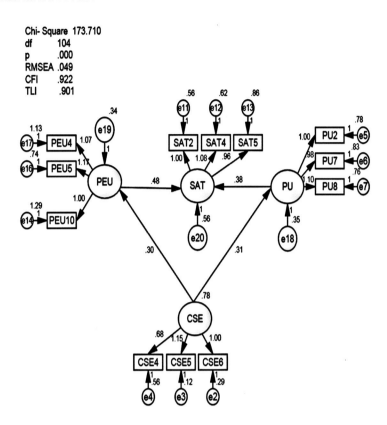

Figure 7 and Figure 8 both indicated that the analysis of this constrained TSM produced another two values:

- Chi-square ($\chi2 = 173.710$) and
- Degree of freedom ($df = 104$),

which were then tested against the unconstrained Chi-square ($\chi2 = 170.229$) and degree of freedom ($df = 100$) values for statistically significant differences. The invariance analysis across the male and female groups resulted in a statistically insignificant change in the Chi-square value, Chi-square ($df = 4$) = 3.481, $p > 0.05$, as revealed in Table 3. This meant that gender did not interact with the exogenous variables of TSM to influence the students' satisfaction in using wireless internet for their learning and research purposes in higher education. As such, it is reasonable to conclude that gender is not a moderating variable for this study.

Table 3. Results of critical value of chi-squared

Models		Chi Squared	D.F.	Critical Value	Chi Squared Change
Moderating Effect of Gender	Unconstrained	170.229	100	9.488 (*p > .05*)	3.481
	Constrained	173.710	104		
			4		

DISCUSSION

The findings of the study have in many ways contributed to the body of knowledge on Technology Satisfaction Model (TSM). Firstly, the hypothesis that perceived ease of use having a positive direct influence on satisfaction stands validated. This was consistent with prior studies conducted by researchers where they found the perceived ease of use with a statistically significant positive direct influence on satisfaction in:

- Using wireless internet (Islam, 2011b; Islam, 2014),
- Online research databases (Islam, 2011a; Islam et al., 2015),
- ICT facilities (Islam, 2016),
- Mobile learning (Lee & Park, 2008),
- E-Learning (Cheok & Wong, 2015) and
- Web digital library (Masrek & Gaskin, 2016).

This finding shows that students' satisfaction in using wireless internet for their learning and research purposes depends on ease of use of this technological service. For instance, if the wireless internet facility is easy to use for students' learning and research purposes in higher education then it will enhance their level of satisfaction, which can lead to academic achievement and success (Kuo et al., 2014). Consequently, this comes in line with earlier studies (Szymanski & Hise, 2000; Dabholkar & Bagozzi, 2002), which found convenience, likewise with the construct ease of use, to be a prominent factor in e-satisfaction. However, in their study, Shamdasani et al. (2008) observed that ease of use mediated by service quality did not show a high influence on satisfaction, and Islam (2016) found that lecturers' ease of use had an indirect influence on their gratification mediated by intention to use of ICT facilities for teaching and research purposes in higher education.

With the revised TSM, the influence of perceived usefulness on satisfaction was found to be validated. This was in congruent with the prior studies done by researchers where they discovered a significant direct impact of students' and lecturers' perceived usefulness on their satisfaction in using:

- Wireless internet service (Islam, 2011b; Islam, 2014),
- Online research databases (Islam, 2011a; Islam et al., 2015),
- Mobile learning (Lee & Park, 2008),
- E-Learning (Cheok & Wong, 2015),
- Web digital library (Masrek & Gaskin, 2016) and
- ICT facilities (Islam, 2016).

This result demonstrates that learners' satisfaction depends on the benefits of wireless internet service. If the wireless internet facility is useful for learning and research purposes in higher education then the learners' satisfaction will be expanded. Researchers also considered the perceived value as perceived usefulness with a positive direct influence on satisfaction (Shamdasani et al., 2008). In another study, Huang (2008) discerned a significant impact of perceived usefulness on consumer satisfaction mediated by their behavioral attitude toward the acceptance of websites. However, The TAG model (Islam, 2016) and ODAS model (Islam, 2011a) exhibited that perceived usefulness had a significant indirect influence on satisfaction mediated by intention to use.

As regards the effect of computer self-efficacy on perceived usefulness and perceived ease of use was discovered in a significant direct path coefficient, thereby validating the hypotheses 3 and 4. These findings were consistent with existing investigations conducted by researchers where they explored the direct influence of computer self-efficacy on perceived ease of use and usefulness (Chow, 2016) in using:

- ICT facilities (Islam, 2016),
- Wireless internet (Islam, 2014; Islam, 2011b),
- Online research databases (Islam et al., 2015; Islam, 2011a) and
- Internet learning resources (Chun, 2014).

Subsequently, computer self-efficacy also had a statistically significant indirect influence on satisfaction mediated by perceived usefulness and perceived ease of use, respectively, stands validated the hypotheses 5 and 6. These results were also similar with previous researches investigated by researchers where they exhibited that computer self-efficacy had significant indirect influence on satisfaction mediated by perceived usefulness and ease of use, respectively (Islam, 2014; Islam, 2016; Islam et al., 2015). The direct and indirect influences of computer self-efficacy confirmed that students' abilities directly increased their usefulness and ease of use of wireless internet and indirectly satisfaction. This means that learners' computer self-efficacy is the most significant latent variable of TSM (Islam, 2014; Islam, 2016; Islam et al., 2015) for assessing their technological satisfaction, usefulness and ease of use in an academic context. However, Ahmad et al. (2010) found that computer self-efficacy indirectly influences faculty's use of computer mediated technology through perceived usefulness and intention to use. Additionally, the TAG model (Islam, 2016) indicated that Malaysian and Chinese lecturers' computer self-efficacy indirectly effects on their intention to use of ICT facilities for teaching and research purposes mediated by perceived usefulness and ease of use, respectively (Islam, 2016). Similarly, the ODAS model (Islam, 2011a) showed the presence of significant indirect relationship between computer self-efficacy and satisfaction through the mediating influence of intention to use online research database.

Concerning the moderating effect of gender, the present study discovered that gender was not a moderating variable of causal structural of TSM in an academic context. This means that gender did not interact with the exogenous variables of TSM to affect the students' satisfaction in using wireless internet technology for their learning and research purposes in higher education. This was obtained after conducting the cross-validation of TSM. The detail findings of cross-validation of TSM have been explained in the result section. In line with these findings, Islam (2011b) found that gender was not a moderating variable, and Ahmad et al. (2010) asserted that gender did not influence faculty's use of technology to facilitate learning and teaching. However, researchers recently explored gender differences in diverse contexts (Chang et al., 2014; Chuang et al., 2015; Khedhaouria & Beldi, 2014).

As evidenced from the revised structural model, the influence of perceived ease of use on students' satisfaction was captured in terms of their easy access to getting technical support from Information Technology Division (ITD) and research materials from online research databases, online course registration and in using wireless internet without having to take recourse to any user manual. However, Islam (2014) revealed that some barriers still persist; these were manifested in the inadequate speed experienced by the students in downloading the materials from the internet. Besides, it was not easy to getting connection to and registration for wireless facility as perceived by the students.

Regarding the influence of perceived usefulness on satisfaction, it was manifested in students getting access to downloading materials from the internet, to obtaining multimedia facilities and to online research databases to further their research. Nevertheless, according to Islam (2014), students articulated their limitations vis-à-vis slower speed compared to the LAN as well as getting wireless internet access from anywhere and anytime in the campus.

Finally, the effect of computer self-efficacy on perceived usefulness, ease of use and satisfaction was limited to their capabilities and requisite skills in using wireless internet facility and online research databases, saving and printing journals or articles, and accessing the database from the IIUM website. Notwithstanding, students described obstacles related to accessing journals from the online research databases (Islam, 2014).

CONCLUSION

In the 21st century human-computer interaction has been rapidly occurred in academic contexts among either learner or educators throughout the globe. In doing so, the present study evaluated human-computer interaction by applying the TSM in a comprehensive public university in Malaysia. The viability of the TSM has been estimated and confirmed by using three-stage of structural equation modeling, namely,

- Confirmatory factor analysis,
- Full-fledged structural model and
- Invariance analyses, which is a unique theoretical, practical and methodological contribution of this study.

The findings of TSM attested that students' satisfaction was directly influenced by perceived ease of use and usefulness in using wireless internet for their learning and research purposes in higher education, and it was also indirectly affected by computer self-efficacy medicated by perceived usefulness and ease of use, respectively. Additionally, computer self-efficacy had a significant direct influence on perceived ease of use and usefulness. And students' computer self-efficacy was the most significant construct of the TSM. The results of cross-validation of the TSM discovered that gender did not interact with the exogenous variables of TSM to affect the students' satisfaction in using wireless internet technology for their learning and research purposes in higher education. Thus, it is reasonable to conclude that gender was not a moderating variable for technology satisfaction in an academic context. Moreover, the TSM was also individually validated for male and female students. As a result, the findings of this study have strong evidence to prove the generalizability of the TSM. Alone this line, the most significant contribution of this study was to utilize the appropriate approaches of invariance analyses for estimating the cross-validation of TSM, which could be useful for future researchers, service providers and academicians. The findings of TSM also could conclude the contemporary definition of research which is the logical integration of ideas as implemented by this study.

LIMITATIONS AND RECOMMENDATIONS

Albeit the research methodology apparently appears valid, reliable and eliciting, only one higher educational institution with a small sample size is used. It is therefore, the research may lack the variation of respondents. A wider research using more organizations with more samples may help to testify the

(TSM) model with a greater acceptability. Critics may generate the questions on its validity showing less number of samples as the excuse. However, usage of internet and the users hold a global pattern; it is thus a great potential for this model to work globally regardless of geographical, economic, social and cultural patterns in a particular country or region.

Based on the findings of TSM, the present study suggests that service providers have to ensure that the wireless internet service provided in higher education is easy and useful to expand learners' satisfaction in using it, especially by focusing on the speed of this technological facility (Nwagwu et al., 2009; Islam, 2011a; Islam 2014). Future researchers, academicians and practitioners should critically observe what are the sub-dimensions that could be considered for computer self-efficacy. A further research on cross-validation of the model could be done to explain the moderating effects of various demographic attributes on students', lecturers' and users' satisfaction. The age, gender, faculties, educational background and nationalities of students might be explored in this regard. In addition, the cross-cultural studies might be practical to provide a better understanding of the TSM.

REFERENCES

Atacan, G., Er, E., & Arifoglu, A. (2013). Public internet access points (PIAPs) and their social impact: A case study from Turkey. *Behaviour & Information Technology*, *32*(1), 14–23. doi:10.1080/014492 9X.2011.582149

Agarwal, R., & Karahanna, E. (2000). Time flies when youre having fun: Cognitive absorption and beliefs about information technology uses. *Management Information Systems Quarterly*, *24*(4), 665–694. doi:10.2307/3250951

Agarwal, R., & Prasad, J. (1998). A conceptual and operational definition of personal innovativeness in the domain of information technology. *Information Systems Research*, *9*(2), 204–215. doi:10.1287/isre.9.2.204

Ahmad, T. B. T., Basha, K. M., Marzuki, A. M., Hisham, N. A., & Sahari, M. (2010). Facultys acceptance of computer-based technology: Cross-validation of an extended model. *Australasian Journal of Educational Technology*, *26*(2), 268–279. doi:10.14742/ajet.1095

Aiken, R. L. (1993). *Personality, theories, research, and applications*. Prentice-Hall Inc.

Aljuaid, N. M. F., Alzahrani, M. A. R., & Islam, A. Y. M. A. (2014). Assessing mobile learning readiness in Saudi Arabia higher education: An empirical study. *The Malaysian Online Journal of Educational Technology*, *2*(2), 1–14.

Ani, O. E. (2010). Internet access and use: A study of undergraduate students in three Nigerian universities. *The Electronic Library*, *28*(4), 555–567. doi:10.1108/02640471011065373

Bandura, A. (1977). Self-efficacy: Toward a unifying theory of behavioral change. *Psychological Review*, *1*(84), 191–125. doi:10.1037/0033-295X.84.2.191 PMID:847061

Bandura, A. (1986). *Social foundations of thought and action: A social cognitive theory*. Englewood Cliffs, NJ: Prentice Hall.

Bandura, A., & Schunk, D. H. (1981). Cultivating competence, self-efficacy and intrinsic interest through self-motivation. *Journal of Personality and Social Psychology*, *41*(3), 586–598. doi:10.1037/0022-3514.41.3.586

Bouzaabia, O., Bouzaabia, R., & Capatina, A. (2016). Determinants of internet use by senior generation: A cross cultural study. *International Journal of Technology and Human Interaction*, *12*(1), 63–83. doi:10.4018/IJTHI.2016010105

Byrne, B. M. (2000). *Structural equation modeling with Amos: Basic concepts, applications and programming*. Mahwah, NJ: Lawrence Erlbaum.

Chang, C., Liu, E. Z., Sung, H., Lin, C., Chen, N., & Cheng, S. (2014). Effects of online college students internet self-efficacy on learning motivation and performance. *Innovations in Education and Teaching International*, *51*(4), 366–377. doi:10.1080/14703297.2013.771429

Chen, Y., & Lan, Y. (2014). An empirical study of the factors affecting mobile shopping in Taiwan. *International Journal of Technology and Human Interaction*, *10*(1), 19–30. doi:10.4018/ijthi.2014010102

Cheok, M., & Wong, S. (2015). Predictors of e-learning satisfaction in teaching and learning for school teachers: A literature review. *International Journal of Instruction*, *8*(1), 75–90. doi:10.12973/iji.2015.816a

Chow, M. (2016). Determinants of presence in 3D virtual worlds: A structural equation modelling analysis. *Australasian Journal of Educational Technology*, *32*(1), 1–18. doi:10.14742/ajet.1939

Chuang, S., Lin, F., & Tsai, C. (2015). An exploration of the relationship between internet self-efficacy and sources of internet self-efficacy among Taiwanese university students. *Computers in Human Behavior*, *48*, 147–155. doi:10.1016/j.chb.2015.01.044

Chun, M. (2014). A study on college students use intention of internet learning resources in Chongqing. *Asian Social Science*, *10*(3), 70–78. doi:10.5539/ass.v10n3p70

Dabholkar, P. A., & Bogazzi, R. (2002). An attitudinal model of technology-based self-service: Moderating effect of consumer traits and situational factors. *Journal of the Academy of Marketing Science*, *30*(3), 184–202. doi:10.1177/0092070302303001

Dash, , M., Pattnaik, A.K., Mohapatra, S., Sahoo, R.C., & Sundar, D. (2011). Using the TAM model to explain how attitudes determine adoption of internet banking. *European Journal of Economics Finance & Administrative Sciences*, *36*, 50–59.

Davis, F., Bagozzi, R. P., & Warshaw, P. R. (1989). User acceptance of computer-technology: A comparison of two theoretical models. *Management Science*, *38*(8), 982–1003. doi:10.1287/mnsc.35.8.982

Davis, F. D. (1989). Perceived usefulness, perceived ease of use and user acceptance of information technology. *Management Information Systems Quarterly*, *13*(3), 319–340. doi:10.2307/249008

Davis, F. D. (1993). User acceptance of information technology: System characteristics, user perceptions and behavioral impacts. *International Journal of Man-Machine Studies*, *38*(3), 475–487. doi:10.1006/imms.1993.1022

Delcourt, M. A. B., & Kinzie, M. B. (1993). Computer technologies in teacher education: The measurement of attitude and self-efficacy. *Journal of Research and Development in Education, 27*(1), 34–41.

Dineva, T., & Koufteros, X. A. (2002). *Self-efficacy and Internet usage-measurement and factorial validity*. Paper presented at the 2002 National Decision Sciences Institute DSI Conference, San Diego, CA.

Dutot, V. (2014). Adoption of social media using technology acceptance model: The generational effect. *International Journal of Technology and Human Interaction, 10*(4), 18–35. doi:10.4018/ijthi.2014100102

Gaudreau, P., Miranda, D., & Gareau, A. (2014). Canadian university students in wireless classrooms: What do they do on their laptops and does it really matter? *Computers & Education, 70*, 245–255. doi:10.1016/j.compedu.2013.08.019

Hair, J. F. Jr, Black, W. C., Babin, B. J., & Anderson, R. E. (2006). *Multivariate data analysis a global perception*. Upper Saddle River, NJ: Pearson Education, Inc.

Hamid, S., Waycott, J., Kurnia, S., & Chang, S. (2015). Understanding students perceptions of the benefits of online social networking use for teaching and learning. *The Internet and Higher Education, 26*, 1–9. doi:10.1016/j.iheduc.2015.02.004

Hanafizadeh, P., Behboudi, M., Koshksaray, A. A., & Tabar, M. J. S. (2014). Mobile-banking adoption by Iranian bank clients. *Telematics and Informatics, 31*(1), 62–78. doi:10.1016/j.tele.2012.11.001

Hashim, F., Alam, G. M., & Siraj, S. (2010). Information and communication technology for participatory based decision-making-E-management for administrative efficiency in higher education. *International Journal of Physical Sciences, 5*(4), 383–392.

Hong, J., Hwang, M., Hsu, H., Wong, W., & Chen, M. (2011). Applying the technology acceptance model in a study of the factors affecting usage of the Taiwan digital archives system. *Computers & Education, 57*(3), 2086–2094. doi:10.1016/j.compedu.2011.04.011

Huang, E. (2008). Use and gratification in e-consumers. *Internet Research, 18*(4), 405–426. doi:10.1108/10662240810897817

International Telecommunications Union. (2010). *Key global telecom indicators for the world telecommunication service sector*. Available at: http://www.itu.int/ITU-D/ict/statistics/index.html

Islam, A. Y. M. A. (2011a). *Online database adoption and satisfaction model*. Lambert Academic Publishing.

Islam, A. Y. M. A. (2011b). Viability of the extended technology acceptance model: An empirical study. *Journal of Information and Communication Technology, 10*, 85–98.

Islam, A. Y. M. A. (2014). Validation of the technology satisfaction model (TSM) developed in higher education: The application of structural equation modeling. *International Journal of Technology and Human Interaction, 10*(3), 44–57. doi:10.4018/ijthi.2014070104

Islam, A. Y. M. A. (2016). Development and validation of the technology adoption and gratification (TAG) model in higher education: A cross-cultural study between Malaysia and China. *International Journal of Technology and Human Interaction, 12*(3), 78–105. doi:10.4018/IJTHI.2016070106

Islam, A. Y. M. A., Leng, C. H., & Singh, D. (2015). Efficacy of the technology satisfaction model (TSM): An empirical study. *International Journal of Technology and Human Interaction, 11*(2), 45–60. doi:10.4018/ijthi.2015040103

Kaba, B., & Osei-Bryson, K. M. (2013). Examining influence of national culture on individuals attitude and use of information and communication technology: Assessment of moderating effect of culture through cross countries study. *International Journal of Information Management, 33*(3), 441–452. doi:10.1016/j.ijinfomgt.2013.01.010

Khedhaouria, A., & Beldi, A. (2014). Perceived enjoyment and the effect of gender on continuance intention for mobile internet services. *International Journal of Technology and Human Interaction, 10*(2), 1–20. doi:10.4018/ijthi.2014040101

Kreijns, K., Vermeulen, M., Kirschner, P. A., van Buuren, H., & van Acker, F. (2013). Adopting the integrative model of behaviour prediction to explain teachers willingness to use ICT: A perspective for research on teachers ict usage in pedagogical practices. *Technology, Pedagogy and Education, 22*(1), 55–71. doi:10.1080/1475939X.2012.754371

Kuo, Y. C., Walker, A. E., Schroder, K. E. E., & Belland, B. R. (2014). Interaction, internet self-efficacy, and self-regulated learning as predictors of student satisfaction in online education courses. *The Internet and Higher Education, 20*, 35–50. doi:10.1016/j.iheduc.2013.10.001

Lee, T. M., & Park, C. (2008). Mobile technology usage and b2b market performance under mandatory adoption. *Industrial Marketing Management, 37*(7), 833–840. doi:10.1016/j.indmarman.2008.02.008

Lee, Y. H., Hsieh, Y. C., & Hsu, C. N. (2011). Adding innovation diffusion theory to the technology acceptance model: Supporting employees' intentions to use e-learning systems. *Journal of Educational Technology & Society, 14*(4), 124–137.

Legris, P., Ingham, J., & Collerette, P. (2003). Why do people use information technology? A critical review of the technology acceptance model. *Information & Management, 40*(3), 191–204. doi:10.1016/S0378-7206(01)00143-4

Lichy, J., & Kachour, M. (2014). Understanding the culture of young internet users in a rapidly changing society. *International Journal of Technology and Human Interaction, 10*(4), 1–17. doi:10.4018/ijthi.2014100101

Liu, S., Liao, H., & Pratt, J. (2009). Impact of media richness and flow on e-learning technology acceptance. *Computers & Education, 52*(3), 599–607. doi:10.1016/j.compedu.2008.11.002

Ma, Q., & Liu, L. (2004). Technology acceptance model: A meta-analysis of empirical findings. *Journal of Organizational and End User Computing, 60*(1), 59–72. doi:10.4018/joeuc.2004010104

Masrek, M. N., & Gaskin, J. E. (2016). Assessing users satisfaction with web digital library: The case of Universiti Teknologi MARA. *The International Journal of Information and Learning Technology, 33*(1), 36–56. doi:10.1108/IJILT-06-2015-0019

Mathieson, K. (1991). Predicting user intention: Comparing the TAM with the theory of planned behavior. *Information Systems Research, 2*, 173–191. doi:10.1287/isre.2.3.173

Mezghani, K., & Ayadi, F. (2016). Factors explaining IS managers attitudes toward cloud computing adoption. *International Journal of Technology and Human Interaction, 12*(1), 1–20. doi:10.4018/IJTHI.2016010101

Moses, P., Wong, S. L., Bakar, K. A., & Rosnaini, M. (2013). Perceived usefulness and perceived ease of use: Antecedents of attitude towards laptop use among science and mathematics teachers in Malaysia. *The Asia-Pacific Education Researcher, 1*(2), Available at: http://link.springer.com/article/10.1007/s40299-012-0054-9

Nwagwu, E. W., Adekannbi, J., & Bello, O. (2009). Factors influencing use of the internet. *The Electronic Library, 27*(4), 718–734. doi:10.1108/02640470910979651

Schepers, J., & Wetzels, M. (2007). A meta-analysis of the technology acceptance model: Investigating subjective norm and moderation effects. *Information & Management, 44*(1), 90–103. doi:10.1016/j.im.2006.10.007

Schunk, D. H. (1991). *Learning theories: An educational perspective*. New York: McMillan Publishing Company.

Shamdasani, P., Mukherjee, A., & Malhotra, N. (2008). Antecedents and consequences of service quality in consumer evaluation of selt-service internet technology. *Service Industries Journal, 28*(1), 117–138. doi:10.1080/02642060701725669

Shittu, A. T., Basha, K. M., Rahman, N. S. N. A., & Ahmad, T. B. T. (2011). Investigating students attitude and intention to use social software in higher institution of learning in Malaysia. *Multicultural Education & Technology Journal, 5*(3), 194–208. doi:10.1108/17504971111166929

Shroff, R. H., Deneen, C. D., & Ng, E. M. W. (2011). Analysis of the technology acceptance model in examining students behavioural intention to use an e-portfolio system. *Australasian Journal of Educational Technology, 27*(4), 600–618. doi:10.14742/ajet.940

Sobel, M. E. (1982). Asymptotic confidence intervals for indirect effects in structural equation models. *Sociological Methodology, 13*, 290–312. doi:10.2307/270723

Sun, H., & Zhang, P. (2006). The role of moderating factors in user technology acceptance. *International Journal of Human-Computer Studies, 64*(2), 53–78. doi:10.1016/j.ijhcs.2005.04.013

Szymanski, D. M., & Hise, R. T. (2000). E-satisfation: An initial examination. *Journal of Retailing, 76*(3), 309–322. doi:10.1016/S0022-4359(00)00035-X

Taylor, S., & Todd, P. (1995). Understanding information technology usage: A test of competing models. *Information Systems Research, 6*(2), 144–176. doi:10.1287/isre.6.2.144

Teo, T. (2009). Modelling technology acceptance in education: A study of pre-service teachers. *Computers & Education, 52*(2), 302–312. doi:10.1016/j.compedu.2008.08.006

Teo, T., & van Schalk, P. (2009). Understanding technology acceptance in pre-service teachers: A structural-equation modeling approach. *The Asia-Pacific Education Researcher, 18*(1), 47–66. doi:10.3860/taper.v18i1.1035

Terzis, V., Moridis, C. N., Economides, A. A., & Rebolledo-Mendez, G. (2013). Computer based assessment acceptance: A cross-cultural study in Greece and Mexico. *Journal of Educational Technology & Society, 16*(3), 411–424.

Thompson, R., Compeau, R. D., & Higgins, C. (2006). Intentions to use information technologies: An integrative model. *Journal of Organizational and End User Computing, 18*(3), 25–47. doi:10.4018/joeuc.2006070102

Venkatesh, V., & Morris, G. M. (2000). Why dont men ever stop to ask for directions? Gender, social influence and their role in technology acceptance and usage behavior. *Management Information Systems Quarterly, 24*(1), 115–139. doi:10.2307/3250981

Venkatesh, V., Morris, G. M., Davis, B. G., & Davis, D. F. (2003). User acceptance of information technology: Toward a unified view. *Management Information Systems Quarterly, 27*(3), 425–478.

Wu, W., Chang, H., & Guo, C. (2008). An empirical assessment of science teacher's intention towards technology integration. *Journal of Computers in Mathematics and Science Teaching, 27*(4), 499–520.

Yousafzai, S. Y., Foxall, G. R., & Pallister, J. G. (2007). Technology acceptance: A meta-analysis of TAM (Part I). *Journal of Modeling in Management, 2*(3), 251–280. doi:10.1108/17465660710834453

Zamani-Miandashti, N., Memarbashi, P., & Khalighzadeh, P. (2013). The prediction of internet utilization behavior of undergraduate agricultural students: An application of the theory of planned behavior. *The International Information & Library Review, 45*(3-4), 114–126. doi:10.1080/10572317.2013.10766379

Zejno, B., & Islam, A. (2012). Development and validation of library ICT sage scale for the IIUM postgraduate students. *OIDA International Journal of Sustainable Development, 3*(10), 11–18.

KEY TERMS AND DEFINITIONS

Computer Self-Efficacy (CSE): In this study, computer self-efficacy refers to the students' beliefs in their computer ability to use the wireless internet for their learning and research purposes in higher education.

Confirmatory Factory Analysis (CFA): The CFA is the first stage of Structural Equation Modeling which is used to validate the measurement models.

Higher Education: Higher education is concerning to college or university where academic subjects (e.g. Bachelor, Master and PhD degrees) are studied at an advance level.

Invariance Analysis: The invariance analysis is the last stage of Structural Equation Modeling which is applicable to test the cross-validation of statistical models using any kind of moderating variables.

Perceived Ease of Use (PEU): In this study, perceived ease of use refers to the students' perception of how easy it is to use the wireless internet service for their learning and research purposes.

Perceived Usefulness (PU): According to the present study, perceived usefulness refers to the students' perception of the benefits derived from using the wireless internet.

Satisfaction (SAT): Satisfaction is defined as the extent to which the usage of technology is consistent with existing values, needs and the experience of students in using wireless internet facility.

Structural Equation Modeling (SEM): The SEM is one of the versatile analytical tools, which is appropriate to develop and validate the statistical models in various aspects of education such as Information and Communication Technology, Business, Economics, Education, Human Sciences, Social Sciences and Science.

Technology Satisfaction Model (TSM): The TSM is a contemporary model which is applicable to assess users' (e.g. learners, educators and consumers) satisfaction in using any kind of innovative technological services either in educational or industrial sectors.

Wireless Internet: The wireless internet is the latest technological innovation which is accessible through laptop, mobile device and personal digital assistant (PDA) to obtain information for teaching, learning, research and communication purposes.

Chapter 10
Continuance Use Intention of Mobile Internet Services:
Does Gender Matter?

Anis Khedhaouria
Montpellier Business School, Montpellier Research in Management, France

Adel Beldi
IÉSEG School of Management (LEM-CNRS 9221), France

ABSTRACT

In this chapter, we investigate the moderating effect of gender on the intention to continue using mobile Internet services (MIS) in an everyday life context. An extended model based on the technology acceptance theory is used to examine gender differences regarding MIS continuance intention in an everyday life context. A survey was conducted among 623 current MIS users to test the hypotheses using structural equation modeling approach. The findings show that female users expressed a stronger need for perceived usefulness and ease-of-use than male users, while male users expressed a significant need for perceived enjoyment. Interestingly, the stronger effect of perceived usefulness in females was contrary to prior TAM research. The observed gender differences suggest that MIS providers should consider gender when advertising and marketing MIS.

INTRODUCTION

Over the last decade, the adoption and the use of mobile Internet services (MIS), i.e., the access to Internet services through handheld mobile devices has surged urgently (Gerpott & Thomas, 2014). According to the International Data Corporation (IDC), the number of worldwide Mobile Internet users is expected to pass the two billions by the end of 2016. A recent review of the information systems (IS) literature shows that gender differences have been always a topic of research interest (Khedhaouria & Beldi, 2014; Khedhaouria, Beldi & Belbaly, 2013). Previous studies show that the qualitative use of both computers and Internet differs significantly between males and females, which may indicate subtle differences in attitudes toward these technologies (Ahuja & Thatcher, 2005; Gefen & Straub, 1997; Venkatesh & Mor-

DOI: 10.4018/978-1-5225-1868-6.ch010

ris, 2000; Venkatesh, Morris & Ackerman, 2000; Lee & Kwon, 2010). Nevertheless, gender differences regarding the use of MIS in everyday life have received little attention in the IS literature (Khedhaouria & Beldi, 2014; Khedhaouria et al., 2013). It has been suggested that MIS use has contributed to equalizing the communicative social integration of males and females much more than computers and fixed Internet, where male users still dominate (Khedhaouria et al., 2013). Understanding gender differences regarding MIS continuance intention in everyday life is therefore important for theory and practice.

MIS are ubiquitous and can be used willingly in everyday life activities as well as in mandatory settings (Lee, Kim, & Kim, 2005; Kim, Gupta, & Jeon, 2013). MIS provide everyday users with wireless access to Internet contents and services such as text messaging, access to large social networks, personal banking, gaming, and much more (Kim & Steinfield, 2004). The main advantages of MIS are mobility and immediacy (Kim, Chan, & Gupta., 2007):

- Internet access anytime, nearly anywhere.

By focusing on gender differences, it may be possible to gain a more nuanced understanding of the motives driving MIS continuance intention in males as opposed to females. While great progress has been made in understanding users' continuance intention (Bhattacherjee, 2001; Bhattacherjee & Premkumar, 2004; Kim et al., 2013), research suggests that low MIS acceptance by users is still a barrier to post-adoption and continuance intention (López-Nicolás, 2008; Lu, Denz, & Wang, 2008; Khedhaouria et al., 2013; Oghuma, Chang, Libaque-Sanez, Park, & Rho, 2015). Hence, the technology acceptance theory (Davis, Bagozzi, & Warshaw, 1989) seems to be useful for our research in order to understand gender differences regarding MIS continuance intention in everyday life. The research question of our investigation is the following:

- Do perceptions regarding MIS continuance intention vary with gender?

Based on the technology acceptance theory, we propose and test a model using data collected from 623 current MIS users. Our model extends the TAM model (i.e., perceived ease-of-use and usefulness) by adding perceived enjoyment as a third predictor because it has been suggested to influence MIS continuance intention in the IS literature (Deng, Turner, Gehling, & Prince, 2010; Khedhaouria et al., 2013). The findings show that female users expressed a stronger need for perceived usefulness and ease-of-use than male users, while male users expressed a significant need for perceived enjoyment. Interestingly, the stronger effect of perceived usefulness in females was contrary to prior TAM research (Venkatesh & Morris, 2000). The observed gender differences suggest that MIS providers should consider gender when advertising and marketing MIS.

Our study makes three contributions to the IS literature. First, it highlights the importance role of perceived enjoyment in MIS continuance intention in everyday life, especially for men users. The ubiquitous of MIS and their increasingly use, show the need to focus on perceived enjoyment as a critical motive for continuance intention. Second, it suggests that IS research should attempt to account for the gender effect on MIS continuance intention in everyday life context. Third, it provides some guidelines regarding how MIS can be designed and customized for gender segments.

The paper unfolds as follows. The next section presents the theoretical foundation for this research. The third section describes the research model and hypotheses. The fourth section discusses the methodology and data analysis techniques used to validate the scales and test the model. The fifth section presents the results. The paper concludes with a discussion of the implications for theory and practice.

THEORETICAL DEVELOPMENT

The Effect of Perceived Enjoyment on IS Continuance Intention

IS behavioral research established that behavioral intention is the major determinant of usage behavior (Kwon & Zmud, 1987). Fishbein and Ajzen (1975) defined behavioral intention as "the strength of one's intention to perform a specific behavior" (p. 288). Behavioral intention is often predicted on the basis of multi-attribute models (Swanson, 1988), which focus on users' motives regarding the various attributes of a technology. The TAM is a multi-attribute model for which the IS continuance intention refers to the post-adoption behavior at an organizational level of analysis (Karahanna, Straub & Chervany, 1999). At an individual level, IS continuance intention leads to continued IS usage behavior and refers to the usage stage where IS use transcends conscious behavior and becomes part of normal routine activity (Liao, Palvia, & Chen, 2009). The TAM predicts users' intentions to continue using an IS based on two motives:

- Perceived usefulness and
- Perceived ease-of-use.

Perceived usefulness is defined as "the degree to which a person believes that using a particular system would enhance his or her job performance"; while perceived ease-of-use is considered as "the degree to which a person believes that using a particular system would be free of effort" (Davis, 1989, p. 320). Most studies based on the TAM are conducted in an organizational context in which the main purposes for using the systems are effectiveness, efficiency, and utility. The studies have been predominantly interested in utilitarian motives, with an emphasis on the useful functionalities provided by IS, and they have thus focused on perceived usefulness as the cognitive source of IT continuance intention (Nysveen, Pedersen, & Thorbjornsen, 2005b). However, when the purpose is to explore MIS continuance intention in the context of everyday life, the TAM can be enriched by other dimensions that take into account both utilitarian and non-utilitarian motives (Deng et al., 2010).

Concepts from uses and gratification research (Katz & Blumler, 1974) can, for example, be added to the TAM in order to extend it to MIS research. Because this type of research focuses on the individual user in everyday life, the general idea is that users seek gratification in media and technology use based on their individual "needs" or "motivations" (Nysveen et al., 2005b). For this reason, uses and gratification research has an instrumental foundation that not only is similar to utilitarian theories of behavioral intention but also encompasses non-utilitarian motives. Uses and gratification studies (Leung & Wei, 2000) have determined several utilitarian motives related to perceived usefulness and ease-of-use, as well as non-utilitarian gratifications related to enjoyment, fun-seeking, and entertainment. Thus, in addition to the traditional antecedents of behavioral intention included in the TAM, uses and gratification research indicates that enjoyment, fun-seeking, and entertainment are significant motivations for MIS continuance intention (Khedhaouria et al. 2013).

Recent hedonic/utilitarian systems research reveals that pleasure and enjoyment should not be overlooked in system designs for everyday life (e.g., Van der Heijden, 2004). Hedonic/utilitarian systems research has its foundation in the context of motivational theory (Deci, 1975). Behavioral intention is thus determined by two fundamental types of motivation:

- Extrinsic and
- Intrinsic (Van der Heijden, 2004).

An extrinsically motivated user is "productivity-oriented" and motivated by what he or she can do with the IT for improving task performance (Kim & Hwang, 2006). Thus, extrinsic motivation can be expected to be the dominant determinant of continuance intention for utilitarian purposes. An intrinsically motivated user is "pleasure-oriented" and motivated to continue the use of the IS for fun and enjoyment (Wakefield & Whitten, 2006). Thus, intrinsic motivation can be expected to be the dominant determinant of MIS continuance intention for hedonic purposes (Deng et al., 2010).

The Effect of Gender on IS Continuance Intention

Table 1 shows the previous studies that examined the effects of gender differences on IT usage. A variety of IS has been examined (e.g., e-mail, on-line shopping, e-learning). However, little attention has been given to the potential moderating effect of gender on the continuance intention for MIS as a contemporary IS. In the IS literature, MIS are considered as a contemporary IS (e.g., Deng et al., 2010; Kim & Steinfield, 2004; Thong, Hong, & Tam, 2006; Khedhaouria et al., 2013).

As shown in Table 1, previous studies, which found significant differences between the sexes, can be divided into those using a theory-based analytic approach and those using a descriptive approach (Lee & Kwon, 2010). The theory-based studies adopted such theories as the TAM, the Theory of Planned Behavior (TPB), and the Expectation-Confirmation Model (ECM). In the descriptive approach, additional evidence for gender differences has been proposed (Bimber, 2000; Imhof, Vollmeyer, & Beierlein, 2007; Li & Kirkup, 2007; Ono & Zavodny, 2005).

Table 1. Summary of previous research on gender differences in IS usage context

Study	Research Object	Background Theory/ Methodology Used	Key Variables	Main Results
Theory-Based Analytic Approach				
Gefen & Straub (1997)	Perception and use of e-mail in the working place	Technology Acceptance Model (TAM)	- Perceived social presence - Perceived usefulness - Perceived ease-of-use	- Women and men differ in their perceptions to use the e-mail - The same mode of communication is perceived differently by the sexes
Venkatesh & Morris (2000)	Gender differences in the overlooked context of individual adoption and sustained usage of technology in the working place	Technology Acceptance Model (TAM)	- Perceived usefulness - Perceived ease-of-use - Subjective norms - Experience - Gender - Behavioral intention	- Men's technology usage decisions are strongly influenced by perceived usefulness -Women are strongly influenced by perceived ease-of-use and subjective norms

continued on following page

Table 1. Continued

Study	Research Object	Background Theory/ Methodology Used	Key Variables	Main Results
Venkatesh, Morris & Ackerman (2000)	Individual adoption and sustained usage of technology in the working place	Theory of Planned Behavior (TPB)	- Attitude toward behavior - Subjective norms - Perceived behavioral control -Behavioral intention	- Men are strongly influenced by their attitude toward using the new technology - Women are strongly influenced by subjective norms and perceived behavioral control
Ahuja & Thatcher (2005)	The influence of the work environment and gender on trying to innovate with IT	- Theory of Trying - Theory of Reasoned Action (TRA)	- Perceptions of the work environment (autonomy, overload) - Gender - Trying to continue innovate	Autonomy interacts with overload to determine trying to innovate with IT. The relationships vary by gender
Ong & Lai (2006)	Perceptions and relationships among the determinants of e-learning acceptance	Technology Acceptance Model (TAM)	- Self-efficacy - Perceived usefulness - Perceived ease-of-use - Behavioral intention to use	Men's computer self-efficacy, perceived usefulness, perceived ease of use, and behavioral intention to use e-learning are all higher than women's
Lee & Kwon (2010)	Continuance intention for on-line shopping services	Expectation and Confirmation Model (ECM)	- Perceived usefulness - Intimacy - Satisfaction - Continuance intention	- Intimacy is more tightly related to continuance use than perceived usefulness - Women are more sensitive to affective factors
Khedhaouria, Beldi & Belbaly (2013)	Continuance intention of MIS	Technology Acceptance Model (TAM)	- Perceived ease-of-use - Perceived usefulness - Perceived enjoyment - Continuance intention	- female users expressed a stronger need for perceived usefulness and ease-of-use than male users - The effect of perceived enjoyment was not significant for either males or females.
Descriptive Based Approach (Continued)				
Bimber (2000)	Differences in men's and women's presence on the Internet	Survey data	- Socioeconomic status - Gender-specific factor	The Internet use gap is the result of both socioeconomics and some combination of underlying gender-specific factors
Ono & Zavodny (2005)	Differences in men's and women's use of computers and the Internet in the United States and Japan and, if so, how this gender gap has changed over time	Micro-data from several surveys during 1997-2001	- Employment status - Type of employment (standard versus nonstandard)	The results indicate that gender differences in IT usage are considerably smaller in the United States than in Japan and in many cases nonexistent in the United States
Li & Kirkup (2007)	Differences in use of, and attitudes toward, Internet and computers generally for Chinese and British students, and gender differences in this cross-cultural context	Survey data	- Internet experience and usage patterns (frequency and internet use) - Internet confidence and skills, attitudes toward the Internet	Men in both countries are more likely than women to use email or chat rooms. Men played more computer games than women. Men in both countries are more self-confident about their computer skills than women
Imhof et al. (2007)	Computer usage	Survey data	- Computer access - Computer use - Computer self-efficacy	User behavior appears to be gender-specific as males spend more time on computer for personal purposes

Source: *(adapted from Lee & Kwon, 2010)*

Research Model and Hypotheses

Our research model is an extension of Technology Acceptance Model to explain and predict MIS continuance intention (Figure 1). The continuance intention is determined by three salient motives:

- Perceived usefulness (PU),
- Perceived ease-of-use (PEOU) and
- Perceived enjoyment (PE).

Furthermore, perceived ease-of-use is a determinant of perceived usefulness and enjoyment. This model assumes that gender differences will moderate the direct relationships between perceptions (PU, PEOU and PE) and MIS continuance intention.

Perceived Usefulness

Perceived usefulness has been regarded as a factor that is positively related to MIS continuance intention (Lee & Kwon, 2010). Hence, we expect that perceived usefulness has an influence on users' MIS continuance intention. Further, the effects of perceived usefulness on IS usage intention are related to instrumental behavioral. Mobile Internet services (MIS) are considered as a variety of IS and they are related to instrumental behavior (Nysveen, Pedersen, & Thorbjornsen, 2005a, Nysveen et al., 2005b). Instrumental behavior represents an extrinsic motivation, that is, motivation based on goal achievement (e.g., recognition or reward) as the main motive for behavioral intention (Deng et al., 2010). Instrumental motives for using MIS may also exist. An instrumental motivation for using mobile chat services, for example, may typically be to receive positive signals from potential boy/girlfriend (Nysveen et al., 2005a). Several studies have reported that men are more driven by instrumental factors than women (Ong & Lai, 2006; Venkatesh & Morris, 2000; Venkatesh et al., 2000). We hypothesize that male users will demonstrate more instrumental motivation than women for using MIS. Thus, it is expected that the

Figure 1. Caption research model

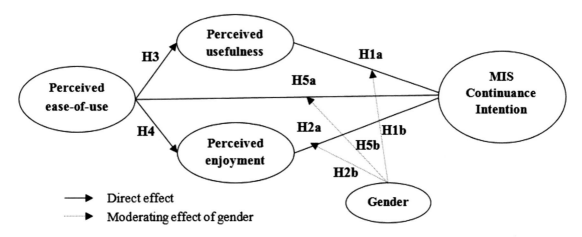

perception of usefulness will have a stronger impact on continuance intention in men than in women. Therefore, the following hypotheses will be tested:

H1a: Perceived usefulness will positively influence MIS continuance intention.
H1b: The effect of perceived usefulness on MIS continuance intention will be stronger for men than for women.

Perceived Enjoyment

Perceived enjoyment stands out as an important motive for continuing to use web portals (Lin et al., 2005). Perceived enjoyment is defined as the extent to which the activity of using the system is perceived to be enjoyable in its own right (Davis, Bagozzi & Warshaw, 1992). If an individual "feels good" using a service, he/she feels intrinsically motivated to continue using it (Lin, Wu, & Tsai, 2005). As mobile Internet services are increasingly used for hedonic purposes, perceived enjoyment can be expected to positively influence MIS continuance intention (Deng et al., 2010). Further, it was found that the direct effect of perceived enjoyment on usage intention is moderated by gender differences (Venkatesh et al., 2000). Women are more likely to value intrinsic factors such as variety and task enjoyment than men (Venkatesh, 1999). It is thus expected that the perception of enjoyment will have a stronger impact on continuance intention in women than in men. Therefore, the following hypotheses will be tested:

H2a: Perceived enjoyment will positively influence MIS continuance intention.
H2b: The effect of perceived enjoyment on MIS continuance intention will be stronger for women than for men.

Perceived Ease-Of-Use

Perceived ease-of-use is an important factor in determining MIS continuance intention (Kim & Steinfield, 2004). Perceived ease-of-use is an assessment of the mental effort involved in using MIS (Nysveen et al., 2005a). MIS that are difficult to access are less likely to be used (Nysveen et al., 2005b). The effect of perceived ease-of-use is mediated by perceived usefulness and perceived enjoyment (Van der Heijden, 2004). The less complex the Internet service is the more useful and enjoyable the user perceives it to be for accomplishing tasks (Moon & Kim, 2001). Therefore,

H3: Perceived ease-of-use will positively influence perceived usefulness.
H4: Perceived ease-of-use will positively influence perceived enjoyment.

Further, the direct relationship between perceived ease-of-use and IS usage intention is moderated by gender, and women experience higher anxiety than men (Venkatesh & Morris, 2000). Nysveen et al. (2005a, 2005b) found that that ease-of-use is a necessity for women's intention to use MIS. They argued that while usefulness is more important in achieving the end-goals of mobile chat services (i.e., extrinsic motivation), ease-of-use is more important in determining satisfaction with the process of text-messaging itself (i.e., intrinsic motivation). Men are more likely to be willing to put in effort to overcome constraints in order to achieve their objectives, without necessarily thinking about or emphasizing the magnitude of the effort involved (Venkatesh et al., 2000). Women, on the other hand, tend to focus on the method used to perform a task, suggesting greater process-orientation. Given the process-orientation of women, perceived ease-of-use is expected to have a powerful influence on MIS continuance intention. Further, evidence suggests that women display somewhat higher levels of technology anxiety, as noted above, and lower technology aptitude than men (Ahuja & Thatcher, 2005). Both technology anxiety and aptitude have been related to perceptions of effort, thus suggesting that constraints to perceived ease-of-use will be more salient to women than to men. We therefore investigate the following hypotheses:

H5a: Perceived ease-of-use will positively influence MIS continuance intention.
H5b: The effect of ease-of-use on MIS continuance intention will be stronger for women than for men.

While the hypotheses (H1a, H2a, H3, H4, and H5a) have been examined in prior IT research, the current study will conduct additional empirical investigation of these hypotheses in the context of MIS continuance intention in everyday life. In addition, this study attempts to extend the TAM by incorporating gender as a potential moderator in the model.

RESEARCH METHOD

Sample and Data Collection

To test our research model and its associated hypotheses, a web-based survey was conducted to collect data from users of Mobile Internet Services among undergraduate and graduate students at a France business school. The model presented in Figure 1 includes four constructs measured by adapting valid and reliable scales used in IS research literature to Mobile Information Systems. The participants indicated their agreement with a set of statements using a 7-point Likert-type scale that ranged from strongly disagree to strongly agree. We measured perceived ease-of-use (PEOU) using four items that we adapted from Wakefield & Whitten's (2006) study. Perceived enjoyment (PE) and usefulness (PU) were measured using, respectively, eight and nine items adapted from the original work of Van der Heijden & Sorensen (2003). Last, we measured continuance intention (CI) using a four-item scale that we adapted from Deng et al.'s (2010) study on MIS. All measures were translated into French by the author and then back-translated into English by an independent native speaker.

Two questionnaires were used to collect the data from students by following the approach undertaken by Deng et al. (2010). The first questionnaire was pilot tested for clarity and relevance on 20 mobile Internet service users, randomly selected from among the students enrolled in the French business school. All 20 students agreed to evaluate the clarity and relevance of the questions for us. After finalizing its format and content, the final questionnaire was posted on a survey website. An e-mail invitation was then sent to over 3,500 undergraduate and graduate students at the two business schools. Interested students were able to click on the link in the e-mail invitation to be directed to the survey website. A screening question was included at the beginning of the survey to determine whether the respondent was using MIS at the time of the survey. The survey website was designed in such a way that only current users could proceed with the survey.

A total of 833 (23.8%) responses were received, and 623 responses were from current MIS users. As Table 2 shows, the current users were 300 women (48.2%) and 323 men (51.8%). The majority of the

Table 2. Sample characteristics

Demographics			Female subgroup		Male subgroup	
			N=300 (48.2%)		N=323 (51.8%)	
			Mean	SD	Mean	SD
Age			22.5	3.2	23.6	4.0
Years of experience with MIS			1.7	1	2.2	1.2

MIS usage frequency per day	Never	Very low	Low	Medium	Frequently	Quite frequently	Very frequently	Total
Female (%)	1%	5%	4.3%	8.7%	14%	15.3%	51.7%	100%
Male (%)	0.3%	3.7%	3.4%	7.4%	15.2%	15.2%	50.5%	100%

respondents were between 21 and 25 years old with a mean age of 22.5 years for female respondents and 23.6 for male respondents.

The respondents had been using MIS from 0.5 to 5 years, with a mean value of 1.7 years for females and 2.2 years for males. In all, 51.7% of the female respondents and 50.5% of the male respondents reported using MIS very frequently every day.

Data Analysis

The present research used both SPSS and AMOS 19.0 to test the measurement and structural model. Frequently used in IS research, AMOS is considered to be more confirmatory in nature and it provides various overall goodness-of-fit indices to assess model fit (Byrne, 2001). It allows one to specify the relationships among both the conceptual factors of interest and the measures underlying each construct, resulting in a simultaneous analysis of

- How well the measures relate to each construct and
- Whether the hypothesized relationships at the theoretical level are empirically true.

Furthermore, AMOS is particularly useful for our study because it provides more rigorous testing of moderation effects (Arbuckle, 2010).

Measurement Model

The measurement model was assessed separately for the full sample and each subgroup (female and male). First, we assessed the degree of multicollinearity across independent variables by following the approach recommended by Hair, Black, Babin, & Anderson (2010). As shown in Table 3, the variance inflation factor (VIF) values are well below. Neter, Wasserman, and Kutner (1990) recommended threshold of 10 (or equivalently, tolerances of 0.1), indicating no serious concerns with multicollinearity in this study.

Last, the psychometric properties of the measurement scales for the first-order factors were assessed in terms of convergent validity, discriminant validity, and reliability for subgroup analyses.

To test convergent validity, we applied principal component analysis with Varimax rotation based on an eigenvalue greater than 1. The extracted variances of the constructs account for:

Table 3. Multicollinearity statistics

Statistic	R²	Tolerance = (1 − R²)	VIF = (1/Tolerance)
Perceived ease-of-use (PEOU)			
PEOU1	0.54	0.46	2.19
PEOU2	0.37	0.63	1.60
PEOU3	0.58	0.425	2.35
Perceived usefulness (PU)			
PU1	0.53	0.47	2.14
PU2	0.59	0.41	2.46
PU3	0.62	0.38	2.64
PU4	0.59	0.41	2.43
Perceived enjoyment (PE)			
PE1	0.65	0.35	2.88
PE2	0.59	0.41	2.44
PE3	0.78	0.22	4.47
PE4	0.63	0.37	2.74
PE5	0.74	0.26	3.88
PE6	0.64	0.36	2.75
PE7	0.67	0.33	3.03
PE8	0.73	0.27	3.68
Continuance intention (CI)			
CI1	0.67	0.33	3.03
CI2	0.54	0.46	2.16
CI3	0.70	0.30	3.33

- 74.5% (full group),
- 73.9% (female subgroup) and
- 75.4% (male subgroup).

Only seven items were dropped because they had loadings below the recommended threshold of 0.70 (Graver & Mentzer, 1999). The resulting factor loadings are shown in Table 4 with all 18 retained items exceeding 0.70 on their corresponding constructs, indicating adequate convergent validity.

To assess the discriminant validity, a good test is to compare the square root of the average variance extracted (AVE) for every construct with the inter-correlations among these constructs (Fornell & Larcker, 1981). The square root of AVE should be greater than the inter-correlation estimates (Hair et al., 2010). The correlation matrix shown in Table 5 indicates that the square roots of AVE on the diagonal are greater than the corresponding off-diagonal inter-construct correlations. This test shows good evidence of discriminant validity.

The reliability of the measurement items was examined using Cronbach's alpha coefficient (Cronbach, 1971) and composite reliability (Hoyle, 1995). Table 5 shows that all the values of Cronbach's alpha

Table 4. Summary of retained items and loadings for Varimax rotation

Retained Items/ Communalities (C) and Loadings	Full Group					Female Subgroup					Male Subgroup				
	C	PEOU	PU	PE	CI	C	PEOU	PU	PE	CI	C	PEOU	PU	PE	CI
Perceived ease-of-use (PEOU)															
1. I found the MIS easy to access	0.70	**0.71**	0.30	0.24	0.23	0.66	**0.70**	0.27	0.26	0.32	0.73	**0.73**	0.31	0.22	0.22
2. The MIS doesn't require a lot of mental effort	0.74	**0.85**	0.07	0.06	0.09	0.79	**0.88**	0.14	0.01	0.06	0.73	**0.84**	0.02	0.10	0.11
3. I found the MIS easy to use	0.78	**0.80**	0.20	0.24	0.21	0.76	**0.79**	0.16	0.22	0.26	0.80	**0.80**	0.24	0.25	0.18
Perceived usefulness (PU)															
4. I evaluate the MIS as efficient	0.70	0.15	**0.76**	0.20	0.24	0.70	0.14	**0.72**	0.21	0.34	0.70	0.14	**0.78**	0.19	0.18
5. I evaluate the MIS as effective	0.74	0.23	**0.77**	0.24	0.21	0.75	0.16	**0.77**	0.19	0.32	0.74	0.28	**0.75**	0.29	0.13
6. I evaluate the MIS as beneficial	0.74	0.18	**0.75**	0.29	0.27	0.79	0.23	**0.80**	0.23	0.20	0.72	0.10	**0.70**	0.33	0.32
7. I evaluate the MIS as productive	0.76	0.10	**0.81**	0.27	0.14	0.82	0.12	**0.84**	0.23	0.15	0.71	0.09	**0.79**	0.26	0.14
Perceived enjoyment (PE)															
8. I evaluate the MIS as exciting	0.71	0.15	0.16	**0.79**	0.18	0.65	0.16	0.14	**0.77**	0.14	0.75	0.16	0.18	**0.81**	0.20
9. I evaluate the MIS as delightful	0.65	0.15	0.16	**0.77**	0.13	0.61	0.13	0.13	**0.75**	0.13	0.69	0.18	0.18	**0.78**	0.12
10. I evaluate the MIS as fascinating	0.81	0.09	0.23	**0.86**	0.05	0.78	0.09	0.25	**0.84**	-0.02	0.84	0.11	0.23	**0.88**	0.09
11. I evaluate the MIS as playful	0.70	0.13	0.16	**0.80**	0.15	0.63	0.10	0.12	**0.75**	0.23	0.77	0.13	0.16	**0.84**	0.14
12. I evaluate the MIS as thrilling	0.79	0.03	0.24	**0.85**	0.09	0.77	0.05	0.24	**0.84**	0.04	0.81	0.03	0.24	**0.86**	0.11
13. I evaluate the MIS as pleasant	0.68	0.19	0.22	**0.73**	0.24	0.69	0.11	0.18	**0.73**	0.32	0.69	0.23	0.24	**0.73**	0.21
14. I evaluate the MIS as amusing	0.71	0.13	0.15	**0.81**	0.16	0.73	0.11	0.13	**0.83**	0.31	0.69	0.15	0.15	**0,78**	0.18
15. I evaluate the MIS as cheerful	0.78	0.08	0.19	**0.85**	0.13	0.78	0.06	0.15	**0.86**	0.15	0.77	0.11	0.21	**0.84**	0.12
Continuance intention (CI)															
16. I intend to continue using the MIS in the future	0.81	0.24	0.27	0.19	**0.80**	0.79	0.21	0.28	0.18	**0.80**	0.83	0.25	0.26	0.20	**0.81**
17. I will always try to use the MIS in my daily life	0.77	0.12	0.21	0.20	**0.82**	0.74	0.11	0.27	0.20	**0.78**	0.76	0.14	0.14	0.20	**0.83**
18. I will keep using the MIS as regularly as I do now	0.85	0.19	0.26	0.20	**0.84**	0.83	0.27	0.29	0.19	**0.80**	0.86	0.13	0.22	0.19	**0.87**
Eigenvalues		1.11	2.35	8.63	1.31		1.02	2.57	8.42	1.29		1.24	2.18	8.84	1.32
% variance extracted	74.5%	6.18	13.06	47.95	7.29	73.9%	5.65	14.25	46.80	7.15	75.4%	6.87	12.10	49.11	7.32

Note: PEOU = perceived ease-of-use; PU = perceived usefulness; PE = perceived enjoyment; CI = MIS continuance intention.

Table 5. Inter-construct correlations, square root of AVE, Cronbach's alpha, and composite reliability

Full Group, Subgroups and Constructs	Cronbach's Alpha	Composite Reliability	Correlation of Constructs[a]			
Full group			PEOU	PU	PE	CI
PEOU	0.81	0.80	**0.76**			
PU	0.87	0.88	0.59	**0.80**		
PE	0.94	0.94	0.48	0.59	**0.83**	
CI	0.87	0.91	0.58	0.65	0.47	**0.88**
Female subgroup						
PEOU	0.79	0.78	**0.74**			
PU	0.87	0.90	0.59	**0.83**		
PE	0.91	0.94	0.46	0.55	**0.81**	
CI	0.87	0.88	0.66	0.69	0.46	**0.85**
Male subgroup						
PEOU	0.81	0.81	**0.77**			
PU	0.86	0.86	0.60	**0.78**		
PE	0.95	0.95	0.50	0.64	**0.84**	
CI	0.88	0.89	0.54	0.61	0.47	**0.85**

Note: [a]Diagonal elements in the inter-construct correlations matrix are the square root of the average variance extracted (AVE). For adequate discriminant validity, diagonal elements should be greater than corresponding off-diagonal elements.

and the composite reliability are well above the suggested 0.70 threshold (Fornell & Larcker, 1981), indicating the high reliability of the retained items.

Following the factor analysis, multiple-group structural equation modeling tested the moderating effect of gender (Hair et al., 2010). The structural model estimate is assessed for moderation by a comparison of two group models. The first group model (or totally free model), called the unconstrained group model, was estimated with path estimates calculated separately for each subgroup (female and male). A second group model, called the constrained group model, was then estimated, with the structural path estimate constrained to be equal between the subgroups. In other words, in the constrained group model, path estimates are maintained constant across structural subgroup models. Comparison of the differences between models with a chi-square difference test (DChi2) indicated whether the model fit significantly decreased (i.e., an increase in chi-square) when the estimates were constrained to be equal. A statistically significant difference between models indicated that the path estimates were different (i.e., model fit was significantly better when separate path estimates were made) and that moderation occurred. If the models were not significantly different, then there is no support for moderation because the structural path estimates were not different between subgroups. Using the multiple-group analysis with AMOS, the DChi2 test and its significance could be calculated (Arbuckle, 2010).

RESULTS

Motives and MIS Continuance Intention

The first research question asked whether perceptions of ease-of-use, usefulness and enjoyment influenced MIS continuance intention. To investigate this question, we examined three models. The full-group model was the baseline model. Females and males were then separated into subgroups. Table 6 shows the fit measures for each model. Structural modelling indicates an acceptable fit of the empirical results with theoretical models.

Figure 2 shows the results of testing the full group model as the baseline model. This model accounts for 48% of the variance of MIS continuance intention, 40% of the variance of perceived usefulness, and 28% of the variance of perceived enjoyment. All path coefficients are significant as hypothesized (PEOU-CI, PU-CI at $p < .001$, and PE-CI at $p < .05$; H1a, H2a, H3, H4 and H5a are confirmed). Thus, perceptions of ease-of-use, usefulness and enjoyment significantly influenced MIS continuance intention in the full group.

Table 6. Fit measures

	Full Group Model	**Female Subgroup Model**	**Male Subgroup Model**
Absolute fit GFI (> 0.90)	0.91	0.91	0.91
RMSEA (< 0.08)	0.06	0.07	0.06
Chi2/df (< 5)	3.90	2.95	2.48
Incremental fit NFI (> 0.92)	0.94	0.94	0.93
CFI (> 0.92)	0.95	0.93	0.96
RFI (> 0.90)	0.92	0.91	0.91
Parsimony fit AGFI (< GFI)	0.88	0.83	0.87
PNFI (> PGFI 0.70)	0.80	0.80	0.80

Figure 2. Caption full group model (baseline model)

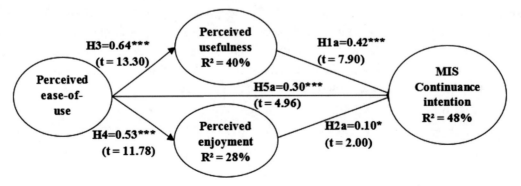

Note: t-values are in parentheses, *p < .05. ***p < .001

Figure 3. Caption female subgroup model

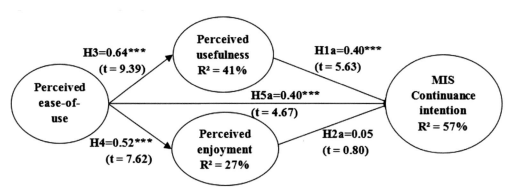

Note: t-values are in parentheses, ***p < .001

Figure 3 illustrates the MIS continuance intention model in the female subgroup. This model accounts for:

- 57% of the variance of MIS continuance intention,
- 41% of the variance of perceived usefulness, and
- 27% of the variance of perceived enjoyment.

The results show an increase in the path coefficient of the direct effect of PEOU on MIS continuance intention (CI) in comparison with the baseline model (from 0.30 to 0.40 at p < .001; H5a is confirmed). The path coefficient of PU-CI shows a decrease in comparison with the baseline model, and exerts a direct significant effect on MIS continuance intention at p = .001 (from 0.42 to 0.40; H1a is confirmed). The other path coefficients, PEOU-PU and PEOU-PE, remain nearly the same in comparison with the baseline model, which exerts a significant indirect effect on continuance intention at p = .001 (H3 and H4 are confirmed). However, contrary to our expectation, the direct effect of PE on MIS continuance intention is not significant at p = .05 (t=0.80 (<1.96); p = .423; H2a is rejected).

Figure 4 presents the MIS continuance intention model within the male subgroup. This model accounts for:

- 41% of the variance of MIS continuance intention,
- 42% of the variance of perceived usefulness, and
- 30% of the variance of perceived enjoyment.

The results show a decrease in the path coefficient of the direct effect of PEOU on MIS continuance intention in comparison with the baseline model (from 0.42 to 0.37 at p < .001; H1a is confirmed). They also show a drop in the path coefficient of the direct effect of PEOU on MIS continuance intention in comparison with the baseline model (from 0.30 to 0.26 at p < .01; H5a is confirmed). The direct effect of PE on MIS continuance intention is significantly different from zero at the 0.05 level (t=1.97; H2a is confirmed). The other path coefficients (PEOU-PU and PEOU-PE) remain nearly the same in comparison with the baseline model, and exert an indirect significant effect on continuance intention at p = .001 (H3 and H4 are confirmed).

Figure 4. Caption male subgroup model

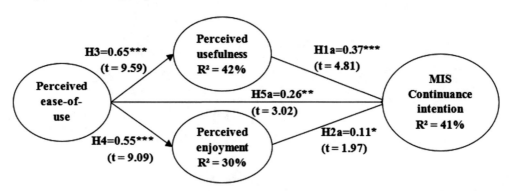

Note: t-values are in parentheses, *p < .05. **p < .01. ***p < .001

It is apparent that gender has a moderating effect on MIS continuance intention, which explains the variation in the path coefficients that represent the direct effects of PEOU, PU and PE on continuance intention. In the subsequent section, we test the moderating effect of gender on MIS continuance intention.

Gender and MIS Continuance Intention

The second research question asked whether the strength of the relationships between perceptions (PEOU, PU and PE) and continuance intention varies by gender. The totally free structural model estimates an identical structural model in both subgroups. The model fit statistics and path estimates for the PEOU-CI, PU-CI, and PE-CI relationships are shown in Table 7. Then a second group model is estimated, the only difference being that the path estimates are constrained to be equal in the two subgroups. These fit results and path estimates are also shown in Table 7. Both models show acceptable fit indices (χ^2/ df, CFI and RMSEA), indicating their overall acceptability. The chi-square difference between models (DChi2) is 32.48 with 19 degree of freedom (df). This is significant (p < .05, p-value = 0.028), indicating that constraining the PEOU-CI, PU-CI, and PE-CI path estimates to be equal between subgroups produces a worse fit. Therefore, the unconstrained totally free model in which the PEOU-CI, PU-CI, and PE-CI relationships are freely estimated in both subgroups is confirmed. This result suggests that gender moderates the relationships between PEOU-CI, PU-CI, and PE-CI.

Looking at the standardized path estimates (B) for the totally free results, we found that the PU-CI and PEOU-CI relationships are significant in both subgroups. Nevertheless, contrary to hypothesis H1b, the effect of perceived usefulness on MIS continuance intention is stronger in the female subgroup (B = 0.40, p < .001) than in the male subgroup (B = 0.37, p < .001). The difference is significant (p < .05, H1b is rejected). The effect of perceived ease-of-use on MIS continuance intention is stronger in the female subgroup (B = 0.40, p < .001) than in the male subgroup (B = 0.26, p < .01). The difference is significant (p < .05, H5b is confirmed). However, the PE-CI relationship is only significant in the male subgroup (B = 0.11, p < .05). The difference in effect is significant (p < .05, H2b is rejected). Thus, it seems that the effect of PU and PEOU on the MIS continuance intention is stronger for women than for men, while PE was determinant for men. Table 8 presents a summary of the hypothesis testing results.

Table 7. Testing for gender as a moderator in the MIS continuance intention model

Model Characteristics	Unconstrained Group Model (totally free for each structural subgroup)	Constrained Group Model (path estimates equal across structural subgroups)	Model Differences (DChi2/Ddf)[b] Significance
Model fit			
χ^2	705.95	738.43	1.71 (32.48/19)
df	260	270	(p-value = .028)*
CFI	0.94	0.94	-
RMSEA	0.051	0.053	-
Standardized path estimates (B)			
PU→CI		-	(p-value = .043)*
Female	0.40***		
Male	0.37***		
PEOU→CI		-	(p-value = .038)*
Female	0.40***		
Male	0.26**		
PE→CI		-	(p-value = .044)*
Female	0.05		
Male	0.11*		

Note: [b]DChi2 = Chi2(constrained group) – Chi2(unconstrained group); Ddf = df(constrained group) -df(unconstrained group). *p < .05. **p < .01. ***p < .001

Table 8. Summary of hypotheses tests

Relationships	Support
H1a: PU-CI	Yes
H1b: PU-CI	No
H2a: PE-CI	No
H2b: PE-CI	No
H3: PEOU-PU	Yes
H4: PEOU-PE	Yes
H5a: PEOU-CI	Yes
H5b: PEOU-CI	Yes

DISCUSSION

The present research addressed the following question:

- "Do perceptions regarding MIS continuance intention vary with gender?"

It did so by investigating the moderating effect of gender on MIS continuance intention in everyday life. An extended TAM model was applied to data from a sample of 623 French MIS users to examine the moderating effect of gender.

The results show that perceived usefulness and perceived ease-of-use significantly influenced MIS continuance intention in the male and female subgroups. However, contrary to our expectation, perceived enjoyment significantly influenced MIS continuance intention only in the male subgroup. The findings also show support for the proposition that the effect of perceptions on MIS continuance intention differs between genders. Female users were strongly motivated by perceived ease-of-use, which confirms previous findings (Ong & Lai, 2006). Interestingly, female users were also more strongly motivated by perceived usefulness than male users, but their perception of enjoyment had no influence on their continuance intention (Khedhaouria et al., 2013). From a theoretical standpoint, this finding is an important contribution since our model accounts for 57% of the variance of MIS continuance intention for female users. This discrepancy with previous findings suggests the importance of focusing on hedonic versus utilitarian purposes (Lee et al., 2009). Our results show that MIS were used specifically for utilitarian purposes rather than hedonic purposes, as the perceived usefulness values are higher than the perceived enjoyment values in both subgroups (Van der Heijden, 2004). When the main purpose was utilitarian, female users expressed a relatively stronger need for perceived usefulness and ease-of-use than male users, while male users expressed a certain need for perceived enjoyment, as well. Thus, including gender as a potential moderator in the TAM helps to better understand the underlying cognitive phenomena related to MIS continuance intention.

The implications of this study are noteworthy for academics and practitioners alike. The results indicate a genuine gender effect on MIS continuance intention. Our research empirically demonstrates that male and female users differ in perceptions regarding MIS continuance intention. This is an important theoretical contribution that can enrich the existing IT literature on the topic. Although certain studies investigated gender effects on IS usage in the workplace (Gefen & Straub, 1997; Venkatesh & Morris, 2000; Venkatesh et al., 2000), these studies are insufficient to account for behavioral intentions toward IS in the context of everyday life, and especially the MIS continuance intention (Khedhaouria et al., 2013). Given the extensive role of MIS in daily life, understanding gender differences in personal technology continuance intention is a recent and important issue (Khedhaouria et al., 2013).

Furthermore, our "counterintuitive" finding that females consider perceived usefulness to a greater extent than males regarding MIS continuance intention. The mobile has contributed to improving the communicative social integration of females much more than computers and Internet, where male users still dominate (Khedhaouria et al., 2013). Our finding highlights a new trend regarding MIS usage. Hence, a better understanding of gender differences in behavioral intention toward MIS can help researchers in developing and testing MIS theories in the future.

From a practical perspective, the academic implications discussed above are instructive and should not be overlooked. Further, given the increasing number of female MIS users, understanding gender differences in MIS continuance intention will be a critical issue in controlling switching behaviors (Ranganathan,

Seo & Babad, 2006). MIS providers should consider the gender of their users when designing and offering MIS. The results show a relatively strong overall effect of perceived usefulness and ease-of-use on MIS female users' intention to continue to use these services for utilitarian purposes. This particular finding tells MIS providers that females are more demanding and that certain basic threshold levels of usefulness must be present for MIS – regardless of their objective – in order for female users to develop positive attitudes and the intention to continue to use them. MIS providers could reduce the number of useful paid services, offer a variety of promotional plans, and provide additional calling minutes to increase female users' usage intentions, which might well compensate any losses (Ranganathan et al., 2006). Moreover, perceived ease-of-use is also revealed to be a significant predictor of female users' intention to continue to use MIS. Consequently, when promoting MIS to female users, MIS providers should particularly highlight aspects relating to "user-friendliness" (Venkatesh & Morris, 2000). By the same token, MIS providers and developers should ensure, through usability pretesting, that all MIS are considered sufficiently easy-to-use for female users (Lee & Benbasat, 2003). Furthermore, as the constraints of mobile terminals, such as small screens, small keypads and slow responses may undermine usage intentions, MIS providers and developers should continue investing in delivering an easy-to-use interface (Wang et al., 2006).

In addition to perceived usefulness and ease-of-use, we also observe that perceived enjoyment has a significant direct effect on male users' intention to continue to use MIS. This finding implies that MIS developers should pay close attention to aspects of enjoyment – like excitement and fun – when designing MIS (Wakefield & Whitten, 2006). Further, MIS providers should take into consideration the importance of playfulness when promoting MIS to men in order to decrease user defection (Khedhaouria et al., 2013).

CONCLUSION

Our work is not free of limitations, and these should be noted. First, we did not control for the types of services or applications that our respondents habitually used (utilitarian and hedonic purposes). Due to the largely unexplored differences between utilitarian applications (e.g., text messaging and payment) and hedonic applications (e.g., network contact and gaming), it is conceivable that gender effects on continuance intention differ depending on the nature of the application (utilitarian versus hedonic). Second, the data were collected from university students with ages ranging from 21 and 25 years old. As age may moderate the effect of perceptions on IS usage (Brown, Dennis, & Venkatech, 2010), we think that more research is needed to examine the generalizability of the results to other users, both younger and older. Last, other factors undoubtedly influence MIS continuance intention but were not included in this study. For instance:

- Personal habit (Limayem, Hirt, & Cheung., 2007),
- Users' inertia (Polites & Karahanna, 2012),
- Past experience (Brown et al., 2010) and
- Cultural customs (Li & Kirkup, 2007) have been shown to influence IS usage. Future research would do well to replicate this study across other European and non-European countries.

This study provides new insight into how gender affects continuance intention for MIS and raises many interesting questions for future research. We hope that it triggers additional theorizing and empirical investigation aimed at a better understanding of MIS users' behavioral intention. As suggested, better knowledge in this area may benefit MIS providers and users alike in their attempt to cope successfully with the challenges brought about by ever more exciting mobile applications.

REFERENCES

Ahuja, M. K., & Thatcher, J. B. (2005). Moving beyond intentions and toward the theory of trying: Effects of work environment and gender on post-adoption information technology use. *Management Information Systems Quarterly*, *29*(3), 427–459.

Arbuckle, J. L. (2010). *User's Guide*. Amos Development Corporation.

Bhattacherjee, A. (2001). Understanding information systems continuance: An expectation-confirmation model. *Management Information Systems Quarterly*, *35*(3), 351–370. doi:10.2307/3250921

Bhattacherjee, A., & Premkumar, G. (2004). Understanding changes in belief and attitude toward information technology usage: A theoretical model and longitudinal test. *Management Information Systems Quarterly*, *28*(2), 229–254.

Bimber, B. (2000). Measuring the gender gap on the Internet. *Social Science Quarterly*, *81*(3), 868–876.

Brown, S. A., Dennis, A. R., & Venkatesh, V. (2010). Predicting collaboration technology use: Integrating technology adoption and collaboration research. *Journal of Management Information Systems*, *27*(2), 9–53. doi:10.2753/MIS0742-1222270201

Byrne, B. M. (2001). *Structural Equation Modeling with AMOS: Basic concepts, Applications, and Programming*. Mahwah, NJ: Lawrence Erlbaum Associates, Publishers.

Chandra, S., Srivastava, S. C., & Theng, Y. L. (2010). Evaluating the role of trust in consumer adoption of mobile payment systems: An empirical analysis. *Communications of the Association for Information Systems*, *27*(1), 351–370.

Chen, S. Y., & Macredie, R. (2010). Web-based interaction: A review of three important human factors. *International Journal of Information Management*, *30*(5), 379–387. doi:10.1016/j.ijinfomgt.2010.02.009

Cronbach, L. J. (1971). Test validation. In *Education Measurement*. Washington, DC: R Thorndike, American Council on Education.

Davis, F. D. (1989). Perceived usefulness, perceived ease of use, and user acceptance of information technology. *Management Information Systems Quarterly*, *13*(3), 319–340. doi:10.2307/249008

Davis, F. D., Bagozzi, R. P., & Warshaw, P. R. (1989). User Acceptance of Computer Technology: A Comparison of Two Theoretical Models. *Management Science*, *35*(8), 982–1003. doi:10.1287/mnsc.35.8.982

Davis, F. D., Bagozzi, R. P., & Warshaw, P. R. (1992). Extrinsic and intrinsic motivation to use computer in the workplace. *Journal of Applied Social Psychology*, *22*(14), 1111–1132. doi:10.1111/j.1559-1816.1992.tb00945.x

Deci, E. L. (1975). *Intrinsic motivation*. New York: Plenum Press. doi:10.1007/978-1-4613-4446-9

Deng, L., Turner, D., Gehling, R., & Prince, B. (2010). User experience, satisfaction, and continual usage intention of IT. *European Journal of Information Systems*, *19*(1), 60–75. doi:10.1057/ejis.2009.50

Fishbein, M., & Ajzen, I. (1975). *Belief, attitude, intention and behavior: an introduction to theory and research*. Reading, MA: Addison-Wesley.

Fornell, C., & Larcker, D. (1981). Evaluating structural equation models with unobserved variables and measurement error. *JMR, Journal of Marketing Research*, *18*(1), 39–50. doi:10.2307/3151312

Gefen, D., & Straub, D. W. (1997). Gender differences in the perception and use of e-mail: An extension to the technology acceptance model. *Management Information Systems Quarterly*, *21*(4), 389–400. doi:10.2307/249720

Gerpott, T. J., & Thomas, S. (2014). Empirical research on mobile internet usage: A meta-analysis of the literature. *Telecommunications Policy*, *38*(3), 291–310. doi:10.1016/j.telpol.2013.10.003

Graver, M. S., & Mentzer, J. T. (1999). Logistics research methods: Employing structural equation modeling to test construct validity. *Journal of Business Logistics*, *20*(1), 33–57.

Hair, J. F., Black, W. C., Babin, B. J., & Anderson, R. E. (2010). *Multivariate data analysis. A global perspective*. Pearson.

Hoyle, R. H. (1995). *Structural equation modeling: concepts, issues and applications. New Delhi, London*. Thousand Oaks, CA: Sage Publications.

Imhof, M., Vollmeyer, R., & Beierlein, C. (2007). Computer use and the gender gap: The issue of access, use, motivation, and performance. *Computers in Human Behavior*, *23*(6), 2823–2837. doi:10.1016/j.chb.2006.05.007

Karahanna, E., Straub, D. W., & Chervany, N. L. (1999). Information technology adoption across time: A cross-sectional comparison of pre-adoption and post-adoption beliefs. *Management Information Systems Quarterly*, *23*(2), 183–213. doi:10.2307/249751

Katz, E., & Blumler, G. (1974). *The Use of Mass Communications: Current Perspectives on Gratifications Research*. Beverly Hills, CA: Sage.

Khedhaouria, A., & Beldi, A. (2014). Perceived enjoyment and the effect of gender on continuance intention for mobile Internet services. *International Journal of Technology and Human Interaction*, *10*(2), 1–20. doi:10.4018/ijthi.2014040101

Khedhaouria, A., Beldi, A., & Belbaly, N. (2013). The moderating effect of gender on continuance intention for mobile Internet services (MIS). *Système dInformation & Management*, *18*(3), 117–142. doi:10.3917/sim.133.0117

Kim, D., & Hwang, Y. (2006). A study of mobile Internet usage from utilitarian and hedonic user tendency perspectives. In *Proceedings of the Twelfth Americas Conference on Information Systems*. Acapulco, Mexico: AIS.

Kim, D., & Steinfield, C. (2004). Consumers' mobile Internet service satisfaction and their continuance intentions. In C. Bullen, & E. Stoher (Ed.), *Proceedings of the Tenth Americas Conference on Information Systems*. Atlanta, GA: AIS.

Kim, H. W., Gupta, S., & Jeon, Y. S. (2013). User continuance intention towards Mobile Internet service: The case of Wimax in Korea. *Journal of Global Information Management, 21*(4), 121–142. doi:10.4018/jgim.2013100107

Kim, H. W. H., Chan, C., & Gupta, S. (2007). Value-based adoption of mobile Internet: An empirical investigation. *Decision Support Systems, 43*(1), 111–126. doi:10.1016/j.dss.2005.05.009

Kwon, T. H., & Zmud, R. W. (1987). Unifying the fragmented models of information systems implementation. In R. J. Boland & R. A. Hirschheim (Eds.), *Critical Issues in Information Systems Research*. New York: John Wiley & Sons.

Lee, I., Kim, J., & Kim, J. (2005). Use contexts for the mobile Internet: A longitudinal study monitoring actual use of mobile Internet services. *International Journal of Human-Computer Interaction, 18*(3), 269–292. doi:10.1207/s15327590ijhc1803_2

Lee, S., Shin, B., & Lee, H. G. (2009). Understanding post-adoption usage of mobile data services: The role of supplier-side variables. *Journal of the Association for Information Systems, 10*(12), 860–888.

Lee, Y., & Benbasat, I. (2003). Interface designs for mobile commerce. *Communications of the ACM, 46*(12), 49–52. doi:10.1145/606272.606300

Lee, Y., & Kwon, O. (2010). Gender differences in continuance intention of on-line shopping services. *Asia Pacific Journal of Information Systems, 20*(3), 51–72.

Leung, L., & Wei, R. (2000). More than just talk on the move: Uses and gratifications of cellular phone. *Journalism & Mass Communication Quarterly, 77*(1), 308–320. doi:10.1177/107769900007700206

Li, N., & Kirkup, G. (2007). Gender and cultural differences in Internet use: A study of China and the UK. *Computers & Education, 48*(2), 301–317. doi:10.1016/j.compedu.2005.01.007

Liao, C., Palvia, P., & Chen, J.-L. (2009). Information technology adoption life cycle: Toward a technology continuance theory (TCT). *International Journal of Information Management, 29*(4), 309–320. doi:10.1016/j.ijinfomgt.2009.03.004

Limayem, M., Hirt, S. G., & Cheung, C. M. K. (2007). How habit limits the predictive power of intention: The case of information systems continuance. *Management Information Systems Quarterly, 31*(4), 705–737.

Lin, C. S., Wu, S., & Tsai, R. J. (2005). Integrating perceived playfulness into expectation-confirmation model for Web portal context. *Information & Management, 42*(5), 683–693. doi:10.1016/j.im.2004.04.003

López-Nicolás, C., Molina-Castello, F. J., & Bouwman, H. (2008). An assessment of advanced mobile services acceptance: Contributions from TAM and diffusion theory models. *Information & Management, 45*(1), 359–364. doi:10.1016/j.im.2008.05.001

Lu, J., Liu, C., Yu, C.-S., & Wang, K. (2008). Determinants of accepting wireless mobile data services in China. *Information & Management*, *45*(1), 52–64. doi:10.1016/j.im.2007.11.002

Lu, J., Yao, J. E., & Yu, C. (2005). Personal innovativeness, social influences and adoption of wireless Internet services via mobile technology. *The Journal of Strategic Information Systems*, *14*(3), 245–268. doi:10.1016/j.jsis.2005.07.003

Moon, J. W., & Kim, Y. G. (2001). Extending the TAM for a World-Wide-Web context. *Information & Management*, *38*(1), 217–230. doi:10.1016/S0378-7206(00)00061-6

Neter, J., Wasserman, W., & Kutner, M. H. (1990). *Applied linear regression models*. Homewood, IL: Academic Press.

Nysveen, H., Pedersen, P. E., & Thorbjornsen, H. (2005a). Explaining the intention to use mobile chat services: Moderating effects of gender. *Journal of Consumer Marketing*, *22*(5), 247–256. doi:10.1108/07363760510611671

Nysveen, H., Pedersen, P. E., & Thorbjornsen, H. (2005b). Intentions to use mobile services: Antecedents and cross-service comparisons. *Journal of the Academy of Marketing Science*, *33*(3), 330–346. doi:10.1177/0092070305276149

Oghuma, A. P., Chang, Y., Libaque-Saenz, C. F., Park, M. C., & Rho, J. J. (2015). Benefit confirmation model for post-adoption behavior of mobile instant messaging applications: A comparative analysis of KakaoTalk and Joyn in Korea. *Telecommunications Policy*, *39*(8), 658–677. doi:10.1016/j.telpol.2015.07.009

Ong, C. S., & Lai, J. Y. (2006). Gender differences in perceptions and relationships among dominants of E-Learning acceptance. *Computers in Human Behavior*, *22*(5), 816–829. doi:10.1016/j.chb.2004.03.006

Ono, H., & Zavodny, M. (2005). Gender differences in information technology usage: A U.S.-Japan comparison. *Sociological Perspectives*, *48*(1), 105–133. doi:10.1525/sop.2005.48.1.105

Polites, G. L., & Karahanna, E. (2012). Shackled to the status quo: The inhibiting effects on incumbent system habit, switching costs, and inertia on new system acceptance. *Management Information Systems Quarterly*, *36*(1), 21–42.

Ranganathan, C., Seo, D., & Babad, Y. (2006). Switching behavior of mobile users: Do users relational investments and demographics matter? *European Journal of Information Systems*, *15*(3), 269–276. doi:10.1057/palgrave.ejis.3000616

Swanson, E. B. (1988). *Information system implementation: Bridging the gap between design and utilization*. Homewood, IL: Irwin.

Thong, J. Y. L., Hong, S., & Tam, K. Y. (2006). The effect of post-adoption beliefs on the expectation-confirmation model for information technology continuance. *International Journal of Human-Computer Studies*, *64*(9), 799–810. doi:10.1016/j.ijhcs.2006.05.001

Van der Heijden, H. (2004). User acceptance of hedonic information systems. *Management Information Systems Quarterly*, *28*(4), 695–704.

Van der Heijden, H., & Sorensen, L. S. (2003). In measuring attitudes towards mobile information services: an empirical validation of the HED/UT scale. In C. U. Ciborra, R. Mercurio, M. De Marco, M. Martinez, & A. Carignani (Ed.). *European Conference on Information Systems*.

Venkatesh, V. (1999). Creating favorable user perceptions: Exploring the role of intrinsic motivation. *Management Information Systems Quarterly*, *23*(2), 239–260. doi:10.2307/249753

Venkatesh, V., & Morris, M. G. (2000). Why dont men ever stop to ask for directions? Gender, social influence, and their role in technology acceptance and usage behavior. *Management Information Systems Quarterly*, *24*(1), 115–139. doi:10.2307/3250981

Venkatesh, V., Morris, M. G., & Ackerman, P. L. (2000). A longitudinal field investigation of gender differences in individual technology adoption decision making process. *Organizational Behavior and Human Decision Processes*, *38*(1), 33–60. doi:10.1006/obhd.2000.2896 PMID:10973782

Wakefield, R. L., Wakefield, K. L., Baker, J., & Wang, L. C. (2011). How website socialness leads to website use. *European Journal of Information Systems*, *20*(1), 118–132. doi:10.1057/ejis.2010.47

Wakefield, R. L., & Whitten, D. (2006). Mobile computing: A user study on Hedonic/Utilitarian mobile device usage. *European Journal of Information Systems*, *15*(3), 292–300. doi:10.1057/palgrave.ejis.3000619

Wang, Y., Lin, H., & Luarn, P. (2006). Predicting consumer intention to use mobile service. *Information Systems Journal*, *16*(2), 157–179. doi:10.1111/j.1365-2575.2006.00213.x

Section 4
What Future is Hidden Behind IS/IT?

Chapter 11
The Fashionable Functions Reloaded:
An Updated Google Ngram View of Trends in Functional Differentiation (1800–2000)

Steffen Roth
ESC Rennes School of Business, France

Carlton Clark
University of Wisconsin – La Crosse, USA

Jan Berkel
Independent Researcher, Puerto Rico

ABSTRACT

Using the updated Google Book corpus dataset generated in July 2012, we analyze the largest available corpus of digitalized books to review social macro trends such as the secularization, politicization, economization, and mediatization of society. These familiar trend statements are tested through a comparative analysis of word frequency time-series plots for the English, French, and German language area produced by means of the enhanced Google Ngram Viewer, the online graphing tool that charts annual word counts as found in the Google Book corpus. The results: a) confirm that the importance of the political system, religion, economy, and mass media features significant change in time and considerable regional differences and b) suggest that visions of economized or capitalist societies are intellectual artifacts rather than appropriate descriptions of society.

INTRODUCTION

In this updated version of one of the first applications of culturomics in sociology (Roth, 2014), we improved readability, incorporated feedback, and drew on the second version of the Google Book corpus dataset to show how big data analysis may check and challenge old familiar self-definitions of modern society. The starting point of our venture remained the distinction between autonomous function systems such as the economy, science, art, religion, etc. In fact, this form of functional differentiation is considered

DOI: 10.4018/978-1-5225-1868-6.ch011

a core concept of modern societies (Leydesdorff, 2002; Beck et al., 2003; Berger, 2003; Vanderstraeten, 2005; Brier, 2006; Baecker, 2007; Kjaer, 2010; Bergthaller & Schinko, 2011; Roth, 2015a). Without functional differentiation, there would be no difference between truth and money, a hospital would be considered the same as a bank, and there would be no sense in the critiques of doping, corruption, or the selling of indulgences. In like manner, the larger part of contemporary definitions and criticisms of modern society would have to do without their most basic categories, since all observations of secularization, economization, and mediatization implicitly refer to an underlying concept of functional differentiation.

Though generally accepted, the idea that particular function systems are more relevant to society than others is not understood without ambiguity. On the one hand, in the light of the fundamental equivalence (Vanderstraeten, 2005; Jönhill, 2012) and autonomy (Tsivacou, 2005; Valentinov, 2012) of the function systems there is no way of arguing that the political system or the economy is essentially more important than religion or sport, per se. On the other hand, there seems to be plenty of empirical evidence of such imbalances in terms of the just mentioned trend observations.

This contradiction can be resolved by stating that it is not despite, but because of their basic equivalence that function systems can be ranked at all because if the function systems were essentially unequal, they would already be ranked and, therefore, could no longer be ranked. In this sense, the function systems can be treated as nominal data that feature a skewed distribution whenever it comes to the analysis of concrete segments of society. Hence, modern societies so far have been defined in terms of different biases to particular function systems with the most prominent cases being the definition of society as capitalist (Roth, 2015b). Though there is still little consensus on the question of whether capitalism results either from the primacy of a particular form of politics or from the primacy of the economy (Risse, 2003; Wallerstein, 2003; Foucault, 2008; Urry, 2010; Lash, 2007; Madra & Adaman, 2014), most people would basically agree on the idea that present societies are subject to an economization of collective goals (Alexander, 1985). This "increasing influence of economic factors and values on the political agenda and other areas of society" (Blumler & Kavanagh, 1999, p. 210) includes the economization of

- Health (Musick, 1999; Cartier, 2003; Ewert, 2009; Brown et al., 2011),
- Art (Velthuis, 2003; Behnke, 2007; Eikhof & Haunschild, 2007; Kjaer, 2010; De Valick, 2014),
- Science (Penders et al., 2009; Berman, 2013),
- Education (Fludernik, 2005; Wilkesmann & Schmid, 2012; Spring, 2015),
- Religion (Robertson, 1992; Wannenwetsch, 2008), and, as a matter of course,
- Society as a whole (Polanyi, 1957; Habermas & McCarthy, 1985; Schmidt, 1993; Altvater & Mahnkopf, 1996; Enderle, 1997; Chomsky, 1999; Sayer, 1999; Finch, 2007; Schimank & Volkmann, 2008).

As a result of this "economic turn" (Smart, 2003) or fethishization of the economy (Foucault, 2008), economization emerges so omnipresent and dominant that even the proliferation of economics is taken for an indicator of economization (Çalışkan & Callon, 2010)[1] or a need of de-economization (Latour, 2004), respectively. Nonetheless, there is also discussion on further forms of trend statements and predictions, which includes sometimes concurrent, sometimes competing definitions of society as:

- Mediatized (Dennis, 1978; Eaman, 1987; Castells, 1996; Chomsky, 1997; Blumler & Kavanagh, 1999; Croteau & Hoynes, 2003; Schulz, 2004; Hjarvard, 2008, 2013; Mazzoleni, 2008; Moon, 2012; Esser & Strömbäck, 2014),

- Politicized (Chomsky, 2000; Blumler & Kavanagh, 1999),
- Militarized (Regan, 1994; Young, 2007; Levy, 2010),
- Intellectualized (Alexander, 1985),
- Or even aestheticized (Blumler & Kavanagh, 1999; Rocha de Oliveira, 2009).

Anything seems to go as long as there is not too much religion involved. Both the economization (Robertson, 1992) and the politicization (Thompson, 2006) of religion seem to be in line with the project of modernity. Any sign of religious recovery, however, apparently understood as a threat to modernity (Martin, 2005; Martin, 2011; Bracke, 2008), even though such a "de-secularization" would not challenge functional differentiation and modernity in a more profound way than a possible "economization of every sphere of existence" (Kane, 2010, P. 81).

In view of the literature, the long-term trends in the discussion of –izations are indeed the politicization and, most prominently, economization, which take place against the background of a requiem for religion and are recently complemented by an emerging media boom.

The problem with the corresponding marginalization of the "other areas of society" (Blumler & Kavanagh, 1999, P. 210) is not only in the fact that "(o)ther social institutions are seen (once again) as mere puppets in the hands of powerful economic trends and actors" (Stehr, 2002, p. 4) or as subjects to the respective political counter-performances, but also in the empirical basis of this discursive bias. So far, the existence of trends is supposed rather than studied. As well, even the few contributions that call for more "observational research" (Blumler & Kavanagh, 1999, p. 225) are so much focused on the analysis of dominant or strong function systems that they do hardly reflect why the respective focus system should be preferred to others and therefore lack the overview Poul Kjaer (2010, p. 532) is interested in the analysis of function systems:

(T)he development of a general theory capable of linking them systematically together. When observed in isolation, the mutual supportive character of these dimensions is not obvious. Only a more general conceptual framework will make it possible to empirically observe to what degree the observed phenomenon constitutes or potentially will be capable of constituting a 'higher order' (...).

In order to approach such a general framework and compensate for the lack of evidence for the respective diagnoses, the present article will consider both the general idea of biased constellations of function systems and the observation of particular trends in the significance of individual function systems. Both are considered hypotheses that still need to be defended.

Subsequent to a theory statement, the present article asks for the empirical validity of the most popular statements of trends in functional differentiation. Namely the secularization, politicization, economization and mediatization of society will therefore be re-conceptualized in terms of hypotheses and tested against the results of a Google Ngram Viewer analysis of the most frequent function system references in the updated second version of the Google Books corpus for the years 1800 through 2000. The results not only show that the importance of individual function systems changes over time and across language areas, but also give reason to believe that popular observations of an increasing importance of the economic systems are intellectual artifacts rather than appropriate (self-) descriptions of society.

THEORY STATEMENT

"Ever since there has been sociological theory it has been concerned with social differentiation" (Luhmann, 1990, p. 423). Differentiation refers to an intrasystem process of subsystem formation (Luhmann, 1977, 1997b). The first known forms of subsystems within society were families and tribes. Families coexisted with other families of the same tribe in the same manner as tribes coexisted with other tribes. As a result, early societies are said to be differentiated into identical and co-equal segments of society. However, in the course of the Neolithic revolution, the situation changed as soon as location decisions condensed to locational advantages and disadvantages in such a way that individual settlements ascended towards centers, while others turned into periphery. This center-periphery differentiation was soon complemented and superposed by stratification, which is commonly associated with the formation of hierarchical social orders, such as the Indian cast system or the Occidental Estates of the realm. Such stratified societies defined persons into ranked hereditary communities and allowed for only limited social mobility, if any at all. Conversely, in the European case, it was mobility that finally changed the static order. Be it the movable types of Gutenberg's printing press, the Central-European rural exodus, or the fact that too many commoners had been granted entry into the gentry, in all cases, the constitutive distinction of nobles and commoners was for its own part superposed by a distinction so fundamental to modernity that animals can no longer be divided in the following way:

a. *Belonging to the Emperor,*
b. *Embalmed,*
c. *Tame,*
d. *Sucking Pigs,*
e. *Sirens,*
f. *Fabulous,*
g. *Stray Dogs,*
h. *Included in the present classification,*
i. *Frenzied,*
j. *Innumerable,*
k. *Drawn with a very fine camelhair brush, et cetera,*
l. *Having just broken the water pitcher,*
m. *That from a long way off look like flies (Borges & Weinberger, 1999 , p. 231).*

In fact, modern man considers it absurd to assume that a siren and a pig represent the same type of animal as soon as they both belong to the emperor or are drawn with the same kind of brush. "Modern society is no longer characterized by a stratification of lineage, clans and families, but by a differentiation of function systems" (Vanderstraeten, 2005, p. 476). Today, society therefore cannot only be differentiated into

1. Similar and equal segments,
2. Similar and unequal centers and peripheries, and
3. Dissimilar and unequal strata, but into
4. Dissimilar and equal function systems, as well (see Figure 1).

Figure 1. Social Differentiation (source: Roth, 2015b:113)

		Equal	
		+	**−**
Similar	**+**	Segmentation (Families, tribes, nations, etc.)	Centralization (Civilizations, empires, etc.)
	−	Functional Differentiation (Economy, Science, Art, etc.)	Stratification (Castes, estates, classes, etc.)

Despite their obvious existence, and despite their importance to modern society, there is still little consensus on necessary and sufficient conditions for the definition of function systems. Nevertheless, when looking at existing working definitions and non-exhaustive lists of function systems (Reese-Schäfer, 1999, p. 176f, 2007, p. 120; Künzler, 1987, p. 327, 1989, p. 100f; Andersen, 2003, p. 159; Stichweh, 2005; Baecker, 1994; Henkel, 2010, p. 183; Luhmann, 1997a, p. 11), a list of 10 function systems can be extracted (Roth and Schütz, 2015):

- Political system,
- Economy,
- Science,
- Art,
- Religion,
- Legal system,
- Health,
- Sport,
- Education, and
- Mass media.

These 10 function systems differentiate society by the binary re-coding of communication according to a specific symbolically generalized communication medium. Each function system applies only one single code, which it also applies exclusively. For example, science, and only science, is all about the medium truth, which is binary coded as true or untrue. Scientific programs and theories decide on when the code of science is properly applied. The function of science is to provide society with ongoing knowledge communication (see Table 1).

While it can be considered impossible to belong to both the estate of the nobles and the estate of the commoners or to two castes at the same time, persons can be included in all of the function systems. This multi-inclusiveness of function system applies to organizations as well, which are, also regarded as:

- Multi-Referent (Tacke, 2001; Simsa, 2001),
- Polyphonic (Thygesen & Andersen, 2007; Andersen & Born, 2007), or
- Multimedia organizations (Roth et al., 2010; Roth 2012; 2014b).

Table 1. The function systems of society

System	Code	Medium	Program (ex.)	Function
Political System	Government/opposition	Power	Ideology	Limitation
Economy	Payment/non-Payment	Money	Price	Distribution
Science	True/untrue	Truth	Theory	Verification
Art	Innovative/imitative	Style	Fashion	Creation
Religion	Immanent/transcendent	Faith	Confession	Revelation
Legal System	Lawful/unlawful	Norm	Law	Standardization
Sport	Success/failure	Achievement	Goal	Mobilization
Health System	Ill/healthy	Illness	Diagnosis	Restoration
Education	Placeable/unplaceable	Vita	Curriculum	Formation
Mass Media	Informative/Non-informative	Medium	Topic	Multiplication

Source: (Roth & Schütz, 2015, p. 24)

Combined with the basic assumption that no function system is essentially more important than the other, the multimedia character of persons, organizations, and further segments of society are the basis of the observation of individual differences in the frequencies of function system references. It is precisely because of the mutual exclusiveness and functional equivalence of the individual function systems that individual persons, organizations, nation states, or cultural areas are likely to feature different frequency distributions of particular function system (p)references. "On this background, it is possible to understand asymmetries, crowding-out effects, and negative externalities between functionally differentiated spheres as a central source of tension and conflict in modern society" (Kjaer, 2010, p. 494). The present article will explore these tension zones and, in doing so, regard society as a system of accessible communications. In this sense, the article takes the language border as a better distinction than national, i.e. geopolitical borders, and will refer to the English, French, and German language areas as societies.

HYPOTHESES

The basic assumption of the functional equivalent and mutually exclusive nature of function systems represents an excellent groundwork for the null hypothesis, which the present article proposes to test. Representing coequal nominal data, function systems can be assumed equally relevant to social systems. The null hypothesis is, therefore, as follows:

- (H0) Function systems relevancies exhibit a uniform distribution in social system.

On the other hand, empirical research seems to indicate an unequal distribution of function system relevancies. The alternative hypothesis reads as follows:

- (H1) Function systems relevancies exhibit an unequal distribution both in the course of time (H1.1) and across cultures (H1.2).

Pursuing the alternative hypothesis and linking to the discourse on major trends in functional differentiation, the article, furthermore, considers the assumed unequal distributions subject to constant change similar to "changes in economic cycles and international competition [that] create preferences for certain kinds of language and explanations" (Cornelissen & Kafouros, 2008, p. 14). The second alternative hypothesis, thus, suggests testing the most popular common senses on trends in functional differentiation:

- *(H2) Societies feature relatively stable trends in functional differentiation, including*
- *(H2.1) the secularization,*
- *(H2.2) the politicization,*
- *(H2.3) the economization, and*
- *(H2.4) the mediatization of society.*

The second hypothesis will be tested against both weak and strong definitions of the respective trends. Trends will, consequently, be analyzed with regard to their incidence in one or several cultural areas as well as to their individual course and their relative importance.

METHOD

The key assumptions proposed in this article are the temporal change of and the intercultural differences in the importance of particular function systems to particular societies. The major problem becomes how to measure this importance in a context that can be expected to allow for somewhat representative information on societies as a whole.

The importance of concepts is often defined in terms of the frequency of their occurrence in given corpora, which is considered "the simplest and most impartial gauge of word importance" (Kloumann et al., 2012, p. 1) or the popularity of objects, ideas, and persons (Ophir, 2010; Bohannon, 2011)2. Given the scope of the present research question and the corresponding scale of the research field, research utilizing the Internet as the largest possible corpus would make sense. Despite the fact that web search engines are said to return word frequency estimates that are highly consistent with established methods (Blair et al., 2002), the problem with Internet word frequency analyses is that the analysis of this most recent media hardly allows for long-term trend analyses. Hence, the present discussion of popular trends in functional differentiation analyses changes the frequency distributions of function system references in the second largest available text data collection.

Since its start in 2004, the Google Books project has digitalized some 15 million of the estimated 115 million books ever published. In 2007, a Harvard research team (Michel et al., 2011) recognized the research potential of the Google Books corpus, performed considerable quality checks, and finally reported the compilation of a representative corpus of more than five million books or 500 billion words covering seven language areas and a time span of 600 years. This corpus was later updated to version 2, issued in July 2012. The development of this enormous dataset soon raised hopes of a golden age of digital humanities (Johnson, 2010), which would open up new types of historical knowledge (Ophir, 2010); it has already given birth to the discipline of culturomics as "the application of high-throughput data collection and analysis to the study of human culture" (Michel et al., 2011, p. 181). The access to the Google Books corpus is facilitated by the Google Ngram Viewer — an open-access interface that allows for trending (Manovich, 2012) in terms of the production of customized time-series plots for entered search terms.

Figure 2. Word frequency shares of Deutschland, England, Frankreich, and USA in the 2009 and the 2012 German Language Google Books Corpus (source: own Google Ngram enquiries)

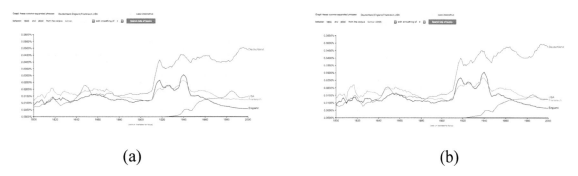

(a)   (b)

In such way, the Google Ngram Viewer can be used to re-present well-known information in a compact and intuitive way (see Figure 2).

In contrasting the two charts combined in figure 2, we find that the patterns of the graphs remain relatively stable between the 2009 and the 2012 versions of the dataset; yet, there are visible differences, too, for example with regard to the performances of the USA and France in the 1990s. Moreover, figure 2 clearly illustrates how the importance of the concepts of Germany, England, France, and the USA varied between the year 1800 and 2000. The graph shows that it was not until the eve of World War I that the concept of Germany became dominant in German books. Furthermore, with regard to Germany, we find top peaks of popularity during the early Nazi era, the Wirtschaftswunder, and the German reunification as well as interim lows after the lost World Wars and in relation to the Protests of 1968. The overall trend, nonetheless, is positive, which is not the case for France and England. Both countries lost relevance after World War II and were overtaken by the USA in the mid-1980s. In this sense, the Google Ngram Viewer also allows for the qualitative analysis of quantitative data, e.g. in terms of the assumption that the USA became more important to Germany and perhaps was the most important occupying power.

Furthermore, the Viewer can be used to detect needs for research as much as for the developing of research questions (see Figure 3-4).

Contrasting the German and the English distribution of the concepts of money (blue), power (red), and love (green) we find that love and money started to feature common characteristics in the English context as of the late 1940s, while love seems to be closer to power than to money in the German context, if at all. Far from representing proof for anything, the presented evidence can, nonetheless, be considered a reason for further research. One big advantage of the updated version of the Google Ngram Viewer is that the tool does to some extent allow for word context analyses now. This is useful in the case of power, since it helps with identifying the frequencies of non-functional meanings such as "electric power" and – if need be – with their exclusion from the sample (which, however, is not required in the present case because of the only marginal performances of non-political meanings of power). Again, a comparison of the present figures 3 and 4 with those in the original article (Roth, 2014) shows that the graphs perform almost identical in the English language case, whereas there are considerable, yet not fundamental, differences in the German language case.

In some cases, a Google Ngram View might even be used for validity tests of more or less prominent hypotheses (see Figure 5-7).

Figure 3. Word frequency shares of money, power, and love in the overall English Language Google Books Corpus 2012 (source: own Google Ngram enquiry)

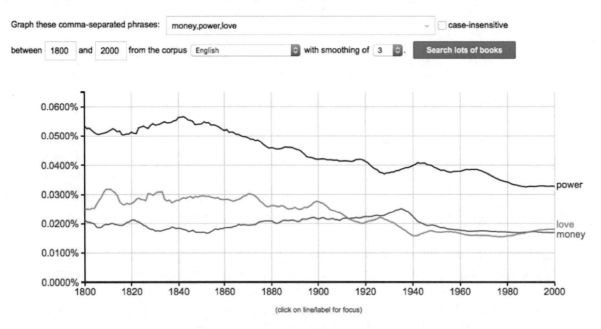

Figure 4. Word frequency shares of Geld, Macht, and Liebe (money, power, and love) in the German Language Google Books Corpus 2012 (source: own Google Ngram enquiry)

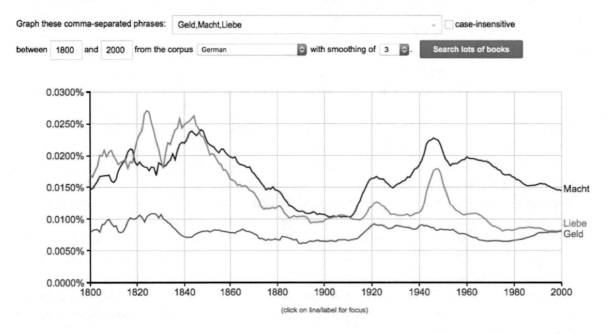

Figure 5. Word frequency shares of globali(z/s)ation and regionali(z/s)ation in the Overall English Language Google Books Corpus 2012 (source: own Google Ngram enquiry)

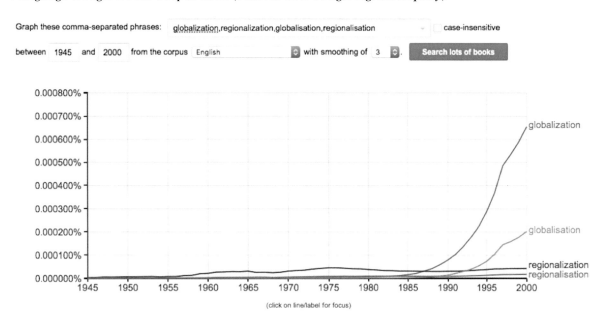

Figure 6. Word frequency shares of globalisation and régionalisation in the French Language Google Books Corpus 2012 (source: own Google Ngram enquiry)

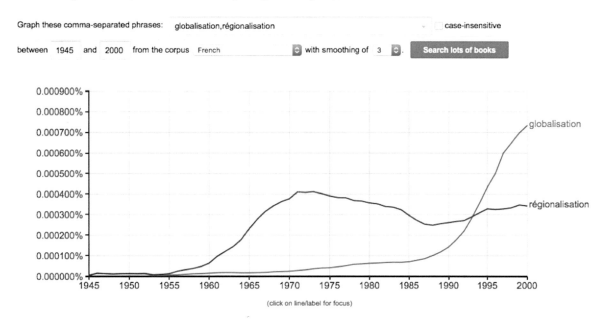

Figure 7. Word frequency shares of globalisierung and regionalisierung in the German Language Google Books Corpus 2012 (source: own Google Ngram enquiry)

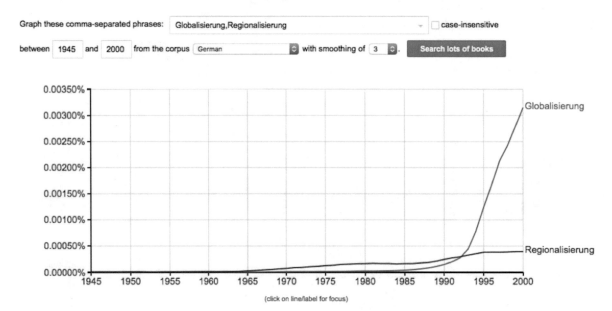

For example, regionalization is sometimes said to be an effect of globalization (Kacowicz, 1999; Amin, 1999; Hurrell, 2007). The Google Ngram View of the respective concepts, however, does not support this idea. Rather, we find evidence for the opposite effect, being that in all the three language areas, the concept of regionalization enjoyed a modest popularity before globalization boomed, which is most evident in the French case, which featured a noticeable trend in regionalization between 1960 and 1975. It is not until the mid-1980s (US-American English) or the early 1990s (British English, French, German), respectively, that the globalization discourse reached the level of the respective regionalization discourses. Moreover, the findings suggest that the globalization discourse could have had its origins in the French discourse and the largest impact on the German discourse. In all these cases, the graphs feature similar patterns in both 2009 and 2012; what seems to have changed are only the absolute word frequencies (see e.g. the German graphs).

Testing its own hypotheses, the present article will focus on the analysis of trends in the 2012 versions of the English, French, and German Google Books 1-gram corpora 1800-2000.[3] Due to the sheer size of the databases concerned, further in-depth analyses will be conducted using the Google Million, an English-language corpus of only one million words designed to fulfill the same representativeness requirements as the larger English version(s), however, with improved handling characteristics.

In this setting, the null hypothesis will be rejected in favor of the alternative hypothesis (H1) when the time-series plots produced by the Google Ngram Viewer feature an unequal distribution of the occurrence frequencies of all function system designations. Moreover, the plots will be analyzed with regard to variations of occurrences in the course of time (H1.1) and across cultures (H1.2).

The hypotheses H2.1-2.4 will be weakly confirmed if the output of the Google Ngram Viewer query supports the respective trend assumptions in at least two out of three language areas. In concrete terms, the plots should display a decrease in the importance of religion (H2.1: secularization) as well as an increase in the importance of the political system (H2.2: politicization), the economy (H2.3: economization), and the media (H2.4: mediatization), respectively. A strong confirmation would, moreover, call for (the loss of) a dominant position in the texture of function system references for all language areas.

Meeting concerns that the function system designations might not represent the most frequent function system reference in the corpus, the Top 2000 1-grams of the Google Million corpus will be scanned for further function system references. The list of the ten most frequent references to function systems relevant to the hypotheses H2.1-2.4 will also be entered into the Google Ngram Viewer and the result compared to the outcome of the query for the names of the function systems.

RESULTS

The ten function systems exhibit unequal occurrence frequencies that vary within and across all the language areas:

In the English case (see Figure 8), at the beginning of the sample period, religion (not the legal system as erroneously reported in the original version) is the most dominant function system followed by art and the political system. A major change to the earlier version of the article is that we replaced policy by political, which is a stronger and more adequate indicator of the importance of the political system. The performance of the political system towards the end of the sample period therefore appears even stronger than in the earlier version. The general picture, however, remains the same: the political system is dominant, followed by health, which overtakes education soon before the millennium. Currently, religion ranks ninth, outperformed even by the formerly marginal economy and mass media system. The performance of the economy is relatively less pronounced in the 2012 data as compared to the 2009 data.

A closer examination of the function systems relevant to the trend hypotheses 2.1-2.4 calls attention to the word frequency shares of the political system, the economy, science, religion, and the mass media system. The decline of religion ($\hat{r} = 0.27$/compared to 0.25 as visually assessed in the earlier version of this article)[4] and the rise of the political system ($\hat{r} = 3.5/3.7$) are the most striking trends. Religion is outperformed by the political system during World War I and by science in the early 1930s, with the latter being a result of slow, but steady growth. At about the same point in time, the formerly marginal economy takes off ($\hat{r} = 3.57/5.00$ between 1930 and 1990). Yet, in 2000 economy and science share about the same numbers of mentions in the Google Books corpus (approximately 100ppm)[5] and are, therefore, both lower-middle ranking function systems:

- The political system (320ppm),
- Health (177ppm) and education (168ppm),
- and Art (119ppm) occupy the first five ranks.

On the verge of the millennium, religion (64ppm) was finally outpaced by the mass media (75ppm). Sport is last (16ppm).

In the French case (see Figure 9), art initially ranks first in front of religion, justice, and the political system. Between World War I and World War II, it was overtaken by the political system, whose increase ($\hat{r} = 5.3/4.9$) to a frequency of 701ppm in 2000 is remarkable (the small counter-trend around 1980 is less pronounced and stable than in the 2009 data). The political system is ranked first uncontestably since the end of the 1920s. In 2000, the political system occurred three times more often than art. As of the

Figure 8. Word frequency shares of the names of the function systems in the overall English Language Google Books Corpus 2012 (source: own Google Ngram enquiry)

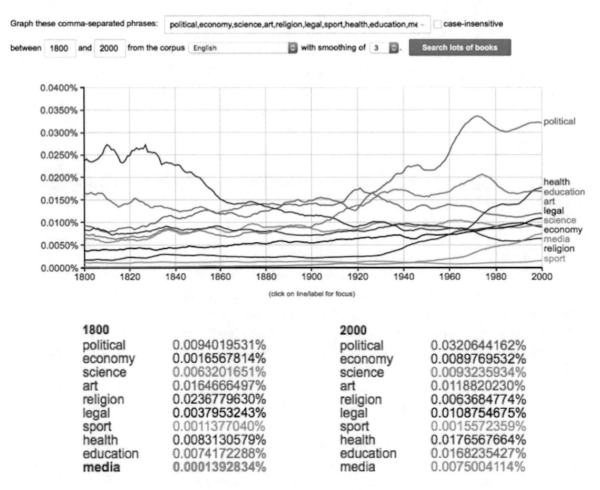

1800		2000	
political	0.0094019531%	political	0.0320644162%
economy	0.0016567814%	economy	0.0089769532%
science	0.0063201651%	science	0.0093235934%
art	0.0164666497%	art	0.0118820230%
religion	0.0236779630%	religion	0.0063684774%
legal	0.0037953243%	legal	0.0108754675%
sport	0.0011377040%	sport	0.0015572359%
health	0.0083130579%	health	0.0176567664%
education	0.0074172288%	education	0.0168235427%
media	0.0001392834%	media	0.0075004114%

late 1920s, after an increase of economic communication, the economy ranks third, closely followed by science, education, the legal system, health, and religion. Mass media and sport come last.

A comparison of the English and the French data uncovers the higher relevance the French function systems have in their corpus. The word *politique*, however, must be considered an exception to this rule because it is both a noun and an adjective. Complemented by the adjective(s), the English and the German political performance would be about the same as the French. Still, it is notable that even *politique_NOUN*, the string used to count only cases in which the ngram politique appears as noun, remains the clear number one in the French corpus in the year 2000 (320ppm). Additionally, despite a considerable decline, second-ranked art (211ppm) is still more important to the French corpus than second and third ranked health and education are to the English.

The German data display the largest variances and the broadest scope of changes within the three language areas. In the early 19th century, Germany seems 'governed' by the legal system as well as science, art, and religion. The latter triad appears to share a common destiny in terms of their collective

Figure 9. Word frequency shares of the names of the function systems in the French Language Google Books Corpus 2012 (source: own Google Ngram enquiry)

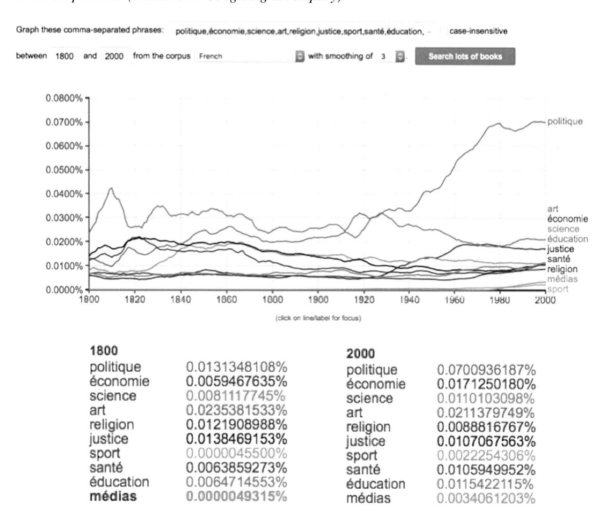

1800		2000	
politique	0.0131348108%	politique	0.0700936187%
économie	0.0059467635%	économie	0.0171250180%
science	0.0081117745%	science	0.0110103098%
art	0.0235381533%	art	0.0211379749%
religion	0.0121908988%	religion	0.0088816767%
justice	0.0138469153%	justice	0.0107067563%
sport	0.0000045500%	sport	0.0022254306%
santé	0.0063859273%	santé	0.0105949952%
éducation	0.0064714553%	éducation	0.0115422115%
médias	0.0000049315%	médias	0.0034061203%

decline up until the 1960s, when science and art finally separated from the downtrend of religion, which appears to have stopped since the 1980s. After a most notable increase ($\hat{f} = 7.9/7.0$), since the early 1960s,

- Politik (290ppm) has ranked first,
- Followed by the legal system (249ppm)
- As well as art and science (141-161ppm).
- Economy (132ppm) is ranked fifth due to an increase in importance dating back to the late 19th century rather than to the late 1920s, like in the case of both the English and the French.

However, there is also a media trend, which started in the mid-1960s, whose calculation in terms of a growth factor does not make much sense because, just like in the case of the English and the French, the media seems to appear from nowhere. In the German case, the same applies to the late 19th century rise of the economy. At least a comparison with the political curve seems revealing to some extent, as

Figure 10. Word frequency shares of the names of the function systems in the German Language Google Books Corpus 2012 (source: own Google Ngram enquiry)

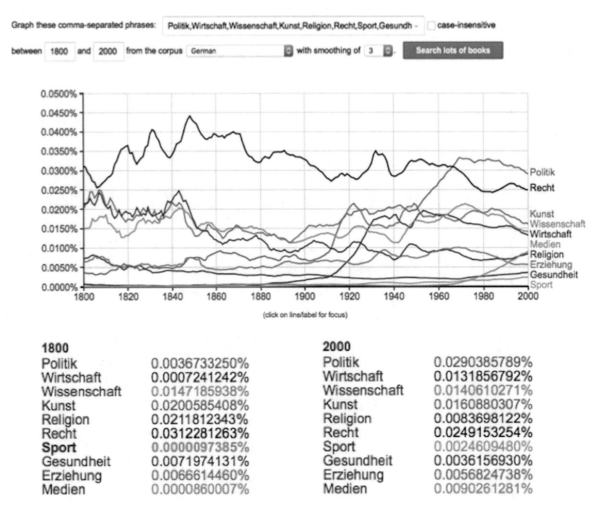

both curves feature a certain parallelism between World War I and the mid-1950s (which, however, appears clearer in the 2009 data).

Interim Discussion

So far, the findings indicate both considerable changes within and significant differences between the language areas. Moreover, with regard to all language areas, the results seem to support the hypotheses H2.1 (secularization) and H2.2 (politicization), even if there is some evidence for the fact that the trends have stopped towards the end of the sample period. Despite considerable increases in the frequencies of all the three designations of the economic system and the mass media system, both systems are still far from being dominant in their respective language areas (see Figure 11). So far, the results would suggest rejecting the hypotheses H2.3 (economization) and 2.4 (mediatization), at least in their strong variant.

Figure 11. Interfunctional comparative profiling of the English, French, and German language area

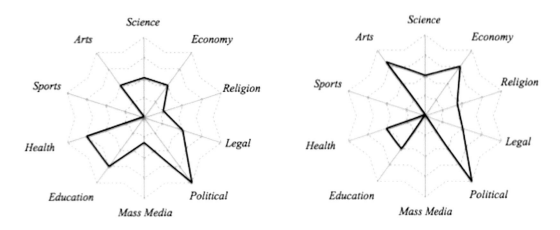

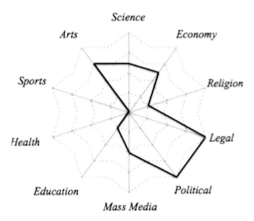

In order to re-test the hypotheses, in particular H2.3 and 2.4, the present article presents the results of an additional analysis.[6] We used a R-program coded by co-author Jan Berkel to extract a word frequency list of the entire English-language Google Ngram corpus data from 2012.[7] For each of the function systems relevant to the hypotheses H2.1-2.4, the ten most frequent references in this list were manually identified and then entered into the Google Ngram Viewer to analyze their performance in the general English corpus using the Google Ngram Viewer (see Figures 12-15).

Just like the performance of the concept itself, the broader view of religion also shows a downtrend of religion that is somehow moderated as of the second half of the 20th century (see Figure 12). The results are in line with the previous multi-language analysis. Contrasting the trend of the religious system and the concept of secularization, the finding is that both graphs move against each other, which is first of all true for God rather than for the other key concepts of the religious system, though the downtrend is featured by all of the ten most important religious ngrams.

Figure 12. Broadband trending the religious system against secularization in the English Language Google Books Corpus 2012 (source: own Google Ngram enquiry)

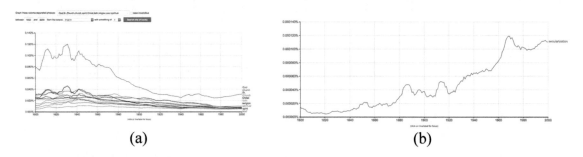

(a)   (b)

Figure 13. Broadband trending the political system against politicization in the English Language Google Books Corpus 2012 (source: own Google Ngram enquiry)

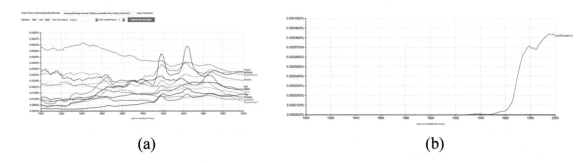

(a)   (b)

Figure 14. Broadband trending the economy against economization and commodification in the English Language Google Books Corpus 2012 (source: own Google Ngram enquiry)

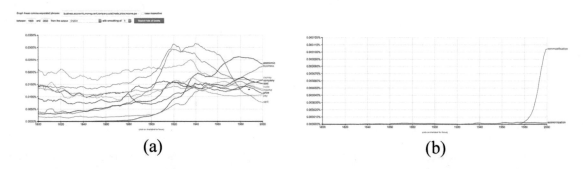

(a)   (b)

Figure 15. Broadband trending the mass media system against mediatization in the English Language Google Books Corpus 2012 (source: own Google Ngram enquiry)

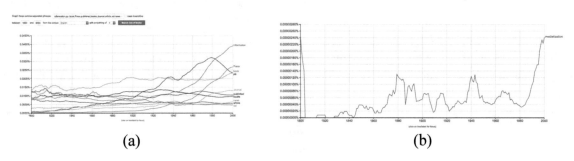

(a)   (b)

The newly identified political references display a stable trend (see Figure 13). The most important political concept, power, is losing importance between 1800-2000, whereas the term political is becoming increasingly important in the 20th century. The overall results mean a significant relativization of the outcome of the previous analysis:

- The upswing of the concept of politicization is not attended by signs of an increasing importance of the political system, which nonetheless appears to be the most dominant function system given the very high word frequencies of the political keywords (ranging from near 100ppm to 570ppm).

Except for the term economic, which starts to rise at about the same time as the German word for economy, the economic frequencies seem to be stagnating or regressing since a sometimes rise in the first half of the 20th century (see Figure 14). Obviously, not starting until the early 1980s, the larger-scale discovery of an economization or commodification of the society might, therefore, have been late, wrong, or both.

As for the mass media system, many keywords feature an upward trend particularly in the second half of the 20th century (see Figure 15). Only "pp.", the abbreviation for pages, displays a downtrend after 1980, thus maybe indicating a changing referencing culture. Apart from this, the findings reinforce the earlier results and add to a greater picture of the evolution of the media system. As a side note, we also find that the lower section of Figure 15 clearly corresponds to the change of the dominant meaning of the concept mediatization, which originally referred to a political reorganization of the Holy Roman Empire and now is used to speculate about socio-cultural change induced by an increasing influence of the mass media system.

Looking at the word frequency shares of each ngram-bundle, again, we find that the economy can hardly be considered more relevant than secularized religion or even the emerging mass media system. The still-dominant political terms achieve twice the scores of the economic terms.

DISCUSSION

The first striking finding of the presented analyses is that the Google Ngram Views of functional differentiation actually react to history, which is true with regard to both the interregional and the regional level. On the one hand, all language areas display a decline of religion as well as clear evidence of the impact of Black Friday on the takeoff of the political system and the economy. On the other hand, the results also reflect particularities related to the histories of the individual languages areas:

- The German time-series plot (see Figure 10) displays a veritable program change for an entire language area from a realm of priests, poets, and philosophers to a national economy. This politico-economic campaign started soon after the death of Karl Marx, which is considerably earlier than in the other two cases.
- In the English and French language area, it was not until Black Friday that the economy became at least moderately relevant.
- In the English case, it seems to be the two World Wars, the Cold War, and de-colonization that led to an uptrend of the political system, which again stopped and moderately declined around GATT Uruguay and Perestroika.

- In the French case, the plot even seems to tell the story of the beginning and end of the Fourth Republic as a struggle of the political and the legal systems[8].

The results, therefore, not only support the hypothesis that modern societies feature an uneven distribution of function system references (H1), but also show that these distributions themselves are subject to changes in time and across cultural borders. The hypotheses H1.1 and H1.2 are, hence, supported by the results.

Both the word frequency plots of the names of the function systems (see Figures 8-10) and the broadband trending of the ten most frequent religious words in the Google Books corpus (see Figure 11) support the secularization hypothesis (H2.1). The dethroning of both the denomination and the most frequent religious terms is evident throughout and across the entire sample(s). Referring to both a state and a trend, the secularization hypothesis can, as a result, be corroborated both in the weak and the strong variant. While the first method also supports the idea of a politicization of the three societies, the politicization hypotheses (H2.2) must be relativized in view of the results of the second. In this sense, the hypotheses can only be defended because of the dominant position the political system (still) takes up in terms of word frequency shares in all of the three societies. In this sense, politicization is a state description rather than a trend statement. As a result, H2.2 is corroborated in its weak variant.

Despite the remarkable growth figures the economic word frequency shares feature in all of the three corpora, the results of both methods suggest rejecting the economization hypothesis (H2.3) in both the strong and the weak variant. In fact, in two cases, the period of the potential trend was rather short (E: 1930-1990; F: 1925-1975). The trends are stopped in all of the three language areas, in none of which the economy ever reached a dominant position throughout the entire 200 years. The only economic term that displays a potentially ongoing uptrend is the term business (see Figure 14). Even this statement, however, has to be relativized because it is true only in the English case.

The mediatization of society (H2.4), in return, however, seems to be an actual trend. Starting in the 1940s (English), 1960s (German), and 1980s (French), the terms media, Medien, and médias feature a modest, but constant uptrend. On a larger scale, the results are also consistent with the analysis of the function system denominations. While the media system never reaches a dominant position in either of the language areas, the trend remains uninterrupted throughout the entire sample period. Even *books* are still popular in books. The mediatization hypothesis is, as a result, weakly corroborated by the present Google Ngram views of functional differentiation.

LIMITATIONS AND FUTURE RESEARCH QUESTIONS

One of the most serious limitations of the first version Google Ngram Viewer was that it did not allow for case-sensitive queries in ngrams. Ngrams also could not be bundled into one single graph, just as the queries could not be for lemmas.[9] Today, the enhanced version of the Google Ngram Viewer can be used to bundle individual ngrams into one graph, in which case, however, the also updated option of case-sensitive research does not apply. Furthermore, the enthusiasm for analyzing combined ngram graphs is limited by the fact that a query may apparently not comprise more than round about 30 ngrams. Still, even in this limited form, the option to compare is attractive (see Figure 16):

Figure 16. Word frequency shares of selected Ngram bundles in the English Language Google Books Corpus 2012 (source: own Google Ngram enquiry)

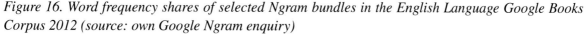

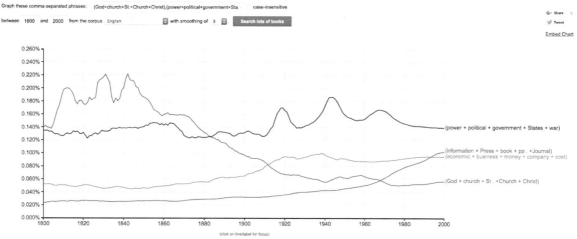

In order to create Figure 16, we entered the following string into the Google Ngram form:

(God+church+St.+Church+Christ),(power+political+government+States+war),(economic+business
+money+company+cost),(information+Press+book+pp.+Journal)

In looking at the performances of the combined keywords relevant to our hypotheses, we find that today's dominant position of the political system is a side-effect of secularization rather than an indicator of an increasing importance of political issues. Furthermore, we see that the economy is far from being a dominant factor. Even within this reduced sample of four out of ten function systems, it is third to the mass media system. This finding contradicts intuitions according to which our lives are dominated by the economic principle(s).

Figure 15 is a fine indicator that further combined ngram queries may well lead to extremely insightful results. Still, however, future research might also be interested in using or developing interfaces that allow for a visualization of trends of keyword bundles comprising more than 30 ngrams. In fact, such tools would be needed to create a compelling chart comparing the performances of robust bundles of 5-10 keywords of all of the 10 function systems of society.

Further critique may come into play with the fact that studying the key media of the Gutenberg Galaxy might not be the key to the emerging Internet society. However, there is evidence that online and offline contents do not differ all that much (Stern, 2004). At the same time, the advantages of a books corpus are evident:

- Book content can be considered subject to stricter selection and, therefore, a better indicator for importance.

Moreover, the Internet corpus does allow for research within the sample period of several hundred years. Further research limits are, as a matter of course, related to restricted language competences and the corpus data size. In fact, it would be best to compare all language areas and analyze 2- or more-grams, e.g. with regard to word co-occurrences, in order to get much deeper context-information. Future research on "Big Data" (Boyd & Crawford, 2012) in general and the present topic in particular could, therefore, call upon international cooperation and access to more powerful computer resources.

Future expeditions in the corpus might then not only open up further and more snapshots of trends in functional differentiation, but also allow for an answer to the question of whether or not functional differentiation is indeed a master trend in present societies. In this sense, an extended Google Ngram View of modern societies could inform on the actual state and trend of modernity itself.

CONCLUSION

The English, French, and German societies actually display politicization, at least in terms of a prevailing, though not trendy, high weight of political communication. A recently re-enforced mediatization can also be observed in all the three cases, albeit as a trend rather than a state description. Secularization seems to characterize both a state (as religion, actually, is not dominant anymore) and a trend, which, however, might have stopped during the last years of the sample period (George, 2005).

The biggest surprise resulting from the presented research certainly is that an analysis of the largest available text corpus does not corroborate the perhaps most prominent state description and trend prediction related to functional differentiation:

The data does not point to an economized or capitalist society.

Starting as a trend in line with the rising popularity of the early socialist movement, the "economization of society" never resulted in a high weight of the economy and stopped rather early (German: 1950's, French: 1970's, English: 1990's).

If it is true that economists "perform" economies, then the presented results also support the idea that economization critics perform economization and that both parties jointly perform an economy bias in social sciences that is incongruent with the average to marginal relevance of the research object. This issue is particularly critical in the context of foresight and futures studies, where it is important to avoid third order risks of giving the right answers to the wrong questions (Roth and Kaivo-oja, in press). Our findings therefore suggest thinking twice before we continue considering economic preeminent issues of present and future societies. In this respect, it is also congruent that the different dictions and notations of economization or commodification are as marginal entries in the English language corpus as misspellings or exotic forenames are. This fact is emphasized not to imply an only marginal relevance of research in economic risks and benefits, but rather as suggestion to consider re-focusing research foci and drawing increased attention to function systems beyond the politico-economic double stars of social science. Maybe even the solution to the present "economic" "crises" is not in more, but rather in less attention to the economy (Roth, 2015b; Roth, in press). In any case, further critiques of economization or economic colonialism necessarily contribute to economization and are, therefore, (drivers of) the problem they try to solve. If high weights of particular function systems are indeed a problem, then vigilance is needed with regard to the political system rather than to the economy. Even more light, however, could be shed on those areas over which the strong interest in (the interplay of) the political and the economic system has casted large clouds throughout the last decades. Apart from a certainly necessary re-cultivation of neglected landscapes of functional differentiation, there is hardly any reason why researchers should be biased to particular function systems and there is even less reason for resentments towards a mediocre function system or for complicity with the most dominant, respectively.

In this sense, the present article gives us a first indication of the transformative power of computer communication. If big data analysis actually corroborates the finding that the idea of an economization of society is an artifact rather than a fact, then this will indeed change the face of modern society.

REFERENCES

Aderhold, J. (2004). *Form und Funktion sozialer Netzwerke in Wirtschaft und Gesellschaft*. Wiesbaden: VS Verlag. doi:10.1007/978-3-322-83386-0

Alexander, J. C. (1985). *Neofunctionalism*. Thousand Oaks, CA: Sage Publications.

Altvater, E., & Mahnkopf, B. (1996). *Grenzen der Globalisierung. Ökonomie, Ökologie und Politik in der Weltgesellschaft*. Münster: Westfälisches Dampfboot.

Amin, S. (1999). Regionalization in response to polarizing globalization. In Globalism and the new regionalism. Palgrave Macmillan. doi:10.1007/978-1-349-27268-6_3

Andersen, N. Å. (2003). Polyphonic Organizations. In T. Hernes & T. Bakken (Eds.), *Autopoietic Organization Theory*. Copenhagen: CBS.

Andersen, N. Å., & Born, A. W. (2007). Heterophony and the Postponed Organization Organizing autopoietic systems. *TAMARA: Journal of Critical Postmodern Organization Science*, 6(1/2), 176–187.

Baecker, D. (1994). Soziale Hilfe als Funktionssystem der Gesellschaft. *Zeitschrift für Soziologie*, 23(2), 93–110. doi:10.1515/zfsoz-1994-0202

Baecker, D. (2007). Communication With Computers, or How Next Society Calls for an Understanding of Temporal Form. *Soziale Systeme*, 13(1-2), 407–418. doi:10.1515/sosys-2007-1-235

Baeza-Yates, R., & Ribeiro-Neto, B. (1999). *Modern information retrieval*. New York: Addison Wesley.

Beck, U., Bonss, W., & Lau, C. (2003). The Theory of Reflexive Modernization. *Theory, Culture & Society*, 20(2), 1–33. doi:10.1177/0263276403020002001

Behnke, C. (2007). Corporate Art Collecting: A Survey of German-Speaking Companies. *The Journal of Arts Management, Law, and Society*, 37(3), 225–244. doi:10.3200/JAML.37.3.225-244

Berger, J. (2003). Neuerliche Anfragen an die Theorie der funktionalen Differenzierung. In H.-J. Giegel & U. Schimank (Eds.), *Beobachter der Moderne. Beiträge zu Luhmanns 'Die Gesellschaft der Gesellschaft*. Frankfurt am Main: Suhkamp.

Bergthaller, H., & Schinko, C. (2011). Introduction: From National Cultures to the Semantics of Modern Society. In H. Bergthaller & C. Schinko (Eds.), *Addressing Modernity. Social Systems Theory and U.S. Cultures*. Amsterdam: Edition Rodopi.

Berman, E. P. (2014). Not Just Neoliberalism: Economization in US Science and Technology Policy. *Science, Technology & Human Values*, 39(3), 397–431. doi:10.1177/0162243913509123

Blair, I., Urland, G., & Ma, J. (2002). Using Internet search engines to estimate word frequency. *Behavior Research Methods*, *34*(2), 286–290. doi:10.3758/BF03195456 PMID:12109025

Blok, A. (2011). Clash of the eco-sciences: Carbon marketization, environmental NGOs and performativity as politics. *Economy and Society*, *40*(3), 451–476. doi:10.1080/03085147.2011.574422

Blumler, J. G., & Kavanagh, D. (1999). The Third Age of Political Communication: Influences and Features. *Political Communication*, *16*(3), 209–230. doi:10.1080/105846099198596

Bohannon, J. (2011). The Science Hall of Fame. *Science*, *331*(6014), 143. doi:10.1126/science.331.6014.143-c PMID:21233362

Bohn, C. (2004). *Clothing as Medium of Communication.* University of Lucerne. Retrieved April 1, 2013, from http://www.unilu.ch/files/clothing-as_medium3.pdf

Borges, J. L., & Weinberger, E. (1999). *Selected Non-Fictions: Jorge Luis Borges.* New York: Viking.

Boyd, D., & Crawford, K. (2012). Critical Questions for Big Data. *Information Communication and Society*, *15*(5), 662–679. doi:10.1080/1369118X.2012.678878

Bracke, S. (2008). Conjugating the Modern/ Religious, Conceptualizing Female Religious Agency. *Theory, Culture & Society*, *25*(6), 51–67. doi:10.1177/0263276408095544

Brier, S. (2006). Construction of Knowledge in the Mass Media. Systemic Problems in the Post-Modern Power-Struggle between the Symbolic Generalized Media in the Agora: The Lomborg Case of Environmental Science and Politics. *Systems Research and Behavioral Science*, *23*(5), 667–684. doi:10.1002/sres.793

Brown, N., Machin, L., & Mcleod, D. (2011). Immunitary Bioeconomy: The Economisation of Life in the International Cord Blood Market. *Social Science & Medicine*, *72*(7), 1115–1122. doi:10.1016/j.socscimed.2011.01.024 PMID:21398003

Burkart, G. (2005). Die Familie in der Systemtheorie. In G. Runkel & G. Burkart (Eds.), *Funktionssysteme der Gesellschaft. Beiträge zur Systemtheorie von Niklas Luhmann.* Wiesbaden: VS. doi:10.1007/978-3-322-80782-3_6

Çalışkan, K., & Callon, M. (2009). Economization, part 1: Shifting attention from the economy towards processes of economization. *Economy and Society*, *38*(3), 369–398. doi:10.1080/03085140903020580

Çalışkan, K., & Callon, M. (2010). Economization, part 2: A research programme for the study of markets. *Economy and Society*, *39*(1), 1–32. doi:10.1080/03085140903424519

Callon, M. (1998). Introduction: The embeddedness of economic markets in economics. In M. Callon et al. (Eds.), *The Laws of the Markets.* Oxford, UK: Blackwell. doi:10.1111/j.1467-954X.1998.tb03468.x

Callon, M. (2007). An Essay on the Growing Contribution of Economic Markets to the Proliferation of the Social. *Theory, Culture & Society*, *24*(7-8), 139–163. doi:10.1177/0263276407084701

Cartier, C. (2003). From home to hospital and back again: Economic restructuring, end of life, and the gendered problems of place-switching health services. *Social Science & Medicine*, *56*(11), 2289–2301. doi:10.1016/S0277-9536(02)00228-9 PMID:12719182

Castells, M. (1996). *Rise of The Network Society*. Cambridge, MA: Blackwell Publishers.

Chomsky, N. (1997). *Media Control. The Spectacular Achievements of Propaganda*. New York: Seven Stories Press.

Chomsky, N. (1999). *Profit over People: Neoliberalism and Global Order*. New York: Seven Stories Press.

Chomsky, N. (2000). *Rogue States: The Rule of Force in World Affairs*. Cambridge, MA: South End Press.

Cornelissen, J. P., & Kafouros, M. (2008). The Emergent Organization: Primary and Complex Metaphors in Theorizing about Organizations. *Organization Studies*, *29*(7), 957–978. doi:10.1177/0170840608090533

Croteau, D., & Hoynes, W. (2003). *Media Society: Industries, Images and Audiences*. Thousand Oaks, CA: Sage.

Davies, M. (2011). *Google Books (American English) Corpus (155 billion words, 1810-2009)*. Available at http://googlebooks.byu.edu/

De Valick, M. (2014). Film Festivals, Bourdieu, and the Economization of Culture. *Revue Canadienne D'études Cinématographiques / Canadian Journal of Film Studies*, *23*(1), 74–89.

Dennis, E. E. (1978). *The media society: evidence about mass communication in America*. Dubuque, IA: Brown.

Eaman, R. A. (1987). *The media society: basic issues and controversies*. London: Butterworth.

Eikhof, D. R., & Haunschild, A. (2007). For Arts Sake! Artistic and Economic Logics in Creative Production. *Journal of Organizational Behavior*, *28*(5), 523–538. doi:10.1002/job.462

Enderle, G. (1997). A Worldwide Survey of Business Ethics in the 1990s. *Journal of Business Ethics*, *16*(14), 1475–1483. doi:10.1023/A:1005866527497

Esser, F., & Strömbäck, J. (Eds.). (2014). Mediatization of Politics: Understanding the Transformation of Western Democracies. Palgrave Macmillan.

Ewert, B. (2009). Economization and Marketization in the German Healthcare System: How Do Users Respond? *German Policy Studies/Politikfeldanalyse*, *5*(1), 21-44.

Finch, J. H. (2007). Economic sociology as a strange other to both sociology and economics. *History of the Human Sciences*, *20*(2), 123–140. doi:10.1177/0952695107077022

Fludernik, M. (2005). Threatening the University—The Liberal Arts and the Economization of Culture. *New Literary History*, *36*(1), 57–70. doi:10.1353/nlh.2005.0019

Foucault, M. (2008). *The Birth of Biopolitics: Lectures at the College de France 1978–1979*. Palgrave Macmillan.

Fuchs, P. (1999). *Intervention und Erfahrung*. Frankfurt am Main: Suhrkamp.

Fuchs, P. (2000). Form und Funktion von Beratung. *Soziale Systeme*, *6*(2), 349–368.

George, S. E. (2005). Believe It or Not: Virtual Religion in the 21st Century. *International Journal of Technology and Human Interaction*, *1*(1), 62–71. doi:10.4018/jthi.2005010103

Habermas, J., & McCarthy, T. (1985). The Theory of Communicative Action, Vol. 2: Lifeworld and System: A Critique of Functionalist Reason. Beacon Press.

Henkel, A. (2010). Systemtheoretische Methodologie: Beobachtung mit Systemreferenz Gesellschaft. In R. John, A. Henkel, & J. Rückert-John (Eds.), *Die Methodologien des Systems*. Wiesbaden: VS. doi:10.1007/978-3-531-92435-9_10

Hjarvard, S. (2008). The Mediatization of Society. *Nordicom Review*, *29*(2), 105–134. PMID:19361120

Hjarvard, S. (2013). *The Mediatization of Culture and Society*. New York: Routledge.

Hurrell, A. (2007). One World? Many Worlds? The Place of Regions in the Study of International Society. *International Affairs*, *83*(1), 127–146. doi:10.1111/j.1468-2346.2007.00606.x

Johnson, C. Y. (2010). In billions of words, digital allies find tale. *The Boston Globe*.

Jönhill, J. I. (2012). Inclusion and Exclusion - A Guiding Distinction to the Understanding of Issues of Cultural Background. *Systems Research and Behavioral Science*, *29*(4), 387–401. doi:10.1002/sres.1140

Kacowicz, A. M. (1999). Regionalization, Globalization, and Nationalism: Convergent, Divergent, or Overlapping? *Alternatives: Global, Local. Political*, *24*(4), 527–555.

Kane, C. L. (2010). Programming the Beautiful. *Theory, Culture & Society*, *27*(1), 73–93. doi:10.1177/0263276409350359

Kjaer, P. F. (2010). The Metamorphosis of the Functional Synthesis: A Continental European Perspective on Governance, Law, and the Political in the Transnational Space. *Wisconsin Law Review*, *2*, 489–1555.

Kloumann, I. M., Danforth, C. M., Harris, K. D., Bliss, C. A., & Dodds, P. S. (2012). Positivity of the English language. *PLoS ONE*, *7*(1), e29484. doi:10.1371/journal.pone.0029484 PMID:22247779

Künzler, J. (1987). Grundlagenprobleme der Theorie symbolisch generalisierter Kommunikationsmedien bei Niklas Luhmann. *Zeitschrift für Soziologie*, *16*(5), 317–333. doi:10.1515/zfsoz-1987-0501

Künzler, J. (1989). *Medien und Gesellschaft. Die Medienkonzepte von Talcott Parsons, Jürgen Habermas und Niklas Luhmann*. Stuttgart: Enke.

Lash, S. (2007). Capitalism and Metaphysics. *Theory, Culture & Society*, *24*(5), 1–26. doi:10.1177/0263276407081281

Latour, B. (2004). *Politics of Nature: How to Bring the Sciences Into Democracy*. Cambridge, MA: Harvard University Press.

Leupold, A. (1983). Liebe und Partnerschaft: Formen der Codierung von Ehen. *Zeitschrift für Soziologie*, *12*(4), 297–327. doi:10.1515/zfsoz-1983-0402

Levy, Y. (2010). The Essence of the Market Army. *Public Administration Review*, *70*(3), 378–389. doi:10.1111/j.1540-6210.2010.02152.x

Lewandowski, S. (2004). *Sexualität in den Zeiten funktionaler Differenzierung. Eine systemtheoretische Analyse*. Bielefeld: Transcript. doi:10.14361/9783839402108

Leydesdorff, L. (2002). The Communication Turn in the Theory of Social Systems. *Systems Research and Behavioral Science*, *19*(2), 129–136. doi:10.1002/sres.453

Luhmann, N. (1977). Differentiation of Society. *The Canadian Journal of Sociology / Cahiers canadiens de sociologie*, *2*(1), 29-53.

Luhmann, N. (1990). The paradox of system differentiation and the evolution of society. In J. C. Alexander & P. Colomy (Eds.), *Differentiation Theory and Social Change: Comparative and Historical Perspectives*. New York: Columbia UP.

Luhmann, N. (1997a). *Die Gesellschaft der Gesellschaft* (Vols. 1-2). Frankfurt am Main: Suhrkamp.

Luhmann, N. (1997b). Globalization or World society: How to conceive of modern society? *International Review of Sociology*, *7*(1), 67–79. doi:10.1080/03906701.1997.9971223

Luhmann, N., & Barrett, R. (2012). *Theory of Society*. Palo Alto, CA: Stanford University Press.

Maass, O. (2009). *Die Soziale Arbeit als Funktionssystem der Gesellschaft*. Heidelberg, Germany: Carl Auer.

Madra, Y. A., & Adaman, F. (2014). Neoliberal Reason and Its Forms: De-Politicisation Through Economisation. *Antipode*, *46*(3), 691–716. doi:10.1111/anti.12065

Manovich, L. (2012). Trending: The Promises and the Challenges of Big Social Data. In M. K. Gold (Ed.), *Debates in the Digital Humanities*. Minneapolis, MN: The University of Minnesota Press. doi:10.5749/minnesota/9780816677948.003.0047

Martin, D. (2005). *On Secularization: Towards a Revised General Theory*. Surrey: Ashgate.

Martin, D. (2011). *The Future of Christianity: Reflections on Violence and Democracy, Religion and Secularization*. Surrey: Ashgate.

Mayntz, R. (1988). Funktionelle Teilsysteme in der Theorie sozialer Systeme. In R. Mayntz, B. Rosewitz, & U. Schimank et al. (Eds.), *Differenzierung und Verselbständigung. Zur Entwicklung gesellschaftlicher Teilsysteme*. Frankfurt am Main: Campus.

Mazzoleni, G. (2008). Mediatization of society. In W. Donsbach (Ed.), *The International Encyclopedia of Communication*. Hoboken, NJ: Wiley.

Michel, J.-B., Shen, Y. K., Aiden, A. P., Veres, A., Gray, M. K., Pickett, J. P., & Aiden, E. L. et al. (2011). Quantitative Analysis of Culture Using Millions of Digitized Books. *Science*, *331*(6014), 176–182. doi:10.1126/science.1199644 PMID:21163965

Moon, Y. B. (2012). The Mediatized Co-Mediatizer: Anthropology in Niklas Luhmanns World. *Zygon: Journal of Religion and Science*, *47*(2), 438–466. doi:10.1111/j.1467-9744.2012.01264.x

Musick, D. W. (1999). Teaching medical ethics: A review of the literature from North American medical schools with emphasis on education. *Medicine, Health Care, and Philosophy*, *2*(3), 239–254. doi:10.1023/A:1009985413669 PMID:11080991

Ophir, S. (2010). A New Type of Historical Knowledge. *The Information Society*, 26(2), 144–150. doi:10.1080/01972240903562811

Penders, B., Verbakel, J. M. A., & Nelis, A. (2009). The Social Study of Corporate Science: A Research Manifesto. *Bulletin of Science, Technology & Society*, 29(6), 439–446. doi:10.1177/0270467609349047

Polanyi, K. (1957). *The great transformation*. New York: Beacon Press.

Reese-Schäfer, W. (1999). *Luhmann zur Einführung*. Hamburg: Junius.

Reese-Schäfer, W. (2005). *Die Moral der Gesellschaft: Paradigm Lost*. Hamburg: Junius.

Reese-Schäfer, W. (2007). *Politisches Denken heute: Zivilgesellschaft, Globalisierung und Menschenrechte*. München: Oldenbourg. doi:10.1524/9783486711288

Regan, P. M. (1994). *Organizing Societies for War: The Processes and Consequences of Societal Militarization*. Westport, CT: Prager.

Risse, T. (2003). The Euro between national and European identity. *Journal of European Public Policy*, 10(4), 487–505. doi:10.1080/1350176032000101235

Robertson, R. (1992). The Economization of Religion? Reflections on the Promise and Limitations of the Economic Approach. *Social Compass*, 39(1), 147–157. doi:10.1177/003776892039001014

Rocha de Oliveira, P. (2009). The Aestheticization of Reality. *The South Atlantic Quarterly*, 108(2), 265–284. doi:10.1215/00382876-2008-033

Roth, S. (2014a). Fashionable functions. A Google ngram view of trends in functional differentiation (18002000). *International Journal of Technology and Human Interaction*, 10(2), 34–58. doi:10.4018/ijthi.2014040103

Roth, S. (2014b). The multifunctional organization: Two cases for a critical update for research programs in management and organization. *Tamara Journal for Critical Organization Inquiry*, 12(3), 37–54.

Roth, S. (2015a). Foreword: Trends in functional differentiation. *Cybernetics & Human Knowing*, 22(4), 5–10.

Roth, S. (2015b). Free economy! On 3628800 alternatives of and to capitalism. *Journal of Interdisciplinary Economics*, 27(2), 107–128. doi:10.1177/0260107915583389

Roth, S. (in press). Growth and function. A viral research program for next organisations[forthcoming]. *International Journal of Technology Management*.

Roth, S. and Kaivo-oja, J. (in press). Is the future a political economy? Functional analysis of three leading foresight and futures studies journals. *Futures*.

Roth, S., Scheiber, L., & Wetzel, R. (2010). *Organisation multimedial: Zum polyphonen Programm der nächsten Organisation*. Heidelberg, Germany: Carl Auer.

Roth, S., & Schütz, A. (2015). Ten systems. Toward a canon of function systems. *Cybernetics & Human Knowing*, 22(4), 11–31.

Sayer, A. (1999). Valuing culture and economy. In L. Ray & A. Sayer (Eds.), *Culture and economy after the cultural turn*. London: Sage. doi:10.4135/9781446218112.n3

Scherr, A. (2001). Soziale Arbeit als organisierte Hilfe. In V. Tacke (Ed.), *Organisation und gesellschaftliche Differenzierung*. Opladen: Westdeutscher Verlag. doi:10.1007/978-3-322-80373-3_10

Schimank, U., & Volkmann, U. (2008). Ökonomisierung der Gesellschaft. In A. Maurer (Ed.), *Handbuch der Wirtschaftssoziologie*. Wiesbaden: VS. doi:10.1007/978-3-531-90905-9_19

Schmidt, C. (1993). On Economization and Ecologization as Civilizing Processes. *Environmental Values*, 2(1), 33–46. doi:10.3197/096327193776679963

Schulz, W. (2004). Reconstructing mediatization as an analytical concept. *European Journal of Communication*, 19(1), 87–101. doi:10.1177/0267323104040696

Schwelger, R. (2008). *Moralisches Handeln von Unternehmen. Eine Weiterentwicklung des Modells und des Ansatzes der Ökonomischen Ethik auf Basis der neuen Systemtheorie und Institutionenökonomik*. Wiesbaden: Gabler.

Simsa, R. (2001). *Gesellschaftliche Funktionen und Einflussformen von Nonprofit-Organisationen*. Bern: Peter Lang.

Smart, B. (2003). An Economic Turn. *Journal of Classical Sociology*, 3(1), 47–66. doi:10.1177/1468795X03003001694

Spring, J. (2015). *The Economization of Education: Human Capital, Global Corporations, and Skills-Based Schooling*. New York: Routledge.

Stehr, N. (2002). *Knowledge and Economic Conduct: The Social Foundations of the Modern Economy*. Toronto: University of Toronto Press. doi:10.3138/9781442676527

Stern, S. R. (2004). Expressions of identity online: Prominent features and gender differences in adolescents World Wide Web home pages. *Journal of Broadcasting & Electronic Media*, 48(2), 218–243. doi:10.1207/s15506878jobem4802_4

Stichweh, R. (2005). *Inklusion und Exklusion: Studien zur Gesellschaftstheorie*. Bielefeld: Transcript.

Tacke, V. (2001). Funktionale Differenzierung als Schema der Beobachtung. In V. Tacke (Ed.), *Organisation und gesellschaftliche Differenzierung*. Wiesbaden: Westdeutscher Verlag. doi:10.1007/978-3-322-80373-3

Thompson, G. F. (2006). Religious fundamentalisms, territories and globalization. *Economy and Society*, 36(1), 19–50. doi:10.1080/03085140601089820

Thygesen, N. T., & Andersen, N. Å. (2007). The polyphonic effects of technological changes in public sector organizations: A system theoretical approach. *Ephemera*, 7(2), 326–345.

Tsivacou, I. (2005). The Ideal of Autonomy from the Viewpoint of Functional Differentiation/Integration of Society. *Systems Research and Behavioral Science*, 22(6), 509–524. doi:10.1002/sres.669

Tyrell, H. (1979). Familie und gesellschaftliche Differenzierung. In H. Pross (Ed.), *Familie - wohin? Leistungen, Leistungsdefizite und Leistungswandlungen der Familie in hochindustrialisierten Gesellschaften.* Reinbeck: Rowohlt.

Urry, J. (2010). Consuming the Planet to Excess. *Theory, Culture & Society, 27*(2-3), 191–212. doi:10.1177/0263276409355999

Valentinov, V. (2012). The Complexity-Sustainability Trade-Off in Niklas Luhmann's Social Systems Theory.[Online first]. *Systems Research and Behavioral Science.*

Vanderstraeten, R. (2005). System and Environment: Notes on the Autopoiesis of Modern Society. *Systems Research and Behavioral Science, 22*(6), 471–481. doi:10.1002/sres.662

Velthuis, O. (2003). Symbolic meanings of prices: Constructing the value of contemporary art in Amsterdam and New York galleries. *Theory and Society, 32*(2), 181–215. doi:10.1023/A:1023995520369

von Rosenberg, F. (2009). *Habitus und Distinktion in Peergroups: Ein Beitrag zur rekonstruktiven Schul- und Jugendkulturforschung.* Berlin: Logos.

Wagner, T. (2006). *Die Soziale Arbeit der Sozialen Arbeit? – Ein kurzer Blick auf die (Selbst-) Beobachtung eines Funktionssystems.* Retrieved April 1, 2013, from http://www.sozialarbeit.ch/dokumente/soziale_arbeit_der_sozialen_arbeit.pdf

Wallerstein, I. (2003). *Decline of American Power: The U.S. in a Chaotic World.* New York: New Press.

Wannenwetsch, B. (2008). Inwardness and Commodification: How Romanticist Hermeneutics Prepared the Way for the Culture of Managerialism — a Theological Analysis. *Studies in Christian Ethics, 21*(1), 26–44. doi:10.1177/0953946808089725

Wilkesmann, U., & Schmid, C. J. (2012). The impacts of new governance on teaching at German universities. Findings from a national survey. *Higher Education, 63*(1), 33–52. doi:10.1007/s10734-011-9423-1

Young, E. S. M. (2007). A Final Period to the Union: The Militarism and Militarization of the United States of America and its Effects on the United States Coast Guard and its People. *Race, Gender, & Class, 14*(3/4), 131–138.

ENDNOTES

[1]   The fade-out of the fact that the proliferation of a scientific discipline represents a process of scientification rather than economization can also be observed in Anders Blok's (2011) reply to Michel Callon's (Callon, 2007; Callon, 1998; Çalışkan & Callon, 2009, 2010) performativity of economics program. Blok is right in pointing out that markets are not only performed by economists, but also by politicians, however, he also takes economists for representatives of the economy and hopes that an ethically guidance of both performers and counter-performers will "generate not only civilized markets, but also civilized politics" (Blok, 2011:271), in the end.

[2]   The present interpretation of word importance does not refer to where word importance is inversely related to word frequency (Baeza-Yates & Ribeiro-Neto, 1999). Such an indexical approach to

[3]   The data from 1500-1800 is likely to feature biases due to insufficient sample sizes: "The oldest works were published in the 1500s. The early decades are represented by only a few books per year, comprising several hundred thousand words. By 1800, the corpus grows to 98 million words per year; by 1900, 1.8 billion; and by 2000, 11 billion" (Michel et al., 2011:176).

word importance would only make sense if the present article was interested in comparing the discriminatory abilities of the concepts involved. All function systems, however, are on the same level of analysis and, therefore, feature the same degree of discriminatory power.

[4]   Fold change of the relative word frequency calculated in terms of the ratio of the word frequency of 2000 and 1800: $\hat{f} = \Theta(2000)/\Theta(1800)$. Due to newly added features, the word frequencies did not have to be visually assessed anymore; rather, we could rely on precise measures as indicated by the enhanced Google Ngram Viewer.

[5]   The abbreviation ppm represents "parts per million", i.e. the relative word frequency per million words in the Google Book corpus. The unit *per million* is used to avoid longer chains of digits after the decimal point. The most common English words account for estimated 45'000ppm in version 1 and measured 46'400ppm in version 2 of the data (4.5%/4.6%: *the*), 30'000ppm/29'400ppm (3.9%/2.9%: *of*) and 23'000ppm/22'800 (2.3%/2.3%: *and*). *Time*, the most frequent noun in the Google Million corpus, has an appearance of 1'160ppm. *Political* (320ppm) hence appears about four times less than *time*.

[6]   In the original version of this article (Roth, 2014), this analysis was based on the English Google Million corpus (only, as other corpora proved unmanageable with the available hardware). First, the 10 separate fractions of this user-friendlier corpus were merged to a 8GB SPSS file. The corpus was then transformed into a ranked word frequency list of books published between 1800 and 2000. The 2,000 most frequent entries of this list were, thereupon, qualitatively analyzed for their function system references. As a first result, some 230 words with a clear function system reference were identified. The only function system missing among the 2,000 most important words of the corpus was sport, with the designation itself as the first reference ranking far beyond the 6,000th position.

[7]   The code will be made available in a work-in-progress article entitle "Futures of a shared memory. A global brain wave measurement (1800-2000)".

[8]   *politique* is both a noun and an adjective; the adding of adjectives like *légal/e* or *juridique*, however, has only minor effects on the big picture.

[9]   A search engine for the Google Books corpus designed by Marc Davies (2011-) allows for these and further options, however, for the American English corpus only.

Chapter 12

Human Digital Immortality:
Where Human Old Dreams and New Technologies Meet

Florin Popescu
University "Politehnica" of Bucharest, Romania

Cezar Scarlat
University "Politehnica" of Bucharest, Romania

ABSTRACT

More or less primitive homo sapiens have always secretly dreamt about, or plainly believed in immortality. All cultures had and still have beliefs, traditions, rituals, legends, old stories, and fairy tales about immortality. Unfortunately, as science and technology progressed, human immortality is a remote ideal yet. In addition, as technology development speeds up, it challenges the social nature of humankind; a possible result is people alienation. It is the purpose of this paper to propose a new prospective: opposed to the common feeling that technology alienates people – in their most intimate nature – the authors believe that modern technologies and human nature (defined by its innermost dream of immortality) converge. The ancient human dream of eternal life can be achieved through technology: i.e. human digital immortality. A day will come when the entire technical capabilities will allow personalities to be copied into a computer. Thus immortality could be provided in a virtualized form, heaven being replaced with a super computer.

INTRODUCTION

More or less primitive *homo sapiens* have always secretly dreamt about, or plainly believed in immortality. All cultures had and still have beliefs, traditions, rituals, legends, old stories, and fairy tales about immortality. For most of the human history, the proverbs have played the role of humankind wisdom repository. Only over the last few centuries it was the role of technology – books by Gutenberg press, then new media by information technology – to extend the human capacity to store and process unimaginable amounts of data.

DOI: 10.4018/978-1-5225-1868-6.ch012

Trends characterizing technological civilization of the 21st century are redefining the relationship between tradition and modernity. While industrial period was defined by a violent rupture in relation with the past, the new digital world is marked by a contrary process. Japanese artist Masamune Shirow, author of the *mangas*[1] of the animated films "Ghost in The Shell" (1995) - directed by Mamoru Oshii, and "Appleseed" (2004) - directed by Shinji Aramaki, state that the virtual world is a more accurate replica of reality and for developing advanced technologies people need to understand and integrate new paradigms in all aspects of the real world (Shirow, 1991).

Confronted with the downfall of a short life – mainly due to diseases and wars – people have always dreamed to live longer, sometimes tending to push this to extreme, towards eternal life. Many legends and writings testify human beings eager to learn about never ending life, about the elixir of youth, the secret of eternal life.

There are different standpoints to understand or to approach immortality (i.e. life vs. death) question:

1. Relative to extension of life:
   a. extension as increase of life expectancy – as result of better quality of life (water and food; living and working conditions; medicines and healthcare services; eco-environment);
   b. life extension as a result of technology direct intervention (either genetics or computer science and information technology) – for shorter or longer time horizons, one-time or repeated interventions;
   c. immortality by progressive life extension;
   d. life indefinitely extended (immortality).
2. Relative to individual life or humankind life (as average life statistically calculated or, more profound, as human species perpetuation).
3. Relative to material or spiritual aspects:
   a. material life;
   b. material heritage;
   c. knowledge heritage;
   d. spiritual heritage;
   e. spiritual life (in religious sense).

All these issues are debateable and, each of them, subject to extended research, discussions, and (interdisciplinary and cross-disciplinary) theories. Table 1 displays several possible combinations – as a matrix model for systematic approach.

Under the sign of this book (*human-technology interaction*), this chapter deals with the issue of individual life extension, mostly in that sense of technology-supported life extension. However, necessary elements of spiritual heritage and knowledge transfer are presented as well.

Table 1. Several issues related to "immortality" question

Immortality question	Individual life	Humankind life
Life extension	Issue: Individual life extension	Issue: Increase in average life expectancy Issue: Human species perpetuation
Immortality	Issue: Immortal individuals	Issue: Immortal humankind

The purpose of this chapter is to propose a new prospective:

- Opposed to the common belief that technology alienates people – in their most intimate nature – the authors believe that modern technologies and human nature, defined by its innermost dream of immortality, converge; the ancient human dream of eternal life can be achieved through technology (i.e. human digital immortality).

The study is focused on four main directions of analysis:

- Firstly, is analysed the immortality perception in mythology all across the Globe, in various civilizations,
- Secondly how genetics addresses immortality,
- Thirdly various ongoing studies and projects about immortality in digital era,
- Fourthly another prospective on immortality (books as means of spiritual immortality) represented by knowledge transfer and,
- Eventually, what will be next...from *Homo Sapiens* to *Homo Optimus*?

Forays into the realm of mythology, the science of genetics, digital technology, knowledge transfer are not performed in order of complexity, but rather in parallel, because since the beginning of this study we asked an appropriate question:

- What technological direction will award immortality?
- Genetics, digital technology or knowledge transfer?

There are enough solid reasons to believe that things will happen somehow in parallel.

The study begins forays into the realm of mythology and genetics because the immortality and the fear of death are themes present for thousands of years in cultures and religions of the world and the evolution of genetics clearly aims to the state of immortality or, for starters, with the unprecedented extension of life.

Consequently, the remaining of this chapter is structured as follows: immortality as seen in antiquity; approaching the immortality concept in terms of genetics or digital technology; immortality as knowledge transfer, followed by conclusions, limitations, and ... further questions (to be read as research avenues).

DREAMING AND THINKING ABOUT IMMORTALITY IN ANTIQUITY

The idea of immortality is present in mythology all across the Globe, taking different forms in various civilizations. There are also certain legends which have the quest of people to achieve this goal as the central focus point. In all of them though, a last minute failure makes immortality to remain just a fairy-tale, a beautiful one though in which people have no right to part in. Four legendary examples of attempts to reach immortality are displayed below.

From childhood memories, we recall the Romanian fairy-tale "Youth without aging and life without death"[2], in which the main character, the Prince Charming (Făt-Frumos in Romanian), from the beginning of the life, is fated to achieve immortality because he chooses to be born only when his father grants him endless youth and life without death. At the age of adulthood, Făt-Frumos enrols in a challenging journey to achieve immortality, a road full of challenges and unseen dangers. As soon as he reaches the enchanted realm of the three fairies, Făt-Frumos is told to never set foot in the Valley of Weeping. Făt-Frumos disregards this advice and thus loses the chance to obtain immortality, a never ending life. The intriguing touch that the imaginary dialogue between Death and Făt-Frumos at the end of the tale is astonishing, even Death admitting that "if you were to be late, even I would have perished". This raises the idea that even death would have an ending in such a brittle world. Behind its beauty, the philosophical elements of the story are also to be underlined.

The ancient inhabitants of Mesopotamia also had a legend about the pursuit of immortality. The legend is called "The Epic of Gilgamesh" (or "Gilgamesh Journey") considered to be a masterpiece of the ancient Assyro-Babylonian literature (Jackson, 1997). The main character, Gilgamesh, touched by the fear of dying after the loss of his friend Enkidu, embarks in a long journey in order to find the herb of immortality. In his journey, he stumbles upon the "water of the dead", a type of water which would have killed anyone who would touch it. Even if he defeats Death, Gilgamesh fails the attempt to reach immortality. Right in the moment when he had the opportunity to obtain immortality, a snake eats the herb, taking away forever the humanity chance to become immortal.

The same failure in obtaining immortality is found in Greek mythology (Hesiod, 1987; Graves, 1955; Burkert, 1977, 1985). The Greeks believed in immortality of their gods and unfading youth – because of the constant use of nectar and ambrosia which renewed their blood (Stoll, 1852). The goddess Tethys tries to grant immortality to her mortal son Achilles, by bathing him in the river Styx. Unfortunately, she forgets to submerge Achilles' heel, making him vulnerable in the face of Death. The only form of immortality granted to people, in Greek mythology is that in which the greatest heroes (Kelsey, 1889, 2012; Kirk, 1970) became constellations after death. Thus, after death, Perseus, Orion, Andromeda become constellations, Castor and Pollux become stars which will form Twins constellation. A beautiful piece of poetry that immerged in astronomy, aiming at immortality.

A final example of a failed attempt to achieve immortality can be found in Norse mythology (Page, 1990; Lindow, 2001; Christopher, 2011). Just like the goddess Tethys from Greek mythology, the goddess Frigg knowing by the tragic end of her son Baldur, asks all the forces of nature to protect him. Although, they swore allegiance to her, she misses a minor detail, a fact that will be fatal to Baldur, the mistletoe, considering it to be without importance. This small detail will be the cause of Baldur's death, proving once again that immortality is a dream forbidden for people.

The main idea of these old legends is that of death being inevitable for people even though religions have met these fundamental aspirations by consoling the idea of the soul immortality and the afterlife, after death, in a world beyond the high threshold, a world in which eternal life is possible. The religion historians tend to agree that all these old legends have common roots.

In this respect, it is relevant to mention that, according to Allen (1978), the orientalist Max Müller[3] claimed as early as 1891 that the most important discovery of the nineteenth century (related to the ancient history of mankind) was this "equation":

Sanskrit Dyaus-pitar = Greek Zeus = Latin Jupiter = Old Norse Tyr

The entire human history is strewn with religious ideas, also artistic and cultural, even with physical trials, some more grotesque and macabre than others, in which the human being would stand the test of time. This is why in so many ways we can talk about immortality.

The famous Romanian philosopher, Lucian Blaga, in his poem "Soul of the Village", gives us a picture of the way in which eternity was portrayed almost a century ago, the ancestral village being used as a metaphor of permanence. Temporality is established as a criterion and the village as a space matrix value. In traditional view, the ancestral village is the territory of the privileged flow slow down time, where eternity found "the cadence" (Blaga, 1924): "Here any thought is slower, / and your heart beats less, /as it would not beat in your chest, / but somewhere, deep, in the earth."

People continued to aspire towards physical immortality, thus after so many centuries in which they could only dream of it, there came the time when we talk about immortality in different terms, as something that in the near future - decades - might be possible. But beyond philosophical considerations or esoteric speculation, it would be interesting to find out what scientists make of this topic. After decades of acquiring outstanding scientific successes, scientists began exploring the vast and miraculous territory called life, seeking what has often been called the "elixir of youth", the biggest dream of humanity representing the final frontier of engineering and technology.

If not more than a century ago, the ancestral village was seen by Romanian philosopher Lucian Blaga as the land of eternity, in the new digital world on the other hand, there are two major research directions in order to understand the human being,

- One biological and the other artificial (i.e. approaching immortality concept in terms of genetics or digital technology – respectively).

Both roads seem to lead inexorably to the emergence of a kind of natural human limitations, intended to cross larger period of time, to achieve Matusalemic life or, why not, immortality.

APPROACHING THE CONCEPT OF IMMORTALITY IN TERMS OF GENETICS

Genetic engineering has made great strides, even colossal over the recent years. And if at the beginning it was considered a term derived from science fiction, genetic engineering has become a prominent part of science, so ground breaking that it is called "synthetic biology" (Calvert, 2010). Synthetic biology is certainly the revolutionary pinnacle in the field of science (Shantharam, 2009). What does genetic engineering represents for immortality, for eternity? There is much to say, but this chapter is trying to provide an intuitive, a fictitious or futuristic perspective towards where humankind is heading.

It seems unbelievable, but the British gerontologist Aubrey de Grey[4] says that the first person who will live to 150 years was already born, and one that will live 1,000 years will be definitely born in less than 20 years (de Grey, 2015). His statements are based on the fact that specialists will have all the necessary means to 'treat' aging body in the next two decades at their disposal. According to de Grey, this will be possible primarily through the elimination of all diseases that affect the human body. He sees future medical check-ups used as a kind of "maintenance" for the body, which will include gene therapies, stem cell therapies, strengthening and boosting the immune system and a number of other medical advanced techniques to maintain the shape of the human body. De Grey describes the aging process as being a lifelong accumulation of various types of diseases that are wearing out the cells. "The idea is to do what we would call periodic restoration of damaged cells before they become corrupted pathological ", explained De Grey (2015).

The idea of extending ones' life is not something new, and or whether it could be extended and how much is still a controversial subject. According to statistics, in each year there is added about three months to ones' life, so whether there will still be controversy on this subject, the trend is clear. In recent decades life expectancy has increased significantly in some developed countries from 70 to 80 years. Based on this information, however, and given the promises made by big investors in "life industry", researchers estimate that, by 2030, a lot of people in civilized countries will live on average 100 years, even 120 years. Worldwide, in 2010, there were about 40,000 centenarians, experts estimating that by 2030 there could be over 1 million centenarians living worldwide (United Nations DoEaSA, Population Division, 2011).

Genetic techniques are advancing more and more in this direction. Organs grown based on our own genes, using stem cells, these procedures have almost zero chance of the organ being rejected by the body (Alterovitz, Muso & Ramoni, 2010). Not far away, perhaps classical surgery will become medical history, humans will no longer need to repair or to extract, but to replace. Stem cell therapies, tissues and bio-artificial organs, genetic therapy appear to fold perfectly on every person desires:

- The eradication of suffering,
- The extension of youth,
- Old age dissolution,
- Supressing death,
- Indefinite prolongation of life expectancy,
- Immortality.

Investigations are underway to identify genetic mechanisms of aging; life expectancy depends on the ability of cells to reproduce without error, to keep their functions unaltered. An accurate reproduction that does not alter the structure or processes of new cells means an accurate replication of DNA (consisting of 46 chromosomes), in other words, the DNA cells should be an exact copy of the initial string. Research has shown that, naturally, the process of copying leaking is inevitable (Jin, 2010). Specifically, during each replication of DNA, a region at the end of each chromosome (called a telomere) shortens a bit. True, at the first cell replication, losses are not significant. However, the "book telomeres" at the end of chromosomes is limited. After several replications, telomere will be increasingly shorter inevitable that will disappear and the copy will not be possible (Sealey & Harrington, 2006).

We may add to this list of methods of intervention in the processes of life and opportunities of medical technologies, imaging techniques (MRI[5] for instance), molecular surgery ("molecular toolbox" interventions) or lasers. Moreover, in recent years there have developed new areas of research which investigate with an unprecedented resolution the processes of cellular life (Howard, Brown & Auer, 2014). It is the so-called science "OMIC AD"[6] that occurred predominantly in this century:

- Genomics (which take into consideration all the information hereditary);
- Proteomics (aiming structure and function of proteins, components of metabolic processes in cells);
- Metabolomics (studying products resulting from the "footprint" of chemical cell cellular processes);
- or areas bordering informatics and biology (studying interactions between proteins, existing types of cells and other molecules, and the consequences of these interactions on cell life).

More and more organs could be grown artificially (Alterovitz et al., 2010) and, overcoming moral, religious constraints or otherwise, we will revive the old, sick or worn. Surely, hospitals will not become workshops with spare parts, but keeping the proportions and simplifying at maximum, we can see things in this way. With new healthy organs people can seriously take to grip with devolution, with biodegradability, with telomeres of cells, with death, in essence. Therefore, we talk about physical survival; actually, definitely, things are not simple. We do not yet know how exactly an organism behaves almost entirely made up of cloned organs. Even if fairly advanced, the research in the field of geriatrics is still in a phase of scientific childhood. The genetic evolution clearly aims to the state of immortality or, for the moment, to unprecedented prolongation of life (Fabian & Flatt, 2011).

Perhaps, the biggest obstacle will be, ultimately, the price. Not everyone will have access to these technologies. They will take probably decades, possibly more, until these processes become accessible to all of us. And then, it might foreshadow a new generation of demigods:

- Not only rich but also eternal youth!

A fracturing of human society that can become deep, dividing the inhabitants of the planet will occur in this case in the future. And so humanity is deeply divided, the differences are much greater than we might think. Access to medicines, to modern medicines is a privilege of the most developed states, other countries still struggling with illness, with misery and underdevelopment. So, who will be the future immortals? It's pretty easy to guess that the rich people of the planet will want to buy time, to buy life and, if possible, youth. A whole set of moral aspects and profession ethics is emerging in this respect.

Concluding, genetics is the science that will change the way of understanding biological limits. All this shows that scientific investigation of life reveals more and more clues on possibilities of manipulating resources and mechanisms of life.

APPROACHING THE CONCEPT OF IMMORTALITY IN TERMS OF DIGITAL TECHNOLOGY

As the authors presented from the beginning of this study, immortality will be performed in parallel by multiple technological directions, immortal man of the future probably wearing at the same time cloned organs and intelligent digital prosthesis, this mix ensuring an extended life compared to current standards.

Somewhat, parallel with research in genetics, inexorably humanity evolves in terms of electronic and digital technologies. Humanity goes deeper into an e-world created by us. More, however, smarter "prosthesis" increasingly becoming a part of our lives. They are even now buds of future immortality, when humans will probably be almost one hundred per cent synthetic.

There are many shocking discussion and statements about a new topic - the disappearance of technology (Kahn, Severson, & Jolina, 2009). According to authors, almost everything that is invented and produced in this area will disappear at a certain point in time. This disappearance, but said improperly, does not mean that we might think at first glance. Technology will restrict in humans. As computers become smaller and smaller, everything will collapse in our own bodies. Various natures of chips will be applied directly to the body or inside the body, intelligent prostheses will be an indissoluble part of us, interacting with our bodies, but especially with the brain and sense organs, the bionic man becomes reality. And from here to the *Singularity of Ray Kurzweil* speaking, it's not such a long way: "information transfer of the entire contents of the brain, the whole consciousness practically into the components of a computer, moving from biological to cyberspace host could provide humans with a type of immortality" (Kurzweil, 2005, p. 215).

Sure, this is limited by certain conditions that may or may not use future functional computers. This sounds complicated now to make sure such a computing power exists, but in the future things will not remain this way. Current development trends of the technology to provide more and more storage space, stunning victories in this direction (*Top 25 Technology Predictions*, by Dave Evans[7]), allows us to believe that the moment humans can move in virtual reality is not so far away. Of course, there are lots of contradictory talks. Let aside the scientific controversies, the spiritualists, religious people, do not place headquartered consciousness in the brain; they see as impossible to preserve (in a simple computer programme) the entire human being, endowed with consciousness structure, with spirit.

Stephen Hawking, one of the most controversial physicists, believes that soon people will become immortal, which will be possible due to the evolution of technology. To make himself understood, the physicist is comparing the human mind with a computer (Hawking, 2013). Technically, the human brains are significantly close to computers, brains functioning in much the same way a computer does, but it is far more powerful than this. Human brain is one of the most fascinating yet not completely explored areas of the human body. This information processor has been the subject of much research study across history (National Institutes of Health, 2014).

The brain is the piece of tissue which directs the planet, in this enigmatic organ lie thinking, memory and feelings; cerebral cortex mysteries are far away from being discovered.

Human brain is composed of specialized cells called neurons that communicate through electrical signals. Each neuron receives electrical signals simultaneously from thousands of other neurons which are "summed up" in a linear manner, and generate electrical signals to other neurons. Parallel architecture for processing information allows the human brain, which operates with signals that propagate in milliseconds to have a capacity of processing information much higher and faster than most modern computers. Our brain is evolving, every day, the brain changes million connections between neurons, opens and rewrites memories and impressions, adds new knowledge etc…(see figure 1).

Penrose[8] (1989) writes that quantum mechanics plays a key role in understanding human consciousness. The human brain can be likened to a bio-quantum computer; it sounds like one of the most beautiful ideas of this book. And you ask yourself: if our mind is marvellous quantum how can we do basic mathematical operations with relatively high numbers?

Conventional computers work with bits - the base of the storage information. A bit can have two states: 0 and 1, therefore, a computer with N bits can be at a time in one of 2^N possible states.

Quantum equivalent of a bit is so-called qubit, which is logical unit storing information in a quantum computer. The fundamental difference from a conventional computer – one that fascinates alike vexing human mind – is that the latter, due to quantum phenomena, it could be found out simultaneously in several states or even in all 2^N states. How is it possible? In theory, a quantum computer works like this: a number of qubits are set in the initial state, to represent the problem to be solved. Then these qubits are manipulated with a finite sequence of logic gates (circuits that perform operations on any processor). This sequence of quantum logic gates is actually called algorithm.

The process ends with a condition which reduces system measurement (the array of qubits) in a single state, i.e. a string of 0 and 1 of length N, which is the solution of the problem. The result is probabilistic and quantum algorithms are often non-deterministic.

Figure 1. Human brain connections (Source: Sott.net)

In theory, those who think that this is possible are encouraged by techniques to compile brain maps. It works as a practical massive transit system, neurons acting as roads leading information from one place to another. At the end of each road they are known as synapses structure that acts like connections that allow us to have a unique set of memories and identity. Some believe that a map of all these connections could simulate what makes us unique. But as we probably imagine, such a map as a digital code would occupy much space. To understand exactly how much - global storage capacity in 2014 was 2.6 billion terabytes. According to International Data Corporation 1.3 billion terabytes would be required to compile the map of human connections (Chorost, 2011).

Another theory says that in the not-too-distant future, the human mind can be stored in a computer, which can be tied to a physical body robot or a virtual world and thus people could live forever (Critchlow, 2015). Critchlow's theory may seem impossible, could have been taken from a science fiction movie, but in a not so distant future, scientists argue that could be possible that someone might exist in a digital machine. According to Critchlow (2015), to boot human brain on a computer, it would need a special computer, capable of storing trillions of connections that exist in the human brain, but if this computer will be designed, people could live forever through it.

If scientists will manage to design a high performance processor with hardware and software designed to suitable accommodate all memories from the human brain, ways of connection and their functions, then, in theory, anyone could live inside the computer. People could live for an indefinite period, even forever, even after their physical body died.

We begin to believe that having a "backup" of our own brain, the memories and experiences, and install it on a computer, could be the best way to leave posterity a sign of our passage on earth. Within certain limits and with patience, this really can be done. In the age of Facebook, iPad and avatars in the virtual reality game "Second Life", even Frankenstein needs an "upgrade", time when he had to seek immortality rooting around the brains of corpses have been gone, from now is enough to sit at the computer and to-grasp program.

It may seem incredible, but in recent years many companies have started investing in the development of cerebral archiving systems sort of copying electronic memories and experiences of people, able to give life to a "digital alter ego" claiming immortality.

Rick Meyer, a researcher at Lifenaut (one of the American companies trying to build the first such digital clone), cited by Geddes (2010), said that "to be able to install yourself in a computer could mean to live forever". On Lifenaut site, for example, it is possible to build (free for now) our own digital alter ego:

- People can upload photos, attach videos, images and the desired text, and answer nearly 500 questions about their personality.

The end result will be an animated avatar image and likeness of our electronic, able to describe, through a voice synthesizer, key moments of our existence. And for those who seem much less, there is the possibility to pay and get more.

Another controversial project which appears, at the first glance, to be the scenario of a science fiction movie belongs to a Russian billionaire[9]. "Human immortality is the next space journey … The goal was to capture public attention. It is true that I have discussions with many of the richest people on earth, but I cannot reveal who they are", said Itskov (2013). He proposed this summer to continue his plans, by addressing the funding application not only to the very wealthy, but the entire business community. The billionaire says that the industry will have to begin the manufacturing of robotic bodies to serve as avatars, computer interfaces which are replacing the brain, so people can control the machines and even to transfer human consciousness through a network between avatars (see figure 2).

He argues that although he does have some degree of hesitation, a change in the evolutionary process is a long-term solution absolutely necessary for the human race to survive. "Not everyone understands the motivation behind this project. I know we can change more by simply changing the way we think. I have no doubt, absolutely none, that this is possible" (Itskov, 2013).

A lot of experts who study the vital functions of the human body, but also some philosophers are asking in what extent someone wants to gain immortality. It might seem bizarre to many, after all their relatives, friends, the entire generation disappeared, and they still live; it might excite some or even provoke repulsion. In addition, the idea of living like an avatar (where a brain with his conscience directs a robot mechanism completely dehumanized) might not tempt anyone. Before we think about immortality, it may worth reflecting on doctor Faust case, which did not bring satisfaction even re-living his own life, twice.

ANOTHER PROSPECTIVE ON IMMORTALITY: BOOKS AS MEANS OF SPIRITUAL IMMORTALITY, BY KNOWLEDGE TRANSFER

The Senegalese musician Baaba Maal, looking at a piece of art exposed by the British artist John Latham at Tate Modern Gallery in London, remembers a West-African proverb: "When an old person dies, a

Figure 2. Towards a new strategy for human evolution (Source: http:GF2045.com)

"The mission of the 2045 Initiative is to ensure the survival of civilization, build a bright future for all mankind, reach new goals and create new meanings and values for humane, ethical and high-tech future" – Dmitry Itskov

whole library dies". The Latham's work is a composition of books, plaster and metal on canvas (see figure 3); the books are painted in twelve different colours and their pages are partly burnt. The books could be opened at different pages – so the work can present multiple facets. The work was completed back in 1960 and it was the subject of an experimental movie produced by Latham – this is why it's named "Film Star".

Figure 3. Fragment of "Film Star" by John Latham (books, plaster and metal on canvas)
Source: Photo taken by C.S., Tate Modern Gallery, London, August 2012.

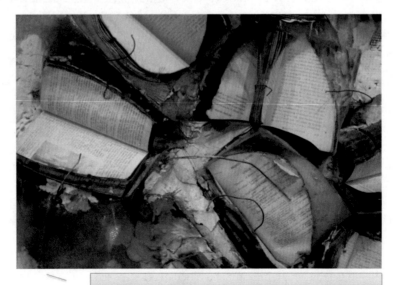

Fragment of "Film Star" by John Latham (books, plaster and metal on canvas)

The African artist explains his vision and feelings in a commentary written under this piece of art (he calls it "The Bigger Picture"): "The idea is that while living, you share your knowledge through your mouth, and when you die it disappears ... all these books – they seem to come from the mind of one person who has used these pages to talk about what he knows ... these books, their different shapes and sizes, represent the history of life, of earth, of humanity ..."

One of the authors (Scarlat, 2015, pp. 36-37) has the opportunity to visit Tate Modern Gallery years ago and, looking at this work, he was marked by the profound message transmitted by the two artists.

Coming back several times, each new visit was a new intellectual – and, maybe, artistic – exercise, contemplation and reflection on the subject of life and [im]mortality, wisdom transmission and knowledge transfer. The antique wisdom transmission from older to younger, from magister to disciple is called nowadays technology transfer.

Besides respected philosophic and artistic considerations made by the above-mentioned artists, ours own is that proverbs are actually unwritten books; the proverbs are the oral alternate option as compared to written books (any type of book, either paper or e-book) to transfer the knowledge and valuable life experiences to the followers.

The knowledge treasure does not die with the burning book (i.e. the one who dies). The African proverb is a metaphor embedded in another metaphor:

- The books may burn but the life lessons and wisdom transmitted from one generation to another, by proverbs, cannot be destroyed; they do not disappear or die. Individuals die but their ideas and wisdom transmitted to the next generations do not.

The proverbs cannot die because they were born together with homo sapiens, and the proverbs will live as long as homo sapiens and his descendants will (Scarlat, 2015, p.37).

Four theses about the oldness and resilience of proverbs could be formulated (Scarlat, 2015, pp.38-39):

- Proverbs existed even before writing symbols were invented;
- Proverbs continued to exist even after the writing systems were elaborated (originally, the proverbs were used mainly for educating the royal and religious elites[10]);
- Yet the proverbs continued to exist after the printed press was invented, and the use of proverbs actually expanded;
- The current development of new media and information & communication technologies did not stop the use of proverbs, they essentially help the proverbs to be used at a larger scale.

Looking back in time, Scarlat (2015, pp.39-43) has developed a matrix model to emphasize five paradoxes of proverbs' dynamics, underlining the role of proverbs in education (originally in elite education, later on in mass and family education), as vehicle of spiritual immortality, by an elementary form of knowledge transfer.

The books are the more advanced means of knowledge and technology transfer. Considering the proverbs as condensed, unwritten, memorized and orally transmitted books, the conclusion is that books in general, by any format (virtual books included), are vehicles of spiritual immortality (as long as human recipients are still there to read ...).

And books are cheaper ...

If peoples' access to healthier water and food, better living and working conditions, better medicines and medical services, newer technologies for life extension (genetics, computer science, information technology) or exploring new living environments (intra- or extra-Terra, outer space) is significantly more and more expensive – the wisdom of proverbs is for free …

WHAT'S NEXT: FROM HOMO SAPIENS TO HOMO OPTIMUS?

For a long time, humans have been considered the pinnacle of evolution; that humanity has achieved its evolutionary peak and nothing to evolve into. Today those who try to foresee the future of mankind and his evolution are thinking of cyborg image, a combination of a biological creature and a technological masterpiece. The scientists are talking about people who will exist in artificial bodies, a man-machine hybrid in which certain body parts can be replaced with artificial parts, things that will lead to an extension of lifetime, even to immortality (Cole, 2013).

The futurologist Ian Pearson believes that a new species, *homo optimus*, is emerging. According to him, those who have not reached 40 years could be part of "electronic immortality" during their lifetime, thoughts and experiences will be stored and kept online for future generations, according to an interview published by *Daily Mail* (Pearson, 2016). He states that, in response to the increased development of technology at all levels, our evolution will go in a completely new direction. This time, the nature won't force us to change, but discoveries and innovations will. "That could lead to weird and wonderful shapes and creations", says the futurologist. He states that by establishing a connection between our brain and the computer, humans could "move" in a body-mind android, and even the whole consciousness could. Basically, he says, that would give us the opportunity to have more existences and identities or to continue to live after biological death. The specialist thinks that although such technologies will be available by 2050, within 20 years of their discovery, they will become sufficiently cheap and widespread. By the end of the century, says dr. Pearson, there will be several types of people, including hybrids of people and cars and people living in android bodies.

CONCLUSION

Immortality and fear of death are themes present for thousands of years in cultures and religions across the world. The ancients believed in a magic potion, a concoction which would grant what man has mostly desired the most, eternal life. The Chinese emperors dreamed to live as long as possible, consuming precious substances, a mix of jade and gold, doing this many times, with fatal consequences. Elizabeth Bathory, a 16th Century Transylvanian Countess called "Lady Dracula" has made an attempt to defeat death, bathing in young girls' blood. Pope Inocentiu the 8th, due to the fact he was too old, tried to increase his longevity by drinking the blood of three young boys, but failing immediately.

Today, the same as always, the attempt to extend life on an indefinite term is still obsessing the wealthy and powerful which have begun to contribute with huge amounts of money different "projects of immortality".

For the moment, regardless of the advancement of medicine or technology, the human life finally reaches the inevitable end, and death will not distinguish between rich and poor. Nevertheless, as we have said, if the peoples' access to better living and working conditions as well as to newer technologies for life extension is significantly more and more expensive (and, consequently, more and more difficult) – the wisdom of proverbs is for free: by their embedded knowledge, the rich and the poor may have equal chances to immortality.

LIMITATIONS AND FURTHER QUESTIONS

Although immortality seems to become a target, modern technologies have proposed new solutions to address the subject in a more realistic manner than mythology or science fiction, often very fascinating. Such technologies do not border on the absurd, instead, they rely on some recent scientific data and research in physics and biology, abandoning conventional processes – excellent in their time, but today they tend to limit the horizon of thought and knowledge.

The idea of cybernetic immortality is to induce our consciousness in a virtual space. Some modern philosophical concepts consider that our world in which we live is a virtual space, and if we come to realize this subsequent passage of a virtual world to another, it would not be unthinkable. If this virtual space will be temporary, as ours, or immortal, it will, of course, depend on software that we do, to get into those spaces. Of course, all these presume that our perceptions, feelings, emotions and our existence are the result of electrical impulses, to whose dominion will handle those able to get up there when we take existence in a virtual world. Thus we ask a normal question:

- Is it possible that man – every person on Earth – to live forever?

Some believe that it is and even want this, some are afraid that it is possible, some hope not and others are convinced that it isn't possible.

The truth is that a passing from a state to the other, from being a mortal creature to that of an immortal presence would be profound, the most severe change ever to take place in the history of mankind. From the right of inheritance and to the pension and insurance system, the whole scaffolding of modern civilization relies on the reality that people do die, after being alive for a period of time. And no matter how tempting the perspective may seem to some, the problems that individual immortality poses are able to make those who are inclined towards this aspect to wonder, do we really want to become immortal?

REFERENCES

Allen, D. (1978). Structure and Creativity in Religion: Hermeneutics in Mircea Eliade's Phenomenology and New Directions. New York: Mouton Publishers.

Alterovitz, G., Muso, T., & Ramoni, M. F. (2010). The challenges of informatics in synthetic biology: From biomolecular networks to artificial organisms. *Journal on Emerging Technologies in Computing Systems Briefings in Bioinformatics*, *11*(1), 80–95. doi:10.1093/bib/bbp054 PMID:19906839

Blaga, L. (1924). Sufletul satului/The Soul of the Village. In *În marea trecere*. Cluj, Romania: Ed. Radio.

Burkert, W. (1985). *Greek Religion*. Blackwell Publishing Ltd and Harvard University Press.

Calvert, J. (2010). Synthetic biology: Constructing nature? *The Sociological Review*, *58*, 95–112. doi:10.1111/j.1467-954X.2010.01913.x

Chorost, M. (2011). *World Wide Mind: The Coming Integration of Humanity, Machines, and the Internet*. New York, NY: Free Press.

Christopher, A. (2011). *Myths of the Pagan North: the Gods of the Norsemen*. London: Continuum.

Cole, D. (2013). *Repairing and replacing Body Parts. What's Next*. National Geographic News.

Critchlow, H. (2015). *Dr. Hannah Critchlow interview*. Retrieved from www.telegraph.co.uk

De Grey, A. (2015). *A roadmap to end aging*. Retrieved on the 23th April 2015 from http://www.ted.com/talks/aubrey_de_grey_says_we_can_avoid_aging

Fabian, D., & Flatt, T. (2011). *The Evolution of Aging*. Nature Education Knowledge, Institute of Population Genetics. *Vetmeduni Vienna Veterinaerplatz*, *1*, A-1210.

Geddes, L. (2010, June). Immortal avatars: Back up your brain, never die. *New Scientist, Issue*, *2763*, 7. doi:10.1016/S0262-4079(10)61706-X

Graves, R. (1955). *The Greek Myths*. Baltimore, MD: Penguin.

Hawking, S. (2013). *Interview*. Retrieved from www.dailymail.co.uk

Hesiod, . (1987). *Theogony*. Indianapolis, IN: Focus, An Imprint of Hackett Publishing Company.

Howard, G., Brown, E., & Auer, M. (2014). *Imaging Life: Biological Systems from Atoms to Tissues*. Oxford University Press.

Ispirescu, P. (1862). *Legende sau Basmele Românilor / Legends or Romanians' Fairy-tales*. Bucureşti: Academic Press.

Itskov, D. (2013). *Global Future 20145 Congress*. New York: Lincoln Center.

Jackson, P. (1997). *The Epic of Gilgamesh* (2nd ed.). Wauconda, IL: Bolchazy-Carducci Publishers, Inc.

Jin, K. (2010). Modern Biological Theories of Aging. Aging and Disease. *US National Library of Medicine*, *1*(2), 72–74.

Kahn, P. H. Jr, Severson, R. L., & Jolina, H. (2009). *The Human Relation with Nature and Technological Nature*. University of Washington.

Kelsey, F. W. (1889). *An Outline of the Greek and Roman Mythology*. Allyn and Bacon. Forgotten Books. (2012). Available at: www.forgottenbooks.org

Kirk, G. S. (1970). *Myth: Its Meaning and Functions in Ancient and Other Cultures*. Berkeley, CA: University of California Press.

Kurzweil, R. (2005). *The Singularity is Near*. New York: Penguin Group.

Larrington, C. (1999). *The Poetic Edda*. Oxford World's Classics.

Lindow, J. (2001). *Norse Mythology: A Guide to the Gods, Heroes, Rituals, and Beliefs*. Oxford, UK: Oxford University Press.

Page, R. I. (1990). Norse Myths (The Legendary Past). London: British Museum & Austin: University of Texas Press.

Pearson, I. (2016). *Dr. Ian Pearson interview*. Retrieved from www.dailymail.co.uk

Penrose, R. (1989). *The Emperor's New Mind: Concerning Computers, Minds and The Laws of Physics*. Oxford University Press.

Scarlat, C. (2015). *Cartea cu proverbe de management / The Book with Management Proverbs*. Bucharest, Romania: Ed. Printech.

Sealey, F., & Harrington, L. (2006). *Telomere DNA Replication, Telomerase and Human Disease*. Department of Medical Biophysics, University of Toronto.

Shantharam, Sh. (2009). *Synthetic Biology. A New Paradigm in the Biotechnology Revolution*. Foundation for Biotechnology Awareness and Education.

Shirow, M. (1991). *Ghost in The Shell*. Academic Press.

Stoll, H. W. (1852). *Handbook of the Religion and Mythology of the Greeks - with a short account of the Religious System of the Romans*. London: Francis & John Rivington. Gilbert & Rivington, Printers.

United Nations DoEaSA, Population Division. (2011). *World Population Prospects: The 2010 Revision*. New York: United Nations.

ENDNOTES

[1]   *manga* = a Japanese type of comic books or cartoons, often violent and/or erotic

[2]   Romanian original: „Tinereţe fără bătrâneţe şi viaţă fără de moarte", Romanian folk fairy-tale, collected and re-counted by Petre Ispirescu (Ispirescu, 1862).

[3]   Müller, Friedrich Max (1823 – 1900): German-born philologist and orientalist, lived and studied in Britain; one of the founders of the Western academic field of Indian studies and the discipline of comparative religion.

[4]   Aubrey de Grey: British researcher on aging; computer scientist, self-taught bio-gerontologist and researcher; chief scientist of *Methuselah Foundation* dedicated to longevity studies; co-authored journal articles with respected scientists in the field.

[5]   MRI: Magnetic Resonance Imaging is a non-invasive imaging technology that produces three dimensional detailed anatomical images without the use of damaging radiation. It is often used for disease detection, diagnosis, and treatment monitoring.

[6]   OMIC AD: The English-language neologism omics informally refers to a field of study in biology ending in -*omics*, such as genomics, proteomics or metabolomics.

[7]   Dave Evans: Chief Futurist, Cisco IBSG Innovations Practice

[8]   Sir Roger Penrose: English mathematical physicist, mathematician and philosopher of science. He is the Emeritus Rouse Ball Professor of Mathematics at the Mathematical Institute of the University

of Oxford; known for his work in mathematical physics, in particular for his contributions to general relativity and cosmology; received several prizes and awards, including the 1988 Wolf Prize for physics, which he shared with Stephen Hawking for their contribution to our understanding of the universe.

[9] The Russian billionaire Dmitry Itskov is the founder of the "2045 Initiative" (*Figure 2*), a non-profit organization focused on researching and developing technologies that can make immortality possible. In 2012, he sent an open letter to more Forbes billionaires, asking them to invest in this project. Although he did not receive any answer in public, the news about "2045 Initiative" began to spread, and discussions about financing with various wealthy people seem to be in progress.

[10] See for example: The Bible, Book of Proverbs.

Chapter 13
Design of Human–Computer Interaction Systems with Directions and Applications:
Human–Computer Interaction

Manoj Kumar
International Engineering Services, India

ABSTRACT

The intention of this chapter is to provide an overview on the subject of Human-Computer Interaction. The overview includes the basic definitions and terminology, a survey of existing technologies and recent advances in the field, common architectures used in the design of HCI systems which includes unimodal and multimodal configurations, and finally the applications of HCI. This chapter also offers a comprehensive number of references for each concept, method, and application in the HCI. Human–computer interaction is considered a core element of computer science. Yet it has not coalesced; many researchers who identify their focus as human–computer interaction reside in other fields. It examines the origins and evolution of three HCI research foci: computer operation, information systems management, and discretionary use. It describes efforts to find common ground and forces that have kept them apart.

INTRODUCTION

Utilizing computers had always begged the question of interfacing. The methods by which human has been interacting with computers has travelled a long way. The journey still continues and new designs of technologies and systems appear more and more every day and the research in this area has been growing very fast in the last few decades. The growth in Human-Computer Interaction (HCI) field has not only been in quality of interaction, it has also experienced different branching in its history. Instead of designing regular interfaces, the different research branches have had different focus on the concepts of multimodality rather than unimodality, intelligent adaptive interfaces rather than command/action based ones, and finally active rather than passive interfaces. This chapter intends to provide an overview on

DOI: 10.4018/978-1-5225-1868-6.ch013

the state of the art of HCI systems and cover most important branches as mentioned above. In the next section, basic definitions and terminology of HCI are given. Then an overview of existing technologies and also recent advances in the field is provided. This is followed up by a description on the different architectures of HCI designs. The final sections pertain to description on some of the applications of HCI and future directions in the field. People have interacted with computers from the start, but it took time for human computer interaction (HCI) to become a recognized field of research. Related journals, conferences, and professional associations appeared in the 1970s and 1980s. HCI is in the curricula of research universities, primarily in computer science, yet it has not coalesced into a single discipline. Fields with researchers who identify with HCI include:

- Human factors and ergonomics,
- Information systems,
- Cognitive science,
- Information science,
- Organizational psychology,
- Industrial engineering, and
- Computer engineering (Rubin et al., 2008).

This article identifies historical, conceptual, and cultural distinctions among three major research threads. One thread extended human factors or engineering psychology to computing. Another developed when mainframes spawned business computing in the 1960s. The third, focused on individual use, arose with minicomputers and home computers and burgeoned with personal computing in the 1980s. Although they share some issues and methods, these research efforts have not converged. They emerged within different parent disciplines, at different times, and comprised different generations of researchers. Approaches, attitudes, and terminology differed. Two computer operation and information systems management embraced the journal oriented scholarly tradition of the sciences; the third comprising cognitive and computer scientists has placed greater emphasis on conference publication. In addition, each thread initially emphasized a different aspect of computer use: mandatory hands-on use, hands-off managerial use, and discretionary hands on use. Designing for a use that is a job requirement and designing for a use is discretionary can be very different activities. These often unvoiced distinctions contributed to the current state of HCI research and may shape its future.

Human tool interaction at the dawn of computing:

- Highly specialized tools were developed through the centuries to support carpenters, blacksmiths, and other artisans.

However, efforts to apply science and engineering to improve the efficiency of work practices became prominent only about a century ago, when time and motion studies exploited inventions such as film and statistical analysis. Frederick Taylor's principles of scientific management had limitations and were satirized in Charlie Chaplin's film Modern Times, but they were applied successfully to assembly line manufacturing and other work practices. World War I training requirements accelerated efficiency efforts in Europe and the US. World War II prompted intense interest in engineering psychology as a result of complex equipment used by soldiers, sailors, and pilots that tested human capabilities. Aircraft ergonomic design flaws for example, in the ejection system's escape hatch led to thousands of casualties. After the war, aviation psychologists created the Human Factors Society. Two legacies of World War II were awareness of the potential of computing and an enduring interest in behavioral requirements for design and training. Early approaches to improving work and what at the time were called man machine interfaces focused on nondiscretionary use. Assembly line workers were hired to use a system; pilots were given planes neither had a choice in the matter. If training was necessary, the workers and pilots were trained. Research goals included reducing training time, but most important was eliminating errors and increasing the pace of skilled performance.

THREE ROLES IN EARLY COMPUTING

ENIAC, arguably the first general-purpose electronic computer in 1946, was 10 feet tall, covered 1,000 square feet, and consumed as much energy as a small town. Once a program was written, several people loaded it by setting switches, dials, and cable connections. Despite a design innovation that boosted vacuum tube reliability by enabling them to be operated at 25 percent normal power, 50 spent tubes had to be found and replaced on an average day.

1945-1958: Managing Vacuum Tubes

Reducing operator burden was a key focus of early innovation:

- Eliminating the need to reset vacuum tubes,
- Facilitating replacement of burned-out tubes, and
- Developing stored-program computers that could be loaded by tape rather than manually with cables and switches.

These endeavors were consistent with the "knobs and dials" human factors tradition. By the late 1950s, one computer operator could do the work that previously required a team. The first engineers to design and build computers chose their vocations.

1958–1965: Transistors Open New Vistas

Early forecasts that the world would need few computers reflected the limitations of vacuum tubes. The arrival of commercial solidstate computers in 1958 led to dramatic change. As computers were deployed more widely, attention to the operators' job increased. Even more significantly, people could envision possibilities that were unimaginable for barn-sized machines of limited capability. Helping operators "In the beginning, the computer was so costly that it had to be kept gainfully occupied for every second; people were almost slaves to feed it." Brian Shackel Low-paid computer operators set switches, pushed buttons, read lights, loaded and burst printer paper; they loaded and unloaded cards, magnetic tapes, and paper tapes, and so on. Teletypes were the first versatile mode of direct interaction.

Early Visions and Demonstrations

In his influential 1945 essay "As We May Think," Vannevar Bush, who helped shape scientific research funding in the US, described a mechanical device that anticipated many capabilities of computers. After transistors replaced vacuum tubes, a wave of creative writing and prototype building by several computer pioneers and experts led to expanded and more realistic visions. J.C.R. Licklider outlined requirements for interactive systems and accurately predicted which would prove easier (for example, visual displays) and which more difficult (for example, natural-language understanding). John McCarthy and Christopher Strachey proposed time-sharing systems, crucial to the spread of interactive computing (Kettebekov & Sharma, 2010). In 1963, Ivan Sutherland's Sketchpad demonstrated:

- Constraints,
- Iconic representations,
- Copying,
- Moving, and
- Deleting of hierarchically organized objects, and object-oriented programming concepts.

Discretion in Computer Use

Our lives are distributed along a continuum between the assembly line nightmare of Modern Times and utopian visions of completely empowered individuals. To use a technology or not to use it:

- Sometimes we have a choice, other times we don't. When I need an answer by phone, I may have to wrestle with speech recognition and routing systems. In contrast, my home computer use is largely discretionary.

The workplace often lies in-between:

- Technologies are recommended or prescribed, but we ignore some injunctions, obtain exceptions, use some features but not others, and join with colleagues to advocate changes in policy or availability.

For early computer builders, their work was more a calling than a job, but operation required a staff to carry out essential but less interesting repetitive tasks. For the first half of the computing era, most hands-on use was by people hired with this mandate. Hardware innovation, more versatile software, and steady progress in understanding the psychology of users and tasks and transferring that understanding to software developers led to handson users who exercised more choice in what they did with computers and how they did it (Duchowski, 2012).

1965–1980: HCI Before Personal Computing

In 1964, Control Data Corp. launched the transistor-based 6000 series. In 1965, integrated circuits arrived with the IBM System/360. These powerful computers, later christened mainframes to distinguish them from minicomputers, brought computing into the business realm. At that point, each of the three roles in computing-operation, management, programming- became a significant profession. Operators interacted directly with computers for routine maintenance, loading and running programs, filing printouts, and so on. This hands-on category can be expanded to include data entry, retrieval, and other repetitive tasks necessary to feed the computer. Managers variously oversaw hardware acquisition, software development, operation, and routing and using output. They were usually not hands-on users. Programmers were rarely direct users until late in this period. Instead, they flowcharted programs and wrote them on paper. Keypunch operators then punched the program instructions onto cards. These were sent to computer centers for computer operators to run. Printouts and other output were picked up later. Many programmers would use computers directly when they could, but the cost of computer use generally dictated an efficient division of labor.

Information Systems

Beginning in 1967, the journal Management Science published a column titled "Information Systems in Management Science." Early definitions of IS14 included "an integrated man/machine system for providing information to support the operation, management, and decision-making functions in an organization" and "the effective design, delivery and use of information systems in organizations."

Programming: Subject of Study, Source of Change

In the 1960s and 1970s, more than 1,000 research papers on variables affecting programming performance were published. Most viewed programming in isolation, independent of organizational context. Gerald Weinberg's landmark The Psychology of Computer Programming appeared in 1971. In 1980, Ben Shneiderman published Software Psychology, and Beau Sheil reviewed studies of:

- Programming notation (conditionals, control flow, data types),
- Practices (flowcharting, indenting, variable naming, commenting), and
- Tasks (learning, coding, debugging).

Programmers changed their own field through invention.

1980–1985: Discretionary use Comes into Focus

In 1980, Human Factors and Ergonomics (HF&E) and IS were focused more on improving efficiency than on augmenting human intellect. In contrast, many programmers were captivated by this promise of computation. Growing numbers of students and hobbyists used minicomputers and microprocessor-based home computers, creating a population of hands-on discretionary users. Twenty years later, the visions early pioneers had of people choosing to use computers that helped them work better began to come true.

The Formation of ACM SIGCHI

In 1980, as IBM prepared to launch the PC, a groundswell of attention to computer user behavior was building. IBM had recently added software to hardware as a product focus. Several cognitive psychologists joined an IBM research group that included John Gould, who had engaged in human factors research since the late 1960s.

CHI and Human Factors Diverge

Despite the initial interdisciplinary cooperation with human factors specialists, most cognitive psychologists were familiar with interactive software but not the human factors research literature. Many had turned to HCI after earning their degrees, when academic psychology positions became scarce. The Human Factors Society did not again cosponsor CHI, and its researchers disappeared from the CHI program committee. Soon, few CHI authors identified themselves with human factors. Reservations about human factors were evident in The Psychology of Human Computer Interaction: Human factors specialists, ergonomists, and human engineers will find that we have synthesized ideas from modern cognitive psychology and artificial intelligence with the old methods of task analysis.

Figure 1 positions some HCI events and topics on a timeline. The top row represents the Human Factors and Ergonomics, predominantly nondiscretionary, HCI focus.

Figure 1. Timeline for events, topics and publications discussed within text

	1905	1915		1945	1955	1965	1975	1985	1995	2005
Human Factors and Ergonomics *Operations & data entry*	Taylor	WWI training	WWI human factors				HFS CSTG	Swiss & Mesier guidelines	HFES CEDM	HFES HPM
							Design of man computer dialogues HUSAT	Psycology of HCI VDU standards		
HCI in MIS *Managerial use*						Human factors		Business graphics	GDSS TAM	SIGCI
									HCI	
Computer – Human Interaction & its antecedents *Discretionary hands on use*			General purpose computer	Bush	Hopper IC based computer	Commercial PC	Sociotechnical & Participatory design	Human interaction with computers Software psycology	DIS95 Commercial www	Emotional design DUX03
	1905	1915		1945	1955	1965	1975	1985	1995	2005

1985–2005: New interfaces, Internet, and the Web

Human computer interaction in the personal computing era has been marked by the spread of Internet and intranet use, graphical user interfaces, and the World Wide Web. Although Internet users doubled annually with remarkable regularity, it required decades to become a significant fraction of the population. Graphics made hard-earned progress through the 1960s and 1970s. In 1981, the Xerox Star was the first product with a full GUI.

HF&E and the Role of Government

Understanding the field of human factors and ergonomics requires a look at the role of government as user and supporter of research and development. HF&E research has responded to military, aviation, and telecommunications interests, with government often leading the way. Bureaucratic needs

- Census,
- Tax,
- Social security,
- Health and welfare,
- Power plant operation,
- Air traffic control,
- Ground control for space missions,
- Military logistics,
- Processing text and
- Voice data for intelligence contribute to government's being the largest consumer of computing.

IS and the Formation of AIS SIGHCI

GUIs did not have a major impact on IS in the 1980s, but business graphics did. Visual display of information affects everyone. HF&E had long addressed manuals and displays, software psychologists considered flowcharts and code organization, and IS focused on the presentation of quantitative data. Bretz (2012) wrote an influential paper that contrasted tables and charts and considered effects of color. IS research included the management of programming in organizations. Also, sociotechnicaland Scandinavian participatory approaches, initiated earlier to bring nondiscretionary users into design, gained recognition.

CHI and the Shifting Focus of Discretionary Use

CHI immediately took up issues raised by GUIs, such as mouse manipulation, visual display of information, and user interface management systems (UIMSs). An influential 2008 analysis by Jaimes and Sebe (2007) concluded that "it is too early to tell" how GUIs would fare. Concluding that GUIs could well prove useful for novices, the authors said "we would not be surprised if experts are slower with Direct Manipulation systems than with command language systems." Experts may well be faster using commands and function keys, but in a rapidly expanding commercial marketplace, novices outnumbered experts. Once they are familiar with an interface, people often do not switch for a promise of better performance if they did, the Dvorak keyboard would be more popular. Experienced users are continually adopting new features and applications. All in all, it was rational to focus on initial experience. More powerful networking and processing led to collaboration support, hypertext and hypermedia, and then mobile and ubiquitous computing.

Evolution of Methods and Theory

Psychologists, who shaped CHI, like those who formed HF&E 30 years earlier, were trained to test hypotheses about behavior in laboratory experiments. Experimental subjects agree to follow instructions for an extrinsic reward. This is a good model for nondiscretionary use, but not for discretionary use. CHI researchers relabeled them "participants," which sounds volitional, but lab findings require confirmation in real-world settings more often than is true for ergonomics studies. Traditional ergonomic goals apply fewer errors, faster performance, quicker learning, greater memorability, and being enjoyable but the emphasis differs. For power plant operation, error reduction is key, performance enhancement is good. Other goals are less critical. In contrast, consumers often respond to visceral appeal at the expense of usability and utility.

HUMAN COMPUTER INTERACTION

Definition of HCI

There is currently no agreed-upon definition of the range of topics which form the area of human-computer interaction. Yet we need a characterization of the field if we are to derive and develop educational materials for it. Therefore we offer a working definition that at least permits us to get down to the practical work of deciding what is to be taught:

- Human-computer interaction is a discipline concerned with the design, evaluation and implementation of interactive computing systems for human use and with the study of major phenomena surrounding them.

From a computer science perspective, the focus is on interaction and specifically on interaction between one or more humans and one or more computational machines. The classical situation that comes to mind is a person using an interactive graphics program on a workstation. But it is clear that varying what is meant by interaction, human, and machine leads to a rich space of possible topics, some of which, while we might not wish to exclude them as part of human-computer interaction, we would, nevertheless, wish to identify as peripheral to its focus. Other topics we would wish to identify as more central.

In this report, we have adopted, as an ACM committee, an appropriate computer science point of view, although we have tried at the same time to consider human-computer interaction broadly enough that other disciplines could use our analysis and shift the focus appropriately. From a computer science perspective, other disciplines serve as supporting disciplines, much as physics serves as a supporting discipline for civil engineering, or as mechanical engineering serves as a supporting discipline for robotics. A lesson learned repeatedly by engineering disciplines is that design problems have a context, and that the overly narrow optimization of one part of a design can be rendered invalid by the broader context of the problem. Even from a direct computer science perspective, therefore, it is advantageous to frame the problem of human-computer interaction broadly enough so as to help students (and practitioners) avoid the classic pitfall of design divorced from the context of the problem.

Because human-computer interaction studies a human and a machine in communication, it draws from supporting knowledge on both the machine and the human side. On the machine side,

- Techniques in computer graphics,
- Operating systems,
- Programming languages, and
- Development environments are relevant.

On the human side,

- Communication theory,
- Graphic and industrial design disciplines,
- Linguistics,
- Social sciences,
- Cognitive psychology, and
- Human performance are relevant.

And, of course, engineering and design methods are relevant.

Field of HCI

The goal of this section is to provide background for this report in terms of some of the major themes and influences that have shaped the field of HCI. In addition, an attempt is made to project some current trends into the near future as a basis for anticipating some of the conditions with which students will be faced upon, or even before, graduation. This section is not intended to provide either an exhaustive history of the past or a full scale "futures projection." It is, rather, to provide a context for the recommendations which follow. Human computer interaction arose as a field from intertwined roots in computer graphics, operating systems, human factors, ergonomics, industrial engineering, cognitive psychology, and the systems part of computer science. Computer graphics was born from the use of CRT and pen devices very early in the history of computers. This led to the development of several human-computer interaction techniques. Out of this line of development came a number of important building blocks for human-computer interaction. Some of these building blocks include the mouse, bitmapped displays, personal computers, windows, the desktop metaphor, and point-and-click editors.

Human-computer interaction is, in the first instance, affected by the forces shaping the nature of future computing. These forces include:

- Decreasing hardware costs leading to larger memories and faster systems.
- Miniaturization of hardware leading to portability.
- Reduction in power requirements leading to portability.
- New display technologies leading to the packaging of computational devices in new forms.
- Assimilation of computation into the environment (e.g., VCRs, microwave ovens, televisions).
- Specialized hardware leading to new functions (e.g., rapid text search).

- Increased development of network communication and distributed computing.
- Increasingly widespread use of computers, especially by people who are outside of the computing profession.
- Increasing innovation in input techniques (e.g., voice, gesture, pen), combined with lowering cost, leading to rapid computerization by people previously left out of the "computer revolution."
- Wider social concerns leading to improved access to computers by currently disadvantaged groups (e.g., young children, the physically/visually disabled, etc.).

Because human-computer interaction involves transducers between humans and machines and because humans are sensitive to response times, viable human interfaces are more technology-sensitive than many parts of computer science. For instance, the development of the mouse gave rise to the point-and-click style of editor interface and the mouse-based graphics program. Partially based on the above trends, we expect a future for HCI with some of the following characteristics:

Ubiquitous Communication

Computers will communicate through

- High speed local networks,
- Nationally over wide-area networks, and
- Portably via infrared, ultrasonic, cellular, and other technologies.

Data and computational services will be portably accessible from many if not most locations to which a user travels.

High Functionality Systems

Systems will have large numbers of functions associated with them. There will be so many systems that most users, technical or non-technical, will not have time to learn them in the traditional way (e.g., through thick manuals).

Mass Availability of Computer Graphics

Computer graphics capabilities such as image processing, graphics transformations, rendering, and interactive animation will become widespread as inexpensive chips become available for inclusion in general workstations.

Mixed Media

Systems will handle

- Images,
- Voice,
- Sounds,

- Video,
- Text,
- Formatted data.

These will be exchangeable over communication links among users. The separate worlds of consumer electronics (e.g., stereo sets, VCRs, televisions) and computers will partially merge. Computer and print worlds will continue to cross assimilate each other.

High-Bandwidth Interaction

The rate at which humans and machines interact will increase substantially due to the changes in:

- Speed,
- Computer graphics,
- New media, and
- New input/output devices.

This will lead to some qualitatively different interfaces, such as virtual reality or computational video.

Large and Thin Displays

New display technologies will finally mature enabling very large displays and also displays that are thin, light weight, and have low power consumption. This will have large effects on portability and will enable the development of paper-like, pen-based computer interaction systems very different in feel from desktop workstations of the present.

Embedded Computation

Computation will pass beyond desktop computers into every object for which uses can be found. The environment will be alive with little computations from computerized cooking appliances to lighting and plumbing fixtures to window blinds to automobile braking systems to greeting cards. To some extent, this development is already taking place. The difference in the future is the addition of networked communications that will allow many of these embedded computations to coordinate with each other and with the user. Human interfaces to these embedded devices will in many cases be very different from those appropriate to workstations.

Group Interfaces

Interfaces to allow groups of people to coordinate will be common (e.g., for meetings, for engineering projects, for authoring joint documents). These will have major impacts on the nature of organizations and on the division of labor. Models of the group design process will be embedded in systems and will cause increased rationalization of design.

User Tailorability

Ordinary users will routinely tailor applications to their own use and will use this power to invent new applications based on their understanding of their own domains. Users, with their deeper knowledge of their own knowledge domains, will increasingly be important sources of new applications at the expense of generic systems programmers (with systems expertise but low domain expertise).

Information Utilities

Public information utilities (such as Compuserve, Prodigy, home banking and shopping, etc.) and specialized industry services (e.g., weather for pilots) will continue to proliferate. The rate of proliferation will accelerate with the introduction of high-bandwidth interaction and the improvement in quality of interfaces.

One consequence of the above developments is that computing systems will appear partially to dissolve into the environment and become much more intimately associated with their users' activities. One can make an analogy to the development of motion power.

The Content of Human-Computer Interaction

The aim in this section is to inventory the current state of results in the field of human-computer interaction. Our object is to delimit the scope of our concerns and to specify the connections with other fields. For convenience, we have loosely arranged the topics in the field into 16 groups (Table 2).

The topics in this table derive from a consideration of five interrelated aspects of human-computer interaction:

- (N) The nature of human-computer interaction,
- (U) The use and context of computers,
- (H) Human characteristics,
- (C) Computer system and interface architecture, and
- (D) The development process.

Although not content areas, per se, and not discussed in the inventory below, project presentations and examinations (P) have been included as a category in this table to stress the importance of having students be exposed to content both through lecture and through the process of actually working on course projects, and in recognition of the fact that in most instructional environments some sort of evaluation of student mastery of content is necessary. Some of the interrelationships among these topics are represented in Figure 2. Computer systems exist within a larger social, organizational and work milieu (U1). Within this context there are applications for which we wish to employ computer systems (U2). But the process of putting computers to work means that the human, technical, and work aspects of the application situation must be brought into fit with each other through human learning, system tailorability, or other strategies (U3). In addition to the use and social context of computers, on the human side we must also take into account the human information processing (H1), communication (H2), and physical (H3) characteristics of users. On the computer side, a variety of technologies have been developed for supporting interaction with humans: Input and output devices connect the human and the machine (C1).

These are used in a number of techniques for organizing a dialogue (C2). These techniques are used in turn to implement larger design elements, such as the metaphor of the interface (C3). Getting deeper into the machine substrata supporting the dialogue, the dialogue may make extensive use of computer graphics techniques (C4).

Complex dialogues lead into considerations of the systems architecture necessary to support such features as:

- Interconnectable application programs,
- Windowing,
- Real-time response,
- Network communications,
- Multi-user and cooperative interfaces,
- And multi-tasking of dialogue objects (C5).

Finally, there is the process of development which incorporates:

- Design (D1) for human-computer dialogues,
- Techniques and tools (D2) for implementing them (D2),
- Techniques for evaluating (D3) them,
- And a number of classic designs for study (D4).

Figure 2. Human-computer interaction

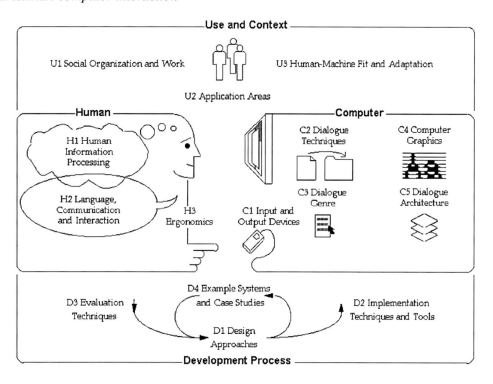

Table 2. Content of HCI

N		The Nature of HCI
	N1	(Meta-)Models of HCI
U		**Use and Context of Computers**
	U1	Human Social Organization and Work
	U2	Application Areas
	U3	Human-Machine Fit and Adaptation
H		**Human Characteristics**
	H1	Human Information Processing
	H2	Language, Communication, Interaction
	H3	Ergonomics
C		**Computer System and Interface Architecture**
	C1	Input and Output Devices
	C2	Dialogue Techniques
	C3	Dialogue Genre
	C4	Computer Graphics
	C5	Dialogue Architecture
D		**Development Process**
	D1	Design Approaches
	D2	Implementation Techniques
	D3	Evaluation Techniques
	D4	Example Systems and Case Studies
P		**Project Presentations and Examinations**

Each of these components of the development process is bound up with the others in a relationship of mutual, reciprocal influence whereby choices made in one area impact upon the choices and the options available in the others. The following inventory of topics contains representative entries relating to all of these aspects of the design and analysis of human-computer interaction systems. This inventory is a current snapshot of topics on which there are results that could be taught. In addition to direct HCI topics, we have included in this inventory results from other disciplines central enough to be taught within courses in HCI. Such a list cannot hope to be complete or even non-controversial, but it should be heuristically useful in the practical business of preparing courses.

Nature of Human-Computer Interaction (N)

Under this heading are overviews of, and theoretical frameworks for, topics in human-computer communication.

1. N1: The Nature of Human-Computer Interaction

- Points of view: HCI as communication, agent paradigm, tool paradigm, the work-centered point of view, human/system/tasks division, supervisory control
- Objectives (e.g. productivity, user empowerment)
- History and intellectual roots
- HCI as an academic topic: journals, literature, relation to other fields, science vs. engineering vs. design aspects

The uses to which computers are put are spoken of as 'applications' in the computer world. These uses and the extent to which the interface (and the application logic in the rest of the system) fits them can have a profound impact on every part of the interface and its success. Moreover, the general social, work, and business context may be important.

2. U1: Social Organization and Work

This heading relates to the human as an interacting social being. It includes a concern with the nature of work, and with the notion that human systems and technical systems mutually adapt to each other and must be considered as a whole.

- Points of view (e.g., industrial engineering, operations research, Rasmussen's cognitive engineering, the Aarhus participatory design approach, Hewitt's open systems)
- Models of human activity (e.g., opportunistic planning, open procedures)
- Models of small-groups, organizations
- Models of work, workflow, cooperative activity, office work
- Socio-technical systems, human organizations as adaptive open systems, mutual impact of computer systems on work and vice versa, computer systems for group tasks, case studies
- Quality of work life and job satisfaction

3. U2: Application Areas

The focus of this section is on classes of application domains and particular application areas where characteristic interfaces have developed.

- Characterization of application areas (e.g., individual vs. group, paced vs. unpaced)
- Document-oriented interfaces: Text-editing, document formatting, illustrators, spreadsheets, hypertext
- Communications-oriented interfaces: Electronic mail, computer conferencing, telephone and voice messaging systems
- Design environments: programming environments, CAD/CAM
- On-line tutorial systems and help systems
- Multimedia information kiosks
- Continuous control systems: process control systems, virtual reality systems, simulators, cockpits, video games
- Embedded systems: Copier controls, elevator controls, consumer electronics and home appliance controllers (e.g., TVs, VCRs, microwave ovens, etc.)

4. U3: Human-Machine Fit and Adaptation

There are several dimensions to this fit and it is possible to place the burden of adjustment in different places: Adjustments can be made:

1. Either at design time or at time of use
2. By either changing the system or the user and
3. The changes can be made by either the users themselves or, sometimes, by the system.

Topics under this heading all relate to changing some component of a socio-technical system so as to improve its fit.

- Alternate techniques for achieving fit
- Nature of adaptive systems, adaptations of human systems that cancel reliability improvements, the nature of error in adaptive redundant systems, empirical findings on user improvisation with routine systems, determinants of successful systems introduction,
- System selection: theories of system adoption
- System adaptation: customization and tailorability techniques
- User selection: compatibilities of user and system characteristics
- User adaptation: ease of learning, training methods (e.g., on-line tutorials), relation to system design
- User guidance: help techniques, documentation, error-handling techniques

It is important to understand something about human information-processing characteristics, how human action is structured, the nature of human communication, and human physical and physiological requirements.

5. H1: Human Information Processing

Characteristics of the human as a processor of information:

- Models of cognitive architecture: symbol-system models, connectionist models, engineering models
- Phenomena and theories of memory
- Phenomena and theories of perception
- Phenomena and theories of motor skills
- Phenomena and theories of attention and vigilance
- Phenomena and theories of problem solving
- Phenomena and theories of learning and skill acquisition
- Phenomena and theories of motivation
- Users' conceptual models
- Models of human action
- Human diversity, including disabled populations

6. H2: Language, Communication and Interaction

Language as a communication and interface médium; Communication phenomena:

- Aspects of language: syntax, semantics, pragmatics
- Formal models of language
- Pragmatic phenomena of conversational interaction (e.g., turn-taking, repair)
- Language phenomena
- Specialized languages (e.g., graphical interaction, query, command, production systems, editors)
- Interaction reuse (e.g., history lists)

7. H3: Ergonomics

Anthropometric and physiological characteristics of people and their relationship to workspace and environmental parameters:

- Human anthropometry in relation to workspace design
- Arrangement of displays and controls, link analysis
- Human cognitive and sensory limits
- Sensory and perceptual effects of CRT and other display technologies, legibility, display design
- Control design
- Fatigue and health issues
- Furniture and lighting design
- Temperature and environmental noise issues
- Design for stressful or hazardous environments
- Design for the disabled

Machines have specialized components for interacting with humans. Some of these components are basically transducers for moving information physically between human and machine.

8. C1: Input and Output Devices

The technical construction of devices for mediating between humans and machines:

- Input devices: survey, mechanics of particular devices, performance characteristics (human and system), devices for the disabled, handwriting and gestures, speech input, eye tracking, exotic devices (e.g., EEG and other biological signals)
- Output devices: survey, mechanics of particular devices, vector devices, raster devices, frame buffers and image stores, canvases, event handling, performance characteristics, devices for the disabled, sound and speech output, 3D displays, motion (e.g., flight simulators), exotic devices
- Characteristics of input/output devices (e.g., weight, portability, bandwidth, sensory modality)
- Virtual devices

9. C2: Dialogue Techniques

The basic software architecture and techniques for interacting with humans:

- **Dialogue Inputs**
  - ○ Types of input purposes (e.g., selection, discrete parameter specification, continuous control)
  - ○ Input techniques: keyboard techniques (e.g, commands, menus), mouse-based techniques (e.g., picking, rubber-band lines), pen-based techniques (e.g., character recognition, gesture), voice-based techniques
- **Dialogue Outputs**
  - ○ Types of output purposes (e.g., convey precise information, summary information, illustrate processes, create visualizations of information)
  - ○ Output techniques (e.g., scrolling display, windows, animation, sprites, fish-eye displays)
  - ○ Screen layout issues (e.g., focus, clutter, visual logic)
- **Dialogue Interaction Techniques**
  - ○ Dialogue type and techniques (e.g., alphanumeric techniques, form filling, menu selection, icons and direct manipulation, generic functions, natural language)
  - ○ Navigation and orientation in dialogues, error management
  - ○ Multimedia and non-graphical dialogues: speech input, speech output, voice mail, video mail, active documents, videodisc, CD-ROM
  - ○ Agents and AI techniques
  - ○ Multi-person dialogues
- **Dialogue Issues**
  - ○ Real-time response issues
  - ○ Manual control theory
  - ○ Supervisory control, automatic systems, embedded systems
  - ○ Standards
  - ○ "Look and feel," intellectual property protection

10. C3: Dialogue Genre

The conceptual uses to which the technical means are put. Such concepts arise in any media discipline (e.g., film, graphic design, etc.).

- Interaction metaphors (e.g., tool metaphor, agent metaphor)
- Content metaphors (e.g., desktop metaphor, paper document metaphor)
- Persona, personality, point of view
- Workspace models
- Transition management (e.g., fades, pans)
- Relevant techniques from other media (e.g., film, theater, graphic design)
- Style and aesthetics

11. C4: Computer Graphics

Basic concepts from computer graphics that are especially useful to know for HCI:

- Geometry in 2- and 3- space, linear transformations
- Graphics primitives and attributes: bitmap and voxel representations, raster-op, 2-D primitives, text primitives, polygon representation, 3-D primitives, quadtrees and octtrees, device independent images, page definition languages
- Solid modeling, splines, surface modeling, hidden surface removal, animation, rendering algorithms, lighting models
- Color representation, color maps, color ranges of devices

12. C5: Dialogue Architecture

Software architectures and standards for user interfaces:

- Layers model of the architecture of dialogues and windowing systems, dialogue system reference models
- Screen imaging models (e.g., RasterOp, Postscript, Quickdraw)
- Window manager models (e.g., Shared address-space, client-server), analysis of major window systems (e.g., X, New Wave, Windows, Open Look, Presentation Manager, Macintosh)
- Models of application-to-dialogue manager connection
- Models for specifying dialogues
- Multi-user interface architectures "Look and feel"
- Standardization and interoperability

The construction of human interfaces is both a matter of design and engineering.

13. D1: Design Approaches

The process of design. Relevant topics from other design disciplines:

- Graphic design basics (e.g., design languages, typography, use of color, 2D & 3D spatial organization, temporal sequencing, etc.)
- Alternative system development processes (e.g., waterfall model, participatory design), lifecycle model, iterative design, choice of method under time/resource constraint
- Task analysis techniques (e.g., field studies, analytical methods), task allocation, market analysis
- Design specification techniques
- Design analysis techniques (e.g., objects and actions)
- Industrial design basics
- Design case studies and empirical analyses of design

14. D2: Implementation Techniques and Tools

Tactics and tools for implementation:

- Relationships among design, evaluation, and implementation
- Independence and reusability, application independence, device independence
- Prototyping techniques (e.g., storyboarding, video, "Wizard of Oz", HyperCard, rapid prototype implementations)
- Dialogue toolkits (e.g., MacApp, NextStep, UIMS's, HyperCard)
- Object-oriented methods
- Data representation and algorithms

15. D3: Evaluation Techniques

Philosophy and specific methods for evaluations:

- Productivity
- Figures of merit (e.g., time, errors, learnability, design for guessing, preference, etc.)
- Usability testing techniques, linking testing to specifications
- Formative and summative evaluation techniques for empirical evaluation, including:
  - field observation methods,
  - participant observation,
  - interviewing techniques,
  - questionnaire design,
  - psychometric methods,
  - video protocols,
  - system logging,
  - experiment design (e.g, concern with sample bias, etc.),
  - methods from psychological and sociological evaluation fields,
  - ethics of working with participants

16. D4: Example Systems and Case Studies

Classic designs to serve as extended examples of human interface design:

- **Command-Oriented**
  - OS/360 JCL (batch-oriented command style, baseline for seeing later improvements)
  - PC DOS (command style interface learned by millions)
  - Airline check-in system (time pressure, ambiguous input, distributed system)
- **Graphics-Oriented**
  - Xerox Star (icon-window interface, generic commands)
  - Apple Macintosh (similar interface over many applications)
  - MacPaint (widely known and available graphics program)
- **Frame-Based**
  - Promis (Rapid response to large set of frames, touch-panel oriented)

- Zog (User-tailorable, rapid-response system, large number of frames, first commercial frame-based system)
- HyperCard (Graphically-oriented frame-based system with user programming language, first mass market frame-oriented system).
- **User-Defined Combinatorics**
  - Unix operating system (strong combinatoric architecture paired with weak human factors)
  - Emacs (language-oriented, large combinatoric command set)
  - Visicalc (a "home-run" application with strong conceptual model that succeeded despite weak human factors)
  - DBaseIII (simple, but successful, user applications generator)
  - Interfaces for untrained, walk-up users:
  - Olympic Message System (practical use of user testing under time pressure)
  - Nintendo Super Mario Brothers (learnable without a manual by grade school children)

The topics listed in this chapter constitute an attempt to inventory the results of HCI and its supporting fields that are available for teaching.

DISCUSSION: CULTURES AND BRIDGES

Despite a significant common focus, there has been limited interaction among the three threads of human-computer interaction research. This has not been for lack of trying. This section outlines some obstacles to interaction and efforts to overcome them. Three communities, two academic cultures:

- The first two HCI disciplines to emerge, HF&E and IS, arisen before discretionary handson use was widespread.

Researchers in each considered both organizational and technical issues. They shared journals; the Benbasat and Dexter paper published in Management Science cited five Human Factors articles. HF&E and IS also sharing the traditional academicculture of the sciences:

- Conferences are venues for work in progress;
- Journals are repositories for polished work.

In contrast, for CHI and other US computer science disciplines, conference proceedings are the final destination for most work. Journals are secondary. Outside the US, computer science retains more of a journal focus, perhaps due to the absence of professional societies that archive proceedings. This circumstance impedes communication across disciplines and continents. Researchers in journal cultures chafe at CHI's rejection rates; CHI researchers are dismayed by the relatively unpolished work at other conferences. Table 1 presents figures obtained from editors of leading conferences and journals. CHI conferences are selective. CHI journals receive fewer submissions despite higher acceptance rates. These patterns were confirmed in interviews. Many CHI researchers state that journals are not relevant. Only about 10 percent of work in CHI-sponsored conferences reaches journal publication. In contrast, a Hawaii International Conference on System Sciences 2004 track Organizer estimated that 80 percent of research

Table 1. Submission and acceptances rates (medians rounded to 10%)

Field	Journals: Annual Submissions	Journals: % Accepted	Conferences % Accepted
Human Factors And Ergonomics	150	30	80
Information Systems	200	10	60
Computer-Human Interaction	50	30	20

there progressed to a journal. A linguistic divide also set CHI apart. HF&E and IS used the term operator; in IS, user could be a manager who used printed computer output, not a hands-on end user. Within CHI, operator was demeaning, user was always hands-on, and end user seemed a superfluous affectation.

Efforts to Find Common Ground

The Human Factors Society was deeply involved with the first CHI conference, but as CHI leaders wrote of human factors' "second class" status and embraced computer science, human factors professionals abandoned CHI. In recent interviews, some recalled feeling that CHI researchers believed incorrectly that they had discovered the topic, ignored human factors contributions, employed usability study methods that were insufficiently rigorous, and seemed more interested in "describing their experiences." Some CHI papers were indeed descriptive, and the widely used "thinking aloud" verbal protocols, introduced to interface design by Clayton Lewis based on the theories of Allen Newell and Herb Simon, were not widely accepted in experimental psychology. The Computer Supported Cooperative Work conference series tried to bridge IS and CHI and met a similar fate. IS participation on the program committee and program, initially one-third, steadily declined. By 2002 no one on the program committee had a primary IS affiliation. In the early 1990s, IS papers were routinely rejected. In interviews, IS researchers said that CSCW reviewers "were not interested in IS contributions" or expected unrealistic effort for conference publications that count little in a field that regards conference papers as work in progress. IS participation in CSCW was disproportionately represented by Scandinavian cooperative or participatory design, which appealed too many in CHI.

Other Activities and Perspectives

Another thread of human–computer interaction research is coalescing as information science, with conferences, journals, and societies that address database use, information retrieval, and the digital evolution of library science. One component of information science research can be traced to office automation efforts that sprang up around minicomputers in the 1970s, between the mainframes that spawned information systems and the PCs of CHI.

DIRECTIONS

Human-computer interaction has been a particularly dynamic field, in large part due to the steady increase in hardware capability. Understanding past and present trends may provide some help in anticipating directions the field could take.

Discretion-Now You See It, Now You Don't

We exercise choice more at home than at work; a lot when buying online, none when confronted by a telephone answering system; considerable when young and healthy, less when constrained by injury or aging. Alternatives disappear:

- Software that was discretionary yesterday is indispensable today, and the need to collaborate forces us to adopt common systems and conventions.

Consider a hypothetical team. In 1985, one member still used a typewriter, others chose different word processors. They exchanged printed documents. One emphasized phrases by underlining, another by italicizing, a third by bolding. In 1995, in order to share documents digitally, group members had to adopt the same word processor and conventions. Choice was curtailed; it had to be exercised collectively.

Looking Ahead: Will Three HCI Fields Endure?

Perhaps not, perhaps HCI goals will be realized only when it ceases to be a field of research altogether. In 1988, Norman wrote of "the invisible computer of the future." Like motors, he speculated, computers would be present everywhere and visible nowhere. We interact with clocks, refrigerators, and cars. Each has a motor, but there is no human–motor interaction specialization.

Human Factors and Ergonomics

Imperatives to improve training, expert performance, and error handling have strong continued support from government and the private sector. David Meister, author of The History of Human Factors and Ergonomics, stresses the continuity of HF&E in the face of technology change: "Outside of a few significant events, like the organization of HFS in 1957 or the publication of Proceedings of the annual meetings in 1972, there are no seminal occurrences … no sharp discontinuities that are memorable.

Information Systems

As IS thrived in the 1990s, other management school disciplines-finance, marketing, operations research, organizational behavior -become more technically savvy. When the bubble burst and enrollments declined, IS was left with a less well-defined niche.

Computer-Human Interaction

This nomadic group started in psychology, obtained a place at the edge of the table in computer science, and is increasingly drawn to information science. Lacking a well-defined academic niche, CHI's identity is tied to its conference, and CHI conference participation has dropped as specialized conferences thrive. The focus on discretionary use is under pressure as technologies appear and spread at an ever-increasing pace. When an emerging technology was slower to attract a critical mass of users, researchers on the topic first contributed to existing conferences and journals.

APPLICATIONS

A classic example of a multimodal system is the "Put That There" demonstration system. This system allowed one to move an object into a new location on a map on the screen by saying "put that there" while pointing to the object itself then pointing to the desired destination. Multimodal interfaces have been used in a number of applications including mapbased simulations,

- Such as the aforementioned system; information kiosks,
- Such as AT&T's MATCHKiosk
- And biometric authentication systems (Oviatt et al., 2010).

Multimodal interfaces can offer a number of advantages over traditional interfaces. For one thing, they can offer a more natural and user-friendly experience. For instance, in a real-estate system called Real Hunter, one can point with a finger to a house of interest and speak to make queries about that particular house. Using a pointing gesture to select an object and using speech to make queries about it illustrates the type of natural experience multimodal interfaces offer to their users. Another key strength of multimodal interfaces is their ability to provide redundancy to accommodate different people and different circumstances. For instance, MATCHKiosk allows one to use speech or handwriting to specify the type of business to search for on a map. Thus, in a noisy setting, one may provide input through handwriting rather than speech. Few other examples of applications of multimodal systems are listed below:

- Smart Video Conferencing (McCowan et al., 2015)
- Intelligent Homes/Offices
- Driver Monitoring (Smith et al., 2013)
- Intelligent Games
- E-Commerce (Kapoor et al., 2007)
- Helping People with Disabilities (Gunes & Piccardi, 2007).

In the following sections, some of important applications of multimodal systems have been presented with greater details.

Multimodal Systems for Disabled People

One good application of multimodal systems is to address and assist disabled people (as persons with hands disabilities), which need other kinds of interfaces than ordinary people. In such systems, disabled users can perform work on the PC by interacting with the machine using voice and head movements. Two modalities are then used:

- Speech and
- Head movements.

Both modalities are active continuously. The head position indicates the coordinates of the cursor in current time moment on the screen. Speech, on the other hand, provides the needed information about the meaning of the action that must be performed with an object selected by the cursor. Synchronization between the two modalities is performed by calculating the cursor position at the beginning of speech detection.

Emotion Recognition Multimodal Systems

As we move towards a world in which computers are more and more ubiquitous, it will become more essential that machines perceive and interpret all clues, implicit and explicit, that we may provide them regarding our intentions. A natural human-computer interaction cannot be based solely on explicitly stated commands. Computers will have to detect the various behavioural signals based on which to infer one's emotional state. This is a significant piece of the puzzle that one has to put together to predict accurately one's intentions and future behaviour. People are able to make prediction about one's emotional state based on their observations about one's face, body, and voice. Studies show that if one had access to only one of these modalities, the face modality would produce the best predictions. However, this accuracy can be improved by 38% when human judges are given access to both face and body modalities together (Pantic et al., 2010). This suggests that affect recognition, which has for the most part focused on facial expressions, can greatly benefit from multimodal fusion techniques. One of the few works that has attempted to integrate more than one modality for affect recognition is (Kapoor et al., 2007) in which facial features and body posture features are combined to produce an indicator of one's frustration. Another work that integrated face and body modalities is (Gunes & Piccardi, 2007) in which the authors showed that, similar to humans, machine classification of emotion is better when based upon face and body data, rather than either modality alone. The authors attempted to fuse facial and voice data for affect recognition. Once again, remaining consistent with human judges, machine classification of emotion as neutral, sad, angry, or happy was most accurate when the facial and vocal data is combined.

Map-Based Multimodal Applications

Different input modalities are suitable for expressing different messages. For instance, speech provides an easy and natural mechanism for expressing a query about a selected object or requesting that the object initiate a given operation. However, speech may not be ideal for tasks, such as selection of a particular region on the screen or defining out a particular path. These types of tasks are better accommodated by hand or pen gestures. However, making queries about a given region and selecting that region are all typical tasks that should be accommodate by a map-based interface. Thus, the natural conclusion is that map-based interfaces can greatly improve the user experience by supporting multiple modes of input, especially speech and gestures. Quickset is one of the more widely known and older map-based applications that make use of speech and pen gesture input. Quickset is a military-training application that allows users to use one of the two modalities or both simultaneously to express a full command. For instance, users may simply draw out with a pen a predefined symbol for platoons at a given location on the map to create a new platoon in that location. Alternatively, users could use speech to specify their intent on creating a new platoon and could specify vocally the coordinates in which to place the platoon. Lastly, users could express vocally their intent on making a new platoon while making a pointing gesture with a pen to specify the location of the new platoon.

Multimodal Human-Robot Interface Applications

Similar to some map-based interfaces, human-robot interfaces usually have to provide mechanisms for pointing to particular locations and for expressing operation-initiating requests. As discussed earlier, the former type of interaction is well accommodated by gestures, whereas the latter is better accommodate by speech. Thus, the human-robot interface built by the Naval Research Laboratory (NRL) should come as no surprise. NRL's interface allows users to point to a location while saying "Go over there". Additionally, it allows users to use a PDA screen as a third possible avenue of interaction, which could be resorted to when speech or hand gesture recognition is failing.

Multi-Modal HCI in Medicine

By the early 1980s, surgeons were beginning to reach their limits based on traditional methods alone. Human hand was unfeasible for many tasks and greater magnification and smaller tools were needed. Higher precision was required to localize and manipulate within small and sensitive parts of the human body. Digital robotic neuro-surgery has come as a leading solution to these limitations and emerged fast due to the vast improvements in engineering, computer technology and neuro-imaging techniques. Robotics surgery was introduced into the surgical area. State University of Aerospace Instrumentation, University of Karlsruhe (Germany) and Harvard Medical School (USA) has been working on developing man-machine interfaces, adaptive robots and multi-agent technologies intended for neuro-surgery. The neuro-surgical robot consists of the following main components: An arm, feedback vision sensors, controllers, a localization system and a data processing centre.

CONCLUSION

Human-Computer Interaction is an important part of systems design. Quality of system depends on how it is represented and used by users. Therefore, enormous amount of attention has been paid to better designs of HCI. The new direction of research is to replace common regular methods of interaction with intelligent, adaptive, multimodal, natural methods. Ambient intelligence or ubiquitous computing which is called the Third Wave is trying to embed the technology into the environment so to make it more natural and invisible at the same time. Virtual reality is also an advancing field of HCI which can be the common interface of the future. This chapter attempted to give an overview on these issues and provide a survey of existing research through a comprehensive reference list. This review of human–computer interaction explores efforts that might benefit from closer coordination but have remained distinct—if anything, moving apart over time. CHI focuses on invention and design; some of its engineering and modeling components have migrated to HF&E. A younger generation has grown up with game consoles and cell phones;

- Communicating with IM and text messaging;
- Developing skills at searching, browsing, tagging, and synthesizing;
- And acquiring multimedia authoring talent via digital cameras and blogs.

However it comes to be defined and wherever it is studied, human– computer interaction is still in its early days.

A commercial software company employee familiar with the human factors community said (in a Sept. 2004 email communication to me from Edie Adams), "After all these years I've concluded that we use the same methods, we study the same things, but we do it to get new ideas, and they do it to improve what already exists." CHI and IS could learn from one another. CHI discovered the limitations of laboratory studies and surveys for understanding discretionary use. Many IS researchers now focused on discretionary use still favor these techniques. IS has a more developed awareness of economic, organizational, and marketing theory and practice than CHI. But strong cultural barriers separate the two. Moore's law ensures that landscapes will shift for some time, providing new forms of interaction to explore, new practices to improve.

REFERENCES

Aggarwal, J. K., & Cai, Q. (2015). Human motion analysis: A review. *Computer Vision and Image Understanding, 73*(3), 428–440. doi:10.1006/cviu.1998.0744

Bretz, E. A. (2012). When work is fun and games. *IEEE Spectrum, 39*(12), 50–58. doi:10.1109/MSPEC.2002.1088457

Campbell, J. P. Jr. (2015). Speaker recognition: A tutorial. *Proceedings of the IEEE, 85*(9), 1437–1462. doi:10.1109/5.628714

Cohen, I., Sebe, N., Garg, A., Chen, L., & Huang, T. S. (2013). Facial expression recognition from video sequences: Temporal and static modeling. *Computer Vision and Image Understanding, 91*(1-2), 160–187. doi:10.1016/S1077-3142(03)00081-X

Duchowski, A. T. (2012). A breadth-first survey of eye tracking applications. *Behavior Research Methods, Instruments, & Computers, 34*(4), 455–470. doi:10.3758/BF03195475 PMID:12564550

Fasel, B., & Luettin, J. (2013). Automatic facial expression analysis: A survey. *Pattern Recognition, 36*(1), 259–275. doi:10.1016/S0031-3203(02)00052-3

Gavrila, D. M. (2009). The visual analysis of human movement: A survey. *Computer Vision and Image Understanding, 73*(1), 82–98. doi:10.1006/cviu.1998.0716

Gunes, H., & Piccardi, M. (2007). Bi-modal emotion recognition from expressive face and body gestures. *Journal of Network and Computer Applications*, *30*(4), 1334–1345. doi:10.1016/j.jnca.2006.09.007

Hayward, V., Astley, O. R., Cruz-Hernandez, M., Grant, D., & Robles-De-La-Torre, G. (2014). Haptic interfaces and devices. *Sensor Review*, *24*(1), 16–29. doi:10.1108/02602280410515770

Jaimes, A., & Sebe, N. (2007). Multimodal human computer interaction: A survey. *Computer Vision and Image Understanding*, *108*(1-2), 116–134. doi:10.1016/j.cviu.2006.10.019

Kapoor, A., Burleson, W., & Picard, R. W. (2007). Automatic prediction of frustration. *International Journal of Human-Computer Studies*, *65*(8), 724–736. doi:10.1016/j.ijhcs.2007.02.003

Kettebekov, S., & Sharma, R. (2010). Understanding gestures in multimodal human computer interaction. *International Journal of Artificial Intelligence Tools*, *9*(2), 205–223. doi:10.1142/S021821300000015X

Khatib, O., Brock, O., Chang, K. S., Ruspini, D., Sentis, L., & Viji, S. (2014). Human-centered robotics and interactive haptic simulation. *The International Journal of Robotics Research*, *23*(2), 167–178. doi:10.1177/0278364904041325

Kirishima, T., Sato, K., & Chihara, K. (2015). Real-time gesture recognition by learning and selective control of visual interest points. *IEEE Transactions on Pattern Analysis and Machine Intelligence*, *27*(3), 351–364. doi:10.1109/TPAMI.2005.61 PMID:15747791

Kuno, Y., Shimada, N., & Shirai, Y. (2013). Look where youre going: A robotic wheelchair based on the integration of human and environmental observations. *IEEE Robotics and Automation*, *10*(1), 26–34. doi:10.1109/MRA.2003.1191708

Legin, A., Rudnitskaya, A., Seleznev, B., & Vlasov, Y. (2015). Electronic tongue for quality assessment of ethanol, vodka and eau-de-vie. *Analytica Chimica Acta*, *534*(1), 129–135. doi:10.1016/j.aca.2004.11.027

McCowan, I., Gatica-Perez, D., Bengio, S., Lathoud, G., Barnard, M., & Zhang, D. (2015). Automatic analysis of multimodal group actions in meetings. *IEEE Transactions on Pattern Analysis and Machine Intelligence*, *27*(3), 305–317. doi:10.1109/TPAMI.2005.49 PMID:15747787

Myers, B. A. (2008). A brief history of human-computer interaction technology. *Interactions (New York, N.Y.)*, *5*(2), 44–54. doi:10.1145/274430.274436

Oudeyer, P. Y. (2013). The production and recognition of emotions in speech: Features and algorithms. *International Journal of Human-Computer Studies*, *59*(1-2), 157–183.

Oviatt, S. L., Cohen, P., Wu, L., Vergo, J., Duncan, L., Suhm, B., & Ferro, D. et al. (2010). Designing the user interface for multimodal speech and pen-based gesture applications: State-of-the-art systems and future research directions. *Human-Computer Interaction*, *15*(4), 263–322. doi:10.1207/S15327051HCI1504_1

Pantic, M., & Rothkrantz, L. J. M. (2010). Automatic analysis of facial expressions: The state of the art. *IEEE Transactions on Pattern Analysis and Machine Intelligence*, *22*(12), 1424–1445. doi:10.1109/34.895976

Riva, G., Vatalaro, F., Davide, F., & Alaniz, M. (2015). *Ambient Intelligence: The Evolution of Technology, Communication and Cognition towards the Future of HCI*. Fairfax: IOS Press.

Rubin, P., Vatikiotis-Bateson, E., & Benoit, C. (2008). Special issue on audio-visual speech processing. *Speech Communication, 26*, 1–2. doi:10.1016/S0167-6393(98)00046-6

Smith, P., Shah, M., & Lobo, N. D. V. (2013). Determining driver visual attention with one camera. *IEEE Transactions on Intelligent Transportation Systems, 4*(4), 205–218. doi:10.1109/TITS.2003.821342

Compilation of References

AACE. (2015). *About AACE*. Retrieved 27/12/2015, 2015, from http://www.aace.org/about.htm

Abner, B. (2015, February 15). *Privacy Settings on Facebook*. Retrieved from https://youtu.be/klMLZKFHFzw

Achecker Website. (2011). Retrieved Mach 2, 2016, from http://achecker.ca/checker/index.php

Aderhold, J. (2004). *Form und Funktion sozialer Netzwerke in Wirtschaft und Gesellschaft*. Wiesbaden: VS Verlag. doi:10.1007/978-3-322-83386-0

Adler. (2014). *Social Media Engagement: The Surprising Facts About How Much Time People Spend On The Major Social Networks*. Available at http://www.businessinsider.com/social-media-engagement-primer-2014-10

Afacan, G., Er, E., & Arifoglu, A. (2013). Public internet access points (PIAPs) and their social impact: A case study from Turkey. *Behaviour & Information Technology*, *32*(1), 14–23. doi:10.1080/0144929X.2011.582149

Agarwal, R., & Karahanna, E. (2000). Time flies when youre having fun: Cognitive absorption and beliefs about information technology uses. *Management Information Systems Quarterly*, *24*(4), 665–694. doi:10.2307/3250951

Agarwal, R., & Prasad, J. (1998). A conceptual and operational definition of personal innovativeness in the domain of information technology. *Information Systems Research*, *9*(2), 204–215. doi:10.1287/isre.9.2.204

Aggarwal, J. K., & Cai, Q. (2015). Human motion analysis: A review. *Computer Vision and Image Understanding*, *73*(3), 428–440. doi:10.1006/cviu.1998.0744

Aguirre, M. E., Mahr, D., de Ruyter, K., Wetzels, M., & Grewal, D. (2012). The Impact Of Vulnerability During Covert Personalization – A Regulatory Mode Approach. *41st EMAC Conference*.

Ahmad, T. B. T., Basha, K. M., Marzuki, A. M., Hisham, N. A., & Sahari, M. (2010). Facultys acceptance of computer-based technology: Cross-validation of an extended model. *Australasian Journal of Educational Technology*, *26*(2), 268–279. doi:10.14742/ajet.1095

Ahuja, M. K., & Thatcher, J. B. (2005). Moving beyond intentions and toward the theory of trying: Effects of work environment and gender on post-adoption information technology use. *Management Information Systems Quarterly*, *29*(3), 427–459.

Aiello, L. M., Barrat, A., Schifanella, R., Cattuto, C., Markines, B., & Menczer, F. (2012). Friendship prediction and homophily in social media. *ACM Transaction on the Web*, *6*(2), 9.

Aiken, R. L. (1993). *Personality, theories, research, and applications*. Prentice-Hall Inc.

Aizpurua, A., Arrue, M., & Vigo, M. (2015). Prejudices, memories, expectations and confidence influence experienced accessibility on the Web. *Computers in Human Behavior*, *51*, 152-160. doi:10.1016/j.chb.2015.04.035

Albrechtsen, E., & Hovden, J. (2010). Improving information security awareness and behaviour through dialogue, participation and collective reflection. An intervention study. *Computers & Security*, *29*(4), 432–445. doi:10.1016/j.cose.2009.12.005

Alexander, J. C. (1985). *Neofunctionalism*. Thousand Oaks, CA: Sage Publications.

Aljuaid, N. M. F., Alzahrani, M. A. R., & Islam, A. Y. M. A. (2014). Assessing mobile learning readiness in Saudi Arabia higher education: An empirical study. *The Malaysian Online Journal of Educational Technology*, *2*(2), 1–14.

Al-Khalifa, H. (2012). The accessibility of Saudi Arabia government Web sites: An exploratory study. *Universal Access in the Information Society*, *11*(2), 201–210. doi:10.1007/s10209-010-0215-7

Allen, D. (1978). Structure and Creativity in Religion: Hermeneutics in Mircea Eliade's Phenomenology and New Directions. New York: Mouton Publishers.

Alloing, C. (2013). *Processus de veille par infomédiation sociale pour construire l'e-réputation d'une organisation. Approche par agents-facilitateurs appliquée à la DSIC de La Poste* (Doctoral dissertation). Université of Poitiers.

Alterovitz, G., Muso, T., & Ramoni, M. F. (2010). The challenges of informatics in synthetic biology: From biomolecular networks to artificial organisms. *Journal on Emerging Technologies in Computing Systems Briefings in Bioinformatics*, *11*(1), 80–95. doi:10.1093/bib/bbp054 PMID:19906839

Altvater, E., & Mahnkopf, B. (1996). *Grenzen der Globalisierung. Ökonomie, Ökologie und Politik in der Weltgesellschaft*. Münster: Westfälisches Dampfboot.

Alvi, S., Downing, S., & Cesaroni, C. (2015). The self and the 'selfie': Cyber-bullying theory and the structure of late modernity. In S. R. Maxwell & S. L. Blair (Eds.), *Violence and crime in the family: Patterns, causes, and consequences* (pp. 383–406). Emerald Group Publishing. doi:10.1108/S1530-353520150000009016

Americans with Disabilities Act of 1990, Amendments Act of 2008

Amer, T. (1991). An experimental investigation of the effects of multi-cue financial information display on decision making. *The Journal of Information Systems*, *5*(2), 18–34.

Amer, T., & Johnson, T. (in press). Information technology progress indicators – Temporal expectancy, user preference, and the perception of process duration. *International Journal of Technology and Human Interaction*.

Amin, S. (1999). Regionalization in response to polarizing globalization. In Globalism and the new regionalism. Palgrave Macmillan. doi:10.1007/978-1-349-27268-6_3

Andersen, N. Å. (2003). Polyphonic Organizations. In T. Hernes & T. Bakken (Eds.), *Autopoietic Organization Theory*. Copenhagen: CBS.

Andersen, N. Å., & Born, A. W. (2007). Heterophony and the Postponed Organization Organizing autopoietic systems. *TAMARA: Journal of Critical Postmodern Organization Science*, *6*(1/2), 176–187.

Andreasson, K., & Snaprud, M. (2014). *The European e-government web accessibility divide*. Paper presented at the Proceedings of the 8th International Conference on Theory and Practice of Electronic Governance.

Ani, O. E. (2010). Internet access and use: A study of undergraduate students in three Nigerian universities. *The Electronic Library*, *28*(4), 555–567. doi:10.1108/02640471011065373

Antheunis, M. L., & Schouten, A. P. (2011). The effects of other-generated and system-generated cues on adolescents perceived attractiveness on social network sites. *Journal of Computer-Mediated Communication*, *16*(3), 391–406. doi:10.1111/j.1083-6101.2011.01545.x

Aral, S., Muchnik, L., & Sundararajan, A. (2009). Distinguishing influence-based contagion from homophily-driven diffusion in dynamic networks. *Proceedings of the National Academy of Sciences of the United States of America*, *106*(51), 21544–21549. doi:10.1073/pnas.0908800106 PMID:20007780

Arbuckle, J. L. (2010). *User's Guide*. Amos Development Corporation.

Arch, A. (2008). *Web Accessibility for Older Users: A Literature Review*. Retrieved 15/11/2015, 2015, from http://www.w3.org/TR/2008/WD-wai-age-literature-20080514/

Argamon, S. A., Koppel, M., Fine, J., & Shimoni, A. R. (2003). Gender, genre, and writing style in formal written texts. *Text*, *23*(3), 321–346. doi:10.1515/text.2003.014

Armano, D. (2010). Why social sharing is bigger than Facebook and Twitter. *Harvard Business Review Blog*. Retrieved from http://blogs.hbr.org/cs/2010/04/why_social_sharing_is_bigger_than_facebook.html

Armstrong, D., Gosling, J., Weinman, J., & Marteau, T. (1997). The place of inter-rater reliability in qualitative research: An empirical study. *Sociology*, *31*(3), 597–606. doi:10.1177/0038038597031003015

Arnold, A.-K., & Garcia, H. (2011). *Generating genuine demand for accountability through communication. The World Bank communication for governance & accountability program (commgap) external affairs*. Washington, DC: World Bank.

ATIA. (2015). *About ATIA - Information*. Retrieved 26/12/2015, 2015, from http://www.atia.org/

Auffray, C. (2013). *Social networks: 20 million French Internet users connect daily*. Retrieved August 17, 2014, from http://www.zdnet.fr/actualites/reseaux-sociaux-20-millions-d-internautes-francais-se-connectent-tous-les-jours-39791743.htm

Aula, P. (2010). Social media, reputation risk and ambient publicity management. *Strategy and Leadership*, *38*(6), 43–49. doi:10.1108/10878571011088069

AWIA. (2015). *Web Accessibility*. Retrieved 26/12/2015, 2015, from https://www.webindustry.asn.au/news-and-events/events/web-accessibility

Back, M., Stopfer, J., Vazire, S., Gaddis, S., Schmukle, S., Egloff, B., & Gosling, S. D. (2010). Facebook profiles reflect actual personality, not self-idealization. *Psychological Science*, *21*(3), 372–374. doi:10.1177/0956797609360756 PMID:20424071

Baecker, D. (1994). Soziale Hilfe als Funktionssystem der Gesellschaft. *Zeitschrift für Soziologie*, *23*(2), 93–110. doi:10.1515/zfsoz-1994-0202

Baecker, D. (2007). Communication With Computers, or How Next Society Calls for an Understanding of Temporal Form. *Soziale Systeme*, *13*(1-2), 407–418. doi:10.1515/sosys-2007-1-235

Baeza-Yates, R., & Ribeiro-Neto, B. (1999). *Modern information retrieval*. New York: Addison Wesley.

Baker, S. M., Gentry, J. W., & Rittenburg, T. L. (2005). Building Understanding of the Domain of Customer Vulnerability. *Journal of Macromarketing*, *25*(2), 128–139. doi:10.1177/0276146705280622

Baltzan, P., & Phillips, A. (2008). *Business driven information systems*. McGraw-Hill/Irwin.

Bamman, D., Eisenstein, J., & Schnoebelen, T. (2014). Gender identity and lexical variation in social media. *Journal of Sociolinguistics*, *18*(2), 135–160. doi:10.1111/josl.12080

Bandura, A. (1977). Self-efficacy: Toward a unifying theory of behavioral change. *Psychological Review*, *1*(84), 191–125. doi:10.1037/0033-295X.84.2.191 PMID:847061

Bandura, A. (1986). *Social foundations of thought and action: A social cognitive theory*. Englewood Cliffs, NJ: Prentice Hall.

Bandura, A., & Schunk, D. H. (1981). Cultivating competence, self-efficacy and intrinsic interest through self-motivation. *Journal of Personality and Social Psychology, 41*(3), 586–598. doi:10.1037/0022-3514.41.3.586

Bandura, A., & Wood, R. (1989). Effect of perceived controllability and performance standards on self-regulation of complex decision making. *Journal of Personality and Social Psychology, 56*(5), 805–814. doi:10.1037/0022-3514.56.5.805 PMID:2724068

Banks, R. (2015). Location based mobile marketing. *Mobile Industry Review*. Available at http://www.mobileindustryreview.com/2015/02/location-based-mobile-marketing.html

Bargh, J. A., McKenna, K. Y., & Fitzsimons, G. M. (2002). Can you see the real me? Activation and expression of the true self on the Internet. *The Journal of Social Issues, 58*(1), 33–48. doi:10.1111/1540-4560.00247

Barkhuus, L., Brown, B., Bell, M., Sherwood, S., Hall, M., & Chalmers, M. (2008). From awareness to repartee: Sharing location within social groups. In *Proceedings of the 2008 Conference on Human Factors in Computing Systems* (pp. 497-506). Florence: ACM Press. doi:10.1145/1357054.1357134

Baumeister, R. F. (1999). Self-concept, self-esteem, and identity. Self-concept, self-esteem, and identity. In V. J. Derlega, B. A. Winstead, & W. H. Jones (Eds.), *Personality: Contemporary theory and research* (2nd ed.; pp. 339–375). Chicago: Nelson-Hall Publishers.

Beard, J., & Dale, P. (2008). Redesigning Services for the Net-Gen and Beyond: A Holistic Review of Pedagogy, Resource, and Learning Space. *New Review of Academic Librarianship, 14*(1-2), 99–114. doi:10.1080/13614530802518941

Bechmann, A., & Lomborg, S. (2012). Mapping actor roles in social media: Different perspectives on value creation in theories of user participation. *New Media & Society, 15*(5), 765–781. doi:10.1177/1461444812462853

Beck, U., Bonss, W., & Lau, C. (2003). The Theory of Reflexive Modernization. *Theory, Culture & Society, 20*(2), 1–33. doi:10.1177/0263276403020002001

Behnke, C. (2007). Corporate Art Collecting: A Survey of German-Speaking Companies. *The Journal of Arts Management, Law, and Society, 37*(3), 225–244. doi:10.3200/JAML.37.3.225-244

Beirut. (2009). *Why do people really tweet? The psychology behind tweeting!* Retrieved April 15, 2016, from http://blog.thoughtpick.com/2009/08/why-do-people-really-tweet-the-psychology-behind-tweeting.html

Bennett, W. L., & Segerberg, A. (2011). Digital media and the personalization of collective action: Social technology and the organization of protests against the global economic crisis. *Information Communication and Society, 14*(6), 770–799. doi:10.1080/1369118X.2011.579141

Benraïss-Noailles, L., & Viot, C. (2012). Social media in recruitment strategies. *French Management Journal, 38*(224), 125–138.

Berger, J. (2003). Neuerliche Anfragen an die Theorie der funktionalen Differenzierung. In H.-J. Giegel & U. Schimank (Eds.), *Beobachter der Moderne. Beiträge zu Luhmanns 'Die Gesellschaft der Gesellschaft.* Frankfurt am Main: Suhkamp.

Bergthaller, H., & Schinko, C. (2011). Introduction: From National Cultures to the Semantics of Modern Society. In H. Bergthaller & C. Schinko (Eds.), *Addressing Modernity. Social Systems Theory and U.S. Cultures*. Amsterdam: Edition Rodopi.

Berman, E. P. (2014). Not Just Neoliberalism: Economization in US Science and Technology Policy. *Science, Technology & Human Values*, *39*(3), 397–431. doi:10.1177/0162243913509123

Bernier, L. (2015). Getting ready for gen Z. *Canadian HR Reporter*, *28*(19), 1–16.

Berthon, P. R., Pitt, L. F., Plangger, K., & Shapiro, D. (2012). Marketing meets Web 2.0, social media, and creative consumers: Implications for international marketing strategy. *Business Horizons*, *55*(3), 261–271. doi:10.1016/j.bushor.2012.01.007

Besson, L. (2004). *Análise político-sociológica do reencontro da sociedade civil brasileira com a cidadania e a democracia segundo a perspectiva da comunicação pública.OLIVEIRA, MJ da C. Comunicação pública*. Campinas: Alínea.

Bhattacherjee, A. (2001). Understanding information systems continuance: An expectation-confirmation model. *Management Information Systems Quarterly*, *35*(3), 351–370. doi:10.2307/3250921

Bhattacherjee, A., & Premkumar, G. (2004). Understanding changes in belief and attitude toward information technology usage: A theoretical model and longitudinal test. *Management Information Systems Quarterly*, *28*(2), 229–254.

Biber, D. (1995). *Dimensions of register variation: A cross-linguistic comparison*. Cambridge, UK: Cambridge University Press. doi:10.1017/CBO9780511519871

Bimber, B. (2000). Measuring the gender gap on the Internet. *Social Science Quarterly*, *81*(3), 868–876.

Bingham, L. B., Nabatchi, T., & OLeary, R. (2005). The new governance: Practices and processes for stakeholder and citizen participation in the work of government. *Public Administration Review*, *65*(5), 547–558. doi:10.1111/j.1540-6210.2005.00482.x

Bisgin, H., Agarwal, N., & Xu, X. (2012). A study of homophily on social media. *World Wide Web (Bussum)*, *15*(2), 213–232. doi:10.1007/s11280-011-0143-3

Blaga, L. (1924). Sufletul satului/The Soul of the Village. In *Ȋn marea trecere*. Cluj, Romania: Ed. Radio.

Blair, I., Urland, G., & Ma, J. (2002). Using Internet search engines to estimate word frequency. *Behavior Research Methods*, *34*(2), 286–290. doi:10.3758/BF03195456 PMID:12109025

Blank, S. (2013). Why the Lean Start-Up Changes Everything. *Harvard Business Review*, *91*(5), 65–72.

Bloch, E. (2012). *Communication de crise et media sociaux. In Collection: Fonction de l'Entreprise*. Paris: Dunod.

Block, R. (Ed.). (1990). *Cognitive models of psychological time*. Florence, KY: Psychology Press.

Blok, A. (2011). Clash of the eco-sciences: Carbon marketization, environmental NGOs and performativity as politics. *Economy and Society*, *40*(3), 451–476. doi:10.1080/03085147.2011.574422

Bloor, M., & Wood, F. (2006). *Keywords in Qualitative Methods: A Vocabulary of Research Concepts*. London: Sage Publications. doi:10.4135/9781849209403

Blumler, J. G., & Kavanagh, D. (1999). The Third Age of Political Communication: Influences and Features. *Political Communication*, *16*(3), 209–230. doi:10.1080/105846099198596

Bohannon, J. (2011). The Science Hall of Fame. *Science*, *331*(6014), 143. doi:10.1126/science.331.6014.143-c PMID:21233362

Bohn, C. (2004). *Clothing as Medium of Communication*. University of Lucerne. Retrieved April 1, 2013, from http://www.unilu.ch/files/clothing-as_medium3.pdf

Borges, J. L., & Weinberger, E. (1999). *Selected Non-Fictions: Jorge Luis Borges.* New York: Viking.

Bosma, H. A., & Kunnen, E. S. (2001). Determinants and mechanisms in ego identity development: A review and synthesis. *Developmental Review, 21*(1), 39–66. doi:10.1006/drev.2000.0514

Bourdet, A.-S. (2016). *Bourdes des sportifs sur les réseaux sociaux: c'est pas moi, c'est mon CM!* Retrieved April 24, 2016, from http://www.lequipe.fr/Football/Article/Bourdes-des-sportifs-sur-les-reseaux-sociaux-c-est-pas-moi-c-est-mon-cm/646602

Bouzaabia, O., Bouzaabia, R., & Capatina, A. (2016). Determinants of internet use by senior generation: A cross cultural study. *International Journal of Technology and Human Interaction, 12*(1), 63–83. doi:10.4018/IJTHI.2016010105

Bovens, M. (2007). Public Accountability. In E. Ferlie, L. E. Lynn Jr, & C. Pollitt (Eds.), *The Oxford Handbook of Public Management.* doi:10.1093/oxfordhb/9780199226443.003.0009

Bovens, M. (2010). Two Concepts of Accountability: Accountability as Virtue and as a Mechanism. *West European Politics, 33*(5), 946–967. doi:10.1080/01402382.2010.486119

Bowker, N., & Tuffin, K. (2003). Dicing with deception: People with disabilities' strategies for managing safety and identity online. *Journal of Computer-Mediated Communication, 8*(2). doi: 10.1111/j.1083-6101.2003.tb00209.x

Boyd, B. K., Bergh, D. D., & Ketchen, D. J. (2010). Reconsidering the Reputation-Performance Relationship: A Resource-Based View. *Journal of Management, 36*(3), 588–609. doi:10.1177/0149206308328507

Boyd, D. M., & Ellison, N. B. (2007). Social network sites: Definition, history, and scholarship. *Journal of Computer-Mediated Communication, 13*(1), 210–230. doi:10.1111/j.1083-6101.2007.00393.x

Boyd, D., & Crawford, K. (2012). Critical Questions for Big Data. *Information Communication and Society, 15*(5), 662–679. doi:10.1080/1369118X.2012.678878

Bracke, S. (2008). Conjugating the Modern/ Religious, Conceptualizing Female Religious Agency. *Theory, Culture & Society, 25*(6), 51–67. doi:10.1177/0263276408095544

Bradbard, D., & Peters, C. (2010). Web Accessibility Theory and Practice: An Introduction for University Faculty. *Journal of Educators Online, 7*(1), n1.

Bradbard, D., Peters, C., & Caneva, Y. (2010). Web accessibility policies at land-grant universities. *The Internet and Higher Education, 13*(4), 258–266. doi:10.1016/j.iheduc.2010.05.007

Bretz, E. A. (2012). When work is fun and games. *IEEE Spectrum, 39*(12), 50–58. doi:10.1109/MSPEC.2002.1088457

Brewer, J. (2004). *Web accessibility highlights and trends.* Paper presented at the 2004 international cross-disciplinary workshop on Web accessibility (W4A). doi:10.1145/990657.990667

Brewer, M. B., & Gardner, W. (1996). Who is this we? Levels of collective identity and self representations. *Journal of Personality and Social Psychology, 71*(1), 83–93. doi:10.1037/0022-3514.71.1.83

Brier, S. (2006). Construction of Knowledge in the Mass Media. Systemic Problems in the Post-Modern Power-Struggle between the Symbolic Generalized Media in the Agora: The Lomborg Case of Environmental Science and Politics. *Systems Research and Behavioral Science, 23*(5), 667–684. doi:10.1002/sres.793

Brown, C. P. (1990). Crimes of the Vault. *Security Management, 34*(1), 31.

Brown, N., Machin, L., & Mcleod, D. (2011). Immunitary Bioeconomy: The Economisation of Life in the International Cord Blood Market. *Social Science & Medicine, 72*(7), 1115–1122. doi:10.1016/j.socscimed.2011.01.024 PMID:21398003

Brown, S. A., Dennis, A. R., & Venkatesh, V. (2010). Predicting collaboration technology use: Integrating technology adoption and collaboration research. *Journal of Management Information Systems, 27*(2), 9–53. doi:10.2753/MIS0742-1222270201

Brown, T. J., Dacin, P. A., Pratt, M. G., & Whetten, D. A. (2006). Identity, intended image, construed image, and reputation: An interdisciplinary framework and suggested terminology. *Journal of the Academy of Marketing Science, 34*(2), 99–106. doi:10.1177/0092070305284969

Bruns, A. (2008). *Blogs, Wikipedia, Second Life, and beyond: From production to produsage.* New York: Peter Lang.

Buchanan, T., Joinson, A. N., Paine, C., & Reips, U. D. (2007). Looking for medical information on the Internet: self-disclosure, privacy and trust. *He@ lth Information on the Internet, 58*(1), 8-9.

Buffardi, L. E., & Campbell, W. K. (2008). Narcissism and social networking web sites. *Personality and Social Psychology Bulletin, 34*(10), 1303–1314. doi:10.1177/0146167208320061 PMID:18599659

Burger, J. D., Henderson, J., Kim, G., & Zarrella, G. (2011). Discriminating gender on Twitter. In *Proceedings of the Conference on Empirical Methods in Natural Language Processing*(pp.1301–1309). Edinburgh, UK: Association for Computational Linguistics.

Burgstahler, S. (2015). Opening Doors or Slamming Them Shut? Online Learning Practices and Students with Disabilities. *Social Inclusion, 3*(6).

Burkart, G. (2005). Die Familie in der Systemtheorie. In G. Runkel & G. Burkart (Eds.), *Funktionssysteme der Gesellschaft. Beiträge zur Systemtheorie von Niklas Luhmann.* Wiesbaden: VS. doi:10.1007/978-3-322-80782-3_6

Burkert, W. (1985). *Greek Religion.* Blackwell Publishing Ltd and Harvard University Press.

Butler, E., McCann, E., & Thomas, J. (2011). Privacy setting awareness on Facebook and its effect on user-posted content. *Human Communication, 14*(1), 39–55.

Byrne, B. M. (2000). *Structural equation modeling with Amos: Basic concepts, applications and programming.* Mahwah, NJ: Lawrence Erlbaum.

Byrne, B. M. (2001). *Structural Equation Modeling with AMOS: Basic concepts, Applications, and Programming.* Mahwah, NJ: Lawrence Erlbaum Associates, Publishers.

Cain, N. M., Pincus, A. L., & Ansell, E. B. (2008). Narcissism at the crossroads: Phenotypic description of pathological narcissism across clinical theory, social/personality psychology, and psychiatric diagnosis. *Clinical Psychology Review, 28*(4), 638–656. doi:10.1016/j.cpr.2007.09.006 PMID:18029072

Çalışkan, K., & Callon, M. (2009). Economization, part 1: Shifting attention from the economy towards processes of economization. *Economy and Society, 38*(3), 369–398. doi:10.1080/03085140903020580

Çalışkan, K., & Callon, M. (2010). Economization, part 2: A research programme for the study of markets. *Economy and Society, 39*(1), 1–32. doi:10.1080/03085140903424519

Callon, M. (1998). Introduction: The embeddedness of economic markets in economics. In M. Callon et al. (Eds.), *The Laws of the Markets.* Oxford, UK: Blackwell. doi:10.1111/j.1467-954X.1998.tb03468.x

Callon, M. (2007). An Essay on the Growing Contribution of Economic Markets to the Proliferation of the Social. *Theory, Culture & Society, 24*(7-8), 139–163. doi:10.1177/0263276407084701

Calvert, J. (2010). Synthetic biology: Constructing nature? *The Sociological Review, 58,* 95–112. doi:10.1111/j.1467-954X.2010.01913.x

Campbell, J. P. Jr. (2015). Speaker recognition: A tutorial. *Proceedings of the IEEE, 85*(9), 1437–1462. doi:10.1109/5.628714

Campbell, M. A. (2005). Cyber bullying: An old problem in a new guise? *Australian Journal of Guidance & Counselling, 15*(01), 68–76. doi:10.1375/ajgc.15.1.68

Campbell, W. K., Bosson, J. K., Goheen, T. W., Lakey, C. E., & Kernis, M. H. (2007). Do narcissists dislike themselves deep down inside? *Psychological Science, 18*(3), 227–229. doi:10.1111/j.1467-9280.2007.01880.x PMID:17444918

Capra, E., Ferreira, S., Silveira, D., & Ferreira, A. (2012). Evaluation of Web Accessibility: An Approach Related to Functional Illiteracy. *Procedia Computer Science, 14*, 36–46. doi:10.1016/j.procs.2012.10.005

Carmon, Z., & Kahaneman, D. (1996). *The experienced utility of queuing: Experience profiles and retrospective evaluations of simulated queues.* Working paper. Durham, NC: Fuqua School of Business, Duke University.

Carniello, M. F. (2015). Proposta Metodológica de Avaliação de Comunicação Governamental Digital. *Revista Observatório, 1*(2), 101–116. doi:10.20873/uft.2447-4266.2015v1n2p101

Carpenter, C. J. (2012). Narcissism on Facebook: Self-promotional and anti-social behavior. *Personality and Individual Differences, 52*(4), 482–486. doi:10.1016/j.paid.2011.11.011

Cartier, C. (2003). From home to hospital and back again: Economic restructuring, end of life, and the gendered problems of place-switching health services. *Social Science & Medicine, 56*(11), 2289–2301. doi:10.1016/S0277-9536(02)00228-9 PMID:12719182

Carver, C., & Scheier, M. (1990). Origins and functions of positive and negative affect: A control-process view. *Psychological Review, 97*(1), 19–35. doi:10.1037/0033-295X.97.1.19

Carver, C., & Scheier, M. (1998). *On the self-regulation of behavior.* Cambridge, UK: Cambridge University Press. doi:10.1017/CBO9781139174794

Castellano, S., & Dutot, V. (2013). Une analyse de l'e-réputation par analogie ou contraste avec la réputation: Une approche par les médias sociaux. *Revue Française du Marketing, 243*, 35–51.

Castellano, S., Khelladi, I., Chipaux, A., & Kuperminc, C. (2014). The Influence of Social Networks on E-Reputation: How Sportspersons Manage the Relationship with Their Online Community. *International Journal of Technology and Human Interaction, 10*(4), 65–79. doi:10.4018/ijthi.2014100105

Castells, M. (1996). *Rise of The Network Society.* Cambridge, MA: Blackwell Publishers.

Castells, M. (2009). *Communication power.* Oxford, UK: Oxford University Press.

Cavil, S., & Sohail, M. (2007). Increasing strategic accountability: A framework for international NGOs. *Development in Practice, 17*(2), 231–248. doi:10.1080/09614520701196004

Chandra, S., Srivastava, S. C., & Theng, Y. L. (2010). Evaluating the role of trust in consumer adoption of mobile payment systems: An empirical analysis. *Communications of the Association for Information Systems, 27*(1), 351–370.

Chang, C., Liu, E. Z., Sung, H., Lin, C., Chen, N., & Cheng, S. (2014). Effects of online college students internet self-efficacy on learning motivation and performance. *Innovations in Education and Teaching International, 51*(4), 366–377. doi:10.1080/14703297.2013.771429

Cheng, S.-T., Chan, W. C., & Alfred, C. M. (2008). Older peoples realisation of generativity in a changing society: The case of Hong Kong. *Ageing and Society, 28*(5), 609–627. doi:10.1017/S0144686X07006903

Chen, S. Y., & Macredie, R. (2010). Web-based interaction: A review of three important human factors. *International Journal of Information Management, 30*(5), 379–387. doi:10.1016/j.ijinfomgt.2010.02.009

Chen, Y., & Lan, Y. (2014). An empirical study of the factors affecting mobile shopping in Taiwan. *International Journal of Technology and Human Interaction, 10*(1), 19–30. doi:10.4018/ijthi.2014010102

Chen, Y., & Zahedi, F. M. (2016). Individuals' Internet Security Perceptions and Behaviors: Polycontextual Contrasts between the United States and China. *Management Information Systems Quarterly, 40*(1), 205–A12.

Cheok, M., & Wong, S. (2015). Predictors of e-learning satisfaction in teaching and learning for school teachers: A literature review. *International Journal of Instruction, 8*(1), 75–90. doi:10.12973/iji.2015.816a

Chomsky, N. (1997). *Media Control. The Spectacular Achievements of Propaganda*. New York: Seven Stories Press.

Chomsky, N. (1999). *Profit over People: Neoliberalism and Global Order*. New York: Seven Stories Press.

Chomsky, N. (2000). *Rogue States: The Rule of Force in World Affairs*. Cambridge, MA: South End Press.

Chorost, M. (2011). *World Wide Mind: The Coming Integration of Humanity, Machines, and the Internet*. New York, NY: Free Press.

Chow, M. (2016). Determinants of presence in 3D virtual worlds: A structural equation modelling analysis. *Australasian Journal of Educational Technology, 32*(1), 1–18. doi:10.14742/ajet.1939

Christopher, A. (2011). *Myths of the Pagan North: the Gods of the Norsemen*. London: Continuum.

Chuang, S., Lin, F., & Tsai, C. (2015). An exploration of the relationship between internet self-efficacy and sources of internet self-efficacy among Taiwanese university students. *Computers in Human Behavior, 48*, 147–155. doi:10.1016/j.chb.2015.01.044

Chun, M. (2014). A study on college students use intention of internet learning resources in Chongqing. *Asian Social Science, 10*(3), 70–78. doi:10.5539/ass.v10n3p70

Chun, R., & Davies, G. (2001). E-reputation: The role of mission and vision statements in positioning strategy. *The Journal of Brand Management, 8*(4), 315–333. doi:10.1057/palgrave.bm.2540031

Claar, C. L., & Johnson, J. (2012). Analyzing home PC security adoption behavior. *Journal of Computer Information Systems, 52*(4), 20–29.

Clarke, J. T., Marks, J. G., & Miller, J. J. (2006). Mind the Gap. *Archives of Dermatology, 142*(7), 927–947. PMID:16847215

Coëffé, T. (2014). *15 Social Networks that have surpassed 100 million users*. Retrieved August 19, 2014, from http://www.blogdumoderateur.com/reseaux-sociaux-100-millions

Cohen, I., Sebe, N., Garg, A., Chen, L., & Huang, T. S. (2013). Facial expression recognition from video sequences: Temporal and static modeling. *Computer Vision and Image Understanding, 91*(1-2), 160–187. doi:10.1016/S1077-3142(03)00081-X

Cohen, J., Cohen, P., West, S., & Aiken, L. (2013). *Applied multiple regression/correlation analysis for the behavioral sciences*. Routledge.

Cole, D. (2013). *Repairing and replacing Body Parts. What's Next*. National Geographic News.

Collins, J. C. (2010). Fortify Your Facebook Privacy Settings: Don't Let the Window into Your Personal Life Sully Your Professional Reputation. *Journal of Accountancy, 209*(6), 42.

comScore. (2011). *It's a Social World. Social Networking Leads as Top Online Activity Globally, Accounting for 1 in Every 5 Online Minutes*. Retrieved April 20, 2016, from http://www.comscore.com/Insights/Press-Releases/2011/12/Social-Networking-Leads-as-Top-Online-Activity-Globally

Conrad, F., Couper, M., Tourangeau, R., & Peytchev, A. (2010). The impact of progress indicators on task completion. *Interacting with Computers, 22*(5), 417–427. doi:10.1016/j.intcom.2010.03.001 PMID:20676386

Cookson, R. (2013). *'Facebook fatigue' stirs investor concern*. Retrieved August 20, 2014, from http://www.ft.com/cms/s/0/8b7ab90e-bc91-11e2-b344-00144feab7de.html#axzz3Ar8SttQN

Cooper, M. (2013). Making online learning accessible to disabled students: an institutional case study. *Approaches to Developing Accessible Learning Experiences: Conceptualising Best Practice, 103*.

Cooper, A., & Reimann, R. (2003). *About face 2.0: The essentials of interaction design*. Hoboken, NJ: Wiley Publishing, Inc.

Cornelissen, J. P., & Kafouros, M. (2008). The Emergent Organization: Primary and Complex Metaphors in Theorizing about Organizations. *Organization Studies, 29*(7), 957–978. doi:10.1177/0170840608090533

Cornwell, B., & Lundgren, D. C. (2001). Love on the Internet: Involvement and mis-representation in romantic relationships in cyberspace vs. real space. *Computers in Human Behavior, 17*(2), 197–211. doi:10.1016/S0747-5632(00)00040-6

Cosley, D., Sosik, V. S., Schultz, J., Peesapati, S. T., & Lee, S. (2012). Experiences with designing tools for everyday reminiscing. *HCI, 27*, 175–198.

Costa, D., Fernandes, N., Neves, S., Duarte, C., Hijón-Neira, R., & Carriço, L. (2013). *Web accessibility in Africa: a study of three African domains. In Human-Computer Interaction–INTERACT 2013* (pp. 331–338). Springer.

Côté, J. E., & Levine, C. G. (2002). *Identity formation, agency, and culture: A social psychological synthesis*. Mahwah, NJ: Lawrence Erlbaum.

Craig, S. L., & McInroy, L. (2014). You can form a part of yourself online: The influence of new media on identity development and coming out for LGBTQ youth. *Journal of Gay & Lesbian Mental Health, 18*(1), 95–109. doi:10.1080/19359705.2013.777007

Crease, M., & Brewster, S. (1998). Making progress with sounds – The design and evaluation of an audio progress bar. In *ICAD98 Proceedings of the 1998International Conference on Auditory Display*. Swinton, UK: British Computer Society, 1–5.

Critchlow, H. (2015). *Dr. Hannah Critchlow interview*. Retrieved from www.telegraph.co.uk

Cronbach, L. J. (1971). Test validation. In *Education Measurement*. Washington, DC: R Thorndike, American Council on Education.

Croteau, D., & Hoynes, W. (2003). *Media Society: Industries, Images and Audiences*. Thousand Oaks, CA: Sage.

Cupach, W. R., & Imahori, T. T. (1993). Identity management theory: Communication competence in intercultural episodes and relationships. In R. L. Wiseman & J. Koester (Eds.), *Intercultural communication competence* (pp. 112–131). Newbury Park, CA: Sage.

Cuvelier, E., & Aufaure, M. A. (2011). A buzz and e-reputation monitoring tool for twitter based on Galois Lattices. In *Conceptual Structures for Discovering Knowledge* (pp. 91–103). Springer Berlin Heidelberg. doi:10.1007/978-3-642-22688-5_7

Dabholkar, P. A., & Bogazzi, R. (2002). An attitudinal model of technology-based self-service: Moderating effect of consumer traits and situational factors. *Journal of the Academy of Marketing Science, 30*(3), 184–202. doi:10.1177/0092070302303001

Dannenberg, R., Cilluffo, F. J., & Cardash, S. L. (2014). *Putin's Russia: A Geopolitical Analysis HSPI Issue Brief 24.* Retrieved March 22, 2016, from https://cchs.gwu.edu/sites/cchs.gwu.edu/files/downloads/Issue%20Brief-Putin's%20 Russia-%20A%20Geopolitical%20Analysis.pdf

DArcy, J., Hovav, A., & Galletta, D. (2009). User awareness of security countermeasures and its impact on information systems misuse: A deterrence approach. *Information Systems Research, 20*(1), 79–98. doi:10.1287/isre.1070.0160

Dash, , M., Pattnaik, A.K., Mohapatra, S., Sahoo, R.C., & Sundar, D. (2011). Using the TAM model to explain how attitudes determine adoption of internet banking. *European Journal of Economics Finance & Administrative Sciences, 36*, 50–59.

Davies, M. (2011). *Google Books (American English) Corpus (155 billion words, 1810-2009).* Available at http:// googlebooks.byu.edu/

Davies, R. (2008, September 26). *Media Perspective: Take a Big Pinch of Salt with What You Read on the Internet.* Retrieved from http://www.campaignlive.co.uk/news/849444/

Davis, F. D. (1989). Perceived Usefulness, Perceived Ease of Use, and User Acceptance of Information Technology. *Management Information Systems Quarterly, 13*(3), 319–340. doi:10.2307/249008

Davis, F. D. (1993). User acceptance of information technology: System characteristics, user perceptions and behavioral impacts. *International Journal of Man-Machine Studies, 38*(3), 475–487. doi:10.1006/imms.1993.1022

Davis, F. D., Bagozzi, R. P., & Warshaw, P. R. (1992). Extrinsic and intrinsic motivation to use computer in the workplace. *Journal of Applied Social Psychology, 22*(14), 1111–1132. doi:10.1111/j.1559-1816.1992.tb00945.x

Davis, F., Bagozzi, R. P., & Warshaw, P. R. (1989). User acceptance of computer-technology: A comparison of two theoretical models. *Management Science, 38*(8), 982–1003. doi:10.1287/mnsc.35.8.982

De Grey, A. (2015). *A roadmap to end aging.* Retrieved on the 23th April 2015 from http://www.ted.com/talks/aubrey_de_grey_says_we_can_avoid_aging

de Souza e Silva, A., & Frith, J. (2012). Mobile interfaces in public spaces: Locational privacy, control, and urban sociality. New York: Routledge.

De Valick, M. (2014). Film Festivals, Bourdieu, and the Economization of Culture. *Revue Canadienne D'études Cinématographiques / Canadian Journal of Film Studies, 23*(1), 74–89.

Dean, D. H. (2008). Shopper age and the use of self-service technologies. *Managing Service Quality, 18*(3), 225–238. doi:10.1108/09604520810871856

Debatin, B., Lovejoy, J. P., Horn, A. K., & Hughes, B. N. (2009). Facebook and online privacy: Attitudes, behaviors, and unintended consequences. *Journal of Computer-Mediated Communication, 15*(1), 83–108. doi:10.1111/j.1083-6101.2009.01494.x

DeCamp, M., Koenig, T., & Chisolm, M. (2013). Social media and physicians online identity crisis. *Journal of the American Medical Association, 310*(6), 581–582. doi:10.1001/jama.2013.8238 PMID:23942675

Deci, E. L. (1975). *Intrinsic motivation.* New York: Plenum Press. doi:10.1007/978-1-4613-4446-9

Delcourt, M. A. B., & Kinzie, M. B. (1993). Computer technologies in teacher education: The measurement of attitude and self-efficacy. *Journal of Research and Development in Education, 27*(1), 34–41.

Dellarocas, C. (2003). The digitization of word of mouth: Promise and challenges of online feedback mechanisms. *Management Science, 49*(10), 1407–1424. doi:10.1287/mnsc.49.10.1407.17308

Dellarocas, C. (2010). Online reputation systems: How to design one that does what you need. *MIT Sloan Management Review*, *51*(3), 33.

Deloitte. (2014). *Global survey on reputation risk*. Reputation@Risk.

DeMartino, I. (2014). *VKontakte (The 'Facebook of Russia') Creator: The Site Is Controlled By Putin's Friends*. Retrieved March 22, 2016, from http://www.business2community.com/social-buzz/vkontakte-facebook-russia-creator-site-controlled-putins-friends-0856559#S43uUUkoLJjdM4tp.99

Deng, L., Turner, D., Gehling, R., & Prince, B. (2010). User experience, satisfaction, and continual usage intention of IT. *European Journal of Information Systems*, *19*(1), 60–75. doi:10.1057/ejis.2009.50

Dennis, E. E. (1978). *The media society: evidence about mass communication in America*. Dubuque, IA: Brown.

Depta, L. (2016). *25 People Sports Social Media Hilariously Called Out, Part 1*. Retrieved April 24, 2016, from http://bleacherreport.com/articles/2630187-25-people-sports-social-media-hilariously-called-out-part-1

Dhopade, P. (2016). How To... Support Generation Z. *Benefits Canada*, *40*(2), 22–23.

Di Felice (2008). D*o público para as redes: a comunicação digital e as novas formas de participação social*. São Caetano do Sul: Difusão, 2008.

Díaz-Bossini, J., & Moreno, L. (2014). Accessibility to Mobile Interfaces for Older People. *Procedia Computer Science*, *27*(0), 57–66. doi:10.1016/j.procs.2014.02.008

Dineva, T., & Koufteros, X. A. (2002). *Self-efficacy and Internet usage-measurement and factorial validity*. Paper presented at the 2002 National Decision Sciences Institute DSI Conference, San Diego, CA.

Dinev, T., & Hart, P. (2004). Internet privacy concerns and their antecedents-measurement validity and a regression model. *Behaviour & Information Technology*, *23*(6), 413–422. doi:10.1080/01449290410001715723

Dixte, M. (2012). *La e-réputation sportive se joue sur tous les terrains*. Retrieved April 20, 2016, from http://blog.youseemii.fr/la-e-reputation-sportive-se-joue-sur-tous-les-terrains

Donaldson, T., & Preston, L. (1995). The stakeholder theory of the corporation: Concepts, Evidence, and Implications. *Academy of Management Review*, *20*(1), 65–91.

Dong, H., McGinley, C., Nickpour, F., & Cifter, A. (2015). Designing for designers: Insights into the knowledge users of inclusive design. *Applied Ergonomics*, *46*, 284-291. doi:10.1016/j.apergo.2013.03.003

Dong, B., Sivakumar, K., Evans, K. R., & Zou, S. (2015). Effect of Customer Participation on Service Outcomes: The Moderating Role of Participation Readiness. *Journal of Service Research*, *18*(2), 160–176. doi:10.1177/1094670514551727

Dos Santos, M. J., Carniello, M. F., & Oliveira, E. A. D. A. Q. (2013). Comunicação digital na gestão pública dos municípios da RMVP: Acesso à informação, transparência e mecanismos de participação. *Revista Brasileira de Desenvolvimento Regional*, *1*(1), 167–184.

Dowling, G. (1994). *Corporate Reputations*. London: Kogan Page.

Duchowski, A. T. (2012). A breadth-first survey of eye tracking applications. *Behavior Research Methods, Instruments, & Computers*, *34*(4), 455–470. doi:10.3758/BF03195475 PMID:12564550

Dutot, V. (2014). Adoption of social media using technology acceptance model: The generational effect. *International Journal of Technology and Human Interaction*, *10*(4), 18–35. doi:10.4018/ijthi.2014100102

Dutta, S. (2010). What's your personal social media strategy? *Harvard Business Review*, *88*(11), 127–130. PMID:21049685

Dwyer, C., Hiltz, S., & Passerini, K. (2007). Trust and privacy concern within social networking sites: A comparison of Facebook and MySpace. *AMCIS 2007 Proceedings*, 339.

Eaman, R. A. (1987). *The media society: basic issues and controversies*. London: Butterworth.

eBIZ. (2016). *Top 15 Most Popular Social Networking Sites*. Retrieved March 18, 2016, from http://www.ebizmba.com/articles/social-networking-websites

Ebrahim, A. (2010). *The Many Faces of Nonprofit Accountability*. Working Paper 10 -069. Harvard Business School.

Ebrahim, A. (2003). Accountability in Practice: Mechanisms for NGOs. *World Development, 31*(5), 813–829. doi:10.1016/S0305-750X(03)00014-7

Ebrahim, A. (2009). Placing the Normative Logics of Accountability in Thick Perspective. *The American Behavioral Scientist, 52*(6), 885–904. doi:10.1177/0002764208327664

Echeburua, E., & de Corral, P. (2010). Addiction to new technologies and to online social networking in young people: A new challenge. *Adicciones, 22*, 91–95. PMID:20549142

Eckert, P. (2008). Variation and the indexical field. *Journal of Sociolinguistics, 12*(4), 453–476. doi:10.1111/j.1467-9841.2008.00374.x

Eijffinger, S. C., & Hoeberichts, M. (2002). Central bank accountability and transparency: Theory and some evidence. *International Finance, 5*(1), 73–96. doi:10.1111/1468-2362.00088

Eikhof, D. R., & Haunschild, A. (2007). For Arts Sake! Artistic and Economic Logics in Creative Production. *Journal of Organizational Behavior, 28*(5), 523–538. doi:10.1002/job.462

Ellison, N., Heino, R., & Gibbs, J. (2006). Managing impressions online: Self-presentation processes in the online dating environment. *Journal of Computer-Mediated Communication, 11*(2), 415–441. doi:10.1111/j.1083-6101.2006.00020.x

eMarketer. (2013). *Tablets, smartphones drive mobile commerce to record heights*. Retrieved from http://www.emarketer.com/newsroom/index.php/emarketer-tablets-smartphones-drive-mobile-commerce-record-heights/

Enderle, G. (1997). A Worldwide Survey of Business Ethics in the 1990s. *Journal of Business Ethics, 16*(14), 1475–1483. doi:10.1023/A:1005866527497

Erikson, E. (1968). *Identity, youth and crisis*. New York: W. W. Norton Company.

Esser, F., & Strömbäck, J. (Eds.). (2014). Mediatization of Politics: Understanding the Transformation of Western Democracies. Palgrave Macmillan.

Etling, B., Roberts, H., & Faris, R. (2014). *Blogs as an Alternative Public Sphere: The Role of Blogs, Mainstream Media, and TV in Russia's Media Ecology*. Retrieved March 24, 2016, from https://cyber.law.harvard.edu/node/95699

EU-FRA. (2015). *People with disabilities*. Retrieved 28/11/2015, 2015, from http://fra.europa.eu/en/theme/people-disabilities

Euromaidan Press. (2014). *Russian aid to Ukraine is actually Russian military, social network reveals*. Retrieved August 20, 2014, from http://euromaidanpress.com/2014/08/11/russian-aid-to-ukraine-is-actually-russian-military-social-network-reveals

Evans, M. (2016). *Social media becomes more of a mobile commerce tool worldwide*. Available at http://www.mobilepaymentstoday.com/blogs/social-media-becomes-more-of-a-mobile-commerce-tool-worldwide/

Ewert, B. (2009). Economization and Marketization in the German Healthcare System: How Do Users Respond? *German Policy Studies/Politikfeldanalyse, 5*(1), 21-44.

Fabian, D., & Flatt, T. (2011). *The Evolution of Aging*. Nature Education Knowledge, Institute of Population Genetics. *Vetmeduni Vienna Veterinaerplatz, 1*, A-1210.

Facebook. (2012). *Safety and Privacy*. Retrieved from http://newsroom.fb.com/content/default.aspx?NewsAreaId=36

Fasel, B., & Luettin, J. (2013). Automatic facial expression analysis: A survey. *Pattern Recognition, 36*(1), 259–275. doi:10.1016/S0031-3203(02)00052-3

Fauconnier, F. (2012). *Prepare a Facebook ad service*. Retrieved November 8, 2013, from http://www.journaldunet.com/ebusiness/le-net/facebook-petites-annonces-1112.shtml

Ferati, M., Raufi, B., Kurti, A., & Vogel, B. (2014). *Accessibility requirements for blind and visually impaired in a regional context: An exploratory study*. Paper presented at the Usability and Accessibility Focused Requirements Engineering (UsARE), 2014 IEEE 2nd International Workshop on. doi:10.1109/UsARE.2014.6890995

Finch, J. H. (2007). Economic sociology as a strange other to both sociology and economics. *History of the Human Sciences, 20*(2), 123–140. doi:10.1177/0952695107077022

Fishbein, M., & Ajzen, I. (1975). *Belief, attitude, intention and behavior: an introduction to theory and research* Reading, MA: Addison-Wesley.

Fleisch, E. (2004). Business impact of pervasive technologies: Opportunities and risks. *Human and Ecological Risk Assessment, 10*(5), 817–829. doi:10.1080/10807030490513838

Fludernik, M. (2005). Threatening the University—The Liberal Arts and the Economization of Culture. *New Literary History, 36*(1), 57–70. doi:10.1353/nlh.2005.0019

Fombrun, C. J. (1996). *Reputation: realizing value from the corporate image*. Boston, MA: Harvard Business School Press.

Fonderie, L. (2012). *Facebook sponsored ads*. Retrieved June 26, 2013, from http://www.lafonderie-idf.fr/facebook-sponsored-ads-3471.html

Fontaine, C., Haarman, A., & Schmid, S. (2006). *Stakeholder Theory of the MNC*. Retrieved April 23, 2016, from http://www.edalys.fr/documents/Stakeholders%20theory.pdf

Fornell, C., & Larcker, D. (1981). Evaluating structural equation models with unobserved variables and measurement error. *JMR, Journal of Marketing Research, 18*(1), 39–50. doi:10.2307/3151312

Foucault, M. (2008). *The Birth of Biopolitics: Lectures at the College de France 1978–1979*. Palgrave Macmillan.

Freshfields Bruckhaus Deringer. (2013). *Containing a crisis. Dealing with corporate disasters in the digital age*. Author.

Frochot, D., & Molinaro, F. (2008). *Livre blanc sur l'e-réputation*. Paris: Les Infostratèges.

Fuchs, P. (1999). *Intervention und Erfahrung*. Frankfurt am Main: Suhrkamp.

Fuchs, P. (2000). Form und Funktion von Beratung. *Soziale Systeme, 6*(2), 349–368.

Fuertes, J., González, Á., & Martínez, L. (2012). Including Accessibility in Higher Education Curricula for ICT. *Procedia Computer Science, 14*, 382–390. doi:10.1016/j.procs.2012.10.044

Gage, D. (1996). Companies need more security training programs, study finds. *Info World Canada, 21*(3), 24–25.

Galitz, W. (2007). *The essential guide to user interface design*. Hoboken, NJ: Wiley Publishing, Inc.

Garcia, A., & Peres, C. (2012). Auditory progress bars: The effects of feedback, endpoint, and free response on estimations of time remaining. In *Proceedings of the Human Factors and Ergonomics Society Annual Meeting 2012*. doi:10.1177/1071181312561335

Gaudreau, P., Miranda, D., & Gareau, A. (2014). Canadian university students in wireless classrooms: What do they do on their laptops and does it really matter? *Computers & Education, 70*, 245–255. doi:10.1016/j.compedu.2013.08.019

Gavrila, D. M. (2009). The visual analysis of human movement: A survey. *Computer Vision and Image Understanding, 73*(1), 82–98. doi:10.1006/cviu.1998.0716

Geddes, L. (2010, June). Immortal avatars: Back up your brain, never die. *New Scientist, Issue, 2763*, 7. doi:10.1016/S0262-4079(10)61706-X

Gefen, D., & Straub, D. W. (1997). Gender differences in the perception and use of e-mail: An extension to the technology acceptance model. *Management Information Systems Quarterly, 21*(4), 389–400. doi:10.2307/249720

George, S. E. (2005). Believe It or Not: Virtual Religion in the 21st Century. *International Journal of Technology and Human Interaction, 1*(1), 62–71. doi:10.4018/jthi.2005010103

Gerpott, T. J., & Thomas, S. (2014). Empirical research on mobile internet usage: A meta-analysis of the literature. *Telecommunications Policy, 38*(3), 291–310. doi:10.1016/j.telpol.2013.10.003

Ghafurian, M., & Reitter, D. (2016). Impatience induced by waiting: An effect moderated by the speed of countdowns. In *Proceedings of the Designing Interactive Systems*. Brisbane, Australia: ACM. doi:10.1145/2901790.2901830

Gilbert, E., & Karahalios, K. (2009). Predicting tie strength with social media. In *CHI '09: Proceedings of the 27th annual SIGCHI conference on Human Factors in Computing Systems* (pp. 211-220). New York, NY: ACM Press. doi:10.1145/1518701.1518736

Gilbertson, T., & Machin, C. (2012). *Guidelines, icons and marketable skills: an accessibility evaluation of 100 web development company homepages*. Paper presented at the international cross-disciplinary conference on web accessibility. doi:10.1145/2207016.2207024

Gillham, B. (2005). *Research Interviewing*. Maidenhead, UK: Open University Press.

Global Web Index. (2013). *Social platforms GWI.8 update: Decline of Local Social Media Platforms*. Retrieved March 13, 2013, from http://globalwebindex.net/thinking/social-platforms-gwi-8-update-decline-of-local-social-media-platforms

GlobalWebIndex (2016). *Social summary. Quarterly report on the latest trends in social networking*. Author.

Goffman, E. (1959). *The presentation of self in everyday life*. New York: Anchor.

Gonçalves, R. (2015). *Fórum para a Sociedade de Informação – Acessibilidade Web*. Retrieved June 20, 2016, from http://www.apdsi.pt/uploads/news/id950/01%20-%20Ramiro%20Goncalves%20-%20Bar%C3%B3metro%20da%20Acessibilidade%20Web%2020132015%20-%20Estado%20da%20Acessibilidade%20Web.pdf

Gonçalves, R., Martins, J., Branco, F., Pereira, J., Rocha, T., & Peixoto, C. (2015). *AccessWeb Barometer: A Web Accessibility Evaluation and Analysis Platform*. Paper presented at the INTERNET 2015 - The Seventh International Conference on Evolving Internet, St. Julians, Malta.

Gonçalves, R., Martins, J., & Branco, F. (2014). A Review on the Portuguese Enterprises Web Accessibility Levels–A Website Accessibility High Level Improvement Proposal. *Procedia Computer Science, 27*, 176–185. doi:10.1016/j.procs.2014.02.021

Gonçalves, R., Martins, J., Branco, F., & Barroso, J. (2013). *Web Accessibility–From the Evaluation and Analysis to the Implementation–The anoGov/PEPPOL Case. In Universal Access in Human-Computer Interaction. User and Context Diversity* (pp. 664–673). Springer.

Gonçalves, R., Martins, J., Pereira, J., Oliveira, M., & Ferreira, J. (2013). Enterprise Web Accessibility Levels Amongst the Forbes 250: Where Art Thou O Virtuous Leader? *Journal of Business Ethics, 113*(2), 363–375. doi:10.1007/s10551-012-1309-3

Gonçalves, R., Martins, J., Pereira, J., Santos, V., & Cota, M. (2013). Can I Access my School Website? Auditing Accessibility of the Portuguese Teaching Institutions Websites. *Journal of Universal Computer Science, 19*(18), 2639–2655.

Gonzalez-Herrero, A., & Smith, S. (2008). Crisis communications management on the Web: How Internet-based technologies are changing the way public relations professionals handle business crises. *Journal of Contingencies and Crisis Management, 16*(3), 143–153. doi:10.1111/j.1468-5973.2008.00543.x

Goodwin, M., Susar, D., Nietzio, A., Snaprud, M., & Jensen, C. (2011). Global web accessibility analysis of national government portals and ministry web sites. *Journal of Information Technology & Politics, 8*(1), 41–67. doi:10.1080/19331681.2010.508011

Gorman, P., Nelson, T., & Glassman, A. (2004). The Millennial Generation: A Strategic Opportunity. *Organizational Analysis, 12*(3), 255–270, 339–340.

Gotsi, M., & Wilson, A. M. (2001). Corporate reputation: Seeking a definition. *Corporate Communications: An International Journal, 6*(1), 24–30. doi:10.1108/13563280110381189

Gouteron, J. (2004). Using the segmentation nostalgia: The age of the internet mediate consumption: Comparative Study of chronological age and subjective age. *The Journal of Management Science: Management and Management, 39*(208), 81–94.

Grau, J. (1984). Security Education: Something to Think About. *Security Management, 28*(10), 25–31.

Graver, M. S., & Mentzer, J. T. (1999). Logistics research methods: Employing structural equation modeling to test construct validity. *Journal of Business Logistics, 20*(1), 33–57.

Graves, R. (1955). *The Greek Myths*. Baltimore, MD: Penguin.

Gray, E. R., & Balmer, J. M. T. (1998). Managing Corporate Image and Corporate Reputation. *Long Range Planning, 31*(5), 695–702. doi:10.1016/S0024-6301(98)00074-0

Greengard, S. (2012). Digitally possessed. *Communications of the ACM, 55*(5), 14–16. doi:10.1145/2160718.2160725

Grimmelikhuijsen, S., & Welch, E. (2012). Developing and Testing a Theoretical Framework for Computer-Mediated Transparency of Local Governments. *Public Administration Review, 72*(4), 562–571. doi:10.1111/j.1540-6210.2011.02532.x

Gunes, H., & Piccardi, M. (2007). Bi-modal emotion recognition from expressive face and body gestures. *Journal of Network and Computer Applications, 30*(4), 1334–1345. doi:10.1016/j.jnca.2006.09.007

Habermas, J., & McCarthy, T. (1985). The Theory of Communicative Action, Vol. 2: Lifeworld and System: A Critique of Functionalist Reason. Beacon Press.

Hair, J. F., Black, W. C., Babin, B. J., & Anderson, R. E. (2010). *Multivariate data analysis. A global perspective*. Pearson.

Hair, J. F. Jr, Black, W. C., Babin, B. J., & Anderson, R. E. (2006). *Multivariate data analysis a global perception*. Upper Saddle River, NJ: Pearson Education, Inc.

Hamada, K., Yoshida, K., Ohnishi, K., & Köppen, M. (2011). Color effect on subjective perception of progress bar speed. In *Proceedings of the Third International Conference on Intelligent Networking and Collaborative Systems*. Iizuka, Japan: Kyushu Institute of Technology. doi:10.1109/INCoS.2011.65

Hamid, S., Waycott, J., Kurnia, S., & Chang, S. (2015). Understanding students perceptions of the benefits of online social networking use for teaching and learning. *The Internet and Higher Education*, *26*, 1–9. doi:10.1016/j.iheduc.2015.02.004

Hanafizadeh, P., Behboudi, M., Koshksaray, A. A., & Tabar, M. J. S. (2014). Mobile-banking adoption by Iranian bank clients. *Telematics and Informatics*, *31*(1), 62–78. doi:10.1016/j.tele.2012.11.001

Hangal, S., Lam, M., & Heer, J. (2011). MUSE: Reviving memories using email archives. In *Proceedings of ACM User Interface Software & Technology (UIST)* (pp.75–84). Santa Barbara, CA: ACM.

Hanson, V., & Richards, J. (2013). Progress on website accessibility?. *ACM Transactions on the Web*, *7*(1), 2. doi:10.1145/2435215.2435217

Hardina, D. (2011). Are Social Service Managers Encouraging Consumer Participation in Decision Making in Organizations? *Administration in Social Work*, *35*(2), 117–137. doi:10.1080/03643107.2011.557583

Hargittai, E. (2010). Digital Na(t)ives? Variation in Internet Skills and Uses among Members of the Net Generation. *Sociological Inquiry*, *80*(1), 92–113. doi:10.1111/j.1475-682X.2009.00317.x

Harper, S., & Chen, A. (2012). Web accessibility guidelines. *World Wide Web (Bussum)*, *15*(1), 61–88. doi:10.1007/s11280-011-0130-8

Harrison, C., Amento, B., Kuznetsov, S., & Bell, R. (2007). Rethinking the progress bar. In *Proceedings of the 20th Annual ACM Symposium on User Interface Software and Technology*. New York, NY: ACM. doi:10.1145/1294211.1294231

Harrison, C., Yeo, Z., & Hudson, S. (2010). Faster progress bars: Manipulating perceived duration with visual augmentation. In *Proceedings of the 28th Annual SIGCHI Conference on Human Factors in Computing Systems*. New York, NY: ACM. doi:10.1145/1753326.1753556

Hashim, F., Alam, G. M., & Siraj, S. (2010). Information and communication technology for participatory based decision-making-E-management for administrative efficiency in higher education. *International Journal of Physical Sciences*, *5*(4), 383–392.

Hawking, S. (2013). *Interview*. Retrieved from www.dailymail.co.uk

Hayward, V., Astley, O. R., Cruz-Hernandez, M., Grant, D., & Robles-De-La-Torre, G. (2014). Haptic interfaces and devices. *Sensor Review*, *24*(1), 16–29. doi:10.1108/02602280410515770

Hearit, K. M. (1999). Newsgroups, activist publics, and corporate apologia: The case of Intel and its Pentium chip. *Public Relations Review*, *25*(3), 291–308. doi:10.1016/S0363-8111(99)00020-X

Hecht, M. L. (1993). A research odyssey: Towards the development of a communication theory of identity. *Communication Monographs*, *60*(1), 76–82. doi:10.1080/03637759309376297

Hecht, M. L., Warren, J., Jung, J., & Krieger, J. (2004). Communication theory of identity. In W. B. Gudykunst (Ed.), *Theorizing about intercultural communication* (pp. 257–278). Newbury Park, CA: Sage.

Henkel, A. (2010). Systemtheoretische Methodologie: Beobachtung mit Systemreferenz Gesellschaft. In R. John, A. Henkel, & J. Rückert-John (Eds.), *Die Methodologien des Systems*. Wiesbaden: VS. doi:10.1007/978-3-531-92435-9_10

Hennig-Thurau, T., Gwinner, K. P., Walsh, G., & Gremler, D. D. (2004). Electronic word-of-mouth via consumer-opinion platforms: What motivates consumers to articulate themselves on the Internet? *Journal of Interactive Marketing, 18*(1), 38–52. doi:10.1002/dir.10073

Henry, S., Abou-Zahra, S., & Brewer, J. (2014). *The role of accessibility in a universal web.* Paper presented at the 11th Web for All Conference. doi:10.1145/2596695.2596719

Henry, S. (2002). *Understanding web accessibility. In Constructing accessible web sites* (pp. 6–31). Springer. doi:10.1007/978-1-4302-1116-7_2

Herring, S. C., & Paolillo, J. C. (2006). Gender and genre variation in weblogs. *Journal of Sociolinguistics, 10*(4), 439–459. doi:10.1111/j.1467-9841.2006.00287.x

Hesiod, . (1987). *Theogony.* Indianapolis, IN: Focus, An Imprint of Hackett Publishing Company.

Hess, D. (2007). Social reporting and new governance regulation: The prospects of achieving corporate accountability through transparency. *Business Ethics Quarterly, 17*(03), 453–476. doi:10.5840/beq200717348

Heylighen, F., & Dewaele, J. (2002). Variation in the contextuality of language: An empirical measure. *Foundations of Science, 7*(3), 293–340. doi:10.1023/A:1019661126744

Higgins, E. T. (1987). Self-discrepancy: A theory relating self and affect. *Psychological Review, 94*(3), 319–340. doi:10.1037/0033-295X.94.3.319 PMID:3615707

Hildebrandt, M. (2008). Ambient intelligence, criminal liability and democracy. *Criminal Law and Philosophy, 2*(2), 163–180. doi:10.1007/s11572-007-9042-1

Hilty, L. M., Som, C., & Koehler, A. (2004). Assessing the Human, Social and Environmental. Risks of Pervasive Computing. *Journal of Human and Ecological Risk Assessment, 10*(5), 853–874. doi:10.1080/10807030490513874

Hjarvard, S. (2008). The Mediatization of Society. *Nordicom Review, 29*(2), 105–134. PMID:19361120

Hjarvard, S. (2013). *The Mediatization of Culture and Society.* New York: Routledge.

Hogan, B. (2010). The presentation of self in the age of social media: Distinguishing performances and exhibitions online. *Bulletin of Science, Technology & Society, 30*(6), 377–386. doi:10.1177/0270467610385893

Hogg, M. A., Terry, D. J., & White, K. M. (1995). A tale of two theories: A critical comparison of identity theory with social identity theory. *Social Psychology Quarterly, 58*(4), 255–269. doi:10.2307/2787127

Hogg, M., & Abrams, D. (1999). Social identity and social cognition: Historical background and current trends. In D. Abrams & M. Hogg (Eds.), *Social identity and social cognition* (pp. 1–25). Malden, MA: Blackwell Publishers.

Hohenstein, J., Kahn, H., Canfield, K., Tung, S., & Cano, R. (2016). Shorter wait times: The effects of various loading screens on perceived performance. In *Proceedings of the 2016 CHI Conference Extended Abstracts on Human Factors in Computing Systems.* doi:10.1145/2851581.2892308

Hojjat, S. K., Golmakani, E., Bayazi, M. H., Mortazavi, R., Khalili, M. N., & Akaberi, A. (2015). Personality traits and identity styles in methamphetamine-dependent women: A comparative study. *Global Journal of Health Science, 8*(1), 14–20. doi:10.5539/gjhs.v8n1p14 PMID:26234975

Holtgraves, T. (2011). Text messaging, personality, and the social context. *Journal of Research in Personality, 45*(1), 92–99. doi:10.1016/j.jrp.2010.11.015

Hong, J., Hwang, M., Hsu, H., Wong, W., & Chen, M. (2011). Applying the technology acceptance model in a study of the factors affecting usage of the Taiwan digital archives system. *Computers & Education*, *57*(3), 2086–2094. doi:10.1016/j.compedu.2011.04.011

Howard, G., Brown, E., & Auer, M. (2014). *Imaging Life: Biological Systems from Atoms to Tissues*.Oxford University Press.

Howe, N., & Strauss, W. (2000). *Millennials rising: The next great generation*. New York: Random House.

Hoyle, R. H. (1995). *Structural equation modeling: concepts, issues and applications. New Delhi, London*. Thousand Oaks, CA: Sage Publications.

Huang, E. (2008). Use and gratification in e-consumers. *Internet Research*, *18*(4), 405–426. doi:10.1108/10662240810897817

Humphreys, L. (2012). Connecting, coordinating, cataloguing: Communicative practices on mobile social networks. *Journal of Broadcasting & Electronic Media*, *56*(4), 494–510. doi:10.1080/08838151.2012.732144

Hurrell, A. (2007). One World? Many Worlds? The Place of Regions in the Study of International Society. *International Affairs*, *83*(1), 127–146. doi:10.1111/j.1468-2346.2007.00606.x

Hurter, C., Girouard, A., Riche, N., & Plaisant, C. (2011). Active progress bars: Facilitating the switch to temporary activities. In *Proceedings of the 2011 Annual Conference on Human Factors in Computing Systems*. New York, NY: ACM, (pp.1963–1968). doi:10.1145/1979742.1979883

Husson, T. (2014). *The Smartphone & Tablet Experience webinar*. Forrester Research.

IAAP. (2015). About IAAP. Retrieved 26/12/2015, 2015, from http://www.accessibilityassociation.org/

Iacobelli, F., Gill, A. J., Nowson, S., & Oberlander, J. (2011). Large scale personality classification of bloggers. In *Proceedings of Affective Computing and Intelligent Interaction:Fourth International Conference* (pp. 568–577). Memphis, TN: Springer-Verlag.

IFOP. (2012). *Observatoire des Réseaux Sociaux*. Retrieved March 16, 2013, from http://www.ifop.com/media/poll/2050-1-study_file.pdf

Imahori, T. T., & Cupach, W. R. (2005). Theorizing about intercultural communication. *Sage (Atlanta, Ga.)*.

Imhof, M., Vollmeyer, R., & Beierlein, C. (2007). Computer use and the gender gap: The issue of access, use, motivation, and performance. *Computers in Human Behavior*, *23*(6), 2823–2837. doi:10.1016/j.chb.2006.05.007

Ind, N., Iglesias, O., & Schultz, M. (2013). Building Brands Together: Emergence and Outcomes of Co-Creation. *California Management Review*, *55*(3), 5–26. doi:10.1525/cmr.2013.55.3.5

International Telecommunication Union. (2015). *ICT facts and figures*. Geneva: ITU.

International Telecommunications Union. (2010). *Key global telecom indicators for the world telecommunication service sector*. Available at: http://www.itu.int/ITU-D/ict/statistics/index.html

Internet, P. (2013). *Pew Internet: Social Networking (full details)*. Retrieved March 15, 2013, from http://pewinternet.org/Commentary/2012/March/Pew-Internet-Social-Networking-full-detail.aspx

Ireland, M. E., & Mehl, M. R. (2014). Natural language use as a marker of personality. In T. M. Holtgraves (Ed.), *Oxford Handbook of Language and Social Psychology* (pp. 201–218). Oxford, UK: Oxford University Press.

Islam, A. Y. M. A. (2011a). *Online database adoption and satisfaction model*. Lambert Academic Publishing.

Islam, A. Y. M. A. (2011b). Viability of the extended technology acceptance model: An empirical study. *Journal of Information and Communication Technology, 10*, 85–98.

Islam, A. Y. M. A. (2014). Validation of the technology satisfaction model (TSM) developed in higher education: The application of structural equation modeling. *International Journal of Technology and Human Interaction, 10*(3), 44–57. doi:10.4018/ijthi.2014070104

Islam, A. Y. M. A. (2016). Development and validation of the technology adoption and gratification (TAG) model in higher education: A cross-cultural study between Malaysia and China. *International Journal of Technology and Human Interaction, 12*(3), 78–105. doi:10.4018/IJTHI.2016070106

Islam, A. Y. M. A., Leng, C. H., & Singh, D. (2015). Efficacy of the technology satisfaction model (TSM): An empirical study. *International Journal of Technology and Human Interaction, 11*(2), 45–60. doi:10.4018/ijthi.2015040103

ISO 9241-171:2008. (2008). *Ergonomics of human-system interaction -- Part 171: Guidance on software accessibility.* Retrieved April 2, from http://www.iso.org/iso/home/store/catalogue_ics/catalogue_det ail_ics.htm?csnumber=39080

ISO. (2003). *TS 16071: 2003: Ergonomics of human-system interaction–Guidance on accessibility for human-computer interfaces.* Geneva, Switzerland: International Standards Organisation.

ISO. (2006). *9241-110: 2006. Ergonomics of human system interaction-Part 110: Dialogue principles.* ISO.

ISO. (2008). *9241-171 (2008) Ergonomics of humansystem interaction--Part 171: Guidance on software accessibility.* ISO.

ISO/TS 16071:2003. (2003). *Ergonomics of human-system interaction -- Guidance on accessibility for human-computer interfaces.* Retrieved March 30, from http://www.iso.org/iso/catalogue_detail.htm?csnumber=30858

Ispirescu, P. (1862). *Legende sau Basmele Românilor / Legends or Romanians' Fairy-tales.* București: Academic Press.

Issa, T. B. T., & Isaias, P. (2016). Internet factors influencing generations Y and Z in Australia and Portugal: A practical study. *Information Processing & Management, 52*(4), 592–617. doi:10.1016/j.ipm.2015.12.006

Itskov, D. (2013). *Global Future 20145 Congress.* New York: Lincoln Center.

Iwata, H., Kobayashi, N., Tachibana, K., Shirogane, J., & Fukazawa, Y. (2013). Web accessibility support for visually impaired users using link content analysis. *SpringerPlus, 2*(1), 116. doi:10.1186/2193-1801-2-116 PMID:23667799

Jackson, P. (1997). *The Epic of Gilgamesh* (2nd ed.). Wauconda, IL: Bolchazy-Carducci Publishers, Inc.

Jacobs, A., & Wilford, R. (2010). Listen First: A Pilot System for Managing Downward Accountability in NGO. *Development in Practice, 20*(7), 797–811. doi:10.1080/09614524.2010.508113

Jaeger, P. (2004). The Social Impact of an Accessible E-Democracy Disability Rights Laws in the Development of the Federal E-Government. *Journal of Disability Policy Studies, 15*(1), 19–26. doi:10.1177/10442073040150010401

Jafar, M. J., & Abdullat, A. (2011). Exploratory analysis of the readability of information privacy statement of the primary social networks. *Journal of Business & Economics Research, 7*(12).

Jäger, U. (2014). *Managing Social Businesses: Mission, Governance, Strategy and Accountability.* Basingstoke, UK: Palgrave MacMillan.

Jaimes, A., & Sebe, N. (2007). Multimodal human computer interaction: A survey. *Computer Vision and Image Understanding, 108*(1-2), 116–134. doi:10.1016/j.cviu.2006.10.019

James, E.H. & Wooten, L.P. (2011). Crisis Leadership and Why It Matters. *European Financial Review*, 60-64.

James, E. H., & Wooten, L. P. (2005). Leadership as (Un)usual: How to display competence in times of crisis. *Organizational Dynamics*, *34*(2), 141–152. doi:10.1016/j.orgdyn.2005.03.005

Jennings, G. (2005). 'Interviewing: a focus on qualitative techniques. In B. Ritchie & P. Burns (Eds.), *Tourism Research Methods: Integrating Theory with Practice* (pp. 99–118). Cambridge, UK: CABI. doi:10.1079/9780851999968.0099

Jin, K. (2010). Modern Biological Theories of Aging. Aging and Disease. *US National Library of Medicine*, *1*(2), 72–74.

Johnson, C. Y. (2010). In billions of words, digital allies find tale. *The Boston Globe*.

Johnson, B. R. (2007). *A mixed-methods study of the influence of generational consciousness on information privacy concern*. ProQuest.

Joinson, A. N. (2001). Self-disclosure in computer-mediated communication: The role of self-awareness and visual anonymity. *European Journal of Social Psychology*, *31*(2), 177–192. doi:10.1002/ejsp.36

Joinson, A. N., Reips, U. D., Buchanan, T., & Schofield, C. B. P. (2010). Privacy, trust, and self-disclosure online. *Human-Computer Interaction*, *25*(1), 1–24. doi:10.1080/07370020903586662

Jones, B., Temperley, J., & Lima, A. (2009). Corporate reputation in the era of Web 2.0: The case of Primark. *Journal of Marketing Management*, *25*(9-10), 927–939. doi:10.1362/026725709X479309

Jönhill, J. I. (2012). Inclusion and Exclusion - A Guiding Distinction to the Understanding of Issues of Cultural Background. *Systems Research and Behavioral Science*, *29*(4), 387–401. doi:10.1002/sres.1140

Jordan, L. (2007). A rights -based approach to accountability. In Global Accountabilities: participation, pluralism, and public ethic (pp. 151-167) New York: Cambridge University Press.

Jung, M., Sirkin, D., Turgut, M., & Steinert, M. (2015). *Displayed uncertainty improves driving experience and behavior: The case of range anxiety in an electric car*. UI Impact on Performance & Decisions. CHI 2015, Seoul, Republic of Korea. doi:10.1145/2702123.2702479

Kaba, B., & Osei-Bryson, K. M. (2013). Examining influence of national culture on individuals attitude and use of information and communication technology: Assessment of moderating effect of culture through cross countries study. *International Journal of Information Management*, *33*(3), 441–452. doi:10.1016/j.ijinfomgt.2013.01.010

Kacowicz, A. M. (1999). Regionalization, Globalization, and Nationalism: Convergent, Divergent, or Overlapping? *Alternatives: Global, Local. Political*, *24*(4), 527–555.

Kahn, P. H. Jr, Severson, R. L., & Jolina, H. (2009). *The Human Relation with Nature and Technological Nature*. University of Washington.

Kane, C. L. (2010). Programming the Beautiful. *Theory, Culture & Society*, *27*(1), 73–93. doi:10.1177/0263276409350359

Kaplan, A., & Haenlein, M. (2010). Users of the world, unite! The challenges and opportunities of social media. *Business Horizons*, *53*(1), 59–68. doi:10.1016/j.bushor.2009.09.003

Kaplan, A., & Haenlein, M. (2011). The early bird catches the news: Nine things you should know about micro-blogging. *Business Horizons*, *54*(2), 105–113. doi:10.1016/j.bushor.2010.09.004

Kapoor, A., Burleson, W., & Picard, R. W. (2007). Automatic prediction of frustration. *International Journal of Human-Computer Studies*, *65*(8), 724–736. doi:10.1016/j.ijhcs.2007.02.003

Karahanna, E., Straub, D. W., & Chervany, N. L. (1999). Information technology adoption across time: A cross-sectional comparison of pre-adoption and post-adoption beliefs. *Management Information Systems Quarterly, 23*(2), 183–213. doi:10.2307/249751

Karkin, N., & Janssen, M. (2014). Evaluating websites from a public value perspective: A review of Turkish local government websites. *International Journal of Information Management, 34*(3), 351–363. doi:10.1016/j.ijinfomgt.2013.11.004

Kasriel, D. (2012). Protecting privacy in our digital age: A growing consumer priority. *Passport: Euromonitor International, 1*.

Katz, E., & Blumler, G. (1974). *The Use of Mass Communications: Current Perspectives on Gratifications Research.* Beverly Hills, CA: Sage.

Katz, K., Larson, B., & Larson, R. (1991). Prescription for the waiting-in-line blues: Entertain, enlighten, and engage. *Sloan Management Review, 32*(2), 44–53.

Kearney, A. T. (2011). *The Sports Market; Major trends and challenges in an industry full of passion.* Retrieved April 20, 2016, from https://www.atkearney.com/documents/10192/6f46b880-f8d1-4909-9960-cc605bb1ff34

Kelsey, F. W. (1889). *An Outline of the Greek and Roman Mythology.* Allyn and Bacon. Forgotten Books. (2012). Available at: www.forgottenbooks.org

Kettebekov, S., & Sharma, R. (2010). Understanding gestures in multimodal human computer interaction. *International Journal of Artificial Intelligence Tools, 9*(2), 205–223. doi:10.1142/S021821300000015X

Khantzian, E. J. (2003). Understanding addictive vulnerability: An evolving psychodynamic perspective. *Neuro-psychoanalysis, 5*(1), 5–21. doi:10.1080/15294145.2003.10773403

Khatib, O., Brock, O., Chang, K. S., Ruspini, D., Sentis, L., & Viji, S. (2014). Human-centered robotics and interactive haptic simulation. *The International Journal of Robotics Research, 23*(2), 167–178. doi:10.1177/0278364904041325

Khedhaouria, A., & Beldi, A. (2014). Perceived enjoyment and the effect of gender on continuance intention for mobile internet services. *International Journal of Technology and Human Interaction, 10*(2), 1–20. doi:10.4018/ijthi.2014040101

Khedhaouria, A., Beldi, A., & Belbaly, N. (2013). The moderating effect of gender on continuance intention for mobile Internet services (MIS). *Système dInformation & Management, 18*(3), 117–142. doi:10.3917/sim.133.0117

Kieke, R. (2006). Survey shows high number of organizations suffered security breach in past year. *Journal of Health Care Compliance, 8*(5), 49–68.

Kietzmann, J. H., Hermkens, K., McCarthy, I. P., & Silvestre, B. S. (2011). Social media? Get serious! Understanding the functional building blocks of social media. *Business Horizons, 54*(3), 241–251. doi:10.1016/j.bushor.2011.01.005

Kim-Choy, C., & Holdsworth, D. K. (2012). Culture and behavioural intent to adopt mobile commerce among the Y Generation: Comparative analyses between Kazakhstan, Morocco and Singapore. *Young Consumers, 13*(3), 224–241. doi:10.1108/17473611211261629

Kim, D., & Hwang, Y. (2006). A study of mobile Internet usage from utilitarian and hedonic user tendency perspectives. In *Proceedings of the Twelfth Americas Conference on Information Systems.* Acapulco, Mexico: AIS.

Kim, D., & Steinfield, C. (2004). Consumers' mobile Internet service satisfaction and their continuance intentions. In C. Bullen, & E. Stoher (Ed.), *Proceedings of the Tenth Americas Conference on Information Systems.* Atlanta, GA: AIS.

Kim, H. W. H., Chan, C., & Gupta, S. (2007). Value-based adoption of mobile Internet: An empirical investigation. *Decision Support Systems, 43*(1), 111–126. doi:10.1016/j.dss.2005.05.009

Kim, H. W., Gupta, S., & Jeon, Y. S. (2013). User continuance intention towards Mobile Internet service: The case of Wimax in Korea. *Journal of Global Information Management*, *21*(4), 121–142. doi:10.4018/jgim.2013100107

Kimmons, R., & Veletsianos, G. (2014). The fragmented educator: Social networking sites, acceptable identity fragments, and the identity constellation. *Computers & Education*, *72*, 292–301. doi:10.1016/j.compedu.2013.12.001

King, N. (2004a). *Using Interviews in Qualitative Research. In Essential Guide to Qualitative Methods in Organizational Research* (pp. 11–22). London: Sage Publications.

King, N. (2004b). *Using Templates in the Thematic Analysis of Text. In Essential Guide to Qualitative Methods in Organizational Research* (pp. 256–270). London: Sage Publications.

King, N., & Horrocks, C. (2010). *Interviews in Qualitative Research*. London: Sage Publications.

Kirishima, T., Sato, K., & Chihara, K. (2015). Real-time gesture recognition by learning and selective control of visual interest points. *IEEE Transactions on Pattern Analysis and Machine Intelligence*, *27*(3), 351–364. doi:10.1109/TPAMI.2005.61 PMID:15747791

Kirk, G. S. (1970). *Myth: Its Meaning and Functions in Ancient and Other Cultures*. Berkeley, CA: University of California Press.

Kirkpatrick, J. (2006). Protect your business against dangerous information leaks. *Machine design, 78*(3), 66.

Kirkup, G. (2010). Academic blogging: Academic practice and academic identity. *London Review of Education*, *8*(1), 75–84. doi:10.1080/14748460903557803

Kitzinger, J. (1994). The methodology of focus groups: The importance of interactions between research participants. *Sociology of Health & Illness*, *16*(1), 103–121. doi:10.1111/1467-9566.ep11347023

Kjaer, P. F. (2010). The Metamorphosis of the Functional Synthesis: A Continental European Perspective on Governance, Law, and the Political in the Transnational Space. *Wisconsin Law Review*, *2*, 489–1555.

Klapproth, F. (2010). Waiting as a temporal constraint. In J. A. Parker, P. A. Harris & C. Steineck (Eds.), Time: Limits and Constraints (pp. 179-198). Leiden, The Netherlands: Koninklijke Brill NV. doi:10.1163/ej.9789004185753.i-378.70

Kloumann, I. M., Danforth, C. M., Harris, K. D., Bliss, C. A., & Dodds, P. S. (2012). Positivity of the English language. *PLoS ONE*, *7*(1), e29484. doi:10.1371/journal.pone.0029484 PMID:22247779

Koops, B. J., Hildebrandt, M., & Jaquet-Chiffelle, D. O. (2010). Bridging the accountability gap: Rights for new entities in the information society? *Minnesota Journal of Law Science & Technology*, *11*(2), 497–561.

Kortum, P., Peres, S., & Stallmann, K. (2011). Extensible auditory progress bar design: Performance and aesthetics. *International Journal of Human-Computer Interaction*, *27*(9), 864–884. doi:10.1080/10447318.2011.555310

Kozinets, R. V. (2016). Amazonian Forests and Trees: Multiplicity and Objectivity in Studies of Online Consumer-Generated Ratings and Reviews, A Commentary on de Langhe, Fernbach, and Lichtenstein. *The Journal of Consumer Research*, *42*(6), 834–839. doi:10.1093/jcr/ucv090

Kramer, A. (2010). An unobtrusive behavioral model of gross national happiness. In: *Proceedings of the Conference on Human Factors in Computing Systems* (pp. 287–290). Atlanta, GA: ACM. doi:10.1145/1753326.1753369

Krämer, N. C., & Winter, S. (2008). Impression management 2.0. The relationship of self-esteem, extraversion, self-efficacy, and self-presentation within social networking sites. *Journal of Media Psychology*, *20*(3), 106–116. doi:10.1027/1864-1105.20.3.106

Kreijns, K., Vermeulen, M., Kirschner, P. A., van Buuren, H., & van Acker, F. (2013). Adopting the integrative model of behaviour prediction to explain teachers willingness to use ICT: A perspective for research on teachers ict usage in pedagogical practices. *Technology, Pedagogy and Education, 22*(1), 55–71. doi:10.1080/1475939X.2012.754371

Kuczerawy, A., & Coudert, F. (2010, August). Privacy settings in social networking sites: Is it fair? In *IFIP PrimeLife International Summer School on Privacy and Identity Management for Life* (pp. 231–243). Springer Berlin Heidelberg.

Kuno, Y., Shimada, N., & Shirai, Y. (2013). Look where youre going: A robotic wheelchair based on the integration of human and environmental observations. *IEEE Robotics and Automation, 10*(1), 26–34. doi:10.1109/MRA.2003.1191708

Künzler, J. (1987). Grundlagenprobleme der Theorie symbolisch generalisierter Kommunikationsmedien bei Niklas Luhmann. *Zeitschrift für Soziologie, 16*(5), 317–333. doi:10.1515/zfsoz-1987-0501

Künzler, J. (1989). *Medien und Gesellschaft. Die Medienkonzepte von Talcott Parsons, Jürgen Habermas und Niklas Luhmann*. Stuttgart: Enke.

Kuo, Y. C., Walker, A. E., Schroder, K. E. E., & Belland, B. R. (2014). Interaction, internet self-efficacy, and self-regulated learning as predictors of student satisfaction in online education courses. *The Internet and Higher Education, 20*, 35–50. doi:10.1016/j.iheduc.2013.10.001

Kurzweil, R. (2005). *The Singularity is Near*. New York: Penguin Group.

Kuss, D. J., & Griffiths, M. D. (2011). Online social networking and addiction—A review of the psychological literature. *International Journal of Environmental Research and Public Health, 8*(9), 3528–3552. doi:10.3390/ijerph8093528 PMID:22016701

Kuzma, J. (2010). *Global E-government web accessibility: a case study*. Academic Press.

Kuzma, J., Yen, D., & Oestreicher, K. (2009). *Global e-government web accessibility: an empirical examination of EU, Asian and African sites*. Academic Press.

Kuzma, J. (2009). Regulatory compliance and web accessibility of UK parliament sites. *Journal of Information Law & Technology, 2*, 1–15.

Kwon, T. H., & Zmud, R. W. (1987). Unifying the fragmented models of information systems implementation. In R. J. Boland & R. A. Hirschheim (Eds.), *Critical Issues in Information Systems Research*. New York: John Wiley & Sons.

La Barbera, D., La Paglia, F., & Valsavoia, R. (2009). Social network and addiction. *Cyberpsychology & Behavior, 12*, 628–629. PMID:19592725

Lamarre, A., Galarneau, S., & Boeck, H. (2012). Mobile Marketing and Consumer Behavior Current Research Trends. *International Journal of Latest Trends in Computing, 3*(1), 1–9.

LaRose, R., & Rifon, N. J. (2007). Promoting i-safety: Effects of privacy warnings and privacy seals on risk assessment and online privacy behavior. *The Journal of Consumer Affairs, 41*(1), 127–149. doi:10.1111/j.1745-6606.2006.00071.x

Larrington, C. (1999). *The Poetic Edda*. Oxford World's Classics.

Lash, S. (2007). Capitalism and Metaphysics. *Theory, Culture & Society, 24*(5), 1–26. doi:10.1177/0263276407081281

Latour, B. (2004). *Politics of Nature: How to Bring the Sciences Into Democracy*. Cambridge, MA: Harvard University Press.

Lazar, J., Beavan, P., Brown, J., Coffey, D., Nolf, B., Poole, R., & Weber, K. (2010). *Investigating the accessibility of state government web sites in Maryland. In Designing Inclusive Interactions* (pp. 69–78). Springer.

Lee, I., Kim, J., & Kim, J. (2005). Use contexts for the mobile Internet: A longitudinal study monitoring actual use of mobile Internet services. *International Journal of Human-Computer Interaction*, *18*(3), 269–292. doi:10.1207/s15327590ijhc1803_2

Lee, S., Shin, B., & Lee, H. G. (2009). Understanding post-adoption usage of mobile data services: The role of supplier-side variables. *Journal of the Association for Information Systems*, *10*(12), 860–888.

Lee, T. M., & Park, C. (2008). Mobile technology usage and b2b market performance under mandatory adoption. *Industrial Marketing Management*, *37*(7), 833–840. doi:10.1016/j.indmarman.2008.02.008

Lee, Y. H., Hsieh, Y. C., & Hsu, C. N. (2011). Adding innovation diffusion theory to the technology acceptance model: Supporting employees' intentions to use e-learning systems. *Journal of Educational Technology & Society*, *14*(4), 124–137.

Lee, Y., & Benbasat, I. (2003). Interface designs for mobile commerce. *Communications of the ACM*, *46*(12), 49–52. doi:10.1145/606272.606300

Lee, Y., & Kwon, O. (2010). Gender differences in continuance intention of on-line shopping services. *Asia Pacific Journal of Information Systems*, *20*(3), 51–72.

Legin, A., Rudnitskaya, A., Seleznev, B., & Vlasov, Y. (2015). Electronic tongue for quality assessment of ethanol, vodka and eau-de-vie. *Analytica Chimica Acta*, *534*(1), 129–135. doi:10.1016/j.aca.2004.11.027

Legris, P., Ingham, J., & Collerette, P. (2003). Why do people use information technology? A critical review of the technology acceptance model. *Information & Management*, *40*(3), 191–204. doi:10.1016/S0378-7206(01)00143-4

Leitner, M., & Strauss, C. (2008). *Exploratory case study research on web accessibility*. Springer. doi:10.1007/978-3-540-70540-6_70

Leitner, M., Strauss, C., & Stummer, C. (2015). Web accessibility implementation in private sector organizations: Motivations and business impact. *Universal Access in the Information Society*, 1–12.

Lenhart, A., Purcell, K., Smith, A., & Zickuhr, K. (2011). *Social Media and Young Adults*. Pew Internet & American Life Project. Retrieved from the Internet on February 2011 at http://www.pewinternet.org/Reports/2010/Social-Media-and-Young-Adults.aspx

Leung, L., & Wei, R. (2000). More than just talk on the move: Uses and gratifications of cellular phone. *Journalism & Mass Communication Quarterly*, *77*(1), 308–320. doi:10.1177/107769900007700206

Leupold, A. (1983). Liebe und Partnerschaft: Formen der Codierung von Ehen. *Zeitschrift für Soziologie*, *12*(4), 297–327. doi:10.1515/zfsoz-1983-0402

Levy, Y. (2010). The Essence of the Market Army. *Public Administration Review*, *70*(3), 378–389. doi:10.1111/j.1540-6210.2010.02152.x

Lewandowski, S. (2004). *Sexualität in den Zeiten funktionaler Differenzierung. Eine systemtheoretische Analyse*. Bielefeld: Transcript. doi:10.14361/9783839402108

Leydesdorff, L. (2002). The Communication Turn in the Theory of Social Systems. *Systems Research and Behavioral Science*, *19*(2), 129–136. doi:10.1002/sres.453

Liao, C., Palvia, P., & Chen, J.-L. (2009). Information technology adoption life cycle: Toward a technology continuance theory (TCT). *International Journal of Information Management*, *29*(4), 309–320. doi:10.1016/j.ijinfomgt.2009.03.004

Liarte, S. (2013). Image de marque et Internet: Comprendre, éviter et gérer leffet Streisand. *Décisions Marketing*, *69*(69), 103–110. doi:10.7193/dm.069.103.110

Lichy, J. & Kachour, M. (2014). Understanding the culture of young Internet users in a rapidly changing society. *International Journal of Technology and Human Interaction, 10*(4), 1-18.

Lichy, J. (2011). Internet user behaviour in France and Britain: Exploring socio-spatial disparity among adolescents. *International Journal of Consumer Studies, 35*(4), 470–475. doi:10.1111/j.1470-6431.2010.00955.x

Lichy, J. (2012). Towards an International Culture: Gen Y Students and SNS? *Active Learning in Higher Education, 13*(2), 101–116. doi:10.1177/1469787412441289

Lichy, J., & Kachour, M. (2014). Understanding the culture of young internet users in a rapidly changing society. *International Journal of Technology and Human Interaction, 10*(4), 1–17. doi:10.4018/ijthi.2014100101

Lichy, J., & Kachour, M. (2016). Understanding how students interact with technology for knowledge-sharing: The emergence of a new social divide in France. *International Journal of Technology and Human Interaction, 12*(1), 90–112. doi:10.4018/IJTHI.2016010106

Liébana-Cabanillas, F., Ramos de Luna, I., & Montoro-Ríos, F. (2015). User behaviour in QR mobile payment system: The QR Payment Acceptance Model. *Technology Analysis and Strategic Management, 27*(9), 1031–1049. doi:10.1080/09537325.2015.1047757

Limayem, M., Hirt, S. G., & Cheung, C. M. K. (2007). How habit limits the predictive power of intention: The case of information systems continuance. *Management Information Systems Quarterly, 31*(4), 105–137.

Li, N., & Kirkup, G. (2007). Gender and cultural differences in Internet use: A study of China and the UK. *Computers & Education, 48*(2), 301–317. doi:10.1016/j.compedu.2005.01.007

Lin, C. S., Wu, S., & Tsai, R. J. (2005). Integrating perceived playfulness into expectation-confirmation model for Web portal context. *Information & Management, 42*(5), 683–693. doi:10.1016/j.im.2004.04.003

Linder, K., Fontaine-Rainen, D., & Behling, K. (2015). Whose job is it? Key challenges and future directions for online accessibility in US Institutions of Higher Education. *Open Learning: The Journal of Open, Distance and e-Learning*, 1-14.

Lindow, J. (2001). *Norse Mythology: A Guide to the Gods, Heroes, Rituals, and Beliefs*. Oxford, UK: Oxford University Press.

Lin, K. Y., & Lu, H. P. (2011). Why people use social networking sites: An empirical study integrating network externalities and motivation theory. *Computers in Human Behavior, 27*(3), 1152–1161. doi:10.1016/j.chb.2010.12.009

Lin, M. P., Ko, H. C., & Wu, J. Y. W. (2011). Prevalence and psychosocial risk factors associated with internet addiction in a nationally representative sample of college students in Taiwan. *Cyberpsychology, Behavior, and Social Networking, 14*(12), 741–746. doi:10.1089/cyber.2010.0574 PMID:21651418

Li, S., Yen, D., Lu, W., & Lin, T. (2012). Migrating from WCAG 1.0 to WCAG 2.0–A comparative study based on Web Content Accessibility Guidelines in Taiwan. *Computers in Human Behavior, 28*(1), 87–96. doi:10.1016/j.chb.2011.08.014

Liu, H. (2007). Social network profiles as taste performances. *Journal of Computer-Mediated Communication, 13*(1), 252–275. doi:10.1111/j.1083-6101.2007.00395.x

Liu, S., Liao, H., & Pratt, J. (2009). Impact of media richness and flow on e-learning technology acceptance. *Computers & Education, 52*(3), 599–607. doi:10.1016/j.compedu.2008.11.002

Livingstone, S. (2008). Taking risky opportunities in youthful content creation: Teenagers use of social networking sites for intimacy, privacy and self-expression. *New Media & Society, 10*(3), 393–411. doi:10.1177/1461444808089415

Lopes, R., Gomes, D., & Carriço, L. (2010). *Web not for all: a large scale study of web accessibility.* Paper presented at the 2010 International Cross Disciplinary Conference on Web Accessibility (W4A). doi:10.1145/1805986.1806001

Lopes, R., Van Isacker, K., & Carriço, L. (2010). *Redefining assumptions: accessibility and its stakeholders. In Computers Helping People with Special Needs* (pp. 561–568). Springer. doi:10.1007/978-3-642-14097-6_90

López-Nicolás, C., Molina-Castello, F. J., & Bouwman, H. (2008). An assessment of advanced mobile services acceptance: Contributions from TAM and diffusion theory models. *Information & Management, 45*(1), 359–364. doi:10.1016/j.im.2008.05.001

Lorca, P., Andrées, J., & Martínez, A. (2012). Size and culture as determinants of the web policy of listed firms: The case of web accessibility in Western European countries. *Journal of the American Society for Information Science and Technology, 63*(2), 392–405. doi:10.1002/asi.21650

Loroz, P. S., & Helgeson, J. G. (2013). Boomers and Their Babies: An Exploratory Study Comparing Psychological Pro files and Advertising Appeal Effectiveness across Two Generations. *Journal of Marketing Theory and Practice, 21*(3), 289–306. doi:10.2753/MTP1069-6679210304

Luck, E., & Mathews, S. (2010). What Advertisers Need to Know about the iYGeneration: An Australian Perspective. *Journal of Promotion Management, 16*(1-2), 134–147. doi:10.1080/10496490903574559

Lüders, M. (2007). *Being in mediated spaces. An enquiry into personal media practices* (Doctoral Thesis). University of Oslo, Norway.

Lüders, M. (2008). Conceptualizing personal media. *New Media & Society, 10*(5), 683–702. doi:10.1177/1461444808094352

Luhmann, N. (1977). Differentiation of Society. *The Canadian Journal of Sociology / Cahiers canadiens de sociologie, 2*(1), 29-53.

Luhmann, N. (1990). The paradox of system differentiation and the evolution of society. In J. C. Alexander & P. Colomy (Eds.), *Differentiation Theory and Social Change: Comparative and Historical Perspectives.* New York: Columbia UP.

Luhmann, N. (1997a). *Die Gesellschaft der Gesellschaft* (Vols. 1-2). Frankfurt am Main: Suhrkamp.

Luhmann, N. (1997b). Globalization or World society: How to conceive of modern society? *International Review of Sociology, 7*(1), 67–79. doi:10.1080/03906701.1997.9971223

Luhmann, N., & Barrett, R. (2012). *Theory of Society.* Palo Alto, CA: Stanford University Press.

Lu, J., Liu, C., Yu, C.-S., & Wang, K. (2008). Determinants of accepting wireless mobile data services in China. *Information & Management, 45*(1), 52–64. doi:10.1016/j.im.2007.11.002

Lu, J., Yao, J. E., & Yu, C. (2005). Personal innovativeness, social influences and adoption of wireless Internet services via mobile technology. *The Journal of Strategic Information Systems, 14*(3), 245–268. doi:10.1016/j.jsis.2005.07.003

Luo, X., & Liao, Q. (2007). Awareness Education as the key to Ransomware Prevention. *Information Systems Security, 16*(4), 195–202. doi:10.1080/10658980701576412

Maass, O. (2009). *Die Soziale Arbeit als Funktionssystem der Gesellschaft.* Heidelberg, Germany: Carl Auer.

Madden, M., Lenhart, A., Cortesi, S., Gasser, U., Duggan, M., Smith, A., & Beaton, M. (2013). Teens, social media, and privacy. Pew Research Center, 21.

Madra, Y. A., & Adaman, F. (2014). Neoliberal Reason and Its Forms: De-Politicisation Through Economisation. *Antipode, 46*(3), 691–716. doi:10.1111/anti.12065

Maister, D. H. (2005). *The psychology of waiting lines*. Retrieved from www.davidmaister.com

Malbon, J. (2013). Taking Fake Online Consumer Reviews Seriously. *Journal of Consumer Policy*, *36*(2), 139–157. doi:10.1007/s10603-012-9216-7

Mander, J. (2015). *North America lags for smartphone ownership*. Available at http://www.globalwebindex.net/blog/north-america-lags-for-smartphone-ownership

Mankoff, J., Fait, H., & Tran, T. (2005). *Is your web page accessible?: a comparative study of methods for assessing web page accessibility for the blind*. Paper presented at the SIGCHI conference on Human factors in computing systems. doi:10.1145/1054972.1054979

Mannheim, K. (1952). The Problem of Generations. In P. Kecskemeti (Ed.), *Essays on the Sociology of Knowledge* (pp. 276–322). London: Routledge & Kegan Paul.

Manovich, L. (2012). Trending: The Promises and the Challenges of Big Social Data. In M. K. Gold (Ed.), *Debates in the Digital Humanities*. Minneapolis, MN: The University of Minnesota Press. doi:10.5749/minnesota/9780816677948.003.0047

Ma, Q., & Liu, L. (2004). Technology acceptance model: A meta-analysis of empirical findings. *Journal of Organizational and End User Computing*, *60*(1), 59–72. doi:10.4018/joeuc.2004010104

Marcia, H. E. (1980). Identity in adolescence. Handbook of Adolescent Psychology, 9(11), 159-187

Marques, L. F. C., Guilhermino, D. F., de Araújo Cardoso, M. E., da Silva Neitzel, R. A. L., Lopes, L. A., Merlin, J. R., & dos Santos Striquer, G. (2016, July). Accessibility in Virtual Communities of Practice Under the Optics of Inclusion of Visually Impaired. In *International Conference on Universal Access in Human-Computer Interaction* (pp. 14-26). Springer International Publishing. doi:10.1007/978-3-319-40250-5_2

Marshall, C. C., & Shipman, F. M. (2011). Social media ownership: Using twitter as a window onto current attitudes and beliefs. *Proceedings of the Conference on Human Factors in Computing Systems* (pp. 1081–1090). Vancouver: CHI 2011. doi:10.1145/1978942.1979103

Martin, D. (2005). *On Secularization: Towards a Revised General Theory*. Surrey: Ashgate.

Martin, D. (2011). *The Future of Christianity: Reflections on Violence and Democracy, Religion and Secularization*. Surrey: Ashgate.

Martinez, J. (2012). Facebook Unveils Privacy Education Feature for New Users. *Hillicon Valley: The Hill's Technology Blog*. Retrieved from http://thehill.com/policy/technology/265639-facebook-unveils-privacy-education-feature-for-new-users

Martínez, A., De Andrés, J., & García, J. (2014). Determinants of the Web accessibility of European banks. *Information Processing & Management*, *50*(1), 69–86. doi:10.1016/j.ipm.2013.08.001

Martins, D. (2012). *E-réputation marques et sportifs: les JO plus « sociaux » que l'Euro*. Retrieved April 24, 2016, from http://www.synthesio.com/fr/blog/francais-e-reputation-marques-et-sportifs/

Masrek, M. N., & Gaskin, J. E. (2016). Assessing users satisfaction with web digital library: The case of Universiti Teknologi MARA. *The International Journal of Information and Learning Technology*, *33*(1), 36–56. doi:10.1108/IJILT-06-2015-0019

Massari, L. (2010). Analysis of MySpace user profiles. *Information Systems Frontiers*, *12*(4), 361–367. doi:10.1007/s10796-009-9206-8

Mathieson, K. (1991). Predicting user intention: Comparing the TAM with the theory of planned behavior. *Information Systems Research, 2*, 173–191. doi:10.1287/isre.2.3.173

Matzat, U., Snijders, C., & van der Horst, W. (2009). Effects of different types of progress indicators on drop-out rates in web surveys. *Social Psychology, 40*(1), 43–52. doi:10.1027/1864-9335.40.1.43

Mayntz, R. (1988). Funktionelle Teilsysteme in der Theorie sozialer Systeme. In R. Mayntz, B. Rosewitz, & U. Schimank et al. (Eds.), *Differenzierung und Verselbständigung. Zur Entwicklung gesellschaftlicher Teilsysteme*. Frankfurt am Main: Campus.

Mazzoleni, G. (2008). Mediatization of society. In W. Donsbach (Ed.), *The International Encyclopedia of Communication*. Hoboken, NJ: Wiley.

McCowan, I., Gatica-Perez, D., Bengio, S., Lathoud, G., Barnard, M., & Zhang, D. (2015). Automatic analysis of multimodal group actions in meetings. *IEEE Transactions on Pattern Analysis and Machine Intelligence, 27*(3), 305–317. doi:10.1109/TPAMI.2005.49 PMID:15747787

McGuire, W. J., McGuire, C. V., Child, P., & Fujioka, T. (1978). Salience of ethnicity in the spontaneous self-concept as a function of ones ethnic distinctiveness in the social environment. *Journal of Personality and Social Psychology, 36*(5), 511–520. doi:10.1037/0022-3514.36.5.511 PMID:671213

McPherson, M., Smith-Lovin, L., & Cook, J. M. (2001). Birds of a feather: Homophily in social networks. *Annual Review of Sociology, 27*(1), 415–444. doi:10.1146/annurev.soc.27.1.415

Meister, M., Pias, M., Topfer, E., & Coulouris, G. (2008). Application Scenarios for Cooperating Objects and their Social, Legal and Ethical Challenges. In *Adjunct Proceedings of First International Conference on The Internet of Things*.

Mendelson, A., & Papacharissi, Z. (2010). Look at us: Collective narcissism in college student Facebook photo galleries. In Z. Papacharissi (Ed.), *The networked self: Identity, community and culture on social network sites*. Routledge.

Mensch, S., & Wilkie, L. (2011). Information security activities of college students: An exploratory study. *Academy of Information and Management Sciences Journal, 14*(2), 91.

Mezghani, K., & Ayadi, F. (2016). Factors explaining IS managers attitudes toward cloud computing adoption. *International Journal of Technology and Human Interaction, 12*(1), 1–20. doi:10.4018/IJTHI.2016010101

Michel, J.-B., Shen, Y. K., Aiden, A. P., Veres, A., Gray, M. K., Pickett, J. P., & Aiden, E. L. et al. (2011). Quantitative Analysis of Culture Using Millions of Digitized Books. *Science, 331*(6014), 176–182. doi:10.1126/science.1199644 PMID:21163965

Miles, M. B., & Huberman, A. M. (1994). *Qualitative Data Analysis: An Expended Sourcebook*. Thousand Oaks, CA: Sage Publications.

Milicevic, M., Zubrinic, K., & Zakarija, I. (2008). Dynamic approach to the construction of progress indicator for a long running SQL queries. *International Journal of Computers, 4*(2), 489–496.

Miller, S. (2011). *Lessons in social media brand reputation: observing athletes on Twitter*. Retrieved April 24, 2016, from http://www.cision.com/us/2011/06/brand-reputation-social-media/

Milne, S., Sheeran, P., & Orbell, S. (2000). Prediction and intervention in health-related behavior: A meta-analytic review of protection motivation theory. *Journal of Applied Social Psychology, 30*(1), 106–143. doi:10.1111/j.1559-1816.2000.tb02308.x

Miñón, R., Moreno, L., Martínez, P., & Abascal, J. (2014). An approach to the integration of accessibility requirements into a user interface development method. *Science of Computer Programming, 86*, 58–73. doi:10.1016/j.scico.2013.04.005

Miyazaki, A. D., & Fernandez, A. (2001). Consumer perceptions of privacy and security risks for online shopping. *The Journal of Consumer Affairs, 35*(1), 27–44. doi:10.1111/j.1745-6606.2001.tb00101.x

Moon, J. W., & Kim, Y. G. (2001). Extending the TAM for a World-Wide-Web context. *Information & Management, 38*(1), 217–230. doi:10.1016/S0378-7206(00)00061-6

Moon, Y. B. (2012). The Mediatized Co-Mediatizer: Anthropology in Niklas Luhmanns World. *Zygon: Journal of Religion and Science, 47*(2), 438–466. doi:10.1111/j.1467-9744.2012.01264.x

Moore, M. M. (2012). Interactive media usage among millennial consumers. *Journal of Consumer Marketing, 29*(6), 436–444. doi:10.1108/07363761211259241

Moovweb. (2016). *7 Mobile Commerce Trends for 2016*. Available at http://www.moovweb.com/blog/mobile-commerce-trends-2016/

Moran, M., Seaman, J., & Tinti-Kane, H. (2012). *Blogs, wikis, podcasts, and Facebook: How today's higher education faculty use social media*. Boston, MA: Pearson Learning Solutions.

Moses, P., Wong, S. L., Bakar, K. A., & Rosnaini, M. (2013). Perceived usefulness and perceived ease of use: Anteced ents of attitude towards laptop use among science and mathematics teachers in Malaysia. *The Asia-Pacific Education Researcher, 1*(2), Available at: http://link.springer.com/article/10.1007/s40299-012-0054-9

Moynihan, D. P. (2003). Normative and instrumental perspectives on public participation citizen summits in Washington, DC. *American Review of Public Administration, 33*(2), 164–188. doi:10.1177/0275074003251379

Mucchielli, A. (1991). *Les méthodes qualitatives, Que sais-je*. Paris: Presses Universitaires de France.

Mukherjee, A., & Liu, B. (2010). Improving gender classification of blog authors. In: *Proceedings of the Conference on Empirical Methods in natural Language Processing* (pp. 207–217). Association for Computational Linguistics.

Munichor, N., & Rafaeli, A. (2007). Numbers or apologies? Customer reactions to telephone waiting-time fillers. *The Journal of Applied Psychology, 92*(2), 511–518. doi:10.1037/0021-9010.92.2.511 PMID:17371095

Muñoz-Leiva, F., Hernández-Méndez, J., & Sánchez-Fernández, J. (2012). Generalising user behaviour in online travel sites through the Travel 2.0 website acceptance model. *Online Information Review, 36*(6), 879–902. doi:10.1108/14684521211287945

Murphy, H. C., Chen, M.-M., & Cossutta, M. (2016). An investigation of multiple devices and information sources used in the hotel booking process. *Tourism Management, 52*, 44–51. doi:10.1016/j.tourman.2015.06.004

Murtaza, N. (2012). Putting the Lasts First. *The Case for Community-Focused and Peer-Managed NGO Accountability Mechanisms, 23*, 109–125.

Musick, D. W. (1999). Teaching medical ethics: A review of the literature from North American medical schools with emphasis on education. *Medicine, Health Care, and Philosophy, 2*(3), 239–254. doi:10.1023/A:1009985413669 PMID:11080991

Myers, B. A. (2008). A brief history of human-computer interaction technology. *Interactions (New York, N.Y.), 5*(2), 44–54. doi:10.1145/274430.274436

Myers, M. D. (1997, June). Qualitative Research in Information Systems. *Management Information Systems Quarterly, 21*(2), 241–242. doi:10.2307/249422

Nadkarni, A., & Hofmann, S. G. (2012). Why do people use Facebook? *Personality and Individual Differences*, *52*(3), 243–249. doi:10.1016/j.paid.2011.11.007 PMID:22544987

Neter, J., Wasserman, W., & Kutner, M. H. (1990). *Applied linear regression models*. Homewood, IL: Academic Press.

Newman, M., Groom, C., Handelman, L., & Pennebaker, J. (2008). Gender differences in language use: An analysis of 14,000 text samples. *Discourse Processes*, *45*(3), 211–236. doi:10.1080/01638530802073712

Ngai, E. W. T., & Gunasekaran, A. (2007). A review for mobile commerce research and applications. *Decision Support Systems*, *43*(1), 3–15. doi:10.1016/j.dss.2005.05.003

Nielsen, J., & Loranger, H. (2006). *Web usability*. New Riders.

Nietzio, A., Olsen, M., Eibegger, M., & Snaprud, M. (2010). *Accessibility of eGovernment web sites: towards a collaborative retrofitting approach*. In *Computers Helping People with Special Needs* (pp. 468–475). Springer. doi:10.1007/978-3-642-14097-6_75

Noh, K., Jeong, E., You, Y., Moon, S., & Kang, M. (2015). A study on the current status and strategies for improvement of web accessibility compliance of public institutions. *Journal of Open Innovation: Technology, Market, and Complexity*, *1*(1), 1–17. doi:10.1186/s40852-015-0001-0

Norberg, P. A., Horne, D. R., & Horne, D. A. (2007). The privacy paradox: Personal information disclosure intentions versus behaviors. *The Journal of Consumer Affairs*, *41*(1), 100–126. doi:10.1111/j.1745-6606.2006.00070.x

Norton, S. (2015). *Forrester: Mobile Phone and Tablet E-Commerce to More Than Double by 2018*. Available at Wall Street Journal online edition: http://blogs.wsj.com/cio/2014/05/12/forrester-mobile-phone-and-tablet-e-commerce-to-more-than-double-by-2018/

Nosko, A., Wood, E., & Molema, S. (2010). All about me: Disclosure in online social networking profiles: The case of FACEBOOK. *Computers in Human Behavior*, *26*(3), 406–418. doi:10.1016/j.chb.2009.11.012

Nowson, S., Oberlander, J., & Gill, A. J. (2005). Weblogs, genres and individual differences. In B. G. Bara, L. Barsalou, & M. Bucciarelli (eds.) *Proceedings of the 27th Annual Conference of the Cognitive Science Society*, (pp. 1666–1671). Lawrence Erlbaum Associates.

Nunnally, J. C. (1978). *Psychometric Theory*. New York: McGraw-Hill.

Nwagwu, E. W., Adekannbi, J., & Bello, O. (2009). Factors influencing use of the internet. *The Electronic Library*, *27*(4), 718–734. doi:10.1108/02640470910979651

Nysveen, H., Pedersen, P. E., & Thorbjornsen, H. (2005a). Explaining the intention to use mobile chat services: Moderating effects of gender. *Journal of Consumer Marketing*, *22*(5), 247–256. doi:10.1108/07363760510611671

Nysveen, H., Pedersen, P. E., & Thorbjornsen, H. (2005b). Intentions to use mobile services: Antecedents and cross-service comparisons. *Journal of the Academy of Marketing Science*, *33*(3), 330–346. doi:10.1177/0092070305276149

Odom, W., Sellen, A., Harper, R., & Thereska, E. (2012). Lost in translation: Understanding the possession of digital things in the Cloud. In *Proceedings of the Conference on Human Factors in Computing Systems* (pp. 781–790). Austin, TX: ACM. doi:10.1145/2207676.2207789

ODwyer, B., & Unerman, J. (2007). From functional to social accountability: Transforming the accountability relationship between funders and non governmental development organisations. *Accounting, Auditing & Accountability Journal*, *20*(3), 446–471. doi:10.1108/09513570710748580

ODwyer, B., & Unerman, J. (2010). Enhancing the role of accountability in promoting the rights of beneficiaries of development NGOs. *Accounting and Business Review*, *40*(5), 451–471. doi:10.1080/00014788.2010.9995323

Oghuma, A. P., Chang, Y., Libaque-Saenz, C. F., Park, M. C., & Rho, J. J. (2015). Benefit confirmation model for post-adoption behavior of mobile instant messaging applications: A comparative analysis of KakaoTalk and Joyn in Korea. *Telecommunications Policy*, *39*(8), 658–677. doi:10.1016/j.telpol.2015.07.009

Oh, L., & Chen, J. (2014). Determinants of employees intention to exert pressure on firms to engage in web accessibility. *Behaviour & Information Technology*, *34*(2), 108–118. doi:10.1080/0144929X.2014.936040

Ohtsubo, M., & Yoshida, K. (2014). How does shape of progress bar effect time evaluation. *IEEE 2014 International Conference on Intelligent Networking and Collaborative Systems*. Salerno, Italy: University of Salerno. doi:10.1109/INCoS.2014.85

OKeeffe, G. S., & Clarke-Pearson, K. (2011). The impact of social media on children, adolescents, and families. *Pediatrics*, *127*(4), 800–804. doi:10.1542/peds.2011-0054 PMID:21444588

Okenyi, P. O., & Owens, T. J. (2007). On the anatomy of human hacking. *Information Systems Security*, *16*(6), 302–314. doi:10.1080/10658980701747237

Ong, C. S., & Lai, J. Y. (2006). Gender differences in perceptions and relationships among dominants of E-Learning acceptance. *Computers in Human Behavior*, *22*(5), 816–829. doi:10.1016/j.chb.2004.03.006

Ono, H., & Zavodny, M. (2005). Gender differences in information technology usage: A U.S.-Japan comparison. *Sociological Perspectives*, *48*(1), 105–133. doi:10.1525/sop.2005.48.1.105

ONU. (2008). *World Population Prospects: The 2008 Revision*. Retrieved 15/11/2015, 2015, from http://www.un.org/esa/population/publications/wpp2008/wpp2008_highlights.pdf

Ophir, S. (2010). A New Type of Historical Knowledge. *The Information Society*, *26*(2), 144–150. doi:10.1080/01972240903562811

Orwell, G. (1949). *Nineteen Eighty-Four. A novel*. New York: Harcourt, Brace & Co.

Ory, W. (2009). *La réputation de l'entreprise ne se limite pas à Internet*. Retrieved April 24, 2016, from http://www.marketing-professionnel.fr/outil-marketing/reputation-entreprise-depasse-internet-perception-globale-marque.html

Oshkalo, A. (2014). *Odnoklassniki.ru rebrands into OK*. Retrieved July 11, 2014, from http://www.russiansearchtips.com/category/social-media-in-russia/

Oudeyer, P. Y. (2013). The production and recognition of emotions in speech: Features and algorithms. *International Journal of Human-Computer Studies*, *59*(1-2), 157–183.

Oviatt, S. L., Cohen, P., Wu, L., Vergo, J., Duncan, L., Suhm, B., & Ferro, D. et al. (2010). Designing the user interface for multimodal speech and pen-based gesture applications: State-of-the-art systems and future research directions. *Human-Computer Interaction*, *15*(4), 263–322. doi:10.1207/S15327051HCI1504_1

Page, R. I. (1990). Norse Myths (The Legendary Past). London: British Museum & Austin: University of Texas Press.

Pantic, M., & Rothkrantz, L. J. M. (2010). Automatic analysis of facial expressions: The state of the art. *IEEE Transactions on Pattern Analysis and Machine Intelligence*, *22*(12), 1424–1445. doi:10.1109/34.895976

Papacharissi, Z. (2009). The virtual geographies of social networks: A comparative analysis of Facebook, LinkedIn and ASmallWorld. *New Media & Society*, *11*(1-2), 199–220. doi:10.1177/1461444808099577

Paquerot, M., Queffelec, A., Sueur, I., & Biot-Paquerot, G. (2011). L'e-réputation ou le renforcement de la gouvernance par le marché de l'hôtellerie? *Management & Avenir*, (5), 280-296.

Pascual, A., Ribera, M., Granollers, T., & Coiduras, J. (2014). Impact of Accessibility Barriers on the Mood of Blind, Low-vision and Sighted Users. *Procedia Computer Science*, *27*(0), 431–440. doi:10.1016/j.procs.2014.02.047

Patil, S., Norcie, G., Kapadia, A., & Lee, A. (2012). Check out where I am! Location-sharing motivations, preferences, and practices. In *Proceedings of Conference on Human Factors in Computing Systems*(pp. 1997-2002). Austin, TX: ACM.

Paul, C., Komlodi, A., & Lutters, W. (2015). Interruptive notifications in support of task management. *International Journal of Human-Computer Studies*, *79*, 20–34. doi:10.1016/j.ijhcs.2015.02.001

Pearce, K. E., & Kendzior, S. (2012). Networked authoritarianism and social media in Azerbaijan. *Journal of Communication*, *62*(2), 283–298. doi:10.1111/j.1460-2466.2012.01633.x

Pearson, I. (2016). *Dr. Ian Pearson interview*. Retrieved from www.dailymail.co.uk

Peesapati, S. T., Schwanda, V., Schultz, J., Lepage, M., Jeong, S., & Cosley, D. (2010). Supporting everyday reminiscence. In *Proceedings of Conference on Human Factors in Computing Systems* (pp. 2027–2036). Atlanta, GA: ACM.

Peevers, G., McInnes, F., Morton, H., Matthews, A., & Jack, M. (2009). The mediating effects of brand music and waiting-time updates on customers satisfaction with a telephone service when put on-hold. *International Journal of Bank Marketing*, *27*(3), 202–217. doi:10.1108/02652320910950196

Pelet, J.-É., Khan, J., Papadopoulou, P., & Bernardin, E. (2014). *Determinants of effective learning through social networks systems: an exploratory study. In Higher Education in the MENA Region: Policy and Practice*. IGI Global.

Penders, B., Verbakel, J. M. A., & Nelis, A. (2009). The Social Study of Corporate Science: A Research Manifesto. *Bulletin of Science, Technology & Society*, *29*(6), 439–446. doi:10.1177/0270467609349047

Penrose, R. (1989). *The Emperor's New Mind: Concerning Computers, Minds and The Laws of Physics*. Oxford University Press.

Perrin, A. (2015). *Social networking usage: 2005-2015*. Pew Research Center. Retrieved April 24, 2016 from http://www.pewinternet.org/2015/10/08/2015/Social-Networking-Usage-2005-2015/

Phinney, J. S. (1990). Ethnic identity in adolescence and adulthood: A review of research. *Psychological Bulletin*, *108*(3), 499–514. doi:10.1037/0033-2909.108.3.499 PMID:2270238

Pinkerton, M. (2015, May 5). *How to Make a Facebook Page Secure*. Retrieved from https://youtu.be/sWPV7DPWxzY

Polanyi, K. (1957). *The great transformation*. New York: Beacon Press.

Polites, G. L., & Karahanna, E. (2012). Shackled to the status quo: The inhibiting effects on incumbent system habit, switching costs, and inertia on new system acceptance. *Management Information Systems Quarterly*, *36*(1), 21–42.

Power, C., Freire, A., Petrie, H., & Swallow, D. (2012). *Guidelines are only half of the story: accessibility problems encountered by blind users on the web*. Paper presented at the SIGCHI conference on human factors in computing systems. doi:10.1145/2207676.2207736

Pratt, J. A., Hauser, K., Ugray, Z., & Patterson, O. (2007). Looking at human–computer interface design: Effects of ethnicity in computer agents. *Interacting with Computers*, *19*(4), 512–523. doi:10.1016/j.intcom.2007.02.003

Prensky, M. (2001). Digital natives, digital immigrants. *NCB University Press*, *9*(5), 1–6.

PricewaterhouseCoopers. (2011). *Changing the game. Outlook for the global sports market to 2015*. Author.

PricewaterhouseCoopers. (2014). *Consommateurs connectés. La distribution à l'ère digitale. 4ème étude mondiale sur les web-acheteurs.* Author.

PricewaterhouseCoopers. (2016). *Global total retail survey. They say they want a revolution.* Author.

Pujol, J. (2014). *Generation Y prefer the malls to shop online.* Retrieved August 15, 2014, from http://pro.01net.com/editorial/622412/la-generation-y-prefere-les-centres-business-to-e-purchases

Putnam, C., Wozniak, K., Zefeldt, M., Cheng, J., Caputo, M., & Duffield, C. (2012). *How do professionals who create computing technologies consider accessibility?* Paper presented at the 14th international ACM SIGACCESS conference on Computers and accessibility. doi:10.1145/2384916.2384932

Quarterly, M. E. (2016). *Ecommerce Quarterly, Q4.* Available at monetate.com/research/

Ramsey, G., & Venkatesan, S. (2010). Cybercrime strategy for social networking and other online platforms. *Licensing Journal, 30*(7), 23–27.

Ranganathan, C., Seo, D., & Babad, Y. (2006). Switching behavior of mobile users: Do users relational investments and demographics matter? *European Journal of Information Systems, 15*(3), 269–276. doi:10.1057/palgrave.ejis.3000616

Rao, D., Yarowsky, D., Shreevats, A., & Gupta, M. (2010). Classifying latent user attributes in Twitter. In *Proceedings of the 2nd International Workshop on Search and Mining User-Generated Contents* (pp. 37-44). New York: ACM. doi:10.1145/1871985.1871993

Raskin, R., & Terry, H. (1988). A principal-components analysis of the Narcissistic Personality Inventory and further evidence of its construct validity. *Journal of Personality and Social Psychology, 54*(5), 890–902. doi:10.1037/0022-3514.54.5.890 PMID:3379585

Raufi, B., Ferati, M., Zenuni, X., Ajdari, J., & Ismaili, F. (2015). Methods and Techniques of Adaptive Web Accessibility for the Blind and Visually Impaired. *Procedia: Social and Behavioral Sciences, 195*, 1999–2007. doi:10.1016/j.sbspro.2015.06.214

Rau, P., Zhou, L., Sun, N., & Zhong, R. (2014). Evaluation of web accessibility in China: Changes from 2009 to 2013. *Universal Access in the Information Society*, 1–7.

RecoverReputation. (2016). *Who Should Manage Your Online Reputation For Athletes, Tennis Players.* Retrieved April 24, 2016, from http://www.recoverreputation.com/who-should-manage-your-online-reputation-for-athletes-tennis-players/

Reese-Schäfer, W. (1999). *Luhmann zur Einführung.* Hamburg: Junius.

Reese-Schäfer, W. (2005). *Die Moral der Gesellschaft: Paradigm Lost.* Hamburg: Junius.

Reese-Schäfer, W. (2007). *Politisches Denken heute: Zivilgesellschaft, Globalisierung und Menschenrechte.* München: Oldenbourg. doi:10.1524/9783486711288

Regan, P. M. (1994). *Organizing Societies for War: The Processes and Consequences of Societal Militarization.* Westport, CT: Prager.

Reid, L.G., Vanderheiden, G., Cooper, M., & Caldwell, B. (2008). *Web Content Accessibility Guidelines (WCAG) 2.0.* W3C.

Reisz, S. (2005). Knowledge and Vigilance: Key Ingredients to Information Security. *Catalyst*, 18-23.

Restrepo, E., Benavidez, C., & Gutiérrez, H. (2012). The Challenge of Teaching to Create Accessible Learning Objects to Higher Education Lecturers. *Procedia Computer Science, 14*, 371–381. doi:10.1016/j.procs.2012.10.043

Rezgui, Y., & Marks, A. (2008). Information security awareness in higher education: An exploratory study. *Computers & Security*, *27*(7), 241–253. doi:10.1016/j.cose.2008.07.008

Ringlaben, R., Bray, M., & Packard, A. (2014). Accessibility of American University Special Education Departments Web sites. *Universal Access in the Information Society*, *13*(2), 249–254. doi:10.1007/s10209-013-0302-7

Risse, T. (2003). The Euro between national and European identity. *Journal of European Public Policy*, *10*(4), 487–505. doi:10.1080/1350176032000101235

Riva, G., Vatalaro, F., Davide, F., & Alaniz, M. (2015). *Ambient Intelligence: The Evolution of Technology, Communication and Cognition towards the Future of HCI*. Fairfax: IOS Press.

Roberts, J., Crittenden, L., & Crittenden, J. (2011). Students with disabilities and online learning: A cross-institutional study of perceived satisfaction with accessibility compliance and services. *The Internet and Higher Education*, *14*(4), 242–250. doi:10.1016/j.iheduc.2011.05.004

Robertson, R. (1992). The Economization of Religion? Reflections on the Promise and Limitations of the Economic Approach. *Social Compass*, *39*(1), 147–157. doi:10.1177/003776892039001014

Robinson, L. (2007). The cyberself: The self-ing project goes online, symbolic interaction in the digital age. *New Media & Society*, *9*(1), 93–110. doi:10.1177/1461444807072216

Rocha de Oliveira, P. (2009). The Aestheticization of Reality. *The South Atlantic Quarterly*, *108*(2), 265–284. doi:10.1215/00382876-2008-033

Rocha, T., Bessa, M., Gonçalves, R., Peres, E., & Magalhães, L. (2012). Web Accessibility and Digital Businesses: The Potential Economic Value of Portuguese People with Disability. *Procedia Computer Science*, *14*, 56–64. doi:10.1016/j.procs.2012.10.007

Rogers, C. (1951). *Client centered therapy*. Boston: Houghton Mifflin.

Ropars, F. (2016). Blog du Modérateur [online] 11 février. Retrieved March 24, 2016, from http://www.blogdumoderateur.com/usage-reseaux-sociaux-11-18-ans/

Roth, S. and Kaivo-oja, J. (in press). Is the future a political economy? Functional analysis of three leading foresight and futures studies journals. *Futures*.

Roth, S. (2014a). Fashionable functions. A Google ngram view of trends in functional differentiation (18002000). *International Journal of Technology and Human Interaction*, *10*(2), 34–58. doi:10.4018/ijthi.2014040103

Roth, S. (2014b). The multifunctional organization: Two cases for a critical update for research programs in management and organization. *Tamara Journal for Critical Organization Inquiry*, *12*(3), 37–54.

Roth, S. (2015a). Foreword: Trends in functional differentiation. *Cybernetics & Human Knowing*, *22*(4), 5–10.

Roth, S. (2015b). Free economy! On 3628800 alternatives of and to capitalism. *Journal of Interdisciplinary Economics*, *27*(2), 107–128. doi:10.1177/0260107915583389

Roth, S. (in press). Growth and function. A viral research program for next organisations[forthcoming]. *International Journal of Technology Management*.

Roth, S., Scheiber, L., & Wetzel, R. (2010). *Organisation multimedial: Zum polyphonen Programm der nächsten Organisation*. Heidelberg, Germany: Carl Auer.

Roth, S., & Schütz, A. (2015). Ten systems. Toward a canon of function systems. *Cybernetics & Human Knowing*, *22*(4), 11–31.

Rothschild, P. C. (2011). Social media use in sports and entertainment venues. *International Journal of Event and Festival Management*, *2*(2), 139–150. doi:10.1108/17582951111136568

Rowatt, W. C., Cunningham, M. R., & Druen, P. B. (1998). Deception to get a date. *Personality and Social Psychology Bulletin*, *24*(11), 1228–1242. doi:10.1177/01461672982411009

Rubin, P., Vatikiotis-Bateson, E., & Benoit, C. (2008). Special issue on audio-visual speech processing. *Speech Communication*, *26*, 1–2. doi:10.1016/S0167-6393(98)00046-6

Russian Internet Forum. (2012). *Российский Интернет Форум. Выходные данные. Дизайн и разработка - Internet Media Holding.* Retrieved November 06, 2012, from http://2012.russianinternetforum.ru/get/40074/876/

Sage, K. D., & Baldwin, D. (2015). Childrens Use of Self-Paced Slideshows: An Extension of the Video Deficit Effect? *Journal of Research in Childhood Education*, *29*(1), 90–114. doi:10.1080/02568543.2014.978919

Samuel, P. (1992). Accountability in public services: Exit, voice and control. *World Development*, *20*(7), 1047–1060. doi:10.1016/0305-750X(92)90130-N

Sánchez-Gordón, M., & Moreno, L. (2014). Toward an integration of Web accessibility into testing processes. *Procedia Computer Science*, *27*, 281–291. doi:10.1016/j.procs.2014.02.031

Sanderson, J. (2011). To tweet or not to tweet: Exploring Division I athletic departments social-media policies. *International Journal of Sport Communication*, *4*(4), 492–513. doi:10.1123/ijsc.4.4.492

Santarosa, L., Conforto, D., & Neves, B. (2015). Teacher Education and Accessibility on E-Learning System: Putting the W3C Guidelines into Practice. *Teaching Education*, *4*(01).

Sareah, F. (2015). *Interesting Statistics for the Top 10 Social Media Sites.* Retrieved March 17, 2015 from http://smallbiztrends.com/2015/07/social-media-sites-statistics.html

Sarraf, S., & Tukibayeva, M. (2014). Survey page length and progress indicators: What are their relationships to item nonresponse? *New directions for institutional research, 161*, 83–97. Retrieved from http://wileyonlinelibrary.com

Sarrel, M. (2010). Stay Safe, Productive on Social Networks. *eWeek*.

Sayago, S., & Blat, J. (2009). *About the relevance of accessibility barriers in the everyday interactions of older people with the web.* Paper presented at the 2009 International Cross-Disciplinary Conference on Web Accessibililty (W4A). doi:10.1145/1535654.1535682

Sayer, A. (1999). Valuing culture and economy. In L. Ray & A. Sayer (Eds.), *Culture and economy after the cultural turn*. London: Sage. doi:10.4135/9781446218112.n3

Scarlat, C. (2015). *Cartea cu proverbe de management / The Book with Management Proverbs.* Bucharest, Romania: Ed. Printech.

Schacter, D. L., Norman, K. A., & Koutstaal, W. (1998). The cognitive neuroscience of constructive memory. *Annual Review of Psychology*, *49*(1), 289–318. doi:10.1146/annurev.psych.49.1.289 PMID:9496626

Schepers, J., & Wetzels, M. (2007). A meta-analysis of the technology acceptance model: Investigating subjective norm and moderation effects. *Information & Management*, *44*(1), 90–103. doi:10.1016/j.im.2006.10.007

Scherr, A. (2001). Soziale Arbeit als organisierte Hilfe. In V. Tacke (Ed.), *Organisation und gesellschaftliche Differenzierung*. Opladen: Westdeutscher Verlag. doi:10.1007/978-3-322-80373-3_10

Schimank, U., & Volkmann, U. (2008). Ökonomisierung der Gesellschaft. In A. Maurer (Ed.), *Handbuch der Wirtschaftssoziologie*. Wiesbaden: VS. doi:10.1007/978-3-531-90905-9_19

Schler, J., Koppel, M., Argamon, S., & Pennebaker, J. W. (2006). Effects of age and gender on blogging. In *Proceedings of AAAI Spring Symposium on Computational Approaches for Analyzing Weblogs* (pp.199–205). AAAI.

Schmalz, D. L., Colistra, C. M., & Evans, K. E. (2015). Social media sites as a means of coping with a threatened social identity. *Leisure Sciences: An Interdisciplinary Journal*, *37*(1), 20–38. doi:10.1080/01490400.2014.935835

Schmidt, C. (1993). On Economization and Ecologization as Civilizing Processes. *Environmental Values*, *2*(1), 33–46. doi:10.3197/096327193776679963

Schoeman, F. D. (1984). *Philosophical dimensions of privacy: An anthology*. Cambridge University Press. doi:10.1017/CBO9780511625138

Schulz, W. (2004). Reconstructing mediatization as an analytical concept. *European Journal of Communication*, *19*(1), 87–101. doi:10.1177/0267323104040696

Schunk, D. H. (1991). *Learning theories: An educational perspective*. New York: McMillan Publishing Company.

Schwartz, H. A., Eichstaedt, J. C., Kern, M. L., Dziurzynski, L., Ramones, S. M., Agrawal, M., & Ungar, L. H. et al. (2013). Personality, gender, and age in the language of social media: The open-vocabulary approach. *PLoS ONE*, *8*(9), e73791. doi:10.1371/journal.pone.0073791 PMID:24086296

Schwartz, R., & Halegoua, R. G. (2014). The spatial self: Location-based identity performance on social media. *New Media & Society*, *17*(10), 1643–1660. doi:10.1177/1461444814531364

Schwelger, R. (2008). *Moralisches Handeln von Unternehmen. Eine Weiterentwicklung des Modells und des Ansatzes der Ökonomischen Ethik auf Basis der neuen Systemtheorie und Institutionenökonomik*. Wiesbaden: Gabler.

Seale, J. (2013). *E-learning and disability in higher education: accessibility research and practice*. Routledge.

Seale, J., & Cooper, M. (2010). E-learning and accessibility: An exploration of the potential role of generic pedagogical tools. *Computers & Education*, *54*(4), 1107–1116. doi:10.1016/j.compedu.2009.10.017

Sealey, F., & Harrington, L. (2006). *Telomere DNA Replication, Telomerase and Human Disease*. Department of Medical Biophysics, University of Toronto.

Selwyn, N., & Stirling, E. (2016). Social media and education ... now the dust has settled. *Learning, Media and Technology*, *41*(1), 1–5. doi:10.1080/17439884.2015.1115769

Sen, A., & Mendes, R. (2000). *Desenvolvimento como liberdade*. São Paulo: Companhia das Letras.

Serra, L., Carvalho, L., Ferreira, L., Vaz, J., & Freire, A. (2015). Accessibility Evaluation of E-Government Mobile Applications in Brazil. *Procedia Computer Science*, *67*, 348–357. doi:10.1016/j.procs.2015.09.279

Severino, S., & Craparo, G. (2013). Internet addiction, attachment styles, and social self-efficacy. *Global Journal of Psychology Research*, *1*, 9–16.

Shah, B. P., & Shakya, S. (2007). Evaluating the web accessibility of websites of the central government of Nepal. ACM Press. doi:10.1145/1328057.1328154

Shamdasani, P., Mukherjee, A., & Malhotra, N. (2008). Antecedents and consequences of service quality in consumer evaluation of selt-service internet technology. *Service Industries Journal*, *28*(1), 117–138. doi:10.1080/02642060701725669

Shantharam, Sh. (2009). *Synthetic Biology. A New Paradigm in the Biotechnology Revolution.* Foundation for Biotechnology Awareness and Education.

Shaw, J. (2009). The Erosion of Privacy in the Internet Era. *Harvard Magazine*, 38–43.

Shekhawat, D., & Rathore, P. S. (2014). Internet usage in college: A comparison of users and non users in relation to self-esteem and satisfaction with life. *Indian Journal of Positive Psychology*, *5*(2), 216–222.

Shenton, Z. (2015). *David Beckham reveals he has full control over son Brooklyn's social media accounts.* Retrieved April 24, 2016, from http://www.mirror.co.uk/3am/celebrity-news/david-beckham-reveals-full-control-6472971

Shirow, M. (1991). *Ghost in The Shell.* Academic Press.

Shittu, A. T., Basha, K. M., Rahman, N. S. N. A., & Ahmad, T. B. T. (2011). Investigating students attitude and intention to use social software in higher institution of learning in Malaysia. *Multicultural Education & Technology Journal*, *5*(3), 194–208. doi:10.1108/17504971111166929

Shneiderman, B., Plaisant, C., Cohen, M., & Jacobs, S. (2009). *Designing the user interface: Strategies for effective human-computer interaction* (5th ed.). Upper Saddle River, NJ: Prentice Hall.

Shroff, R. H., Deneen, C. D., & Ng, E. M. W. (2011). Analysis of the technology acceptance model in examining students behavioural intention to use an e-portfolio system. *Australasian Journal of Educational Technology*, *27*(4), 600–618. doi:10.14742/ajet.940

Siano, A., Vollero, A., & Palazzo, M. (2011). Exploring the role of online consumer empowerment in reputation building: Research questions and hypotheses. *Journal of Brand Management*, *19*(1), 57–71. doi:10.1057/bm.2011.23

Simon, B. (2004). *Identity in modern society. A social psychological perspective.* Oxford, UK: Blackwell.

Simonson, I. (2015). Mission (Largely) Accomplished: Whats Next for Consumer BDT-JDM Researchers. *Journal of Marketing Behavior*, *1*(1), 9–35. doi:10.1561/107.00000001

Simsa, R. (2001). *Gesellschaftliche Funktionen und Einflussformen von Nonprofit-Organisationen.* Bern: Peter Lang.

Siponen, M. T. (2000). A conceptual foundation for organizational information security awareness. *Information Management & Computer Security*, *8*(1), 31–41. doi:10.1108/09685220010371394

Smart, B. (2003). An Economic Turn. *Journal of Classical Sociology*, *3*(1), 47–66. doi:10.1177/1468795X03003001694

Smith, A. (2015). U.*S. Smartphone Use in 2015.* PewResearchCenter. Available at http://www.pewinternet.org/2015/04/01/us-smartphone-use-in-2015/

Smith, B. (2014). *The instant messaging shootout: BBM, WhatsApp, Line, WeChat and Viber.* Retrieved August 17, 2014, from http://gearburn.com/2014/03/the-instant-messaging-shootout-bbm-whatsapp-line-wechat-and-viber/

Smith, C. (2015). The surprising facts about who shops online and on mobile. *Business Insider.* Available at http://www.businessinsider.com/the-surprising-demographics-of-who-shops-online-and-on-mobile-2014-6

Smith, H. J. (1993). Privacy policies and practices: Inside the organizational maze. *Communications of the ACM*, *36*(12), 104–122. doi:10.1145/163298.163349

Smith, K., Mendez, F., & White, G. L. (2014). Narcissism as a predictor of Facebook users privacy concern, vigilance, and exposure to risk. *International Journal of Technology and Human Interaction*, *10*(2), 78–95. doi:10.4018/ijthi.2014040105

Smith, P., Shah, M., & Lobo, N. D. V. (2013). Determining driver visual attention with one camera. *IEEE Transactions on Intelligent Transportation Systems*, *4*(4), 205–218. doi:10.1109/TITS.2003.821342

Smyrnaios, N. (2011). *Social networks: reflection of cultural differences?*. Retrieved December 17, 2012 from http://www.inaglobal.fr/numerique/article/les-reseaux-sociaux-reflet-des-differences-culturelles#intertitre-8

Snead, J. T. (2013). Social media use in the U.S. Executive branch. *Government Information Quarterly*, *30*(1), 56–63. doi:10.1016/j.giq.2012.09.001

Sobel, M. E. (1982). Asymptotic confidence intervals for indirect effects in structural equation models. *Sociological Methodology*, *13*, 290–312. doi:10.2307/270723

Sobkowicz, P. (2013). Quantitative Agent Based Model of User Behavior in an Internet Discussion Forum. *PLoS ONE*, *8*(12), e80524. doi:10.1371/journal.pone.0080524 PMID:24324606

Socialbakers. (2016). *David Beckham Facebook statistics*. Retrieved April 20, 2016, from http://www.socialbakers.com/statistics/facebook/pages/detail/84218631570-david-beckham

Soman, D., & Shi, M. (2003). Virtual progress: The effect of path characteristics on perceptions of progress and choice. *Management Science*, *49*(9), 1229–1250. doi:10.1287/mnsc.49.9.1229.16574

Song, C., & Lee, J. (2016). Citizens' Use of Social Media in Government, Perceived Transparency, and Trust in Government. *Public Performance & Management Review, 39*(2).

Spence, P. R., Lachlan, K. A., Spates, S. A., & Lin, X. (2013). Intercultural differences in responses to health messages on social media from spokespeople with varying levels of ethnic identity. *Computers in Human Behavior*, *29*(3), 1255–1259. doi:10.1016/j.chb.2012.12.013

Sponcil, M., & Gitimu, P. (2013). Use of social media by college students: Relationship to communication and self-concept. *Journal of Technology Research*, *4*, 1–13.

Spring, J. (2015). *The Economization of Education: Human Capital, Global Corporations, and Skills-Based Schooling*. New York: Routledge.

Statista. (2015). *U.S. mobile retail commerce revenue 2013-2019, by device*. Available at http://www.statista.com/statistics/249894/mobile-retail-commerce-revenue-in-the-united-states-by-device/

Statista. (2016a). *Leading social networks worldwide as of April 2016, ranked by number of active users (in millions)*. Retrieved April 20, 2016, from http://www.statista.com/statistics/272014/global-social-networks-ranked-by-number-of-users/

Statista. (2016a). *Statistics and facts about mobile social networks*. Available at http://www.statista.com/topics/2478/mobile-social-networks/

Statista. (2016b). *Distribution of time spent on social media content in the United States as of December 2015, by platform*. Available at http://www.statista.com/statistics/444986/social-content-platform-time-usa/

Statista. (2016b). *Most viewed YouTube channels worldwide as of March 2016, by monthly views (in millions)*. Retrieved April 20, 2016, from http://www.statista.com/statistics/373729/most-viewed-youtube-channels/

Statista. (2016c). *Most popular Facebook fan pages as of April 2016, based on number of fans (in millions)*. Retrieved April 20, 2016, from http://www.statista.com/statistics/269304/international-brands-on-facebook-by-number-of-fans/

Steel, E., & Vascellaro, J. E. (2010). Facebook, MySpace confront privacy loophole. *The Wall Street Journal, 21*.

Stehr, N. (2002). *Knowledge and Economic Conduct: The Social Foundations of the Modern Economy.* Toronto: University of Toronto Press. doi:10.3138/9781442676527

Stern, S. R. (2004). Expressions of identity online: Prominent features and gender differences in adolescents World Wide Web home pages. *Journal of Broadcasting & Electronic Media, 48*(2), 218–243. doi:10.1207/s15506878jobem4802_4

Stewart, K. A., & Segars, A. H. (2002). An empirical examination of the concern for information privacy instrument. *Information Systems Research, 13*(1), 36–49. doi:10.1287/isre.13.1.36.97

Stichweh, R. (2005). *Inklusion und Exklusion: Studien zur Gesellschaftstheorie.* Bielefeld: Transcript.

Stoll, H. W. (1852). *Handbook of the Religion and Mythology of the Greeks - with a short account of the Religious System of the Romans.* London: Francis & John Rivington. Gilbert & Rivington, Printers.

Stone, J. (2014). *Russian Internet Censorship, Social Media Crackdown Make It Easy for Putin to Stay Popular.* Retrieved 02 March, 2016, from http://www.ibtimes.com/russian-internet-censorship-social-media-crackdown-make-it-easy-putin-stay-popular-1651078

Stone, A. R. (1996). *The war of desire and technology at the close of the mechanical age.* Cambridge, MA: MIT Press.

Sumner, C., Byers, A., & Shearing, M. (2011). Determining personality traits & privacy concerns from Facebook activity. *Black Hat Briefings*, 1–29.

Sun, H., & Zhang, P. (2006). The role of moderating factors in user technology acceptance. *International Journal of Human-Computer Studies, 64*(2), 53–78. doi:10.1016/j.ijhcs.2005.04.013

Sutko, D. M., & de Souza e Silva, A. (2011). Location-aware mobile media and urban sociability. *New Media & Society, 13*(5), 807–823. doi:10.1177/1461444810385202

Swanson, E. B. (1988). *Information system implementation: Bridging the gap between design and utilization.* Homewood, IL: Irwin.

Szymanski, D. M., & Hise, R. T. (2000). E-satisfation: An initial examination. *Journal of Retailing, 76*(3), 309–322. doi:10.1016/S0022-4359(00)00035-X

T/A Initiative. (2016). Retrieved from www.transparency-initiative.org/about/definitions

Tacke, V. (2001). Funktionale Differenzierung als Schema der Beobachtung. In V. Tacke (Ed.), *Organisation und gesellschaftliche Differenzierung.* Wiesbaden: Westdeutscher Verlag. doi:10.1007/978-3-322-80373-3

Tajfel, H., & Turner, J. C. (1979). An integrative theory of intergroup conflict. In W. G. Austin & S. Worchel (Eds.), *The social psychology of intergroup relations* (pp. 33–47). Monterey, CA: Brooks/Cole.

Tapscott, D. (1998). *Growing up digital: The rise of the net generation.* New York: McGraw-Hill.

Taylor, B. (2015). *5 ways the smartphone is conquering the tablet.* Available at http://www.pcworld.com/article/2889275/phones/5-ways-the-smartphone-is-conquering-the-tablet.html

Taylor, R. J. (2015). *3 Steps for Location-Savvy Social Media Marketing.* Available at http://www.convinceandconvert.com/social-media-strategy/social-location/

Taylor, S. (1995). The effects of filled waiting time and service provider control over the delay on evaluations of service. *Journal of the Academy of Marketing Science, 23*(1), 38–48. doi:10.1007/BF02894610

Taylor, S., & Todd, P. (1995). Understanding information technology usage: A test of competing models. *Information Systems Research, 6*(2), 144–176. doi:10.1287/isre.6.2.144

Teens & Social Networks Study. (2010). *Objective: To understand teens' experience with social networking and communities*. Retrieved December 17, 2012, from http://fr.scribd.com/doc/33751159/Teens-Social-Networks-Study-June-2010

Teo, T. (2009). Modelling technology acceptance in education: A study of pre-service teachers. *Computers & Education, 52*(2), 302–312. doi:10.1016/j.compedu.2008.08.006

Teo, T., & van Schalk, P. (2009). Understanding technology acceptance in pre-service teachers: A structural-equation modeling approach. *The Asia-Pacific Education Researcher, 18*(1), 47–66. doi:10.3860/taper.v18i1.1035

Terzis, V., Moridis, C. N., Economides, A. A., & Rebolledo-Mendez, G. (2013). Computer based assessment acceptance: A cross-cultural study in Greece and Mexico. *Journal of Educational Technology & Society, 16*(3), 411–424.

The Armchair Athletes. (2016). *Online Reputation Management*. Retrieved April 24, 2016, from http://www.thearmchairathletes.com/services/online-reputation-management/

Thelwall, M. (2008). Homophily in MySpace. *Journal of the American Society for Information Science and Technology, 60*(2), 219–231. doi:10.1002/asi.20978

Thomas, L., MacMillan, J., McColl, E., Hale, C., & Bond, S. (1995). Comparison of focus group and individual interview methodology in examining patient satisfaction with nursing care. *Social Sciences in Health, 1*, 206–219.

Thompson, G. F. (2006). Religious fundamentalisms, territories and globalization. *Economy and Society, 36*(1), 19–50. doi:10.1080/03085140601089820

Thompson, R., Compeau, R. D., & Higgins, C. (2006). Intentions to use information technologies: An integrative model. *Journal of Organizational and End User Computing, 18*(3), 25–47. doi:10.4018/joeuc.2006070102

Thong, J. Y. L., Hong, S., & Tam, K. Y. (2006). The effect of post-adoption beliefs on the expectation-confirmation model for information technology continuance. *International Journal of Human-Computer Studies, 64*(9), 799–810. doi:10.1016/j.ijhcs.2006.05.001

Thoreau, H. D. (1854). *Walden*. Springer.

Thornberg, R. (2015). School bullying as a collective action: Stigma processes and identity struggling. *Children & Society, 29*(4), 310–320. doi:10.1111/chso.12058

Thumin, N. (2008). 'It's good for them to know my story': Cultural mediation as tension. In K. Lundby (Ed.), *Digital storytelling, mediatized stories: Self-representations in New Media* (pp. 85–104). New York: Peter Lang.

Thygesen, N. T., & Andersen, N. Å. (2007). The polyphonic effects of technological changes in public sector organizations: A system theoretical approach. *Ephemera, 7*(2), 326–345.

Tifferet, S., & Herstein, R. (2012). Gender differences in brand commitment, impulse buying, and hedonistic consumption. *Journal of Product and Brand Management, 21*(3), 176–182. doi:10.1108/10610421211228793

Tom, G., & Lucey, S. (1997). A field study investigating the effect of waiting time on customer satisfaction. *The Journal of Psychology, 131*(6), 655–660. doi:10.1080/00223989709603847

Trewin, S., Cragun, B., Swart, C., Brezin, J., & Richards, J. (2010). *Accessibility challenges and tool features: an IBM Web developer perspective*. Paper presented at the 2010 international cross disciplinary conference on web accessibility (W4A). doi:10.1145/1805986.1806029

Tsivacou, I. (2005). The Ideal of Autonomy from the Viewpoint of Functional Differentiation/Integration of Society. *Systems Research and Behavioral Science, 22*(6), 509–524. doi:10.1002/sres.669

Tufekci, Z. (2008). Grooming, gossip, Facebook and MySpace. *Information Communication and Society*, *11*(4), 544–564. doi:10.1080/13691180801999050

Turkle, S. (1995). *Life on the screen: Identity in the age of the internet*. New York: Simon and Schuster.

Turner, J. C., Hogg, M. A., Oakes, P. J., Reicher, S. D., & Wetherell, M. S. (1987). *Rediscovering the social group: A self-categorization theory*. Basil Blackwell.

Turner, J. C., & Oaks, P. J. (1986). The significance of the social identity concept for social psychology with reference to individualism, interactionism, and social influence. *The British Journal of Social Psychology*, *25*(3), 237–252. doi:10.1111/j.2044-8309.1986.tb00732.x

TwitterData. (2014). *Insights into the #WorldCup conversation on Twitter*. Retrieved April 20, 2016, from https://blog.twitter.com/2014/insights-into-the-worldcup-conversation-on-twitter

Tyrell, H. (1979). Familie und gesellschaftliche Differenzierung. In H. Pross (Ed.), *Familie - wohin? Leistungen, Leistungsdefizite und Leistungswandlungen der Familie in hochindustrialisierten Gesellschaften*. Reinbeck: Rowohlt.

United Nations DoEaSA, Population Division. (2011). *World Population Prospects: The 2010 Revision*. New York: United Nations.

Urry, J. (2010). Consuming the Planet to Excess. *Theory, Culture & Society*, *27*(2-3), 191–212. doi:10.1177/0263276409355999

USACM. (2015). *Web Accessibility*. Retrieved 26/15/2015, 2015, from http://usacm.acm.org/accessibility/category.cfm?cat=23&accessibility

Valentinov, V. (2012). The Complexity-Sustainability Trade-Off in Niklas Luhmann's Social Systems Theory.[Online first]. *Systems Research and Behavioral Science*.

Valenzuela, S. (2013). Unpacking the use of social media for protest behavior: The roles of information, opinion expression, and activism. *The American Behavioral Scientist*, *57*(7), 920–942. doi:10.1177/0002764213479375

Valenzuela, S., Arriagada, A., & Scherman, A. (2012). The social media basis of youth protest behavior: The case of Chile. *Journal of Communication*, *62*(2), 299–314. doi:10.1111/j.1460-2466.2012.01635.x

van de Pas, J., & van Bussel, G.-J. (2015). 'Privacy Lost - and Found?' The information value chain as a model to meet citizens' concerns. *Electronic Journal of Information Systems Evaluation*, *18*(2), 185–195.

van der Geest, T., & Velleman, E. (2014). Easy-to-read Meets Accessible Web in the E-government Context. *Procedia Computer Science*, *27*, 327–333. doi:10.1016/j.procs.2014.02.036

Van der Heijden, H., & Sorensen, L. S. (2003). In measuring attitudes towards mobile information services: an empirical validation of the HED/UT scale. In C. U. Ciborra, R. Mercurio, M. De Marco, M. Martinez, & A. Carignani (Ed.). *European Conference on Information Systems*.

Van der Heijden, H. (2004). User acceptance of hedonic information systems. *Management Information Systems Quarterly*, *28*(4), 695–704.

van Rooij, S., & Zirkle, K. (2016). Balancing pedagogy, student readiness and accessibility: A case study in collaborative online course development. *The Internet and Higher Education*, *28*, 1–7. doi:10.1016/j.iheduc.2015.08.001

VanderPlas, S., & Hofmann, H. (2016). Spatial reasoning and data displays. *IEEE Transactions on Visualization and Computer Graphics*, *22*(1), 459–468. doi:10.1109/TVCG.2015.2469125 PMID:26390492

Vanderstraeten, R. (2005). System and Environment: Notes on the Autopoiesis of Modern Society. *Systems Research and Behavioral Science*, *22*(6), 471–481. doi:10.1002/sres.662

Vasquez-Colina, M. D. (2005). *Relationships among demographic variables, organizational culture, interpersonal self-efficacy and perceived job performance*. Academic Press.

Veletsianos, G. (2012). Higher education scholars participation and practices on twitter. *Journal of Computer Assisted Learning*, *28*(4), 336–349. doi:10.1111/j.1365-2729.2011.00449.x

Veletsianos, G. (2013). Open practices and identity: Evidence from researchers and educators social media participation. *British Journal of Educational Technology*, *44*(4), 639–651. doi:10.1111/bjet.12052

Veletsianos, G., & Kimmons, R. (2013). Scholars and faculty members lived experiences in online social networks. *The Internet and Higher Education*, *16*(1), 43–50. doi:10.1016/j.iheduc.2012.01.004

Velthuis, O. (2003). Symbolic meanings of prices: Constructing the value of contemporary art in Amsterdam and New York galleries. *Theory and Society*, *32*(2), 181–215. doi:10.1023/A:1023995520369

Venkatesh, V. (1999). Creating favorable user perceptions: Exploring the role of intrinsic motivation. *Management Information Systems Quarterly*, *23*(2), 239–260. doi:10.2307/249753

Venkatesh, V. L., Thong, J., & Xu, X. (2012). Consumer Acceptance and Use of Information Technology: Extending The Unified Theory Of Acceptance and Use of Technology. *Management Information Systems Quarterly*, *36*(1), 157–178.

Venkatesh, V., & Morris, G. M. (2000). Why dont men ever stop to ask for directions? Gender, social influence and their role in technology acceptance and usage behavior. *Management Information Systems Quarterly*, *24*(1), 115–139. doi:10.2307/3250981

Venkatesh, V., Morris, G. M., Davis, B. G., & Davis, D. F. (2003). User acceptance of information technology: Toward a unified view. *Management Information Systems Quarterly*, *27*(3), 425–478.

Venkatesh, V., Morris, M. G., & Ackerman, P. L. (2000). A longitudinal field investigation of gender differences in individual technology adoption decision making process. *Organizational Behavior and Human Decision Processes*, *38*(1), 33–60. doi:10.1006/obhd.2000.2896 PMID:10973782

Vernette, E., & Hamdi-Kidar, L. (2013). Co-creation with consumers: Who has the competence and wants to cooperate? *International Journal of Market Research*, *55*(4), 2–20. doi:10.2501/IJMR-2013-047

Vessey, I. (1991). Cognitive fit: A theory-based analysis of the graphs versus tables literature. *Decision Sciences*, *22*(2), 219–240. doi:10.1111/j.1540-5915.1991.tb00344.x

Viard, R. (2016). *Ranking Social Networks*. Retrieved March 24, 2016, from http://www.webmarketing-conseil.fr/classement-reseaux-sociaux/

Vigo, M., & Harper, S. (2014). A snapshot of the first encounters of visually disabled users with the Web. *Computers in Human Behavior*, *34*, 203–212. doi:10.1016/j.chb.2014.01.045

Villar, A., Callegaro, M., & Yang, Y. (2013). Where am I? A meta-analysis of experiments on the effects of progress indicators for web surveys. *Social Science Computer Review*, *31*(6), 744–762. doi:10.1177/0894439313497468

Volkmann, C., Tokarski, K. O., & Ernst, K. (2012). *Social entrepreneurship and social business. An Introduction and Discussion with Case Studies*. Wiesbaden: Gabler.

von Rosenberg, F. (2009). *Habitus und Distinktion in Peergroups: Ein Beitrag zur rekonstruktiven Schul- und Jugendkulturforschung*. Berlin: Logos.

W3C website. (2012). *Introduction to Web Accessibility*. Retrieved Mach 23, 2016, from http://www.w3.org/WAI/intro/accessibility.php

W3C website. (2016). *Designing for Inclusion*. Retrieved Mach 1, 2016, from https://www.w3.org/WAI/users/Overview.html

W3C. (1999). *Web Content Accessibility Guidelines 1.0*. Retrieved 25/11/2015, 2015, from http://www.w3.org/TR/WAI-WEBCONTENT/

W3C. (2005). *Introduction to Web Accessibility*. Retrieved 15/11/2015, 2015, from http://www.w3.org/WAI/intro/accessibility.php

W3C. (2008). *Web Content Accessibility Guidelines (WCAG) 2.0*. Retrieved 25/11/2015, 2015, from http://www.w3.org/TR/WCAG20/

W3C. (2015). *About W3C*. Retrieved 25/11/2015, 2015, from http://www.w3.org/Consortium/

Wagley, J. (2008). Social Sites: More Foe Than Friend? *Security Management, 52*(5), 54.

Wagner, T. (2006). *Die Soziale Arbeit der Sozialen Arbeit? – Ein kurzer Blick auf die (Selbst-) Beobachtung eines Funktionssystems*. Retrieved April 1, 2013, from http://www.sozialarbeit.ch/dokumente/soziale_arbeit_der_sozialen_arbeit.pdf

WAI. (2005). *Web Accessibility Initiative (WAI)*. Retrieved 25/11/2015, 2015, from http://www.w3.org/WAI/

Wakefield, R. L., Wakefield, K. L., Baker, J., & Wang, L. C. (2011). How website socialness leads to website use. *European Journal of Information Systems, 20*(1), 118–132. doi:10.1057/ejis.2010.47

Wakefield, R. L., & Whitten, D. (2006). Mobile computing: A user study on Hedonic/Utilitarian mobile device usage. *European Journal of Information Systems, 15*(3), 292–300. doi:10.1057/palgrave.ejis.3000619

Walker, P. (2002). Understanding Accountability: Theoretical Models and their Implications for Social Service Organizations. *Social Policy and Administration, 36*(1), 62–75. doi:10.1111/1467-9515.00270

Wallerstein, I. (2003). *Decline of American Power: The U.S. in a Chaotic World*. New York: New Press.

Walther, J. B., Van Der Heide, B., Kim, S. Y., Westerman, D., & Tong, S. T. (2008). The role of friends appearance and behavior on evaluations of individuals on Facebook: Are we known by the company we keep? *Human Communication Research, 34*(1), 28–49. doi:10.1111/j.1468-2958.2007.00312.x

Wang, H.-Y., & Wang, S.-H. (2010). User Acceptance Of Mobile Internet Based On The Unified Theory Of Acceptance And Use Of Technology: Investigating The Determinants And Gender Differences. *Social Behavior and Personality, 38*(3), 415–426. doi:10.2224/sbp.2010.38.3.415

Wang, Y., & Haggerty, N. (2011). Individual Virtual Competence and Its Influence on Work Outcomes. *Journal of Management Information Systems, 27*(4), 299–333. doi:10.2753/MIS0742-1222270410

Wang, Y., Lin, H., & Luarn, P. (2006). Predicting consumer intention to use mobile service. *Information Systems Journal, 16*(2), 157–179. doi:10.1111/j.1365-2575.2006.00213.x

Wannenwetsch, B. (2008). Inwardness and Commodification: How Romanticist Hermeneutics Prepared the Way for the Culture of Managerialism—a Theological Analysis. *Studies in Christian Ethics, 21*(1), 26–44. doi:10.1177/0953946808089725

Warren, J. (2007). *Service User and Carer Participation in Social Work*. Glasgow, UK: Learning Matters Ltd.

Warren, S. D., & Brandeis, L. D. (1890). The right to privacy. *Harvard Law Review, 4*(5), 193–220. doi:10.2307/1321160

Wartick, S. L. (2002). Measuring corporate reputation: Definition and data. *Business & Society*, *41*(4), 371–393. doi:10.1177/0007650302238774

Waters, S., & Ackerman, J. (2011). Exploring privacy management on Facebook: Motivations and perceived consequences of voluntary disclosure. *Journal of Computer-Mediated Communication*, *17*(1), 101–115. doi:10.1111/j.1083-6101.2011.01559.x

Web site WAI. (2016). *Web Accessibility Initiative (WAI)*. Retrieved Mach 5, 2016, from http://www.w3.org/WAI

WebAIM. (2015). *About WebAIM*. Retrieved 27/12/2015, 2015, from http://webaim.org/about/

Weingart, P. (1999). Scientific expertise and political accountability: Paradoxes of science in politics. *Science & Public Policy*, *26*(3), 151–161. doi:10.3152/147154399781782437

Weiss, L., Rafaeli, A., & Munichor, N. (2008). Proximity to or progress toward receiving a telephone service? An experimental investigation of customer reactions to features of telephone auditory messages. *Advances in Consumer Research. Association for Consumer Research (U. S.)*, *35*, 791–792.

Wellens, L., & Jegers, M. (2014). Beneficiary participation as an instrument of downward accountability: A multiple case study. *European Management Journal*, *32*(6), 938–949. doi:10.1016/j.emj.2014.03.004

Wentz, B., Lazar, J., Stein, M., Gbenro, O., Holandez, E., & Ramsey, A. (2014). Danger, danger! Evaluating the accessibility of Web-based emergency alert sign-ups in the northeastern United States. *Government Information Quarterly*, *31*(3), 488–497. doi:10.1016/j.giq.2014.02.010

Whetten, D. A. (2006). Albert and Whetten revisited: Strengthening the concept of organizational identity. *Journal of Management Inquiry*, *15*(3), 219–234. doi:10.1177/1056492606291200

White, M. G. (2012). *What Types of Social Networks Exist?* Retrieved April 20, 2016, from http://socialnetworking.lovetoknow.com/What_Types_of_Social_Networks_Exist

White, G. L. (2012). Information Security Education Relationships on Incidents and Preventions: Cyber Assurance Literacy Needs. In *Proceedings of the Information Systems Educators Conference ISSN* (Vol. 2167, p. 1435).

White, G. L. (2015). Education and Prevention Relationships on Security Incidents for Home Computers. *Journal of Computer Information Systems*, *55*(3), 29–37. doi:10.1080/08874417.2015.11645769

White, J. M., Wampler, R. S., & Winn, K. I. (1998). The Identity Style Inventory: A revision with a sixth-grade reading level (ISI-6G). *Journal of Adolescent Research*, *13*(2), 223–245. doi:10.1177/0743554898132007

White, J., Goette, T., & Young, D. (2015). Measuring the Accessibility of the US State Government Web Sites. *Communications of the IIMA*, *5*(1), 4.

WHO. (2014). *Disability and health*. Retrieved 15/11/2015, 2015, from http://www.who.int/mediacentre/factsheets/fs352/en/

Wijayaratne, A., & Singh, D. (2010). Is there space in cyberspace for distance learners with special needs in Asia? A review of the level of Web accessibility of institutional and library homepages of AAOU members. *The International Information & Library Review*, *42*(1), 40–49. doi:10.1080/10572317.2010.10762841

Wilkesmann, U., & Schmid, C. J. (2012). The impacts of new governance on teaching at German universities. Findings from a national survey. *Higher Education*, *63*(1), 33–52. doi:10.1007/s10734-011-9423-1

Wilkinson, D. (2016). *Who are 'Generation Z' and what it means for your organisation*. Retrieved March 23, 2016, from https://www.linkedin.com/pulse/who-generation-z-what-means-your-organisation-david-wilkinson

Wittmann, M. (2015). Modulations of the experience of self and time. *Consciousness and Cognition, 38,* 172–181. doi:10.1016/j.concog.2015.06.008 PMID:26121958

Wu, D., Ray, G., & Whinston, A. B. (2008). Manufacturers Distribution Strategy in the Presence of the Electronic Channel. *Journal of Management Information Systems, 25*(1), 167–198. doi:10.2753/MIS0742-1222250107

Wu, W., Chang, H., & Guo, C. (2008). An empirical assessment of science teacher's intention towards technology integration. *Journal of Computers in Mathematics and Science Teaching, 27*(4), 499–520.

Xia, F., Hsu, C., Liu, X., Liu, H., Ding, F., & Zhang, W. (2015). The power of smartphones. *Multimedia Systems, 21*(1), 87–101. doi:10.1007/s00530-013-0337-x

Xie, I., Babu, R., Jeong, W., Joo, S., & Fuller, P. (2014). *Blind Users Searching Digital Libraries: Types of Help-seeking Situations at the Cognitive Level.* Academic Press.

Xu, H., Dinev, T., Smith, J., & Hart, P. (2011). Information privacy concerns: Linking individual perceptions with institutional privacy assurances. *Journal of the Association for Information Systems, 12*(12), 798.

Yao, D., Qiu, Y., Huang, H., Du, Z., & Ma, J. (2011). A survey of technology accessibility problems faced by older users in China. *Universal Access in the Information Society, 10*(4), 373–390. doi:10.1007/s10209-011-0222-3

Yao, M. Z., Rice, R. E., & Wallis, K. (2007). Predicting user concerns about online privacy. *Journal of the American Society for Information Science and Technology, 58*(5), 710–722. doi:10.1002/asi.20530

Yarkoni, T. (2010). Personality in 100,000 Words: A large-scale analysis of personality and word use among bloggers. *Journal of Research in Personality, 44*(3), 363–373. doi:10.1016/j.jrp.2010.04.001 PMID:20563301

Yesilada, Y., Brajnik, G., & Harper, S. (2011). Barriers common to mobile and disabled web users. *Interacting with Computers, 23*(5), 525–542. doi:10.1016/j.intcom.2011.05.005

Yi, Y. (2015). Compliance of Section 508 in public library systems with the largest percentage of underserved populations. *Government Information Quarterly, 32*(1), 75–81. doi:10.1016/j.giq.2014.11.005

Yoon, C., Hwang, J. W., & Kim, R. (2012). Exploring Factors That Influence Students' Behaviors in Information Security. *Journal of Information Systems Education, 23*(4), 407.

Young, E. S. M. (2007). A Final Period to the Union: The Militarism and Militarization of the United States of America and its Effects on the United States Coast Guard and its People. *Race, Gender, & Class, 14*(3/4), 131–138.

Young, J. (2013). A conceptual understanding of organizational identity in the social media environment. *Administration in Social Work, 14,* 518–530.

Young, K. (1999). Internet addiction: Evaluation and treatment. *Student BMJ, 7,* 351–352.

Yousafzai, S. Y., Foxall, G. R., & Pallister, J. G. (2007). Technology acceptance: A meta-analysis of TAM (Part I). *Journal of Modeling in Management, 2*(3), 251–280. doi:10.1108/17465660710834453

Yu, D., & Parmanto, B. (2011). U.S. state government websites demonstrate better in terms of accessibility compared to federal government and commercial websites. *Government Information Quarterly, 28*(4), 484–490. doi:10.1016/j.giq.2011.04.001

Zakay, D., & Hornik, J. (1991). *How much time did you wait in line? A time-perception perspective* (Working Paper No. 20/91). Tel Aviv, Israel: The Leon Recanati Graduate School of Business Administration, Tel Aviv University.

Zamani-Miandashti, N., Memarbashi, P., & Khalighzadeh, P. (2013). The prediction of internet utilization behavior of undergraduate agricultural students: An application of the theory of planned behavior. *The International Information & Library Review*, *45*(3-4), 114–126. doi:10.1080/10572317.2013.10766379

Zap, N., & Montgomerie, C. (2013). *The status of web accessibility of Canadian universities and colleges: A follow-up study 10 years later.* Paper presented at the World Conference on Educational Multimedia, Hypermedia and Telecommunications.

Zeichick, A. (2008). Facebook's Combinatorial Challenge. *Technology Review*, *111*(4), 47.

Zejno, B., & Islam, A. (2012). Development and validation of library ICT sage scale for the IIUM postgraduate students. *OIDA International Journal of Sustainable Development*, *3*(10), 11–18.

Zhao, O. J., Ng, T., & Cosley, D. (2012). No forests without trees: Particulars and patterns in visualizing personal communication. *Proceedings of iConference* (pp. 25–32). Ontario: ACM.

Zhao, X., Salehi, N., Naranjit, S., Alwaalan, S., Voida, S., & Cosley, D. (2013). The many faces of Facebook: Experiencing social media as performance, exhibition and personal archive.*Proceedings of Conference on Human Factors in Computing Systems* (pp. 1-10). Paris: ACM. doi:10.1145/2470654.2470656

About the Contributors

T. S. Amer is the Arndt Professor of Business in The W. A. Franke College of Business at Northern Arizona University. He received his Ph.D. from The Ohio State University in 1989. Professor Amer teaches accounting information systems, managerial and cost accounting. His current research interests include the implications of information technology on human decision making and human/computer interactions. Professor Amer has published in Contemporary Accounting Research, Auditing: A Journal of Practice and Theory, The Journal of Information Systems, The International Journal of Technology and Human Interaction, Interacting with Computers, and Advances in Accounting Information Systems.

Maria José Angélico Gonçalves is Professor of Scientific area of Computer Science in ISCAP (School of Accountancy and Administration of Porto of Polytechnic Institute of Porto), PhD with honor in Component-Based Software Engineering - Human Machine Interfaces, University of Vigo. She is a researcher at CICE (Research Centre for Communication and Education), ISCAP, and a collaborate researcher at CEPESE (Research Centre for the Study of Population, Economics and Society Centre), Porto University. She is developing many research activities concerning the integration of the Information Technologies and Communication in higher education context and organizational context. She has been a member of the Program and Scientific Committee of several conferences. She serves as Member of the Editorial Board and referee for many scientific journals. In addition, she has published numerous papers in various international journals and conferences. She can be reached at mjose@iscap.ipp.pt

Adel Beldi, PhD in Management Science is Associate Professor at the IESEG School of Management Lille-Paris and Lille Economy and Management (LEM-CNRS), France. He obtained his PhD degree in management from South Paris University and a Research Master degree from Paris-Dauphine University. He conducted extensive research on issues relating to the adoption, implementation and use of Enterprise Resources Planning (ERP). His research findings have been published in peer reviewed journals in Information Systems and Management such as the Journal of International Business and International Journal of Project Management. He is also the author of several articles and book chapters on CRM implementation.

Jan Berkel is an independent software engineer with over 10 years of work experience in international IT companies and start-ups such as SoundCloud, Trampoline Systems and Cegetel SA. He is an active open source contributor and occasional speaker at conferences.

Frederico Branco is Assistant Professor at the University of Trás-os-Montes and Alto Douro and Member of INESC TEC research center. He has published over 30 articles in journals and event proceedings. It is involved in several academic works, as dissertation guidance and final grade projects. Participates in several research projects. His professional career goes through the industry in which over 20 years has been involved in various planning and implementation projects of Information Systems, with particular focus on agri-food and services sectors. Currently holds several functions of senior management in the areas of Operations, Information Systems and Quality Management.

Sylvaine Castellano is an Associate Professor of Management at Paris School of Business. She graduated with a Doctoral degree in Management from the University of Luxembourg. She is the Head of the Management & Strategy research department in Paris School of Business. Her research interests mainly include institutional and competitive dynamics as well as entrepreneurship in the sport, wine and luxury industries. She particularly published articles related to the concepts of reputation, e-reputation, legitimacy, status, heritage and retro-industries.

Carlton Clark is a Lecturer in the Department of English at the University of Wisconsin—La Crosse (USA). He was awarded a PhD in rhetoric from Texas Woman's University. His current research fields include social systems theory and US-China relations.

Ramiro Gonçalves is an Associate Professor with Habilitation at University of Trás-os-Montes e Alto Douro, in Vila Real, Portugal, and a Senior Researcher at INESC TEC Associated Laboratory, Porto, Portugal. Ramiro is currently the Executive Director of the PhD degree in Informatics and has around 150 publications (including book chapters, Scientific Citation Index journal articles, as well as publications in refereed conference proceedings).

A. Y. M. Atiquil Islam is currently working as a Research Fellow at the University of Malaya. He did a multidimensional PhD by combining two faculties, namely, Education and Computer Science & Information Technology under the Institute of Graduate Studies, University of Malaya (UM). He obtained his Master of Education in IT from the International Islamic University Malaysia (IIUM). In his field of specialization, he developed and validated three models, namely, Online Database Adoption and Satisfaction (ODAS) Model, Technology Satisfaction Model (TSM) and Technology Adoption and Gratification (TAG) Model. With regard to leadership, Dr. Islam has proved his abilities as a chief executive in few business and social organizations since 2002 to 2007. Leading from the front, he has conducted several workshops on the application of Structural Equation Modeling, SPSS and Rasch Measurement during 2010 to 2016. Beside this, He is involved as a committee member in conducting national and international conferences. Dr. Islam has also presented and published many papers in the international conferences (Japan, Singapore, Hong Kong, Taiwan, China and Malaysia) and journals including a book (Germany) and chapter in a book (IIUM Press). Moreover, he has been engaged with many collaborative research projects in conducting quantitative research in higher education by applying Structural Equation Modeling (SEM) and Rasch Model in Malaysia, China, Saudi Arabia, Oman, South Korea, Philippine, Hong Kong and Bangladesh. He is an editor of Asian Journal of Education and e-Learning (AJEEL) and reviewer of The Australian Educational Researcher. His research interests are in the arena of Quantitative Modeling, ICT in Education, Information System, Assessment and Evaluation, Quality in Higher Education and Tourism.

Todd Johnson is a Senior Lecture of Computer Information Systems at The W. A. Franke College of Business at Northern Arizona University. After earning his MBA in 2003 from NAU, Todd has been teaching in the CIS area. His research interests include human/computer interaction, and Enterprise Resource Planning software systems. He currently teaches classes ranging from freshman level Introduction to Computer Systems, through MBA courses encompassing advanced Excel and business analytics. His primary teaching interests include ERP systems, analytics, computer networking, and computer security.

Maher Kachour, PhD in the field of applied mathematics specializing in statistics, from IRMAR, University of Rennes, France. Currently employed as enseignant-chercheur (research professor) at IDRAC Research, Maher is the project leader for developing corporate software for online recruitment across 10 campus locations and an elected member of the research steering group focusing on 'Rethinking Business Models'. Based within IDRAC Research (Lyon), his present focus of research includes Business Models and applications, integer-valued time series, and statistical distributions. Maher teaches Statistical Analysis, Research Methodology and Introduction to Business Models.

Anis Khedhaouria is Associate Professor at Montpellier Business School. He holds a PhD from the University of Annecy (France) and his major topics of research are creativity, innovation, and entrepreneurship management. He has published his research in several peer reviewed journals such as Applied Psychology, Small Business Economics, Journal of Business Research, Journal of Knowledge Management, International Journal of Technology and Human Interaction, Learning Organization.

Insaf Khelladi is an Assistant Professor at ICN Business School (Nancy). Her thesis is about the individual investor behavior. Her research interests include financial & mobile marketing, investor & consumer behavior, and entrepreneurship. Insaf holds an MBA in Global Finance, from IAE Nice, and a BA in financial economics from Algiers University. She has been working for ten years in managing development projects within several international organizations (ex: IFC, World Bank, UNDP).

Manoj Kumar received his PhD in Mechanical Engineering from the Indian Institute of Technology, Delhi, India. He is presently working as Director, International Engineering Services, H.No.: 87A, RZI - Block, West Sagarpur, New Delhi - 110046, India. He has authored or co-authored over 80 research papers in journals and conferences.

Jessica Lichy, PhD in the field of online consumer behaviour in a cross-cultural context, CEISR (Centre for European & International Studies Research, University of Portsmouth, GB). Currently employed as enseignant-chercheur (research professor) at IDRAC Research, and Erasmus visiting professor at St Petersburg State Polytechnic University (Russia), Satakunta University (Finland), UCLan (UK), University of Chester Business School (UK), University of Greenwich Business School (UK) and the Cork campus of IDRAC (Ireland). Based in Lyon (France), present focus of research includes business models applied to digital marketing and international consumer behaviour, innovative pedagogy and monitoring trends in Internet user behaviour. Member of the Academy of Marketing and EDiNEB (Education Innovation in Business & Economics), other disciplines of interest include the impact of culture in the use of social media, technology-enhanced learning in higher education, and research methodology. Reviewer for International Journal of Consumer Studies and Behaviour & Information Technology. Jessica teaches e-business, CCM, International Marketing and Research Methods.

José Martins Is currently an Invited Assistant Professor at the University of Trás-os-Montes and Alto Douro, Invited Assistant at the Polytechnic Institute of Bragança and Member of INESC TEC research center. He has published over 40 articles in indexed journals and event proceedings. Currently he is supervisor for several Master Degree dissertations and PhD thesis. During his research career he has participated in several research projects and is currently a member of a research project aimed at studying the use, adoption and consequences of using IST to the tourism activities in Douro Valey. During his professional career José has also worked as an information systems and technologies senior consultant where he directly participated in several international projects. At the presente time José Martins dedicates most of his time to his lectures and to his research activities where he tries to understand the variables and (in)direct impacts of ICT adoption at individual and firm levels.

Erika Melonashi holds a PhD degree in Psychology from the University of Sheffield, UK and is currently Associate Professor in Psychology at the European University of Tirana. Prof. Assoc. Melonashi is also Research Track Leader at the Doctoral School of the University and Lecturer at the Department of Education.

Francis A. Méndez-Mediavilla is an Assistant Professor of Statistics in the McCoy College of Business Administration at Texas State University-San Marcos. He received his Ph.D. from Rutgers University, New Jersey, in 2005. He has published more than 15 scholarly articles. Some of his manuscripts have been published in the Journal of Applied Statistics, the British Journal of Management, and the International Journal of Technology and Human Interaction. He is a member of the American Statistical Association, the Institute of Mathematical Statistics, and the Decision Sciences Institute. His current research interests include non-parametric inference, time series forecasting, survey sampling, and computational statistics.

Panagiota Papadopoulou holds a BSc (hons.) in Informatics from the University of Athens, an MSc (distinction) in Distributed and Multimedia Information Systems from Heriot-Watt University and a PhD in Information Systems and E-commerce from the University of Athens. She teaches at undergraduate and postgraduate courses at University of Athens, Harokopio University, Hellenic Open University and others, works in European and national research projects and provides evaluation and consulting services for public organisations. She has published in international journals such as the European Journal of Information Systems and has authored the book New Technologies and Management Information Systems. Her research interests include trust, e-commerce, social networks and information systems.

Carlos Miguel Carvalho Peixoto is a master degree in Computer Engineering from the University of Tras-os-Montes and Alto Douro (UTAD), Portugal. Currently frequents a Informatic PhD at the same university and is also a researcher at the Institute for Systems and Computer Engineering, Technology and Science (INESC TEC) on the Web Accessibility Barometer project. His main research interests areas is web accessibility, social networking and information systems.

Florin Popescu is a Phd candidate at University "Politehnica" of Bucharest, Romania – is currently working for Minister of Defense in the areas of: Information Superiority (Communication & Information Systems), Surveillance & Reconnaissance, Space, Cyber Defence. Holding master degree in Managerial Communication, as well as bachelor degrees in military telecommunications field and international business, He has authored several researches/articles published in international journals. His areas of interest vary from Defence R&T to project management, to organization strategy and technology entrepreneurship. He can be reached at popescuveve@gmail.com

Steffen Roth is Assistant Professor of Management and Organization at the ESC Rennes School of Business as well as Visiting Professor at the International University of Rabat and the Yerevan State University. He was awarded a PhD in management from the Chemnitz University of Technology and holds another PhD in organizational sociology from the University of Geneva. He was a visiting professor at the University of Cagliari and the Copenhagen Business School. His research fields include organizational theory, social differentiation, ideation and crowdsourcing, and culturomics.

Cezar Scarlat is a Professor of Entrepreneurship, Management and Strategy at University "Politehnica" of Bucharest, Romania – is currently the Director of Doctoral School of Entrepreneurship, Business Engineering and Management associated with Faculty of Entrepreneurship, Business Engineering and Management - FAIMA. Holding master degrees in electronics engineering, and international business as well as a PhD degree in Management and Industrial Engineering from University "Politehnica" of Bucharest, he currently teaches Entrepreneurship, Project management, and Management courses at his home university and abroad (Finland, Belgium, Portugal) as exchange or visiting professor. He serves as committee member of numerous international conferences as well as member of the editorial board for several referred prestigious international journals (as Industrial Management & Data Systems - IMDS, Expert Systems with Applications – ESWA). He has authored several books and manuals, and more than one hundred articles published in international journals. Over last two decades, he actively participated and managed more than thirty education and research projects. His areas of interest vary from economic models and local development, to project management, to business management and marketing, to organization strategy, and technology entrepreneurship. He can be reached at cezarscarlat@yahoo.com

Amélia Ferreira da Silva is adjunct professor at School of Accounting and Administration of Porto, Polytechnic Institute of Porto. Her teaching areas are Cost Accounting; Management Accounting; and Strategic Management Accounting. In 2011, she finished PhD in Accounting, at University of Vigo, Spain. She has several participations in international conferences; scientific publications in international journals, and collaborates as reviewer with main international journals. She investigates- Her research interest are mainly in Decision making process; Accounting and management control in healthcare; Business Failure Prediction.

Anabela Martins Silva is currently assistant professor at the Department of Management, School of Economics and Management, University of Minho. She holds a PhD in Accounting. Her teaching areas include a range of courses in the areas of Cost Accounting; Management Accounting; Management Control and Performance Evaluation; Balanced Scorecard and Activity Based Costing. She integrated a research team in a quality management project applied to the healthcare sector. She has published in relevant journals and participated in several international conferences. Currently, she is the director of the Degree in Accounting. She is also a member of the executive committee of the Master in Accounting and the Master Management Units of Health.

Karen H. Smith is Associate Professor of Marketing in the McCoy College of Business Administration at Texas State University. She holds Bachelor and Master degrees in Economics from Baylor University and a Ph.D. in Marketing from the University of Texas at Austin. Prior to her academic career, she worked in the banking industry. Her research interests include consumer behavior and social marketing. Her published research covers topics such as smoking behavior, anti-smoking advertising, effects of nutrition information on fast food choices, and green marketing. Her most recent research examines privacy and security risks of consumers who use Facebook.

Sandrina Teixeira is an Adjunct Professor at School of Accounting and Administration of Porto, Polytechnic Institute of Porto, Portugal. Since 2013 has Coordinator of the Digital Marketing Masters and of the Degree in Business Communication. Between 2013-2014 has Coordinator of the Degree in Marketing. She is responsible by various courses, such as: unit of Marketing and Advertising Communication, Development of Multimedia Content, Seminars in the Digital Marketing Masters. She got a PhD at University Vigo of Communication, Advertising and Public Relation, in 2011. Her research interests are in digital communication, transparency in public administration and new consumers. Her supervised several master degree dissertations, was arguer in various proofs masters in various institutions of higher education and presided several master juries degrees.

Garry L. White is an Associate Professor in the Computer Information Systems department at Texas State University in San Marcos, Texas. He holds a MS in Computer Sciences from Texas A & M University – Corpus Christi and a PhD in Science Education, emphasis in Information Systems, from The University of Texas at Austin. Professional Certifications from the Institute of Certified Computer Professionals (ICCP) and (ISC)2 include C.D.P, C.C.P., C.S.P, Expert in Security Systems, and CISSP. He has been on the Texas State University faculty since 1997. His research are in the areas of privacy and information security issues. He has published papers in journals such as the Journal of Computer Information Systems and International Journal of Information Security and Privacy. Conference proceedings include the Decision Sciences Institute and the Computer Information Systems Conference. Recently, he taught a graduate course in Information Security at the University of Ludwigshafen of Applied Sciences, Ludwigshafen, Germany. He has served as President of the Alamo Chapter of the International Information Systems Security Certification Consortium.

Index

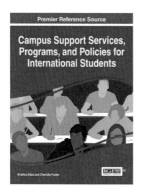

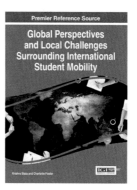
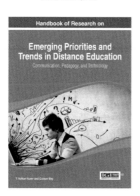
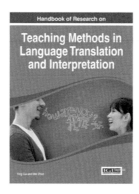

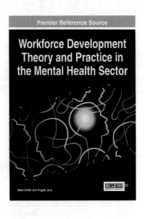
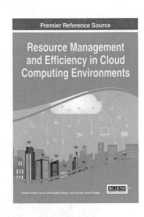

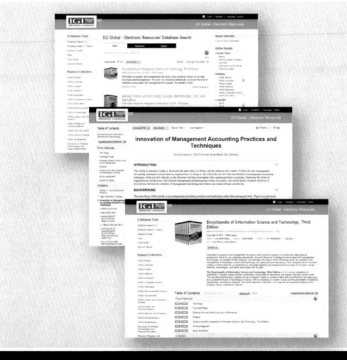